A History of Rome

A HISTORY OF
ROME

FOURTH EDITION

MARCEL LE GLAY
late of la Sorbonne

JEAN-LOUIS VOISIN
University of Bourgogne

YANN LE BOHEC
University of Lyon III

Translated by
ANTONIA NEVILL

Preface and new material by
DAVID CHERRY
Montana State University

Additional material by
DONALD G. KYLE
University of Texas at Arlington

Preface and new material by
ELENI MANOLARAKI
University of South Florida

WILEY-BLACKWELL
A John Wiley & Sons, Ltd., Publication

Edition history: Presses Universitaires de France (*Histoire Romaine*, 1e in French, 1991; 2e, 1994); Blackwell Publishers Ltd (1e in English, 1996; 2e, 2001); Blackwell Publishing Ltd (3e, 2005)

Blackwell Publishing was acquired by John Wiley & Sons in February 2007. Blackwell's publishing program has been merged with Wiley's global Scientific, Technical, and Medical business to form Wiley-Blackwell.

Registered Office
John Wiley & Sons Ltd, The Atrium, Southern Gate, Chichester, West Sussex, PO19 8SQ, United Kingdom

Editorial Offices
350 Main Street, Malden, MA 02148-5020, USA

9600 Garsington Road, Oxford, OX4 2DQ, UK

The Atrium, Southern Gate, Chichester, West Sussex, PO19 8SQ, UK

For details of our global editorial offices, for customer services, and for information about how to apply for permission to reuse the copyright material in this book please see our website at www.wiley.com/wiley-blackwell.

Library of Congress Cataloging-in-Publication Data

Le Glay, Marcel.
  [Historie romaine. English]
  A history of Rome / Marcel Le Glay, Jean-Louis Voisin, Yann Le Bohec ; new material by David Cherry, Donald G. Kyle ; preface and new material by Eleni Manolaraki ; translated by Antonia Nevill. – 4th ed.
       p. cm.
  Includes bibliographical references and index.
  ISBN 978-1-4051-8327-7 (pbk. : alk. paper) 1. Rome–History. I. Voisin, Jean-Louis.
II. Le Bohec, Yann. III. Cherry, David, Dr. IV. Title.
  DG209. L3613 2009
  937–dc22

                                                                          2008036231

A catalogue record for this book is available from the British Library.

Set in 10/13 pt Sabon by SNP Best-set Typesetter Ltd., Hong Kong
Printed and bound in Singapore by Fabulous Printers Pte Ltd

01 2009

CONTENTS

PLATES

FIGURES AND MAPS

Figures

Maps

CHRONOLOGIES, GENEALOGIES, AND BOXES

Chronologies

Genealogies

Boxes

PREFACE TO THE FOURTH EDITION

I wish to thank Wiley-Blackwell for inviting me to work on this book, with which I have been familiar as a student, instructor, and reviewer. The initial project had called only for an expansion of the coverage of the late Republic, but Al Bertrand, to whom I am very grateful, encouraged me to add, edit, and rearrange materials throughout the book. Warmest thanks to Jinyu Liu and Lee Brice for our discussions on the late Republic, and to Barbara Duke and Fiona Sewell for including me in the production part of the process.

I have tried to follow closely the excellent editions of David Cherry and Donald Kyle, who expanded the narrative with literary evidence while balancing the biases of ancient authors with modern interpretations of events. To this end I discuss various texts, both prose and poetry, keeping with the previous editors' emphasis on social and cultural history. Plates and maps have been added to illustrate the development of the Empire and provide some iconographic context for imperial ideology. Brief discussions of inscriptional evidence have been included as comparanda to the literary record. Conversely, several now dated discussions from the 1991 edition have been deleted to make room for these materials, and the "Guide to Further Reading" has been again brought up to date.

Over the past three editions citations of prose texts have differed widely; the original authors favored Latin titles and a basic book and chapter citation without section numbers, even for specific quotations. Subsequent editions featured some English titles, and section numbers in new citations but not in the older ones. I have simplified citations throughout by using exclusively Arabic numerals and English titles, and by reverting to the basic book and chapter indication of the first edition. My rationale is that section numbers are routinely omitted or diverge in English translations; basic book and chapter numbers are generally uniform in Loeb, Penguin, Oxford, and other translations, even in electronic form, all of which are used in survey classes as supplements to this textbook. Again following Cherry and Kyle, I have cited or modified Loeb translations for these texts.

Eleni Manolaraki
September, 2008

PREFACE TO THE THIRD EDITION

I am grateful to Blackwell, and especially to Al Bertrand, for giving me another opportunity to try to improve this book, and to Donald Kyle for contributing several new sections on Roman spectacles, including triumphs, festivals, celebrations, games, and gladiatorial combat. New, also, are the sections on Romanization and on the sources for Roman history.

Coverage of the late Republic has again been expanded, this time to include more extensive treatment of the reforms of the Gracchi, the wars against Jugurtha and Mithridates, the career of Pompey, and the accomplishments (and failings) of Julius Caesar. The section in chapter 2 that treats of the earliest history of the city of Rome has been revised to incorporate new interpretations of the archaeological evidence for its development. And the "Guide to Further Reading" has been brought up to date.

David Cherry
January, 2004

PREFACE TO THE SECOND EDITION

The enthusiastic response that greeted this book's publication (in English) in 1996 has made it both possible and desirable to expand and to update it. This second edition incorporates a number of improvements, many of them suggested by readers, including a more extensive treatment of the causes of the First Carthaginian War, and of Hannibal's purposes on the eve of the Second. Coverage of the period of the late Republic has been expanded to include Pompey's arrangements in Syria and Palestine 64–63 BC, the story of Caesar's conquest of Gaul, and a more detailed examination of the political developments of 63–44 BC that forever changed the shape of the Roman world – the so-called conspiracy of Catiline, the purposes and behavior of the First Triumvirate, the causes and course of the civil war between Caesar and Pompey.

To remedy what was probably the most obvious inadequacy of the first edition, a new section entitled "Private Life: Women and Family" has been added to chapter 6. It examines, among other things, the structure and demography of the Roman family, and the so-called "emancipation" of women in the late Republic, including changes in the rules that governed marriage and divorce.

New, also, is the "Guide to Greek and Roman Writers," which is intended to provide readers with both a broad overview of the nature of the surviving literature and an introduction to the characteristics of individual authors and their works. The "Guide to Further Reading" has been brought up to date. And two maps have been added, one of the city of Rome in the early third century BC (chapter 4), the other showing Roman conquests in the period 148–30 BC (chapter 5).

David Cherry, 2000

PREFACE TO THE FIRST EDITION

No work of this kind, intended for students, has existed until now. There has been a growing need for a book that will clearly and effortlessly give them the basic knowledge they need in order to flesh out the analytical criticisms of texts and documents they have to produce, and to derive the maximum benefit from the specialized courses available to them.

In order to meet this double target in a volume of reasonable size and handy format, we have emphasized events, but without neglecting ideas. We have chosen to present a chronological and factual narrative, but not at the expense of civilization, institutions, and economic and social problems, which all have their place.

We have not pursued originality at all costs. We sometimes give our personal points of view, but we avoid argument. Nor have we set out to write a textbook as the term is usually understood. We were thinking rather of a volume of *initiation* into the history of Rome. Hence our use of sources to persuade readers that nothing can compare with reading the documents. Here too, of course, as in the exposition of events, choices have constantly been made – often quite drastically. A glossary supplies definitions of words not explained in the text, and of some Latin terms that can be translated only approximately.

We have added an extensive guide to further reading, and the text contains a large number of maps (which does not mean that there is no need to refer to good atlases). The history of mankind cannot be understood without constant reference to the realities of geography.

Rome cannot be isolated from Greece. Their contacts were numerous well before the Roman political grip on the Greek-speaking world and the Hellenistic cultural grip on Rome. The Empire was a Roman universe (*imperium Romanum*), but it was composed of two civilizations, the Latin West and the Greco-Latin East, which separated in late antiquity to center around Rome and Constantinople.

We are jointly responsible for the book as a whole, with part I edited by M. Le Glay, part II by J.-L. Voisin, and part III by Y. Le Bohec.

It will be good if students become familiar with this enthralling history of a small town which became the capital of the greatest and most enduring empire history has known. If they find in it matter for reflection, that will be even better.

The authors

ABBREVIATIONS

Most Romans had two or more names – the first name or *praenomen* and the name of the *gens* (clan), the *nomen*. There could also be a third name or *cognomen*. The commonest *praenomina* are generally abbreviated: A. = Aulus; C. = Gaius; Cn. = Gnaeus; D. = Decimus; L. = Lucius; M. = Manius; M. = Marcus; P. = Publius; Q. = Quintus; Ser. = Servius; Sex. = Sextus; Sp. = Spurius; T. = Titus; Ti. = Tiberius.

INTRODUCTION

The Sources for Roman History

The sources that survive to describe the history of the Roman world are incomplete and often inadequate, their survival and recovery a matter largely of chance. There are a great many questions about the Roman world that simply cannot be answered. The sources are, broadly speaking, of two types: written and material. The written sources are preserved on a variety of media, including manuscripts, inscriptions, papyri, and coins.

The written record

There were no written documents at Rome before about 600 BCE, when the Romans adopted consonantal writing. And much of what was produced in the sixth and fifth centuries was destroyed in 390 BCE, when Rome was sacked by the Celts. The history of Rome did not begin to be systematically recorded until near the end of the third century BCE, at a time when Rome had already established itself as the dominant power in the Mediterranean region.

The earliest historians were mostly senators, who were, not surprisingly, interested mainly in public affairs, and who relied extensively on legends and oral traditions, the family records of the nobility, and the annalistic accounts compiled by the colleges of priests. Their works survive only in fragments. The early history of Rome, as it has come down to us, is preserved mainly in the works of writers, such as Livy (59 BCE–17 CE or 64 BCE–12 CE) and Dionysius of Halicarnassus (c.60/55–after 7 BCE), who lived a very long time after the events they describe.

In every period, history was considered to be a branch of literature, not scholarship. It was meant to serve as a store-house of moral lessons, and a practical guide for the politically active class. Style was generally more important than strict adherence to the facts. After the collapse of the Republic, historical writing was focused even more narrowly on the city of Rome, with little attention paid to the larger Roman world, except where it intersected with the doings of the emperors and their courts, about which there was a seemingly insatiable curiosity.

From at least the time of Augustus (27 BCE–14 CE), information was officially controlled. Access to the truth became increasingly difficult.

Inscriptions

Epigraphy is the study of texts inscribed on durable materials, such as stone, bronze, lead, pottery, or walls (*graffiti*). Hundreds of thousands of inscriptions have been recovered from across the Roman world, mostly from the western half of the Empire, and mostly from the period 1–250 CE. They shed light on virtually every aspect of Roman life. Hundreds of official documents are preserved, including laws and treaties, decrees of the Roman Senate, edicts of magistrates, pronouncements of the emperors, calendars, customs tariffs, and milestones. Inscriptions are an important source of information about the economic and social history of the Empire, about the army and the nature of military life, and about religious institutions and practices, including the spread of Christianity in the Roman world.

There are also a great many honorary and commemorative inscriptions, which can be used to reconstruct careers, family relationships, or patterns of military recruitment. It is worth emphasizing, however, that commemorative inscriptions provide information only about that part of the population which used stone inscriptions, and really only about that part of the stone-using population which both could afford a permanent memorial, and was thought, or considered itself, to deserve one. In most areas, it seems, that was a fairly large part of the population. But it would be foolish to think that the poor are not massively under-represented in the epigraphic record.

Papyri and other documents

In many parts of the Roman world, papyrus was used as a kind of writing paper. It was produced by pressing together two thin transverse strips cut from the papyrus plant and laid side by side. With the exception of military documents, which everywhere were written in Latin, almost all of the surviving papyri are in Greek. Most come from Egypt, where the exceptionally dry climate has helped to preserve them. Other significant find spots are Dura-Europus on the Euphrates, Nessana in the Negev, a cave in the Judaean desert, a tomb in Macedonia, and a villa at Herculaneum, where the papyrus was carbonized in the eruption of Vesuvius in 79 CE.

Unlike inscriptions, papyri were not intended to be permanent. Most of them are concerned with the routine business of everyday life: private letters, contracts, financial records, wills, petitions, legal decisions, tax records, shopping lists. One (*P. Oxy.* iii.745) records the tragic death of an 8-year-old slave boy, Epaphroditus, who leaned too far out of an upstairs window to see the castanet dancers at a festival.

The Romans wrote also on wooden tablets, the surfaces of which were thinly waxed or sometimes just smoothed. The two most important surviving collections are the financial records of a man named Lucius Caecilius Jucundus, which were recovered at Pompeii, and a set of letters and other military documents that was found in the 1970s at Vindolanda, just south of Hadrian's Wall.

Other records are preserved on ostraca, or potsherds, which were widely used as a form of inexpensive writing material, particularly, it seems, in the eastern Mediterranean, and especially for tax receipts.

Coins

Coins began to be minted around 300 BCE, originally only in bronze but soon after also in silver and gold. In the period of the Republic, they were issued only at intervals, and for specific needs, like war; it was not until the time of Augustus that they began to be produced in a regular way. From the late Republic, coins were often used for propaganda, to advertise accomplishments or official programs.

Through their iconography and legends, coins are an important source of information about military and political events, foreign policy, the administration of the provinces, economic developments, and religious institutions, including the imperial cult. They indicate what certain buildings and monuments looked like. Collectively, they constitute a kind of portrait gallery of the emperors and their wives. Their geographic distribution can be used to reconstruct trade patterns, especially across the frontiers. And buried hoards of coins may sometimes date localized periods of political unrest or invasion.

The material record

The unwritten archaeological record consists of the buildings and other structures that survive above ground or that have been excavated by archaeologists, as well as the artifacts and other finds associated with them. For a very long time, archaeology in the Mediterranean world concentrated on uncovering or excavating urban areas and grand monuments, sometimes with more enthusiasm than attention to detail. What was not monumental was often neglected or destroyed. A more scientific archaeology was developed in the late nineteenth century and in the early part of the twentieth, mostly in connection with the excavation of military sites in the north-west provinces of the Empire.

Archaeology often used to be called the "handmaid" of the written sources. It is now widely understood that the material record is itself a primary source, which sometimes complements the literary evidence, and sometimes contradicts it. At the same time, it is worth emphasizing that archaeology deals only with material remains: even under the best of circumstances, it can tell us only what was physically present at a certain place at a certain time.

Rome and the Mediterranean

The site, development, and entire history of Rome were to a large extent influenced by geography. Of the three great Mediterranean peninsulas, the Italian was the most favored: its central position between the Greek and Iberian peninsulas, together with the fact that, while it has the smaller land mass, and extends farther into the sea, it is solidly attached to the European continent by the rich Po valley, made it the fruitful meeting-ground for trading and cultural movements between the eastern and western Mediterranean, and similarly between peoples from the north and those living around the sea.

The eastern half of the Mediterranean was for thousands of years at the heart of brilliant civilizations, and sometimes great empires, contending for mastery of the seas and trade routes: in the south, the Egyptian Empire of the Pharaohs; in the east, the Phoenician cities dominating the coastal areas; in the north, the Mycenaeans, who inherited the civilization of Crete. Between 1500 and 1000 BCE, the Mycenaeans reached the coasts of Sicily, southern Italy, Etruria, and the Adriatic (hence in Homer's *Odyssey* the sometimes very precise descriptions of Italian shores). And as early as the eleventh century BCE, those able traders, the Phoenicians, must in their turn have penetrated the western Mediterranean. At all events, in the eighth century they established trading settlements in Sicily, Sardinia, and North Africa (Utica, Carthage), and on the Iberian peninsula (Cadiz). On the site of Rome itself a colony of people from Tyre managed to install itself as early as the eighth or seventh century in the area that became the Forum Boarium (livestock market). The Greeks followed and rivaled the Phoenicians, and not only in Sicily and southern Italy; their colonizing movements also reached southern Gaul (Marseilles was founded around 600 BCE by Phocaeans from Asia Minor), and then the Iberian peninsula.

The western half of the Mediterranean was fringed by peoples of great diversity, generally living in tribes or racial groups, with a mainly agricultural economy, and a culture and religion reflecting their daily preoccupations and their activities as warriors.

In the coastal regions of the Maghreb (present-day Algeria, Morocco, and Tunisia), the settled, wheat-eating Berber peoples (Libyans, Numidians, Moors) did not live as completely on the "fringes of history" as has been thought; they could have had contact with Sicily to the east and the Iberian peninsula to the west, and in any case certainly had contact with the Phoenicians: Punic civilization (or that of the Phoenicians of the west) was imposed in eastern Tunisia by wealthy Carthage, and elsewhere in the form of trading settlements scattered along the coastline, as far as the borders of Cyrenaica to the east, and to the west at least as far as the south of present-day Morocco.

The Iberian peninsula, where the fertile coastal plains are in striking contrast with the highlands of the interior, was occupied by peoples with widely different civilizations. Iberians, Celtiberians, and the Celtic populations of the north-west grouped around their hill forts had scarcely anything in common apart from their devotion to their war leaders and their religious nature. As early as the eighth century BCE, the large mining centers were active, notably in the Guadalquivir valley (kingdom of Tartessus). These were what attracted the Phoenicians, followed by the Greeks.

In southern Gaul, the Ligurian and Celto-Ligurian peoples of the east, and the Iberians and Celtiberians of the west, who were sometimes grouped in confederations, and often led by an aristocracy of chiefs acknowledged by the collective whole, were brought into contact with the Greek world as early as the seventh century BCE by Rhodian traders and by the Phocaean colonists from Marseilles, who subsequently spread as far as Ampurias (*emporion* = trading post) in the west, and Nice (Nikaia) and Antibes (Antipolis) in the east. Trading relations were also formed with the Greeks of Magna Graecia (the Greek cities in southern Italy) and with the Etruscans.

The hinterland or continental mainland must not be overlooked, because of the great migrations of peoples which on more than one occasion brutally interrupted the history of the Italian peninsula and transformed its population. In the immediately pre-Christian millennia, the movements of peoples that affected territories later influenced by Rome and its culture are particularly:

- in the south, the activities of the peoples of the sea and desert;
- in the north, Indo-European, and notably Celtic, invasions.

The "peoples of the sea," raiders of uncertain origin, sailed into the eastern Mediterranean in the second millennium BCE. Leaving aside the legendary traditions which sometimes obscure history, there is textual and archaeological evidence of the settlement, as early as the Bronze Age, of the Ibero-Ligurians, and in Sicily of the Sicani and Siculi (perhaps one and the same race of conquerors). It is possible that the Siculi were the original population of Italy.

As for the desert peoples, from around 1500 BCE they were the "Equidians," horse-breeders and wagon-drivers who, having become excellent horsemen (the Gaetuli and Garamantes), were the ancestors of the Tuaregs. Their presence in the Sahara and their activities as warriors and traders had a great influence on the history of the Maghreb, which was often governed by the relations between nomads and settled tribes.

In the north, in the second millennium BCE, it was Indo-European invasions that brought to the Mediterranean countries peoples who practiced cremation, and used horses and wagons. It is difficult to reconstruct and date their movements. There are records of the existence of vast fields of cinerary urns in Silesia and Pannonia (present-day Hungary) from around 1300–1200 BCE. After the year 1000 this civilization of urn-fields gradually dwindled until the eighth century BCE. At that point the Hallstatt civilization (named after an archaeological site at Hallstatt in Styria) triumphed in the first Iron Age. In Italy, the Latins were probably the first of the Indo-European peoples to arrive in the peninsula.

Only a part of them settled in Latium, while others went off to Sicily. When they adopted a settled way of life, they practiced body burial. Early in the fifth century BCE, when the Hallstatt culture was in its final stages, there appeared a new civilization, known as that of La Tène (after the name of a Swiss archaeological site); it corresponded with the second Iron Age. This was the era of the Lady of Vix (an ancient skeleton discovered at the site) and the formation of a Gaulish "nationality," characterized by original art forms, highly developed craftsmanship, and its own religion, which mingled deified animal and natural forces and anthropomorphic divinities, its rites and myths preserved through the oral teachings of the Druids.

The arrival of the Indo-Europeans was one of the major events in the history of the West. It had profound repercussions on the peopling of Italy.

The Origins of the "Roman Miracle"

The Roman achievement, sometimes referred to as the "Roman miracle," consisted of this: a small town in Latium began by dominating other Latin townships, then established its authority over the Italian peninsula before going on to impose itself on the Mediterranean world and beyond for at least eight centuries. Of all the questions raised by Rome's historic destiny, the question of its origins immediately comes to the fore. It is all the more interesting, but also all the more difficult, because of the numerous legends that surround it (for instance, Roma, daughter of Telephus, himself the son of Herakles/Hercules, who would make Rome an Etruscan town; or Romos, son of Ulysses, who would make it Greek). The origin of the Latin town is not in fact mentioned in any dependable historical document.

PART I

FROM THE ORIGINS TO THE EMPIRE

1

ITALY BEFORE ROME

In the middle of the eighth century BCE, the time traditionally considered as the foundation date of Rome, Italy was a patchwork of peoples, some long settled, others still on the move. Among these peoples, two became established and rapidly dominated the north and south of the peninsula: the Etruscans and the Greeks. From early on, both peoples influenced deeply the budding township that later became Rome, the center of a Mediterranean empire. With the Phoenicians who set up their trading posts and the Greeks who established colonies, the East gained predominance in the western half of the Mediterranean basin.

1.1 | The Peoples of Prehistoric Italy

Several elements survive from the pre-Indo-European, Mediterranean inhabitants of Italy, who were mainly aboriginals and immigrants from overseas. The Ligures were primitive mountain-dwellers, settled north of Etruria on the shores of the Gulf of Genoa and in the Maritime Alps. The Sicani were Sicilian aboriginals who had been pushed back to the south-western part of the island (around Gela and Agrigentum) by the Siculi. These had come from the Italian peninsula in the thirteenth or eleventh century BCE. According to other traditions, however, the Sicani and the Siculi were closely related or even identical peoples. Most historians agree that the Siculi have a fundamentally Mediterranean background: their matriarchal customs, traces of which remain in the rites of sacred prostitution practiced later in the sanctuary of Aphrodite on Mount Eryx, were foreign to the customs of Indo-European populations. They seem to have been closely related to the Oenotri, the Chones, the Morgates, and the Itali (originally only the "toe" of the peninsula, modern Calabria, was called *Italia*). These names were given to the indigenous populations of southern Italy by Greek authors, who regarded them all as *Pelasgi* (a name given by Greek historians to the prehistoric inhabitants of Greece). Dionysius of Halicarnassus, who wrote *Roman Antiquities* in Greek, claimed that the Italians were Greek in origin, an obviously incorrect generalization.

A pre-Indo-European substratum therefore existed, but it was not homogeneous, despite traces of a linguistic community. Some historians hold that these peoples (Pelasgi, Ligures, Siculi, Oenotri, etc.), who, according to the epic poet Virgil, were at the origin of primitive Rome, boil down to a single unity tracing to Arcadia, in the central Peloponnese. In his epic poem the *Aeneid*, Virgil traces the beginnings of Rome to an Arcadian foundation. Although such legends and literary fictions are neither factual nor accurate, they still reflect historical events and developments, as well as the social and cultural responses to these processes. The Arcadians certainly played an effective role in the colonization of southern Italy, from where the Arcadian legends reached Latium.

Following the Indo-European invasions into the greater part of Europe, Iran, and India (in the second millennium), new transalpine peoples came to settle in Italy, often overlaying older, indigenous strata. These can be roughly categorized into the following groups:

- The Veneti in the region of the Po delta. Of Illyrian origin, according to the fifth-century BCE Greek historian Herodotus, they maintained close relations with the coastal regions of the western Adriatic. Inscriptions from this area document the use of an archaic Indo-European language.
- The Celtic populations (Insubres, Cenomani, Boii, Lingones, and Senones). These infiltrated massively from the north-west, between the sixth and fourth centuries. They dominated the Po valley so greatly that, for centuries, Romans

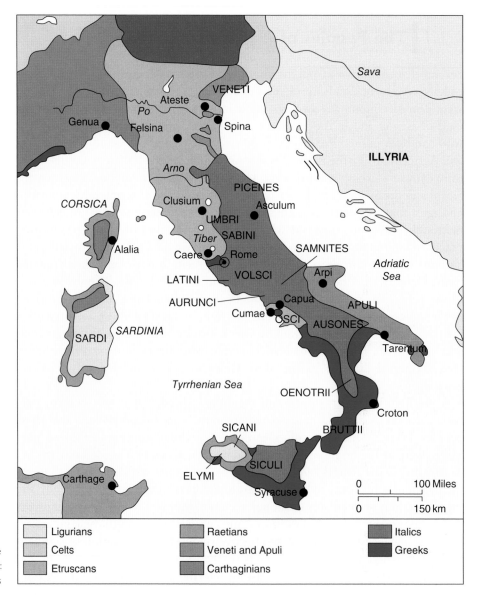

Map 1.1 Italy in the eighth century BCE: the Italic peoples

called this area Cisalpine Gaul ("Gaul on this side of the Alps"). Their influence and culture spread as far as Etruscan Felsina (Bologna), which became a gateway from the Po valley to Etruria (modern Tuscany).

■ The Umbri, who for a time were dominant in central Italy, occupied the hinterland of the Adriatic coast as far as the upper Tiber. Their Osco-Umbrian language is known notably from seven bronze plaques found near Iguvium (modern Gubbio), which provide a key to their rituals and divinities.

■ The Piceni followed the Umbri on the same coast and settled in the region of Ancona.

- The Sabines and Samnites adjoined the Latini on the east and south-east. These populations, known as "Sabelli," were joined by the Marsi on the borders of Lake Fucinus, the Volsci in the Pontine plain, and the Campani in the Naples region, where they encountered the Osci and the Ausoni, who had settled there before them.
- On the Adriatic coast to the south were the Frentani, the Apuli, and, around Tarentum, the Iapygians or Messapians, whose Illyrian origin, attributed to them by the early authors, is indicated by a study of the names of both places and peoples.
- On the western coast to the south were the Lucani and Bruttii, who overlay the indigenous strata of Oenotri, Chones, Morgates, and Itali.
- In the midst of all these peoples, the Latini occupied only the plain of central Italy between the Tiber and the Alban Hills. It is a plain dotted with hills, capable of providing refuge and defense, giving onto the Tyrrhenian sea by way of a coast that is difficult to access. This coast is linked to the hinterland by the Tiber, a navigable river which played an essential role in the choice of Rome's site. In proto-historic Italy, the Latins were probably the oldest and certainly the most important Indo-European peoples who had migrated to the peninsula. Excavations of the burial sites of Lavinium and Antium have revealed hut-shaped cinerary urns, dating between 1000 and 875 BCE. Similar objects have been found in the pit tombs on the site of the Roman Forum. The rite of body burial only gradually replaced cremation. Archaeological findings in the small towns of Latium suggest the primacy of Alba over Rome, which is also attested by literary sources.
- To the north, beyond the Tiber, stretched the land of the Etrusci (or Tusci), whom the Greeks called *Tyrrhenoi*. The origin of this people remains mysterious and controversial. Did they come from the north or the east? (The land of Urartu, modern Armenia, has been suggested as a place of origin, on the basis of the same cauldrons with griffons' heads which have been found there as in Etruria.) Or were they aboriginals who integrated various cultural influences? Perhaps they were not a new people, but rather a new civilization which developed in an indigenous setting. One thing is certain: by the early seventh century, the Tusci had become strongly established in Etruria, and their sphere of influence extended beyond the River Silarus (Sele) in the Salerno region in Campania. In fact, Etruscan inscriptions found in Volturnum (Capua) and Pompeii suggest their colonization of that region. Their influence to the north, as far as the Po valley, is suggested by abundant evidence of their culture and their creation of Etruscan towns such as Felsina and Melpum (Milan).

1.2 | The Cultures of Prehistoric Italy

The cultures and way of life in early Italy were less varied than the peoples themselves. Except in the Apennines, where primitive mountain-dwellers lived, livestock breeding and agriculture developed better means of survival than the older practices of hunting and fishing. The seasonal movement of livestock into higher or lower plains for pasturing became a central rural activity. This was due to the climate and soil of Italy, one sixth of which is mountainous and grassland. This practice either predominated or, as in Tuscany and central Italy, complemented agriculture. There, in the spring, the flocks gave place to crops. From Latium the flocks moved annually toward rich Umbria. This movement of people and animals was followed by trade between the two regions, which was aided by the easy transportation through the Tiber. Trade relationships, in turn, precipitated conflicts between the two regions.

On the other hand, there was a wide variety of languages, some of which show marked affinities among them. Mostly they belonged to the Indo-European family, one of them at least of a very archaic branch. Indo-European was indeed an enduring cultural element. Latin, for example, preserved Indo-European words designating the most ancient forms of religious, constitutional, and family life expressed in Indo-European: e.g. *rex* (king), *flamen* (priest), *pater* (father), *mater* (mother).

Closely akin to Latin is Faliscan. Venetan is known from inscriptions on votive stone slabs (*stelae*) found in the town of Este in the Veneto region. Umbrian is attested by the bronze tablets from Iguvium; and its relative, Oscan, was used by all the peoples of the south-west. The Sabines, Marsi, Volsci, and Piceni similarly had their own dialects.

Ligurian stood outside these Indo-European languages, but borrowed elements from them. There was also Messapian or Iapygian, which is connected to Illyrian. And there was also, of course, Etruscan, to which we will turn below.

Etruscan culture

Among this mix of cultures in the Italy in the eighth century BCE, Etruscan culture stands out by virtue of its progress and artistic brilliance. First, it was an urban civilization. In an Italy of villages, Etruria alone had towns. These were ritually founded and endowed with enclosing walls, gates, and temples built in stone. These features were later adopted by Romans in the development of their own towns. Etruria was composed roughly of a federation of 12 city-states with magistrates who, in the event of grave danger, would make themselves subject to a **dictator** (*macstrna = mastarna*). This later happened in Rome, at the end of the reign of the first of the Tarquins, with the coming to power of Servius Tullius, whose original name was allegedly Mastarna. State structure, of course, implies political and social institutions. Governed first by kings (*lucumons*) surrounded by *fasces*, symbols of their authority, and adorned with well-known insignia (the gold crown and scepter surmounted by an eagle), the Etruscan peoples replaced them in the fifth century with annual magistrates (*zilath*). This practice too was adopted by the Romans, and the Roman officers known as **praetor**s perhaps correspond broadly to these ancient Etruscan magistracies. Certainly, there was a similar political change in Rome from monarchy to republic in the early fifth

dictator: Magistrate appointed legally with full powers, but for a specified period (less than six months) and in order to accomplish a precise task, when grave danger threatened the state.

fasces: A bundle of rods bound round an axe. Carried by the lictors accompanying the magistrates *cum imperio* (senior magistrates with civil and military powers).

praetor: Senior magistrate specially responsible for justice. Performed some of the functions of the consuls in their absence.

century. Etruscan society was patrician and almost feudal: a class of nobles formed the oligarchy of the *principes* (wealthy land-owners who held power in the cities), until the rural plebeians forced their way in. Below was an immense class of slaves (though they could be emancipated and, once freed, could join the followers of the great men).

Moreover, the Etruscan civilization was materially and technically advanced, unlike those of other areas in Italy. Thanks to an advanced knowledge of hydraulics, the Etruscans practiced drainage and irrigation. Furthermore, skilled craftsmen, familiar with Greek techniques, constructed for the Etruscans shafts and tunnels to exploit the deposits of tin, copper, and iron which abounded in Etruria. Together with the iron from the island of Elba, these Etruscan minerals were widely traded. Among their most remarkable products were arms, tools, and domestic furnishings in bronze and iron (mainly mirrors and small chests), and pottery showing high levels of ceramic technique, such as *impasto* (thickly laid paint) and *bucchero nero* (black luster).

The Etruscans enjoyed an unchallenged primacy in three fields, the best known and most enigmatic of which was religion. The Etruscan religion was a revealed religion, and a religion of books (not of "the" Book, like the Bible of the Hebrews). The sacred books of the prophets, of whom the chief was Tages, laid down the Etruscan religion. They prescribed the rules concerning rituals and the life of states and of men (*libri rituales*), the manner of interpreting thunder and lightning (*libri fulgurales*), and the art and method of observing the entrails of sacrificial victims (*libri haruspicinales*). They also provided the knowledge necessary to conduct a person into the next world (*libri acheruntici*). The Etruscan religion was highly ritualistic, as indicated by the bronze liver of Placentia (Piacenza). This artifact features an image of the sky marked out in compartments bearing the names of the gods, and was used as a reference for examining the livers of animals offered to the gods. The Etruscans formed a pantheon similar to that of the Greeks: a leading Triad (Tinia = Jupiter, Uni = Juno, Menrva = Minerva) was venerated in tripartite temples (as the temple of Jupiter Capitolinus later in Rome). This was followed by deities roughly corresponding to the Greek Olympians but infused with elements of Italian animism and local folklore: Voltumna/Vertumnus, "the first of the gods of Etruria," according to Varro, Turan = Aphrodite, Fufluns = Dionysos, Turms = Hermes, Sethlans = Hephaistos, Hercle = Herakles, Maris = Ares, Nethuns = Neptune, etc.

In their conception of the after-life, the Etruscans were influenced by the Middle East and Greece. Their "Paradise" was a place of coolness, music, and banquets; their "Hell" a place of melancholy and grief, of suffering and tortures for the wicked, a place where two monstrous spirits reigned, half-man half-beast, Charun (related to the Greek Charon) and Tuchulcha (see the Tarquinian tomb of Orcus, or Hades). However, the evil funerary divinities could be appeased by the blood of combatants (a rite considered to be related to the gladiatorial fights, as we shall see below). Hence there are scenes of funerary combat on the frescos of Etruscan tombs.

Plate 1.1   Liver of Piacenza: bronze model of a liver of a sheep, made in Etruria and used for divination. The concave surface features a complex combination of principles of cosmology, hepatoscopy, and religious mythology, and it is our only source for several obscure divinities of the Etruscan pantheon. Third to second century BCE. Museo Civico, Piacenza. akg-images/ Bildarchiv Steffens

Etruscan art was also sophisticated and highly influenced by Hellenism, which it introduced into central Italy. That influence appears particularly in:

- Sculpture of statues (e.g. the Apollo of Veii) and bas-reliefs, statuettes, tripods, and candelabra in bronze, and the painted terracotta decoration covering the temples. Starting in the fourth century, the decorating of sarcophagi and cinerary urns with mythological reliefs became the general practice.

Plate 1.2 Etruscan tomb painting: Ceres, the goddess of grain, with armed attendants. Sixth century BCE. C. M. Dixon

- Painting, known particularly through the frescos in tombs, notably at Tarquinii.
- Pottery: alongside the Greek vases, mainly Attic, revealed in the thousands by the necropoleis, elegant native pottery developed. Greek vases were both imported and produced locally, for example the seventh-century water pots of Caere.

Etruscan architecture was no less splendid than Etruscan art. Rome was informed by it in three areas: town planning (checkerboard layout and enclosing walls in freestone, in immense polygonal bond, or rectangular bond, known as *opus quadratum*); the construction of temples (rectangular in plan, with a

Plate 1.3 Etruscan terra-cotta sarcophagus: husband and wife reclining on a couch. Caere (Cerveteri), sixth century BCE. C. M. Dixon

tripartite cella on a podium, and architectural decoration in polychrome terracotta); and the arrangement of tombs (either a funeral chamber topped by a tumulus and decorated with frescos, or a tomb made of rock, decorated and filled with precious objects). The great princely tombs of the seventh century (Regolini-Galassi at Caere, Bernardini and Barberini at Praeneste) feature rich furnishings (gold, ivory, vases).

The Etruscan language, which bears, naturally enough, the traces of borrowings from Greek and Italic dialects, is not considered to be an Indo-European tongue – linguistic connections have been explored with Basque, Caucasian, and (mainly) pre-Hellenic dialects. It is known to us through some 10,000 inscriptions, unfortunately for the most part very short, late-period epitaphs, which do not allow for much progress in our knowledge of the language. The Pyrgi inscriptions (bilingual golden tablets, in Etruscan and Punic) have not cast as much light on the Etruscan language as was hoped.

The Etruscan alphabet, disseminated throughout Italy, became the model by which Italy became literate.

Plate 1.4 Fresco from tomb in Caere (Cerveteri): the Etruscan god Turms carrying off the soul of a deceased woman. His wings and sandals correspond to the garb of Greek Hermes (Mercury), messenger of the gods and usher of souls into the Underworld. Sixth century BCE. Louvre museum, Paris. (C) RMN/Hervé Lewandowski

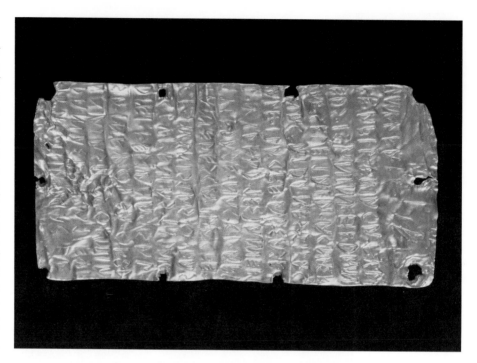

Plate 1.5   One of the Pyrgi Tablets. The three golden leaves of the Tablets record a diplomatic exchange between an Etruscan and a Tyrian king, in both Phoenician and Etruscan. The bilingual inscription provides evidence of Phoenician and Punic influence in Italy, and has cast some light on the mysteries of Etruscan theology and language. Late sixth century BCE. Antiquarium of Pyrgi, Santa, Italy akg-images/ Erich Lessing.

1.3 | The East's Influence on the West

While the Etruscans settled north of the Tiber and rapidly extended their power as far as the Po valley in the north and Campania in the south, two other peoples were gaining a foothold in Italy: the Phoenicians and the Greeks. Their settlements indicate the strength of the eastern expansion and influence in the western Mediterranean.

Phoenician settlement and culture

At least as early as the eleventh century BCE, Phoenician navigators from Tyre and Sidon had reconnoitered the African and Iberian coasts. The costly silver and ivory objects recovered from the great tombs of Etruria were actually imported from Phoenicia. Additionally, objects manufactured in Italy follow on Phoenician models and ranges of images borrowed from the Middle East. These artifacts reveal clearly an eastern influence on Etruscan civilization in the eighth–seventh centuries. And the presence of Phoenician traders is attested not only in Sicily, Sardinia, and Malta, but in the eighth–seventh centuries in Rome itself, where a colony of Tyrians was able to settle in the area of the Forum Boarium. The founding of the Ara Maxima Herculis, the earliest altar to Hercules in Italy,

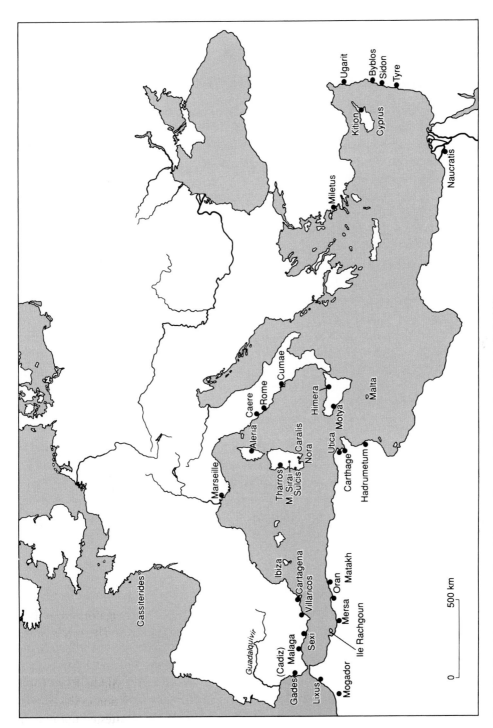

Map 1.2 Phoenician expansion (from J. Heurgon, *Rome et la Méditerranée occidentale*, PUF, 1980)

has been linked with the presence of Tyrian merchants and the worship of the Tyrian Baal-Melqart.

The Greeks in Italy and Sicily

The Greek colonization in the West is better known than that of the Phoenicians. Greek migrations, mainly in southern Italy and Sicily, are confirmed by both writings and archaeological findings. The Greek influence on the people of the Italian peninsula constituted one of the major events in the history of the Mediterranean in the first millennium BCE.

As in the Aegean and on the borders of the Black Sea, Greek colonization began in the Tyrrhenian Sea during the eighth century. Cumae appears to have been both the northernmost and the oldest of the Greek colonial foundations in Italy (c.770), followed by Ischia (c.740; see the so-called "Nestor's cup" from Pithecusae). Other settlements, first of Chalcidian origin, next Megarean, Corinthian, Achaean, and Lacedaemonian, and then Rhodian, Cretan, and Ionian (from Asia Minor), were established, on the one side between Cumae and Rhegium (Reggio di Calabria), and on the other (the instep of the "boot") as far as Tarentum and beyond, as well as along the whole perimeter of Sicily (which the Greeks called *Trinacria*, "triangular"). The density of settlement was such that, in the second century BCE, the Greek historian Polybius used the name *Megale Hellas* (Great Greece) to define the Hellenized south of Italy, which was translated into Latin as *Magna Graecia*. In fact, the name must go back to the sixth century.

In Sicily

After Cumae, the Chalcidians founded Naxos, Leontini, and Catana, and then, in order to dominate the Sicilian straits, they founded Zancle and (on the mainland) Rhegium; the Megareans established their settlements at Megara Hyblaea (c.750) and later at Selinus (c.650); the Corinthians installed themselves at Syracuse (c.733); and the Rhodians and Cretans at Gela and Acragas (Agrigentum).

In southern Italy

It was mainly the Achaeans, the Laconians, and the Locrians who settled at Sybaris (c.750), Croton, Metapontum, Siris, Tarentum (c.706), and Locri (c.673). The indigenous populations, who in some places simply coexisted and in others actively cooperated with the Greek settlers, were all more or less affected and acculturated by them, even as they in turn influenced the newcomers with their own practices. Archaeologists and historians study this interaction between the two cultures through monuments, sculptures, paintings, and especially pottery, emphasizing the degree of the work's "native" characteristics and its imitation of Greek models.

The Greek influence spread through the coastal areas to the hinterland, where the Chalcidians, for instance, must have introduced the culture of the olive tree

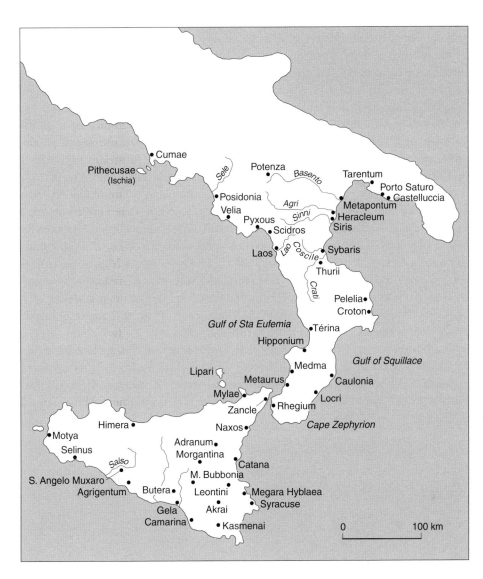

Map 1.3 Greek colonization (from J. Heurgon, *Rome et la Méditerranée occidentale*, PUF, 1980)

into central Italy. Eventually it touched Rome, and various traditional tales reflect a Roman tendency to parallel, and emulate, Greek history. For example, the traditional date of Rome's founding (754/753 BCE) roughly coincides with the date given for the settlement of the Achaeans in Sybaris (750). Similarly, the chronology for the expulsion of the last Etruscan king from Rome (509 BCE) coincides with the fall of Sybaris, the wealthiest city in Magna Graecia, and the victory of Harmodius and Aristogeiton over the Pisistratid tyrants of Athens.

These symbolic connections suggest clearly an interaction between the Romans and the Greeks of Magna Graecia, Sicily, and even the Greek mainland, as early as the seventh century. Proto-Corinthian and then Corinthian pottery found on the Palatine, and in the Forum in particular, prove these strong ties. The Greeks, like the Etruscans, had a profound influence on budding Roman culture, on its law, institutions, art, and religion. The discovery at Lavinium of a dedication to the Dioscuri, in Greek, demonstrates that Tarentum or Locri (centers of the worship of Castor and Pollux) had contacts in Latium, very close to Rome, already at the end of the sixth century or beginning of the fifth. The philosopher and mathematician Pythagoras stands out for his enduring spiritual influence. He emigrated from Samos to Croton in about 530 and died at Metapontum. He was regarded by Herodotus as the wisest and most learned of men, and his doctrine inspired the model government of Archytas at Tarentum (428–347 BCE), who aimed to follow the Platonic doctrine of a "philosopher in power." Pythagoras' influence quickly spread throughout Italy and thus to Rome. His popularity is suggested by the fact that Numa Pompilius, the second king of Rome, was said to have been Pythagoras' disciple, despite the chronological impossibility (discussed by Plutarch in his *Life of Numa*). At all events, Pythagoreanism, and later neo-Pythagoreanism, left their mark on Roman thinking.

In addition to art, Roman literature also owes much to that of Greece, either by direct contact or through the channel of Magna Graecia: the first epic and tragic poets came from Tarentum and Apulia (Livius Andronicus, Ennius, Pacuvius) or from Capua (Naevius); and Roman comedy was invented by Epicharmus, a Sicilian.

Rome was thus born in an Italy whose peoples had complex origins, and amid populations that were very mixed, but dominated by two advanced civilizations, Etruscan and Greek.

2

THE FORMATION
OF ROME

From Romulus to the Tarquins

It is still difficult to say anything certain about the origins of Rome, which are clouded in legend. Information reported in the literary sources about the period before the sixth century comprises of legends and traditions broadly reflecting historical events and developments. Against this fictionalized and literary background, the archaeological record provides some chronological landmarks. New discoveries in the Forum and on the Palatine suggest that the literary tradition about early Rome may be more credible than is sometimes supposed, especially for the period after about 600 BCE.

2.1 | Latin and Sabine Kings

The legends recounted by early Greek and Latin authors about events that alleg-edly occurred in the area of Rome before the formal founding of the city (placed by tradition in 754/753 BCE) are essential in understanding how Romans con-structed their national identity and past. Greek authors write of an Arcadian, Evander, who about 60 years before the Trojan War settled on the left bank of the Tiber. There he was welcomed by Faunus, king of the aborigines, he installed himself on the Palatine and subsequently received Herakles (Hercules) on the Forum Boarium. A central foundation hero is Aeneas, who, after the fall of Troy (variously dated 1193 and 1184 BCE), also took refuge in Latium. Latin authors, notably Fabius Pictor, the first Roman annalist (c.200), tell the story of Romulus and Remus, the twins reared by a she-wolf, who founded the city on a hill. These legends were gradually interwoven, embellished, and later given a comprehensive literary setting by Livy in his monumental *History of Rome* and by Virgil in his epic *Aeneid*. Aeneas and Romulus are the most important foundation heroes in these various myths and narratives.

According to the legends, Aeneas, son of Anchises and Venus, founded Lavin-ium. His son was Ascanius, whom the Romans called Iulus to consecrate him as the ancestor of the Julii (the family of Julius Caesar and the first Roman emperor, Augustus). Iulus Ascanius founded Alba Longa, the head of a confederation of villages in Latium known as the Latin League. Romulus, his descendant (some regard him as the grandson of Aeneas), founded Rome. He and his brother Remus, twin sons of the god Mars and Rhea Silvia, an Alban Vestal, came from Alba to the banks of the Tiber, and founded the city between 754 and 748, on April 21, the date held to be its day of birth (*dies natalis*).

Archaeology provides a more concrete approach, with results that sometimes confirm this legendary backdrop. In 1907 the foundations of huts were discov-ered on the Palatine, near the spot where Romans preserved the memory of Romulus' house (*casa Romuli*). These indicated that the huts were rectangular in plan, with rounded corners, and measured about 4.8 by 3.4 m. The bases were hollowed out of the tuff of the hillside to between 0.4 and 0.5 m in depth. Holes dug around the perimeter marked the spots where the posts supporting the roof had been sunk. The walls would have been made of reeds coated with clay. Outside, a channel collected water and drained it away. In the middle was a larger hole, for the central supporting post, around which there are often traces of the hearth. Lastly, on one side, usually to the south, the door cavity survives. Now, in eighth–seventh-century tombs excavated near the Forum, terra-cotta hut-urns serving as ossuaries have been found whose shape corresponds to the general aspect attributed to these "Romulean" dwellings. Furthermore, pottery picked up from the bases of the huts is dated by specialists to as early as the middle of the eighth century, that is, the traditional foundation date of Rome. It disappears around 575 BCE, with the primitive hut replaced by the different architecture of

Plate 2.1 She-wolf with Romulus and Remus. The original figures of the twins were destroyed in the late Republic; new ones were added during the Renaissance. C. M. Dixon

Plate 2.2 Ceramic hut-shaped urn. This type of cinerary urn is one of the most typical ossuaries of Etruria and Latium in the ninth to eighth centuries BCE. The shape, which represents the home of the deceased, provides us with a model for the domestic architecture of the ancient huts in Rome. Museo Gregorimo Etrusco: inv 15396. Vatican Museums Photo

the Etruscan era, a more permanent and larger construction. It can now be said with some degree of confidence that the huts date probably to the first half of the eighth century.

Other hut bases were discovered in another part of the Palatine, under the imperial palace of the Flavians (end of the first century CE). These apparently belonged to another village, since there was a tomb between the two sites marking the boundaries between the living and the dead. Others were sited at the location of the future Forum. In 1988 another small nucleus of dwellings was found. And it now appears that the early settlement on the Palatine was protected by an enclosing wall, constructed probably in the eighth century, and thus had a real organization of the kind usually attributed only to the era of the Etruscan kings.

Very little burial evidence survives from the tenth and ninth centuries in Rome, largely because of later building. Elsewhere in Latium, at the same period, burials often included prestige goods, an indication perhaps that an elite class had begun to emerge, one that was wealthy enough to import metals. Burial sites in Rome from the eighth and seventh centuries are generally few, probably more because of destruction of the material record than because of any significant cultural or social change. Of the 41 eighth–seventh-century tombs excavated early in the twentieth century on the site of the Forum, some took the form of circular pits containing cinerary urns, the others rectangular trenches for body burials, the latter dating to the seventh century. The burial ground ceased to be used at the beginning of the sixth century, a date that obviously marks an important moment in the development of Rome. A number of seventh-century female graves have been identified in other parts of Latium, many of which contained spinning equipment.

Other tombs were found on the Quirinal and Esquiline hills. The material contained in them, much like that recovered in eighth- and seventh-century graves in other parts of Latium, included weapons, helmets, shields, and even a battle chariot, and shows that here we are dealing with a different people, a race of warriors who buried their dead, and against whom the inhabitants of the Palatine and the Velia must have had to protect themselves with outer defensive walls.

Among these inhabited areas, one on the Palatine and its slopes stands out. Dominating the valley of the future Forum on one side, and on the other the corridor separating the hill from the Tiber, where the livestock market was later established (Forum Boarium), its topography played a vital historical role:

> It is not without good reason that gods and men chose this place to build our city: these hills with their pure air; this river which brings us produce from the interior and allows sea convoys to come upstream; a sea handy to our needs, but far enough away to guard us from foreign fleets; our situation in the very center of Italy. All these advantages shape this most favored of sites into a city destined for glory. (Livy, 5.54)

Livy emphasizes the strategic importance of the Tiber and of the hills located nearby. The river valley facilitated movement and trade (especially in salt) up into the Apennines. The Palatine hill was small enough to be defended easily, but large enough to accommodate a growing settlement. The Capitoline hill was easily defended, too, and thus it was made into a kind of citadel during the time of the kings. Livy elsewhere mentions the Tiber Island (Insula Tiberina). This tiny island provided the lowest fording-point above the mouth of the river for shepherds and their flocks. In the event of danger, they could take refuge in the nearby hills, especially the Palatine, setting up their dwellings and raising their defenses. The island also provided an overland line of communication and trade between Etruria and Latium, but this route was not fully exploited until the sixth century. The site was located, too, in a kind of cultural frontier zone, between the Etruscans, Faliscans, and Latins. Additionally, the local geology provided stone (mainly soft tufas) suitable for building, as well as volcanic sands for making mortar.

The historical events on the Palatine and the other hills of Rome in the middle of the eighth century are shrouded in legend. It seems very likely that the Palatine was indeed the cradle of Rome. Some said that Romulus was the son of Aeneas, or the son of Latinus, king of Latium, and a Trojan woman called Roma. Others claimed that he was the offspring of the god Mars and a daughter of Aeneas, Lavinia. He was also said to be the grandson of a king of Alba. Plutarch, who recounts all these legends in his *Life of Romulus*, compares them with those surrounding Theseus, the hero who founded Athens. However, while Theseus is portrayed as a hero who brought about the federation of the inhabitants of Attica around one city, which became Athens, Romulus is rather different. Unlike Theseus, who is an independent mythological figure surrounded by other legends unrelated to the foundation of Athens, Romulus is only associated with the foundation of Rome. Romulus was probably born of a later identification of the god Quirinus (as a deified Romulus) and of the Roman need for a city-founder in the Greek style. It is possible that Romulus was simply a leader of bands of migrants, perhaps from Latium, living on stockbreeding and brigandage. Rome's *dies natalis*, April 21, was also, it may be noted, the feast of Pales, the patron deity of flocks, when the *Parilia* or *Palilia* was celebrated. Her name derives from the same root as the Palatine's.

Equally legendary is the list of the seven kings of royal Rome: this number was first proposed by Fabius Pictor, who claimed that the royal period lasted 245 years, or seven generations of 35 years. Inspired by the legends, a pattern was elaborated which stressed dualism as an important element in Roman thought:

- the twins, Romulus and Remus, the chosen one and the outcast;
- the association of Romulus, the Latin, and Titus Tatius, king of the Sabines, whose agreement sealed the amity of the two peoples;
- the succession of Romulus by Numa Pompilius, i.e. the political founder followed by the religious founder (Numa was regarded as the inventor of the Roman religion).

This dualism was presented as foreshadowing the republican consular rule of two men (diarchy), the patrician–plebeian division, and the duality of certain sacerdotal colleges. The alternation of Latin and Sabine kings in the first four kings of Rome, intended to preserve the joint rule of Romulus and Titus Tatius, also seems to support the Roman emphasis on dualistic patterns.

The great Indo-European historian and linguist Georges Dumézil (1898–1986) attempted to explain Rome's earliest times through his "theory of the three functions." In his view, the history of the earlier Roman kings is pure myth. The legends of early Rome simply reflect a tripartite division common to all the political, social, and religious systems of the Indo-European peoples. Three hierarchized bodies represented and secured three basic societal functions: religious sovereignty, military power, and productive force. From that came a society composed of those who held politico-religious power (kings, magistrates, priests), and their god Jupiter, god of sovereignty; those who ensured military protection, with Mars, god of war; and those with the ability to produce (farmers, shepherds, craftsmen), with Quirinus as their patron god. From that very ancient state of affairs there survived in Rome the college of the three major *flamines* (priests of a single god): of Jupiter, Mars, and Quirinus. As for the kings, they expressed first the doubling of political and religious sovereignty (Romulus and Numa respectively), then warrior power (Tullus Hostilius), and lastly economic prosperity and social concerns (Ancus Marcius).

Among all these suggestions and speculations, what can be regarded as certain?

1 First, foundation legends were formed gradually, built up on elements of Italic folklore, with influence from Greek historiography and etiological explanations. These produced a kind of Vulgate of the origins of Rome, with divergent and overlapping versions. In 296, the fable of the twins suckled by the she-wolf was already established, as indicated by the dating of a bronze group featuring this scene.

2 Next, the traditional date of the *Parilia*, April 21, 754/753 BCE, is merely a symbolical moment. Rome was founded through the long and complex processes of migration, urbanization, and inhabitation: the erection of huts, clustering in groups of villages around the Palatine, the building of a wall protecting the villages of the seven original hills (Palatium, Velia, Fagutal, Germal, Oppius, Caelius, and Cispius), embracing the Palatine, Esquiline, Velia, and Caelian, but not the Capitol, Quirinal, or Viminal. Remains of walls discovered at the foot of the Palatine could date back to this era in the seventh century, or possibly even to the eighth.

3 Lastly, the way of life of the earliest historic occupants of the site of Rome was essentially pastoral: a civilization of shepherds who followed the totemic cult of the wolf and the ancient rite of the *Lupercalia*.

The great moment in the history of Rome's earliest times occurred when it came under the rule of the Etruscans in the sixth century, for that was the origin of its birth as a town.

flamines: College of 15 priests attached to the worship of a divinity: 3 major *flamines* (Jupiter, Mars, and Quirinus) and 12 minor. In Italy and provincial towns, the *flamines* administered the imperial cult.

lupercalia: February 15, when animals were sacrificed in the Lupercal (the cave where the she-wolf was supposed to have suckled Romulus and Remus); the festival combined fertility and purificatory rituals, and included flagellation. The Luperci or priests of Lupercus were a fraternity of 12 (later 24) priests attached to the worship of Faunus.

Figure 2.1   Rome at the end of the royal era

2.2 | Etruscan Rome

The birth of Rome as both town and organized state was linked with Etruscan settlement in southern central Italy and the accession in Rome of a dynasty from Etruria. Writing in the first century BCE, the historian Sallust remarked on this change when he bluntly contrasted the Latino-Sabine royal epoch with that of the foreign "arrogant tyranny" that followed (*The Conspiracy of Catiline* 6).

The birth of the town

As we saw, the Etruscans had developed an urban civilization. They had even organized their 12 peoples of Etruria around a federal center, Volsinii, a wealthy and powerful town. As early as the sixth century, their imperialism led some of them to the banks of the Tiber, their presence attested at the foot of the Palatine in the *vicus Tuscus* (Etruscan quarter). The beginnings of the new dynasty also date back to the sixth century, when the population of Rome may have reached 20,000–30,000. According to tradition, it was forged by the king Tarquin the Elder and continued by Servius Tullius and Tarquin the Proud. Despite ambiguities surrounding the exact names and chronology of these kings (especially for the final phase of their dominion), archaeology confirms a strong Etruscan presence in Rome. Numerous *bucchero* vases, found in houses and burial sites, suggest steady commercial relations with Etruria. Inscriptions in Etruscan accompanying various articles prove that the shepherds' villages of the nascent Rome opened up to new activities, in both craftsmanship and trade. New social formations developed alongside the old aristocracy of the **quirites**. The rapid development of this led to the classification of Rome into five classes according to wealth, credited traditionally to the sixth king of Rome, Servius Tullius. Both legend and archaeological evidence from Rome indicate the military activity of Etruscan mercenaries originally from Vulci, Tarquinii, and Veii.

quirites:
Denomination of the Roman people, i.e. members of the civilian body: as opposed to *milites*, which designated citizens under arms.

The main contribution of Etruscan domination of Rome, however, was the development of urban technology: the real foundation of Rome as a city can properly be dated to the sixth century and two major public projects:

Plate 2.3 Cloaca Maxima, at its outlet to the Tiber. Most of what survives dates to the time of Augustus. C. M. Dixon

1   The drainage of marshy areas is one of the most original features of Etruscan activity. Canals were dug in the lower Po valley, the Tuscan Maremma, and doubtless even in the Pontine marshes (Pliny the Elder, *Natural History* 3.120). In Rome itself, the damp valley of the Forum was dried out; one, and possibly two, attempts were made to pave it. Especially spectacular was the construction of the Cloaca Maxima, the huge drain that emptied into the Tiber downstream from the Pons Aemilianus (the present-day Ponte Rotto). Pliny the Elder writes "It is said that Tarquin made the tunnel large enough to allow the passage of a wagon loaded with hay" (*Natural History* 36.108). A boom in agriculture followed in Latium and Campania, bringing about profound changes in rural life, such as the creation of large estates.

2   The introduction of new masonry techniques resulted in vast works of urban development. A preoccupation with urban defense (shared by the towns in Etruria as well as Greek cities) is obvious in the construction of an enclosing wall. Two successive walls were built: their traces are still visible in Rome. The first, dating from the sixth century, was built in blocks of well-shaped and regularly laid sedimentary tuff from the Roman countryside. This original wall partly collapsed, either by rapid disintegration or during the seizure of Rome by the Gauls in 390. At all events, it was rebuilt in certain places, and in others repaired with less-well-cut blocks of tuff known as *grotta oscura*, from the territory of Veii (which was conquered by Rome in 396). According to Livy, this new wall dated from 378. It must therefore have been erected following the sack of Rome.

When the damp valley of the area of the Forum had been dried out, the site was floored with flagstones. The archaic huts and cemeteries were replaced by a public square, signaling the center of a city-state (parallel to the *agora* of Greek cities).

In the sixth century, at the same time as rich votive deposits of statuettes, tiny altars of Etruscan origin, and high-quality Greek vases, new temples also appeared. These places of worship, with their polychrome terra-cotta ornamentation, helped to give Rome an air of urban splendor. Among them was a temple dedicated, according to tradition, to the goddess Fortuna by Servius Tullius, who was especially attached to this cult. At the end of Etruscan domination, the construction of religious buildings increased: in 509 the temple of Jupiter Capitolinus, in 497 the temple of Saturn, north of the Forum, in 496–493 the temple of Ceres, and in 495 the temple of Mercury. It is an indication that the elite was increasingly willing, and perhaps eager, to spend its wealth conspicuously on the development of monumental public architecture.

All these material transformations were, of course, linked with profound political, social, and spiritual changes – in short, with the birth of a state.

Formation of the state

The true foundation of a city (*urbs*: the very word seems to be Etruscan in origin) lies in its urbanization, that is, in the organization of a state, with its administrative framework and its social and political institutions.

The essence of that achievement in Rome is attributed to the Servian reforms, of which Livy (1.43) and Dionysius of Halicarnassus (4.16) have left a very exact picture, so that of the three Etruscan kings Servius Tullius is the best known. According to some, he was a foreigner, a former slave (*servus*), who had become the son-in-law of Tarquin thanks to the latter's wife Tanaquil, a capable woman who subsequently facilitated his rise to power. According to others, notably the Etruscologist emperor Claudius, he was a mercenary, perhaps Etruscan, named Mastarna (= dictator), a friend of the princes of Vulci, and gained mastery of Rome after eliminating the faction of the Tarquins. At all events, it was he who was credited with the organization of Rome into a state.

Administrative framework

Increased and modified by the arrival of the Etruscans, the *populus* in Rome had been divided into tribes and **curiae**, based primarily on ethnic origin. The three ancient tribes were the *Ramnes* (Latins, or, in Dumézil's view, those who enjoyed political and religious primacy), the *Tities* (Sabines, or farmers), and the *Luceres* (Etruscans or warriors). The new Servian constitution created tribes on a territorial basis. There were four urban tribes, corresponding to the four areas of Rome (the *Palatina*, *Esquilina*, *Collina*, and *Suburana*), and some 10 rural tribes for its territory, the *ager Romanus*. The number of these rural tribes naturally increased with every Roman conquest, so that by the middle of the third century there were 31 rural tribes. From the time of the Servian reforms, all citizens were compulsorily attached to a tribe by tribal area, where, according to Dionysius of Halicarnassus (4.14), they had to be domiciled and pay their taxes. Because of this, the curial system vanished and a new social classification appeared.

curia: A voting group in the *comitia curiata*. Also, the customary meeting place of the Senate in the Forum. There was also a *curia* in Pompey's theater on the Campus Martius. In the colonies and townships in the provinces, the meeting place of the municipal council, generally in the open on the Forum.

The Servian social organization

According to the clan or **gens** system, each of the three tribes was divided into 10 *curiae*. There were thus 30 *curiae*, bearing specific names. This number-based system is known from the works of the polymath Varro, and its details cannot be ascertained without a doubt. Certainly however, the Servian reforms, which aimed to integrate newcomers into the social structure, replaced the old curial organization. The new system was based on residence and wealth, and involved a *census*, a registration of all free persons living in Roman territory, and of their property. In this social classification the distribution of political rights was based on wealth. A distinction was made between five classes of citizens: the first

gens (pl. gentes): A Roman clan or group of families linked by a common name and by a belief in a common ancestor.

comprised those who possessed capital of at least 100,000 *asses* (an *as* was originally a pound weight in uncoined copper, but was gradually reduced in weight); the second, capital of 75,000; the third 50,000; the fourth 25,000; and the fifth 11,000. This assessment in *asses* does not in fact correspond with the economic data of the period, when wealth was measured in, roughly, acres of land (*jugera*) and head of livestock (*pecunia*, from *pecus* = flock; later the word came to mean money). It would not have been established on these monetary bases until the second century BCE.

So the *census* system, recalling Cleisthenes' tribal reform in Athens (the abolition of four ancient tribes and establishment of 10 new ones), became the dominant form of demographic classification. Politically, it found expression in the centuriate assembly (***comitia centuriata***), to which we shall return. It also defined the new military organization.

comitia centuriata: Assembly of the people, gathered for the election of senior magistrates, voting on laws and justice. Voting was by centuria, according to classes established on the basis of their wealth at the time of the census.

Servian military organization

Livy (1.42) carefully noted the parallel between civilian and military rights and duties. Each of the five classes of citizens was divided into *centuriae* (groups of 100 men), half of whom had to serve in the regular army (the *juniores* aged between 17 and 45) and the other half in the reserves (the *seniores*, aged between 46 and 60), all equipped and fed at their own expense. This division had two consequences: those whose *census* was lower than 11,000 *asses* (these were the *capite censi*, literally "counted by head") were largely exempt from military service. Orphans, slaves, freed slaves, and citizens who had been stripped of their civic rights were also exempt. Military service (*militia*) was both a duty and a right of the classified citizen who retained his civic rights. On the other hand, military rights and duties in this civic army varied according to class, that is, according to financial status:

- From the first class, 18 *centuriae* of horsemen (*equites*) and 80 *centuriae* of foot soldiers (*pedites*) were recruited, armed at their own expense with offensive and defensive weapons.
- From the three following classes came 20 *centuriae* apiece of more lightly armed foot soldiers, two *centuriae* of engineers, and two of musicians. The fifth class provided 30 *centuriae* of men armed with slings.
- There was also a single, non-combatant *centuria* of those who did not possess any property but registered only their persons in the *census* (they were *capite censi*).

There were thus 193 *centuriae* in total, in which the first class occupied a pre-eminent position. This privileged status of the first class was also reflected in the political organization.

Box 2.1 Servian military organization

Class	Census	Centuriae	Juniores	Seniores	
1	100,000	equites	12	6	18
		pedites	40	40	80
2	75,000		10	10	20
3	50,000		10	10	20
4	25,000		10	10	20
5	11,000		15	15	30
				Engineers	2
				Musicians	2
				Capite censi	1

Political organization

As the *centuria* was both a military and a voting unit, it is obvious that the first class, with its 98 *centuriae*, held an absolute majority in centuriate assemblies. The *comitia centuriata* were thus dominated by the wealthier citizens. Many of these belonged to the **patrician** order, a kind of hereditary nobility, which reserved for itself the great priestly offices and extensive land ownership. It kept the army supplied with officers and was surrounded by followers and dependants (*clientes*, or "clients"), whom their **patron** protected in return for a pledge of loyalty (*fides*) and support in his political aspirations. For example, when the *gens* of the Claudii left its original, Sabine territory to settle in Roman territory, it is said to have come with some 5,000 clients. Under the kings, the centuriate assembly, even the first class, was not independent. The assembly gathered fully armed at the sound of the trumpet to support royal plans for the state, war, and the distribution of booty.

Even though restricted, the power to make such decisions belonged to the combatant section of the citizens. This emphasis on the military aspect of political life in the royal era is strongly characteristic of the period of Etruscan domination, especially toward the end, under the last king, Lucius Tarquinius Superbus. According to ancient sources, Tarquin achieved power by means of a violent usurpation.

The end of Etruscan domination

Tarquin's seizing power by force against the will of the *patres*, and his relying on the support of the people, had already assimilated him to Greek "tyrants." By denying burial to Servius Tullius, notes Livy, he committed the grave offence of sacrilege. His subsequent behavior further accentuated parallels with such tyrants.

patrician: Originally a member of the *de facto* nobility providing senators (*patres*), then a member of the nobility by birth, for whom access to certain priesthoods and the consulate was initially reserved. The republican patriciate was defined and formed in the fifth century BCE.

patron: Important personage with whom, by a bilateral commitment, individuals (*clientes*) or public collectives (cities, peoples, provinces) were linked. The patron ensured the daily security and legal defense of his clients, who in return owed him respect, help, and their votes. He acted as intermediary between the state and the public collectives to whom he was patron.

Ancient authors drew the parallels, especially since Tarquin was considered contemporary with the Pisistratid tyrants of Athens. Dionysius of Halicarnassus (4.41) in particular denounced three of his tyrannical actions:

1 his creation of a personal armed guard composed of Romans and foreigners, "ensuring his constant security against any traps that might be set for him";
2 his hostility to the aristocracy and withdrawal into himself, his contempt for (or fear of) the public, his way of dealing with matters of state on his own or with a few private advisers, for whom his favors were reserved;
3 his ambition to form personal bonds with other families, even among those foreign to the town; his concern to increase the town's appearance by a policy of great public works, which also brought him the support of the needy lower classes.

According to ancient sources, the rape of the noble matron Lucretia by Tarquin's son, Sextus Tarquinius, pushed the aristocracy's hostility too far. Their opposition brought about the revolution led by Lucius Junius Brutus. Brutus was traditionally considered the hero who, in the words of the historian Tacitus (*Annals* 1.1), "established liberty and the consulate." The deposed Tarquin appealed for help to Lars Porsenna, the Etruscan king of Clusium, probably in 509–508, but Porsenna's intervention was unsuccessful. Fleeing to Tusculum, Tarquin finally died in Cumae in 495. The foundation of the Republic is of uncertain date, perhaps 504, or as late as 480–475.

The story of Lucretia's rape provides us with a legendary backdrop and a symbolic etiology for actual historical events. The expulsion of the Tarquins must have been caused by much more than the actions of Brutus, who might or might not be a fabricated character. Tarquin's departure was the result of the decline of Etruscan power, the awakening of the Italic peoples, internal movements in the colonies of Magna Graecia (e.g. the destruction of Sybaris, a Greek colony in the golf of Tarentum), and the result of a rising of the aristocracy (patriciate) of Rome against foreign domination.

Cicero and Tacitus claim that the expulsion of the kings brought the Republic, which was synonymous with liberty. Authors emphasize the last phase of the royal epoch, particularly the tyrannical nature and foreign origin of the last king. In the first century BCE, the profound horror of royalty still fed republican rhetoric and proved fundamental in the assassination of Julius Caesar. As we shall see, Caesar's adopted son Octavian (Augustus), who became the first emperor of Rome, took particular pains in order not to appear royal in his presentation or actions.

Conclusion: Rome and the Etruscans

The influence of the Etruscans on the development of early Rome appears to consist mainly of three things: a relatively short-lived period, corresponding more or less to the sixth century, when Etruscan aristocrats exercised political power at Rome; a more lasting change in religious practices and institutions; and a transformation of sorts in material culture, marked by the widespread use of certain kinds of Etruscan-made goods, like *bucchero* pottery, a development that in turn may have contributed to the emergence of a merchant and artisanal class in Rome.

2.3 | The Religion of Archaic Rome

This is a difficult and disputed area. Since our literary sources come from a much later date, the historian has to tread carefully among moralizing evocations of a distant past, and the works of systematizing theologians and inventive mythographers. For example, the Chant of the **Salii** (priests of Mars), a kind of rhythmic litany recited by the brotherhood of the 12 Salii during the ceremonies of the cult of Mars, is known only through fragments quoted by Horace, Quintilian, and Varro; but it seems to have been an old ritual in archaic language that the priests themselves no longer understood. With rare exceptions, literary texts of religious interest are much later than the ancient epoch. This is the case with the oldest and most important liturgical calendar, that of Antium (modern Anzio), which is datable to the late second or early first century BCE. Nevertheless, it seems to have preserved references to ancient festivals belonging to the pre-Etruscan Italic time, even if their liturgical development took place in the Etruscan era. It is thus a document that reveals something of the religious feelings, beliefs, and rites of the Romans in the seventh–sixth centuries.

> **Salii, Salians:** Fraternity of 12, later 24 priests of Mars and Quirinus. They opened and closed the war cycle of the year: March–October.

Archaeological findings are particularly valuable in reconstructing archaic religion. It is now realized that about the end of the seventh century the earliest huts in the southern part of the area of the Forum were destroyed. They were replaced by an area of beaten earth that was marked by a low, rectangular stone pillar (*cippus*) and thus intended for ritual purposes. A tile-covered edifice was then built there, and was itself replaced around 580 by a larger, decorated construction, identified as the **Regia** (dwelling of the king). Nearby, a contemporary well lay very close to the site of the future temple of Vesta. So we have traces of a place of public worship, replaced by the Regia. This location is associated with a sacred area devoted to Vesta, the goddess of fire, whose worship involved an important role for water. Obviously, the person of the king was closely associated with religion.

> **Regia:** Abode of the king on the Forum, near the temple of Vesta, and then frequently the dwelling of the *pontifex maximus*. Religious center of Rome.

At the other end of the site of the Forum, toward the north-east, a space (called the *Comitium*) was cleared for political and judiciary purposes, and between 625 and 600 a building was constructed (perhaps the first *Curia Hostilia*). Then around 580 came the establishment of a place of worship, probably the Volcanal, the sanctuary of fire (like the temple of Vesta at the southern end of the Forum). A *cippus* discovered in this location contains the word *rex* and ritual instructions. Here again we find signs of public worship and the presence of the king in a religious context.

Lastly, the discovery on the Capitol of a votive deposit datable to the late seventh or early sixth century BCE, and linked therefore with a building other than the later temple of Jupiter, indicates again the existence at this time of places of public worship in or about Rome.

From all this we may gather that even at this very early date public worship was already organized, that it was officiated at several places in the town, and that the king was very much a presence in the sacred domain.

Religion before the Etruscan domination

After the manner of other Mediterranean peoples, the Romans probably believed in the existence of mysterious higher forces inhabiting nature around them. It is likely that the Earth (Tellus, Terra mater), in which they laid their dead and which provided them with the means of life, was regarded as the generator of all life, giving rise to religious practices of a naturalist and earthy nature, enriched no doubt by Indo-European conceptions of the world. A very early calendar that we know of, which includes a distinction between "profane" days (*dies fasti*), dedicated to action, and "sacred" days (*dies nefasti*), reserved for the gods and intended to ensure the effectiveness of the work or war of the days of action, may date back to those distant times.

As in the Aegean basin, the ancient Romans must also have honored various animals, plants, and other natural objects, seeing them as the incarnations of higher forces or simply as divine symbols, without any suggestion of totemism or animal, object, or plant gods. The goat personified the god Faunus, and at the time of the *Lupercalia* (February 15) in honor of this god of fertility, the priests of Lupercus would run round the Palatine, stripped to the waist, their lower parts covered with a goatskin. Jupiter Lapis was incorporated in the flint or the thunderbolt; Jupiter Terminus, in the boundary stone. Sacred woods, such as Furrina on the Janiculum, were devoted to ancient divinities.

The development of this practical, animistic, Earth-oriented religion comprised of many components: first Italic, a mingling of practices from the conquering Indo-European peoples (notably Latins), with borrowings from the subjected indigenous Mediterranean peoples, and additions from those peoples neighboring on Latium (Umbrians, Osci, Volsci, etc.); second Etruscan, even before the sixth-century conquest; and third Greek, either through direct contact or channeled via the Etruscans, who were profoundly Hellenized even in the sixth century.

Italic components

The religion of the pre-Etruscan era was characterized by the coexistence of two religious influences. The first, indigenous and Mediterranean, was dominated by the telluric deities of fertility: chthonic divinities responsible for fertility and fruitfulness, mostly female deities, versions of the Earth Mother, but also male gods. Thus Quirinus appears to have reigned over the traditionally Sabine lower slopes of the towering hill later called the Quirinal. Summanus, god of night lightning, and Terminus, god of boundaries, dominated the Capitol, on whose slopes Veiovis and Saturn, god of fertility, were ensconced. Italy in its entirety was probably consecrated to Saturn, who, according to legend, sought refuge there after he was dethroned by his son Jupiter (authors often refer to Italy as *Saturnia*). Saturn's dethronement has been interpreted as the mythological reflection of the influx of the Indo-European peoples and their gods into Italy. On the basis of literary, ritual, and priestly survivals (notably the pre-eminence of the three *flamines* of Jupiter, Mars, and Quirinus), Georges Dumézil stressed the enthronement of the gods in pre-Etruscan Rome in a divine trinity matching the functional division of society at that time: Jupiter, god of the luminous sky; Mars, fighting god and god of fighters; and Quirinus, god of peace and prosperity, the protector of production.

Etruscan and Greek components

The Etruscans seem to have been responsible for the organization of public worship in Rome itself, once it had become an urban state. This was arranged around the expression of three major concerns: fecundity, victory, and death:

1 The purpose of the earliest rituals was to ensure the fertility of the land, and the fruitfulness of flocks and families. Thus there were the *Parilia* (or *Palilia*) and the *Lupercalia*, in honor, respectively, of Pales and Faunus, pastoral deities; the *Fordicidia*, when 30 in-calf cows were offered to the Earth; and the December *Saturnalia*, which commenced the "cereal crop cycle."
2 Among the warrior rites, in March there were the dances of the Salii, the horse races of the festival of *Equirria*, and the purification ceremonies of the festivals of *Quinquatrus*, for weapons, and *Tubilustrium*, for battle trumpets, while in October the close of activities was marked by fresh purification ceremonies (*Armilustrium*, *Tigillum sororium*, *October equus*).
3 February was devoted to the dead (*Parentalia*, *Feralia*), and was also the month of purifications (*Lupercalia*, *Regifugium*).

Personal religion centered on the worship of domestic deities such as the Lares and the Penates, as well as that of the **Genius** (guardian deity).

Genius: A god's power of creation. Each man also had his protective genius, as each woman had her *Juno*.

As early as the beginning of the sixth century, Roman religion came under Greek influence, though it is difficult to separate Greek and Etruscan elements. From Latium came the cults of Minerva and of the Dioscuri, and from Sicily, the cult of Ceres. Pythagoreanism brought a more spiritual aspect to religious thinking and rites. Therefore, Rome's religion in the sixth–fifth centuries BCE appears to differ considerably (although partly) from that of earlier times.

Roman religion in the sixth and fifth centuries

The pantheon

Capitoline Triad:
Jupiter, Juno, and
Minerva, the triad that
replaced the initial
triad of Jupiter, Mars,
and Quirinus.

inauguration: When
the augurs took the
auspices to consecrate
the investiture of a
magistrate, or the
opening of a temple
or a public place
(= dedication).

Calends: The first
day of the month;
belonged to Janus.

Nones: Day of the
month: the 7th in
March, May, July, and
October; the 5th in
other months.

Ides: Day of the
month: the 15th in
March, May, July, and
October; the 13th in
the other months.

rex sacrorum: First
of the Roman priests,
successor to the kings,
from whom he
inherited religious
authority.

**pontiffs
(pontifices):** College
of six, later nine, and
then 16 priests with
the duty of
administering sacred
and family law,
religious jurisdiction,
and keeping the
Annales.

vestals: College of
six priestesses whose
duty was to watch
over the flame, the
guarantee of Rome's
power.

augurs: College of
priests skilled in
interpreting the flight
of birds, and from
that determining the
will of the gods.

The early trinity of Jupiter, Mars, and Quirinus gave way to that of Jupiter Maximus Optimus, Juno, and Minerva. The cult, first established on the Quirinal, was subsequently transported to the Capitol, which had become Rome's sacred hill, and thus these gods are often referred to as "the **Capitoline Triad**." The first true temple constructed in Rome was on this hill and, according to the ancients, was **inaugurated** in 509. Built in the Etruscan manner, it consisted of a tripartite cella. It featured sacred statues in polychrome terra-cotta, and architectural decoration of terra-cotta plaques embellished with painted reliefs. Jupiter, identified with the Etruscan Tinia by way of the Greek Zeus, is worshiped as the chief of the gods: he pledges abundance (*Ops*), he is supremely good (*Optimus*), supremely great (*Maximus*), and master of the divine and the human world. Juno, already venerated in central Italy as a chthonic goddess, a form of the Earth Mother and likened to the Greek Hera and the Etruscan Uni (wife of Tinia), becomes Juno Regina, with many attributes. However, Juno is primarily the goddess of women and safeguards the bonds of marriage. Minerva, identified with the Etruscan Menrva and Greek Athena, is the goddess of intelligence and spiritual activity, overseeing the arts and craftsmen.

Ritual and the organization of the priesthoods

The ritual of the origins was codified in a calendar. In addition to the standard **Calends** (first day of the month), the **Nones** (5th or 7th), and the **Ides** (13th or 15th), 45 annual festivals were arranged by month, classified in cycles: the war cycle from March to October, the cycle of the dead and purifications in February (the last month of the year), and the agricultural and pastoral cycle (the former more prominent than the latter), from April to December.

The organization of the celebrations and strict observance of their rites were tied to the establishment of the priesthoods (attributed by legend to Numa). The priests – religious officials – were individual or collegial, and were organized in hierarchies. At their head and honored above all the rest came the "king of the sacred" (*rex sacrorum*), the priest of Janus, a patrician appointed for life. Then came the three major *flamines*, the *flamen Dialis* (the priest of Jupiter), the *flamen Martialis* (Mars), and the *flamen Quirinalis* (Quirinus) (survival of an original divine trinity), and the 12 minor *flamines*, again each attached to a particular cult. The great **pontiff** (*pontifex maximus*) was in charge of the college of pontiffs, and later became the chief authority of the Roman religion. There were also two functional colleges: that of the **Vestals** for the worship of Vesta, and that of the **augurs**, who specialized in observing the heavens and interpreting **auspices**. Next came the college of the *epulones*, whose duty was to organize and supervise sacred banquets, and the college of the "men in charge of sacrifices,"

Plate 2.4 Colossal statue of Minerva, Roman goddess of handicrafts. National Archaeological Museum, Rome. C. M. Dixon

auspices: Signs of the divine will, observed by the augurs in a *templum*, a "space marked out" with the help of a curved stick (*lituus*).

epulones: College of seven priests whose duty was to organize the sacred banquets (*epula*); created in 196 BCE.

sodales, sodalities: Colleges of priests, generally attached to the worship of archaic divinities: Arvales, Luperci, Salians.

Arval Brethren: A college of 12 priests, devoted to the worship of Dea Dia, a corn deity.

fetiales: College of 20 diplomat-priests entrusted with international affairs: declarations of war, making of peace and treaties.

haruspices: Of Etruscan origin, college of 60 councilors (later priests) who were specialists in examining the entrails of sacrificial victims, notably the liver and heart.

an important body which helped spread the Greek sacrificial rituals and thus transform religious feeling. In addition there were the *sodales*, fraternities who specialized in preserving archaic rites: the Luperci, the 12 **Arval Brethren** (cult of Dea Dia), the 12 Salii, and the 20 *fetiales*, who imparted a sacred character to declarations of war and peace treaties. The Etruscans introduced the *haruspices*, whose specialty was interpreting lightning and the entrails of sacrificial victims.

New gods and temples

New divinities were introduced into Rome: Minerva, the Dioscuri, and Ceres were followed by Diana, who came from Aricia on Lake Nemi (Diana Nemorensis); Fortuna of Praeneste, similarly revered in Antium and several towns in Latium; Hercules, the personification of the Punic Melqart and the Greek Herakles; Mercury, patron of trade, who represented the Greek Hermes. Under Greco-Etruscan influence, old Italic deities were transformed. Liber Pater, for example, god of fruitfulness, was assimilated to the Etruscan Fufluns and

Box 2.2 Festival calendar: The three principal cycles

The cycle of purifications and the dead

(a) February 15: *Lupercalia*, festival of Faunus, protector god of flocks; purification of the city.
    February 13–21: *Parentalia* and *Feralia*, in honor of the family dead.

(b) March 16–17: Procession of the *Argei*; the Vestals throw wicker effigies into the Tiber (= sacrifice of purification; cf. the Hebrew scapegoat).

(c) May 9–11: *Lemuria*, to appease the *lemures* (= ghosts, phantoms).

The cycle of war

(a) March 1: The Salii bring out the shields of Mars, god of war.
    March 14: *Equirria*, dedication of the cavalry horses to Mars.
    March 17: *Agonium*, sacrifice to Mars.
    March 19: *Quinquatrus*, dedication of weapons to Mars, and festival of Minerva.
    March 23: *Tubilustrium*: dedication of the trumpets to Mars.

(b) October 15: *October equus*, sacrifice of a horse to Mars.
    October 19: *Armilustrium*, purification of weapons. Originally marked the end of campaigns.

The agrarian cycle

(a) March 17: *Liberalia*, festival of Liber and Libera, god and goddess of generative functions. Assumption of the *toga virilis* (toga of manhood).
    April 15: *Fordicidia*, festival of Tellus. Sacrifice of in-calf cows.
    April 19: *Cerialia*, festival of Ceres, who ensures germination.
    April 21: *Parilia/Palilia*, festival of Pales, protective goddess of flocks.
    April 23: *Vinalia*, festival of new wine.
    April 25: *Robigalia*, festival of Robigus, who prevents corn from "rust."
    April 29: *Floralia*, festival of Flora, who brings crops into flower.

(b) August 21: *Consualia*, festival of Consus, god of grain stores.
    August 25: *Opalia*, festival of Ops, goddess of plenty.

(c) December 11: *Agonium*, sacrifice of a victim.
    December 15: *Consualia*, festival of Consus.
    December 17: *Saturnalia*, festival of Saturn, god of fecundity; the Earth at rest is celebrated. Beginning of the liturgical year of the Arval Brethren (cult of Dea Dia, goddess of fecundity).

Thracian Dionysus and thus became Bacchus, god of wine and resurrection. Similarly, Ceres, an expression of the Earth Mother, was assimilated, under the influence of Sicily and Magna Graecia, to Demeter, the goddess of cereal crops and the mysteries.

In this way a "national" religion was born, turning Rome into a sacred city, conscious of its religious superiority and adept at using it to its political advantage.

3

THE YOUNG REPUBLIC

The Fifth and Fourth Centuries BCE

Rome achieved that urban culture and statehood that enabled it to benefit from the influences of Greek civilization, and then to experience its first expansion just when Etruscan power began to decline and rivalries broke out among the Greek colonies. Nevertheless, the history of the two centuries following the expulsion of the Tarquins remains obscure, and only the main events can be ascertained with relative confidence. This is due to the scarcity of literary and archaeological sources, and the vanity of the families (*gentes*) who wanted to rewrite history in order to endow themselves with glorious ancestors.

Despite these difficulties, it is possible to follow the tumultuous birth of the Republic, marked chiefly by the institution of the consulship and the first battles against the peoples of Latium. The period is characterized by internal struggles within the Roman state, as well as by conflicts with its neighbors. Thus, between 450 and 390 Rome was seeking a balance in both areas. This balance was reached by the organization of its political institutions and by the formation of a new body of "nobles." Both processes involved long conflicts and difficulties.

3.1 | The Birth of the Republic and the Struggle of the Orders

Around 296, the pontiffs began to keep and display annual records (*Annales*) with the lists of eponymous magistrates (*Fasti consulares*), in order to establish a reliable dating system. For the preceding period they drew up lists filled with fictional ancestors of the great men of their own era. Thus, the history of the Republic's beginning, recounted somewhat incoherently by Livy, was all the more falsified because certain influential men had their family name figure in it associated with the advent of "liberty" and the first expansion of the town. However, it is possible to observe how the republican system, after several decades of uncertainty, gradually took shape amid social conflict and wars in Latium.

> **Annales:** Annual account of events concerning Rome and Roman life drawn up by the pontiffs and recorded on whitened boards set up in the Regia. Included records of magistrates and events of cult importance.

Thirty years of uncertainty

According to annalistic records, the period 509–474 was rich in important political and military events:

- 509: Departure of Tarquin under pressure from L. Junius Brutus. Livy begins the second book of his *History of Rome* proclaiming, "I shall now retrace the political and military history of a free Rome, under magistrates elected for a year and under laws whose authority exceeds that of men." The Romans saw a close bond between the departure of the Etruscans, the end of royalty, and the advent of the Republic.
- 508: War against Tarquin, who had raised troops at Veii and Tarquinii. Intervention of Porsenna at Tarquin's request. Having taken Rome, Porsenna was subsequently defeated near Aricia by the Latins in alliance with the Cumaeans.
- 501: Threat of the Latin League against Rome, which chose a dictator aided by a master of cavalry (*magister equitum*). In 496, the victory of Rome over the Latins at Lake Regillus near Tusculum (gained allegedly with the miraculous help of the Dioscuri) brought about an alliance between the Latin League and Rome, placing Rome on an equal footing with the Latins. Strengthened by this alliance, the Romans were able to fend off incursions by the Aequi and Volsci.
- Then conflicts in Rome between the **plebeians** and the patricians began, a development or process referred to today as the "struggle of the orders." In 494, the plebeians withdrew to the Sacred Mount to protest against heavy debts and their lack of representation in the republican system. In response, the patricians released some of the plebeians from their debts and conceded some of their power by creating the office of the tribune of the people. At that time (according to a certainly anachronistic view), agrarian laws were

> ***plebs*, plebeians:** Political grouping, which appeared in 494/493 BCE, of all those in Rome, of any class, who opposed the patrician organization of the state. Made up of rich and poor, patrons and clients, native Romans and foreigners (Latins, Sabines, etc.) who had come into the city. At first their sole point in common was their opposition to the privileges of the patricians. Subsequently plebeian *gentes* were formed, in opposition to the patrician *gentes*. At the end of the Republic, the word defined the common people.

adopted for a more equitable distribution of the public land (*ager publicus*) among citizens.

- Rome found itself engaged in difficult wars against its powerful neighbor, Veii. In 476, having defeated the Veians on the Janiculum, Rome took full advantage of its victory. Two years later, in 474, the Etruscans were vanquished at Cumae by the Cumaeans and their Syracusan allies.

Modern critics have attempted to sort out fact from fiction in the annalistic records, including historical concealments, errors, and connivances on the part of the *gentes*. The main and undisputed historical event, however, is the move from a sacred royalty to a regime in which power was exercised, collegially or not, by magistrates appointed for a fixed period of time. This was not, incidentally, a purely Roman occurrence; the replacement of the *rex* by a single, supreme magistrate or by groups of magistrates (praetors or **consuls**) was a phenomenon common to numerous towns in Latium, Etruria, and the Osco-Umbrian territory. After the expulsion of kings from Rome, it appears that power was exercised first by a *praetor maximus*. This man, named M. Horatius, is said to have dedicated the temple of Jupiter Capitolinus in 509. At the time, *praetor* meant magistrate; and *maximus* implies that there were several. In fact, Rome was doing no more than borrowing the Etruscan institution of the *zilath* (= in Latin, *praetores*). Later, probably in 449, following the decemvirate, two consuls were substituted for the praetors: this was a specifically Roman innovation. The consular office, annual and collegial, became the defining institution of the Republic.

consul: Head of state under the Republic; survived under the Empire with reduced powers. The office was annual and collegial: two consuls under the Republic; two ordinary and eponymous consuls plus normally two substitute consuls under the Empire.

External wars

Archaeological discoveries in Latium, at Lanuvium, Satricum (40 km south of Rome), and Falerii (Città Castellana), show that there, as in Etruscan country (Veii, Tarquinii), Etrusco-Greek workshops produced religious statues and architectural ornamental terra-cottas of high quality right up until 480–475. These symptoms of an architectural and religious fever of Etruscan and Greek inspiration prove that the influence in Latium of these two cultures remained predominant in spite of the conflicts.

These conflicts were, of course, connected with questions of frontiers. Rome's territory, the *ager Romanus*, must have extended to around the fifth or sixth *mille* (thousand paces), particularly toward the Alban Hills: each year the festival of the *Ambarvalia* was marked by a sacrifice celebrated in shrines erected at about the fifth *mille* of every Roman road, the most famous of which was in the sacred grove of the Arvales on the Via Campana. North of the Tiber, the Roman territory encompassed the lands dominated by the Romilii and the Fabii families. Toward the Alban Hills, it included the towns of Bovillae and Alba and the lands of the Papirii bordering on Tusculum. Seaward, the infertile ager Solonius extended toward the hinterland of Ardea and Aricia. To the north-east, the territory was contested between the Romans and the Sabines, and protracted wars between the two are a landmark in Roman history of this period. Frontier problems arose with neighboring Latin towns (Ardea, Aricia, and above all Tusculum, which seems to have been pre-eminent at the beginning of the fifth century), as well as the Etruscans in the north-west.

These various conflicts can be summarized in the following wars:

- With the Latins: in 496 the Roman victory at Lake Regillus brought about the conclusion of a treaty of peace and military alliance between Rome and the Latin communities, setting Rome on an equal footing with them (493).
- Against the Volsci, with the help of the Latins, who were joined by the Hernici, a people wedged between the Aequi and the Volsci.
- Against the Sabines, whose incursions had increased. These lasted until 448, and began again 150 years later.

By defending itself staunchly against its powerful neighbors, Rome began to establish its authority in Latium. And it did so in spite of occasionally bitter internal conflicts.

Internal difficulties

Since the expulsion of the Tarquins had been due partly to the action of patrician families hostile to the Etruscan Kings, with the backing of the people, it was commonly thought that the patricians were at first the only ones exercising the office of magistrate, only later yielding their prerogatives to the plebeians. Recent work has shown that, on the contrary, the plebeians entered history as a political force just after that date. The patriciate, a senatorial nobility formed as early as the seventh century from powerful families who had emerged from the *patres* (forefathers; the word was also used to designate senators), was a socially coherent body, assured by hereditary title of certain monopolies, notably religious. The plebeians, on the other hand, represented an extremely diverse group of all those who did not belong to the elite, in other words those who were neither patricians nor their clients but for the most part small property owners, artisans, and shopkeepers (classes of persons especially numerous in the Aventine quarter, on the banks of the Tiber, the site of the *emporium*, the first port installation). Shortly after the expulsion of the kings from Rome, these plebeians found themselves in difficulties. Bad harvests and even a shortage of food (hence the appeal to agrarian deities in 496–493) added to the increasing problem of debts, contracted by small property owners at extortionate rates; and a slowing down of business occurred, noticeable in the pottery-vessel trade (hence perhaps the appeal to Mercury in 495).

A close and critical scrutiny of the *fasti* reveals the presence of 12 plebeian consuls between the years 509 and 486, including Spurius Cassius, who imposed the alliance of 493 on the Latin League.

tribunes of the plebs: College of 10 magistrates whose task was the protection of the *plebs*; they were inviolable (*sacri*) and had the right of intercession (= veto) over decisions of the magistrates, with the exception of dictators. Starting with Augustus, the emperor held the power of the tribunes (*tribunicia potestas*).

It seems that in fact the period 509–486 was marked by intense political agitation. Notably, there was the withdrawal (*Secessio*) of the plebeians to the Aventine and to the Sacred Mount across the Anio. It was a dangerous secession for the patricians, who were thus deprived of their manual workers, as well as for the state, threatened with the creation of a rival state that might ally itself with Rome's enemies, since many plebeians were of foreign origin. It is supposed to have been followed by the appointment of the first **tribunes of the** *plebs*, two at first, then in 471 four, according to Diodorus, who seems to consider these four to be the earliest.

An examination of the *fasti* also reveals that between 485 and 461 only one plebeian managed to become consul. This suggests a patrician tightening of control over the plebeians, corresponding with the accession to power of the mighty family of the Fabii (then engaged in a war against Veii).

These internal struggles and conflicts among the patricians and the plebeians, combined with pressure from external wars, led to the appointment of the decemvirate in the middle of the fifth century BCE.

3.2 | The Decemvirs and their Task

decemviri, decemvirs: Legislators who replaced the consuls in 451 and 450 BCE; the compilers of the Law of the Twelve Tables.

The creation of the **decemvirate** marked a decisive moment in the history of Roman institutions and civilization. In order to obtain a written code of law and a status that together would put an end to the arbitrary nature of the consular power and of the privileges of the patricians, the plebeians engaged in a long struggle. According to tradition, they organized their own people's assembly based on the territorial tribes (four for the town and 21 for the rural areas). These meetings of the plebs (*concilia plebis*), called together by the tribunes, began to make decisions. Again according to tradition, in 462 a tribune, Terentilius Harsa, led a campaign to obtain "written laws establishing the ***imperium***," in other words, the limits of consular power. In the end, the patricians yielded.

imperium: Sovereign civil and military power; under the Republic was held by dictators, consuls, and praetors. Under the Empire, only the emperor could hold it; he could delegate it.

The college of decemvirs

In 451 and 450, the consular *fasti* interrupt their regular listings and note the advent of a college of 10 extraordinary magistrates, elected, invested with consular authority, and charged with the task of "making laws so that liberty shall be equal for all, from the highest to the lowest" (Livy 3.31, 3.34). The tribunes of the *plebs* stepped down together with the consuls to allow the decemvirs to perform their task. The decemvirs thus obtained full powers to draw up a legal code. As they had not completed their task at the end of their annual term, a second decemvirate was elected in May 450 and included plebeians. The integrity of the first group of men was matched by the abuses of the second. In 449, they tried to make their power permanent. Against them, the *plebs* had to resort to a new secession to the Aventine, and a revolution drove them out of office.

The work of the decemvirs, now recognized as genuine, was of exceptional importance. Ten tables of law were drawn up in 451; two more in 450. According to Livy (5.34), they contained "the source of all private and public law." Legal experts consider that in the twelve tables, Rome developed its most important legislative monument before the compilations of Justinian.

Before the laws were drawn up, it seems that embassies were sent to Greece for consultation and advice. It is extremely probable that the laws were inspired not only by Solon's Athenian legislation, but also by that of the lawgivers Zaleucus of Locri and Charondas of Thurii, two towns in Magna Graecia. The laws were exhibited in the Forum on 12 bronze tables, and memorized by all young Romans – that was still so in Cicero's time, in the first century BCE. They are known only through mutilated fragments, which, however, allow an appreciation of the whole.

A legal code

The task of the legislators was to ensure that the law would be equal for all citizens. As indicated by their title (*decemviri legibus scribundis*), it was also a matter of replacing the "oral law" of traditional practices by specific written laws. Henceforward were established:

- The personal rights of citizens. Property ownership and the family were recognized as fundamentals of the social order. A distinction was established between *proprietas* (ownership, property) and *possessio* (exclusive use or enjoyment). The law dictated that, after certain customary time limits, *possessio* could become *proprietas*. The law governing the acquisition of property varied according to whether rural land and livestock were involved (*res mancipi*) or other forms of wealth. In the first case there had to be a special verbal contract (*mancipatio*) performed in the presence of witnesses. The focus of the laws on matters of agricultural property and rights reveals the essentially rural character of Roman society and economy.

  The laws also defined major crimes: theft, attacks on crops, bearing false witness. Guardianship and the order of inheritance were formalized. Within the family, the limits of paternal authority were fixed. The father of the family ruled no longer the extended family (*gens*), but only his own household (wife and children); his power was reduced; and a certain amount of female emancipation was provided for. The father still had the right to sell, repurchase, and resell his child, up to three times; after that the child was emancipated.

- Relations between citizens and the system of justice. State justice was made accessible to all. In any conflict, the injured party had to try to settle matters with the guilty party; if an agreement was impossible, it was permissible to resort to a kind of talionic law (an eye for an eye). The dates, times, and places prescribed for a court appearance had to be announced to the parties involved. And procedural time limits were fixed.

Resort to the death penalty was rendered more difficult. Religious concerns were also included in the tablets: the curse phrase *sacer esto* ("let him be taboo!") cut the condemned man off from the community and consigned him to the infernal gods. The state of insolvent debtors was improved, but laws concerning debtors who had been sentenced remained harsh.

sacer: Sacred, thus reserved for the gods (as opposed to profane), whence taboo, sacrosanct (e.g. the tribunes of the *plebs*).

A constitutionally important feature was that the death sentence could be pronounced only by the sovereign assembly of the people, that is, the *comitia centuriata*. Thus, for common law crimes (murder by sorcery, arson, false witness causing death) and political crimes, consular criminal jurisdiction disappeared. The consuls kept only their coercive, administrative, and policing power – they therefore retained their armed bodyguards, or lictors, who implemented their right of arrest and summons.

proletarii, proletarians: Those whose only belongings were their offspring (*proles*).

■ The status of the citizen. The laws established a distinction between the propertied classes and those without any land or other assets (*proletarii*) rather than between patricians and plebeians. As regards the latter, the last two law tables prohibited marriage between members of the patriciate and members of the *plebs*. This indicates a reaction on the part of the nobles to the rise of the *plebs*. This arrangement, which Cicero considered "inhuman," was revoked in 445 by the Canuleian law.

Political institutions

Once drawn up by the decemvirs, the laws of the twelve tables were submitted to the *comitia centuriata*, who approved them by vote, thus creating the first "voted law" (*lex rogata*). That decisive action guaranteed the legislative function of the people's assembly (*populus* = the whole body of citizens as distinguished from the *plebs*). By their action, the *comitia* created by Servius Tullius entered the republican constitutional process.

The laws of the twelve tables had immediate consequences for the institutions of state proper, and mainly its magistracies. These consequences were realized in the Valerian-Horatian laws of 449.

The *leges Valeriae-Horatiae*

aediles: Patrician (curule) and plebeian magistrates, who superintended the provisioning of Rome, trade, markets (especially weights and measures), public games, roadways, sanitation, and police.

The restoration of the Republic in 449 brought two consuls to power, L. Valerius and M. Horatius, who according to tradition got three laws passed by which the Roman constitution became patricio-plebeian.

1   The inviolability of the tribunes was recognized and confirmed: "Anyone who strikes the tribunes of the *plebs* or the **aediles** [their assistants] will be consigned to Jupiter, and his goods will be sold to the benefit of Ceres, Liber, and Libera." The guilty person was thus accursed.

2   Official authority was recognized for *plebiscita*, that is, decisions of the *concilia plebis*, acknowledged as decisions of the *populus* assembled in **comitia tributa**. Actually, plebiscites gained the force of law only after 286 (Hortensian law).

3   Consular sovereignty was renounced. It became illegal in the future to create a new magistracy without appeal to the people.

Two additional innovations were:

1   the introduction of consular collegiality;
2   official acknowledgment of tribunician *intercessio* or veto: if the tribunes were unanimous, they could block a decision of the consuls which they considered contrary to the interests of the *plebs*. Only the dictator, during his short-lived *imperium*, could escape the tribunes' *intercessio*.

The three Valerian-Horatian laws sealed the gains won by the *plebs*, and patrician Rome gave up the sovereignty of the consular *imperium*. It is understandable that Polybius should have dated the second founding of the Roman constitution from this point.

One fundamental matter was still not settled: plebeian access to the consulship, the supreme magistracy. Nothing prohibited it – but nothing permitted it. Claiming their right to it by tradition (the *mos maiorum* or ancestral right), the patricians firmly intended to preserve their monopoly. The *plebs*, for its part, mobilized to break that monopoly.

3.3 | In Search of Equilibrium: 449–312 BCE

Examination of the *fasti* reveals the struggle of the *plebs* against the patriciate on this matter of plebeians attaining the consulship. Their conflict lasted until 367, the date of the Licinio-Sextian compromise.

Patrician resistance and plebeian demands

From 449 to 446 only patricians occupied places in the consular colleges. In 445, one plebeian was to be found. Between 444 and 441, once again only patricians were consuls. In 440 and 439, two plebeians crept in. But from 438 to 435 only patricians were appointed. The patricians tried to sidetrack plebeian demands for the consulship. They instituted military tribunes with consular power (that is, armed with the *imperium*), a magistracy which was open to plebeians but which, at the end of the term of office, did not confer the right to the same privileges as the consulship, namely the consular title, a place of honor in the **Senate**, the purple toga, and the right to display portraits of ancestors (*ius imaginum*).

---

comitia tributa: Plebeian assembly charged with the election of aediles, tribunes, and quaestors, and voting on plebiscites. Voting was by tribe.

Senate: Assembly of 300 members, then 600 under Sulla, 900 under Caesar, again 600 from Augustus, composed of former magistrates, a list of whom was drawn up every five years by the censors, later by the emperor, who carried out the *lectio senatus* (calling the roll). It was the government of the republican state. Under the Empire it maintained its prestige, but its role diminished to the point where it became Rome's municipal council.

From 444 – though the college of that year was contested: one patrician and two plebeians – to 432, there seem to have been three of them in each college. The number rose to four from 426 to 406 and became six from 405 to 367.

According to some authors, the institution of the military tribunate was in response less to political demands than to military needs, especially the necessity to wage war on various fronts. And indeed, as we shall see, Rome in this period found itself facing numerous enemies and grappling with increasingly important wars.

Rome and its enemies

From 444 until 290 serious and sequential conflicts broke out in Latium, with Veii, with Gaulish invaders, and in Campania.

1   In Latium, Rome, which had been placed on an equal footing with the Latin League and was linked with Aricia by a treaty of alliance, was made arbiter

Plate 3.1   Gallic prisoner with hands bound. Roman bronze statuette, first century BCE. British Museum. C. M. Dixon

in 444 in a conflict between Aricia and Ardea. It took advantage of that to award itself the territory of Corioli, which opened up the Pontine plain.

2   Conflict broke out around 437 with Veii, the southernmost of the Etruscan cities. The cause was the city of Fidenae, which Veii held in order to control the salt route (Via Salaria) and the grain trade between Campania and Etruria, and which Rome wanted to acquire. This important site was captured in 435. Subsequently, Rome attacked Veii itself, and won it after a siege lasting 10 years (406–396), led by the dictator M. Furius Camillus. According to the legend, Camillus evoked (*evocatio*, from the Latin *e(x)-vocare*, "to call out") Juno-Uni, the tutelary goddess of the Vei, to leave the town before it was sacked by the Romans. Veii was destroyed and its land annexed by Rome.

> **evocatio:** Religious ceremony intended to compel a divinity to abandon the city he or she protected in order to take up residence in the city that wanted to extend a welcome.

In 398, Rome had to wage war against Volsinii and Tarquinii. At that time, Volsinii was the religious center of the Etruscan confederation (the *fanum Voltumnae*). Rome had to break off hostilities and make peace in 390, at the time of the first Gaulish invasion.

3   The first half of the fourth century BCE was marked by a historical phenomenon of major political and psychological importance for Rome: the second wave of Celtic invasions.

The civilization of the second Iron Age (known as that of La Tène), which had spread through Europe at the end of the fifth century, was national and, led by an enterprising peasantry enticed by the rich valley lands and the sunshine of the southern countries, and by their reputation for wealth, was intent on conquest. Perhaps driven on as well by other peoples, between 390 and 329 these tribes undertook three movements in Italy. The first, between 390 and 380, ended in the capture of Rome. Roman tradition has provided an account of the event, as detailed as it is suspect. Led by Brennus, the Gauls are said to have defeated first the Etruscans near Clusium, then the Romans on the banks of the Allia, a tributary of the Tiber, before seizing Rome itself. Installed in the Forum, they were yet unable to take the Capitol, which was defended by Manlius. Sacked and held to ransom, Rome, it is said, was occupied from July 18, 390, until the following February. Livy's account, however, does not match the list of eponymous magistrates, and today the capture of Rome tends to be dated no earlier than 381. In the end the Gauls retreated, themselves threatened by the Veneti and Alpine peoples. The Gauls' capture of Rome had lamentable consequences for the historian of early Rome, because of the destruction of monuments and archives.

The Gauls descended a second time in around 358–354, and a notable event during this incursion was the capture of Felsina, to which the Boian Celts gave the name Bononia (Bologna). The invaders ventured into Latium, and some bands as far as Apulia. Confronted by the Romans mobilized by Camillus, they retreated, ravaging Etruria on their way.

A third wave of invaders surged south in around 347–343. Rome was again threatened, but was saved by the dictator L. Furius. In 332–329, one last Gaulish threat hung over Latium, but this time Rome, which had become master of Latium and Campania, imposed a 30-year peace on the Gauls.

The wars against the Gauls played an important part in the construction of a Roman national identity, the emergence of leading military men, and the conceptualization of the *tumultus Gallicus* as a barbarian threat against all established rules. This collective memory was still vivid in Roman political thought in the first century BCE, when Caesar conquered and Romanized Gaul.

4   Between 380 and 291, after succeeding in intimidating Tusculum into accepting a *foedus aequum* (treaty of alliance between equals), which was followed by the submission of those Latin towns that had been recalcitrant, the conquest of the lands of the Volsci, and the capitulation of Tibur, Rome turned its attention to Campania. Master of Latium, Rome found itself neighbor to the Samnites, who, since the fifth century, had formed a Campanian state. Its capital, Capua, had developed from a simple agricultural center into a large town. In 354, a peace agreement was reached between the Romans and the Samnites. However, just 13 years later, in 341, the first of the three Samnite Wars took place.

Chronology 3.1	The three Samnite Wars
341	First Samnite War:
327–304	Second Samnite War.
298–291	Third Samnite War.

In these wars, Roman successes and victories were far from assured: in 321, after their defeat in the Caudine Forks, a narrow mountain pass near Beneventum, two vanquished Roman legions passed ceremonially under a yoke of Samnite spears. In 295, in the battle of Sentinum in northern Umbria, the general P. Decius Mus consecrated himself to the underworld and plunged into the enemy ranks on horseback, in return for Rome's victory (this ritual is known as *devotio*). Once the submission of the Samnites was achieved, these wars resulted in:

devotio: Ceremony during which a general devoted (offered) himself and his army to the *Manes* (benevolent spirits) and the Earth by reciting a formula, dictated to him by the *pontifex maximus*, to ward off a major peril to the army and obtain victory from the gods on the occasion of a battle.

- the turning of Capua into a federated municipality (in 334), prior to its annexation between 318 and 312;
- the dissolution of the Latin League and the setting up of Roman colonies in Latium – the port of Ostia was founded in 335;
- the creation of a Roman–Campanian state by agreement between the Roman and Capuan aristocracies, with a shared army and a Roman Senate that welcomed the great Campanian families, notably the Atilii, whose dynamism helped to commit Rome to a maritime policy;
- entry into direct contact with both the Greek cities of Magna Graecia (Tarentum, for example) and the Italic peoples who were in open conflict with those cities. This contact swiftly drew Rome toward the south;

▪ contact with Punic Carthage. The Carthaginians had long maintained connections with the Etruscans, mainly with the town of Caere, of which Pyrgi was the port (home of the bilingual Pyrgi tablets). Rome made an alliance with Caere (later a Roman *municipium*, a free town subject to Rome) and in 348 concluded a treaty with Carthage – the first, according to Diodorus Siculus (Livy mentions it, but without saying that it was the first). Polybius, on the other hand, dates the first Roman–Carthaginian treaty to 509 BCE. The issue at hand was demarcating the trading and colonization zones of each of the two parties: Rome could not trade in either Sardinia or Africa, except in Carthage, but could do so in Carthaginian Sicily.

These external difficulties and conflicts combined with political instability and patrician–plebeian rivalry in Rome led to the compromise found in the Licinio-Sextian plebiscite of 367.

The Licinio-Sextian compromise of 367 and its consequences

As we have seen, the political situation in Rome had been somewhat confused since 444. After 377, political dissent was exacerbated by the activities of two tribunes of the *plebs*, C. Licinius and L. Sextius, who held the office for 10 years. Licinius and Sextius boycotted elections and used their veto to weaken the power of the patricians and benefit the plebeians. On several occasions, the Senate appealed to a dictator to compose matters. Eventually, an informal coalition of new men, composed of lesser patricians and eminent, politically active plebeians, was formed. The Senate accepted the famous Licinio-Sextian plebiscite of 367, which settled the following three questions:

1 the question of debts, by means of legislation against usury, the institution of a moratorium, and a reduction of current debts;
2 the agrarian question, by limiting the extent of possession of lands of the *ager publicus*, that is, lands that had been conquered and annexed and had thus become the property of the Roman people;
3 the question of access to the consulship. This was the main point of the reform. The consulship was re-established. It was now specified that one of the two consuls must be a plebeian. L. Sextius was the first plebeian consul elected as such, and C. Licinius the third (in 364). This decision was a milestone in the history of the Republic's institutions. For the first time, plebeian access to the supreme office was codified.

The establishment of republican public offices

Immediately after their capitulation to plebeian demands, the patricians reacted by imposing new magistracies, reserved for their own members and endowed

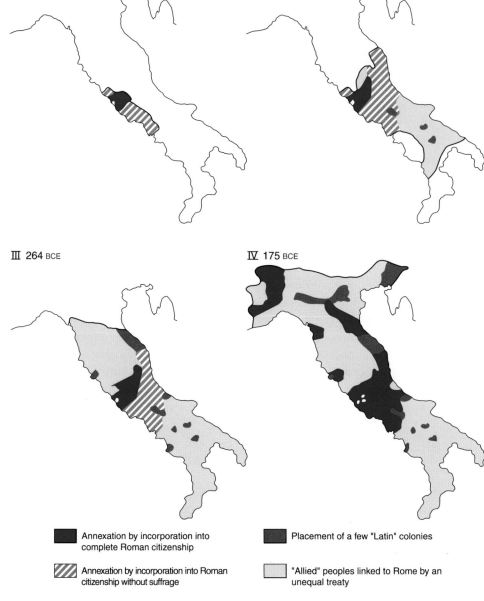

I 334 BCE

II 290 BCE

III 264 BCE

IV 175 BCE

| | Annexation by incorporation into complete Roman citizenship | | Placement of a few "Latin" colonies |
| | Annexation by incorporation into Roman citizenship without suffrage | | "Allied" peoples linked to Rome by an unequal treaty |

Map 3.1 The conquest of Italy and organization of territories (from M. Humbert, *Institutions politiques et sociales de l'Antiquité*, Dalloz, 1989)

with powers taken from the consuls. However, during the following decades, the plebeians managed to obtain access to these too.

- The praetorship for a judiciary magistrate was created in 366. The office was held at first by a single magistrate, who was in charge of civil justice and criminal jurisdiction. He was armed with a civil and military *imperium*, but one inferior to that of the consuls (he was entitled to only six lictors, as opposed to 12 for the consuls). The plebeians gained access to this office in 356.
- The curule aedileship was introduced, an office entrusted to two magistrates of patrician origin whose duties were to oversee, together with the aediles of the *plebs*, the provisioning of Rome, major festivals, and market regulations. The office was opened to plebeians in 364.
- In 356, plebeians were similarly eligible for the dictatorship, an office with sovereign but temporary power, its limit fixed by the accomplishment of a specific task. In 351 the **censorship** too was opened to plebeians. This office had been created in 443 to carry out a five-yearly *census* of citizens and their assets. Lastly, in 300, the office of the *pontifex maximus*, last stronghold of patrician monopoly, yielded. The *plebs* thus ended up in triumph everywhere. By the end of the fourth century all offices were open to both patricians and plebeians.

censor: Magistrate charged with the task of conducting a *census* every five years of citizens and their possessions, and of drawing up a list of senators.

The advent of a new nobility

This settlement in Roman society gave the Republic, at least in principle, a balance of power among its constituents. Polybius (6.11–18) provides a detailed, and idealized, description of this "mixed" constitution, discussing what he sees as the equitable division of powers among the consuls, the senate, and the people.

This political system was the result of the struggle of the orders as well as changes within the patrician and plebeian bodies themselves. There appears to have been a decline of the old patriciate complemented by an emergence of less conservative patrician families, such as the Fabii, who no longer disdained to ally themselves with plebeian families (C. Licinius himself seems to have become the son-in-law of a Fabius). At the same time, certain plebeian families began to stand out, acquiring wealth and authority. Thus a "center party" was formed at the same time as there developed in society a new nobility, both patrician and plebeian. This was composed of those with an ancestor in their family who had held curule magistracies, so called because their holder was entitled to sit on the **curule seat** (aedileship, praetorship, and, above all, consulship).

curule seat: Folding X-shaped seat, reserved for senators.

This new state of affairs naturally brought its own consequences. The Senate was no longer under firm patrician control. The plebeians had a secure place in it. Plebiscites vested with the authority of the senators (*auctoritas patrum*) were the equivalent of laws. And at some time between 318 and 313, the Ovinian plebiscite widened the powers of censors (among whom there had been plebeians since 351) for drawing up the list of senators (the *album senatorium*).

This long history of the *plebs*' political conquests in the fourth century was completed with the great censorship of Appius Claudius Caecus (the Blind) in 312. One of the most celebrated personalities in Roman history, descended from Attius Clausus, the Sabine founder of the *gens Claudia*, Caecus was the first to give this family that prominence which rendered it still illustrious under the Empire. A man of vast culture, author of *Sententiae* in Saturnian verse, he made himself famous by two important institutional actions: getting the sons of emancipated slaves (freedmen) admitted to the Senate, and then reorganizing the composition of the tribes so as to enable the lower classes (the *humiles*) and freedmen to be included in them. This open-minded patrician was symbolic of the new nobility then gaining power. Furthermore, by having the Via Appia built from Rome to Capua, Caecus was expressing the ambitions of those Romans who were aspiring to the expansion of Rome toward Magna Graecia.

3.4 | The Republic's Institutions at the End of the Fourth Century

After the decemviral reforms and the plebeian victories that followed them, the institutions of Rome remained those of an aristocratic republic governed by the Senate. Magistrates ran the state administration, while the assemblies of the people exercised their power in the election of magistrates and by voting on laws.

The magistrates

Since Rome lacked a written constitution, magistracies were established as and when they were needed. They were hierarchized, specialized, elective, collegial, and annual (in order to avoid a relapse to personal, tyrannical power).

The only ones that were not elected magistracies were the dictator, his master of cavalry, and the *interrex*. Dictatorship was a formal magistracy, but exceptional because of its time limitation (it was confined to the accomplishment of a precise mission and by no means allowed to last longer than six months). A single dictator, without a colleague, was appointed by the consuls on the decision of the Senate, to exercise his office only in the civil domain. In military matters he was represented by a master of cavalry, chosen by himself. With his 24 lictors, the dictator held simultaneously the legal authority and power (*imperium*) of the two consuls. He thus had sovereign power, though this did not abolish the other magistracies – they were merely subject to his authority for a limited period. And he was not subject to the *intercessio* of the tribunes. Though recourse to the dictatorship was frequent in the fifth and fourth centuries, it became rare in the third, except during the Punic Wars, after which it disappeared until the first century BCE. The *interrex* was appointed by patrician senators in the event of the abrupt death or resignation of both consuls. His remit – which lasted only five days – was to have new consuls elected and pass the auspices on to them. Those magistracies which required no election were also exceptions to the rule of annual tenure. So too was the censorship, which lasted 18 months and was confirmed only every five years.

The ordinary magistrates (censors, consuls, praetors, aediles, tribunes, and **quaestors**) were thus all elected by people's assemblies. The censors and the senior magistrates *cum imperio*, that is, with both civil and military power, jurisdictional and coercive, implying the right to take the auspices (consuls and praetors), were elected by the *comitia centuriata*. Minor magistrates (aediles, tribunes, and quaestors) were elected by the *comitia tributa*.

> **quaestor:** Minor magistrate whose special task was finance.

Box 3.1 Roman magistracies

- Dictatorship: exceptional and for a limited period. Assistance of a "master of cavalry" for military affairs.
- Censorship: every five years. Duration: 18 months.
- Senior magistracies (with civil and military power): annual and collegial:
  - = consulship
  - = praetorship
- Minor magistracies (civil power): annual and collegial:
  - = aedileship
  - = tribunate of the *plebs*
  - = quaestorship

The office of the censors was created in 443. These two magistrates were compulsorily former consuls, but had no *imperium* and no lictors. Their mission was threefold. First, they took a *census* of citizens, whom they had to classify, and their possessions, which they had to assess in order to determine the political rights and military duties of each one. At the close of the *census*, which took place every five years, the censors also performed the **lustrum**, a sacrifice of expiation and purification. Second, the censors established the list of senators *(album senatorium)*, with the related right of exclusion for infamy, a power conferred by the Ovinian plebiscite. Third, they managed the state's patrimony, in particular in the renting out of the *ager publicus* (the collective property of the Roman people, formed from military conquests), the allocation of public lands, the construction and maintenance of public buildings, etc. They were also the state's high moral authority.

> **lustrum:** Five-yearly purification performed by the censors after carrying out the *census*; hence the space of five years (*lustrum*) between two purifications.

The two consuls were in some ways the presidents of the Republic. They held the *imperium domi militiaeque*, that is, the *imperium domi*, a sovereign political, judicial, and coercive power within the sacred boundaries of Rome (the

pomoerium: Sacred boundary of Rome. The land that lay inside it could not receive the tombs of the dead, temples to foreign gods, or the army except for triumphs. Magistrates with *imperium* lost it by crossing the boundary.

pomoerium), and the *imperium militiae*, a sovereign military and jurisdictional power outside the boundaries of the city.

The praetorship was held by a single praetor, from 366, entrusted with civil jurisdiction (*praetor urbanus*), coupled with another magistrate, after 242, in charge of lawsuits between Roman citizens and foreigners, or between foreigners residing in Rome (*praetor peregrinus*). Others were created later for provincial administration.

At the time of their creation, in 493, the aediles were at first plebeian. Later, in 366, two curule aedileships were created, patrician to start with and then open to the *plebs*. The aediles had no *imperium*. Their function was to look after the provisioning of Rome, and to care for markets, public order, and the public games.

The four quaestors, dating from the earliest days of the Republic, had chiefly financial powers, in particular concerning the administration of the public treasury (*aerarium*). In the third century, two other quaestors were made responsible for the issuing of currency. Later, others were sent to Sicily and Sardinia.

cursus honorum: Ascending order of Roman magistracies. The political career ladder.

The tribunes of the *plebs* were magistrates somewhat apart from the hierarchy of the other magistracies (**cursus honorum**). Compulsorily plebeian originally, tribunes enjoyed a sacrosanct or inviolable person and exercised a major power (only dictators and censors could escape it). Their power of veto could be exercised against any decision by other magistrates, and their power of *auxilium* allowed them to safeguard any citizen who placed himself under their protection. In the following centuries, as we shall see, tribunes often used their veto and their right to convene the assembly to serve their own political agenda, or that of their patrons.

The people's assemblies

The people's assemblies brought together the entire *populus*, i.e. the whole civic community of the *quirites*. Roman citizenship, whether original (that of the *ingenui*) or acquired by emancipation (for *liberti*), consisted of an ensemble of (unevenly distributed) rights and duties. At the end of the fourth century, the whole of the Roman citizen body numbered between 200,000 and 250,000 (adult males), and citizens acted within three assemblies of unequal importance.

comitia curiata: Ancient assembly of the people (voting was by *curia*), which retained only a religious role; it conferred the *imperium* on magistrates.

The *comitia curiata* or curiate assembly was a relic of the royal epoch, when citizens were grouped in 30 *curiae*. It no longer met, except for formalities – voting on the *lex de imperio*, or law of investiture of magistrates, was its principal function. Early in the Republic the *curiae* were replaced in the proceedings of the assembly by 30 lictors. Thus it may be seen how much this institution had deteriorated.

The *comitia centuriata* or centuriate assembly was the most important of the people's assemblies. It represented the *populus* divided into five classes and 193 *centuriae*, each of which was a voting unit. As we have seen, the first class, with its 98 *centuriae* and the richest citizens, enjoyed an absolute majority. That privilege was further strengthened through a voting practice by virtue of which the *centuria* called upon to cast the first vote (known as a prerogative) was always chosen, randomly, from the 18 equestrian *centuriae* of the first class. The vote of that first *centuria* most frequently influenced that of the following *centuriae*, and when a majority was obtained, voting stopped. In practice, the second class voted only rarely, and the third only in very exceptional circumstances. The *comitia centuriata* elected senior magistrates, military leaders, and censors; and they voted on important laws, such as constitutional laws, formally declared war, etc.

The *comitia tributa* or tribal assembly, reorganized in 312 by Appius Claudius, represented the *populus* divided into "tribes," originally actual tribes but by then tribally denominated groups of individuals, henceforward including laborers and other less privileged citizens (the *humiles*). It elected minor magistrates and voted on plebiscites. It also had judicial competence in matters concerning a public crime for which the penalty did not exceed a fine.

The council of the *plebs* (*concilium plebis*) stood apart from the two assemblies. It was an assembly of the *plebs* only, convened by a tribune. From the time when plebiscites gained the force of law, there was a tendency to merge it with the tribal assembly, which was convened, and thus presided over, by a magistrate with *imperium*, and in which plebeians were broadly in the majority.

The Senate

The Senate was the supreme council of the Republic. Although at the end of the fourth century it did not yet have the fundamental role it played after the Second Punic War, Cicero's words may already be applied to it: "Our ancestors made the Senate the guardian, the defender, the protector of the state; they wanted the magistrates to be the ministers, so to speak, of this imposing Council" (*Speech on Behalf of Publius Sestius* 117).

Since the Ovinian law of c.318–313, the composition of the Senate had been in the hands of the censors, who, choosing from among "the best," revised the list of its 300 members every five years. Its members (the *seniores* or *patres*) were largely former senior magistrates (former censors, consuls, praetors) – later, former curule aediles could also enter, and later still, former tribunes. Meeting at the summons of a higher magistrate, who presided over the session, the senators gave their opinion on every matter submitted to them. The first man invited to speak was the **princeps senatus**, the leader or senior man in the Senate, a patrician and former censor. Then other senators could have their turn to speak, in order of their former office. Once each member's opinion (*sententia*) had been given, the senators proceeded to vote. The decision, expressing the state's supreme authority (*auctoritas*), was a **senatus consultum** (or decree of the senate), advice which virtually bound the magistrates.

The authority of the Senate, though still not general, already covered a wide field. Besides the decrees, the Senate influenced greatly the transformation of

princeps senatus:
Leader of the Senate. Inscribed first on the official list drawn up by the censors, and had the privilege of speaking first at meetings of the Senate. Under the Empire, the emperor was *princeps senatus*.

senatus consultum:
Decision of the Senate which, under the Empire, had the force of a law. In the event of major danger, under the Republic, the *senatus consultum ultimum*, or ultimate senatorial decree, gave full powers to the consuls.

Plate 3.2   Relief depicting senators. Ancient Art & Architecture Collection

plebiscites into laws, the supervision of the magistrates' activities, and the supreme control of finances, international affairs, general administration, and justice. In essence, the Senate guided the policies of Rome. However, as it gradually became open to people outside the old nobility, and later to Italians and non-Italians, it faced mounting challenges in keeping a coherent and unanimous front in the face of Roman expansion.

4

THE GROWTH OF
THE REPUBLIC

War and Conquest in the Third Century BCE

On the brink of the third century BCE, after the Third Samnite War, there was only one state from the Tiber to Cumae and from the Tyrrhenian Sea to Lake Ficino. Furthermore, Rome seemed to have contained its internal political conflicts with well-balanced institutions. Although in the social field struggles had not been completely resolved, its territorial expansion was already allowing for an economic development that would grow still further, and a military strength capable of coping with the conquests opening up before it. Rome found itself increasingly involved in Italian affairs, notably in the south. Roman contacts with the Greek world multiplied, precipitating a Hellenization of art and religion and an increasingly active engagement in Mediterranean affairs. Perhaps inevitably, Roman interests clashed with the Carthaginian interests which largely dominated in the western Mediterranean. From that conflict arose a struggle between Rome and Carthage which, by its duration, its bitterness, the means employed, and the successive involvement of nearly all the inhabitants of the Mediterranean shores, assumed the dimensions of a decisive step in the formation of the modern West.

4.1 | Economy, Society, Army

The Roman economy relied mainly on agriculture and pasture. As in all ancient civilizations, the rural economy was the backbone of Roman life, and this remained a subsistence economy. Given the richness of Campania's fields and groves, the formation of a Roman–Campanian state was therefore an important event economically as well as politically. In Latium crop-growing and pasture were vital, with the seasonal movements of flocks and herds spreading out toward Sabine territory. Medium-sized and small properties seem to have been in the majority at that time. It was not until the end of the third century that the massive arrival of slaves and the first consequences of foreign wars contributed to the formation of the first large-scale properties.

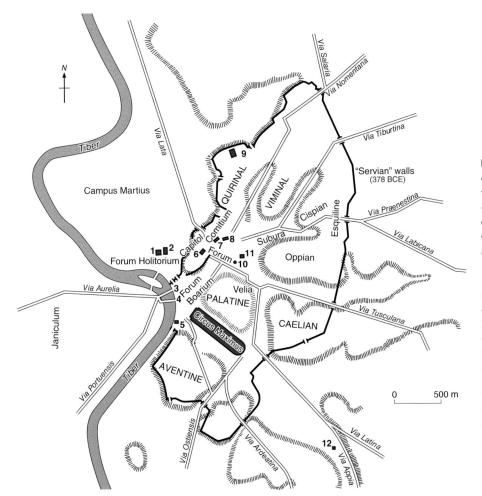

Figure 4.1 The city of Rome in the early third century BCE (after F. W. Walbank et al. (eds.), *The Cambridge Ancient History*, 2nd edn, CUP, 1989, vol. 7, pt. 2) 1 temple of Apollo (431 BCE   2 temple of Bellona (296 BCE) 3 Aemilian bridge 4 Sublician bridge 5 temple of Ceres (493 BCE)   6 temple of Saturn (497 BCE) 7 Rostra (338 BCE) 8 temple of Janus 9 temple of Quirinus (293 BCE) 10 temple of Vesta 11 Regia 12 tomb of the Scipios

Nevertheless, as we have seen, as early as the end of the sixth century, the excessive borrowing by small owners had created a massive debt problem for Rome. And, in the middle of the fifth century, the laws of the twelve tables had intervened in questions of property to defend the rights of citizens against the powerful.

On the economic plane, the great event of the first third of the third century was the appearance of Roman coinage, its creation reflecting Rome's development and the new direction of its economy. The origins of the striking of coinage lay in the cities of Asia Minor in the seventh century BCE. Rome struck its first coins in the early third century BCE, during the war with Pyrrhus, king of Epirus. This was a bronze coinage (the *aes grave*). The monetary unit was the *as*, weighing one Roman pound (324 g); this unit was divided into 12 ounces, with further sub-units. The creation of this coinage must have been related to the institution in 289 of the *triumviri monetales*, a college of three young magistrates in charge of issuing the money. Their office was situated on the Capitol, near the temple of Juno, the goddess henceforth called upon to watch over this establishment, as she had watched over Rome and warned it of threatening dangers. (Livy, 5.47, tells how the Capitoline geese raised the alarm at the time of the Gauls' attack, thus alerting the Romans; the goose was the symbolic attribute of the goddess.) Thus Juno Moneta gave her name to the "monetary" institution. This monetary unit survived until the Second Punic War. Notably, about 235, the prow of a ship figured on the reverse side of the Roman *as*, the symbol of Roman ambition for maritime domination.

Another important date in the history of Roman coinage was 269, which saw the minting of silver coinage in Rome. But it was not until the Second Punic War, or, more precisely, about the year 214, that a metrological system was established with equivalence for bronze and silver coinage. The silver denarius, worth 10 bronze *asses*, appeared at that time, replacing the silver *quadrigatus* (thus named from featuring Jupiter in a four-horse chariot, or *quadriga*), which had too large a value. Rome thus possessed a light currency, making transactions easier. The requirements of war, intensified by the creation of a fleet, quickly caused financial strain. It proved necessary to revalue the denarius at 16 *asses*. Moreover, monetary manipulations began which affected the metal standard of silver coinage. However, with the denarius, integrated with a coherent and Mediterranean-wide metrological system, Rome was furnished with a currency that was accepted in foreign trade circuits. Moneychangers' shops were set up on the Forum.

From the middle of the fourth century, Roman society, especially Roman high society, underwent important changes, with the formation of a new nobility, mentioned above, and with the gradual introduction of new men into the ruling classes. There was an Italianization of these classes, to the advantage of Sabines (M. Curius Dentatus), Campanians (the Atilii), Etruscans (the Volumnii and Ogulnii), and Umbrians (the Sempronii). The families of the Furii, Quinctii, and Papirii from Tusculum had already been integrated into Latium. These newcomers brought a fresh energy to the ruling classes. The Campanians in particularly played such an active role in Roman politics in the Mediterranean and southern Italy that they could be said to have made the early Punic Wars their own affair.

Box 4.1 The birth of Roman currency

- In the beginning, valuation in head of livestock (*pecus*), hence the word *pecunia* = wealth in livestock, then money, fortune, riches.
- Gradual appearance of bronze ingots (*aes rude*), subsequently stamped with a mark, the bull (*aes signatum*).
- 289 BCE: appearance of bronze coinage (*aes grave*) with the faces of Janus and Minerva; creation of the college of three magistrates responsible for the minting of these coins (the *triumviri monetales*).
- 269 BCE: issue in Rome of silver didrachma, depicting Hercules, and the she-wolf suckling the infants Castor and Pollux, then a deified Rome (Dea Roma) and Victory holding a palm.
- About 214 BCE: issue in Rome of the silver denarius, one denarius = 10 bronze *asses*.

The Roman army that fought in the service of these policies, and no doubt determined how they should be carried out, had been forged during the wars of the fourth century on the basis of the Servian directions. It thus remained founded on property qualification in the sense that only the five propertied classes were obliged to do service, with, as we have seen, the heavier weapons and the monopoly of the cavalry conferred on wealthy citizens of the first class; the *proletarii* and *capite censi*, with very rare exceptions, were exempt. It was a national army: service (*militia*) was both a right and a duty of the citizen; and unlike the Greek armies, it included no mercenaries. At the end of the third century allied contingents were introduced into the army, provided by the subject cities and peoples of Italy. It was usually made up of four legions, raised only for the campaign period, that is, during the clement weather between the months of March and October. Each legion consisted of 3,000 heavily armed foot soldiers, 1,200 more lightly armed *velites*, and 300 horsemen. These were distributed equally in two consular armies. Weapons and tactics became established during the course of the wars. Thus it was during the Samnite Wars that the Romans acquired the custom of breaking up the massed body of the legion (perhaps influenced by the tactical arrangement of the Greek phalanx), dividing it into more flexible units, the maniples, composed of two centuries, each containing 60 men. The legionaries were provided with a wooden-handled javelin with a long slender point (*pilum*) and an oblong shield (*scutum*). From the war against Pyrrhus they seem to have borrowed the art of organizing and fortifying their camps (developing the technique to a perfection that earned the admiration of Polybius), as well as certain principles of maneuver on the field of battle. But their command remained far inferior to that of the professional strategists in the Greek world. Furthermore, at the beginning of the third century, they still had no fleet at their disposal.

Polybius acknowledged that the Roman army was pre-eminent on two counts: the personal worth of the soldiers and their intensive training.

4.2 | The Conquest of Central and Southern Italy

The years 348–338 marked a crucial period in Rome's march toward mastery of the peninsula and a maritime commitment. Its good relations with Caere, at the time Italy's largest city, probably attracted Rome to look toward the open seas. After 291 (end of the Third Samnite War), the new means available to the Roman–Campanian state encouraged it to expand its power.

Rome and central Italy

The Sabine region was still independent, but because of its geographical position its territory was often crossed by both Roman soldiers and Roman traders. In 290, M. Curius Dentatus, consul at the time, ravaged it as far as the Adriatic. The land was annexed, its towns received prefects to administer them, and the confiscated lands were colonized – thus a Latin colony was established at Hadria (Atri).

Shortly afterwards, the Senonian Gauls attacked Arretium (Arezzo) in Etruria. They were eventually driven out, but not until they had neared Volsinii. Pushed back as far as the sea, they lost part of their territory to Rome. A Roman colony was installed at Sena Gallica in 283, and later, in 268, another at Ariminum (Rimini). This brought about the annexation of a large part of the *ager Gallicus* between Ancona and Rimini.

Meanwhile, back in Etruria, the towns were ravaged by class struggles between the democrats and the aristocrats, the latter generally supported by Rome. Their territories were gradually lost to Rome and they themselves became "federated" cities (*foederatae*), that is, bound to Rome by a treaty. A Roman colony was settled at Cosa, and in 265 Volsinii was captured and destroyed. It was the end of great Etruria.

Roman territory, which had covered 5,000 km^2 after the Latin War, now extended over 27,000 km^2.

Rome and Pyrrhus, king of Epirus

In the first quarter of the third century, Rome, though busy in central and north central Italy, found itself engaged in the complex affairs of southern Italy, through the rivalries of Greek colonies there and their problems with the indigenous populations.

In 284, Thurii, the rival of Tarentum, appealed to Rome for help in resisting the Lucani. A Roman consul, dispatched to the site, set up a garrison in the city, a move that inclined Croton, Locri, and Rhegium to join with the Romans, but failed to settle the internal discord – the parties continued to tear one another apart, the pro-Roman aristocrats opposing the anti-Roman democrats.

Two years later, in 282, Tarentum sent an army to Thurii to drive out Rome's partisans. This caused Rome to intervene in 281 by dispatching an army that ravaged the Tarentine territory. Tarentum made an appeal to Pyrrhus of Epirus. In 296, at the age of 23, this young king of Epirus had inherited a very poor, mountainous country, wedged between Illyria, Macedon, Thessalia, and Aetolia. After modernizing his country's pastoral economy and its army, he had stepped up military intervention in Macedon and Thessalia. Having become king of both countries, and thus having doubled his territory and population, he imagined himself to be master of Greece and, like a new Alexander, intended for a great destiny. After all, it seems that among the last projects of Alexander the Great himself had been a planned military operation in the West. Having been driven out of Macedon, Pyrrhus was delighted to respond to Tarentum's appeal. He aspired to unite the Greek cities of Magna Graecia, reconcile them with the indigenous peoples of the interior, and thus establish a powerful new kingdom, whence he could set off to reclaim Macedon.

He landed at Tarentum in the spring of 280, with 25,000 men and a number of elephants. These beasts dumbfounded the Romans at their first encounter with them below the walls of Heraclea, where the Epirots gained their initial victory. This success led Pyrrhus into Campania, where he had a failure at Capua. A second victory came at Ausculum, but he again failed to gain advantage from it (hence the expression "Pyrrhic victory"). Negotiations followed between Rome and Pyrrhus, and in 278, concerning the protection of Sicily, between Rome and Carthage. In fact Pyrrhus landed in Sicily. Proclaimed king of Syracuse, then master of Agrigentum, he entered the area of the island controlled by Carthage. His failure at Lilybaeum, the Carthaginian threat, and the rebellion of Sicilians crushed by taxes caused him to re-embark in 275, first for Italy, and then, driven out by the revolt of the Greek cities, for Epirus, leaving Tarentum with a garrison, which remained there two years. In 272 he was killed at the siege of Argos, allegedly struck down by a tile thrown by an old woman from the top of her house.

This war opened new areas of influence, enabling Rome to complete its grasp on southern Italy.

The capture of Tarentum: 273–272 BCE

After the defeat of Pyrrhus, Rome had no real rival left in Italy. The region of Lucania was the first to yield, and a Roman colony was settled there at Paestum in 273. Next, Tarentum, with its riches and its strategic position, became a point of contest among the Romans, who sent an army, and the Carthaginians, who sent a fleet. In 272, Millo, head of the garrison, handed the citadel over to the Romans on condition that he and his supporters be given free exit to Epirus.

Plate 4.1   War-
elephant. Roman
terra-cotta plaque.
C. M. Dixon

triumph: A public
processional entrance
of a general into
Rome in celebration
of military victory.

Tarentum received its "liberty," that is, the status of a free town but with a
Roman garrison in its citadel. It had to pay heavy compensation, and the **triumph**
of the two consuls in Rome featured a parade of all the statues, paintings, and
other marvels seized from the town. Rome had thus reduced the only city in
southern Italy capable of competing with it.

There followed the submission of the whole of southern Italy, with its Greek
and indigenous populations. It is noteworthy that from this time on, the name
"Italia," which had hitherto designated first Calabria and then southern Italy,
was extended to cover the entire peninsula.

It is easy to see that the war with Pyrrhus and the capture of Tarentum brought
Rome face to face with Carthage, an army face to face with a navy. The First
Punic War was simply a matter of time. But before approaching that chapter of
Roman and Mediterranean history, it is appropriate to examine another conse-
quence of the direct contacts established with the Greek world: the Hellenization
of Rome's art and religion.

4.3 | The Hellenization of Art and Religion

Contrary to what is sometimes said, there had been no deep Hellenic influence
in Rome in the seventh century BCE; the presence of proto-Corinthian and then

Corinthian pottery articles in the archaic tombs proves trading, rather than cultural, interactions. The first Hellenization is datable to the third century. It was the fruit of contacts begun with the Greeks of Magna Graecia, and with the Etruscans, themselves influenced by Greek culture. Throughout the fourth century, Rome had not looked beyond central Italy. When its horizons expanded, Rome, and the whole of central Italy, reaped the benefits of the Greek civilization.

Art

At the end of the fourth century and the beginning of the third, honorific statues, and even equestrian statues, began to appear in the Forum. They were in bronze, or so it seems, for they have not survived. And there is every reason to think that they came from the Greek cities of southern Italy. It is known that in 275,

Plate 4.2 Relief depicting victory of a gladiator announced by a trumpeter. The other waits for judgment on his life. First century BCE. Ancient Art & Architecture Collection

M. Curius Dentatus, in his triumphal procession celebrating his victory over Pyrrhus and the Samnites, put on show some "Tarentine delights" *(deliciae Tarentinae)* which included old pictures. It is also known that the capture of Tarentum in 272 was followed by the looting of the town's works of art, for which it was renowned, especially its chased and embossed metalwork. But it is difficult to say what the influence of those works was on Roman art of the period, and all the more so because Rome in the third century was still largely a rural town, with simple, traditional architecture. The temples, to which the greatest care was given, for they were consecrated to the gods, were built either of light materials (which have totally vanished) or in volcanic tuff, with terra-cotta architectural decoration. However, it should be noted that even in 296 the terra-cotta quadriga of the temple of Jupiter Capitolinus was replaced by another in bronze, offered by the Ogulnii brothers, who also commissioned the famous bronze she-wolf for the Lupercal, the cultic cave on the Palatine. The 2,000 bronze statues seized by the consul M. Fulvius at Volsinii, doubtless looted from the sanctuary of the *fanum Voltumnae*, came to adorn the twin temples of Fortuna and Mater Matuta (the Lady of the Morning) in the Forum Boarium. But, clearly, that was merely decorative addition, foreign to the architecture.

In Italy, and especially in the south, the Greek imprint had become ever more noticeable. Thus, at Paestum, the "temple of Peace" (probably built in 273 at the time of the settlement of the Latin colony) includes elements borrowed from classical Greek tradition, for instance a frieze in the Doric style featuring panels ornamented with a figure. During the course of the third century such influences traveled through central Italy and reached Rome.

Literature

At the beginning of the third century, trade relations and religious influences encouraged Romans to communicate in Greek. Greek was also the language of international relations. In 281, a Roman ambassador sent to Tarentum made a speech in Greek (which allegedly caused some sniggering). In the first half of the century, Greek language began to penetrate more visibly into Rome, mainly with the arrival of Greek-speaking prisoners of war reduced to slavery. In 272, Livius Andronicus, while still a child, arrived in Rome with other *Graeculi* ("little Greeks"), as they were called with a certain scorn. He was the first epic poet to write in Latin, though on Greek subjects. He translated the *Odyssey*, presenting Odysseus (Ulysses) as an Italic hero, the mediator between Greece and Italy. Thus Livius Andronicus endowed Rome with its first national epic. Moreover, he created Latin theater. He may have used Greek models in doing so, but it was none the less a great moment in Roman literary history. The second half of the third century witnessed the appearance of the first generation of Latin literature.

Religion

The goddesses of Eleusis – Demeter and Kore – who had meanwhile become the Sicilian goddesses bestowing fertility, had been introduced into Rome as early as the beginning of the fifth century BCE. Installed on the Aventine, Demeter, identified with the Roman Ceres, was adopted by the plebeians as their divine protectress. The temple of Ceres became the religious center of the *plebs*. Later came Hera of Argos, the goddess with the pomegranate, symbol of fecundity and immortality, who, like Ceres, protected the fruits of the earth. From the Heraion of the Silarus (Sele) her cult traveled toward Latium as far as Lanuvium, Tibur, and Falerii. Some Greek characteristics were also evident in the temple of Hercules installed on the Forum Boarium.

In the first half of the third century, the Hellenization of Roman religion was advanced in three ways.

1   By the introduction of a new divinity. In 293, following a plague (*pestilentia*, probably malaria) and on the indication of the **Sibylline Books,** an embassy went to Epidaurus to seek the god Asklepius/Aesculapius, to whom a temple was dedicated on the Tiber Island in 291. He definitively dethroned the old Latin Apollo, until then venerated as a healing god (Apollo medicus). Around 180, the cult of his daughter or consort Hygea, assimilated to the Italic Salus, came to join him.

2   By the introduction of a funeral rite, of apparently Etruscan origin, which had taken root in Magna Graecia, chiefly at Capua: the ***munus***, a bloody fight which took place above the tomb of the deceased, who was to be revived by the blood of the combatants. In Rome, the first *munus* was organized in 264 on the Forum Boarium – three pairs of men fought. We shall return to the origins of gladiatorial games extensively at the end of this chapter.

3   Through the influence of Pythagoreanism and Orphism. The latter was a way of thinking rather than a theological doctrine or religion. It was expressed in collections of sacred verses and oracles attributed to Orpheus, as well as in forms of prayers inscribed on gold leaves which we refer to as "Orphic tablets." The engraved Orphic formulas, such as those found on plates of gold exhumed from tombs at Thurii and Petelia in Magna Graecia, were to help the dead find their way in the Underworld. They were "passports for the next world," distributed in the name of the mythical hero who descended to the kingdom of Hades/Pluto to bring back his beloved Eurydice. It is difficult to say whether these mystical and soteriological influences had touched Roman minds as early as the first half of the third century. However, their presence in Rome at least marked the beginning of a movement that later profoundly transformed Roman religious sensibilities – although less, it should be said, than the repercussions of the Punic Wars.

Sibylline Books: Collection of prophecies attributed to the Sibyl, preserved by the *Quindecimviri sacris faciundis,* who were specialists in the interpretation of these writings. From 38 BCE they were kept in the Palatine temple of Apollo.

***munus* (pl. munera):** A duty or obligation to the dead, often in the form of funeral games; an arena spectacle (combat of gladiators or beasts).

Chronology 4.1	Greek and eastern gods in Italy and Rome
Seventh century BCE	Melqart (Hercules) in Rome on the Forum Boarium(?).
528–509	Introduction of the cult of Apollo from Cumae. The Sibylline Books are purchased from the Sibyl.
Sixth–fifth centuries	Eastern-style Minerva at Lavinium (Latium).
495	Hermes (Mercury) introduced into Rome by Greek traders; temple of Mercury dedicated there.
493	Dedication of the temple of Ceres on the Aventine: cult introduced from Sicily. Influence of Etrusco-Greek cult of Dionysus?
484	Dedication of the temple to the Dioscuri (Castores), who were "evoked" from Tusculum on the occasion of the battle of Lake Regillus.
431	Dedication of Apollo's temple, on the Campus Martius (Field of Mars).
293	After a *pestilentia* (outbreak of contagious disease), introduction of Asklepius/Aesculapius: temple dedicated on the Isola Tiberina in 291.
249	Hades (Dis Pater) and Proserpine are honored in the first secular games, known as those of Tarentum (*ludi Tarentini*).
217–216	Vow to the Erycine Venus (Aphrodite of Mount Eryx in Sicily), Greco-Punic.
212	Sacrifice with Greek rites and annual games in Greek style in honor of Apollo (*ludi Apollinares*).
April 4, 204	Arrival at Ostia and installation on the Palatine of the Black Stone of Pessinus (the baetyl of Cybele, Phrygian Great Mother of the gods).
	Creation of the *ludi Megalenses*.
April 10, 191	Dedication of the temple of the Great Mother of the gods (Cybele) on the Palatine.
186	Scandal of the Bacchanalia.
181	Dedication of the temple to the Erycine Venus at the Colline gate, fêted by prostitutes.
180	Hygea, or Hygiea (Salus), daughter or consort of Aesculapius, joins him on the Isola Tiberina.
	Destruction of the "Pythagorean books" discovered at the foot of the Janiculum.
175	Expulsion of the Epicurean philosophers from Rome.
146	"Evocation" to Rome of the Carthaginian Tanit.
139	Expulsion of eastern astrologers from Rome.
105	A Serapeum (altar to Serapis) is attested at Pozzuoli in Campania.
Late second century	First Iseum (altar to Isis) attested at Pompeii.
82	Introduction into Rome by Sulla of the Cappadocian cult of Mâ.
59–48	Official destruction of the Isis-Serapis altars on the Capitol.
43	Vow of a temple to Isis.
33	Expulsion from Rome of the Chaldean magi.

4.4 | The Punic Wars

Rome fought three wars against Carthage between 264 and 146 BCE. These wars constitute major events in the history of Rome and the Mediterranean basin.

Chronology 4.2	The Punic Wars
264–241	First Punic War
218–201	Second Punic War
149–146	Third Punic War

The First Punic War: 264–241 BCE

Our sources for this first war are Polybius (Book 1), Livy, Diodorus Siculus (fragments 22-4), and Cassius Dio (through the Byzantine historian Zonaras). All of them based their accounts on a Greek historian from Agrigentum, Philinos (a contemporary of Hannibal and favorable to the Carthaginians) and on the *Annals* of Fabius Pictor.

Essentially, the conflict arose from the clash of economic interests. The Carthaginians wished to protect the maritime and commercial basis of their power while the Romans explored, and increasingly committed themselves to, a policy of expansion outside Italy.

Carthage, founded at the end of the ninth century BCE by Phoenicians from Tyre, had built up a trading empire in eastern North Africa (present-day Tunisia), along the coasts of that part of Africa, in the south of Spain, and in the islands of the western Mediterranean basin. The reach of the Punic influence into Sicily and Tarentum eventually caused it to collide with Roman interests.

Carthage's strength lay above all in its navy. For its land forces, it resorted largely to mercenaries, and since the war with Pyrrhus had borrowed his use of elephants.

Rome, as we have seen, remained essentially a land-based power. It possessed an army of drafted citizens, joined gradually by allied contingents.

Until 273/272, relations between these two powers, the one well established, the other emerging, had managed to keep a precarious balance. Agreements, the first perhaps concluded in 509, and two other, more certain pacts in 348 and 278, had temporarily accommodated their interests. In 278, during the war against Pyrrhus, the two states had undertaken not to conclude an agreement with him unless they did so together, and Carthage, hoping to keep the king on Italian territory, had promised Rome ships and money. Nevertheless, in 273/272 a menacing Carthaginian fleet came and moored facing the port of Tarentum, watching enviously as the Roman army undertook the siege.

The immediate cause of the war, however, and therefore also of Rome's first military intervention outside Italy, was the double-dealing of the Mamertines ("sons of Mars"), a group of former Campanian mercenaries who several years earlier had seized control of the strategically located city of Messina, in northeast Sicily, from which they routinely launched plundering expeditions into Syracusan territory. In 265, the king of Syracuse, Hiero II, responded by attacking the Mamertines, who appealed to Carthage for assistance, and then, fearing that the Carthaginians intended to stay, asked the Roman Senate for both military aid and an alliance. Most of the senators were, according to Polybius, reluctant to agree, not least because they felt that an alliance with the Mamertines would be undignified. Others warned that if the Romans failed to act, the Carthaginians would rapidly conquer Syracuse and subjugate the whole of Sicily: the Carthaginians, Polybius has them say, would be "dangerous neighbors for them, surrounding them and threatening all parts of Italy." After a long debate, the Senate decided not to honor the Mamertines' request. But the consul Appius Claudius Caudex took the issue directly to the popular assembly, which voted to help them.

According to Polybius, Appius Claudius persuaded the assembly by reminding them of "the clear and considerable advantage that each individual might expect," that is, the certain prospect of booty. Without excluding this popular motivation, we can add to it strategic considerations, according to which a pre-emptive first strike against Carthaginian interests in Sicily might preclude a larger and more dangerous war in Italy. This defensive imperialism was probably combined with the desire of ambitious aristocrats to win military glory and with a collective demand for spoils and other material gains.

A war began that lasted for 23 years. Its course was marked by indecisive battles on land and later at sea: in Sicily around Messina and then Agrigentum, and at Mylae (Milazzo, west of Messina), the first Roman naval victory, won by C. Duilius; in Africa, with the astonishing but unsuccessful expedition of C. Atilius Regulus, carried out in 256 against the advice of the Roman elders; and lastly in the Tyrrhenian waters, where, after a serious naval defeat at Drepanum in 249, leading to an immense effort being put into shipbuilding, the Romans won a victory in the Aegates Islands, forcing a peace in 241.

This first Punic War (which the ancients sometimes referred to, more correctly, as the Sicilian war) had important consequences.

First, most of Sicily became a Roman province. The Carthaginians had to quit the entire island, as well as the Lipari islands, lying between Sicily and Italy.

In Carthage, weakened by the defeat and by the payment of a heavy war indemnity, the First Punic War brought in its wake a social revolt, together with a war against their own disgruntled Numidian and Libyan mercenaries (from the winter of 241/240 to the beginning of 237). Rome profited from this war by seizing Sardinia in 238. In 237, to save Carthage and restore its might, the Punic general Hamilcar Barca undertook the conquest of Spain. There he succeeded in setting up a Barcine Empire, to which his successor Hasdrubal gave an almost monarchic structure with a capital at Carthago Nova (New Carthage, modern Cartagena). Hamilcar's son, Hannibal, took over this territory, organized after the manner of Hellenistic kingdoms, and, starting in 221, he began the course which led to the Second Punic War.

Another outcome of the First Punic War was the birth of Rome's naval power, an event supremely important for the future. Until then Rome had been a city of "landlubbers." But already at the end of the fourth century it had been noticed how much there was to gain by the possession of a fleet: in 311, at a time when it had only the vessels of its allies and maritime colonies at its disposal, Rome appointed two admirals (*duoviri navales*). Now the necessities of a war fought against the naval might of Carthage compelled the creation of a countervailing naval force. Rome achieved this through a massive and expensive program of shipbuilding. As early as 260, the consuls had at their disposal a squadron of 100 quinqueremes and 20 triremes. It was also a time of Roman technical and strategic inventions, the most remarkable of which was the grapnel, which to some extent transformed naval battles into a war of foot soldiers on the sea.

This invention was responsible for the first naval success achieved by the Romans, at Mylae in 260. It subsequently inspired them to launch into military and trading expeditions in the Mediterranean. With the acquisition of the two islands of Sicily and Sardinia, Rome gained two important stepping-stones on this path.

The Second Punic War: 218–201 BCE

After 23 years of armed peace, war resumed because Hannibal, emerging from the great aristocratic Barcine family, became Carthage's military strategist.

Rome, meanwhile, had become master of Italy. After four years of fighting (226–222), it had established itself solidly in Cisalpine Gaul through Cn. Scipio's occupation of Mediolanum (Milan), by building roads, and by the installation in 218 of two Latin colonies beyond the Po, at Cremona and Placentia.

Meanwhile, too, Hannibal had been preparing for the war some think he eagerly desired. Livy preserves a fanciful story, in which Hannibal's father, Hamilcar Barca, instills in his young son a burning hatred for Rome, and makes him solemnly swear to avenge Roman treachery. But there were other causes at play, larger than one man's ambition. Carthaginian military and diplomatic successes in Spain had brought them, by 220, to the region of Saguntum. This was a city allied to Rome by a treaty of mutual protection, but well to the south of the River Ebro, which Rome had declared in 226 as the northern limit of Carthaginian expansion in Spain. At the urging of Saguntum, the Senate sent an embassy to Hannibal to warn him against attacking the city. Angered by what he no doubt considered to be Roman meddling, Hannibal wrote to Carthage for advice. Soon after (early in 219), he laid siege to Saguntum. It was not until early in the following year, however, after Saguntum had already fallen – the Romans having stood idly by – that the Senate responded, by sending a delegation to Carthage to demand Hannibal's surrender. The Carthaginians opted for war. In May of 218, knowing that he was no match for Roman naval power, and understanding

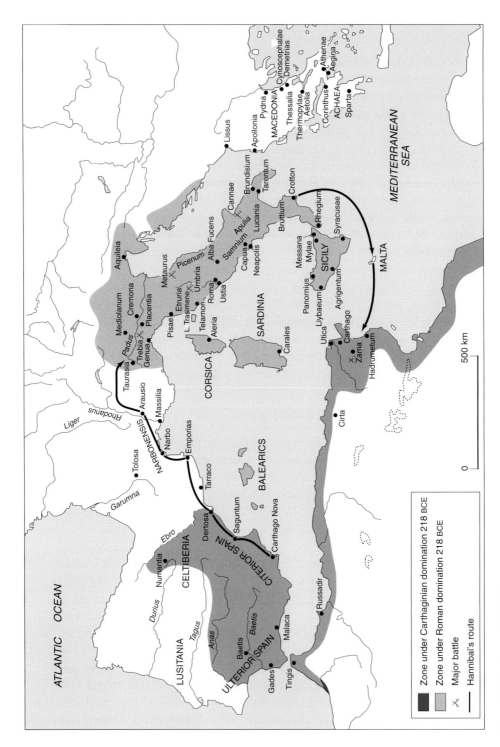

Map 4.1 The Second Punic War

ATLANTIC OCEAN

MEDITERRANEAN SEA

LUSITANIA
CELTIBERIA
ULTERIOR SPAIN
CITERIOR SPAIN
NARBONENSIS
BALEARICS
CORSICA
SARDINIA
SICILY
MALTA
MACEDONIA
ACHAEA

Durius
Tagus
Anas
Baetis
Baetis
Ebro
Garumna
Liger
Rhodanus

Numantia
Gades
Tingilis
Malaca
Russadir
Carthago Nova
Saguntum
Dertosa
Tarraco
Emporias
Narbo
Tolosa
Massilia
Araussio
Taurasia
Genua
Trebia
Placentia
Cremona
Mediolanum
Padus
Aquileia
Pisae
Etruria
L. Trasimene
Telamon
Aleria
Carales
Metaurus
Picenum
Umbria
Roma
Ustia
Alba Fucens
Samnium
Capua
Neapolis
Apulia
Lucania
Cannae
Brundisium
Tarentum
Bruttium
Crotton
Rhegium
Messana
Mylae
Panormus
Syracusae
Liybaeum
Agrigentum
Utica
Carthago
Zama
Hadrumetum
Cirta
Lissus
Apollonia
Thessalia
Pydna
Cynoscephalae
Demetrias
Thermopylae
Aetolia
Corinthus
Athenae
Aegina
Sparta

500 km
0

Zone under Carthaginian domination 218 BCE
Zone under Roman domination 218 BCE
Major battle
Hannibal's route

perhaps that his best chance of success lay in establishing a single front, ideally in Italy, Hannibal set out for the Alps.

This war, lasting 17 years, has often been called the "Hannibalic War," so much was it dominated by the personality and exploits of this great general. Unlike the first war, it was not confined largely to the place where it began – in this case Spain, with the siege of Saguntum – but raged over Italy, which was ravaged for over 15 years by Carthaginian armies living off the land. Then it reached Africa, where, repeating Regulus' exploits but with more success, P. Cornelius Scipio landed and terminated the war in a final battle, at Zama in 202. These events touched even the Greek world, where the First Macedonian War was the direct result of the Roman–Punic struggle.

Three phases may be distinguished in the development of hostilities.

Carthaginian operations in Italy, and Rome's difficulties: 218–211/210

Hannibal was banking on a rebellion by the Cisalpine Gauls. And indeed, though at first restrained by the action of the consul P. Scipio, many of them abandoned Rome after its defeats at the Ticinus and the Trebia. After the further defeat at Lake Trasimene, even part of Picenum followed the victorious Hannibal. However, Hannibal failed to raise the peoples of central Italy (Marsi, Maruccini, Paeligni); the ravages inflicted by his troops tended rather to set the countryside against him. That failure spurred him on to enter Campania, where he hoped that Capua would defect to him and where, as master of fertile lands, he counted on setting up a bridgehead with Carthage. His hopes were dashed at first. But the Roman defeat at Cannae in 216 had formidable consequences, provoking further serious defections from the Roman cause:

- In southern Italy, where, besides those among the Bruttians, Lucanians, and Samnites, there was the even more serious defection of Capua and several Campanian towns. Despite the Roman–Campanian state, Capua sided with Hannibal. A treaty concluded in 215 even planned for the sharing of Italy between Capua and Carthage should the Romans be defeated, and in 214 a project was born for a Carthaginian state in southern Italy. At Tarentum, occupied by a Roman garrison, treachery delivered the gates of the town into the Carthaginians' hands. Metapontum and Thurii followed the example.
- In Sicily, where the death of the aged Hiero II of Syracuse, one of Rome's allies, allowed Hannibal to proceed with his intrigues there. That caused the Romans to attack Syracuse, which was besieged, in vain, for eight months in 214. A Carthaginian army was able to land and seize Agrigentum. This was the signal for a Sicilian uprising. This necessitated the presence of a Roman army there which would have been very useful on the mainland (the war in Sicily lasted until 209), and depleted Rome's grain supplies since Sicily was a major supplier of corn.

- Lastly in Sardinia, where the natives rebelled after Cannae. Here, Ti. Manlius, thanks to his good knowledge of the country, was able rapidly to overcome the Sardinian rebels, taking prisoner the Carthaginian Hanno, who had come to give them support – in 215 nearly everything seemed settled there.

Rome itself was, however, never in mortal danger. Despite these defections, and the threats that twice hung over the capital, its safety was ensured by the unshakeable loyalty of central Italy, the unyielding attitude of the Senate, and the support of the *populus*.

The reconquest of Italy: 211–206

Beginning in 213, Rome's main objective was to reconquer Campania, and punish Capua and the Samnites for supporting Hannibal. Not without difficulty, and in spite of two serious defeats, in that year the consuls managed to surround Capua with a double entrenchment. The siege lasted until 211. Capua's fall was the start of Rome's regaining full control of Italy.

In southern Italy Despite an attempt by Hannibal to break the siege by coming and camping for five days before Rome (before having to withdraw in order to

Chronology 4.3	The Second Punic War

219/218	Siege of Saguntum by Hannibal. Declaration of war by Rome.
218	Hannibal marches from Spain to southern Gaul and crosses the Alps.
	Roman defeat on the Ticinus.
	Roman defeat at the Trebia.
217	Roman defeat at Lake Trasimene.
216	Roman defeat at Cannae.
216/215	Hannibal at Capua.
215	Agreement between Hannibal and Philip of Macedon.
214	The Romans reoccupy Samnium.
212/211	Siege of Capua and recapture of the town by the Romans.
211	Hannibal marches on Rome, then beats a retreat.
211/210	Roman victories at Syracuse and Agrigentum.
210–206	Scipio's successes in Spain.
209	Recapture of Tarentum by the Romans.
207	Hannibal's brother Hasdrubal arrives in Italy. He is beaten on the Metaurus.
205	The decemvirs decide to bring the Black Stone of Pessinus to Rome, to introduce the cult of Cybele, protectress of the Trojans, "ancestors" of the Romans.
204	Scipio lands in Africa.
202	Scipio's victory at Zama.
201	Peace with Carthage.

get back to Bruttium), Capua, deserted by the Carthaginians, was finally taken by the Romans. According to Livy, the chief citizens were killed or imprisoned, the populace sold into slavery, and the city's status reduced to that of a rural town.

The years 210–209 were not free from distress for Rome, but there was also a rallying of support: the treasury was empty; but the senators, appealed to by the consul Laevinus, poured their gold and silver into the public coffers. Meanwhile, the allies began to show signs of weariness: in 209, 12 Latin colonies declared themselves exhausted of both men and money, and refused the loans demanded; but 18 others said they were prepared to make any sacrifice.

Rome punished forcefully the other reconquered areas. Bruttians and Lucanians were debarred from recruitment to the legions and saw their lands confiscated to the advantage of the Roman colonies. Similarly, in Campania, those towns which had allied themselves with Hannibal lost their territories. Thus was formed the *ager Campanus*, some 60,000 ha of the richest lands in Italy placed at the disposal of the Roman Senate.

In 209, Q. Fabius Maximus managed to regain Tarentum, which was sacked, and 30,000 of its inhabitants sold into slavery. The punishments visited on Capua and Tarentum put an end to all attempts at defection.

End of the war in Sicily This was the work of Claudius Marcellus, who finally seized Syracuse after three years of siege. Looting and pillaging took place on an immense scale, but there were few massacres. The Greek physicist, engineer, and mathematician Archimedes, whose engineering inventions had helped stall the Roman attack for a while, was killed by a Roman soldier while solving a geometry problem. The consul M. Valerius Laevinus took Agrigentum in 209, and restored peace in Sicily and its production of corn for Rome. The year 209 marks the end of Greek Sicily; from then on the island was entirely Roman.

End of the Sardinian revolt The two legions left by Rome had to confront another large uprising, and then pacify the Sardinians, who periodically heard rumors of the arrival of a Carthaginian fleet. Order was restored between 209 and 207, and the island participated in equipping the expeditionary force of Scipio, who was making ready for his departure for Africa.

The Roman offensive: 206–201

After the successes of 209–207, Rome still experienced some difficult moments, in particular with the arrival in Italy of two other Punic armies. Hasdrubal, Hannibal's brother, caused some disturbance in Cisalpine Gaul and Etruria on his way to reinforce Hannibal, but he was defeated and killed at the battle of Metaurus. Mago, Hannibal's younger brother, landed in Liguria in 205. At first he managed to subdue some Italian cities and bring them to the Carthaginian side, but he was defeated in 203, and then recalled to Carthage following Scipio's landing.

P. Cornelius Scipio's landing in Africa was the great event of the last phase of the war. Since 210, the young Scipio had been attracting everyone's attention. Dispatched as proconsul (literally "acting as a consul") to Spain (before he had held any other important office), he had recaptured Carthago Nova and, while holding both it and Saguntum – the two principal maritime bases in the western Mediterranean – he put an end to the Barcine empire and made the crossing to Africa possible. Elected consul for 205, after a rough political battle in which supporters and adversaries of an African expedition opposed one another in the Senate, he obtained the province of Sicily, with the right to cross over to the African continent.

He left for Africa in 204 with two legions and their auxiliaries, 35,000 men in all, relying heavily on the help of the Numidian king Massinissa, with whom negotiations had long been going on. He landed near Utica and in the spring of 203 won a victory over the Punic forces. Carthage recalled first Mago, and then Hannibal, who landed near Hadrumetum (Susa) in the autumn. While attempts at negotiations were proceeding, Scipio made intensive preparations, drilling his troops in a tactic based on that of his opponent. With the decisive assistance of the Numidian cavalry, he won his great victory at Zama (near Ksar Toual Zammel in present-day Tunisia) on October 29, 202.

Peace negotiations, disastrous for Carthage, were concluded in the spring of 201. Carthage handed over all but 10 of its war vessels and all its elephants, and pledged itself to pay 10,000 talents over 50 years and not to make war on others without Rome's agreement.

Consequences of the Second Punic War

Despite the enormous human losses, the war had important repercussions in the growth of Rome and Italy, reaching far beyond 201.

First, it forced Rome to provide itself with a powerful military apparatus. Before 218, it had normally maintained between six and eight legions, or between 25,000 and 33,000 men. Between 217 and 203, it mobilized up to 28 legions, i.e. some 120,000 men, added to which were the troops supplied by allies and the men employed in the navy. This unprecedented military effort understandably brought financial difficulties. But Rome took advantage of these to provide itself with a light currency, making its transactions easier.

Next, those testing years brought about a singular strengthening of Roman institutions. The Senate, which had been the soul of the resistance, now enjoyed immense prestige. Its authority (*auctoritas*) covered all important decisions and acts in political life. Decimated by the first disasters (80 senators were killed at Cannae), it was brought up to strength by a *lectio senatus*. Henceforth, a strict hierarchy was established for recruitment to the Senate: choice was made first, by order of seniority, among former curule magistrates (consuls, praetors), and then among former aediles, tribunes, and quaestors. It thereby became truly an assembly of former magistrates directing the policies of magistrates, thus gaining further prestige.

lectio senatus: A reading or calling of the roll of the senators, carried out by the censor, who could strike from the list the names of those he considered unworthy.

Also, the war produced magistrates and generals of great worth, men who, often armed with extraordinary powers, had acquired or displayed personal renown, great ability, and vast ambition. This was notably so in the case of P. Cornelius Scipio Africanus, who was the first to bear the title of *imperator* (commander-in-chief, victorious by the grace of the gods). The power of these men, based sometimes on the will of the people more than on that of the Senate, foreshadowed the rise of the great *imperatores* of the first century BCE.

Plate 4.3 Athlete making a lustration. Roman votive relief, second century BCE. Capitoline Museum, Rome. C. M. Dixon

The First Macedonian War (215–205) was also a repercussion of the Second Punic War. The young king Philip V had wanted to profit from Rome's troubles by taking back Illyria, where Rome had established settlements. In 215, he made an agreement with Hannibal, engaging with him to force Rome to give up its Illyrian protectorate. Rome, busy in Italy, responded by making a treaty of alliance with the Aetolians, enemies of the Macedonians in Greece. Eventually, in 205, the Peace of Phoinike was negotiated, by which Rome kept its bridgeheads in Illyria. The peace apparently consisted of a general pact of non-aggression between the Romans and Philip, effectively depriving Hannibal of Macedonian help.

In fact, Rome found itself increasingly involved in Balkan affairs while at the same time it now had important interests in Spain and the western Mediterranean. A new chapter of its history was opening, which included a third war with Carthage.

4.5 | Gladiatorial Combat: Rise and Early Development

gladiator: A skilled, trained, and well-armored weapons fighter who performed in public combats against another gladiator. Various types (Samnite, *Retiarius*, etc.).

While the earliest **gladiators** may have been prisoners of war forced to fight to the death at funerals, by the late Republic a gladiator (from *gladius*, the "Spanish sword" used by Roman soldiers from the late third century BCE) was a skilled, trained, and well-armored weapons fighter who performed in public combats against another gladiator. Gladiatorial combats were carefully arranged between well-matched opponents to provide the entertaining elements of suspense and unpredictability. Even with the well-designed protective armor, militaristic gladiatorial duels involved a significant chance of injury and death; but they have been misunderstood as fights, necessarily and sadistically, "to the death." Some scholars now interpret these combats as shows or entertainments put on by trained and talented performers; and, however distasteful it might be, we can consider gladiatorial shows a Roman spectator sport. Like fighting cocks or pit bulldogs, the gladiators came to represent or symbolize their masters and fans, providing vicarious self-validation of Roman militarism and machismo.

The historical context: militarism and Roman culture

amphitheater: Venue for gladiatorial combats and animal spectacles (e.g. the Colosseum (Flavian Amphitheater) at Rome). Included arena, subchambers, and seating for spectators.

All studies recognize militaristic imagery as a consistent feature of the appeal of gladiators. With weapons and armor, with training and skill in fighting, with the danger of injury and death, gladiatorial combat unquestionably had military overtones. Stressing the metaphor of gladiators as soldiers, scholars have felt that the arena turned war into a game or drama in the domesticated battlefield of the **amphitheater**, set up in memory of Rome's warrior traditions.

Stoic and elitist literary sources criticized the emotionalism of spectators, but often praised the gladiator's soldierly discipline and acceptance of death through training. Gladiators supposedly provided emotional conditioning for the soldier-citizen. Cicero (*Tusculan Disputations* 2.17) declares that, like Roman soldiers of old, gladiators show discipline and a desire above all to please their masters; offering an education in facing pain and death, they sustain wounds, and when defeated they offer their necks for the death blow, and die with honor.

Origin, exposure, and adaptation

Older works assumed that Rome adopted gladiators from the Etruscans as a form of funerary human sacrifice, and sixth-century Etruscan tomb paintings do depict a blindfolded man with a club being attacked by a large dog and attended by a masked figure named Phersu with a whip or leash. However, there are no certain depictions of gladiators in early Etruscan art, and at most the Phersu game was a precursor to Roman beast combats. While it is unlikely that gladiatorial combats per se came to Rome solely through Etruscan influence, the Etruscans did give Romans their preference for foreign, slave, or captive performers, and also their conviction that good citizens watched rather than performed in public games.

Most scholars now favor an early fourth-century origin for gladiators in Campania (west central Italy in the general area of Naples and Cumae). Campanian tomb paintings (especially from Paestum, south-east of Pompeii, c.370–340 BCE) and vase paintings seem more obviously to depict armed single combats and even referees, and sources refer to combats at Campanian banquets. Campanian funeral games apparently included gladiatorial fights in which elite volunteers competed for prizes but originally fought only to the point of first bloodshed.

Realistically, the origin of Roman gladiatorial combats is probably not a historical question answerable in terms of a single original location or context. Combats and blood sports of various kinds simply were too widespread in antiquity. Before the first recorded gladiatorial fight in 264 BCE Rome had already been exposed, directly or indirectly, to all the suggested original influences (e.g. rituals of sacrifice and condemnation, grand funerals, Homeric prototypes, single combats, scapegoats, etc.). Early Rome itself was already familiar with public executions of criminals, animal sacrifices in festivals, and countless acts of brutality in war. Moreover, the adoption of imported cultural features usually involves cultural adaptation: some negotiation or cultural give-and-take. Whatever the precursors before and beyond Rome, the best approach is to concentrate on the more immediate context of Rome's adoption, adaptation, and development of gladiatorial combats into culturally distinctive spectacles.

Romans became familiar with Campanian gladiatorial combats in 308 BCE when the Romans and Campanians won a battle against Samnites, who fought with plumed helmets, and greaves on their left leg. As Livy (9.40) says, after the victory, the Romans adorned the Forum with the captured arms to honor their gods "while the Campanians, in consequence of their pride and in hatred of the Samnites, equipped after this fashion the gladiators who furnished them entertainment at their feasts, and bestowed on them the name of Samnites." The Romans did not immediately adopt Campanian-style gladiatorial entertainments, but they were exposed in 308 to elements of later gladiatorial shows: Samnite gladiatorial armor, staged combats, and the term "Samnite" – like "gladiator" later – as a hateful insult.

The earliest recorded gladiatorial combat at Rome was over 40 years later, in 264, when the sons of Decimus Junius Brutus gave a gladiatorial show to honor their dead father. This *munus* (a duty, tribute, or obligation to the dead) was a modest affair with only three pairs of gladiators, and it was held in the Forum Boarium, not even in the main Forum (Livy, *Epitomes* 16; Valerius Maximus 2.4). This probably was simply a forced combat, possibly to the death; there is no mention of later standard elements (e.g. prizes, a special facility, training and skills, the granting of respite or *missio*, possible manumission). Perhaps this first combat was simply a trial balloon, a novelty in an age of expansion when Rome was experimenting widely with spectacular entertainments.

> **missio:** Release from combat, public decision (of sparing or killing defeated gladiator) at end of combat.

The Romans had encountered but not adopted gladiatorial combats in 308, but did adopt them by 264. In the interim much had changed. Rome had completed the conquest of Italy, which had highlighted military virtues and leadership; and the political Struggle of the Orders between the plebeians and patricians was over. Adjusting politically, the Roman elite reformulated itself as the "nobles" (*nobiles*), a class of descendants of office holders. No longer able to rely simply on birth, this elite restored the deferential tendencies of the masses by competitive demonstrations of their generosity and worthiness for leadership. The provision of military displays in triumphs, beast shows, and *munera* at funerals became essential features of popular politics.

Cannae and gladiatorial ideology

A crucial stage in Roman attitudes to gladiators took place in the wake of Hannibal's defeat of Rome at the battle of Cannae in 216 BCE. When Cannae brought a national crisis of mass despair and depleted manpower, the Senate declined a Carthaginian offer to ransom Roman freeborn prisoners of war from the battle. Instead, Livy (22.57) says, Rome proclaimed a new levy of troops and even turned to using slaves. With money from the treasury, they purchased 8,000 young, sturdy slave volunteers, outfitting them with armor and weapons that had been taken from earlier enemies and publicly displayed as spoils of war. The slave volunteers swore an oath to serve courageously as long as the enemy was in Italy. Rome preferred slaves, selected for their fighting potential and equipped with the dedicated spoils of earlier wars, to free men who had already surrendered and broken their oaths. Roman tradition stressed a hierarchical social order based on freedom, land-ownership, and military service, but Cannae forced Rome to appreciate that even slaves – selected and sanctified by a voluntary oath – could serve Rome, like gladiators, by fighting and by inspiring others to military virtue.

Cannae crystallized the ideology of military virtue, of enlistment, endurance, and elevation that Rome traditionally expected of its soldiers in battle and came to demand of gladiators in the arena. Hannibal strengthened Rome's desire to demonstrate publicly that poor fighters would be punished and good soldiers, of whatever origin, would be rewarded. Cannae left a legacy of insecurity, a need for reassurance through brutality, a willingness to see moral examples beyond the ranks, and an approval of the elevation of the lowly by demonstration of martial virtue (*virtus*) and willingness to face death. According to Roman values, those who contributed to the needs of the state, as soldiers or as gladiators, deserved privileges. After Cannae, Romans embraced the notions of gladiatorial self-elevation and merited *missio*, which became crucial to the later combats. The arena's military morality plays re-enacted the lessons of Cannae: gladiators faced death in the arena like those slave volunteers and like Roman heroes who died in battle.

Sources do not record any gladiatorial combats between 264 and 216 BCE, but after Cannae gladiatorial spectacles at Rome escalated dramatically: 22 pairs in 216, 25 pairs in 200, 60 pairs in 183, etc. The imagery suited an age of continuing and expanding warfare, warfare that provided a ready supply of bellicose and foreign prisoners of war to turn into slaves and gladiators.

The preparation of gladiators

Rome's earliest gladiators probably included violent criminals and rebellious slaves; but foreign prisoners of war made the best gladiators, and the battlefield was the best source of supply. Complete social outsiders without rights or privileges, captives with some skill and experience were enslaved and underwent further training and conditioning to become combative but controlled performers in Roman arenas. The main early types of gladiators (Samnites, Thracians, and Gauls; see chapter 6, section 6.2, "Spectacles in the Late Republic," and chapter 11, section 11.6, "Spectacles and the Roman Empire") were named after historical military foes of early Rome, for early prisoners of war apparently were forced to fight with their own equipment in their own ethnic style. Rome had fought and defeated such enemies, but old fears and distrust persisted.

Under the Republic gladiators were owned privately, organized in groups (*familiae*), and prepared (and sometimes owned) by trainers (*lanistae*). Sometimes former gladiators themselves, these disreputable figures were viewed by society as on the same level as procurers and undertakers. Gladiatorial training facilities or schools (*ludi*) arose, notably at Capua and sites around the Bay of Naples (from at least the late second century). As remains of the gladiatorial barracks at Pompeii and the Ludus Magnus (the imperial school) at Rome show, gladiators lived in small cells, but they were not routinely chained or locked up. To prepare them for the arena, and to protect their investment, the owners gave

flamilia: Group of gladiators under a trainer (*lanista*).

ludi: Public games or shows; gladiatorial schools.

them modest but healthy food, medical attention, and regular exercise through their training.

Upon entering a gladiatorial school, recruits swore an oath "to be burned by fire, bound in chains, to be beaten, to die by the sword." All these, except the last, were severe affronts to the dignity of a citizen and the integrity of his body. This "voluntary" ritual promise mitigated Rome's responsibility and guilt. Whatever their origins, gladiators were all equal as slaves, bound by their oath. Knowing that they could distinguish, redeem, elevate, and save themselves only by skill and courage, gladiators embraced a militaristic *esprit de corps* and took professional pride in fighting – and if necessary dying – with courage and discipline. They were motivated by the desire to perform well, win rewards and fame, and achieve freedom, and also by the fear of failure – of defeat and dishonor as well as of death – in the arena.

Although some Romans of status entered the arena (see p. 246, below), such a citizen's proper role was to produce the shows, control the performers, and decide whether they had fought well enough to be spared. Romans identified not with the actual individual gladiator, a lowly, despicable foreigner, but rather with the skills and virtue that Rome gave to him through training and demanded that he display – or else.

Roman attitudes to gladiators

As gladiatorial entertainment at Rome emerged in the middle Republic (264–133 BCE) and as it became increasingly politicized and professionalized in the late Republic (133–31), the image of gladiators became ambivalent. The Romans themselves were puzzled by the inconsistency between the fighters' base and vile social status and the growing popular appeal of these impressive performers of the arena. Romans feared and loathed gladiators for their lowly or alien social origins or their heinous crimes, but they also associated them with glory, military virtue, discipline, and eroticism. Accordingly, the Christian writer Tertullian (*On Spectacles* 22) later saw the Romans as inconsistent, fickle and confused:

> look at their attitude to ... gladiators [*arenarios*] ... to whom men surrender their souls and women their bodies as well, for whose sake they commit the sins they blame; on one and the same account they glorify them and they degrade and diminish them. ... The perversity of it! They love whom they lower; they despise whom they approve; the *art* they glorify, the *artist* they disgrace.

Gladiators might achieve fame, wealth, or freedom by fighting successfully, but even free, former gladiators lived beyond the edge of respectable society. As Tertullian remarks and law codes attest, even if they became freedmen, they were barred from certain offices and even some cemeteries. Like actors, criminals, debtors, prostitutes, gravediggers, and other disreputable figures, gladiators were branded with the indelible *infamia* (a moral stigma and a legal status of diminished rights) associated with their performances.

Conclusion: a Roman entertainment

Rather than being regularly offered by the state according to the calendar of festivals, gladiatorial combats were provided occasionally by noble families as a privately funded addition to grand funeral rites. Combats became more lavish and popular in the late Republic, but they were not regularized and the tie to recent aristocratic deaths was not broken until the time of Julius Caesar.

Historically, the symbolic dynamics of the gladiatorial combat – what its actions and participants meant to the Romans beyond the demonstration of the status of the provider – cannot be separated from the military and political context of the middle and late Republic. This included recurring, brutal warfare, anxiety persisting from Cannae, the use of military captives as performers, and the growing appreciation of their impressive and entertaining military virtues in the arena. Gladiators were introduced at Rome perhaps as a novelty, and did not become understood in Roman terms until nearly 50 years later, in 216. Their combats became more and more appreciated, however ambivalently, under the late Republic until they were fully institutionalized by Augustus.

5

CONSEQUENCES OF CONQUEST

The Second Century BCE

After the death of Alexander the Great (323 BCE), the most important historical phenomenon for the future of the West was the gradual transition from Rome as city in Italy to Rome as capital of a Mediterranean empire. Between the end of the Second Punic War (201) and the annexation of Egypt (31–30), Rome conquered territories by means of its armies and diplomacy, in both the "barbarian" West and the Hellenistic East. Rome thus became the most powerful and enduring territorial empire in antiquity. But – and this is another essential historical phenomenon – while for the first time the West laid hands on the East, the eastern (Hellenistic) civilization penetrated deeply into the West. The result was a common cultural language and community of Greco-Roman interaction, which stands at the basis of modern western traditions. It is therefore necessary to address the question of Roman imperialism and its consequences.

5.1 | What Was Roman Imperialism?

Regardless of how imperialism was understood and rationalized by Romans, there is little doubt that Rome became a conquering power with a positive will for conquest and territorial expansion. The word *imperium* is truly Latin, just as the concept it covers is really and initially Roman. And this concept led to the first true and lasting attempt at universal domination. Some eminent historians (Theodor Mommsen, Maurice Holleaux, Ernst Badian) consider that Roman imperialism was defensive rather than offensive. According to their interpretation, Rome responded to wars that were forced upon it – in sheer self-defense; the Roman Senate, in particular, had no expansionist policy. According to other critics, however, the conquests were desired by all in Rome: by senators for the financial resources and social prestige necessary for their careers, by equestrians with an eye to financial exploitation of the conquered lands, and by ordinary citizens enticed by the prospect of looting and a share in the spoils. Polybius begins his history by admiring the unprecedented achievement of Rome "to extend its domination over nearly all the inhabited world, and that in under fifty-three years" (1.1). Writing in the second century BCE, long before Rome was the enormous empire it would become under the emperors, Polybius pronounces the future on the basis of the present: "Rome has subjugated more than just a handful of peoples. It has conquered almost the entire universe, so that there is no one today who can resist it and, in years to come, none can hope to surpass it" (1.2).

The problem of Roman imperialism was posed even in antiquity, as Polybius exemplifies. A Greek born about 200 BCE and deported to Italy after the victory of Pydna (168), Polybius meditated on the reasons for Roman successes, providing in his (universal) *History* a profound reflection on Rome, its past, its actions, and its destiny. A member of the Roman aristocratic world, and in particular of the literary circle around P. Cornelius Scipio Aemilianus (adopted grandson of Scipio Africanus), Polybius took a deterministic and elitist view of Roman success. He explained and, to a large extent, justified Rome's domination by the excellence of its "mixed" constitution, by the superiority of its army, and by what he saw as the superiority of the Roman state "in the domain of religious concepts" (8.56). In the political morality of the ancient world, anyone with any superiority whatsoever over his neighbors had the right, if not the duty, to make use of it. International law did not oppose the notion of "might is right." Thus, in the view of ancient authors such as Polybius, the superiority of the Roman people (*maiestas populi Romani*) largely legitimized Rome's domination (*imperium populi Romani*).

Following Polybius, historians of the seventeenth and eighteenth centuries (Bossuet and Montesquieu among others) and even the twentieth (such as Gaetano De Sanctis) argued for a premeditated, deliberate imperialism, evolved by a Senate constructing vast plans for expansion. In their view, Rome conquered the

Mediterranean basin methodically: Latium first and then Italy, the western half of the Mediterranean next, and the eastern afterwards. This view is open to criticism, given specific instances where Rome did not make use of the opportunity to conquer new territory:

- When it intervened in Illyria in 229 against the pirate state of Queen Teuta, Rome contented itself with simply maintaining bridgeheads there.
- Victorious over Philip V of Macedon at Cynoscephalae in 197, and then over Perseus at Pydna in 168, Rome could have annexed Greece at either time, but it did not do so until 146.
- In Spain, as early as 206, on the fall of the Barcine empire, Rome could have seized the country, whose natives, because of their hatred for the Carthaginians, would have given the Romans a warm welcome. It created a mere two provinces (Hispania Citerior and Hispania Ulterior) only in 197, and later set about a methodical conquest of the peninsula, completed in 19 BCE.
- In Africa, the Romans could have annexed at least the Carthaginian territories in 201. They did not do so until 146, and then contented themselves with what is today the north-east of Tunisia. If Rome had so desired, Egypt could have been annexed in 168; it became a Roman province only in 30, after the victory at Actium.

In fact, given the composition of the Senate and the attitude of the ruling classes, it would seem that hardly anyone in the governing circles of Rome at the end of the third century envisaged a commitment to a resolutely imperialist policy. At the time of the First Macedonian War (215–205), the only preoccupation was to prevent Philip V and Hannibal from joining forces. It was after Zama, between 200 and 198, that Rome really began to take an interest in the affairs of the Greek world. The Second Macedonian War (200–196) is perhaps the first example of a clearly imperialistic campaign. But it is fair to say that, even during the Second Punic War, a few influential senators (the Scipios, for example) had been very much attracted to the idea of Roman expansion. Hannibal himself had played a major role in this: the outrage over the Punic presence on Italian soil, the threat hanging over Rome, and the danger posed by the alliance of Carthage and Macedon were realities that spurred certain senators to cast their gaze overseas. The attack made by Rome against Macedon in 200 was the start of a new policy.

But it was still essentially a defensive imperialism, lacking self-awareness: before 148 the only annexations in the eastern Mediterranean were those of Zacynthos (Zante) and Cephallenia. Nevertheless, it should be noted that in this period, in 188, the Roman imperialist doctrine was explicitly formulated, thanks to the consul Cn. Manlius Vulso, who campaigned to Asia Minor in 189: in his view it was an urgent and absolute necessity for Rome both to ensure peace on land and at sea and to keep the entire East under surveillance. Livy relates Vulsius' exhortation directly to his soldiers to campaign against the Galatian Gauls of

Plate 5.1 Carthaginian silver coin from western Sicily, third century BCE. Ancient Art & Architecture Collection

Asia Minor, and their enthusiastic response to his proposal (Livy 38.12). Rome was to act as a universal "policeman," a policy which would lead to the establishment of protectorates over towns and of client states – and thence to annexation.

The era of annexations began in 148–146: the reduction of Macedon to a Roman province, the capture of Corinth and annexation of Achaea, and lastly the capture and destruction of Carthage signaled the great watershed. Henceforth a conquering brand of imperialism triumphed, leading, in a little over a century, to the formation of the Roman Empire. By 30 BCE, the Mediterranean was virtually a Roman lake.

5.2 | Conquests from 200 to 148 BCE: Defensive Imperialism

As we have seen, Rome's conquests between 200 and 148 were extremely limited. But it is important to follow the way in which the Roman outlook developed through these wars.

The Second Macedonian War: 200–196 BCE

During the Second Punic War, Rome had struck up friendly relations both with Pergamum and with Rhodes, an important trading center. Now, the king of Pergamum and the Rhodians warned that Philip V and Antiochus III of Syria had concluded a secret pact of alliance. Alarmed by this prospect of Macedonian imperialism and remembering the war with Pyrrhus, Rome decided, in 200, to attack the king of Macedon and drive him out of Greece. Roman policy was to guarantee the security of the Italian peninsula, and to that end it now sought to remove the aggressive king Philip from the Greek peninsula. To do so Rome itself turned aggressor. Nevertheless, victorious at Cynoscephalae in 197, Rome took virtually no territorial advantage from its success. One may recall the demonstrations of philhellenism made by the young and brilliant victor of Cynoscephalae, T. Quinctius Flamininus. Flamininus made a declaration of independence for the Greeks, in 196: "The Roman Senate and Titus Quinctius, consul, having vanquished king Philip and the Macedonians, leave free, without garrison, exempt from tribute, and in possession of their traditional laws, Corinthians, Phocidians, Locrians, Euboeans, Phthiot Achaeans, Magnesians, Thessalians, and Perrhaebians." According to Plutarch (*Life of Flamininus* 10), the exhilarated shouts of the Greeks created such disruption in the air that some ravens flying above the assembly fell instantly dead on the ground.

In fact, what the Greeks obtained was not total liberty (*eleutheria*), but rather a range of exemptions. Greece's status was actually that of a client state, a protectorate, with advantages for Rome. As a center of espionage, advance post, and buffer state, "free" Greece would act as a main road and a barrier, an arrangement set to guarantee Italy against the ambitions of Hellenistic monarchs.

By the same token, Rome found itself caught up in this arrangement. In 195, Flamininus was thus compelled to wage war against Nabis of Sparta, and then in 192–189 against the Aetolians, who had allied themselves with Antiochus (battle of Thermopylae, won by M. Acilius Glabrio). The Third Macedonian War followed.

The Third Macedonian War: 171–168 BCE

Philip V, who died in 179, was succeeded by the young Perseus. His keen interest in Greece made him a source of anxiety for Rome; his securing of ties with Syria (he became the son-in-law of Seleucus IV, Antiochus' successor) and his growing dealings with enemies of the king of Pergamum (Rome's friend) made him a threat, though hardly a serious one. Perseus had no desire to fight Rome, but rather to win over the Greeks and the Achaean League in particular. The Romans, however, were concerned that Perseus would destroy Roman political control in Greece. The warnings issued by Eumenes II of Pergamum, who accused Perseus of imperialistic plans in Greece, were given credence by the Senate, which was increasingly bent on managing the affairs of the Greeks. For the second time

Rome decided to intervene. After three indecisive campaigns in 171, 170, and 169, L. Aemilius Paullus won a victory over Perseus at Pydna in June 168.

Following the advice of M. Cato (known as "the Elder"), the Senate was unwilling to annex either Macedon or Illyria (which had allied with Perseus), but it made heavy demands: though proclaimed free, the two kingdoms were carved up and subjected to the paying of tribute; royalty was abolished; that part of Epirus which had betrayed the Roman cause was devastated; and the Greek ruling classes who had failed it were purged. Rome thus continued to refuse any territorial annexation but increasingly behaved as Greece's suzerain.

The beginnings of economic imperialism: 168–148 BCE

As early as the first half of the second century, crowds of Italian businessmen had followed in the legions' footsteps and spread all over Greece, where they were lumped together under the general term *Romaioi*. These *negotiatores* (simultaneously businessmen, traders, and financiers) are known to us through inscriptions from Illyria, Epirus, and Thessalia (there is evidence of a community of Italians in Larissa at the beginning of the second century), and then from Delphi, Boeotia, and especially the Cyclades.

In 166, the Roman Senate took a decision of major importance: to turn the island of Delos into a free port, granting it to Athens as a colony. Thus it rewarded Athens by giving it the holy island of Apollo, and punished the Rhodians, who had tried to mediate between Rome and Perseus during the Second Macedonian War to protect their maritime trade. Aulus Gellius, writing in the second century CE, provides some additional insight into the motives behind the Roman animosity toward Rhodes. He refers to a speech by Cato the Elder to the Senate, in which he attempted to "defend and save our excellent and most loyal allies, against whom many of the most distinguished senators were intently hostile because they wished to plunder and possess their wealth" (*Attic Nights* 6.3). According to Gellius, this speech became so popular that it circulated both separately and as part of Cato's historical narrative *Origines*. This popularity probably corresponds to widespread self-reflection on Rome's imperialistic intentions in the second century BCE.

At any rate, even though Rhodes escaped war, its economy was almost ruined as a result of the Roman actions, while the economic activity on Delos rapidly rose. Indeed, numerous Italian businessmen went to settle there, and Delos quickly became the center of trade between the Hellenic East and the Roman West.

5.3 | Conquests from 148 to 133 BCE: Conscious Imperialism

The years 148–133 mark a historical turning-point. A new brand of imperialism was being forged that would take Rome consciously toward empire. Three events occurred at the beginning of this period, events that, though precipitated by external circumstances, also undoubtedly displayed a new political determination on the part of Roman ruling circles to pursue an imperial course. This change was personified in 148 in Scipio Aemilianus, son of L. Aemilius Paullus and adopted son of the son of Scipio Africanus. Although he was under the required age, Aemilianus was elected consul for the following year.

The annexation of Macedonia: 148–146 BCE

This started with the venture of a certain Andriscus, an obscure Asian mercenary. Passing himself off as the son of Perseus, Andriscus had rallied the majority of Macedonians behind him and found support in Thrace. The praetor Q. Caecilius Metellus launched and led an expedition, reinforced by Pergamum's fleet, and succeeded in bringing about Andriscus' downfall. This time the Senate decided to reduce Macedon to a Roman province. A proconsul, residing in Thessalonica, was placed in charge of it. This was the first Roman province to be formed in the eastern basin of the Mediterranean. But soon other parts of Greece followed the same fate.

The rebellion and submission of Greece: 147–146 BCE

The causes of the rising that occurred in Greece at this time are not entirely clear. Due to social struggles and nationalist agitation, every inter-city quarrel ran the risk of expanding into a generalized conflict (such as the Peloponnesian War of the fifth century BCE). In 151, the return of 300 Achaeans deported after Pydna, "decrepit old Greeks" (to use Cato's words) but filled with hatred of Rome, did little to pacify people's minds. At all events, a row between Athens and Oropus over a question of customs rapidly escalated into a more serious conflict between the Achaeans, appealed to by Oropus, and Sparta, supported by the Roman Senate.

In 147–146, taking advantage of the fact that Rome was busily engaged in Spain and Africa, the Achaean strategist Critolaus, head of the anti-Roman party, promised the lower classes the abolition of debts, and succeeded in getting the vote for war against Sparta, Rome's ally. Two Roman legions, under the command of L. Mummius, were sent to Greece. Operations were short-lived. Critolaus was defeated and killed. His successor, Diaeus, had no better luck at Leucopetra. The last act was played out at Corinth, which had given a poor reception to a Roman embassy. In September 146, L. Mummius seized the town and, carrying out the Senate's official order to "destroy Corinth" (Livy, *Epitomes* 3), delivered it up to the mercy of his soldiers. The inhabitants were massacred or sold as slaves; the town was looted and burnt; the soil was **vowed** to the infernal gods. Great works of art were removed, dispersed, or destroyed. Polybius, who was on the spot, wrote: "I was there; I saw paintings trampled underfoot; soldiers sat down on

vow: Promise which religiously committed whoever made it (*votum susceptum*) and which it was imperative that he carry out (*votum solutum*).

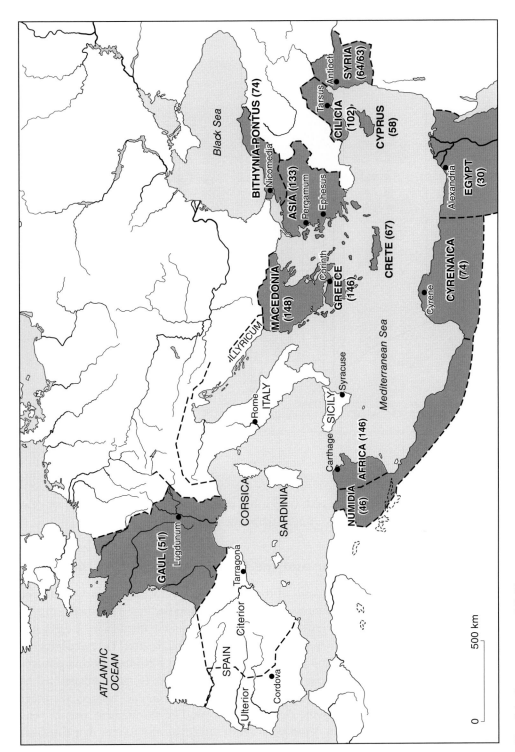

Map 5.1 Roman conquests, 148–30 BCE

Plate 5.2 Temple of Hercules Victor (also known as Temple of Vesta). Located in the Forum Boarium, the temple dates to 120 BCE and is the earliest surviving marble edifice in Rome. Alinari Archives, Florence

them to play dice!" The sack of Corinth marked the end of free Greece. It now became a Roman province under the name Achaea.

The Third Punic War and the fall of Carthage: 150–146 BCE

Several months earlier, in April of the same year, 146, Rome similarly destroyed Carthage. Since 195, Massinissa, the king of Numidia, had been increasing his attacks on Punic territories. Rome's arbitration (under the treaty of 201) had been generally conciliatory toward Carthage, although after 167, doubtless to reward Massinissa for his loyalty, it had been less so – Rome had thus allowed him to gain control of the ports of the Major Syrtis. A Roman embassy led by Cato arrived in the Punic capital in 153 to arbitrate the conflict between Carthage and Massinissa. Struck by the city's prosperity and its rearmament after the end of the Second Punic War, Cato persistently urged on the Senate that Carthage should cease to exist (Plutarch, *Life of Cato the Elder* 27).

Following a Carthaginian counter-attack on the Numidians, Rome declared war against Carthage in 149. Conducted from 147 on by the consul Scipio Aemilianus, it resulted, after a long siege and almost eight days of street fighting

Plate 5.3 Punic tower, Tunisia. © Roger Wood/CORBIS

and massacre, in the fall of the city. In obedience to the Senate's orders, the inhabitants were reduced to slavery or forced to emigrate, the town was burnt (though not totally, as recent excavations have revealed), and the soil was declared taboo (*sacer*), pledged to the gods for destruction. Punic territory (the north-east of Tunisia) became the Roman province of Africa, with Utica as its capital.

Thus, in the space of a few years there was a marked transition from the protectorate system, combined with more or less direct economic control, to a clear and determined pattern of annexation. The protectorate system was, however, by no means abandoned, but continued to grow alongside the system of annexation (the historian Justin relates that Scipio Aemilianus was sent to the East "to inspect the kingdoms of the allies" in 136/135). Meanwhile, the financial aspects of Roman imperialism were developing everywhere through banking, trading, and commercial activities.

Chronology 5.1	Conquests 241–27 BCE

241	Sicily	**119–107**	Balkans
238	Sardinia	**102–101**	Cilicia
227	Corsica	**96–74**	Cyrenaica
197	Creation of two Iberian provinces	**68–67**	Crete
168	Zante and Cephallenia	**64**	Bithynia–Pontus
166	Delos, free port	**64–63**	Syria
148–146	Macedonia	**58–51**	"Long-haired" Gaul (called after its long-haired inhabitants)
146	Achaea		
146	Africa	**58**	Cyprus
133–126	Asia	**46**	Numidia (Africa nova)
123	Majorca	**27**	Egypt (annexed, a full four years after Actium)
121	Transalpine Gaul		

The legacy of Pergamum

The Hellenistic kingdom of Pergamum had been formed in the third century on the west coast of present-day Turkey around the very rich Kaikos valley. Its successive rulers, Philetaerus, Eumenes I, Attalus I, Eumenes II, and Attalus II, had built it up into the most powerful realm in Asia Minor, its ports bursting with traffic and its sumptuously appointed towns dotted by sanctuaries of international renown. Troubled by their neighbors, the kings of Pergamum had maintained excellent relations with Rome. In 188, Eumenes II had placed himself under Rome's protection, but had at the same time preserved political sovereignty. Under Attalus II (159–138), that sovereignty had seeped away. Under his successor, Attalus III (138–133), the Roman hold over Pergamum intensified. In 136, when Scipio Aemilianus visited Pergamum, he behaved as if he were in a conquered country. When Attalus III died in the spring of 133, he bequeathed in his will all his personal wealth and property, including his treasury and the territory of Pergamum, to the Roman people.

This enormous acquisition of new territory had great and immediate consequences in Rome, to which we will return.

5.4 | War and Conquest: 133–96 BCE

Rome's foreign relations in the period after 133 were much more openly and self-consciously expansionist, so much so that we could claim that Rome now had a policy of deliberate imperialism.

Asia: 133–126 BCE

The will of Attalus III, by which he had bequeathed the kingdom of Pergamum to Rome, was quickly ratified by the Senate, which sent out a commission of five senators under Scipio Nasica to look into the affairs of the kingdom. Their work was cut short, however, by a rebellion led by Aristonicus, the illegitimate son of Attalus' predecessor Eumenes, who appealed to the population of the interior by promising, among other things, to free all slaves and to set up a kind of utopian state called the City of the Sun, where everyone would be free and equal. A Roman army was sent against him under the command of Publius Licinius Crassus, who was defeated by Aristonicus and killed while retreating. His successor, Marcus Perperna, consul in 130, defeated and captured Aristonicus, but died shortly afterwards. The final settlement of the kingdom was carried out in 128–126 by a commission of 10 senators led by Manius Aquilius. The bulk of the kingdom was annexed as a new province called Asia (a few of the less fertile eastern districts were handed over instead to local rulers). Some of the Greek cities, including Pergamum itself, were declared to be "free"; many were promised a measure of self-governance. The new province was wealthy, and soon became much sought after by Roman candidates for provincial governorships.

Southern Gaul: 125–118 BCE

In 125, Rome's ally, Massilia (modern Marseilles) appealed to the Romans for help against aggressive neighboring tribes, notably the Saluvii. The Senate sent the consul Fulvius Flaccus, who campaigned against the Saluvii, and also against the Ligurians and Vocontii. His successor, Gaius Sextius Calvinus, consul in 124, captured the Saluvii's largest settlement, near Aquae Sextiae (modern Aix-en-Provence). Alarmed, the Allobroges, who lived between the Rhone and the Isère, and the Arverni, who lived west of the Rhone, began actively to resist Roman encroachment. Both were defeated, however, in 121, the Allobroges by Gnaeus Domitius Ahenobarbus at Vindalium (near Orange), the Arverni by Quintus Fabius Maximus, probably near Valence. The Senate decided to annex southern Gaul as a province, which was originally called Gallia Transalpina ("Gaul on the other side of the Alps"), later renamed Gallia Narbonensis. Under the direction of Domitius Ahenobarbus, a road, the Via Domitiana, was constructed through it to connect Italy and Spain. A few years later, a colony of Roman citizens was set up at Narbo Martius (modern Narbonne).

In 123, to secure the sea routes to Spain, military operations were undertaken against the piratical activities of the Balearic islanders. Colonies of Roman citizens were established at Palma and Pollentia in Majorca. For his efforts, the Roman commander, Quintus Metellus, was awarded a triumph and the cognomen Balearicus.

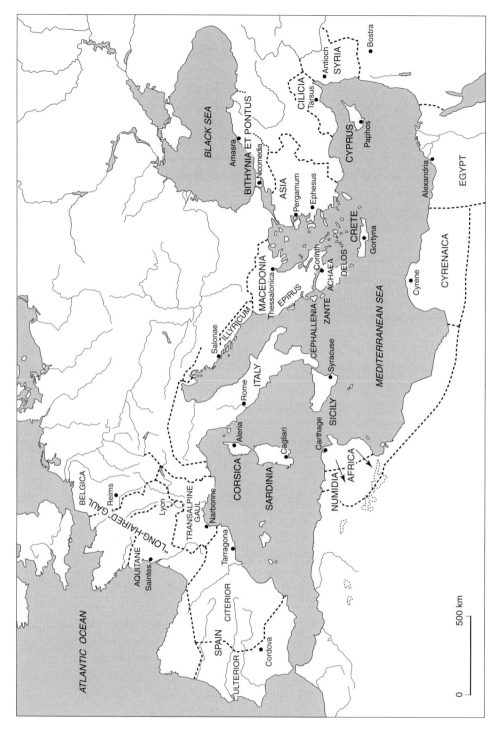

Map 5.2 The Roman Empire in 27 BCE

The Balkans: 119–107 BCE

Attacks on Macedonia's northern frontier by the Scordisci, a Thracian tribe who lived along the lower Save, were repulsed in 119 by Gaius Metellus, thereafter Gaius Metellus Delmaticus. Four years later, Marcus Aemilius Scaurus led a successful expedition against the Taurisci, who lived south of the Drave. In 114, however, the Scordisci defeated a consular army and invaded Greece, penetrating as far south as Delphi. They were gradually reduced, by Gaius Metellus Caprarius, in 113–112, Livius Drusus, in 112–111, and Marcus Minucius Rufus, in 110–107.

Cilicia and Cyrenaica: 102–96 BCE

In 102, to suppress the pirates who were preying upon shipping in the eastern Mediterranean, a Roman expedition was sent to Cilicia, on the south coast of modern Turkey. Most of the pirates' bases were destroyed, and the region was annexed as the new province of Cilicia. Six years later, in 96, the king of Cyrene, Ptolemaeus Physkon, bequeathed his kingdom to the Roman people, whereupon it was declared to be a new province, Cyrenaica.

Two more wars belong to the end of the second century: the war against Jugurtha (112–105) and the German wars (113–101). Because of the direct and immediate consequences of both these wars for power struggles of the late Republic, we shall turn to them in the next chapter.

5.5 | Roman Triumphs: Spectacles of Military Victory

In modern times armies returning from winning wars have often been given grand parades through the streets of cities, and thousands of civilians have turned out to witness and applaud the success of their soldiers and generals. The same social impulse to recognize publicly the contribution of armies and their leaders to the security and prosperity of the state arose naturally at Rome. From its beginning Rome was a warrior state, with armies of soldier-citizens led by consular generals; and military and political power intertwined in the concept of *imperium*, the power to command troops given to leaders by the Roman people. Semi-legendary figures (e.g. Horatius, Cincinnatus, Camillus) offered models of heroism, sacrifice, and victory in defense of Rome, and the increase in warfare put ever more emphasis on the notion of just and divinely sanctioned wars and on the leadership of magnificent generals. Early Rome institutionalized the recognition of successful generals in the awarding of a "triumph" (*triumphus*), a public processional entrance of a general into Rome in celebration of his significant military victory. Roman tradition credited Romulus with celebrating a triumph and founding the custom at Rome (Plutarch, *Life of Romulus* 16), but the first triumph recorded by Livy (1.38) is that of Tarquin the Elder after he defeated the Sabines. According to Livy (30.15), a triumph was the highest honor a Roman could achieve. Many consuls of the Republic were credited with triumphs, and many emperors staged triumphs for themselves. In all, Rome witnessed some 300 triumphs, a military track record of conquest and splendor.

Origins

As with many famous Roman ceremonies, the origins of the triumph remain uncertain. Processions are one of the most fundamental rituals of early communities, and scholars suggest the influence on Rome of Italian, Greek, or, most often and most likely, Etruscan precursors. There were earlier versions of the word in Greek and Etruscan, Etruscan art depicts similar processions, and the Latin peoples seem to have had similar traditions. Interpretations of such processions include Etruscan New Year's celebrations with the king in the role of a god, or festivals of victory, new beginnings, or good fortune. But by the time the practice emerges in Roman history it already combined religious, military, and political elements. The purpose clearly included commemoration of the great victory won by the general; a display of courageous and mighty forces, the booty that he had won, and the lands he had conquered; and the religious agenda of thanking Jupiter for the victory and soliciting his assistance in the future.

There are parallels between triumphs and the lavish funerals of great Romans, in that both ceremonies involved processions and rituals, sacrality, familial honor, orchestrated display, interaction among participants and spectators, and displays of generosity. However, rather than an obligatory honoring of the dead, the triumph was a communal celebration of victory and life, of success and security. The great funeral was a privately organized event (unless officially declared a state funeral and granted state finances), but the triumph, with the Senate granting money for the arrangements, was a public "affair of state."

Probable elements of a triumph under the Republic

The elements and their sequence in the procession apparently changed over time as individual generals made their own adaptations, but references in ancient sources (e.g. Livy, Polybius, Plutarch, Zonaras) suggest a reconstruction of the outlines of the triumph under the Republic. The essential element, the star of the procession, was the victorious general, the *triumphator*. Dressed in elaborate robes that suggested kingship and Jupiter, he rode in a special gilded chariot, one that was designed to look like a round tower, drawn by four horses. In front of the general marched his lictors carrying the *fasces* denoting his *imperium*. The general's sons or family members might accompany him, in the chariot or riding its horses, but all others proceeded on foot. In the chariot with the general was a public slave who held a laurel wreath (or gold crown) over his head and regularly reminded him that he was a mortal, that his glory was temporary. The general was to avoid haughtiness and to remember that his success was assisted by divine favor. However ambiguously, the glory belonged to Jupiter as well as to the mortal general.

The procession included the display of prominent captives, some of whom would be executed later. It was a great honor for the army to capture the leader of the enemy army, and it was reassuring to the masses to know that leaders such as Jugurtha, Vercingetorix, and other famous foes of Rome (Cleopatra making herself an exception) were killed in triumphs. Other prisoners of war in the procession were freed as an act of generosity and were presented as new freedmen of the general. Along with the captives, other impressive and valuable spoils of war were carried or marched, including material objects and animals.

The general's army, which he normally would have disbanded outside the city, joined the parade on this special occasion. Many of the soldiers wore special decorations, weapons, or crowns personally given to them by the general to recognize their valor in battle. In a vein similar to the slave's remarks about mortality, to temper any self-adulation or perhaps to appease the gods, the soldiers chided the general with disrespectful chants. This carnivalesque element of license, which contrasted starkly with the absolute obedience demanded of soldiers on campaign, is typical of festivals of thanksgiving. Also demonstrating an essential aspect of religious thanksgiving, the procession included animals (bulls or oxen) and priests who would conduct a sacrifice. By the early second century BCE the pageantry of the processions was embellished with paintings depicting events from the war, banners, musicians, and torchbearers.

The route of the triumph was hallowed by tradition but it also afforded maximum visibility for the people. After assembling in the Campus Martius, the parade entered the city through a special triumphal gate, which was closed thereafter and was not to be used by others. The procession wound its way through areas of Rome, circling the Palatine hill, before taking the Sacred Way through the Forum to the temple of Jupiter Capitolinus on the Capitol. At the temple the general dedicated his *fasces*, wreathed with laurel leaves, to Jupiter for bestowing his favor on him.

Triumphs at times perhaps evoked mixed feelings among the Romans. The whole procession normally incited popular jubilation, as thousands of spectators filled temporary stands and lined the streets, not only to view the sight but also to applaud and cheer: to interact and be involved in this collective ritual. However, the magistrates and senators, who also marched in front of the general in the triumph, may have felt some level of anxiety. Republican leaders and thoughtful citizens perhaps also had politically ambivalent feelings. This was the only circumstance under which a general was allowed to bring his army into the city, and the potential danger of the situation grew as the Republic weakened. A triumph appropriately acknowledged the conquering general for doing his duty, for serving Rome well; but, as a ritualized demonstration of power, it also dramatically heralded the achievement of a single man, in effect treating him as a king and even a god. As triumphs increased in number and extravagance, the balance between popular gratitude and elite self-representation was threatened.

Regulations

Since a triumph, as the pinnacle of military honors, so flattered and lauded a single general, the state was extremely careful about granting one. By tradition, to be eligible a general, one holding an office with *imperium* and having taken his own auspices (*auspicia*), had to have victoriously conducted a legitimate war in his assigned territory against a foreign foe. Also, he must have secured peace, having won and completed the war in which a minimum of 5,000 enemies were killed. Triumphs thus functioned as visible proof of such deaths.

The process began on campaign at the front, when the troops might proclaim their general *imperator* (roughly equivalent to "supreme commander") if he led them to success, and if they felt he was worthy of a triumph. The general sent a messenger bearing news of his success to Rome, and upon returning to Italy with his army he remained outside Rome and awaited the will of the Senate. The Senate determined whether or not to proceed with a popular vote in the assembly that would permit the general to enter the city with his army while retaining his military command (*imperium*). The Senate traditionally had the power (by procedures and control of the necessary funding) to celebrate a general's success lavishly or to overlook and undermine his achievement. Since the triumph so clearly associated military prowess and political leadership, the Senate was cautious about undermining republican traditions and their own position.

Given the various requirements and steps involved, clearly the awarding or securing of a triumph was heavily politicized. The regulations seem to have grown over time, but they were not consistently upheld. The Senate might chose to grant only a lesser form of triumph, an *ovatio* or procession on foot, as was done for Crassus' defeat of the revolt of Spartacus. Introduced during the First Punic War, a naval triumph (*triumphus navalis*), a similar but smaller procession with an exhibition of prows of ships, might be awarded for a naval victory, but this kind remained rather rare. If not granted a triumph in Rome by the state, a general might finance and stage one on his own outside the city, and some generals essentially coerced the Senate into granting triumphs at Rome, whether they met the formal requirements or not. Pompey, for example, held two triumphs without holding the adequate offices, and Julius Caesar held a triumph for defeating the sons of Pompey in what was a civil, not a foreign, war.

Triumphal grandeur and games

Since the Republic was almost continuously at war, with more distant and sometimes multiple fronts, the number, scale, and components of triumphs became more elaborate and expensive over time. The numerous Greek wars led to numerous triumphs, and to greater Roman exposure, via plunder, to Greek art and culture. After defeating King Philip V of Macedon at Cynoscephalae in 197 BCE, proclaiming the freedom of the Greek states, and receiving abundant honors in Greece, Titus Quinctius Flamininus returned to Rome to celebrate the first three-day triumph, one in which he displayed many thousands of pounds of gold and silver (Livy 34.52). After warring successfully against the Aetolian Confederacy in Greece, Fulvius Nobilior introduced the first performances of Greek athletes and actors in his triumph in 186 (Livy 39.22). The consul Lucius Aemilius Paulus celebrated his victory at Pydna over King Perseus of Macedon in 168 with a grand triumph that lasted three days and included an amount of gold and silver worth 120,000,000 sesterces or more (Plutarch, *Life of Aemilius Paulus* 32–5; Livy 45.40). Regrettably, because generals sought triumphs for personal satisfaction, political prestige, and popularity with the masses, there can be little doubt that at times they provoked attacks and sought out engagements, as in the pacification of Spain, in hopes of accumulating the requisite "body count." An authority on Roman military history suggests that through most of the middle Republic about one consul in every three celebrated a triumph. As Rome's subject territories and its frontiers became more distant, the triumphs visually brought the captured enemy – the foreign and now subdued barbarian – to Rome. Triumphs displayed the rewards, if not the reality, of fighting abroad to citizens who were increasingly removed from actual battles. Polybius (6.15) says that the *triumphator* in effect recreated for citizens the spectacle of his achievements on campaign.

As Rome's frontiers expanded, triumphs came to include the parading of exotic animals from the conquered foreign territories. Soon such animals were exhibited and "hunted" in arenas (in **venationes**), and increasing numbers of war captives were displayed and forced to fight in shows at Rome. Thus the display of beasts and captives as war booty and symbols of the conquest of foreign enemies and lands led to the creation or elaboration of other forms of spectacles. Paid for by the victorious general out of his spoils of war, such shows were put on at the end of triumphal processions, further demonstrating the extent and glory of the victory. Especially by the late Republic, a triumph became an occasion for a great general, enriched by war booty, to offer triumphal games; and triumphal games came to include more forms of entertainment and more lavish distributions of largesse to the people, such as public banquets and distributions of meat.

venatio: Spectacle with beasts, staged as a hunt with hunters or as a combat of beasts against humans or other beasts.

5.6 | The Economic, Social, and Political Consequences of the Conquests

The effects of the conquests were considerable in all aspects of Roman life, altering principally the conditions of the economy, of social life, and of political action. The agrarian reforms of Tiberius and Gaius Gracchus, the slave wars, and the war of Rome's allies (Social War) all stemmed from the growth of empire.

New living conditions in Rome and Italy

The first fruits of the wars and victories reaped in Rome were economic, followed by social and political developments.

First, the newly captured and controlled territories produced an enormous influx of spoils into Rome. "So numerous were the spoils coming from wealthy nations that Rome was incapable of containing the fruits of its victories," notes the historian Florus (*Epitome* 1.18). Tarentum and Syracuse paid a heavy tribute in works of art.

Indemnities imposed on the defeated rulers and the taxes levied on the provinces added to the wealth of spoils. This vast influx of booty and steady flow of gold brought about massive movements of capital in a city hitherto devoted mainly to agricultural activities. They affected wages and the cost of living (generally by an increase at the expense of the poorer classes), but chiefly the financial world (devaluation of the denarius) and overall economic policy.

The long absences of Rome's citizen-soldiers in distant theaters of war, preventing them for many years at a time from working their lands, as well as the army's need for vast quantities of cereals, oil, and wine, resulted in profound changes in Italian agriculture. The influx of slaves taken as prisoners of war (e.g. 50,000 on the capture of Carthage, 140,000 Cimbri and Teutons in 104), and of foreign corn newly made available, also left their mark. The poorer peasants (the majority) had little choice in reacting to the increasing availability of foreign corn and the subsequent devaluation of Italian cereals. Some sold their land and moved into urban centers (hence the creation of a potentially volatile body of urban poor, mainly in Rome), while others shifted their production by planting vineyards and olive groves in addition to (or instead of) grain. These, however, were costly replacements. The selling of land resulted in the merging of many smaller properties into a few great ones, to the advantage of the largest beneficiaries of war (generals and *negotiatores*). Viticulture and olive culture, on the other hand, resulted in a diversification in the crops grown in Italy, and rural activity became more commercial and developed. The organization of large markets obliterated the older practices of "self-sufficiency," that is, the use of produce for domestic consumption and small-scale trade.

The development of a large trading economy was one of the new features of the second century. The opening up of Rome to the outside world, the activities of businessmen, the monetary influx, and increasing needs connected with the new conditions of living drove Romans and Italians to invest in large commercial operations. As early as 218, a *lex Claudia* had attempted to prohibit senators from engaging in any lucrative activity based on trade – a law which they got round by doing business through front men, such as their friends in the equestrian class or their own freedmen. Capital investment and financial loans (frequently

Plate 5.4 Slave-boy named Iunius in a kitchen at Pompeii. C. M. Dixon

at extortionate rates) became a major business of the wealthy. Delos emerged as a great trading center and huge slave market. The Romaioi were actively present in every Mediterranean port, and began forming profitable associations with the companies of tax collectors (*publicani*). The power and influence of the *publicani* on the Roman political system, and especially on the Senate, cannot be stressed enough. In the absence of an organized revenue service for the collection of taxes from its provinces, Rome farmed out tax collection to the company that presented it with the highest bid. Once the *publicani* had paid that amount in advance, they turned to the provincials to make up for it and for additional profit, often using abusive methods to do so. Their practices put tremendous pressure on the provincials, who had little means of reacting. The harmful consequences of the actions of the *publicani* will become clearer in the following chapter, in the context of the first triumvirate.

    The social and political transformations brought about by the conquests were equally important. In rural areas, the flood of slave labor contributed to the creation of a new type of agriculture and, at least in certain regions, to a preference for stockbreeding. In the towns, and particularly in Rome itself, the influx of domestic slaves altered the conditions of family life. In time, slaves were integrated into the urban cultural life, as scribes, doctors, teachers, and other professionals.

publicani: Private individuals who "farmed" public services (*publica*); levying taxes, contracting for public works and for equipping armies and the navy. In the late third century BCE they formed companies and soon large joint stock companies (*societates*).

Another effect of the conquests, and of the profits they accrued, was the formation of municipal elites in Italy's towns. This became noticeable first in central southern Italy, where there was an acceleration in the growth of villages into urban townships. Their growth brought them an administrative status that attracted "new money" businessmen, who made their wealth through commerce and financing (*negotiatores*, or their relatives). These soon became urban benefactors who defended and adorned their towns with defensive walls, forums, and temples.

From the second century on, these municipal elites constituted a reservoir from which part of the equestrians (*equites*) would be recruited, and, in their turn would supply the senatorial order with fresh blood. The struggle between the senatorial and the equestrian classes needs to be introduced here, since another important consequence of the Roman conquests at this time was the rapid social, economic, and political empowerment of the equestrian class in Rome. The equestrian order, whose wealth basis was business rather than land, had formed during the course of the third century between the traditional senatorial nobility (whose prosperity was founded on land-ownership) and the lower classes.

This was not a "middle class" (which did not exist in Rome), but a category of privileged citizens – senators' sons, officers, rich land-owners, publicans – whose membership was signified by their entitlement to a horse supplied and maintained by the state (they were known as *equites equo publico* (literally "horsemen by virtue of a public horse"). In the second century, these equestrians, who still played a paramount voting role in the centuriate assembly, aspired to take a more active part in social and, chiefly, legal affairs. They saw the fact that the courts were in the hands of senators as contrary to their interests. This was especially so when in 149 a *lex Calpurnia* set up permanent tribunals (*quaestiones perpetuae*) charged with judging promagistrates (governors of provinces), with whom many equestrians engaged profitably in provincial trading and financial business. The political power of the equestrians grew ever stronger from the time of the Gracchi. The equestrians gradually provided Rome with the executives and elements of a new society, acquired political power, and, by the end of the first century and the reign of Augustus, began to replace the old-established nobility.

The class conflict between the senatorial and equestrian classes was aggravated by the fact that the senatorial order itself was undergoing internal changes. Senior offices were increasingly confined to a few families, whose ancestors had also held these offices and who had thus bequeathed their prestige to their descendants, known as the *nobiles*. This group was comprised at first of former senior magistrates and their descendants, but by the end of the second century, it was limited to the descendants of former consuls. Therefore the same families (*gentes*) came to monopolize all the high offices. But the appearance of the new senators, the ambitions of the equestrians, and the accumulation of wealth by individuals outside the *nobiles* (and even the senatorial class) began to immobilize this ruling social group.

The tensions created by this increasing disparity between incomes and political weight among the upper social classes were accentuated by troubles among the free lower classes. The conquests had brought certain social benefits to them too, mainly through the development of urban and rural craftsmanship and the boom in small trade thanks to the expansion of Italy's internal and foreign trading. These gains were naturally accompanied by new disadvantages. Those driven from the rural world, small shopkeepers (the *tabernarii*), the jobless, the unemployed professionals, and the victims of slave-labor competition, were seeking opportunities in Rome, forming what many saw as an *infima plebs*: a lowly and dangerous crowd, ready to stir rebellion to improve their own fortunes.

This period also saw the appearance of a social group that proved to be increasingly active economically and politically. These were the freedmen (*liberti*) talented and skilled slaves who had grown close to their masters and thus obtained their emancipation. Having become free citizens, but with reduced political rights, freedmen stayed in the service of their former masters, as their clients and supporters. Thus in the second century "clienteles" were formed serving chiefly the political interests of their patrons – at election times they were their active partisans. When Gaius Gracchus came to the Forum, he was accompanied by some 3,000 friends and clients in procession. The often disruptive activities of clients in Rome's public spaces, and particularly the Forum, became an increasingly important factor in the political life of Rome, as we shall see below.

Out of these new economic, social, and political conditions of life arose great conflicts which deeply marked Rome's history and, to a certain extent, paved the way for the decline of the Republic as early as the beginning of the first century BCE. The new challenges that arose from Rome's conquests became clear in the events surrounding the brothers Tiberius and Gaius Gracchus.

The Gracchi: 133–121 BCE

The reforms introduced by the tribunes Tiberius and Gaius Gracchus in the period 133–121 were intended to solve some of the economic and social problems that had intensified in Italy in the course of the second century, primarily as a result of two developments: an enormous influx of wealth and slaves into Italy after Rome's conquests, and the ruinous effects of military service on the peasant class. These two problems were interconnected: in every period, the bulk of Rome's soldiers had been farmers. In the second century, however, when they were required to serve increasingly long periods overseas, many of them returned home to find that their farms had fallen into disrepair, or that, in their absence, their land had been sold off or expropriated by the wealthy. The politically active class, and the well connected, used the wealth generated by Rome's conquests to buy up property, which, increasingly, they organized into large, plantation-like estates (*latifundia*) and worked mainly by slave labor. With little work to be found in the countryside, the rural poor began to migrate in large numbers to Rome, where employment was scarce and sporadic.

Faced with the very real prospect that a shrinking peasantry would be unable to provide the soldiers Rome needed, a number of senators began to talk openly in the 140s about giving some of Rome's publicly owned land (*ager publicus*) to the dispossessed. The land, which had been acquired mainly during Rome's conquest of Italy, was occupied mostly by squatters (*possessores*), senators among them, who were expected to pay rent to the state. Since, however, Rome did not possess an institutional machinery that would ensure the consistent collection of rents, many of those who were working the land had come to think of themselves as having ownership of it.

Tiberius Gracchus

Tiberius Gracchus came from a prominent background: his grandfather, Scipio Africanus, had defeated Hannibal; his father, Tiberius Sempronius Gracchus, was twice consul (in 179 and 163), and censor in 169; his wife, Claudia, was the daughter of the *princeps senatus*, Appius Claudius Pulcher. According to our sources, while traveling through Etruria as quaestor in 137 Tiberius first became aware of the problems experienced by small farmers because of the growing *latifundia*. He was elected tribune for 133, and, early in his tribunate, he proposed a law that would make it illegal for any one person to possess more than 500 *iugera* (roughly 300 acres) of public land, or for any family to have more than 1,000. However much land they possessed below these limits they were to be allowed to keep rent-free, forever. Whatever was left over would then be distributed to the landless in small parcels, probably of 30 *iugera* (18 acres). Tiberius also proposed that the newly acquired kingdom of Pergamum (bequeathed to the Roman people in the will of Attalus III in that same year) be diverted for solving the agrarian problem. Insofar as it exempted private property, the proposal might have been considered moderate. But those who controlled a lot of public land had a great deal to lose. And many of them were senators.

Expecting a hostile reaction in the Senate, Tiberius took his proposal directly to the popular assembly. And when one of his fellow tribunes, Marcus Octavius, tried to block the proposal, obviously acting on behalf of the Senate, Tiberius arranged for him to be deposed from office. A three-man commission was established to administer the law; it consisted of Tiberius himself, his younger brother Gaius, and his father-in-law, Appius Claudius Pulcher.

In the summer of 133, Tiberius declared himself a candidate for a second tribunate in 132. Re-election was not illegal, and not entirely unprecedented, but his opponents regarded it as proof that he was dangerously ambitious. At a meeting of the assembly on the Capitol, during a discussion of Tiberius' eligibility for a second tribunate, a brawl broke out. When word of it reached the Senate, the chief priest (*pontifex maximus*), Publius Scipio Nasica, gathered together a number of senators and other opponents of Tiberius, and marched to the assembly, where they proceeded to kill Tiberius and about 300 of his followers. The bodies were dumped in the Tiber at night. A court was set up to punish the survivors: many were condemned and executed; others escaped, and were banished without trial. The three-man commission, however, was allowed to continue its work, as Tiberius was replaced by his brother's father-in-law, Publius Licinius Crassus. Some modern historians have interpreted this fact to mean that the Senate objected less to Tiberius' law than to his methods. Additionally, we can speculate that the senators lacked the political will and constitutional power to rescind Tiberius' reforms, which were aggressively supported by the people.

Gaius Gracchus

Tiberius' brother Gaius was elected tribune for 123, and again for 122. He pushed through a series of reforms, the exact order of which is unclear. Among other things, he re-enacted Tiberius' land law, put forward a proposal to establish new colonies in Italy and one, to be called Junonia, at Carthage, and sponsored a law that required the state to provide clothing to soldiers. Most importantly, perhaps, at least in the long term, he carried a law that provided that the state would purchase grain in bulk, store it at warehouses in Rome, and then distribute it in monthly allotments to the citizen population at a price below the market rate.

In the summer of 122, Gaius announced that he would stand for a third tribunate, in 121. But by now his opponents had succeeded in undermining his popularity, and he lost the election. Fearing for his safety, perhaps not without cause, he formed a personal bodyguard. Not long afterwards, a servant of the consul Opimius was killed during a disturbance. The Senate's response was to issue what came to be known as its "ultimate decree" (*senatus consultum ultimum*), which authorized the consuls to take whatever action they deemed necessary to protect the interests of the state. Faced with what amounted to a declaration of martial law, Gaius and his supporters took refuge on the Aventine hill, where they were soon defeated and killed. Some 3,000 of his followers were rounded up and executed, without trial.

The significance of the Gracchi

Though their enemies routinely branded them as demagogues and careerists, there is really no reason to think that the Gracchi were motivated by anything other than a genuine desire to improve the welfare of the Roman people. It can hardly be denied either that responsibility for the violence that ended their careers rests mainly with the Senate. The Gracchi mark a watershed in the political life of the Roman Republic: henceforth, the political class was divided into two, often mutually hostile, factions, the *populares* ("populists") and their rivals, the *optimates* ("best ones"). These were not political parties in the modern sense, but rather unofficial and fluid groups within the wealthy elite. While the *populares* brought political issues directly to the popular assemblies, by-passing senatorial consultation and approval, the conservative *optimates* struggled to maintain the established order through a united senatorial front against popular demands. The

populares: Roman political group, though not an organized party, who worked through and supposedly on behalf of the people, challenging the *optimates* in the Senate.

optimates: Roman political group, through not an organized party. Aristocratic and conservative, members of the Senate, they opposed the *populares*.

struggles between individuals from these two groups are another important factor in the political drama of the late Republic, as we shall see below.

The Gracchi are important for another reason: their deaths, obtained on the pretext of national security, opened the door to the widespread and systematic use of violence in public life, a development which, if it did not cause the fall of the Republic, certainly hastened it.

The slave wars

The several serious slave wars that began their course at this time were basically due to the sheer scale of the slave influx in Italy. At first the slaves came mostly as prisoners of war, but later they were bought in markets like that of Delos. Their number in Italy in the second–first centuries BCE is estimated at between 32 percent and 50 percent of the population. Many of these slaves were treated harshly by their masters, mainly in the rural areas, where in some parts slaves represented as much as 70 percent of the population. Their situation seems to have been especially painful in Sicily, under the iron rule of Greek masters. It was a matter of time before these disaffected slaves clustered around those who were willing to lead a revolt.

The first of these slave wars was in Latium. There slaves employed as shepherds turned to highway robbery, but they were quickly suppressed by the consular armies in 143 and 141. Larger-scale revolts broke out in Sicily (135–132), serious because of both the number of slaves involved and the strength of their organization. According to our sources, the first revolt began in the region of Henna, at the instigation of a certain Eunous, a slave of Syrian origin from Apamea. Eunous claimed to be a soothsayer, a devotee of the Syrian goddess Atargatis, and also called upon Demeter of Henna. There he had himself proclaimed king under the name Antiochus and set up his capital. A fellow fugitive named Achaeus (no doubt deriving his name from his Achaean origin) took a seat in his royal council. Another slave, a Cilician named Cleon, and his brother Comanus gained mastery of Agrigentum and placed themselves under the authority of Eunous. The rebels soon seized Tauromenium (Taormina), Catana, and Messina.

It was not until 134 that Calpurnius Piso succeeded in recapturing Messina and was able, in 133, to begin the siege of Henna. The town fell in 132, Cleon was killed, and so was Eunous, taken by surprise in a cave. This long and difficult war signaled to Rome the slaves' potential for organized rebellion, and the Senate deemed it necessary to send a commission of 10 senators to Sicily, with the task of reorganizing the province. The fear of slaves became a recurrent (and often justified) concern for the Romans in the next few centuries, as they increasingly relied on their labor and lived alongside them.

In 103, there was a rising of slaves in Campania, allegedly the individual undertaking of a Roman equestrian from Capua who was in love with a slave girl. The disturbances, however, reached Sicily. And at this point came the intervention of the Roman – or Italian – plebeians Varius and Salvius. The former had two rich land-owners assassinated by their 30 slaves, while the latter, who claimed to be a seer, became king under the name of Tryphon, and was succeeded by a Cilician, Athenion, who claimed to be an astrologer. After several failures, the consul Aquillius put down the insurrection in 101.

In Italy, the last and most famous of the slave revolts was that of Spartacus in 73. This was different from the others: because of its proximity to Rome, which felt the threat all the more keenly; because of its origin, the actions of a Thracian gladiator which influenced the schools of gladiators in Capua; because of the personality of its leader, Spartacus, who was perceived less as a "barbarian," and perhaps more as Greek; and because of the spontaneous nature of the movement. We will examine this rebellion in the context of the late Republic, in the following chapter.

The conquests of the second century BCE had decisive effects on Rome's political, economic, and social development. Their consequences were equally important in the cultural life of the Romans.

5.7 | Cultural Consequences

Direct contact with Magna Graecia and the Hellenistic world, the influx of foreigners, primarily slaves, into Rome and Italy, the increase in travel and trade throughout the Mediterranean: all these resulted in a transformation of the way of life on the peninsula and mainly in Rome. There in the second and first centuries BCE a startling development is evident in its material culture as well as in the moral, intellectual, and spiritual life of its citizens.

The development of material culture

All aspects of the material culture of the peninsula at this time were affected by a trend toward grandiosity, luxury, and refinement.

In Rome, a town where architecture had largely remained simple and traditional, stone temples were now being built, clearly influenced by Greek architecture, and even adorned with Eastern elements. Between 200 and 175, no fewer than 15 temples were constructed. And between 146 and 121, a new series was built, featuring the Greek marble of Mount Pentelicus and the use of the portico. Other buildings began to give the city the look of a real capital; aqueducts, bridges, and roads enriched the urban plan. A new type of edifice, the basilica, appeared in Rome. The highly ornate Corinthian column became popular. And private houses became larger and more sumptuous. A large number of great *domus* (private mansions) appeared at the end of the second century featuring marble columns, with elegant interior decorations in spacious reception rooms. In the Hellenized south, and then in central southern Italy, temples were built with vast sacred courtyards (*areae*) surrounded by colonnades – the temple of Apollo at Pompeii is a fine example. The most grandiose was the temple of

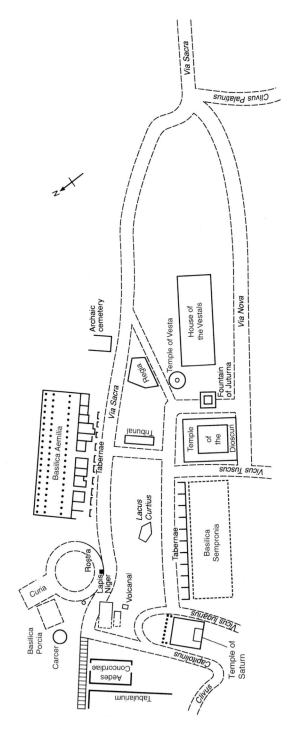

Figure 5.1 The republican Forum

Fortuna Primigenia at Praeneste, built between 110 and 100 and then enlarged and embellished in the time of Sulla. Its great series of tiered terraces leading up to a domed space (*tholos*) housing the sacred statue exuded something of the baroque. Similarly, in the countryside large villas proliferated, with porticoed gardens and gymnasia decorated with Greek works of art.

Matching the growing luxury of the public edifices and private dwellings, there were luxurious developments in the adornments, clothing, and food of the Romans from the second century BCE onwards.

Plate 5.5 Temple of Apollo, Pompeii. The statue of Apollo the Archer is a copy of a bronze statue found at the site, now in the National Archaeological Museum, Naples. C. M. Dixon

Back in 275, the consul P. Cornelius Rufinus had been expelled from the Senate for using a 10-pound silver service for his table (Aulus Gellius, *Attic Nights* 4.8). This episode illustrates the traditional aversion of Romans to luxury and the moral value they ascribed to parsimony. But, in the second century BCE, times had changed. Now engravers, silversmiths, and other craftsmen began to manufacture ornate vases and embellishments for beds and chests using bronze and precious metals. In the same way, the coarse wool tunic was replaced by tunics and togas of linen (from Egypt) and soon of silk (from the Far East). One of the legendarily rich men of Rome was L. Licinius Lucullus, whose life straddles the second and the first centuries BCE. Various episodes surrounding Lucullus illustrate the Romans' new and unapologetic enjoyment of riches and luxury. According to Plutarch, Lucullus offered 200 purple cloaks to a friend requesting only 100 to dress a dramatic chorus. He also entertained lavishly, offering banquets of different cost in specially designated houses throughout the city (*Life of Lucullus* 39, 41). In fact, the transformation of Roman cuisine was one of the first palpable consequences of Rome's Mediterranean conquests. At the beginning of the third century, Romans mocked themselves as *pultiphagi*, porridge-eaters. A century later the palates of the affluent experienced baked goods, peacocks, thrushes, guinea-fowl (from Africa), and pheasants (from the Black Sea). These goods, many of them imported, came with the foreign cooks to prepare them. The comic poet Plautus provides a vivid, if extravagant, image of the changing culinary culture of Rome at this time.

An intellectual, spiritual, and moral revolution

The second half of the third century witnessed the appearance in Rome of the first generation of Latin literature, dominated by the Tarentine Livius Andronicus. In the years 215–160, a second generation was producing new literature, influenced by the historical events of their own time. Naevius wrote a national epic, devoted to an account of the war against Carthage. Roman history was born with Fabius Pictor. The comedies of Plautus blended Greek New Comedy with elements from Italic farce. And, brought to Rome by Cato, Ennius, the first truly national poet, wrote 30,000 lines of an epic titled *Annales*, narrating the history of Rome from the fall of Troy to his own day. From 160 and onwards authors clustered loosely around a literary circle, led by Scipio Aemilianus. Here we find Polybius, Terence, Laelius (the Wise), Pacuvius, the first tragic poet, Accius, perhaps the greatest of Roman tragedians, and Lucilius, creator of the classical Latin satire.

The Hellenization that so profoundly influenced the material culture of the Roman world flowed into its religion and morals through philosophy. We have already seen that, as early as the third century, Greek gods and rites penetrated into the heart of Italy and Rome. The Second Punic War, and what the Romans saw as the profanation of the Italian land by the Punic enemies, precipitated conspicuous developments in religious sensibilities. Two important developments in that field belong to this time. First, the cult of the Phrygian goddess Cybele was brought from Pessinus into Rome in 205/204 BCE. Second, in 186 BCE, an event known today as the Bacchanalian affair revealed the popularity, influence, and perceived social threat of Dionysian mysticism. Following recriminations surrounding the nocturnal and orgiastic celebrations of Bacchus, the Senate feared, according to Livy, a "domestic conspiracy." After brief hearings, a senatorial decree was published, calling for the immediate disbandment of the cult, the destruction of all temples and shrines to Bacchus, the denunciation of anyone involved in these rites, and the punishment of those who would attempt to assist them to escape. Livy, who provides a detailed narrative of these events (39.8-19), relates that the male and female victims of this senatorial decree numbered in the thousands throughout Rome and Italy. Fortunately, we possess a bronze plate documenting this senatorial decree (known as *senatus consultum de Bacchanalibus*) which allows us a comparison with Livy's narrative of this affair.

Orphism and Pythagoreanism, doctrines of purity combined with ascetic practices, also enjoyed some success at this time, and similarly suggest the appeal of mysticism in Rome.

Meanwhile, the permeating Greek influence in Rome popularized the schools of Greek philosophy. Their representatives in the Roman capital, mainly from Athens and Rhodes, increasingly attracted the young and the aristocratic. The school of Stoicism was led by Panaetius of Rhodes. Opposing what he saw as the deterioration of morals, Panaetius recommended the practice of virtue, or rather of the four cardinal virtues: knowledge, justice, self-control, and courage. Epicureanism rivaled Stoicism and, much like it, promoted the concept of a virtuous contentment. Epicureanism, with its atomistic explanation of the physical universe, achieved success in Rome at the end of the second century, and in the next century with Lucretius' *On the Nature of Things*, a didactic epic poem in six books.

These significant shifts and evolutions in the last two centuries of the Republic, the consequence of Rome's expansion, often shocked ancient authors. The denunciation of indulgence as one of the major causes of republican Rome's decline became a commonplace in contemporary and later authors such as Polybius, Sallust, Diodorus Siculus, Seneca, and others. Cato the Elder's opposition to the repeal of the Oppian law is an episode that demonstrates the ambivalence felt about Rome's increasing wealth. This law had been passed in 215 by the tribune Gaius Oppius, to limit women's adornment and extravagance during the Second Punic War. Livy (34.2-4) creatively reconstructs a speech by the consul Cato in 195, during the debate regarding the possible repeal of the now antiquated law. There Cato denounces female luxury as the first step toward the political and social dissolution of the Roman state, and vehemently opposes the repeal.

In the same vein, Sallust, in his *Conspiracy of Catiline* (6–13), provides moral reasons for the decline of the Republic, inveighing against not only the increase of luxury and the lust for pleasure, but also the contempt for the gods and the impious corruption of men in power. A contemporary of Julius Caesar, Sallust lived through the political crisis of the Republic's last century, and he knew well how to describe it. Despite his dramatic and moralistic tenor, Sallust is essentially correct in observing that, together with great cultural influences, Rome's conquests brought deep changes in its traditional political and social life. These changes created conflicts which, already manifest by the end of the second century BCE, would explode in the last century of the Roman Republic.

6

THE LATE REPUBLIC

The First Century BCE

In the view of Sallust and Varro, Gaius Gracchus was at the root of the Civil Wars of the last century of the Republic, an overstatement that does not account for almost a century of civil strife. The reforms of the Gracchi simply exposed, and tried to address, the underlying economical and social consequences of Rome's Italian and Mediterranean conquests. The brutal deaths of the Gracchi and the disturbances surrounding them initiated a paradigm of political violence that evolved into a series of civil conflicts throughout the first century. Six powerful men and their armies dominate this century, and the events of the late Republic largely unfold around the conflicts of these three pairs: Marius and Sulla, Pompey and Caesar, Mark Antony and Octavian. In addition, slave rebellions and the war of the Italian allies against Rome (the "Social War") revealed all the weaknesses of a regime and society established for a city-state, which had meanwhile become a Mediterranean empire of unprecedented dimensions. The last century of the Roman Republic was in many respects a decisive period in Rome's history: not only because it was permeated by physical violence and turmoil in the public sphere, but also because it was a time when traditional values were collapsing, overtaken by new attitudes and a desire for new standards of living.

6.1 | Personal Ambitions and the Civil Wars

The clash of personal political ambitions did not, of course, date from the end of the second century BCE. Previously, however, it had occurred within the framework of public institutions: in the Senate, personal conflicts influenced or precipitated important decisions; in the assemblies, they steered popular votes to certain magistrates at the time of elections. In the first century, however, those with political ambitions felt themselves less and less subject to institutional rules that were enforced with ever decreased effectiveness. Therefore, they were more disposed to seek their achievement outside the settled arrangements for gaining power within the Republic. It was a matter of time before the army became an instrument of personal advancement at the service of these ambitious men.

A new Roman army

The whole military organization, as we have seen, was founded on the Servian constitution. The republican army of the early days had been essentially a national militia based on the *census* and property qualification, drafted for specific campaigns and disbanded once the war was over. Since the third century, however, and especially since the Second Punic War, things had changed. The scope of the wars and the length of those campaigns resulted in the dispossession of the lower classes from their small properties, and, subsequently, their disqualification from military service. Additionally, fear of losing their livelihoods made citizens increasingly reluctant to do their military duty (*militia*), and, consequently, the number of men who could be mobilized from the five classes had become insufficient for Rome's campaigns.

Thus, the necessity of lowering the minimum qualification of the fifth class and admitting the *proletarii* became obvious at the turn of the first century. This development is associated with the military reforms instituted by Gaius Marius in 107. Marius is credited with a number of reforms of the Roman army, including those of its equipment, training, and battle formation. However, his most important reform was a new method of recruitment: volunteers could now enter the legions, to fill the depleted ranks of those drafted according to property qualifications. These volunteer landless or propertyless *proletarii* would be paid in addition to being entitled to a share in the booty, and they would receive an allocation of land at the end of their service. From now on citizens from the lower classes, and especially those from rural areas, would supply the main body of recruits. Thus the army of rich citizens would be increasingly replaced by an army of landless plebeians.

This new demographic make-up had almost immediate consequences in the *esprit de corps* of the army and in its relations with civilian society at large. Beginning with "Marius' mules" (the soldiers' nickname, from carrying all their heavy equipment themselves), armies became professional employees at the service of their commander, from whom they expected their pay and rewards: booty, distributions of gifts at the time of triumphs, and, upon discharge, plots of land to ensure a permanent home and income. The republican national army led into campaigns by the consuls clashed with, blended with, and eventually was replaced by the armies of men like Marius, Caesar, and Octavian (later named Augustus, the first Roman emperor). The loyalty of the soldiers to individual generals as opposed to the Roman state is a defining characteristic of this new army, which can help us explicate the sequential wars of this period. We need therefore to turn to the first of these generals, Gaius Marius.

Marius

G. Marius, an equestrian originally from Arpinum (Arpino) in Latium, owed his rise to his brilliant military skills but also to the political backing of one of the most powerful and wealthy families of Rome, the Caecilii Metelli. Thinking they could use him for partisan purposes, the Metelli advanced Marius into the senatorial class and helped him to become, successively, quaestor, tribune, and praetor (in 115).

Marius' career was propelled by his military excellence, which he had ample opportunity to prove in two very different wars: the war against Jugurtha, in Africa (112–105), and the war against the Germanic tribes of the Cimbri and the Teutones (104–101). Even though both these wars belong technically to the second century, we treat them here because they led to Marius' extraordinary consular career and the events that followed his decline from the highest Republican office.

The war against Jugurtha: 112–105 BCE

In 118, the king of Numidia, Micipsa, died, bequeathing his kingdom to his two sons and to his nephew, Jugurtha, whom he had previously adopted as his son. Soon afterwards, Jugurtha murdered one of his adoptive brothers, and defeated the other, Adherbal, who then fled to Rome to ask for help. The Senate decided to send a commission to Numidia to divide the kingdom: it gave the eastern half to Adherbal, including the capital at Cirta (modern Constantine, Algeria); Jugurtha received the less fertile western part of the kingdom. Unhappy with this settlement, Jugurtha attacked Adherbal in 112, forcing him to hole up in Cirta, which Jugurtha then besieged. Adherbal was eventually forced to surrender the city, after which he was executed, together with a number of Italian merchants who happened to be living there. The Senate declared war, and sent an army to Africa under the command of Lucius Calpurnius Bestia, consul in 111. He persuaded Jugurtha to surrender, in return for the right to remain king of Numidia. To the historian Sallust, the significance of the agreement was clear: Bestia, like other Roman officials before him, had been bribed by Jugurtha. A formal inquiry was undertaken, and Jugurtha was summoned to Rome, where he refused to make a public statement. He soon returned to Africa, remarking, according to Sallust, that Rome was "a city for sale."

The war went on. The commander in 110, the consul Spurius Albinus, achieved little; his brother Aulus was defeated by Jugurtha near Suthul. The command was then handed over to Quintus Caecilius Metellus, consul for 109. Metellus chose Marius as his senior assistant (legate) and took him to Numidia. It is here that Marius began to get popular acclaim through his military career.

Metellus adopted a strategy of wearing down Jugurtha by attacking his strongholds, including Sicca, Zama Regia, and Vaga, which he captured in 108. Jugurtha, however, was able to enlist the help of his father-in-law, Bocchus, king of Mauretania (modern Morocco). So after some two years of campaigning, Metellus appeared to have accomplished little. On the other hand, Marius quickly built a reputation for himself as a hardened soldier and an affable leader, sparing himself no physical labor and sharing the hardships of the rank and file. When he decided to become a candidate for the consulship of 107 against Metellus' advice, Marius caused a break in his relationship with his patrons but nevertheless got himself elected. His election to the consulship was an impressive departure from tradition, alarming to many senators. Marius was a "new man" (*homo novus*), meaning that he had no noble ancestors who had held a senior magistracy. He was conscious that he owed everything to his personal and, above all, military qualities. His humble origins and his popularity with the soldiers ingratiated him with the people, who were opposed to the traditionalism of the senatorial aristocracy.

In 107 Marius' popularity was so widespread in Rome that the centuriate assembly was persuaded to strip Metellus of his command, and promptly handed it over to Marius. It was then that Marius raised new troops by enlisting volunteers, for the first time, from among the *proletarii*. In 106, he defeated Jugurtha and Bocchus near Cirta. With Bocchus' help, Jugurtha was captured the following year, and then displayed in Marius' triumph at Rome in 104. Shortly after, he died in the state prison, the Tullianum. The eastern part of Numidia was handed over to Jugurtha's half-brother, Gauda, and the western half to Bocchus, as a reward for betraying Jugurtha.

Almost simultaneous with the end of the war against Jugurtha, the German wars additionally showcased Marius' military excellence.

The German wars: 113–101 BCE

In 113, two German tribes, the Cimbri and the Teutones, began to migrate south toward Noricum, a region bordering the north-east of the Italian peninsula. Collective fear was fed by rumors about the numbers and strength of the barbarian force and by memories of the capture of the city early in the fourth century. The consul Gnaeus Carbo was sent north to engage them, but was soundly defeated at Noreia (near modern Ljubljana). The Germans, however, decided to move westwards through Switzerland, instead of advancing on the northern frontier of

Italy. They were soon joined by the Tigurini and some other Celtic tribes. By 110, they had reached Gaul. The following year, an army was sent north to protect the province, under the command of the consul Marcus Iunius Silanus. The Germans asked that they be allowed to settle along the frontier. Their request was rejected, however, by the Senate, which was concerned that their presence would constitute an ongoing threat to the security of the province.

Soon after, Silanus was defeated, somewhere, it seems, in the valley of the Rhone. For reasons that are not entirely clear, the Cimbri then turned northwards, while the Tigurini continued to advance to the west. Two years later, they were driven back by the consul Lucius Cassius Longinus. But the victory was short-lived: before the end of 107, Longinus was defeated and killed in an ambush in the Garonne valley. The Cimbri then returned, but were held off for a time by Quintus Servilius Caepio, consul in 106. The following year, however, after receiving reinforcements under the consul Gnaeus Mallius, Caepio was badly defeated at Arausio (modern Orange), with the reported loss of 80,000 soldiers, one of the worst defeats in Roman history. An invasion of Italy seemed imminent.

The disaster of Orange prompted equestrians and plebeians in Rome to effect Marius' re-election as consul for 104, even though he was busy in Africa against Jugurtha, and thus absent from Rome. It was yet another break with tradition, which demanded that the consular candidate be in Rome to stand for the office and that there be a 10-year interval before a second tenure of this office.

Consul once again in 104, Marius set about the task of saving Italy from the danger of the German invasion, and at this juncture more of his army reforms took place. Made consul again each year until 100, he forged a powerful army, introducing a strategic recasting of the legion and a standardization of its weaponry. Finally, Marius won successive victories against the Teutones at Aquae Sextiae in Transalpine Gaul (in 102), and at Vercellae in Cisalpine Gaul (in 101).

Marius had thus held six consulships altogether. Military exigency, his personal ambition, and his widespread reputation as a successful commander had trumped republican institutions and provided him with unprecedented power, prestige, and political influence (*auctoritas*). When he returned to Rome to celebrate his African triumph, in 104, he also staged his entry into consular office. Without laying down the triumphal insignia, he arrived the following day to sit in the Senate, still dressed in the purple mantle of victorious *imperatores*. It was the first time that a military leader had insisted on wearing his triumphal apparel after the triumph. But, despite his creation of essentially a personal army, Marius did not use it to establish himself as a sole ruler. Rather, he allowed himself to be involved in political rivalries and struggles, and even to be led into civil war.

From 100 to 86 BCE: the decline of Marius

Marius' last consulship, in 100, was the beginning of his decline, brought on him by his *populares* friends. These were the tribune Lucius Saturninus and the

THE LATE REPUBLIC 127

praetor Gaius Glaucia, whom Cicero described as "the ordure of the Senate." Following the precedent of the Gracchi, Saturninus proposed, among other items in his ambitious legislative agenda, an agrarian bill. The bill provided land allotments and the foundation of colonies for the veterans of Marius' German wars. These were to take place in the areas newly freed from the Cimbri in northern Italy. Furthermore, according to the same bill, Italian allies would be admitted to these colonies. Anticipating senatorial objection, Saturninus added to his bill a restrictive clause: the senators would have to take an oath to abide by the vote of the assembly, or be expelled from Rome if they opposed it.

Marius, as consul, found himself in a difficult position, with conflicting interests in settling his veterans, supporting his associates, and maintaining his hard-earned status with the senators. Despite his initial refusal to comply, Marius eventually took the oath and advised the Senate to follow his example. When Quintus Metellus refused the indignity of taking the oath, Marius was only too glad to banish his one-time patron from the city. However, the urban poor resented the possibility of allies possessing land and any other privileges that they considered exclusive to themselves, and so, on the day of the vote, riots broke out between them and the Italians who had flocked into Rome to support the law.

In that same year, Saturninus caused additional trouble by enlisting a gang to attack a rival candidate of his friend Gaius Glaucia for the consulship of 99. Disturbed by the public violence, evoking the days of the Gracchi, the Senate passed its ultimate decree, vesting Marius with complete authority to see it that the "Republic comes to no harm." Marius collected an armed force and laid siege to the Capitol, where Saturninus, Glaucia, and their associates had taken refuge. Marius obliged them to surrender and placed them into temporary custody in the Senate house, but they were soon discovered and stoned to death by an angry mob. Everyone considered Marius responsible for the disturbances, and thus the hero of the German wars finished his consular year discredited by both the Senate and the people.

To escape from his intense unpopularity, the following year Marius left Rome for Asia, claiming he wished to offer sacrifices to the goddess that the Romans called "Great Mother" (*Magna Mater*). Plutarch claims that Marius' real purpose was to regain his military glory by stirring up war with the kings of Asia and particularly with Mithridates VI Eupator, king of Pontus (*Life of Marius* 31). In fact Mithridates became one of the most powerful and long-standing enemies of Rome, until his death in 63 BCE. We summarize here the main events of the three wars against Mithridates, and we shall return intermittently to them in their proper timeline.

The wars against Mithridates: 88–63 BCE

Mithridates VI Eupator was king of Pontus, a region in central Asia Minor south of the Black Sea. It was an area rich in metals, made up mostly of villages and royal castles. In 104, at a time when the Romans were preoccupied with the German threat to their northern borders, he embarked upon an ambitious plan to create a kind of Anatolian empire. He first enlisted the help of Nicomedes III, ruler of the neighboring kingdom of Bithynia, who was officially a "friend and ally" of Rome, but tired of the extortionate practices of the Roman moneylenders in his kingdom. The two seized control of Galatia and Paphlagonia, and then advanced against Cappadocia. Ordered by the Senate to leave Cappadocia alone, Mithridates enlisted the help of his son-in-law, Tigranes, king of Armenia, who was persuaded to invade Cappadocia in 93. A year later, however, the former king of Cappadocia, Ariobarzanes, was restored to the throne by Sulla, who was governor of Cilicia. Mithridates patiently waited for another opportunity.

In 90, with the help of Tigranes, Mithridates seized control of both Cappadocia and Bithynia as the Romans were occupied with the Social War (see below). The Senate responded by sending a commission under Manius Aquilius, who eventually compelled Mithridates to withdraw. But Aquilius went further, persuading Nicomedes IV to invade Pontus itself in 88. Nicomedes was quickly defeated; Aquilius was captured and killed. Mithridates advanced through the province of Asia, promising freedom to the Greek cities and canceling all taxes. And then he ordered the slaughter of all the Roman and Italian men, women, and children in the province; as many as 80,000 were killed.

Urged by the democratic faction at Athens to liberate Greece from Roman rule, Mithridates then sent an army across the Aegean under the command of Archelaus, who, after some initial successes, was forced back into Attica. In 87, Lucius Cornellius Sulla (on whom more below) sailed to Epirus with five legions, marched to Athens, and promptly besieged it, bottling up Archelaus in the port at Piraeus. Early in 86, Sulla took the city; Archelaus fled to Thessaly, where Mithridates had sent reinforcements. They met Sulla in battle at Chaeronea, and lost decisively. Mithridates, however, was not ready to give up; he sent another army by sea to Euboea. This, too, was defeated by Sulla, in Boeotia, at Orchomenus. In the summer of 85, Sulla and Mithridates met at Dardanus near Troy. In return for being recognized as the king of Pontus, Mithridates agreed to become a "friend and ally" of Rome, to surrender 70 of his warships, to evacuate all of the territory that he had seized in Asia Minor, and to pay Rome an indemnity of 2,000 talents.

War, of a sort, broke out again in 83, when Lucius Licinius Murena, whom Sulla had left behind in Asia with two legions, launched a series of raids against the territory of Pontus. Eventually defeated in battle by Mithridates, he finally agreed to obey an order from Sulla that he should leave the king alone.

Several years later, in 75, Nicomedes IV, king of Bithynia, bequeathed his kingdom to Rome, which promptly declared it a province. Unwilling to allow the Romans to control the entrance to the Black Sea, Mithridates invaded Bithynia. The command against him was entrusted to the two consuls of 74, Marcus Aurelius Cotta and Lucius Licinius Lucullus (of the legendary wealth), who had been a friend of Sulla. Eager to win military glory, Cotta rushed into battle, was defeated both on land and at sea, and then besieged at Chalcedon. Mithridates himself advanced against Cyzicus, which he began to besiege. But Lucullus soon arrived, and managed to cut off the king's supply-lines, eventually forcing Mithridates to withdraw. At this point, it seems, Lucullus decided that, to defeat Mithridates once and for all, it was necessary to conquer Pontus itself. It required three years of almost continuous warfare (73–70). Mithridates eventually fled to Armenia, where he was given refuge by Tigranes. When Tigranes refused to hand him over, Lucullus decided to invade Armenia. He defeated Tigranes and captured the Armenian capital, Tigranocerta, in 69. But Tigranes and Mithridates escaped to fight again. Defeated in battle for a second time in 68, both escaped once more, Mithridates all the way to Pontus, which he recaptured in 67. Tigranes, meanwhile, invaded Cappadocia. Lucullus pursued Mithridates to Pontus, but his political enemies at Rome had conspired to have him stripped of the command, which was turned over first to Acilius Glabrio, and then to Pompey, who invaded Pontus and defeated Mithridates near Dasteira. Mithridates escaped again, this time northwards, where he spent the better part of the next two years raising additional troops. His supporters, however, began to turn against him, eventually forcing him to take refuge in the citadel at Panticapaeum, where in 63, at age 68, he committed suicide.

Rome's wars against Mithridates were the result of an inevitable clash between two empires, especially since, as we saw, Rome developed a consciously imperialistic ideology over the course of the second century. Marius was among the first to challenge Mithridates, during his trip to the East, allegedly telling him to either become stronger than Rome, or to do its bidding without a word (Plutarch, *Life of Marius* 31). Returning to Rome in 96, Marius built a house near the Forum to put himself back in the public eye. Despite the fact that he had been elected augur in his absence, he tried to restore his previous luster in vain and so he continued to live in retirement.

Sulla

The man who now came to dominate Roman political life, and develop an increasing conflict with Marius, was Lucius Cornelius Sulla. In many ways, Sulla made a lively contrast to Marius. First, unlike Marius, Sulla came from an old patrician family, the Cornelii, and was a supporter of the *optimates*. Sulla had served as Marius' quaestor in 107, during his first consulship and his command in the war against Jugurtha. In fact, Sulla was the one who had persuaded Bocchus, Jugurtha's father-in-law, to betray Jugurtha and hand him over to the Romans, effectively terminating the war in 106. Yet it was Marius who took the credit, and his triumph in 104 probably chagrined Sulla and added to the tension between the two men. Sulla, however, continued to serve on Marius' staff until the end of his campaigns against the Cimbri and the Teutones in 101.

As Marius' career began to decline in 100, Sulla's flourished. As praetor in 97, he impressed the people by the sumptuousness of the "Apollo's games" he gave.

Sulla also touted his special relation to the god Apollo, allegedly carrying with him a golden image of the god whenever he was in battle (Plutarch, *Life of Sulla* 29). As proconsul of Cilicia, Sulla was sent on a mission to the East in 96, to deal simultaneously with Mithridates and the Parthians, Rome's perpetual rivals, on the subject of Armenia. From that emerged a pact of friendship between Rome and Parthia, which boosted Sulla's reputation as a wise diplomat. In 93, Sulla left the East and returned to Rome. There he aligned himself with the senatorial aristocracy, who had been opposed to Marius during his heyday. According to Plutarch (*Life of Sulla* 6), the relationship of the two men was further strained when Bocchus dedicated to the Capitol trophies and artwork featuring himself handing over Jugurtha to Sulla. This episode was the last straw for Marius, and an open clash between the two men was stalled only by the beginning of the Social War.

The Social War: 91–88 BCE

Faced with the secession of some 100,000 men, Rome dispatched its two best generals, Marius and Sulla. The reason for this war was Rome's refusal to grant its Italian allies (*socii*) the Roman citizenship they desired. The question had been first raised as early as after the conquests in the third century. Since that time, Italy had been a confused tangle of territories. Rome conferred unevenly upon them privileges, rewards, rights, and duties, based loosely on their status compared to that of Roman citizens.

Roman citizens, full members of the civic body, participated in all the state's activities; they enjoyed the benefit of civil and legal rights; since 167 (after Pydna) they had been free of direct taxation (*tributum*), and they were entitled to a share in booty, to agrarian allocations, and to distributions of grain. Next came the "Latins," who held a status half-way between that of citizens and that of the allies. Inhabitants of Latin cities and colonies, the Latins shared the civil and legal rights of citizens (rights of contract, commercial, matrimonial), and were liable for certain fiscal and military dues (serving in auxiliary units). But in other respects, they were more like allies, carrying a Latin name but without all the political rights of citizens: in order to vote, they had to come to Rome and vote in a tribe drawn at random for each ballot. They aspired to full citizens' rights.

The allies belonged to a third, even less privileged, category. They were peoples connected with Rome by a treaty that outlined their relations with the capital, which, in most cases, exerted close control over them. Although in general they had remained loyal during the Second Punic War, they had received no reward. Quite the reverse: since 177 they had been excluded from the possession of land which they had helped to win for, or restore to, the Romans. They continued to supply the Roman army with contingents that were indispensable to its wars of conquest.

In 123, Gaius Gracchus had raised the possibility of granting citizenship to the Latins and Latin rights to the allies. Not only did the Senate reject this proposal, but it was decided to expel from the capital those Latins and allies who had no voting rights. The matter resurfaced between 95 and 91, when new measures were taken to counter the infiltration of Latins and Italian allies into the city.

In 91, the tribune M. Livius Drusus proposed a bill (*rogatio*) recommending a law that would grant citizenship to the Italians, as well as a new grain law. Immense hopes were raised among the Italians, but the senatorial oligarchy strongly opposed Drusus. To support him, a group of 10,000 Marsi set off for Rome, intent on sacking the city. They were successfully persuaded to turn back. At the same time, the Senate rejected Drusus' rogation. According to Livy (*Epitomes*), when the Italians realized that Drusus could not keep his promise to give them citizenship, they became bent on defection. Shunned by the senators as the cause of the war, Licinius withdrew and was soon murdered in his home by an unknown person. That gave rise to the revolt of the Marsi, and then of the Samnites, and soon of the whole of central and southern Italy. Thus began the Social War, also known as "the war of the allies" or the "Marsian War." For three years Rome witnessed "the whole of Italy rise up against [it]" (Velleius Paterculus, *History of Rome* 2.15).

This long and bitter struggle has sometimes been compared to the American Civil War. Great atrocities were committed: at Asculum (Ascoli) in Picenum, Roman women were scalped before being put to death; at Grumentum in Lucania, the small Roman garrison and the civilian population were massacred. The allies set up their capital in Corfinium, which they renamed Italica, and established several state institutions. The Marsi and Samnites, the most active of the rebels, issued their own currency to mark their sovereignty and independence from Rome. Among the Marsi this coinage bore the word "Italia," and among the Samnites, in Oscan, "Vitalia."

Pressured by the allies and with an eye always to its interests in Italy, Rome granted the essence of the Italian demands: the *lex Julia de Civitate Latinis Danda* (90) awarded Roman citizenship to all the Latins and to the allies who had not taken up arms, or were willing to lay them down at that time; in the next year, a *lex Plautia Papiria* added new tribes to the *comitia* as new communities were granted citizenship. In December 89, the war seemed to have ended – though in a few places it was prolonged until 88.

The allies had thereby won, at least in principle. The question remained of how to integrate the new citizens (*novi cives*) into the civic body. Given the voting process in the assembly (*comitia*) and the numbers of new citizens involved, their voting power would increase according to how many Roman tribes they were distributed in. The more tribes they were assigned to, the wider their influence in the elections. Seeing the danger of their presence in all or many of the 35 tribes, the Senate wanted to enroll them in only a few. Hence arose difficult disputes between *populares* and *optimates*. A senatorial decree in 84 conceded their enrollment in 35 tribes. By 70/69, under pressure from the *populares*, the related *census*-taking operations were completed – revealing that the adult male citizens at that time numbered 910,000, twice as many as before the war.

The main consequences of the Social War, besides the enlargement of the citizen body, were, first, the wide diffusion of Roman law and the quickening of the process of Romanization in the peninsula. Only the Cisalpine region remained apart, still a province and administered as such until the time of Caesar. Second, enormous clienteles were formed in Italy, for instance that of Cn. Pompeius Strabo (father of Pompey the Great) in Picenum, where he owned vast properties. And finally, with the entry into the ruling classes of Rome of citizens from the Italian cities and colonies, a new society began to form: moving gradually and determinedly into the magistracies and the Senate, these new Italian Romans would eventually take over from the old Roman families. The deep institutional and social changes brought on by this expansion of citizenship found both advocates and opponents. One of the more immediate results of the war, however, was the outbreak of violent hostilities between Marius and Sulla.

The break between Marius and Sulla: 88 BCE

During the Social War, the fortunes of the two men had diverged even further. According to Plutarch (*Life of Marius* 33), the war added as much to Sulla's reputation and power as it took away from Marius, who was already past his prime. As soon as this war ended, another danger reared its head, and, with it, the conflict between Marius and Sulla came to a head.

Alarmed by the increasing Roman presence and influence in Anatolia, Mithridates invaded it to "liberate" the province of Asia from Roman control. He then ordered regional overseers and satraps to execute Roman and Italian expatriates throughout Asia. As we saw above, around 80,000 people were massacred in Ephesus, Pergamum, Tralles, and other Greek cities in Asia Minor. This incident, sometimes referred to as the "Asiatic Vespers," prompted the Senate to decide on an expedition against Mithridates. As soon as the decision was made, the Senate was immediately faced with a potentially explosive dilemma.

Who would take command of the expedition to be mounted against Mithridates? Sulla, elected consul for 88, had the legal right to wage that war. He had also ensured the favor of the powerful Metelli by marrying one of their family, Caecilia Metella. Marius, however, at the time a private citizen and 72 years old, was not about to accept the legality of Sulla's right to command the campaign. Nostalgic about his old military prestige and looking forward to the prospect of booty, he convinced the tribune Publius Sulpicius Rufus to propose to the assembly that Sulla's commission be rescinded and offered to himself instead. Most senators objected, and the consuls declared a cessation of public business (*iustitium*) to stop the assembly from meeting. Rufus, however, caused a riot by inviting an armed gang of his supporters into the Forum, forcing the consuls to withdraw the *iustitium*. He then called the assembly and managed to push his bill through by filling the *comitia* with newly enfranchised Italian allies. Even though Marius possessed no institutional basis for this command, he was still seen as an experienced general and at an advantage because of his knowledge of the king. Besides, he had the support of the *populares*.

As he was preparing for his departure to the East, Marius sent two military tribunes to take command on his behalf of six expeditionary legions stationed in Nola, Campania. Sulla managed to get there first, and then successfully urged the legionaries to resist this change of command; indeed, as soon as they arrived on the scene, the two tribunes were stoned to death. Sulla then coolly proceeded to lead these legions to Rome. Fighting between the supporters of the two men broke out in the streets, at the end of which a victorious Sulla proceeded to the Senate house and forced the senators to reassign the command of the Mithridatic War. He also effected the banishment of Marius, who meanwhile managed to escape to Campania. Though captured at Minturnae, where he was in hiding, Marius again managed to escape, fleeing to Ischia. From there he reached Africa and rejoined his loyal veterans from the Jugurthine war, who had been allocated land there through Marius' efforts.

Sulla's march against Rome is a momentous turning-point in Roman history. For the very first time, a Roman general led a state army into the sacred precinct of the city, to ensure the success of his plans. Even though it can be argued that Sulla was merely defending the legitimacy of his initial commission of the Mithridatic War, the fact remains that he set an example of political transgression and abuse of military authority that others would soon follow.

After Sulla's departure for Asia to deal with Mithridates, Marius plotted his return as the *populares* regained power in Rome. He landed in Etruria, recruited volunteers, and joined forces with Lucius Cornelius Cinna, one of the leaders of the *populares*. After taking Ostia, he occupied the Janiculum and, at the end of 87, he took control of Rome. His siege of the city, horrifying in the heat of summer, was followed by terrible reprisals against Sulla's supporters, who were executed en masse. Marius forced the senators to revoke his banishment, while Sulla was declared a public enemy and his reforms and laws invalid. Marius and Cinna were elected consuls for 86: it was Marius' seventh time, a number which he claimed had been prophesied to him when he was young. Just two weeks later, however, Marius died and Cinna was left in sole control for the next few years (87–84). Marius' extraordinary career, and his even more spectacular decline and disgrace, left a deep mark in the collective consciousness of his contemporaries. Plutarch (*Life of Marius* 34) remarks that the sight of the elderly Marius exercising in the Campus Martius in preparation for the campaign against Mithridates caused some to pity him "for his greed and ambition, because, even though he had become very wealthy from being indigent, and greatest from being small, he did not know how to set limits to his fortune."

Meanwhile Sulla defeated Mithridates' generals in Greece (86–85) and drove him from Asia; then, eager to return to Italy, Sulla made peace with him (85), concluding what became known as the First Mithridatic War. When Sulla's return became known, there was a short period of relative calm, dominated by the fear of reprisals. But then the violence resumed even more fiercely. Landing at

Brundisium (Brindisi) in the spring of 83, Sulla found himself confronted by a senatorial army, commanded by the consuls and with the mission of applying the senatorial decree which, at Cinna's instigation, had outlawed him. After bitter fighting which lasted through the summer of 83 and then the spring and summer of 82, Sulla gained control of Rome on November 1, at the battle of the Colline gate, just outside the walls of the city. The casualties were between 50,000 and 70,000 in the two armies, and 3,000 were executed among the 12,000 prisoners whom Sulla assembled on the Campus Martius.

The great proscription of 82 BCE

Sulla also carried out a decimation of Rome's ruling circles. He compiled a list of those he considered enemies of the state (that is, his personal enemies) and published it in the Forum. This was the first "proscription list" (*proscribere* means both "to put on display" and "to condemn") of the late Republic, which consisted of:

- the display in public places of an edict of the proconsul justifying the measures taken, before enumerating them;
- a ban on any shelter or help given to the named individuals, the threat of death for those who broke the ban, a reward of 40,000 sesterces for the denouncer or murderer of a proscribed person, and, similarly, emancipation for slaves who did so;
- a list of 80 members of senatorial rank, all Marian magistrates or former magistrates. A second and then a third list appeared subsequently with a further 440 names.

There were appalling scenes in Rome and Italy, notably at Praeneste, which had dared to resist Sulla in 83/82. Other abuses included the scandalous transfers of property (the confiscated possessions of the proscribed), and egregious acquisitions of wealth from the same source. Similarly, Sulla settled his own veterans on lands confiscated from those he had proscribed.

In 80, at the height of Sulla's power, Marcus Tullius Cicero (on whom more below) made his entrance into public life. At the time only 27 years old, he defended his first criminal case in court and began to build his reputation as a successful orator. The case was complicated, and entangled in the dangerous Sullan politics: a man named Sextus Roscius, from the Umbrian city of Ameria, was charged with parricide in a plot orchestrated by Chrysogonus, one of Sulla's freedmen. Among other manipulations, Chrysogonus' plot involved entering the name of Roscius' father posthumously in Sulla's proscription lists, thus making his estate fair game for confiscation. Cicero, realizing that this was a ruse to defraud Roscius of his rightful patrimony, made a tactful case against Chrysogonus and his associates without offending Sulla, and obtained the acquittal of his client.

Sulla's dictatorship: 82–79 BCE

Once Sulla had completed the eradication of his enemies, he set about his political program. A *lex Valeria* conferred the dictatorship on him. The office of dictator, previously voted only in emergencies and with maximum tenure of six months, was first given to Sulla without a time limit. This appointment was considered all the more outrageous because no one had assumed this office for 120 years, since the days of the Second Punic War. The *lex Valeria* granted Sulla:

- the legalization of his past actions;
- the power of life and death;
- the right to dispose of the conquered kingdoms;
- the right to share out the lands of the *ager publicus* and create colonies. This he did in Etruria, Umbria, Latium, Campania, and Corsica (at Aleria). It was a means of rewarding his troops and building up clienteles for himself.

The senatorial decree conferring on Sulla practically limitless power could be considered the conceptual paradigm for the law delegating sovereign authority (*lex de imperio*), on which imperial power would later be based. On the other hand, Sulla's contemporaries did not necessarily see in this law a paradigm of absolute monarchy. Given the circumstances, the senatorial priority was to stabilize the state. Reflecting on the *lex Valeria*, Cicero argues that "this most hateful law" had only one excuse: that it was forced upon Sulla by the times, rather than by his own ambition (*On the Agrarian Law* 3.2).

The years 81–80 were marked by political and self-publicizing activity on Sulla's part. He restored to the Senate some of its lost powers, and even strengthened its authority by a series of measures he introduced: bills tabled by tribunes were to be submitted for prior senatorial approval, and the tribunes' right of veto was reduced. This has led some historians to see Sulla as a defender of the senatorial class. On the other hand, as we have seen, Sulla eliminated many senators by proscription, and subsequently raised the number of the Senate's members from 300 to 600. These new members were primarily equestrians from his own extensive clientele. He also made the quaestorship an automatic qualification for membership in the Senate, and raised the number of quaestors to 20. In addition, he re-established the previous statutory gap of 10 years between two tenures of the same office, which Marius had flouted conspicuously with five successive consulships (104–100). Sulla also introduced a new measure, according to which a magistrate had to wait for two years before being elected for the next office up in the *cursus honorum*. He firmly delineated the trajectory of the *cursus*, making the quaestorship a prerequisite for the praetorship, and, likewise, the praetorship a prerequisite for the consulship. Thus he hoped to prevent unqualified individuals from standing for the consulship.

Sulla's reforms in the field of law were generated in the same spirit of both senatorial restoration and personal control over it. He reduced the judiciary power of the equestrians, restoring court juries to the senators. He also established new courts to deal with specific offences, and institutionalized sharper distinctions between civil and criminal law.

After celebrating a sumptuous triumph in 81, he surrounded himself with a train of 24 lictors (consuls had only 12). In addition to his devotion to Apollo, Sulla advertised himself as the protégé of Venus. In his correspondence with Greeks he used the title *Epaphroditus* ("protected by Aphrodite–Venus"), translated by the Romans as *Felix* ("fortunate, blessed by the gods"). By invoking the protection of a divinity to serve his political ideology, Sulla set up an example for future generals (and emperors) to construct their personal relationships with various gods.

Finally, around 80, Sulla became tired and ill. Perhaps believing that he had restored order to Rome and reinstated its institutions, or, faced with new opposition and having no desire to resort to fresh violence, in that year (or in 79 according to some) he abdicated all power. He withdrew from public life and began to write his memoirs, but died in 78, in his sixtieth year.

As indicated by Cicero's comment on the *lex Valeria*, Sulla's legacy continued to divide the body politic of Rome for decades. For some he was a tyrant *par excellence*. But one cannot overlook his senatorial and legislative work, and that of urban renewal, both in Rome itself and in many towns in Italy, notably in Pompeii, where he created a *colonia Cornelia Veneria*. Additionally, Sulla enjoyed respect from his contemporaries for abdicating from office of his own will. According to our sources, once he had returned the consular elections to the hands of the people, he refused to even approach the assembly during their vote. Instead, he walked around the Forum as a private citizen, open to anyone who wished to challenge him on his previous career as a dictator (Plutarch, *Life of Sulla* 34; Appian, *Civil Wars* 1.103–4). Certainly his confident abdication and the fact that he was not harmed afterwards indicate a certain collective acceptance, if not approval, of his actions. On the other hand, his two marches on Rome, his proscriptions, and the abuses that followed injured irreparably the existing institutions, and particularly the Senate. The destructive path that Sulla blazed was soon followed by other ambitious generals, notably Gnaeus Pompey and Julius Caesar.

The rise of Pompey: 79–61 BCE

Pompey was born of equestrian rank in 106 or 105, the son of Gnaeus Pompeius Strabo, who controlled Picenum during the Social War, and from whom Pompey inherited a vast number of followers. Pompey had sided with Sulla when he landed in Brundisium in 83, and had helped him reclaim Italian communities from Marian supporters and veterans led by Marius' son. Pompey also fought the Marians in Sicily and Africa (82–81), where his soldiers gave him the title *Magnus*, "the Great" (a clear emulation of Alexander the Great). For his ruthlessness he acquired another nickname, "the teenage butcher." The early part of his career was also the beginning of a long-standing rivalry with another ambitious man who had also helped Sulla in his return to Italy. This was Marcus Licinius Crassus, who, after fleeing Cinna's proscriptions in Rome, had also joined Sulla on his return to Brundisium. Crassus had led Sulla's right wing at the Colline gate, where he won the battle for him when the center of the formation, led by Sulla himself, nearly collapsed. Yet Crassus' career was overshadowed by that of Pompey, who, among his other extraordinary honors, was proclaimed *imperator* by Sulla himself (Plutarch, *Life of Crassus* 6).

It is indicative of the shifting loyalties of the late Republic that Pompey, Sulla's favorite, backed the ambitious nobleman Marcus Aemilius Lepidus for the consulship of 78, even though Lepidus was openly hostile to Sulla. As soon as Lepidus became consul, he proposed measures canceling or opposing Sulla's constitutional arrangements: to renew the sale of subsidized grain at Rome, to return land that Sulla had confiscated, and to restore the powers of the tribunate. After he was elected, however, Lepidus went even further, and tried to stir up a rebellion, first in Etruria, and then in Gaul. Early in 77, the Senate declared him a public enemy. The command of the war against Lepidus was entrusted to Quintus Lutatius Catulus (Lepidus' colleague in the consulship of 78) and to Pompey, though he had yet to hold any elected office. Defeated by Catulus, and then by Pompey at Cosa in Etruria, Lepidus managed to escape to Sardinia, but died from disease soon afterwards. Pompey was then given the opportunity to prove his military skills outside Italy. In 77 he was sent to Spain, where Quintus Sertorius, governor of Nearer Spain (Hispania Citerior), was posing a serious threat to Rome.

The revolt of Sertorius in Spain: 83–72 BCE

Sertorius had had an adventurous career, from surviving the battle of Arausio in 105, to fighting under Marius in the battle of Aquae Sextiae in 102, to his efforts to contain the atrocities committed by Marius' and Cinna's armies upon their capture of Rome in 87. Appointed as proconsul of Spain in 83, Sertorius set on building an independent state in the Roman model (including a Senate made of his friends), with a considerable following among the native population. He defeated the governor of Further Spain (Hispania Ulterior) in 80, and he subsequently forged an alliance with the pirates who operated along Spain's Mediterranean coast. In 77, Pompey was sent against him. The following winter (76–75), Sertorius entered into negotiations with Mithridates, asking for money and ships in return for recognizing the king's claim to Bithynia and Cappadocia. The war dragged on, with varying fortunes on both sides, until 72. That year, with his support rapidly eroding through the rivalries of his commanders, Sertorius was murdered by one of his own lieutenants, Marcus Veiento Perperna.

Soon afterwards, Perperna was defeated and killed by Pompey, who stayed in Spain until 71. Then, his return to Italy provided him, quite by accident, with another opportunity to claim military glory and prestige. This was the revolt of Spartacus.

The revolt of Spartacus: 73–71 BCE

Our sources agree that Spartacus was a Thracian who had once served as an auxiliary in the Roman army, but it is not clear how he was enslaved and trained as a gladiator in Capua. In 73, Spartacus and a Gaul named Crixus broke out of the gladiatorial school with 78 associates and fled to the nearby Mount Vesuvius. Gradually joined by several hundred rural slaves, shepherds, and even freeborn impoverished discontents, Spartacus assembled a force of 70,000. The rebels then formed two groups, one commanded by Spartacus and the other by Crixus. Thus organized, they pillaged southern Italy. Spartacus, however, intended to repatriate the slaves to their home countries, while Crixus had no plans to leave Italy.

In 72, a terrified Senate dispatched both consuls against the rebels, and Crixus was killed in battle. Spartacus then began to march north, as if he wanted to cross the Alps and take the Gallic slaves home. After crossing Picenum, he defeated the Cisalpine governor at Modena. Changing his tactics, he turned south toward Lucania, perhaps hoping to take the maritime route out of Italy. It was then that Crassus was given extraordinary command and six legions to suppress Spartacus. Crassus complemented this senatorial army with legions raised from his own funds, one of the many expenses that earned him the title of the richest man in Rome. With 10 legions in all, he drove the slave army to the strait of Messina. There Spartacus in vain tried to ensure a passage to Sicily with the help of pirates. When they failed to carry out their promises Spartacus was seemingly cornered, but he managed to escape in the winter of 72–71.

Finally, in 71, Crassus' legions defeated the stranded slave army in Lucania. Spartacus was killed in battle, and Crassus had 6,000 of his followers crucified along the Appian way (Via Appia) from Capua to Rome. A few thousand survivors made it to Etruria, where they were cut down by Pompey on his way back from Spain. It was an extraordinary coincidence for him: after Sertorius' death and, ironically, at the instigation of Crassus himself, the Senate had recalled Pompey to help Crassus with the rebellion. By tying up the loose ends, Pompey was able to write to the Senate claiming that "Crassus had defeated the fugitives in open battle, but that he himself had pulled out the very root of the war" (Plutarch, *Life of Crassus* 11). The Senate added insult to Crassus' injury by awarding him a lesser triumph "on foot" (an *ovatio*) for his suppression of Spartacus, while Pompey celebrated a regular *triumphus* for his victory over Sertorius (on the conditions and implications of these celebrations, see p. 106).

Plate 6.1 Scene from a play, with masked actors: a magician and his clients. The mosaic, signed by Dioscurides of Samos, is from Cicero's villa at Pompeii. National Archaeological Museum, Naples. C. M. Dixon

Pompey's joint consulship with Crassus: 70 BCE

Though neither had much reason to trust the other, Pompey and Crassus decided to work together to advance their interests: among other things, each wanted to be consul in 70. Unlike Crassus, who had been praetor, Pompey had still not held any of the requisite elected offices. Additionally, being only 35 years old, Pompey did not even meet the minimum age qualification for the consulship (42) as set up by Sulla. But he had an army positioned outside Rome. Faced with the implicit but real threat of military violence and remembering all too well Sulla's march on Rome, the Senate caved in. Pompey ran for the consulship and was elected with Crassus as his colleague. They quickly did away with what was left of Sulla's constitutional settlement. And then, to the surprise of everyone, they retired into private life.

The rise of Caesar: 85–67 BCE

Gaius Julius Caesar, the man who would eventually defeat the great Pompey in a civil war, did not have a similarly glorious rise to power. The chronology of his early career is not entirely clear, but its main events can be summarized here with relative confidence. He was born in 100 to the *gens Julia*, which claimed descent from Iulus Ascanius, the son of Rome's founder, Aeneas. The controversy about the origins of his family *cognomen*, Caesar, is the first among many legends surrounding his person. Relevant speculation includes the birth of one of his ancestors through "Caesarian" section (Latin *caesus*, "cut open") or his own thick head of hair (Latin *caesaries*) as possible origins of this name.

Despite their ancient pedigree, the Caesar branch of the Julian family was not politically influential (a Lucius Julius Caesar had been the last consul, in 90). Yet their strong connections with the Marian party greatly helped advance Caesar throughout the early sixties. His father's sister, Julia, was the wife of Marius, who thus became Caesar's uncle. In fact the career of Caesar senior (he became praetor, governor of the province of Asia, and commissioner of a veterans' colony in Cercina, Etruria) was the result of Marius' power and influence. When his father died in 85, Caesar became the head of his family at age 16. The following year, probably at Cinna's instigation, he was nominated for the highest priesthood of Jupiter (*flamen Dialis*). One of the many restrictions for the sanctity this office was that its holder be married to a patrician, who would serve the cult in her capacity as the *flamen*'s wife. Caesar then promptly broke off his engagement with Cossutia, a woman from an equestrian family, and was married to Cornelia, Cinna's daughter.

It is not certain whether Caesar was actually inaugurated into this priesthood, but his Marian connections made him an instant enemy of Sulla. Upon his return to Rome after the Mithridatic War, Sulla insisted that Caesar divorce Cornelia on pain of his life. Caesar refused and went into hiding instead, but his life was spared through the intervention of the Vestals and several members of his mother's family (the Aurelii) who were supporters of Sulla. Self-exiled from Rome, he had a brief military career in the province of Asia, but returned soon after Sulla's death in 78. Since his family property had been confiscated by Sulla, he lived frugally in one of the most impoverished neighborhoods of Rome, the Subura. He made his living as a lawyer in criminal cases and he seems to have been a very skilled orator, judging from Cicero's praise (*Brutus* 248–55). In 75 he traveled to Rhodes, to study rhetoric with Cicero's teacher, Apollonius of Molon. On his way there he was captured by Cilician pirates, an early episode in his life that ancient biographies underline as symbolic of his nature: claiming that he was worth more than they were asking, Caesar proposed a higher ransom to the pirates than the one they were asking themselves. And while his staff were sent away to collect it, he cheerfully assured the pirates that soon he would capture and crucify them – which is exactly what he did soon after his release.

quindecimviri sacris faciundis: College of two (*duumviri*), later ten (*decemviri*), then 15 (*quindecimviri*) priests charged with custody and interpretation of the Sibylline Books, the worship of Apollo, and overseeing foreign cults established in Rome.

While he was in Rhodes (74), Mithridates invaded Bithynia. On his own initiative and at his own expense, Caesar raised a small band of auxiliaries and expelled the king's agents from the province of Asia. By providing Lucullus with precious time to organize his army and attack Pontus, Caesar earned a reputation for himself in Rome.

Returning there (73), Caesar was invited to join the college of pontiffs. Comprised of 15 lifetime members, the ***quindecimviri sacris faciundis***, this college had the superintendence of all religious worship in Rome, both public and private. When one of the 15 members of the college died, the *pontifices* themselves nominated their new colleague (a process known as *cooptatio*). At the time, the pontifical college comprised of members of the senatorial nobility and friends of Sulla. Impressed with Caesar's emerging prestige, they trusted that his Julian pedigree would fit with their own political traditions. But their hopes were soon dashed. In the next few years, Caesar's activities revealed his opposition to Sulla's policies, branding him as a supporter of the *populares*. In 73 (or 72) he became military tribune (*tribunus militum*), the first office voted to him by the people. He fervently supported the restoration of the tribune's powers, which had been severely curtailed by Sulla. In 70 he urged the tribune of the people to propose the recall of the exiled supporters of Lepidus (among whom was Cornelia's brother) and also spoke himself to the assembly in support of the proposed law. Pompey and Crassus, who, as consuls that year, revived the powers of the tribunate, certainly must have seen in Caesar an energetic ally.

In 69 Caesar entered the senatorial *cursus honorum* by serving as quaestor under the governor of Further Spain. That same year, he cleverly turned a family incident into a political opportunity: both his aunt Julia and his wife Cornelia died, and Caesar delivered their funeral oration in the Forum. There he proudly reminded his audience that Julia was descended from Venus herself, and shocked the senators by carrying in the funeral procession images of Marius, which had been banned by Sulla years before. In 67, after his quaestorship, he was admitted to the Senate and in the same year he married Pompeia, Sulla's granddaughter by his daughter Cornelia. It was an important juncture in his political career. His first marriage had aligned him with the *populares*; his second with the conservative *optimates*. It was clear that Caesar was an extremely clever, bold, and ambitious man, who would take any opportunity to establish himself as a powerful agent in the Republic. In 65, as aedile, he dazzled the people with lavish gladiatorial spectacles, theatrical performances, and public banquets.

Pompey's campaigns in the East: 67–62 BCE

Meanwhile, Pompey's career began to thrive. In 67, one of the tribunes, Aulus Gabinius, proposed that something should be done about the pirates of the Mediterranean. Based in Cilicia in southern Asia Minor, these brigand fleets raided common maritime routes, jeopardizing the transportation of grain to Rome. With an eye to Pompey, Gabinius made the following suggestion: someone of consular rank should be given a special command in the Mediterranean for three years, with authority equal to that of a provincial governor for 80 kilometers inland, and a vast force of ships and soldiers. The Senate protested against such unprecedented power being given to a single individual, but Pompey had considerable popular support, and the measure was eventually enacted. No one before Pompey had been vested with such great authority and resources. His army of 120,000 infantry, 4,000 cavalry, and 270 ships, as well as his delegation of specific patrol areas to his commanders (the Straits of Gibraltar, Africa, Sardinia, and Corsica, the Greek islands, Lycia, Pamphylia, Cyprus, etc.), enabled him to guard the entire basin at once. Pompey divided the Mediterranean into two basic halves, and then, with a squadron of 60 ships, cleared the western half of pirates in 40 days. Turning his attention to the eastern half, he defeated the pirates at sea off the coast of Cilicia near the mountain Coracesium, which was their stronghold. Pompey's lightning campaign was over in less than three months.

Rome had meanwhile renewed the war against Mithridates, who, encouraged by the distractions afforded by Sertorius and Spartacus, had renewed hostilities against Rome by occupying Bithynia (Third Mithridatic War, 75–65). The command of the war had been given to L. Licinius Lucullus but was then stripped from him and handed over to the consul Manius Acilius Glabrio in 67. The law effecting this change was proposed by the same tribune, A. Gabinius, who gave Pompey the command against the pirates. Early in 66, the tribune Gaius Manilius proposed a law extending Pompey's already extraordinary command over the Mediterranean to include the whole of Roman Asia until he ended the war against Mithridates. Manilius' bill would effectively render Pompey as powerful as a Roman governor. The Senate again opposed Pompey's assumption of powers greater than those he already possessed. However, Cicero, who was now praetor, successfully supported Manilius' proposal (the oration *On the Manilian Law* is one of Cicero's few speeches out of the courtroom). In his efforts he was joined by Caesar, the only important nobleman who supported Pompey. Both men had their own agenda for advocating Pompey's commands in 67 and 66. Cicero wished to flex his political muscle with the Senate by courting the good will of the people, who favored Pompey and were certain to vote for him regardless of senatorial objections. Caesar also wanted to ingratiate himself with the people, and perhaps to set a voting precedent in his own future interests (Plutarch, *Life of Pompey* 25; Cassius Dio 36.43). Both men sought the favor of Pompey, who had gained power and prestige in the revolts of Sertorius and Spartacus. In any event, Manilius' bill was passed, Pompey was given the command against Mithridates, and he immediately left for the East.

Following on Lucullus' groundwork, Pompey quickly drove Mithridates' forces to the eastern end of the Black Sea and took all of his territory except Armenia. He promptly invaded Pontus and defeated Mithridates near Dasteira. He also fined him 6,000 talents, and continued his pursuit of Mithridates as far as Crimea, where the king committed suicide in 63.

Pompey's settlement in the East

Pompey then set about reorganizing the whole of Rome's eastern frontier, creating a continuous line of provinces from the Black Sea to Syria, which he now annexed as a new province.

With Mithridates defeated, Pompey set out for Syria, which had been in a state of considerable disorder since 69, when Antiochus XIII was restored to the throne of the decrepit Seleucid Empire: cities had been seized by tyrants; the depredations

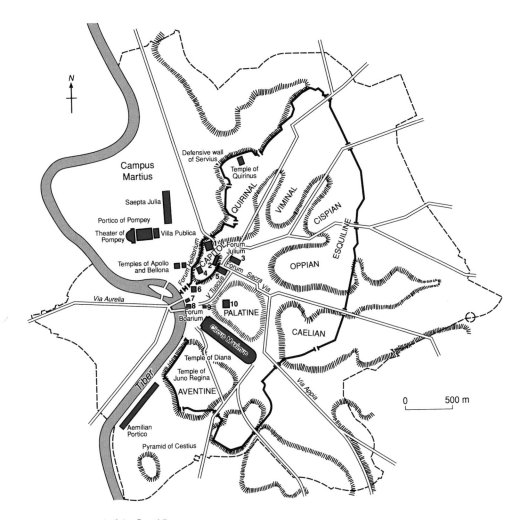

Figure 6.1   Rome at the end of the Republic
1 Temple of Juno Moneta   2 Tabularium   3 Basilica Aemilia   4 Temple of Jupiter Capitolinus   5 Basilica Iulia   6 Temples of Furtuna and of Mater Matuta   7 Temple of Portunus   8 Temple of Hercules Olivarius   9 Ara maxima   10 Temple of Cybele or Magna Mater

of pirates and highwaymen had gone virtually unchecked. Pompey's solution was characteristically direct – he declared Syria to be a Roman province. Deputations arrived meanwhile from Palestine, bearing gifts from Hyrcanus and Aristobulus, the sons of Jannaeus, who had been warring since 67 for the throne of the Maccabees. Pompey's lieutenant Gabinius had earlier intervened in favor of Aristobulus, who was supported by the Sadducees and was now under siege in Jerusalem. But Pompey chose instead to support Hyrcanus, who had the backing of the Pharisees and was thought to be more pro-Roman than his brother. Aristobulus agreed to submit, but his followers refused, and barricaded themselves in the Temple quarters of Jerusalem, which Pompey was therefore obliged to besiege (for three months). He recognized Hyrcanus as high priest and ruler, but not king, of Judaea.

The eastern borders of these provinces were to be guarded by client kingdoms, like Galatia and Paphlagonia, which would function as a kind of buffer zone against the Parthian Empire. The result was that Rome's strategic frontier extended all the way to the Euphrates and the Syrian desert. These regions were not under the direct political and military control of Rome, but controlled indirectly through their native rulers, who were dependent on Rome for their kingdoms. Pompey also founded or restored a large number of cities in Bithynia, Pontus, Asia, and Syria, equipping them with Greek political institutions and customs. Once he completed his eastern settlement, Pompey returned home, with greater wealth, prestige, and military glory than any Roman before him. Near the end of 62, he landed at Brundisium amid great speculation about what he would do next. But to the surprise of almost everyone, he dismissed his troops and withdrew into private life, emerging only once in 61, to celebrate his third triumph.

During Pompey's absence in the East, a brief but serious crisis occurred in Rome, in 63, which is known as Catiline's conspiracy. Despite the fact that it was quickly contained by Cicero, the consul for that year, this incident further exposed the vulnerability of republican institutions as well as the simmering conflicts among various social classes in Rome.

Catiline's conspiracy: 64–62 BCE

In 64, an impoverished young noble, Lucius Sergius Catilina, campaigned for the consulship of 63, on a platform calling for the cancellation of debts, and with the backing of Caesar and Crassus. Catiline lost to Cicero, who, despite being a new man, was supported by a client base that he had built through his career as a lawyer. In 63, after failing again to win the consulship for the next year, Catiline hatched a conspiracy to take control of the city. An uprising was planned for October 28, when Rome would be set on fire and leading senators put to death. But Cicero got wind of it and publicly denounced Catiline in the Senate, rousing such hostility against him that Catiline left the city. He fled to Etruria, where his fellow conspirator Lucius Manlius was raising an army. Once Cicero found out Catiline's destination, he persuaded the Senate to issue its "ultimate decree," vesting him with absolute power, and to declare war against Catiline.

Meanwhile, the conspirators in Rome undermined their cause by trying to recruit to it a Gallic tribe, the Allobroges. An embassy of the Allobroges happened to be in the city, to protest against the abuses of their provincial governor. One of Catiline's associates, Publius Cornelius Lentulus, who was praetor at the time, promised them relief if they would join the conspiracy against Rome. The Allobroges, however, revealed Lentulus' overtures to their patron in Rome, who in turn informed Cicero. With their help, Cicero organized the interception of letters from five conspirators to the Allobroges. As soon as he got hold of them, he presented this hard evidence to the Senate.

Once the five conspirators were arrested, a spirited debate followed on whether or not they should be executed without trial. Two men took the lead in this debate: Caesar, opposing the death penalty, and Marcus Porcius Cato (nicknamed "the Younger"), who supported it. In the footsteps of his great-grandfather, Cato the Elder, the Younger Cato was a vehement traditionalist who did not tolerate any challenge to the senatorial control of the state. His arguments won the Senate's support over those of Caesar, and, without delay, Cicero made arrangements for the death penalty. Lentulus was forced to abdicate his office, and all the conspirators died by strangulation in the Tullianum. A proudly self-satisfied Cicero was proclaimed father of his country, and reveled in what he considered to be the peak of his career. But the constitutionality of his actions was almost immediately questioned: execution of a Roman citizen without trial was illegal, and the high profile of the conspirators made their rushed punishment even more problematic. Public opinion would soon be manipulated against Cicero (as we shall see below). For the time being, the execution of Lentulus and his associates practically extirpated the conspiracy in Rome. In January 62, Catiline and his army fought with two senatorial legions near the town of Pistoia, Etruria, where he himself was killed in battle.

Our two main sources for this conspiracy, four speeches *Against Catiline* by Cicero and the historical monograph *The Conspiracy of Catiline* by Sallust, condemn Catiline for attempting the violent overthrow of the government with his army of destitute debauchees. However, the political and moral picture is not as clear as Cicero, in particular, presents it as being. Catiline's support base cut across social class inside and out of Rome, including senators, equestrians, ordinary citizens, and even women, freedmen, and fugitive slaves. One of the common grievances among these divergent groups was the problem of debt, which had become increasingly pressing since the second century BCE. What Cicero interprets as the moral degeneration of the impoverished, the dispossessed, and the indebted can be seen as their effort to gain access to the wealth increasingly concentrated in the hands of the few. Sallust, writing his monograph about 20 years after the events, presents Catiline in the economic, social, and cultural context of his time, thus affording us a slightly more balanced view of his rebellion than that of Cicero. Sallust also recreates the debate between Cato and Caesar (*The Conspiracy of Catiline* 51–2), whom he singles out from his contemporaries as two exceptionally gifted and diametrically opposed personalities. Sallust's contrasting of Caesar's popularity and generosity with Cato's frugality and severity (*The Conspiracy of Catiline* 54) draws a vivid portrait of the two men.

The First Triumvirate: 60–54 BCE

What we call today "the First Triumvirate" is an unofficial and initially covert political alliance among Pompey, Crassus, and Caesar. The events that led to this partnership were largely coincidental, but the rampant ambitions that under-pinned them had long been in the making. After serving in Rome as praetor (62), Caesar returned to Further Spain in 61 as propraetor, where he won a consider-able military reputation with victorious campaigns against the Lusitanians. In 60, he returned to Rome eager both to hold a triumph for his Spanish victories and to submit his candidacy for the consulship of 59. His combined political and military aspirations are hardly surprising. According to Suetonius, during his quaestorship in Spain (in 69) Caesar wept bitterly when he saw a statue of Alexander the Great in the temple of Hercules at Gades: it reminded him that Alexander's accomplishments had far outdone his own at the same age (*Julius Caesar* 7). His victory over the Lusitani must have underlined to him that it was finally his time to assume the supreme office of the Roman state.

However, Caesar was faced immediately with a protocol difficulty: as we have seen already (chapter 5), a commander about to celebrate a triumph was forbid-den to enter the city before the day of the event. He therefore asked the Senate for permission to declare his candidature for the consulship *in absentia*. Most senators were alarmed at the prospect of Caesar as consul. At the instigation of Cato they refused Caesar's request, certain that he would prefer the glory of his triumph to the uncertainty of his consular candidacy. Then, surprisingly, Caesar forfeited his triumph and entered Rome to declare himself as a candidate.

Pompey, meanwhile, had been pressing his own demands since his return from the East two years previously. He wanted his arrangements there to be officially ratified by the Senate, and land to be given to his veterans. The Senate, in an effort to curtail his power, was stalling in satisfying his demands even as it enjoyed the immense revenues that Pompey had brought back from his eastern settlement.

At about the same time, Crassus too was making an unsuccessful case to the Senate on behalf of certain clients of his. These were tax collectors (*publicani*) who had won the bid for collecting taxes from Asia. Realizing that the actual tax revenue from that province was less than the bid they had paid to secure this commission, the *publicani* were trying to persuade the Senate to revise the terms of their contract. The Senate turned them down, in the process snubbing Crassus, who supported their plea.

Thus, at this juncture, three powerful men who had every reason to antagonize each other found their ambitions equally obstructed by the conservatism of the Senate. It was because of the Senate's uncompromising and, in many ways, short-sighted position that these three agreed to form the political alliance which we call the First Triumvirate. This private agreement was consolidated (in 59) by the marriage of Pompey to Caesar's only daughter, Julia, the daughter of Cornelia.

Having joined their resources and influence, the three men secured their diverse goals: Caesar was elected consul for 59, and, with blatant disregard of his partner in the consulship (who had been elected with the help of conservative senators precisely to counter Caesar), he pushed through the assembly the requests of his own two partners. First, Pompey's eastern settlement was ratified and his veterans were given land. Additionally, Crassus' clients, the *publicani*, received a partial but significant refund of their initial bid to the Senate. The Triumvirs were essentially running the state, to the dismay of many senators, including Cicero. Because of his previous support of Pompey, Cicero was invited to join the Triumvirate, but he declined on senatorial principle. Whether he believed in it realistically or wishfully, Cicero in his speeches supported the ideal of an agreement between senators and equestrians (*concordia ordinum*) and, similarly, an accordance of all the "good" citizens (*consensus omnium bonorum*). Regardless of their social status and wealth, these *boni* would be loyal to the state and support actively its supreme political instrument, the Senate. Since the Triumvirs represented the exact opposite of this political and moral orthodoxy, it was a matter of time before Cicero fell foul with them.

In 59, the Triumvirs enlisted one of the tribunes of 58, Publius Clodius, to act as their agent. Clodius was an old enemy of Cicero, who had long waited for an opportunity to harm him. The feud between the two traces back to 62, and is entangled between fact and anecdote. In December of that year, Clodius had disguised himself as a woman to attend an all-female ritual in honor of the "Good Goddess" (Bona Dea) celebrated by the Vestals and patrician women. This ritual was traditionally held at the home of the chief priest in the college of the pontiffs, the *pontifex maximus*. Caesar had been elected to this office the previous year, 63. According to one version, Clodius and Pompeia were having an affair, and it was she who had smuggled him into her house. Others speculate that Clodius merely wanted to see Pompeia, with whom he was in love, or even that he was trying to play a prank. Either way, Clodius had to flee Caesar's house when his cover was revealed by a slave. Because this scandal constituted an impiety compromising his office, Caesar immediately divorced Pompeia, despite proclaiming her innocent, for not being above suspicion.

Clodius, who was soon identified and prosecuted in 61 for sacrilege, claimed that he had been out of town on the night in question. But Cicero demolished this alibi, testifying that Clodius had in fact visited him in his house only a few hours before the incident. Nevertheless, the jury voted for Clodius' acquittal, probably after both bribery and intimidation.

Thus Cicero acquired a dangerous and powerful enemy, who, in 58, finally got his chance for revenge. Clodius stirred the controversy about Cicero's execution of Catiline's associates without trial, claiming that he had abused the Senate's ultimate decree. Cicero did not wait to be formally prosecuted but left for Macedonia, and Clodius then had him officially declared an exile.

In the same year Caesar too left Rome to take up his proconsular duties as governor of Transalpine Gaul. Soon after Caesar's departure, Clodius launched a series of public attacks on Pompey. Some believe this was done at the request of Caesar or Crassus; others suggest that Clodius was simply too opportunistic to maintain any loyalty to those who had helped him get elected. Clodius challenged Pompey to account for his eastern settlement, and he even sent a gang of his supporters to attack Pompey personally. Insulted and terrorized, Pompey hid out in his house for several months, and organized a rival gang of armed thugs under the leadership of Titus Annius Milo, tribune for 57. Pompey also advocated to the Senate Cicero's recall from exile, and secured the popular vote for his return through Milo and his colleague in the tribunate, Publius Sestius. Pompey's reasons for his newfound support of Cicero are not entirely clear. Besides responding to Clodius' provocation by bringing back his enemy, Pompey probably realized that Cicero still had the authority to stabilize the volatile situation. This had been further exacerbated by a protracted grain shortage and subsequent popular riots.

Upon his return in the summer of 57 Cicero indeed tried to mend both the political climate and his personal relationship with the Triumvirs, by getting Pompey appointed manager of the grain supply for five years. However, as the shortage continued, Pompey became a convenient scapegoat for the people and even more vulnerable to the growing attacks on the Triumvirate in the Senate. Additionally, the street fighting of the rival gangs of Clodius and Milo was a new low in the public violence that had gripped Rome's political life since the Gracchi. As Pompey found himself in the eye of the storm, Caesar was fighting a series of successful campaigns against the native peoples beyond his province. His wars brought the whole of Gaul under Roman control, with far-reaching consequences for his own career, his relationship with Pompey, and the fall of the Republic.

Caesar's conquest of Gaul: 58–51 BCE

In the beginning of his *Commentaries on the Gallic War*, Caesar stated confidently that northern Gaul (which the Romans called Gallia Comata, "long-haired Gaul") was divided into three ethnically distinct regions, each with its own language, laws, and institutions. In the south-west, between the Garonne and the Pyrenees, lived the Aquitani; the center was home to various Celtic tribes such as the Aedui and Sequani; and the north was inhabited by the Belgae, mixed tribes of Celts and Germans. The Gauls were primarily an agricultural people who lived mostly in villages or small towns. There were a few mining and manufacturing centers on major rivers and trade routes, and several hilltop fortresses in the interior, including Bibracte (near Autun), Gergovia (near Clermont-Ferrand), and Alesia (near the headwaters of the Seine). The largest political unit was the tribal state (*civitas*), a loose confederation of more or less independent clans, which often fought among themselves.

When Caesar arrived in Transalpine Gaul in the spring of 58, the Helvetii of western Switzerland had begun to migrate west to escape the aggression of their Germanic neighbors, the Suebi. They had already assembled at the banks of the Rhône, having burnt their homes and villages behind them. Caesar refused to let them cross. Why he wanted to make war on the Helvetii is unclear: we might suppose that he saw in them an opportunity to win military glory; perhaps he genuinely believed that they were a threat to the security of the province. After some minor skirmishes, the Helvetii were decisively defeated at Bibracte. Envoys

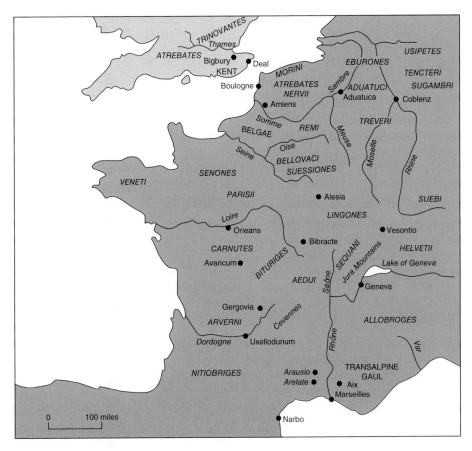

Map 6.1 The tribes and regions of Gaul and southern Britain, 58–50 BCE (from Antony Kamm, *Julius Caesar: A Life*, Routledge 2006)

now arrived from many parts of central Gaul to request Caesar's help against Ariovistus, king of the Suebi, whose rudeness at a subsequent meeting with Caesar afforded him a suitable pretext for war. Somewhere along the eastern slopes of the Vosges (perhaps near Cernay), Ariovistus' army was routed; the survivors fled to the Rhine; Ariovistus died shortly afterwards. When news reached Caesar in 57 that the Belgae were making military preparations, he advanced against them. Short of supplies, and overcome by mutual jealousies, they gradually dispersed. By the end of 57, the greater part of Gaul had been overrun.

In 56, while his lieutenants Quintus Sabinus and Publius Crassus reduced Normandy and Aquitania, Caesar marched against the Veneti, in Brittany. He had their leaders executed and the rest of the population sold into slavery. His next victims were the Usipetes and Tencteri, who had been driven across the Rhine by the Suebi. When they refused his offer of land east of the Rhine, he defeated them, and slaughtered their women and children. Late in the summer of 55, he launched his first attack on Britain, eager, perhaps, to lay claim to its reported mineral wealth. The invasion was short-lived, accomplishing little more than the submission of some tribal leaders in Kent. He returned in 54, defeated a Kentish army near Canterbury, and overwhelmed some Belgic tribes who had combined their forces under Cassivellaunus, king of the Catuvellauni.

By 52, Gaul was restless. A national uprising swept across much of central Gaul, led by the Arvernian chief Vercingetorix, at whose hands Caesar suffered his first real defeat, at Gergovia. Later, near Dijon, he met up again with Vercingetorix, whom he forced into the hilltop fortress of Alesia. Though a large relief army came to his aid (250,000 according to Caesar), Vercingetorix was eventually forced to surrender. Six years later, he was displayed in Caesar's triumph, and then executed. It is clear that Caesar's conquest of Gaul was made easier by the lack of political cohesion among the Gauls, and by the absence, until Vercingetorix, of an effective leader. It is undeniable that, in opening up central Europe to the Roman civilization, Caesar changed the history of the western world.

Estrangement among the Triumvirs: 56–53 BCE

Caesar's protracted absence in Gaul, the mounting glory of his conquests, the standing rivalry between Pompey and Crassus, and a mutual distrust among the three men were quickly eroding the Triumvirate. At Caesar's instigation, the partners met at Luca (modern Lucca), in April 56. There they managed to patch up their differences, agreeing, among other things, that Pompey and Crassus would be consuls in 55. Another important decision arrived at in that conference was that Caesar's command in Gaul should be renewed for another five years. Similarly, Pompey received a five-year term in Spain and Crassus an equivalent position in Syria. Unlike Caesar and Crassus, who exercised their commands in person, it was agreed that Pompey would stay in Rome to oversee the grain supply, governing his province through authorized representatives (*legati*). Soon afterwards the Triumvirate collapsed altogether, when Julia died in childbirth (54), severing the kinship between Caesar and Pompey, and Crassus was then killed (53) fighting the Parthians at Carrhae in Mesopotamia.

Caesar and Pompey on the road to war: 53–49 BCE

Violence and disorder had now become commonplace at Rome, so much so that the consular elections of 53 had to be postponed. Early the next year, Clodius was murdered by Milo, and, in the rioting that followed his funeral, the Senate house was burned down. A desperate Senate voted its ultimate decree, and agreed to appoint Pompey sole consul for 52. Meanwhile, the fates of Caesar and Pompey began to diverge openly. Caesar continued to amass wealth and power from his Gallic conquests, offending the sensibilities of the senators, while Pompey found himself in their most conservative faction by marrying, soon after Julia's

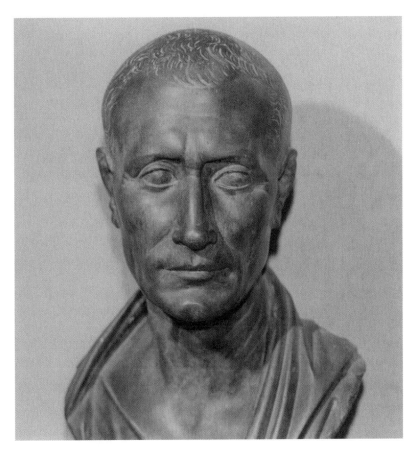

Plate 6.2 Bust of
Julius Caesar. Vatican
Museum. C. M. Dixon

death, into the family of the Metelli. With their relationship increasingly strained
throughout 50, both men began to prepare, if not openly, for war.

In December of that year, Caesar's command in Gaul was about to expire, and
the Senate was beginning to debate the question of his successor. Then the tribune
Marcus Scribonius Curio (at the instigation of Caesar himself) forced the Senate
to vote on his proposal that Caesar would relinquish his arms and command
(*imperium*) in Gaul, if Pompey did the same for his command in Spain. The
proposal was enthusiastically received by both the senators (370 voted for, and
only 22 against) and the people, who showered Curio with garlands and flowers
for his attempt to avert war. The senators were equally mistrustful of both men,
but Pompey made the better impression: he had been present in Rome throughout
this time, he was connected to the senatorial aristocracy, and he gallantly declared
that he would relinquish his own command as soon as Caesar did the same. In
short, Pompey was considered more loyal to the Republic, particularly by those

who had resented Caesar's popular measures and highhanded ways during his consulship (Appian, *Civil Wars* 2.29).

Despite Curio's protests that Pompey should show good will by abdicating his command first, the two consuls asked Pompey to defend the state and handed him two legions. Ironically, both these legions had been sent from Caesar to defend the Roman province of Syria from a Parthian invasion, but had remained in Italy awaiting developments. One of the two was actually Pompey's, who had lent it to Caesar for his Gallic campaigns but then requested it for the defense of Syria. Caesar's compliance with Pompey's request had effectively deprived Caesar of two legions, marking one more break in the deteriorating relationship between the two men throughout 50.

In January 49, another Caesarian tribune, Marcus Antonius (Mark Antony), forced the consuls to read a letter from Caesar agreeing to the terms of Curio's earlier proposal. But the consuls, with the support of an increasingly resolute Pompey, refused to allow the matter to come to a vote. Instead, they proposed that Caesar disband his army immediately, or be declared a public enemy; the motion was passed, but vetoed by Antony. All opportunities for reconciliation had been exhausted, and war seemed inevitable. On January 7, the Senate issued its ultimate decree, and Antony was warned to leave Rome. He and Curio promptly left the city and joined Caesar. A few days after the Senate's issue of the ultimate decree, Caesar marched from Ravenna south to Ariminum with a single legion; in doing so he crossed the Rubicon river, the boundary between Cisalpine Gaul and Italy. This now famous crossing was an open and irreversible declaration of war.

Technically speaking, it was Caesar who was responsible for starting the war. But it is not certain how much either he or Pompey truly wanted it. Conservative senators played a decisive role in egging Pompey on against Caesar. They were led by Cato, who represented the most traditionalist faction of the Senate and would not settle for anything less than its absolute supremacy. His views were often extremely idealistic; Cicero confided to his friend Atticus that "although he [Cato] has the best intentions and supreme loyalty, meanwhile he harms the Republic because he declaims his opinions as if he lived in Plato's Republic rather than in the cesspool of Romulus" (*Letters to Atticus* 2.1). However, to an extent, Cato's principles were legitimate and valid. Despite the heavy blows to its power and prestige, in the collective consciousness the Senate still remained the supreme constitutional authority, identified with the state itself. Pompey also wished to defend the Senate, both to satisfy his ambition for military glory, and in the belief that he was truly fighting for the right cause. On the other hand, Caesar believed that he too had made enough efforts toward reconciliation through Curio and Antony, whose tribunicial rights had been simply trampled on by an obstinate Senate. Certainly it seemed that it was not principles that were at stake, but the honor and prestige of powerful and ambitious men; but we do not have to see their ambitions, willful delusions, and ideals as mutually exclusive motives for the Civil War.

Chronology 6.1	The life of Caesar

July 13, 101 BCE (?)	Birth of C. Julius Caesar in Rome.
84	He marries Cornelia, Cinna's daughter. Appointed priest of Jupiter (*flamen Dialis*).
83	Birth of his daughter Julia.
80–78	Army service in Asia, then Cilicia.
78	Return to Rome.
75	Journey to Rhodes; taken prisoner by pirates.
72	Military tribune and *pontifex* (priest).
69	Funeral eulogy for his aunt Julia. He defies the Senate by having effigies of Marius paraded in procession. Quaestor in Further Spain (Hispania Ulterior).
67	Rapprochement with Pompey and Crassus. He marries Pompeia, Sulla's granddaughter. Superintendent of the Via Appia.
65	Curule aedile; he gives sumptuous games (the *ludi Romani*) and a *munus* (gladiatorial fights) of 320 pairs of combatants.
63	Elected praetor at 38 (minimum age), he appears as leader of the *populares*. Elected *pontifex maximus*.
62	Praetor. The Clodius scandal; he repudiates Pompeia.
61	Propraetor in Further Spain.
60	First Triumvirate of Caesar, Pompey, and Crassus.
59	Consul, great activity. He marries Calpurnia, daughter of L. Calpurnius Piso; Pompey marries Caesar's daughter Julia. The *lex Vatinia* confers the government of Cisalpine Gaul on him for five years, with three legions, then Transalpine Gaul, with a fourth legion.
58–51	Proconsul in Gaul: the conquest of the Gauls:
	58 campaign against the Helvetii and Ariovistus;
	57 rising of the Belgae; campaign against the Suessiones and Nervii;
	56 campaign in Brittany, Normandy, and Aquitaine. Gaul appears to be conquered;
	55 crossing of the Rhine and the Channel;
	53 revolt in north Gaul; second crossing of the Rhine;
	52 deals with general insurrection led by Vercingetorix; defeat at Gergovia, victory at Alesia;
	51 the last rebellions; general pacification.
56	Renewal of the First Triumvirate at Lucca, with Pompey and Crassus.
54	Death of Caesar's mother and daughter.
50	Caesar stripped of his powers; break with Pompey; the Senate decides to recall him.
January 49	Crossing of the Rubicon, frontier between Cisalpine Gaul and Italy. March on Rome, evacuated by Pompey. Siege of Marseilles and campaign in Spain against supporters of Pompey. Dictator for 11 days.
48	Caesar's second consulship. Victory at Pharsalus over Pompey (August). Pompey murdered. Siege and capture of Alexandria (October 48–March 47); Egypt a protectorate.
47	Lightning campaign against Pharnaces, king of the Bosporus; victory of Zela (August). Return to Rome: dictator for a year.
46	Campaign against Pompey's supporters in Africa: victory of Thapsus (April); in Spain: victory of Munda (March 45). Caesar's third consulship. Dictator for 10 years.
45	Fourth consulship. Triumphs and honors from the Senate.
44	Fifth consulship. New honors, notably divine. Life dictatorship. Assassination (Ides of March).

Civil War: 49–46 BCE

By openly declaring war against Pompey and the Senate, Caesar put himself in the ethically weak position of the unjust aggressor. Moreover, the majority of the Senate was against him, and Pompey's armed forces greatly outweighed his. Pompey controlled most of Italy, Spain, and the East. Surprisingly however (or perhaps not, given the irrelevancy of senatorial ideals to them), the Italian communities went over to Caesar, relieved that he did not take any lives or damage their property. It is indicative of Caesar's growing popularity that the only notable stand against him, at Corfinium, ended with the commander, Lucius Domitius Ahenobarbus, being handed over to Caesar by his own men. By refusing to punish anyone at Corfinium Caesar diplomatically exercised, and advertised, his lenience (*clementia*). His treatment of Ahenobarbus and his soldiers won him both the battle of impressions and new forces from Ahenobarbus' army.

Seeing that popular opinion was becoming increasingly favorable toward Caesar, Cicero proposed to send messengers to him offering reconciliation, but his call went unheeded. After just two months, Pompey decided to abandon the peninsula and cross over to Greece. There he hoped to amass forces loyal to him from his eastern campaigns, and only then make a stand against Caesar.

Since Caesar had no fleet, he went instead to Spain, to face the Pompeian legions. He defeated them in less than three months, and then he too crossed the Adriatic. Meeting a part of Pompey's army in Dyrrhachium, he began building a series of forts around it, but Pompey's forces broke through and almost routed Caesar's army. Now on the offensive, Pompey shadowed Caesar as he moved southwards, and eventually offered battle in Pharsalus, Thessaly, in August 48. There Pompey's army was defeated and he fled to Egypt, where he hoped to be receive refuge and reinforcements from the king, Ptolemy XIII, who was only 15 years old at the time.

Ptolemy, however, was urged by his advisers not to support a lost cause against the now powerful Caesar, and so he had Pompey murdered as soon as he landed in Egypt. Caesar arrived in pursuit a few days later. There he was greeted with Pompey's head, which prompted his vengeance for the disrespect shown Pompey (Appian, *Civil Wars* 2.86).

Caesar then lingered in Alexandria, partly because he became captivated by the king's 18-year-old sister, Cleopatra, whom he helped to reclaim her throne from Ptolemy. Meanwhile, in October 48, in his absence, he was appointed dictator for a year. Caesar left Egypt in 47, establishing Cleopatra as sole queen of Egypt. At the time she was pregnant with a son whom she later named Caesarion (Greek for "little Caesar"). After a brief and successful campaign in the East against Pharnaces, son of Mithridates, Caesar returned to Rome in the same year.

Early in 46, he sailed to the province of North Africa. There the remaining Pompeians had regrouped to make another stand, using the capital city, Utica, as their stronghold. While Caesar was besieging Thapsus the Pompeian army

arrived, only to be annihilated. Utica surrendered, and many of Pompey's supporters committed suicide to avoid what they considered the indignity of Caesar's
clementia. Cato, who had been the staunchest opponent of Caesar throughout
his career (and particularly during the critical year 50), committed suicide in
Utica, thus gaining posthumously the nickname *Uticensis*. It was the Stoic death
of a man who came to symbolize the senatorial ideals, and even the Republic
itself. Many Roman authors, senators themselves, consider the two practically
indistinguishable. After Cato's death Cicero wrote a eulogy entitled *Cato*, to
which Caesar felt compelled to respond with a treatise entitled *Anti-Cato*. Writing
more than a century later, the poet Lucan evokes in his epic Cato's name as
shorthand for the lost Republic: "the victorious cause was pleasing to the gods,
the defeated one to Cato" (*Civil War* 1.128).

When news of Caesar's victory at Thapsus reached Rome, he was appointed
dictator for 10 years. There were few complaints, and most of those seem to have
been directed at his decision to install Cleopatra and Caesarion in his house on
the Janiculum (in 46).

In the meantime, Pompey's son Sextus escaped from Thapsus to Spain with a
few survivors to join his older brother Gnaeus, who had fled there earlier. There
they built up a sizeable army, joining their own resources to Pompey's veterans,
the survivors of Pharsalus, and even native Spanish and Celtiberian allies.
However, by the end of 46 Caesar was on location, having made the journey in
less than a month. In the spring of 45 he won a hard victory at Munda (near
modern Cordoba), where Gnaeus was killed (we shall return to Sextus below).
Caesar then returned to Rome, where he remained until his death.

Some of the events of this Civil War are narrated by Caesar himself in a
three-volume account known today as *Commentaries on the Civil War*. This
narrative covers the events of the first two years of the war, roughly from Caesar's crossing of the Rubicon to his mediation between Cleopatra and Ptolemy
XIII for the throne of Egypt. Unsurprisingly, both this work and his earlier
Commentaries on the Gallic War (in seven volumes) relate heavily biased versions of Caesar's political ideology and military savvy, but nevertheless they
comprise our most detailed and authoritative sources for both these wars. The
comparison of Caesar's account with parallel narratives, both contemporary and
later (Cicero's letters and speeches, several biographies by Plutarch, Suetonius'
biography of Caesar, Appian's *Roman History*, and the narratives of Velleius
Paterculus and Cassius Dio), provides complementary, conflicting, or mutually
confirming perspectives on Caesar's career in this decade (58–49). Certainly, one
of Caesar's purposes in writing these works was to provide the raw material for
historical narratives. His commentaries were fascinating to contemporary
authors, including Cicero, who considered them daunting to future historians
on the subject (Suetonius, *Julius Caesar* 56). The pseudo-Caesarian narratives
The Alexandrian War, *The African War*, *The Spanish War*, and book eight of
the *Gallic War* suggest the appeal and challenge of both commentaries to
aspiring historians.

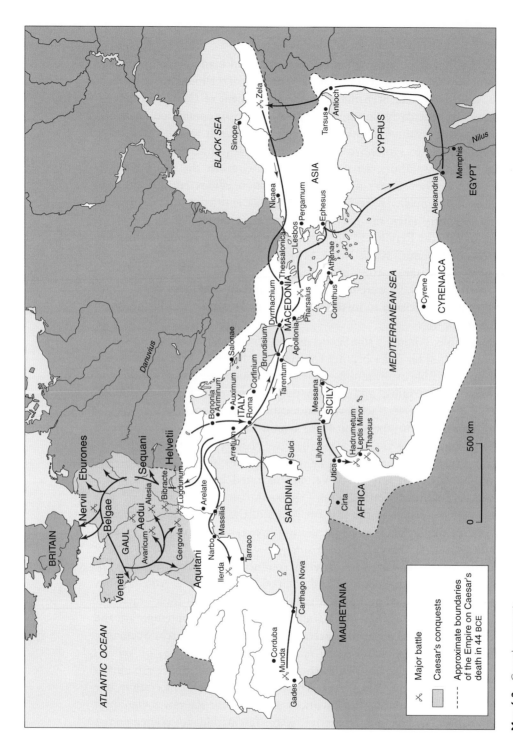

Map 6.2 Caesar's conquests

The dictatorship of Caesar: 48–44 BCE

Though he seems to have taken little pleasure from administration, Caesar enacted a remarkably large number of reforms in the period 48–44, mostly in the intervals between his military campaigns. Perhaps his best-known and longest-lasting reform was that of the calendar (in 46) that is still called "Julian" after him. Before Caesar's reform, the solar year and the calendar year diverged so much that, as Plutarch notes (*Life of Caesar* 59), the priests alone knew what time of the year it was. They would suddenly insert an entire month into the calendar to align the solar and calendar years, a practice dating to the reign of Numa. By assigning 365 days to the calendar year and by inserting a leap day in February every four years, Caesar effected this alignment. He also introduced several measures to relieve the debts accrued during the economic collapse of the Civil War, and he passed a law to check extravagance (like most such measures, it seems to have had little effect). Additionally, he increased the number of magistrates and the size of the Senate, mainly by introducing senators from Italian communities and even from the provinces of Spain and Gaul. The influx of these "foreigners," who had become Roman citizens only recently, was particularly offensive to those senators who viewed the *curia* as the exclusive grounds of the Roman aristocracy.

Caesar also provided the city with new buildings, including a new forum (Forum Julium) to the north-east of the old Forum Romanum, a basilica (Basilica Iulia), and a public library. The purpose of his lavish public projects (many of which were left unfinished at his death) was to ingratiate himself with the people, to restore and improve the capital, and, of course, to celebrate himself as its undisputed head. He also planned to build a new road over the Apennines, and to deepen the harbor at Ostia. And, in order to settle his veterans, he founded or planned no fewer than 20 colonies, mainly in Spain and North Africa.

Other measures were intended to improve the condition of the provinces. Caesar abolished the tax-collection system in Asia that relied on the often predatory exactions of the *publicani*, and replaced it with a fixed land tax; a similar system was set up in Sicily. He also tried to break down some of the barriers that separated Italy from the provinces, both by encouraging Romans to settle in the provinces and by giving Roman citizenship to provincials, sometimes to entire towns, like Gades (Cadiz) and Olisipo (modern Lisbon).

Caesar was also planning to strengthen the security of Rome's north-eastern frontier by attacking the Dacian king Burebistas. He planned too an invasion of Parthia, a campaign that he expected would keep him away from Rome for three years. A few days before he was to leave, however, on the Ides (15th) of March, 44 BCE, he was murdered in front of the Senate house, stabbed by the praetors Marcus Junius Brutus and Gaius Cassius Longinus, Brutus' brother-in-law. The mystique that had surrounded him throughout his life only grew when a comet was sighted a few days after his death (Suetonius, *Julius Caesar* 88; Seneca, *Natural Questions* 7.17).

Without a doubt, Caesar's assassination was motivated by a widespread fear and resentment of his growing power and his attendant disregard for senatorial traditions. By overshadowing the Senate and the magistrates, Caesar had become dangerously powerful. Because he knew that his power rested ultimately on his soldiers, Caesar only minimally tried to cloak it in various constitutional forms. He was *pontifex maximus* from 63, and augur from 47: he was well positioned, therefore, to control the state's religious institutions. He was consul in 48, and from 46 to 44. The dictatorship was given to him in various forms and for varying periods of time; early in 44, however, he declared himself dictator "for life" (*dictator in perpetuo*), a legend he also had inscribed on coins bearing his image. It was the first time in Roman history that a living ruler was portrayed on coinage. Other unprecedented honors were bestowed upon him, especially in the last months of his life. The month Quinctilis was renamed Iulius (July). He was given the title "father of his country" (*parens patriae*). His statue was placed in the temple of Quirinus; a second was set up on the Capitol near those of Rome's seven kings; a third showed him with a globe beneath his feet. A temple was built to celebrate his *clementia*; a new college of priests was established, the Julian Luperci; a priest was appointed in his honor. His enemies in the Senate probably colluded in voting him these extraordinary privileges, aiming to increase the collective resentment against him (Plutarch, *Life of Caesar* 57). Thus they would provide themselves with the moral and political justification they knew they would need to engineer his downfall.

It is uncertain whether Caesar wished to be king or not. Several incidents in the early part of 44 suggest that he was laying the groundwork for it, trying to gauge the public feeling. A diadem that someone had placed on his statue was removed by two tribunes, Flavus and Marullus, who announced that they would punish anyone who referred to Caesar as king. And they actually prosecuted a number of people who addressed Caesar as king (*rex*) when he was returning from the Alban Mount. According to Cassius Dio (44.10), Caesar made light of this proclamation, but he later arranged for both tribunes to be removed from office and the Senate. At the festival of the Lupercalia on February 15, he refused a crown that was ceremoniously offered to him by his colleague in the consulship, Antony. Would he have accepted it, if the crowd had urged him to do so? Cicero, in one of his invectives against Antony (*Philippics* 2.85), describes the great consternation of the people who witnessed this episode, suggesting that it was only their loud laments and protests that kept Caesar from assuming the kingship then and there.

In the end, we must admit that there is really no way to know whether Caesar truly aspired to become a *rex* in the sense of the early kings of Rome. What is clear is that many had come to resent his power. The senatorial conspiracy led by Brutus and Cassius involved as many as 60 men, many of whom had served Caesar in one capacity or another. Others, including Brutus and Cassius, had sided with Pompey during the Civil War but had been pardoned by Caesar. The conspirators killed Caesar in the name of liberty (*libertas*). What they got instead was a new civil war.

6.2 | Toward a New Order

The period 44–31 is framed by two major events: Caesar's assassination and the victory of Octavian over Antony and Cleopatra at Actium. These two events encompass a time of immense importance in the history of Rome: the end of dictatorship, a 13-year crisis, the end of the Civil Wars, and Octavian's establishment of a personal regime at the head of which he ruled as the restorer of peace. It was the end of the senatorial Republic, with its boast of *libertas*, and the advent of a new regime commonly known as the Empire or the Principate. Even though it had been long in the making, the conventional date for its beginning is considered to be January 16, 27, when Octavian was awarded the title "Augustus" by the Senate, as well as extraordinary military and political authority. This event, known as "the settlement of 27 BCE," inaugurated a new political system, social order, and culture. It is the Principate (of Augustus and his successors) that gave Rome the aesthetic grandeur and cultural importance that it holds to this day.

Events following Caesar's death: 44–43 BCE

The conspirators had planned to throw Caesar's corpse into the Tiber and proclaim the return of liberty by declaring all his measures null and void. They expected that they would be immediately hailed as liberators not only by the Senate, but also by the people of Rome. However, they underestimated Caesar's charismatic appeal and his long-standing popularity with the people, which he had cultivated up until the end of his life through benefactions, public works, and debt settlements. When the news of his assassination spread through the city, the conspirators were confronted by hostile crowds and were forced to take refuge on the Capitol. Antony, now the sole consul, went into hiding in his house on the Esquiline. Marcus Aemilius Lepidus, who had been the dictator's master of cavalry (*magister equitum*), remained on the Forum, close to his troops, who were massed on the Tiber island. Anxiety and fear reigned everywhere.

From March 15, 44, to the autumn of 43, after some vacillation, alliances gradually shifted.

Immediately following Caesar's death, Antony seized the moment offered by the power vacuum. He persuaded the Senate to declare a general amnesty without annulling any of Caesar's actions, so that the city would not descend into complete disorder. A few days later, however, Antony turned Caesar's funeral into a political opportunity for himself. Delivering a dramatic eulogy in the Forum, Antony expressed indignation at the murder and he further incensed the crowds by reading Caesar's will: he had left 300 sesterces to each Roman citizen and his magnificent gardens as a public park. His posthumous generosity so inflamed the people that they spontaneously cremated Caesar's body and began riots against the conspirators. Within a month, and amidst the general hostility, the conspirators were forced to leave Rome. Brutus and Cassius traveled eastwards and began to raise money and an army in Greece to defend the republican cause. Antony, on the other hand, stayed in Rome, where he obtained Caesar's papers, will, and riches, and presented himself as his political heir.

At that time, Caesar's 18-year-old great-nephew, Octavius, learned of his great-uncle's death in Apollonia, Illyricum. When he found out that Caesar in his will had appointed him his "first heir" and had adopted him, he sailed to Italy and visited his adoptive father's veterans, who welcomed him as Caesar's successor. He recruited 3,000 men from among them, and began to challenge openly Antony's claims to Caesar's legacy. In order to further declare his authority and legitimacy as Caesar's sole political heir, he changed his name to Gaius Julius Caesar Octavianus (hence the name Octavian, which is used for him until 27 BCE; after 27, he is referred to as Augustus).

Soon after Octavian's return in Rome, Antony realized that the young man constituted a serious threat to his own ambitions. Antony stalled when Octavian asked him to pay the bequest of 300 sesterces from the money that he had appropriated from Caesar's widow, Calpurnia. Octavian then paid this amount from his own funds, a clearly antagonistic gesture towards Antony that earned him great favor with the people. Despite the occasional and superficial reconciliations between the two men, it was clear that Antony was losing ground.

Genealogy 6.1	**Octavian–Augustus' parentage**

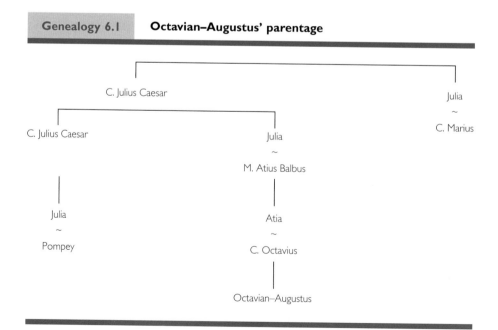

The battle of Mutina: 43 BCE

Eventually Octavian and Antony clashed openly, in the battle of Mutina (Modena). As consul in 44, Antony had been assigned the province of Macedonia for 43. However, in the summer of 44 he managed (through the tribunes) to exchange it for that of Cisalpine Gaul. This province was more profitable and closer to Rome than Macedonia, and thus doubly appealing to Antony, who wished to maintain an advantage over Octavian. The term of the current governor, Decimus Brutus, was expiring at the end of that year, but Antony left Rome in November to assume his command a full two months earlier. Decimus Brutus, however, refused to give up his post and instead retired to the fortified town of Mutina under arms. He was supported by the Senate because he had been one of the conspirators in Caesar's assassination (he was a relative of Marcus Brutus), and because his tenure represented the senatorial legitimacy that Antony was trampling on so conspicuously.

At this time, Cicero deployed his rhetorical skill and experience to champion Octavian's cause as foil to Antony's power. A harsh exchange between Antony and Cicero in September 44 was followed by 14 invective speeches that Cicero wrote against Antony, denouncing him as an enemy of the state. These speeches abound with Ciceronian stock accusations of Antony's cruelty, sexual profligacy, and eccentric indulgences, and much of his slander against Antony evokes his portrait of Catiline 20 years previously. Known as *Philippics* (in imitation of Demosthenes' speeches against Philip II of Macedonia, father of Alexander the Great), these speeches are heavily biased but nevertheless invaluable sources for Antony's career under Caesar and the events immediately after Caesar's death.

In his letters and speeches from this period Cicero often stressed Octavian's youth ("a noble young man, or rather a boy," *Philippics* 4.3), to reassure the senators about his docility. Undoubtedly Cicero entertained no illusions about Octavian's motives or his potential to harm the Republic. However, having identified Antony as a greater threat, he secured for Octavian the grant of propraetorian power, beginning on January 1, 43. Thus he legitimized Octavian's previously unconstitutional command of his private army composed of Caesar's veterans. Now an official representative of the Republic, Octavian joined the senatorial army led by the consuls Aulus Hirtius and Gaius Pansa and moved against Antony in Mutina.

After a series of battles in April, Antony was defeated and withdrew to the south of Transalpine Gaul (modern Provence) where he formed an alliance with Lepidus. Meanwhile, the two consuls in command of the senatorial armies had died in the battle of Mutina, and Octavian refused to hand them to Decimus Brutus, as per the instructions of the Senate. Now in command of eight legions in total, Octavian was hailed as *imperator* by his troops. Confident in his strength he marched on Rome, seized the state treasury, which he distributed among his men, organized elections, and got himself elected consul. This was another blow to the already crumbling Republic.

The Second Triumvirate: 43–32 BCE

To the shock of Cicero and the Senate, Octavian then arranged a private recon-ciliation with Antony, a remarkable reversal that was facilitated by Lepidus. Following a meeting near Bononia (Bologna) in November, the three men reached an agreement: a triple magistracy was instituted for five years for Antony, Octavian, and Lepidus, to be renewed in 37. This meeting was the basis of what we call "the Second Triumvirate." Before the end of November, the assembly in Rome voted the Triumvirs supreme legislative and judicial power for five years. The law passed on that day (*lex Titia*) vested the three men with full authority to reconstitute the state (*Triumviri reipublicae constituendae*). Thus, whereas the First Triumvirate (in 60) had been a secret and illicit arrangement, the second was publicly sanctioned. The passing of the *lex Titia* is indicative of how social attitudes were quickly conforming to political developments that were at odds with republican principles.

The immediate consequences of the second Triumvirate were:

- A new proscription. The Triumvirs sent paid assassins with the task of execut-ing 17 opponents in Rome. Antony personally arranged for the murder of Cicero, ordering "the hands that had written the *Philippics*" to be cut off and displayed in the forum together with his head (Plutarch, *Life of Cicero* 48). A list was displayed publicly as at the time of Sulla's proscription. Then there was a second list. There appear to have been 300 victims in all: 150 senators and 150 equestrians. The chief victims were senators, but several more had already left Rome with Brutus and Cassius.
- The division of the Roman world among the Triumvirs. Lepidus received southern Gaul and the Iberian provinces, with three legions; Antony received northern Gaul (Gallia Comata) and Cisalpine Gaul, with 20 legions; and Octavian Africa, Sicily, and Sardinia, with 20 legions. Italy remained undi-vided, and the East was for the time being in the hands of Brutus and Cassius.
- War against Caesar's murderers. In order to recover the East, with its wealth of men and money, Octavian and Antony set out together eastward, by the Via Egnatia. They met the joint armies of Brutus and Cassius near Philippi, Macedonia, and defeated them in October 42. First Cassius and then Brutus committed suicide. Writing more than a century after these events, Tacitus marks succinctly this decisive moment (*Annals* 1.2): "after the slaughter of Brutus and Cassius there were no more Republican armies." Even though it is difficult to pinpoint an exact moment marking the end of the Republic, certainly the deaths of Brutus and Cassius mark formally the end of senatorial opposition to the essentially private armies of ambitious generals.

After Philippi, the Triumvirs controlled the East. Then they negotiated a new distribution, out of which Lepidus came out on the losing end: he yielded southern

Gaul to Antony (who now became master of the whole of Gaul) and Spain to Octavian, who added it to Sicily and Sardinia. Lepidus was left with Africa as his only province. The Italian peninsula was too important to be divided.

The Triumvirs also carved out missions for themselves: Antony would raise money and troops in the East, resources necessary for a resumption of Caesar's plans against the Parthians. Another motivation for the Parthian campaign was the desire to avenge the defeat and death of Crassus in 53. Octavian, on the other hand, had to return to Italy and face two daunting tasks. First, he had to deal with Sextus Pompey, son of Pompey the Great. Fleeing from Spain after the death of his brother Gnaeus in the battle of Munda (45), Sextus had occupied Sicily since 44, ravaging the coast of Italy with his pirate fleet. He had amassed a considerable force composed of his father's veterans, those who had escaped the proscriptions from Rome, those fleeing the Italian communities that the Triumvirs had assigned as prizes for the soldiers, and even runaway freedmen and slaves. Natives from Africa and Spain had also joined Sextus' rather formidable navy of pirates. Octavian now had to eliminate or negotiate with Sextus. A second urgent matter for Octavian was the allocation of land to the veterans of Philippi and the settlement of colonies.

The deal between Octavian and Antony seemed uneven: Antony kept for himself the East with its riches and dreams of glory and profit. Octavian undertook difficult responsibilities, but he had the advantage of his easy access to Rome. Thus he was in a better position to develop and disseminate his own ideology in the capital, and control the public responses to it. With Lepidus away in Africa, the cautious alliance between Octavian and Antony was already beset with smoldering discord.

The first signs of discord: 42–36 BCE

The war of Perusia: 41–40 BCE

Octavian first had to resolve the problem of the veterans, to whom land in Italy had been promised. The dislocation and distress caused in Italian communities by his land confiscations is reflected in Virgil's first *Eclogue*, his first published poem in 41 BCE. A dialogue between two recently dispossessed farmers, it is considered as reflecting his personal experience of the confiscation of his family estate at Mantua.

Antony's supporters made Octavian's task no easier. Lucius Antonius, Antony's brother, and consul for 41, took advantage of the collective resentment at the confiscations to stir up a war against Octavian. Lucius claimed that he wished to abolish the rule of the Triumvirate and restore the Republic and that Antony would gladly abandon his partnership with Octavian and Lepidus. Lucius was aided by Antony's wife, Fulvia, "a woman with no mind for spinning or housekeeping, who did not condescend to control a private citizen, but wished to lead a leader and command a commander" (Plutarch, *Life of Antony* 10). Octavian managed to blockade Lucius' forces in Perusia (Perugia), and cut off the forces that Fulvia had sent to his aid. Rather than starve to death, Lucius surrendered (in 40), and both he and Fulvia were pardoned by Octavian. Sling bullets have been recovered from Perusia, which were hurled by both sides during that siege. They are inscribed with obscene messages and sketches insulting their intended recipients Lucius, Fulvia, and Octavian. These inscriptions provide us with valuable information about the propaganda of both sides, and about Roman conceptualizations of gender and power.

The treaty of Brundisium: 40 BCE

Throughout the events that led to the war of Perusia, Antony had remained in the East, hedging his bets by taking no responsibility for the actions of Lucius and Fulvia against Octavian. However, he was forced to respond to a clear provocation by Octavian, just a few months after the end of the Perusine war. When Antony's governor in Gaul died that summer, Octavian immediately took control of his army, as well as that of Spain, which was also Antony's province. Having acquired a total of 11 legions and two large provinces, Octavian dismissed Antony's officers from their commands, substituted his own, and returned to Rome. It was a major loss of territory and power for Antony, who returned to Italy to find the harbor at Brundisium closed to him by Octavian's troops. Greatly angered at this blatant insult, he landed anyway and laid siege to the port. When Octavian arrived soon after, a battle between the two seemed imminent. But the soldiers on both sides, many of whom had served together under Caesar, refused to fight and left the generals little choice but to patch up their differences. Their agreement is known as the treaty of Brundisium (October 40). This treaty added Transalpine Gaul to Octavian's command in the West, and confirmed Antony's control of the East and Lepidus' position in Africa. When they returned to Rome, the two men sealed their arrangement with Antony's marriage to Octavian's sister, Octavia (Fulvia had died soon after the Perusine war). Virgil's fourth *Eclogue*, which was written about this time, is thought to reflect the collective hope for "a grand order of the ages" (*Eclogues* 4.5), a new era of peace and stability.

Negotiations and war with Sextus Pompey: 39–36 BCE

After the renewal of the Triumvirate with the treaty of Brundisium, Octavian resumed his task of dealing with Sextus Pompey. But when he prepared to move against Sextus, the popular reaction at Rome, where food shortages and riots had become commonplace, forced Octavian instead to negotiate. In the summer of 39, the Triumvirs met with Sextus at Misenum (near Naples). There they persuaded him to abandon his blockade of the Italian coast by letting him keep Sicily, and by adding Corsica and Sardinia to his control. In return, Sextus would send to Rome monthly a stipulated amount of grain. This agreement is known as the treaty of Misenum.

Sextus, Octavian, and Antony parted on good terms. According to Plutarch (*Life of Antony* 32) and Appian (*Civil Wars* 5.73), Sextus gallantly passed on an excellent opportunity to have them both murdered aboard his ship. But the treaty of Misenum proved immediately fragile. Sextus grew disillusioned over the Triumvirs' promise to surrender the Peloponnese to him, and his exasperation grew when Octavian suddenly divorced Sextus' relative Scribonia on the very day she gave birth to a daughter, Julia.

In 38, with Sextus having resumed his piracy, Octavian advanced against him, but was soundly defeated in a naval battle off the coast of southern Italy. By 36, Octavian was prepared to try again. While Lepidus occupied western Sicily, Octavian lost another naval engagement, this time off the coast of eastern Sicily. But his admiral, Marcus Vipsanius Agrippa, was able to destroy much of Sextus' fleet at Naulochus, near the Strait of Messina. Sextus fled to Asia, where he was murdered in 35 on Antony's orders.

After Sextus' elimination, Lepidus, who had benefited the least from the Triumvirate, claimed Sicily for himself. Octavian arrived in Sicily to reproach Lepidus, who ordered him to leave. But Octavian slipped into his camp, and persuaded Lepidus' soldiers to desert to himself. Lepidus was now stripped of his Triumviral powers, and forced into retirement at Circeii (modern promontory of San Felice Circeo). However, Octavian allowed him to retain his fortune and the office of *pontifex maximus*, which he had held since Caesar's death in 44. When Lepidus died in Circeii in 12 BCE, Octavian himself (then Augustus) succeeded him in that office.

After Sextus' defeat in 36, Octavian was received as a victor in Rome and was vested with tribunician powers and sacrosanctity. With his 45 legions (about 300,000 men) and a fleet of 600 vessels, he was now the unchallenged master of the West.

Growing tensions between Octavian and Antony: 43–33 BCE

As we saw, the arrangements of the Second Triumvirate in 43 had seemed most advantageous to Antony, who assumed the prestigious command of the eastern part of the Empire. However, throughout the 30s, his frequent travels between the two parts of the Empire, his liaison with Cleopatra, and, above all, Octavian's clever maneuvering prevented Antony from establishing himself in the East as solidly as Octavian was doing in the seat of the Empire, Italy.

During his first stay in the East, Antony's chief concern had been to raise money for his veterans, which he did by imposing onerous levies on the towns and through other oppressive demands. During his time in Alexandria (41–40), he began a relationship with Cleopatra of Egypt, which was cut short by his rapid journey to Italy after the Perusine war. As we saw, a war between Octavian and Antony was averted at this point through the treaty of Brundisium and Antony's marriage to Octavia. After Brundisium, the trouble caused by Sextus Pompey kept Antony from returning to the East and beginning his Parthian campaign, which he assigned instead to his deputy Publius Ventidius.

Antony was present at the treaty of Misenum in 39, after which he went to Athens with Octavia. In the spring of 38 he was again preparing for his Parthian campaign, when Octavian asked him to come to Brundisium for a consultation on the renewed war with Sextus. But when Octavian failed to arrive for their meeting, an outraged Antony returned to Athens, where he continued preparations for his Parthian campaign. Ventidius' successes in the East were certainly frustrating to his own ambitions (Cassius Dio, 49.21). Meanwhile, the five-year term of the Triumvirate expired in 38. In the spring of 37, Octavian and Antony met at Tarentum, in a climate of suspicion and rivalry which they tried to dispel with grand gestures of mutual trust (Appian, *Civil Wars* 5.94). At Tarentum, Octavia played an important role in reconciling her brother to her husband, at least for the present. The two men renewed their pact for another five years, and agreed on an exchange of forces. Antony presented Octavian with 120 of the ships in his entourage, for Octavian's mere promise of 20,000 legionaries for the Parthian campaign. Their agreement is known as the treaty of Tarentum.

After the treaty of Tarentum, Antony again left for the East, leaving Octavia in Italy. While he was in Syria he sent for Cleopatra. When she arrived, Antony acknowledged the twins she had borne him in 40, essentially conceding a spousal role for her. In 36, Antony finally resumed his Parthian campaign. He secured the support of the king of Armenia, Artavasdes, and together they invaded the Parthian territory of Media. But when the Parthians countered by attacking Artavasdes' forces, he quickly withdrew to Armenia, leaving Antony to fend for himself. Antony was then forced to withdraw from Media, losing nearly one quarter of his men in the process. Even though it was not entirely his fault, the defeat was nevertheless generally attributed to Antony, in the very year that Octavian shone by eliminating Sextus Pompey in Naulochus.

Antony soon resumed his efforts to reclaim resources and prestige from his eastern campaigns. In 35 he successfully attacked Armenia, to punish Artavasdes for his desertion the previous year. He annexed Armenia as a Roman province, and returned to Alexandria in 34. There Antony celebrated a triumph for his conquest of Armenia, complete with the parade of the captured Artavasdes in chains. A few days later, Antony and Cleopatra, ceremonially enthroned as king and queen, bestowed titles, territories, and even Roman provinces upon their three children: the twins Alexander Helios and Cleopatra Selene and the two-year-old Ptolemy Philadelphus. Cleopatra and Caesar's son Caesarion were crowned as joint rulers of Egypt, Caesarion as "king of kings" and Cleopatra as "queen of kings." These proclamations and bequests are known as the "donations of Alexandria."

Antony's Alexandrian triumph and the donations of Alexandria caused a fatal rift in his relationship with Rome, which was under Octavian's political and ideological control. A triumph was, above all, a Roman prerogative, a cultural product for the consumption of the urban crowds of Rome. Such a celebration outside Rome was an implicit challenge to the cultural supremacy and the national feeling of the Romans: "this above all distressed them, that he was donating to the Egyptians the fine and formal rituals of their country, for the sake of Cleopatra," comments Plutarch (*Life of Antony* 50). Indeed, Antony's prolonged and public affair with the queen provided constant fodder for his denigration by Octavian's camp. As the relationship between the two men gradually deteriorated, the specter of Cleopatra was utilized to warn against the imminent danger posed to Rome by Antony's "orientalization." In the war of ideas and representations that followed, Antony was relentlessly presented as Cleopatra's minion, who wanted to make Alexandria the capital of the Empire and share the East with the queen and their children.

Moreover, the personal kinship between Octavian and Antony both suffered from and further fueled their political confrontation. Octavia had been a diplomatic link between the two men, just as Caesar's daughter Julia had consolidated the pact between Caesar and Pompey. It was partly through Octavia's mediation that her brother and her husband had renewed their pact with the treaty of Tarentum in 37 (Plutarch, *Life of Antony* 35; Appian, *Civil Wars* 5.93; Cassius Dio 48.54). In 35, as Antony was preparing for his Armenian campaign in Alexandria, Octavia left Rome bringing troops, gifts, and supplies for his soldiers. But when she arrived in Athens, she received a letter from Antony asking her to leave the supplies there and return to Rome. This was essentially an embarrassing repudiation of a Roman matron by her husband, who was now openly living with a foreign woman as his wife. Octavia returned to Rome, and stoically refused Octavian's request to divorce Antony and move out of their house. Instead, she continued to raise his children by Fulvia in addition to their own two daughters. It was widely speculated that it was Octavian himself who had led his sister into this public humiliation, in order to gain a plausible pretext for a war. Antony's treatment of Octavia, and her own response to this incident, certainly succeeded in stirring the public feeling in Rome against Antony.

After his separation from Octavia, his triumphal parade, and the donations of Alexandria, Antony had little influence in Rome. In 34, a letter that he sent to the Senate requesting ratification of his arrangements in the East was conspicuously ignored. In the following year, Octavian intensified his propaganda against him. On January 1, 32, he officially announced the split, and Antony confirmed it by formally divorcing Octavia. Octavian responded by getting hold of Antony's will, which had been left with the Vestals. Some senators protested against Octavian's blatant disregard of the protocol surrounding such documents, but Octavian proceeded to have the testament read in the Senate. In was then revealed that Antony had made provisions for his children by Cleopatra, and had ordered to be buried at her side. These directives seemed to confirm Octavian's allegations that Antony wished to move the capital of the Empire to Alexandria.

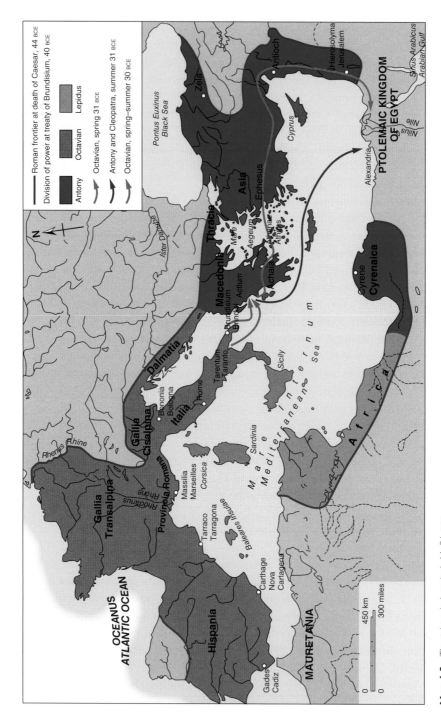

Map 6.3 The triumviral period, 44–31 BCE

The war of Actium: 32–31 BCE

The year 32 was a difficult one for Octavian. With the Triumvirate officially dissolved, he had no legal authority and took the precaution of leaving Rome, where his enemies were preparing his impeachment. At the beginning of February, he reacted by making a bid for power: he returned to Rome, convened the Senate, and, surrounded by soldiers, laid before the senators his grievances against Antony. The consuls, who supported Antony, were panicked and fled to Ephesus with 300 senators.

In July 32, by senatorial decree, war was declared on Cleopatra, and Antony was stripped of all his powers. Both sides prepared. In the East, a powerful army and fleet, mainly Egyptian, were assembled, while intensive propaganda was put out against Octavian. In the West, Octavian had himself elected consul for 31. Then, he obtained, first in Italy and then in the western provinces, the swearing of an oath of loyalty to him (not to the state). This was a gesture of great significance: besides giving him command of the war, this oath committed entire regions to him personally, and essentially made the West his clientele. A no less intensive propaganda on his behalf accused Antony of every possible turpitude.

The two sides clashed in the Adriatic on September 2, 31, at the entrance to the Gulf of Ambracia, at Actium, below a promontory dominated by a temple to Apollo. It is a much-debated event, regarded by some as a tough battle, and by others as involving no real engagement between the two navies. In any event, Cleopatra suddenly decided to return to Alexandria, and Antony followed her after ordering his army to retreat to Macedonia and then Asia. In 30, Octavian arrived in Alexandria, blockaded the imperial palace and demanded their surrender. Antony committed suicide, and Cleopatra did the same a few days later to avoid her humiliating display and ceremonial execution in Octavian's triumph. Caesarion and Antyllus (Antony's older son by Fulvia) were hunted down and executed. Egypt was annexed as a Roman province.

Augustan poets celebrated Actium as a great and decisive military victory on land and at sea, won through the intervention of Apollo, and bringing the era of the Civil Wars to a close. However, it was less a strategic turning-point and more a political and psychological victory, inaugurating a new order. The new order revealed, and reinforced, the profound social and cultural transformations that had taken place in attitudes during the 13 years preceding Actium.

6.3 | Social and Cultural Transformations

Cicero recounts that when Antony tried to place the royal diadem on Caesar (the infamous incident of the Lupercalia of 44), there was a loud groan throughout the forum and, when Caesar refused it, the people shouted their approval. "In this way, criminal, you tested what the Roman people could bear and endure," Cicero protests (*Philippics* 2.85). Less than 20 years later, largely the same body politic acquiesced in, and even welcomed, the idea of Octavian as sole ruler. In order to understand Octavian's successful assumption of the extraordinary commands and powers that led to his victory at Actium we must first sketch the changes that had occurred in society, social life, the ideology of political power, and even the concept of life during the 17 years between these two events. These were part of a development that had started well before that time.

Social changes in the late Republic

All classes of society found themselves affected by the upheavals. Among the ruling classes, the strongest positions were beginning to be occupied by the "new senators" who had emerged from the municipal elites of Italy and the western provincial elites. These replaced the old aristocracy, which was also decimated by the Civil Wars and proscriptions. This was particularly apparent in the entourage of Octavian: almost all of his consuls were Italians, as was Agrippa, his loyal admiral who had won both Naulochus and Actium for him. The equestrians too now crowded at the top, having advanced continuously since Pompey and Caesar, whose councils had been filled with them. The proscriptions of senators had been the occasion of considerable profit for the equestrians. Maecenas, an Etruscan aristocrat, close friend of Octavian–Augustus, and patron of a literary circle, preferred to remain an equestrian when he could have gained access to the senatorial class. His prestige and satisfaction with his status are indicative of the growing confidence and influence of the equestrian class.

Among the lower classes the changes were equally significant, with centurions promoted to municipal Senates and sometimes even to the equestrian order, and freedmen occupying increasingly privileged positions in economic and social life. The career of the poet Horace is indicative of this social mobility. In a poem from his first collection, published in the mid-30s (*Satires* 1.6), Horace expresses his gratitude to his patron, Maecenas, for not snubbing him because his father was a humble freedman. The beneficiaries of social advancement would become keen partisans of Octavian, as the rift between him and Antony grew throughout the thirties.

Spectacles in the late Republic: festivals, celebrations, and games

circus: Racetrack for chariot racing (e.g. the Circus Maximus at Rome). Chariots started from starting gates (*carceres*) and raced seven laps down and back around a central barrier (*euripus*) and conical turning posts (*metae*).

An important catalyst in the changing social attitudes of these years was the clever use of spectacle and entertainment to shape the public feeling. In order to gauge the political significance of spectacles, it is essential to examine these events diachronically in their proper historical and cultural context. Competitive and violent, cultured and coarse, native and imported, Roman spectacles (of the stage, **circus**, and arena) were increasingly lavish, popular, and politically charged in the late Republic. Spectacles (*spectacula*) were public shows, spectacular in scale and action, things meant to be seen and worth seeing, put on by elite representatives of the community to reinforce the social order, which included their own status.

From early times Rome celebrated festivals or holidays (*feriae*) concerned with fertility and harvest, fields and **lustration** (ritual purification). These rustic ceremonies (e.g. Saturnalia, Lupercalia) were moved into the emerging city, held close to temples and shrines, and added to the official festival calendar. The fundamental rite was the sacrifice of domesticated animals to honor the gods. Like other ancient peoples, the Romans felt that they were dependent on the good will of the gods, so they regularly and ritually offered blood sacrifices publicly for the welfare of the community.

Roman games (*ludi*) were the shows or contests that arose as part of the celebrations or religious rites that were acts of communal thanksgiving to the gods for military success or deliverance from crises. Inherently popular, they increased over time and became annual and state-financed, and civic officials organized them as supplements to traditional festivals. *Ludi* usually included *ludi circenses* or chariot races, begun, according to tradition, in the Circus Maximus by the Etruscan king Tarquin the Elder. Other shows, *ludi scaenici* or theatrical performances, also credited to Etruscan influence, took place on early temporary stages before the development of permanent theaters in the late Republic. The *Ludi Romani*, the oldest games, begun in 366, and the *Ludi Apollinares*, instituted during the Second Punic War, presented both circus and theater games. Some old state festivals, such as the *Ludi Magni Votivi*, probably originated as triumphal games vowed by generals to Jupiter before a campaign. Unlike these festival games, which were organized by the state to honor the gods, the more notorious blood sports (*munera*) with gladiators were organized privately under the Republic and held by relatives to enhance the funerals of nobles.

lustration:
Performance of a purificatory ceremony, e.g. of a body of people, a piece of land, a city.

Chariot racing in Rome

Rome had horse races in festivals from very early times, including a race in the Games of Mars (with the October Horse sacrifice), and there may have been early chariot races in the Campus Martius; but horse races were not part of the formal contests of the Republic, and the chariot races soon moved to the Circus Maximus. The Romans (e.g. Livy 1.35) credited Tarquin the Elder (616–579 BCE) with institutionalizing chariot racing at Rome: Livy says he planned out the Circus Maximus and assigned places for temporary wooden stands for the elite. Originally, the site in Murcia valley between the Palatine and Aventine hills was simply a natural, reasonably level area, about which temporary stands were erected, as in Etruscan sport. Tarquin's contribution probably was to alter the course of a stream underground, drain the area, and hold regular races on the site.

There is debate about the relative influences of Etruscan, Greek, and Latin traditions on Roman chariot racing. Etruscan influence is apparent in the costumes and techniques, and in Rome's disinclination for horse races. Greek

factions: Professional
chariot racing business
associations; groupings
of spectators
according to the
"color" or team they
supported.

influence on the facility is indicated by early similarities to the Greek hippodrome, but other features (e.g. **factions**, central barrier, starting stalls, seven laps, position of finish line) seem distinctively Roman, although most of these features are not well known until the late Republic. In sum, it seems that, from the monarchy on, Roman chariot racing combined a Greek competitive aspect with an Etruscan emphasis on spectatorship and with distinctive Roman organization.

Ludi circenses with chariot races were institutionalized in the fourth century (366 BCE), with many others to follow, so the Circus Maximus developed architecturally during the Republic. The primary function of the circus, and the focus of its elaborated architectural design (under the Empire; see chapter 11), was as a venue for chariot races. However, as a spectator facility, it was also used for numerous spectacles, including beast and gladiatorial shows and triumphal games; but as these grew they presented problems (e.g. of animal control), so many non-equestrian events shifted to amphitheaters when they were developed in Rome at the end of the Republic.

Organization by colors: firms, teams, and fans   The earliest circus entries may have been made by individuals, as in Greece, but the Republic saw the development of a system of professional chariot racing associations (probably after the Second Punic War, though unattested until the seventies BCE). With the formal institution of regular public funding for races, the factions (*factiones*, teams and colors) responded to the need for more efficiency and professionalism in the staging of races. While their origins are uncertain, the factions clearly were privately owned and operated businesses, led by private executives. Well entrenched and self-contained by the first century, with stables and headquarters in the Campus Martius, the factions owned the chariots, horses, stables, equipment, and staff; and they were paid for the use of all the necessary elements by the producers, called editors (*editores*), who financed the races. These elaborate organizations recruited or purchased and trained an array of functionaries from drivers to wheelwrights. As shown in mosaics, some (*sparsores*) threw water on the horses, and others (*hortatores*) called out strategies or encouragement from horseback or on foot.

Although two-horse chariots are known, teams usually consisted of 4, 6, 8, or 12 four-horse chariots (*quadrigae*). Teams were identified by their colors (worn by the charioteers and loyal fans): red, white, green, and blue, with the greens and blues as the dominant and most mentioned colors under the Empire. Tertullian (*On Spectacles* 9.50) felt that the four colors represented the four seasons, and that the circus, with the colors and its cultic decorations, was, in effect, a pagan religious center.

In both aspects, as businesses and in the form of the colors used to mark teams and show fan loyalty, factions endured for centuries. Although they developed and elaborated the physical setting of chariot racing, the early emperors generally respected these traditions.

Hunts in the arena: cruelty to animals as entertainment?

The great beast spectacles (*venationes*) of Rome must be understood in the changing context of Rome's history from humble rural roots to imperial power. As well as having native hunting traditions, Romans regularly killed animals in blood sacrifices. Also, in certain festivals early Romans hunted, baited, or abused local animals. In the games of the ancient Italian fertility goddess Ceres, foxes with burning brands tied to their tails were let loose in the Circus Maximus; and the games of Flora, an ancient Italian fertility goddess of flowers and vegetation, included hunts of harmless small wild animals (roe deer and hares) staged in the Circus. When beast shows became an official part of state festivals in 169 BCE, customs such as the games of Ceres and Flora no doubt made Romans more receptive to the spectacular carnage in the arena.

Once introduced in association with triumphs, shows with beasts became more and more popular, leading to their inclusion in regular festivals. In 275 BCE M. Curius Dentatus exhibited four elephants, taken from Pyrrhus at Beneventum, in his triumph. In 251 the proconsul, Lucius Caecilius Metellus, brought 142 elephants to Rome and exhibited them as spoils of war in the Circus Maximus, arranging a mock battle with slaves. In 186 Marcus Fulvius Nobilior in his triumph at Rome held a hunt with lions and panthers. In 169 the curule aediles P. Cornelius Scipio Nasica and P. Lentulus exhibited 63 African wild beasts, 40 bears, and some elephants in circus games, thus introducing beasts shows into state festivals. As Livy (44.18) commented, "magnificent displays were on the increase."

At first foreign animals apparently were merely displayed as curiosities and not killed, but in time the beasts were pitted against each other or were routinely hunted and killed. Early hunters (*venatores*) were foreign professionals, imported to demonstrate their skills and equipment in hunting exotic animals. (A later group, the *bestiarii*, were beast handlers and beast fighters.) Since Romans saw hunting in the wilds as a good preparation for warfare, they felt that exposure to the blood and death of animals in hunts in the arena offered similar benefits.

Beast shows expanded in size as they spread from state festivals and triumphs to funeral games during the late Republic. Usually held in the Forum and Circus Maximus, they later found another home in the amphitheater. Later hunts expanded even further with imperial excesses, and they outlived the decline and fall of gladiators and of Rome itself.

Greek games in Rome

Through exposure to Etruscan and Greek customs, the early Romans were familiar with basic sporting contests, such as running, wrestling, and boxing, which they probably practiced outside the city in the Campus Martius. However, they were culturally suspicious of the influence of serious Greek athletics, especially because of its public nudity. As noted, in addition to beasts and actors, M. Fulvius Nobilior, in his triumph in 186 BCE in the Circus Maximus, put on the first athletic contests with imported Greek athletes, who probably demonstrated the events of the Greek pentathlon for the first time at Rome. Unlike the introduction of gladiators and beast fights, this experiment did not catch on quickly. Even when Sulla in 80 BCE transferred most of the events of the Greek Olympics of that year to Rome, and when M. Aemilius Scaurus possibly added games with athletes to the regular festival calendar in 58, Greek athletics could not rival the normal events of the arena and circus. Although Greek athletic contests were included in some of the great triumphal shows of the first century BCE, they remained exceptional and suspect at Rome.

Gladiators as professional performers

In the late Republic, ambitious leaders used gladiators in shows with increasing numbers and frequency. Gladiators became professional entertainers, and Romans became knowledgeable and attentive sports fans who recognized skilled performances. Politicians responded to the people's desire for shows, and performances developed a hierarchy of craft or entertainment value, with gladiators as star attractions. Gladiatorial shows were spectacularly appealing and politically effective. For example, in 122 BCE Gaius Gracchus, seeking popular support as tribune, took down the barriers built around an arena in the Forum for a gladiatorial show and opened spectatorship without payment to all Romans. The dynamics of a collapsing Republic in the Civil Wars did not create, but accelerated, an ongoing process of elevation: privileges for gladiators increased in the late Republic and early Empire, which also saw the development of specialized, monumental facilities for preparation and performance. The escalation of spectacles brought more glory and better treatment to gladiators, leading to the ambivalent feelings so often noted in sources of the late Republic and early Empire.

Romans increasingly appreciated gladiators as models of martial virtue and as specialized providers of mass entertainment. Death and victory were perhaps the only options for the first gladiators, but later gladiators were granted improved chances of survival, and even fame and wealth. Sparing losers probably arose as a way for spectators to express appreciation, or as an economic measure by *editores* not wanting to lose their investments in such valuable resources. The first reference to awarding the *rudis* – the wooden sword symbolizing release from the arena – is from Cicero (*Philippics* 2.29). By his time gladiators were skilled artisans, essential stars in Rome's entertainment industry, performers to be elevated and not just eliminated.

Despite their early and continuing vile social origins, gladiators were becoming talented professionals who were trained and recompensed (by contracted wages or prizes won). They were fighters specializing in certain weapons, expert craftsmen who bound themselves by a sacred oath to train, suffer, and fight with decorum until killed or released. What had been scorned as servitude came to be acclaimed as an art. The fame of the actors and the virtues of the actions became increasingly inconsistent with the social origins and status of the group. Hence the symbolic paradox of the gladiator, the elevation, glamour and privileges given to debased men. The root of the ambivalence was the enduring disjunction between the Roman view of the type of people who were gladiators – an aboriginal and persisting prejudice – and the growing status, privileges, and glory won by professional gladiators. (See also chapter 4.)

Gladiators and soldiers

With the escalation of gladiatorial combats in the late Republic, the images and worlds of the gladiator and soldier were increasingly correlated. Rutilius Rufus as consul in 105 BCE began the practice of using gladiatorial trainers to instruct landless army recruits. The Roman defeat at Arausio by the Cimbri and Teutones in 105 was the worst since Cannae in 216, and the Romans in crisis turned to Marius and to gladiatorial instructors.

Under the Republic gladiators wore essentially the same equipment as soldiers (helmet, shield, sword), and various types (e.g. Samnites, Thracians, Gauls, *Provocatores*) fought against opponents of the same type. The most popular type under the late Republic seems to have been the Samnite, a heavily armed figure, with helmet, sword, a guard on the right arm, and probably a greave on his left leg. *Provocatores* also fought with a greave and arm guard, but they also had a partial breastplate, a medium-size oval shield, a short, straight sword, and a helmet with large neck and cheek guards, and with feathers at its sides (the latest army model in the Augustan period).

While Romans admired the military prowess of gladiators, they did not see gladiators as Roman soldiers. Rather, gladiators were still seen as threatening outsiders, "others," not the ideal, patriotic, landholding citizen-soldiers of early Rome. There was no Roman type of gladiator because producers would not have risked – and crowds would not have tolerated – the possible defeat of a fighter representing Rome.

When the gladiators' revolt led by Spartacus turned into the slave war of 73–71 BCE, it traumatized Rome. Whatever his origins, Spartacus was trained by Rome as a gladiator, and he and other skilled warriors became rebel soldiers against Rome: a complete perversion of 216, when slaves were trained by Rome to be soldiers for Rome. Although the war was initially disdained as merely a matter of slaves and gladiators, Rome grudgingly had to respect the virtues of Spartacus' army. Florus (2.8) says that Spartacus' men fought to the death as befitted men led by a gladiator, and that Spartacus died bravely "as became a general." Rome's ambivalence about gladiators was like its feelings about its greatest enemies: Rome wanted to crush and dominate them but they were granted respect for their military skills and fighting spirit.

Games and the crisis of the Republic

From the third century BCE through the late Republic and into the early Empire, political opportunism, imperial resources, and social needs greatly expanded spectacles into public entertainments. By the late second and increasingly in the first century BCE rival generals and magistrates further enlarged and conflated existing spectacles, and imported or invented variations, to display their power and to court popular support. Great generals, such as Sulla and Pompey, put on grander and more complex shows, using funeral and triumphal honors and the festival calendar as excuses. Some votive games were institutionalized as regular annual games, such as the *Ludi Victoriae Sullae* from 81 and the *Ludi Caesaris* from 46 BCE, and the number of days of festivals at Rome grew accordingly.

In 81 Sulla held a great triumph in which he displayed rich and exotic spoils from the war against Mithridates. To make a political statement, his procession also included political exiles and their families (who had left Rome when the Marians took control of the city), who were told to proclaim him "savior" and "father." At the end of the triumph he gave a speech and asked the people to give him the surname Felix: the fortunate one (Plutarch, *Life of Sulla* 34). Plutarch adds that Sulla held feasts for the people with vintage wines and with so much food that large quantities of leftovers had to be thrown into the Tiber. Later, when his wife Metella died, he honored her with a gladiatorial spectacle. Sulla stepped down from his dictatorship but others learned about political violence and spectacular extravagance from Sulla's career.

The actual activities, the range of spectacular and often violent performances, were becoming very similar in funeral *munera* and triumphal *ludi*. In theory or pretext *munera* under the Republic had always been associated with death and funerary honors, but now aspiring politicians clearly had to provide violent spectacles, whether officially in *ludi* or unofficially in *munera*. Laws of 67 and 63 BCE forbade electoral corruption by means of giving gladiatorial shows, banquets, or cash within two years of one's standing for office, but candidates side-stepped the law. As magistrates, especially aediles, knew, the production of lavish shows was politically expedient and even necessary. In 51 BCE Cicero was governor of Cilicia and his friend Caelius, elected as aedile at Rome for 50, wrote to him repeatedly, pleading for him to supply him with leopards so that he could put on an impressive show and thus gain political mileage. Violent spectacles were so prominent in society that many politicians in the 60s and 50s even used gangs of gladiators for personal protection.

Pompey and Julius Caesar: magnificence and munificence

Pompey's third and most magnificent triumph, in September of 61 BCE, after his victory over Mithridates of Pontus, celebrated his victory over three continents. Appian provides abundant details on this, the most lavish triumph Rome had yet seen. In the procession were wagons full of gold and treasures, over 300 enemy leaders and generals, and painted scenes of victories. Pompey in a bejeweled chariot wore the supposed cloak of Alexander the Great.

In 55 Pompey dedicated his theater (Rome's first stone theater) in the Campus Martius with several stage and musical shows and athletic performances. He also put on hunts in the Circus Maximus for five days, in which 20 elephants and 500 or 600 lions and some 400 other African beasts died. A letter from Cicero to a friend who missed the show (*Letters to his Friends* 7.1) scorned the killing of the beasts, especially the hunt of elephants on the last day.

> But what pleasure can it possibly be to a man of culture, when either a puny human being is mangled by a most powerful beast, or a splendid beast is transfixed with a hunting spear? And even if all this is something to be seen, you have seen it more than once; and I, who was a spectator, saw nothing new in it. The last day was that of the elephants, and on that day the mob and crowd was greatly impressed, but manifested no pleasure. Indeed the result was a certain compassion and a kind of feeling that that huge beast has a fellowship with the human race.

Despite Cicero's supposed reaction, the shows of 55 overall were a popular success, and it would take Julius Caesar to outdo Pompey.

In numerous ways the career of Julius Caesar signaled the end of the Republic and the need for a transition to empire. In the history of the spectacles as well, Caesar was innovative in scale, context, and content. Caesar understood the political advantages of generously giving entertainments to the people, and the lesson was not lost on his successor. Fully appreciating the political potential of the arena, Caesar broke the restriction of gladiatorial *munera* to funerals, and he expanded and experimented with diverse spectacles. He got past the need for the recent death of a male relative: in 65, as aedile, he held games for his long-dead (20 years earlier) father with gladiators, stage-plays, and a combat between criminals with silver weapons and beasts. He kept gladiatorial troops at Capua and assembled so many gladiators at Rome in 65 that a bill was passed limiting the number that a person could keep in the city to 320 pairs (Suetonius, *Julius Caesar* 10). The excuse was concern about gladiator revolts but the true concern was Caesar's pursuit of excess popularity.

Caesar's great triumphs of 46 BCE

After the Civil Wars, Caesar's triumphal games in August of 46 BCE trumped even those of Pompey. Caesar celebrated five triumphs (for Gaul, Egypt, Pontus, Libya, and Spain; Suetonius, *Julius Caesar* 37–9), four of them in one month, and he showered largesse on his soldiers and the citizens of Rome, including banquets and doles of meat. As Suetonius details, the triumphal games in September of 46, which also celebrated the consecration of Caesar's temple of Venus Genetrix, were the grandest Rome had yet seen, a truly spectacular combination of theatrical, equestrian, athletic, and gladiatorial events held in several sites in front of large crowds (*Julius Caesar* 39):

He gave entertainments of diverse kinds: a combat of gladiators and also stage plays in every ward of the city . . . as well as races in the circus, athletic contests, and a sham sea-fight [a *naumachia*]. . . . [military dances, theatrical events, equestrian contests, and the Game of Troy (an equestrian performance) also were held]. . . . Combats with wild beasts were presented on five successive days, and last of all [in the Circus Maximus] there was a battle between two opposing armies, in which five hundred foot-soldiers, twenty elephants, and thirty horsemen engaged on each side. . . . [three days of athletic competitions took place in the Campus Martius]. . . . For the naval battle a pool was dug in the lesser Codeta and there was a contest of ships. . . . Such a throng flocked to all these shows from every quarter, that . . . the press was often such that many were crushed to death, including two senators.

Caesar added a gladiatorial combat in the Forum to his games in 46, with the excuse that it was for his daughter Julia, who had died eight years before. He made significant provisions (Suetonius, *Julius Caesar* 26):

[While fighting in Gaul earlier] he announced a combat of gladiators and a feast for the people in memory of his daughter, a thing quite without precedent. . . . He gave orders too that whenever famous gladiators fought without winning the favor of the people, they should be rescued by force and kept for him. He had the novices trained, not in a gladiatorial school by professionals, but in private houses by Roman equestrians and even by senators who were skilled in arms, earnestly beseeching them, as is shown in his own letters, to give the recruits individual attention and personally direct their exercises.

Clearly, Caesar saw the usefulness of gladiators.

Furthermore, as well as a hunt with 400 lions and the first display of a giraffe at Rome, Caesar's spectacles compounded many earlier activities (e.g. gladiators, stage-plays) with new variations such as athletic contests, Thessalian bullfighting, the Game of Troy, and mock battles both on land and on water.

Also in his triumphal spectacles of 46 BCE, Julius Caesar gave the first naumachy (*naumachia*) or mock sea battle at Rome. The term applied both to the artificial sites and to the spectacles: the large, shallow basins with banks of seats for spectators, and the naval battles (re-enactments with actual ships of famous non-Roman battles) staged thereon with large numbers of forced combatants. Caesar had a special basin dug in the Campus Martius, and 4,000 oarsmen and 2,000 fighters in costume recreated a battle between Tyrians and Egyptians. Rather than harmless military displays or even combats of professional gladiators, these staged battles on water (or on land) were spectacular mass executions of captives.

The escalation of spectacles was seemingly out of control and too much was focused on Caesar himself. After Caesar's assassination, Augustus faced and dealt with the problem, turning a divisive political competition into a cohesive imperial institution.

naumachia: A staged naval battle; the basin dug for such a show.

Private life: women and family

The reordering of social hierarchies had important consequences also for the position of women. A number of women of the politically active class were able to assert themselves in ways that were highly visible, and that seem not to have been possible in an earlier age, though even now they met with widespread disapprobation. Sempronia, whose husband was one of the consuls of 77, is said to have been involved in Catiline's conspiracy; she is described by Sallust (*Conspiracy of Catiline* 25) as smart, funny, and well-read, but altogether too skilled at singing and dancing. The "Lesbia" to whom the poet Catullus proclaims his devotion was, in real life, Clodia, sister of Publius Clodius, tribune in 58, a married woman so notorious for her very public love affairs that Cicero could claim, apparently with a straight face, that her home served merely as a cover for "lust, extravagance, and every kind of unheard-of vice" (*In Defense of Caelius* 57). Male society, we might suppose, will have been more comfortable lauding the accomplishments of a woman like Turia, who is said to have risked her own safety to rescue her husband from the clutches of the Triumvirs, and who may be the unidentified woman who was memorialized in a eulogy delivered by her husband, and later inscribed on stone at Rome (the so-called *Laudatio Turiae*), that also extols her more conventional attributes – modesty, obedience, affability, agreeableness, dedication to wool-working, sober dress. What Turia, or any other woman, might have thought of her husband's characterization of her is, unfortunately, unknown.

It is difficult to know also whether the public conduct of women like Sempronia and Clodia, whose exploits our sources take a considerable and unconcealed pleasure in recounting, should be understood to signal a broader change in the roles of women who were not part of the wealthy, governing class. No one, of course, would maintain that the behavior of ordinary British women is described by the conduct of the women of the royal family. In the absence of evidence to the contrary, we might suppose that the lives of most lower-class women, including slaves, were not so very different from what they had been. Freeborn women continued to scratch out a living as laundresses, weavers, butchers, and fish-sellers, or in one of the occupations that are recorded on inscriptions at Pompeii: bean-dealer, nail-seller, brick-maker, even stonecutter. A number of poor women worked as waitresses in taverns, where they were probably expected, or obliged, to engage in prostitution on the side. In fact, for a lot of unskilled working-class women, prostitution was the only way to make a living, however inadequate. Many worked out-of-doors in the public archways (*fornices*). Slave women were employed mostly in the homes of the wealthy, cooking, cleaning, weaving – in short, doing whatever they were told to do, which sometimes meant submitting to the sexual demands of their owners.

It has been suggested that it was also mainly among the poorer classes that newborn children were abandoned (in the Roman term, "exposed"), left in public places – either because their parents were unable to care for them or because they were unwanted – usually, it seems, with the expectation (or hope) that they would be found and raised as slaves. Many undoubtedly died. Apologists for the Romans have sometimes minimized the extent of the practice, but the evidence is conclusive: it was both widespread and widely accepted. It is reasonably clear also that daughters were abandoned more often than sons, perhaps because they might some day need a dowry, and could therefore be seen to be a potential drain on the family's financial resources. It is a cruel and often unremarked irony that the very institution of dowry, which served as the means by which some women acquired a measure of independence within marriage, may have condemned others to slavery.

It is unlikely that anything had a greater effect on the lives of upper-class women than the changes that occurred in marriage and divorce, mainly, it seems, in the period between about 150 and 50 BCE. Where it had previously been customary for a woman to marry in such a way that she passed into the control of her husband, who then exercised over her a legal authority not unlike that of a father over his daughter, by the time of Cicero, if not earlier, most marriages were arranged so that instead of becoming subject to her husband's authority, the wife remained under her father's power. Why the shift happened is unclear. It is tempting, but probably wishful thinking, to suggest that it occurred because women wanted it to. Modern commentators are inclined to think that it was the product of an increasingly widespread desire to prevent women's share of their fathers' estates from passing out of their natal families. Whatever the explanation, the effect was to give women considerably more independence in marriage. It continued to be the case, however, even into the second century CE, that a woman's consent to marriage was not legally required. (It was sufficient that her father, or guardian, approve.) And wives were, on average, it seems, about 10 years younger than their husbands – a disparity that, in the view of some moderns, is likely to have made them psychologically and emotionally subordinate. There is little reason to believe either that male expectations were now considerably less rigid or restrictive than they were in the time of Cato, who once complained publicly that women were violent and uncontrollable, and went on to say that if wives were ever given the same rights as their husbands, they would be unbearable.

An even more dramatic change took place in the rules governing divorce. For much of the period of the Republic, only husbands could initiate a divorce, and then only in certain circumstances. Originally, according to a law that our sources attribute to Rome's legendary founder, Romulus, divorce was permitted only in the event of poisoning (which probably means that the wife had taken or drunk something to induce an abortion), tampering with the keys, or wine-drinking (which was more or less synonymous with adultery). Sometime in the third century BCE, a man named Carvilius Ruga was allowed to divorce his wife on the grounds that she was barren (inability to conceive was generally assumed to be the wife's failing). By the time of Cicero, however, divorce was easily accomplished, by either wife or husband, generally without financial penalties, and for almost any reason. It was, if the disapproving moralists of the Augustan age are to be believed, fairly common, at least in the political class. But though wives now possessed the right to end a marriage, few actually seem to have done so, maybe because women had very few opportunities to make an independent living, and perhaps also because custody of children was normally awarded to their father.

The legal independence of women was somewhat constrained also by the institution of guardianship. Like prepubescent children whose fathers had died, every adult woman who was not in her husband's control, or under her father's power – because she had either outlived him or been released from it – was required by law to have a guardian (*tutor*), whose main function was to authorize financial transactions she entered into that might result in loss to her (the signing of a contract, for example). The legal sources are explicit about the reasons women were thought to need guardians: they lacked judgment, and were easily duped. In most cases, it appears that the guardian was either the woman's husband or a male relative (often, it seems, an uncle). By the time of the late Republic, however, guardianship had become something of a formality, at least in some cases, so that an increasing number of women were able to manage their financial affairs more or less independently. And from the time of Augustus, freeborn women who had given birth to three children, and freedwomen who had given birth to four, were released from guardianship altogether.

In law, and probably often in fact, a woman's place in the home was emphatically subordinate to that of the *paterfamilias*, the male head of the household, who possessed almost unlimited authority over everyone who lived in it. He had the right to dissolve his children's marriages, and even to execute them (thankfully, few actual instances are recorded, and some of them are probably unhistorical). Those who were under his power (*potestas*) owned nothing in their own name; anything they acquired belonged to him. Under the law, then, it was theoretically possible for a senator whose father had not formally released him from his authority to be unable even to sign a contract.

potestas: Power, especially civil (executive) powers of a magistrate, inferior to *imperium*.

In practice, however, the power of the *paterfamilias* was limited, in at least two ways. First, what the sources refer to as the "family council," which appears to have been made up of male relatives and to have served as a kind of advisory group to the *paterfamilias*, may sometimes have acted as a check on his authority. Second, and more importantly, the demography of the Roman family, which can now be reconstructed thanks to the pioneering studies of Richard Saller (and others), indicates that most Romans were probably not subject to their fathers' control at those times in their lives when they are most likely to have wanted to make independent decisions. Comparative evidence drawn from other, better-documented pre-industrial societies suggests that average life-expectancy at birth in the Roman world was probably of the order of 25 to 30 years. Infant mortality was undoubtedly very high: more than one-quarter of newborns are likely to have died before their first birthday. Half or more of all children probably did not survive past the age of 10. Those who did will have lived, on average, another 35 to 40 years. It is reasonably clear also that men's average age at marriage in the Roman world was, compared to many other pre-industrial societies, relatively late. Analysis of funeral inscriptions suggests that most men probably married in their late twenties and most women in their late teens or early twenties, so fathers could often be up to 40 years older than their children. This comparatively large generation gap, when combined with the figures given above for average life-expectancy at birth, means, among other things, that probably only one fifth of men, and fewer than half of all women, were still under their father's power at the time they got married. And more than 95 percent of men will have been free from their father's control by the time they turned 40.

It may also be doubted that the traditional picture of the Roman household as consisting of several nuclear families ruled by an authoritarian, elderly patriarch corresponds, in any very precise way, to the realities of Roman family life. The image is derived mainly from what survives of Roman private law, easily our largest source of information about the family. But legal rules do not always reflect social practice. The literary sources, including Cicero, suggest that it was very unusual for adult sons to live with their fathers, or for adult brothers to set up a common household. And the many surviving funeral inscriptions on which the relationship between the commemorator and the deceased is identified rarely record extended family relationships (grandparents, aunts and uncles, cousins). What really mattered to the Romans, it seems, were the relationships of the nuclear family, of husband and wife, and of parent and child.

It is impossible to determine (or even to estimate) the average size of a Roman family. The evidence that we do possess about the number of children the Romans had is entirely anecdotal, and tends to report the exceptional, like Gaius Crispinus Hilarus of Fiesole, who is said to have made a sacrifice at the Capitol in Rome on April 9, 5 BCE, together with his 8 children, 27 grandchildren, and 18 great-grandchildren. It is notoriously difficult also to determine what attitudes or sentiments may have characterized the relationship of parent and child. It seems now to be fashionable to maintain that the Romans generally attached little value to children, and then mainly for the adults that they would grow up to be, or in the expectation that they would support their parents in old age. The philosophically minded, like the emperor Marcus Aurelius, were inclined to categorize children with barbarians, slaves, and animals, on the grounds that they were all irrational. But the grief expressed on tombstones set up to commemorate children is, in many cases, undeniably genuine. It was not uncommon for adults to show interest, and even to take pleasure, in the behaviors of childhood. Among the wealthy, about whom we are best informed, it seems to have been expected that fathers would play an active role in the education of their sons, especially when they were young. And small children were often referred to as *deliciae*, "sweethearts."

Intellectual life

In the cultural field, new lines of development appeared in sharp contrast with republican traditions.

One striking feature was the decline in the art of oratory. Hortensius and Cicero, the great representatives of senatorial and court debates, were gone. The circumstances that had given rise to them had changed. Octavian, with his increasingly firm hold on the Senate, gradually rendered senatorial oratory obsolete. There were no more political opportunities for speeches such as Cicero's scathing *Philippics*, or even orations such as *On the Manilian Law*, Cicero's endorsement of Pompey's command in the East. Instead, aspiring authors turned to history (Sallust, Cornelius Nepos, Livy), science, and erudition (Varro). At this time, Latin poetry too found a voice among young Italian intellectuals, who flocked to Rome eager to respond to the new order: Virgil (from Mantua), Horace (from Venusia in Apulia), Cornelius Gallus (from Forum Iulii, modern Fréjus), Ovid (from Samnium), Tibullus (from the Tivoli region), and Propertius (from Umbria).

Since the era of Caesar, when the Epicurean philosopher Philodemus of Gadara had been much esteemed, a political and learned Epicureanism had spread in high society, and a moral and a less informed Epicureanism among the people. In Rome, peace was the principal aspiration. Civil war became more than ever an object of horror. Peace, and above all peace among citizens, was regarded as

Plate 6.3 Virgil, seated, holds a copy of the *Aeneid*; he is flanked by the muses Clio and Melpomene. Roman mosaic from Tunisia, second to third century CE. Bardo Museum, Tunis. C. M. Dixon

the supreme good, bringing with it order and prosperity. The deliverer of these blessings would be a "savior."

Because Roman religion was inextricably linked to political and civic life, its developments also reflect the cultural quest for renewal at this time. We have seen to what extent the *imperatores* (from Marius and Sulla to Caesar) had appealed to the patronage of deities, especially Venus. Caesar had even enjoyed the benefit of being officially deified during his lifetime, as voted by the Senate at the beginning of 44. After his death, he had been recognized (in July 44) as *divus Julius* and admitted among the gods of Olympus. A *lex Rufrena* of 42 seems to have organized cultic practices for Caesar throughout Italy (the date and content of this law are much disputed, however).

Octavian was fully conscious of this background when he accumulated priest-hoods, and he greatly encouraged the perception that he was favored by the gods. Early in his career, he assumed various religious offices. He was made pontiff in 48 by Caesar, augur between 42 and 40, and a member of the college of quinde-cimvirs in 37. He subsequently became a member of the *fetiales*, of the Arval Brethren, and of the Titian Brethren (*sodales Titii;*), before being elected *pontifex maximus* in 12, after Lepidus' death. He thus sanctified his powers and, through them, his person. As victor at Philippi in 42, he proclaimed that he avenged his adopted father's death (an act of filial duty, *pietas*), and he pledged a temple to Mars the Avenger. After his victory over Sextus Pompey in 36, he vowed a temple to Apollo, his appointed protector. Built on the Palatine, this became Rome's most luxurious temple.

Octavian thus turned to his advantage his contemporaries' hopes for peace and their anxieties in the face of Antony's "orientalizing" ambitions. With consum-mate skill in his self-representation, and with the effective support of his entou-rage, Octavian appeared in the eyes of all as the protégé of Apollo, the young god of order, the arts, and youth, the complete opposite to Dionysus–Bacchus, Antony's patron and god of orgiastic excess. Fighting with the West against the East, Octavian established for himself the image of the savior of traditional Rome, the restorer of ancestral values threatened by the oriental mirages of a "new Dionysus," the ally of troublesome Egypt. Octavian knew how to play on national feeling and war-weariness.

Writing more than a century after Actium, the senator historian Tacitus sum-marizes and explicates how Octavian's pervasive control at all levels of society slowly became monarchical power (*Annals* 1.2): "when he had seduced the sol-diery with gifts, the people with grain, and everyone with the sweetness of leisure, he rose up gradually and drew to himself the duties of senate, magistrates, and laws – without any adversary." In the next chapter we examine Actium and its aftermath as inaugurating Octavian's gradual transformation into emperor Augustus.

PART II ROME, MASTER OF THE WORLD

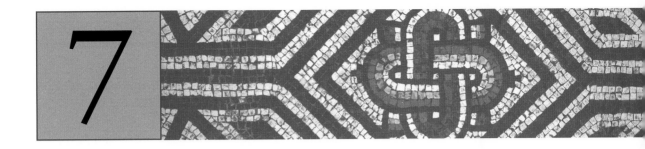

7

THE ROMAN WORLD IN 31–28 BCE

Actium, a victory of political ideology and national morale as much as a military success, took its place in the mythology of Octavian–Augustus as the moment when he was presented by the gods to men: "the ship of Augustus [floated] in full sail under the sign of Jupiter . . . Phoebus . . . rose above the stern of Augustus' ship" (Propertius, *Elegies* 4.6.21–7). But Actium was neither a predetermined victory nor the last step of the war.

7.1 | Actium and its Aftermath

On the evening of September 2, 31 BCE, the prospects for Octavian's camp were encouraging rather than assured. Antony and Cleopatra had fled with part of their fleet. Another part was still intact, sheltering in the Gulf of Ambracia, and there had still been no engagement with Antony's land army. Octavian was determined to obtain a decisive victory and bring the war to an end.

Ending the war

The next day, Antony's fleet surrendered. A week later his deserted legions rallied to Octavian. The sailors and legionaries were incorporated into the armed forces of Octavian. For Antony that meant the loss of Greece, Macedonia, and Asia Minor, for they were thus left defenseless. Octavian went to Samos, but at the end of the autumn he was recalled to Italy because of a simmering military

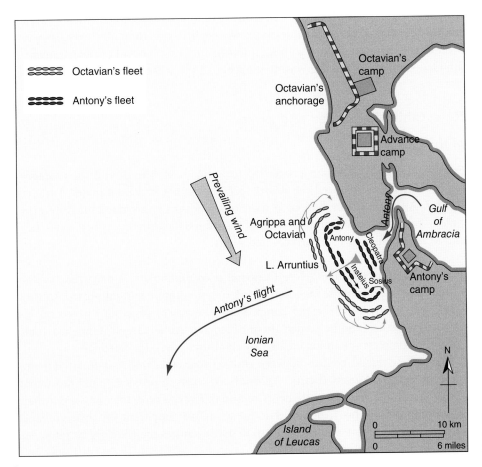

Map 7.1 The battle of Actium, September 2, 31 BCE

rebellion and a reported plot. Meanwhile, returning to Alexandria, Cleopatra made unrealistic plans: to settle in Spain, to carve out a realm for herself in India. Antony, deserted by his Cyrenaican legions, went to Alexandria, where he lived in near-isolation.

At the beginning of the year 30, Octavian returned to the East, received the backing of the king of Judaea, and, from Syria, made preparations for the invasion of Egypt. He had two armies: one in the West led by C. Cornelius Gallus, the other in the East led by himself. Cleopatra, trying to preserve the throne for her children, attempted to negotiate with Octavian, who was determined, however, to possess the treasure of the Ptolemies. She had a mausoleum prepared in which she threatened to have herself incarcerated and burnt together with the treasure if her conditions were rejected. At the end of July, Octavian's cavalry was at the gates of Alexandria. Despite an initial success, Antony was betrayed and subsequently defeated on August 1. Believing the queen to be dead, he stabbed himself to death. Octavian played for time, negotiated with Cleopatra, put her out of action, and gained control of the treasure. A few days later, to avoid being put on display in the triumph of Octavian, Cleopatra committed suicide.

Cleopatra's son by Caesar, Caesarion, and Antony's son from Fulvia, Marcus Antyllus, were executed. Egypt was reduced to a province, though with a special status: Cornelius Gallus, an equestrian, was its first governor, and senators were prohibited from going there without authorization. At the end of the summer of 30, Octavian left Egypt. He was now master of the whole Mediterranean basin.

Re-establishing order and peace

In the East

From Alexandria, Octavian proceeded to Syria, Asia Minor, and then Greece. On his way he reorganized the Roman territories that had been under Antony's control. Antony's policy had been judicious, and Octavian maintained its principles – to consolidate frontiers, to have regard for the differences between cities, and to make allies of local princes and kings.

- Consolidating frontiers. Here Octavian used diplomacy. It mattered little to him whether or not the kingdoms bordering the empire had supported Antony. He was ready to make the compromises necessary to ensure peace on his eastern borders. So he settled the problems of Armenia and untangled some of the complex situations created by rivalries among the Parthians.
- Respecting the differences between cities. Those cities that had declared themselves against Antony (Beirut, Aphrodisias) received privileges, and those that he had plundered had their debts remitted. Everywhere, they preserved their autonomous status (Antioch, Laodicea), as was apparent on their coinage. Many cities in Asia and Syria began to date events in their history by reference to the battle of Actium.

Plate 7.1 Cleopatra and her son Caesarion make offerings to the goddess Hathor. The relief is on a wall of the temple of Hathor at Dendera. C. M. Dixon

- Forming alliances. Although a few recalcitrant sovereigns were deposed and put to death (Alexander of Emesa), the majority rallied in support fairly quickly in order to secure their chances of being pardoned. Many rulers (Herod of Judaea, Amyntas in Galatia, Archelaus in Cappadocia) submitted and swore loyalty to Octavian.

On January 1, 29, while at Samos, Octavian assumed his fifth consulship. It was the first of many subtle steps that would transform him from Octavian into the revered Augustus, the first emperor of Rome.

In the West

By way of Greece (he put Sparta back on its feet and gave it the task of organizing the Actium games), Octavian returned to Rome at the beginning of the summer of 29. Fortunately, we possess a supremely important document for the events surrounding Octavian's rise to imperial power and the senatorial and popular responses to him in Rome. This is a marble inscription found in a temple of Rome and Augustus in Ancyra (modern Ankara, Turkey), capital of the province of Galatia. Often referred to as *monumentum Ancyranum* but more commonly known as *Res Gestae* (literally, "accomplished things"), this document is Augustus' political testament in his own words. Augustus had deposited this document with the Vestals, along with his private and public wills. He left instructions that a copy of the *Res Gestae* be set up in bronze tablets in front of his mausoleum on the Campus Martius, but those tablets have not been recovered. Copies of the *Res Gestae* were also distributed in the provinces, and throughout the twentieth century fragments were recovered, mainly in Asia Minor. However, the inscription from Ancyra is to date the most complete version of Augustus' narrative. With the benefit of hindsight after several decades in power, Augustus provides an authoritative first-person narrative of his accomplishments, beginning with his raising an army in 44 BCE and the battle of Mutina the following year. In a way, Augustus' *Res Gestae* can be seen as the literary legacy of Caesar's commentaries, one of the many precedents set by Caesar that Augustus elaborated and honed throughout his imperial career.

The *Res Gestae* contain precious information about those first two years after Actium while Octavian was still consolidating and legitimizing his power in Rome. According to this document, the Senate and people awarded Octavian exceptional honors: his name was written into the ancient song of the Salii, the priestly college dedicated to the cult of Mars. His actions were ratified by a special disposition, tribunician power was granted to him for life (in 30) and with a wider scope than for the tribunes of the *plebs*. Finally, on January 11, 29, the doors of the temple of Janus in the Forum, which were kept open anytime Rome was at war, were closed by a decision of the Senate. Augustus proudly stressed that it was only the third time in the history of Rome that these doors had been closed.

On August 13, 14, and 15, Octavian celebrated a triple triumph, over Illyria, Actium, and Egypt. Three days later he dedicated the temple to the Divine Julius on the Forum, on the very spot where the dictator's body had been burnt in March 44. And on August 28, the Curia Julia was opened. Henceforth in the Senate's meeting hall there stood a statue of Victory and an altar dedicated to the goddess. The purpose was to remind everyone of Actium and its victor.

The miracle of Actium

Immediately after the battle which rendered him master of the world, Octavian had two trophies erected: one in the temple of Apollo guarding the entrance to the Gulf of Ambracia; the other, opposite, on the actual site of his camp. The latter trophy, instead of being placed under the care of Venus or Victory, was raised to Mars, Neptune, and Apollo. It was a way of showing plainly that victory had been won both on land and at sea. Actium became a central part of the ideology surrounding Augustus. It was supported by a series of political and religious measures and was fed by literary and artistic media.

Political and religious measures

First it was necessary to give thanks to Apollo, Octavian's guardian deity, so the Senate took the decision to build a temple to Apollo on the Palatine near his residence. Second, facing Actium, the free, autonomous Greek city of Nicopolis ("the town of Victory") was founded to serve as an immortal monument. The vast territory allotted to it accented its symbolical importance. And near the town, a great shrine was dedicated to Apollo, containing a sacred grove and a stadium and gymnasium intended for the celebration of games that were to be put on an equal footing with the Olympic Games (the first were held in 28). Lastly, coins were minted bearing the figure of Victory carrying trophies.

Literary and artistic media

As a central part of Augustan ideology, Actium and its aftermath are featured prominently in the works of Virgil, Horace, and Propertius, a poetic triad that reflects complex responses to this event. Virgil (*Aeneid* 8.675–728) describes Actium as a total victory on land and at sea, an event of cosmic proportions and significance: he portrays Octavian as imposing on the stern of his vessel, a double flame springing from his temples, Caesar's worthy heir and the savior of his country. His victory, depicted as a triumph of the orderly West over the chaotic East, has been aided by nature itself (wind, waves, animals) and by the nation's gods (Venus, Neptune, Minerva, Mars, and, above all, Apollo and Jupiter, whose earthly deputy Octavian is). This triumphal feeling is countered elsewhere in the *Aeneid* with somber reflections on the human cost of war and victory. Similarly Horace, in his famous Cleopatra Ode (*Odes* 1.37), rejoices at the newfound liberty after the victory at Actium ("now we must drink and dance with free feet," he says), but also suggests his respect for the dignified suicide of the Egyptian queen. In the same vein, Propertius professes his wonder at the splendid temple to Apollo on the Palatine, but he does so within the context of a rather un-heroic literary work: this is an erotic elegy dedicated to his real or fictional mistress Cynthia (*Elegies* 2.31).

This ensemble of responses connected with Actium reveals the main themes and challenges of an "Octavian" ideology, holding the idea of victory at its core.

This was to be the heart of the imperial mystique. Octavian owed his victory directly to the Olympians and the auspices in his possession. By skillfully emphasizing the defense of Hellenism in the face of Egyptian barbarism, drawing a parallel between Salamis and Actium, Octavian opened up the possibility of reconciling the Greek East and the West. This blending of myth and history, East and West, is a central theme in Virgil's *Aeneid*. There Aeneas's son Ascanius leads the "Trojan games" on the shores of Actium (5. 596–603).

7.2 | Rome and Italy

At the very idea that Cleopatra might set up an oriental monarchy in Rome, which Octavian's propaganda had put about, the whole of Italy rose up and gathered around its protector: in 32 it swore an oath of loyalty supporting the Actium campaign. This almost unprecedented act turned all citizens into clients of Octavian. This patron–client relationship gave Octavian an immense power base but also created responsibilities on his part. Upon his return from Actium and in the years that followed, he developed a major project for the restoration of Rome and Italy.

The restoration of Rome

The city was old. Behind it lay seven centuries of history. For a long time a city of peasants, it had undergone profound transformations affecting the surroundings and way of life of its population of citizens, slaves, freedmen, and foreigners. With its 800,000 (perhaps 1,000,000) inhabitants, it was the largest conurbation in the ancient world. For that reason, it was far from being a safe, clean, let alone grandiose city, comparable with the great cities of the East, or a worthy capital of the world and a suitable abode for its conquerors. Conscious of this disparity, Caesar had desired to ennoble the city and improve living conditions. His assassination meant these plans were shelved, and the subsequent Civil Wars and disturbances added to the problems created by Rome's haphazard and antiquated layout.

The problems of Rome's urban landscape

- The city was no longer contained by the Servian defensive wall, which it largely overflowed, especially into the area across the Tiber. As a result, the old administration, with its four areas, was outdated. Rome was an open town.
- Provisioning was no longer adequate and, as the war against Sextus Pompey had shown, this inadequacy could become crucial if supplies of the staple food, wheat, were disrupted. There was also insufficient water.

- Public safety was practically non-existent: fire was a constant concern (in 31 the Circus Maximus was burnt down), as was the flooding of the Tiber (the last occurred after the death of Caesar). Theft, murder, and popular disturbances were quite common, given the absence of an organized police force.
- Ancient buildings, which constantly needed repairs and maintenance, had long been neglected.
- Traffic in the city was extremely difficult and congested. Rome had never had any town-planning system and buildings were erected randomly. There was a shortage of space and the Forum was too small.

Caesar's works and projects

The dictator had realized the urgent need for reorganizing the city. In 45, he had issued a municipal regulation concerning the cleaning, maintaining, and paving of the streets. And in order to gain more urban space, he had planned to make maximum use of the Campus Martius, even at the price of diverting the course of the Tiber. He had already embarked on a transformation of the capital with a vast program of building and rebuilding. His most important projects were the Basilica Julia, Comitium, Curia Julia, Forum Julium, Villa Publica, Saepta Julia, expansion of the Circus Maximus, and a plan for a theater. Interrupted by his death and the Civil Wars that followed, much of this work was still unfinished at the time of Actium.

Octavian's public projects

Although he abandoned certain of Caesar's enterprises (diverting the river), Octavian pursued others (linking the Forum and the Campus Martius) and completed the construction of what Caesar had started (the Curia Julia was opened in 29, the planned theater would become the theater of Marcellus, etc.). Moreover, he undertook various other works, as a matter of fulfilling vows (the temple of Mars Ultor, pledged in 42, that of Apollo on the Palatine, pledged in 36 and completed in 28), as reconstructions and restorations (the temple of Apollo Sosianus in 34/33, the portico of Octavia perhaps in 33, repairs to 82 temples in the year 29 using the Egyptian booty), or as constructions of entirely new buildings (his own mausoleum in 29). According to Suetonius (*Augustus* 28), he proudly claimed that he had found Rome a city of bricks and left it a city of marble.

Octavian also actively encouraged private citizens to provide public buildings and amenities. The building activity of Agrippa in 33 was a fine example of such benefaction. Agrippa gave priority to the water supply to the capital: he added two aqueducts to the existing four, restored the latter to good working order, increased the number of water-supply points, renovated the drainage system, and reorganized the water services, all at his own expense.

In order to maintain popular support, Octavian paid great attention to everything connected with Rome's provisioning: in 29, he distributed 400 sesterces to each of 250,000 beneficiaries, and in 28 arranged exceptional distributions of grain. Lastly, as we shall see below, he began a policy of providing spectacles and amusements (the first stone amphitheater was constructed in the capital). In the early twenties BCE, Rome was taking shape as a truly imperial city.

Italy

For the first time in almost a century, Italy (the peninsula plus the Cisalpine region) saw an end to civil war, brigandage, and general disorder. Following Actium, and upon his return from the East at the end of 31, Octavian encountered some difficulty in imposing order in Italy. Towns in Italy loyal to Antony (like Bologna) were punished, as well as his supporters among the Italian senators and gentry. But the feeling of a political and spiritual unity that had manifested itself at the time of the oath in 32 had been strengthened by the victory at Actium, resulting in a blended feeling of Italian and Roman patriotism. It is true that, with the exception of a few Alpine tribes, all free men in Italy already had Roman citizenship and enjoyed important privileges long before Actium. But this unity of citizenship and shared privilege did not necessarily involve a "nationalistic" loyalty to Rome. Italian Romans were primarily attached to their place of origin (colony or *municipium*). Rome, whose Senate administered Italy as a federation of cities, remained physically and emotionally distant from their political consciousness. Each region preserved its individuality: Etruscan was still spoken in Etruria, Greek in Magna Graecia, Oscan in Samnium, even though Latin was gradually prevailing throughout Italy.

But in the wake of Actium, Italy owed its dazzling revolution to the renewal of its political class. That was due to a triple phenomenon: the demographic disappearance or weakening of the families of the old nobility; the rise of new Roman nobles; and the appearance of a fresh generation of "new men," for the most part Italian, who gathered around Octavian. Frequently very rich, these new men were the ones who made up the young victor's most fervent supporters. The fact that none of the great writers who contributed to the legend of Actium originated in Rome suggests this victory of a new Italy over an old Rome.

In the economic field, efforts begun before Actium and stimulated by the arrival of the eastern booty began to bear fruit. The last Civil Wars had accelerated the changes initiated in the preceding century: the numbers of small land-owners continued to decline; tree crops (olives) and livestock (sheep) developed to the detriment of cereal crops. Despite these shifts, however, agriculture remained a subsistence economy with some growing specialization and diversification of produce. Land plots of every type and size (*latifundia*, small and medium properties) were worked by various methods (direct land development, use of slave labor, indirect farming by tenants, and sharecropping). The only real novelty was the appearance of a new category of colonists, no longer free workers but slaves to whom the slave-owner rented land as if they were free men. Following the death of Caesar, Octavian had first faced the problem of settling veterans in Italy,

Plate 7.2   Main street at Pompeii. C. M. Dixon

with all the contentious confiscations and redistributions of property it involved. With the demobilization after Actium he faced it again.

7.3 | The Provinces

Rome in 30 BCE possessed a Mediterranean empire consisting of all the countries directly or indirectly subject to its laws. Some of its provinces traced back to the Punic Wars (Sicily, Sardinia), while others were only recently acquired (Egypt). Each was governed according to the particular status it had been given at the time of its annexation. This Roman world was thus extraordinarily varied, and though it largely lacked unity and coherence these were not necessarily desired or imposed. On an empire-wide scale, two major geographical and cultural groups can be roughly distinguished, the very ones in confrontation at Actium. The eastern half of the Mediterranean, where Greek was spoken, possessed a certain cultural cohesion of practices and customs which were Greek or Hellenized, particularly so in major urban centers. In the western half, Latin was the language largely used. Romans viewed their neighbors to the West as barbarians, in urgent need of civilization that was tantamount to their Romanization. The lack of a distinct and homogenous tradition in this western part (as opposed to the eastern one) rendered their acculturation by Rome a relatively easy and rapid, if often uneven, process.

The West

Sicily, Sardinia, and Corsica

Sicily was the oldest Roman province. After a period of prosperity between 43 and 36, Octavian punished those cities that had helped Sextus Pompey before his defeat by Octavian and Agrippa off Naulochus. The province gradually recovered. Six colonies were founded in the coastal zones, but the ruined hinterland went to great estate-owners. In the mid-first century BCE the Sicilian Diodorus (Siculus) of Agyrium wrote a work titled *Historical Library*, an ethnographical and historical narrative covering much of the Mediterranean world and beyond (Greece, Europe, Egypt, Mesopotamia, India, Scythia).

Sardinia and Corsica had been strategically important during the Civil Wars, but they seem to have remained peaceful and obscure under Augustus.

The two Spains

There were four influences at work in the Spanish provinces of Nearer and Further Spain: that of the old Iberian civilizations, the Greek influence around Emporia (modern Ampurias), the Punic influence on the south coast, and the Celtic on the south-east coast. Since 39 they had had a single administration. Romanization was very uneven. It was strong in the south (no other province had as many colonies of citizens) but weak elsewhere, leading to constant local revolts. In the north-west, the regions inhabited by the Astures and the Cantabri possessed vast mineral wealth, and Rome was therefore particularly keen on conquering them. The decade 39–29 BCE was punctuated by military interventions in the area. The Spanish campaigns (29–19) completed the domination of Rome over the province of Spain. Established in 25, the colony of Emerita Augusta (Mérida) became an important cultural center in the western part of the empire.

Africa

As early as 40, the two African provinces (Africa vetus, the former territory of Carthage, annexed in 146, and Africa nova, the former kingdom of Numidia, annexed in 46 after Thapsus) were combined under the authority of the same governor. This proconsul resided in Carthage, which was refounded as a Roman colony and reinforced by the arrival of 3,000 new colonists. The territory he

Plate 7.3 Theater of Emerita Augusta (Mérida) in Spain, built by Agrippa in 18 BCE. akg-images/Bildarchiv Monheim

administered stretched from the Minor Syrtis as far as the River Ampsaga (the Rummel Wadi), around which lay a land that enjoyed a certain autonomy, the Cirtian confederation (centered on Cirta). Romanization was limited outside the urban centers of Carthage, the coastline (Utica), and the interior (Cirta itself), due to the strong indigenous and Punic traditions and the military instability of the area (the southern fringes of the province were ravaged by tribal wars and were never as secure as the interior).

However, three triumphs *ex Africa* were celebrated between 34 and 28. In this province, the threat to the Roman interests came from the west (from the tribe of the Musulamii), from the south (from the tribe of the Gaetuli), and from the east (from the nation of the Garamantes). The importance of these African lands was immense: as grain-growing regions, they could provide for Rome's food supplies. To the west of the Ampsaga lay Mauretania. On the death of the Moorish king Bocchus II, his kingdom came under the direct administration of Rome, represented by prefects. So it remained until 25 BCE, when it was entrusted to Juba II, the son of the king defeated at Thapsus.

Transalpine Gaul

For almost a century there had been a Roman presence here. But until Caesar, Romanization had been relatively meager. Octavian continued the process, founding colonies (Béziers in 36, Orange in 35, Fréjus after Actium) and residing there for a time (39–38). If one compares the excessive demands made on it in the pre-Caesarian period with the treatment it began to receive under Caesar, it is understandable that the transalpine area should have pledged a solid attachment to Caesar's adoptive son.

Celtic Gaul

Celtic Gaul was quickly adapted to the Roman presence, despite the sporadic risings among the Treveri (31–30), the Morini (29), and the Aquitani (28). Caesar's expeditions had left the country so weak and drained that the peace that the Roman presence brought was certainly much needed, if not wholeheartedly desired. In 40 (and until the beginning of 37), Agrippa had re-established order and undertaken the development of the new province. A military show of strength, combined with a skillful policy of alliances with the Germanic peoples of the left bank of the Rhine, had sheltered the country from the incursions of the Germani from across the river. Moreover, the Caesarian foundations of Nyon, Lyons, and Augst blocked the access routes to the Rhône valley, which had been the favored passage to Italy for Germanic invaders. Roman policy was no longer exclusively Mediterranean. By preventing Gaul from being drawn into the Germanic sphere, Rome extended its influence deep into the European mainland.

Illyricum

This province, the pivotal point of the two Mediterranean basins, had been almost lost in the period after the death of Caesar. As part of the treaty of Brundisium it had been allocated to Octavian, who in a series of hard-fought campaigns reconquered the country and even penetrated into Pannonia (35–33). However, as was the case in other Roman provinces, only the coastal regions remained under firm Roman control.

All in all, Rome held on with fair success to its western conquests. The only significant threats to them came from the nomads of the southern parts of the African territories and the Germani east of the Rhine.

The East

Octavian's first concern, as we have seen, was to reorganize the East. He embarked on it to gain the confidence of the populations who had supported Antony, while simultaneously dissociating himself in public opinion from Antony's eastern

Plate 7.4 Triumphal arch built c.20 CE to commemorate the campaigns of the Second Gallica legion. Orange, France. C. M. Dixon

practices. He accomplished this by preserving Roman forms of government, by setting up or maintaining vassal states, and by annexation or diplomacy. Thus he effected the least possible break between the Roman provinces.

Macedonia

Macedonia, the oldest Roman province on the eastern side, was of great strategic importance. It served as a shield for Achaea, which it protected against the barbarians of the north. Moreover, it controlled the Via Egnatia, which provided a vital link between West and East, the first big strategic route built outside Italy. Octavian immediately strengthened this province through diplomacy (placing a subject king, Cotys, on the throne of Thrace, to the north-east of the province) and through the settlement there of veterans of Philippi. Military intervention was also used, quite effectively: in 29–28 the governor of Macedonia, M. Licinius Crassus (grandson of the Triumvir), repulsed an invasion of the native tribes of the Bastarnae and Getae, and launched victorious counter-operations in the region. We shall return to this episode in chapter 8.

Achaea

This province had been practically ruined through inter-state conflicts, the Roman Civil Wars, the passage of troops, looting, the burden of taxes, and the recruitment of soldiers. By taking prompt action after Actium, Octavian gave the towns new hope: around 30 BCE, a new town plan for Corinth was laid down; Patras also received his attention; Sparta was rewarded for its loyalty; and Nicopolis was founded to celebrate the victory at Actium. Outside these urban centers, however, the rural areas remained in a poor state, exploited by affluent land-owners.

Asia, Bithynia, and Syria

Between 31 and 29, Octavian made two stays in Asia and Bithynia. At the time of Actium these provinces had enthusiastically given him their support. In 29, they requested authorization to award Octavian divine honors. Syria was a mosaic of territories of different status (cities, principalities, tetrarchies) more or less closely linked with Rome. This province had undergone changes under Mark Antony and was pacified after Actium, preserving throughout a cultural and administrative diversity. The preservation of a series of vassal kingdoms (Galatia, Cappadocia, Paphlagonia, Commagene, Judaea, Armenia Minor, Pontus, etc.) ensured the connection between Syria and the provinces of Asia and Bithynia, and between Syria and Egypt. On the death of each sovereign, annexation took place, for the most part without clashes, almost as a natural course.

Egypt

In the aftermath of the conquest of Egypt, two problems arose for Octavian: to ensure its security and to organize the new province. Military expeditions in Upper Egypt began in 30. The administration of this province was unusual, not least because of its importance as a grain source for Rome. In 30, with the exception of the Greek cities (Alexandria, Ptolemais, and Naucratis), its territory was placed under the management of an equestrian, a unique exception to the administration of other territories by senators. And the outlines of Octavian's policy for Egypt began to emerge: to preserve, at least on the surface, the respect due to tradition; to disengage himself from the power of the priests and from customs deemed too alien or unseemly for a Roman; and to make sure that Rome controlled the heart of the Egyptian system. Thus he preserved almost in its entirety the traditional administration, but Romanized his coronation name, breaking with a thousand-year-old tradition. For "Pharaoh Octavian" was declared to exercise his office in the name of a power that belonged to him alone, which no longer owed anything to Egypt and its traditions: he was pharaoh as *autokrator*, that is, in the name of the *imperium* conferred on him by the Senate and people of Rome.

Cyrenaica, Crete, and Cyprus

Tossed from one camp to another in the Civil Wars, these relatively recent provinces found stability after Actium. Crete was grouped with Cyrenaica. In 58 BCE, Cyprus had been stripped of its independence because its king, Ptolemy, had allegedly helped the pirates whose depredations had aggravated the wars against Mithridates. Ptolemy committed suicide and the island was then added to the province of Cilicia. After Actium, Cyprus was detached from Egypt.

In August 29, as Octavian celebrated his triple triumph in Rome, the world he dominated was no longer the one that had existed two years earlier. There was the Roman world before Actium, and the Roman world after Actium. Was it an official break? Perhaps. Ancient historians, such as Cassius Dio, regarded it as fundamental – an opinion shared by many moderns.

7.4 | Boundaries and Frontiers

Beginning in the years 76–75 BCE, the increasingly frequent appearance of the globe on Roman coins indicates plainly that Rome saw itself as the conscious champion of order in the world. Augustus could pride himself justifiably on having reached the limits of the world. Yet the Romans realized that much remained just beyond their geographical and military reach. Their connections with that part of the world were numerous, primarily commercial, and often belligerent.

On the fringes of the Roman world

In the north: Britain

Caesar had twice crossed the English Channel and landed in Britain. Since then, contacts between the island and Roman provinces had been rare. But they did exist. Rome followed the political transformations brought about by the wars between the British kingdoms. In 34, 27, and 26, Octavian planned expeditions against the Britons. By contrast, Ireland remained undisturbed by the Romans.

In the north-east: Germania

For the early authors, the term "Germania" covered the territories extending from the valleys of the Rhine and Danube to the North Sea and the Baltic. Its eastern frontiers were not defined, but modern scholars agree that the valley of the Vistula was probably the eastern boundary. Even before Caesar crossed the Rhine, Roman traders had ventured into those regions. And following him, Agrippa was the second Roman to cross the river at the head of an army. But until the Augustan era nothing is known of the frontier system. It seems likely, however, that the Rhine had almost no true defense. At the most it may be supposed that, during his stay in 39–38, Agrippa had established the tribe of the Ubii on the left bank of the Rhine, in the area of the future Cologne, to hold in check the tribes from across the Rhine. The movements of these western Germani (the peoples between the Rhine and the Elbe: the Suevi or Suebi, Canninefates, Chatti, Frisii, Marcomanni, Quadi, Batavi, etc.) were in certain cases becoming stabilized. Their expansion henceforward was to the west into the Celtic region and to the east into the territory of other, eastern Germani, themselves on the move from the Baltic toward the south-east, along the Elbe and the Oder.

The Alpine peoples

These peoples controlled the passage between Italy, Celticum, and Raetia (in particular the two passes of the Little St Bernard and the Great St Bernard, used by numerous Roman traders) and between Italy and Transalpine Gaul. Divided among themselves by tribal conflicts, and keeping away from foreign influences, they lived by working a few mines and breeding livestock.

The Danube basin

In the western part were Celtic peoples (in Raetia and Noricum) and Germanic tribes; in the central part, Illyrians (Dalmatians and Pannonians) and more Celtic peoples; farther east, Thracians (Moesians, Getians, Dacians) and Germani (Bastarnae). These Germani launched raids into the Roman provinces of the Balkans (for instance in Macedonia in 29–28), and organized themselves into kingdoms and leagues.

In the East: Parthians and Arabs

Parthia Since the defeat and death of M. Licinius Crassus at Carrhae in 53 BCE, the Romans had regarded Parthia as their chief rival empire. Caesar and Antony had both tried to keep the Parthians in check. Apart from their conflicting imperialistic plans, there were two sources of strife between Rome and the Arsacid Empire: Armenia, constantly at stake between the two powers, and the Syrian frontier. The Parthian empire, which had provided itself with a new capital (a new town, Ctesiphon), controlled one of the essential stages of the silk route, which passed through its territory.

The Arabs The Nabataean Arabs lived on the caravan routes converging on Petra, an immense distribution center of luxury products originating from the Indian, Arabian, and African worlds. The Kingdom of the Nabataeans was, in Roman eyes, the gateway to an idyllic country, Arabia felix ("fruitful Arabia," modern Yemen), and the land of the Gerraei, "the richest of all peoples," as Strabo called them – countries that fascinated Rome because of their wealth and importance in international trade.

In the south: Nubia and the Sahara

Nubia Lower Nubia was occupied by pillaging nomads from the eastern desert, the Blemmyes, who threatened Egypt from time to time. Farther south lay the Ethiopian kingdom of Meroe (present-day Sudan), a centralized kingdom strong enough to launch military operations as far as Roman Egypt. It was the southernmost land in Africa known to the Greeks and Romans, and was an important trading post between the Mediterranean world and sub-Saharan Africa. Gold and slaves made their way through it toward Aswan and Alexandria.

The Sahara There is no specific word in Latin to designate this great desert. Latin writers spoke of the "lonely places" or "wilderness." The Nasamones lived near the eastern and southern shores of the Major Syrtis; the Garamantes farther west, in Fezzan; the Gaetuli led their nomadic life on the borders of Numidia and Mauretania; and still further west came the Pharusi. All were nomadic shepherds, their territories poorly known to the writers, with vaguely defined boundaries. They occasionally harassed the settled inhabitants of their regions, particularly those in the coastal towns and, with caravans of donkeys and mules, crisscrossed the northern fringes of the desert. The Nasamones sometimes went as far as Chad and the Niger.

Beyond the frontiers

The Slavs, Balts, and Finns Living to the east and north of the Germanic peoples, the Slavs, Balts, and Finns were unknown to the Romans at the time of Augustus. In the first century CE, however, the Slavs first appear in Pliny the Elder (the Veneti of the Vistula) and the Balts and Finns in Tacitus (the Estes and the Fenni).

The Sarmatae The Sarmatians, Iranian nomads, lived to the east of the Bastarnae, though they were moving west and south, and in 30–29 BCE they intensified their incursions across the Danube even as far as Macedonia. They were sometimes called the Scythians.

India and China If we are to believe Strabo, shortly after the annexation of Egypt, 120 vessels passed the straits of Bab el-Mandeb at the southern end of the Red Sea, the gateway of the sea route to India. Some went as far as the Ganges. And as early as the end of Augustus' Principate, large quantities of pottery from Arezzo made an appearance in the region of Pondicherry on the south-east coast of India. Direct relations with China, the country of the Seres, though very limited, existed from the last quarter of the first century BCE.

This world, still restricted and compartmentalized, eventually assumed a new cohesion under the Augustan Principate, to which we now turn.

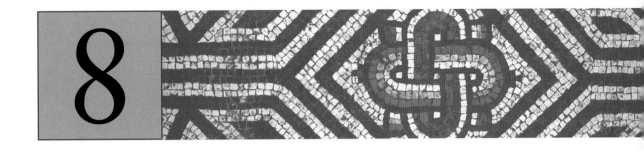

8

AUGUSTUS

The Birth of the Imperial Regime: 29 BCE–14 CE

On August 19, 14 CE, at Nola in Campania, the emperor Augustus died in his seventy-sixth year. All Italy wept for the man who prided himself on having re-established peace on land and at sea, on having "expanded all the provinces of the Roman people situated on the frontiers of nations which were not subject to our Empire," as Augustus himself stated in his *Res Gestae* (26). According to Suetonius (*Augustus* 28), the emperor had desired but one reward: to be considered the author of the best of regimes. In Rome, the senators outdid one another in heaping honors on the deceased emperor. One even proposed designating the entire period from the day of his birth till the day of his death "the age of Augustus" (Suetonius, *Augustus* 100). Augustus had clearly revolutionized the Roman state and had begun a new era in history. From leader of a victorious faction in civil war, he had slowly and subtly transformed himself into the "first man" of a new regime which the Romans understood (or appeared to understand) as the Principate, the Republic, and the state. Even more extraordinary was that Augustus had accomplished this not by creating a new constitutional position for himself, or even by proclaiming himself a perpetual dictator, but through the gradual concentration of republican offices and titles in his own person, with the agreement, or acquiescence, of the Senate and the people. Romans came to recognize themselves in this regime, visualizing their place in the universe and the mission entrusted to them by Providence. Virgil expresses this concept clearly in his *Aeneid*, which quickly became canonized as the great national epic of Rome: "You, O Roman, reflect that your role is to lead the nations by your authority; for this is your skill, and also to keep peace under your control, to be merciful to those you have subjected and to humble the arrogant" (*Aeneid* 6.851–3).

8.1 | The Formation of the Principate

Historians disagree over the exact moment that the Principate was born. Augustus' victory at Actium (31 BCE), his triple triumph in Rome (29 BCE), his first and second constitutional settlements with the Senate (27 and 23 BCE) have all been proposed as starting points. Our inability to pinpoint a precise moment reveals the essential nature of Augustus' monarchical government: operating behind an ambiguous and complex institutional façade, the Principate was not born but emerged progressively, dominating the very core of the republican system, the Senate. Augustus' successors only built on, and strengthened, what he had put in place during his 44-year reign (starting from Actium). However, even before Augustus established his rule, there were four factors in place that seem to have prepared, and abetted, the formation of his regime.

The Hellenistic model In the eastern half of the Mediterranean basin, the city-state of Rome had come into contact with the monarchies born out of the division of Alexander's empire. These kingdoms, with their complex bureaucratic administration, consisted of Greek and eastern elements. Their sovereigns depended on the collective acceptance of their power as absolute and theocratic. As the inhabitants of the eastern side of the Mediterranean were accustomed to the idea of a large empire led by one man alone, Italian soldiers, traders, and civilians at large were also becoming familiar with the monarchic model. The *imperatores* or generals themselves, at least since Scipio Africanus, had remained fascinated by the image of Alexander the Great. As indicated in the episode of Caesar's weeping before a statue of Alexander in Spain (Suetonius, *Julius Caesar* 7), Octavian's adopted father was no exception to this ambition. While in Alexandria (in 30) Octavian himself placed on public display the coffin containing the body of the great Alexander, which he had removed from its vault, and showed his veneration by laying a crown of gold upon it and scattering flowers. When asked if he also wanted to inspect the tomb of the Ptolemies, he replied that "he had wanted to see a king, not corpses" (Suetonius, *Augustus* 18). Furthermore, on his return from Egypt, it was on the model of Alexander's tomb that Octavian undertook the construction of his own mausoleum in the northern part of the Campus Martius. Circular in shape, this imposing tomb (87 m in diameter) made a grand statement about the monarch and his dynasty. In addition, in his Forum in Rome, two pictures represented episodes from Alexander's life, and it is thought that a colossal statue of the emperor as Alexander adorned the *curia*.

The extent of the conquests By the middle of the first century BCE, the Republic had conquered an immense territorial empire, claiming its right to universal domination. But the lack of an organized civil service for the administration of the provinces had led to their rapacious exploitation by governors and tax collectors. Unsurprisingly, provincials felt little attachment, if not bitter resentment,

(a)

Plate 8.1 Great Cameo of France, Gemma Augustea, and Blacas Cameo celebrating Augustus, various members of the Julio-Claudian family (living and deceased), and imperial conquests **(a)** Cameo of France, 37–41 CE. Cabinet des Médailles, or Cabinet de France, Bibliothèque nationale de France, Paris. Bibliotheque Nationale, Paris, France/The Bridgeman Art Library **(b)** Gemma Augustea, 37–41 CE. Kunsthistorisches Museum, Vienna. Kunsthistorisches Museum, Vienna, Austria/The Bridgeman Art Library **(c)** Blacas Cameo, 14–20 CE. British Museum, London. ©The Trustees of the British Museum. All rights reserved

(b)

(c)

toward Rome. Exhausted by the abuses of their governors, the passivity of the Senate, and the unreliability of Roman laws, the provinces did not object to a centralized government under one man. It is reasonable to think that sooner or later conquests would make the structures of republican government unsuitable. Ancient authors (Strabo, Florus, Cassius Dio) agree that the technical and administrative difficulties resulting from this system, together with the need to stabilize Roman territory and provincial resources, necessitated changes in the nature of government. A solution to the provincial problem became both available and obvious: just as Rome was the center of power, power could be held only in the hands of a single person.

Exhaustion of the republican institutions Torn apart by civil wars, rival generals, and powerless senators, republican institutions had proven incapable of protecting the state and the safety of its people. Cicero's death at the hands of the second Triumvirate (43) was a major turning-point in the collapse of senatorial authority. After this event, no project, reform, or program had kindled the enthusiasm of supporters of the senatorial Republic. These proposed no remedy other than a return to an earlier state. Even the murderers of Caesar, who claimed to have restored the liberty of the Republic through their act, could not rally popular support. Since the near-extinction of the old republican aristocracy no one, with the exception of Octavian, had been able to call up a popular response to the claim that he was defending liberty. Dating around the events of Actium, Tibullus' protest against war and his hymn of the peaceful countryside (*Elegies* 1.10) reflect the collective mistrust of the military values of the Republic which had led to decades of bloodshed.

The evolution of attitudes People were becoming familiar with monarchical ideas. It was thus agreed that the victors owed their success to their good fortune, a gift from the lord of the gods granted on the intervention of a guardian deity, Venus. And it was right, therefore, that these exceptional men should receive earthly honors that went beyond the customary norms. People began to pray to the gods for the well-being of an *imperator*, as if the well-being of the state and the Roman people depended on that of one man alone. Changes too in notions concerning the ideal life opened the door to a monarchical order. Whereas formerly the citizen had found his happiness in and through public life, henceforward he sought it far from the Forum, in the peace of rural life or by giving up his life to the service of a general. The gradual obliteration of the civic process brought the disappearance of public debates and orators. As we saw, instead of political oratory, poetry emerged as a new medium of public expression which explored and responded to the new regime. Virgil, Horace, Propertius, and other poets belonged to a literary circle sponsored by C. Maecenas, a close friend and adviser to Octavian–Augustus. Furthermore, the traditional concept of inevitable decline, linked with the theory that, like human beings, cities undergo a biological cycle (birth, growth, maturity, decline, death), was countered by the idea that "a city must be formed in such a way that it is eternal" (Cicero, *The Republic* 3.23) Co-opting such rhetoric, Octavian–Augustus offered hope of a new order that would ensure peace and break the cycle of violence and civil war – a hope shared by all.

The teachings of the philosophical schools More than Platonism, more than Stoicism, more even than the political reflections of Cicero, Epicureanism presented the institution of monarchy as a great development for mankind. The disciples of Epicurus looked on it as a regime in which the citizen, relieved of the concern of participating directly in government, could devote himself entirely to the cultivation of his inner life, avoiding the snares of competition and rivalry that littered the public arena. Several testimonies to that proposition have come down to us. One of the most striking consists of fragments of a political treatise, *The Good King according to Homer*, written by Philodemus of Gadara, possibly in 45 BCE, arguing that good kings *could* exist. Enlightened by wise counselors, it is the duty of the good king to be moderate, to make sure that his personal conduct conforms to the rules of morality, to show himself to be just toward men and pious toward the gods, and to see that unity and peace exist between his subjects.

Therefore, under the influence of various factors, Roman society was ready to surrender to the providential man whose virtues would ensure peace. But these aspirations needed to be strengthened skillfully through the construction of a monarchical ideology tailored to Roman principles, through an institutional and social compromise.

Institutional compromise: 29–23 BCE

Obstacles and advantages

The triumph of 29 meant the end of the war against Cleopatra and a return to a legal state, the nature of which was in dispute. If he chose to institute a monarchical regime openly, Octavian would have to overcome a number of formidable obstacles.

- The title of king, or anything that might be a reminder of it, was the first of these. The very word *rex*, the name of Romulus, or Caesar's near coronation at the Lupercalia of 44 were memories that still retained sufficient emotional charge in Rome to incite an assassination. The Ides of March told a cautionary tale against royal ambitions.
- Although its power was significantly weakened, the Senate, guardian of ancestral custom (*mos maiorum*), had preserved its prestige. Some of the senatorial families had held the *res publica* as their own personal property for decades, and even centuries. To overlook it, or in any way fall foul of it, would be to expose oneself to the hostility of the great families and their clienteles.

- The reputation and personality of Octavian did not go unchallenged. His father C. Octavius, initially an equestrian, had been the first in his family to follow the *cursus honorum*. His humble family origins inspired malicious gossip. According to Suetonius (*Augustus* 2), Antony taunted Octavian claiming that his great-grandfather was a freedman and a rope-maker from the countryside near Thurii. Octavian was accused of owing his success to Caesar, an accusation leveled against Antony too, in 43. Octavian's personal military accomplishments, looked at in a certain light, appeared somewhat bland, and were indeed criticized. And it was still remembered that during the Civil Wars he had been a ruthless faction leader.

- The institutional position of Octavian was ambiguous for the present and uncertain for the future. Since 32, his Triumviral powers had in theory ceased. Three elements of power thus remained to him: the consulship, which he had occupied each year since 31 but which conferred no military responsibility on him; the sacrosanctity of the tribunes of the *plebs*, and tribunician power (i.e. the power of the tribunes without actually being one), both for life, received respectively in 36 and 30; and the oath of loyalty sworn to him by Italy and the western provinces in the autumn of 32.

The precariousness of Augustus' institutional position in these early years can be seen in his brief and subtle conflict with M. Licinius Crassus. As governor of Macedonia, Crassus (grandson of the Triumvir) defeated the tribes of the Getae and Bastarnae to the south of the Danube in 29–28 BCE, and killed their king, Deldo, in battle. According to custom, his victory guaranteed the grant of a triumph. But Crassus also claimed his right to the *spolia opima* ("rich spoils"), an ancient honor awarded to a Roman commander who had personally slain the enemy leader. This involved the ritual dedication of the enemy's captured armor to a temple of Jupiter, a remarkable privilege that had been earned extremely rarely in Roman history (Plutarch, *Life of Marcellus* 8). Clearly, Crassus' claim to the right of the *spolia opima* posed a serious challenge to Augustus' military primacy. So his request was blocked on a technical argument: as we saw in chapter 5, to be eligible for a triumph the victorious general had to have taken his own auspices (*auspicia*) before embarking on his campaign. The argument leveled against Crassus was that he, as a proconsul, was fighting not under his own auspices, but under those of the consul, Augustus himself. Not only did Crassus not dedicate the *spolia opima*, but soon after this incident he disappears from the record. The very fact that this event is alluded to rather than explicitly narrated in our sources (see, for example, a passing mention in Cassius Dio, 51.24) probably reflects Augustus' success in containing it. His silencing of Crassus is indicative of a policy that the ***princeps*** observed throughout his career, namely the submission of individual generals and their conquests under his own name. His support by the army was the essence of his supreme power and he was therefore determined to maintain it.

princeps (pl. *principes*): Simply, "first" or "leader." The word was used generally to denote a man of great prestige and authority. In the senate, influential men such as Caesar or Cicero could at times act as *principes*, by speaking first on the topic discussed and thus influencing subsequent debate.

Augustus was reluctant to seek the ambiance of monarchy, but he held some considerable advantages were he to claim its substance.

- He was the adoptive son of a god, the deified Julius Caesar. This prestigious relationship linked him not only to Caesar, the only *divus* in Rome, but also to Caesar's ancestress Venus Genetrix. Augustus strongly promoted this divine lineage. In 29, the temple of the Divine Julius was dedicated in the Forum, and the new *curia*, the Curia Julia, begun by Caesar, was inaugurated: before the façade of the temple was a platform decorated with the prows (*rostra*) of the ships captured at Actium; at the far end of the Curia there was a statue of Victory brought back from Tarentum by Octavian, and before it an altar, making it an object of worship. These monuments celebrated the father and at the same time underlined the merits of the son.

- He stood at the head of a formidable and (as Antony's soldiers had rallied to him) single army of over 60 legions, as well as all the auxiliary troops. Although he quickly demobilized more than half of his legionaries and settled the veterans, his military power remained overwhelming.

- He was immensely rich. His expenditure between 30 and 29 BCE has been estimated at 1,000 million sesterces. That fortune came partly from inheritances from both his natural father and his adoptive father, partly from the confiscation of lands and sales of enemy possessions, and mainly from the Egyptian booty. He was the richest man of his time and could practice a policy of public benefaction on a grand scale.

- In 43 BCE, Octavian had been acclaimed *imperator*. In 40, he had transformed this honorific title into a permanent part of his name, attaching it to his person, doubtless to advertise his primacy of honor and his superior power.

- He presented himself simultaneously as a man of victory and a man of peace. Apart from his triumph in 29, a series of initiatives taken by the Senate conferred on him this double merit while he was in the East. On January 1, 29, the Senate gave its *auctoritas* to all his acts up to that date, and on January 11 the doors of the temple of Janus were closed for the third time in the history of Rome, signifying universal peace. In addition, Octavian was saluted with the title "savior of the state." An arch in his honor was erected in the Forum, between the temple of the Divus Julius and the temple of Castor. The words *Respublica conservata* ("Republic sustained") were inscribed on his triumphal arch. On the day of his triumph, when according to tradition the magistrates and the Senate headed the procession, for the first time it was the *imperator*, Octavian, who led it.

So Octavian enjoyed numerous advantages. He knew how to use these skillfully, taking decisions, or seeing that they were taken, apparently with the sole aim of restoring the past. At the same time he tested out innovations of a seemingly minor nature but of decisive importance for the balance of power within the state. His political genius lay precisely in his grasp of the fact that, the better

rostra: A platform from which speakers delivered their addresses, situated near the Curia under the Republic and subsequently moved farther west. Decorated with the prows of boats captured at the Battle of Antium (338 BCE), whence its name *rostra* (cutwaters).

to establish his personal power, he had to preserve the Republic, and even to consolidate the veneer of its institutions in order to empty them of their content. Between 28 and 23 BCE, slowly and with pragmatism, an advantageous institutional compromise was pieced together.

The forms of the compromise

In 28, Octavian inaugurated his sixth consulship, with Agrippa as his colleague. There was no military expedition – the two consuls stayed in Rome the whole year. Vested with censorial powers, they took a *census* (the last dated back to 70 BCE), in which 4,063,000 citizens were listed. As part of the census, Augustus effected a deep revision of the Senate (*lectio senatus*). Through this *lectio*, though the Senate's numbers still topped 600 members, 190 senators were taken out of the senatorial rolls. Moreover, this *lectio* had Octavian himself appointed head of the Senate (*princeps senatus*). He could now steer the Senate's decisions, since he would be the first to give his opinion when its deliberations got under way. In the same year, several moral and sumptuary laws were enacted, increasing advantages for those who followed political and social conformity. The Republic of former years appeared to be restored: the coinage of the year 28 celebrated Octavian as the champion of republican liberty, *libertatis reipublicae vindex*.

At least, that is what Octavian proclaimed. On January 13, 27, he "transferred the Republic from [his] power into that of the Senate and the Roman people" (*Res Gestae* 34). It was ostensibly an abdication: Octavian handed over all his powers to the Senate – which, however, at once begged him to stay. Historians still wonder about the motives and sincerity of this renunciation: was it a sincere abdication, a clever maneuver, a sense of duty pushed to the point of sacrifice, the conscious fulfillment of a historic mission of restoration, or a piece of collusive role-playing? The possibilities are numerous, and not mutually exclusive. At all events, an accommodation was reached marking a disposition of what was essentially an imperial authority. In response to the Senate's pleas, Octavian accepted only a special commission vesting him with the authority of a proconsul over certain provinces. But these were the provinces where the bulk of the legions were stationed, so that he now possessed the legal authority he had lacked but with little diminishment in military power. Augustus' proconsular *imperium* (the nature of which is still not entirely clear) was specified to last for only 10 years, but in fact it would be renewed seamlessly from one decade to the next, until his death. The Senate, on the other hand, kept the management of mostly pacified provinces with no army. The distribution of provinces between the *princeps* and the Senate was thus far from balanced. Moreover, there is evidence of imperial intervention in senatorial provinces, as is the case with the five edicts of Augustus at Cyrene, regulating matters for the senatorial provinces of Crete and Cyrenaica. His interference could not be rejected: the Cyreneans expressed their gratitude to Augustus for his concern.

On January 16, 27 BCE, three decrees complemented the awarding of the *imperium*. The first accorded Octavian the title "Augustus." The titles of "Romulus" and "Quirinus" were originally proposed but turned down, because they carried too strong an evocation of royal power. "Augustus," by contrast, was a new term, borrowed from religious vocabulary. For Suetonius it was linked with augury; for Livy it was contrasted with *humanus*. The title achieves its full value when associated with the word *auctoritas*, signifying thus the holder of supreme authority. Both "Augustus" and *auctoritas* are connected to the verb *augere* ("to increase"), implying the idea that Octavian's authority and intentions were "augmented" by a superior and divine quality, and/or that he himself was the "increaser" of the Empire. Whether etymologically sound or not, the connection too with the priestly office of *augur* was hard to miss. Yet even before the assumption of this extraordinary title, Augustus was already more than a mere man: "At that time," he wrote, "I was above everyone in authority (*dignitas*), but I had no more power (*potestas*) than any of my colleagues in my various magistracies" (*Res Gestae* 34). In this way, his *auctoritas* ensured that his powers were superior to those of other magistrates. He thus became Imperator Caesar Divi filius Augustus, indicating his *imperium* by his *praenomen*, his divine kinship with his adoptive father, whose *cognomen* (Caesar) became a family name, and his new quality by the name Augustus.

The second decree awarded him the laurels and the civic crown, to honor his triumph and his role as savior of his fellow citizens. By virtue of the third decree, a golden shield was hung in the Curia, inscribed with the words *virtus* (bravery), *clementia* (leniency), *iustitia* (justice), *pietas* (piety, filial duty). *Virtus* was the quality of a true citizen-soldier and here designated the excellence of the one who possessed it. *Clementia* evoked Caesar and suggested magnanimity (especially toward the defeated), moderation in the use of power, and leniency to the errors of others. *Iustitia* represented justice and equity. And *pietas* embraced all that each man owed to the deities, his family, and his *civitas*. Since the time of Scipio Africanus, those four virtues had been the ideal virtues of the Roman man. Thus, by drawing on various political, philosophical, and religious elements, Augustus was able to present himself merely as the *princeps senatus*, the "first man" in the senate (appointed so in 28 BCE; see *Res Gestae* 7), while in reality his power and authority far exceeded that of any leading senator in the Republic.

Between 27 and 23 BCE, Augustus strengthened his powers in practice without creating new offices for himself. He asked only to retain the consulship, which he assumed each year, thus enabling him to exercise a kind of supervision over Rome, Italy, and the various other magistrates.

Augustan government: 23 BCE–14 CE

The new regime seemed to be established; so much so that Augustus was able to leave Rome for three years (27–24). However, in 23 the weakness of a system in which everything depended on the person of the emperor was exposed. First, disturbances linked with the trial of a provincial governor gave rise to a conspiracy in which the emperor's colleague in the consulship was compromised. This immediate crisis was resolved, but a feeling of unease remained. This was aggravated by the rapid decline in Augustus' health, seemingly to the point of death. The great uncertainty created by these two events, either of which might have precipitated renewed dissension and civil war, brought about some important constitutional modifications to the regime, which is known as the "second settlement" (the first being the one in 27) or "the settlement of 23 BCE."

In the first place, Augustus gave up the consulship – he resumed it only twice, in 5 and 2 BCE, in order to present his grandsons and heirs to the people. It has often been thought that, in return, he had the benefit of an *imperium maius et infinitum*, an *imperium* exercised over the whole Empire, but that he did is not at all certain: his renewable proconsular *imperium*, together with his accumulated personal *auctoritas*, would have sufficed to afford him powers of that scope. From 23 onward Augustus was therefore, in the absence of the consulship, no longer a magistrate in the technical sense of the term. He refused the dictatorship, life censorship, and consulship in perpetuity offered to him by the Senate and people, and accepted only special duties that were to some extent detached from the magistracy that supported them: the power of censorship in 19, 18, and 12, and the consular power for life, given to him in 19. By refusing the permanent consulship, Augustus left open both consular posts as rewards for his clients and associates instead of monopolizing one himself.

His abandonment of the consulship was more than compensated for by the formal confirmation of his tribunician power, received officially on July 1, 23 (it was renewed each year on the same date, and the number of the renewal served to enumerate the years of his reign). Though not a tribune of the *plebs* (he was not eligible, being patrician), Augustus now possessed all the tribunes' powers: sacrosanctity of his person, veto over other magistrates, the right to convene the Senate, the right to propose laws, and the right to aid citizens in distress (*ius auxilii*). Better still, above that of all other tribunes, this power not only applied to the capital but extended to all of the Empire and its inhabitants. The *tribunicia potestas*, *imperium*, and *auctoritas* from that time onward constituted the basis of the new regime.

The final additions were made in 12 BCE, when, on the death of Lepidus, Augustus was elected *pontifex maximus*, and in 2 BCE, when he was hailed as "father of his country" (*pater patriae*) by the Senate and people, thus becoming a kind of patron on an imperial scale. These became the main features of Augustus' Principate, which later emperors developed only slightly, according to their own personalities and circumstances. The institutions of the Republic (Senate, magistracies, *comitia*) remained; Augustus presented himself as merely a citizen. Remaining outside the state's institutions, he allowed them to continue functioning in their normal manner. But if he thought he should intervene he did so, and decisively. Two administrations and two powers were superimposed, that of the emperor and that of the Senate. But the imperial power always had the last word.

Symbolically, the dividing line between the age of the Republic and the Augustan age may be seen in the celebration of the Secular Games (*Ludi Saeculares*) of 17 BCE. These games marked the end of one *saeculum*, or era (defined as the utmost span of a human lifetime), and the beginning of the next, an event calculated to occur every 100 years. They had taken place in 348, 249, and 146. But the Civil Wars had prevented the holding of the games in the forties. By holding them in 17 (with the *saeculum* recalculated as 110 years), Augustus was both observing and deeply reshaping this tradition, with the certainty that he was opening a new age. Horace's *Secular Hymn*, written for this occasion, is simultaneously a hymn to Apollo and Diana and a celebration of Augustus, "the famous progeny of Anchises and Venus" (*Secular Hymn* 50). We shall return to the Secular Games below, in the context of Augustus' policy on spectacles and entertainment in Rome.

8.2 | The Emperor and his Entourage

Augustus

The man

Although there is no lack of literary and visual representations of Augustus, it is difficult to picture him. His portraits, which range over a whole lifetime, are almost all deliberately idealized. The literature sometimes presents us with opposing views, reflecting Augustus' elusive nature. For example, Tacitus (*Annals*

Chronology 8.1   **Biography of Octavian–Augustus until 44 BCE**

63   Born in Rome, on September 23. His father, C. Octavius, who died in 59, was a *homo novus*. His mother, Atia, was a niece of Caesar, who took an interest in her son at an early age and introduced him to Roman life – he entered the college of pontiffs in 48. Caesar also watched over his education, which was carefully conducted. Strong bonds of affection existed between the young man and his great-uncle.

46   Caesar had Octavian take part in his African triumph even though he had not been in the campaign. It was a way of designating him his heir.

45   He fought at Caesar's side against Pompey's supporters in Spain. In September, without telling him, Caesar adopted him and made him his heir.

44   He was in Apollonia in Epirus, as much to complete his studies as to prepare for the campaign against the Parthians, when he learned of the dictator's assassination. He decided to avenge him, and, in reply to his mother, who tried to dissuade him, he quoted a passage from the *Iliad*: "May I die now, for they have killed my friend and I was not there to defend him." He was in Rome by May. There then began one of the greatest political ventures ever: having set out to avenge his adoptive father, Octavian established a regime that was to last five centuries and left its decisive imprint on the history of mankind.

Plate 8.2 Detail from the Ara Pacis Augustae, a great marble altar consecrated July 4, 13 BCE, on the Campus Martius, Rome. It depicts members of the imperial family. C. M. Dixon

1.9-10) relates an alleged debate among those present at Augustus' funeral, anonymous speakers arguing for two contrasting perspectives on his accomplishments. Other narratives (e.g. Suetonius' *Augustus*) abound with stock expressions which should contain a germ of truth: good looks, frail health, self-control, energy, hard work, efficiency, organizational ability, simplicity of life in his Palatine residence, strong will, prudence, morality, and a healthy amount of pleasures and indulgences. Augustus was certainly a complex man whose greatness and genius shone most brilliantly in the preparation, realization, and utilization of political action.

His political ideas were inspired by the Caesarian legacy and adapted to circumstances in order to win and preserve power. They grew stronger during the course of his reign, and reached their pinnacle in an elevated and austere concept of the function of the state. Yet even before this majestic plane was achieved, an early "Augustan" ideology and mission emerged, which is manifested in literature (mainly Virgil and Horace) and, later, in the arts. Poets, architects, sculptors, and artists of every kind placed themselves at the ruler's service, to celebrate Rome's second birth, the return of prosperity, the reign of perpetual youth, and the majesty

Plate 8.3 Female figure from the eastern façade of the Ara Pacis, variously identified as a personification of Mother Earth (Tellus), Venus Genetrix, Ceres, Italy, or Peace. The infants, animals, vegetation, and nymphs flanking the central figure evoke the peace, fertility, and material prosperity of Augustus' rule. 13–9 BCE. Museum of Ara Pacis, Rome. akg-images/Pirozzi

of the *Imperator*. The themes of this ideology were peace (as expressed in the Ara Pacis Augustae), social order, a return to the four Roman virtues of bravery, leniency, justice, and piety, featured on the golden shield (see above), the restoration of traditional religion, the grandeur of Rome, and the defense of *libertas*. In all styles and at all levels of artistic achievement, these themes appeared again and again: the power of visual and literary imagery was put to use to announce the dawn of a new golden age, when happiness would not be given freely and without cost, but earned by effort and devotion to the affairs of the state.

His family

Augustus had become engaged in political life through his family; now he engaged his family in his political struggles. Traditionally, the upper classes had used the bonds of marriage to seal political alliances, and Augustus did the same through-out his career to neutralize possible opposition and, later, to ensure his succession. Thus, as we already saw, he married his sister Octavia to Antony to consolidate the treaty of Brundisium (40); in 25, he had his only daughter Julia married to his nephew Claudius Marcellus, marking him out as his preferred successor. When Marcellus died he had her married to Agrippa, and, when he died too, he forced his stepson Tiberius to separate from his wife in order to marry Julia (12 BCE). Ten years later, and following a mysterious affair (her adultery and/or a plot against him), Augustus exiled Julia in the island of Pandateria, where she died of sickness and malnutrition a few months after Augustus himself (Tacitus, *Annals* 1.53). In the use he made of his relatives, Augustus was exercising both his supreme political power and his full rights as head of his family (*paterfamilias*).

Augustus' third wife, Livia, whom he had married in 38, became an important force in the imperial house. She belonged by birth and marriage to the prominent *gens Claudia*. She divorced her husband while she was pregnant in order to marry Augustus, who had himself just separated from Scribonia. According to Suetonius (*Gaius* 23), her great-grandson Gaius (Caligula) called Livia "Ulysses in petti-coats." She exercised subtle but decisive influence on dynastic affairs, particularly through her constant promotion of her sons Tiberius and Drusus as Augustus' successors. Augustus adopted her in his will, under which she became "Julia Augusta." The name of Augustus' imperial family (Julio-Claudians) comes from the merging of Livia's *gens* with his own.

His associates

Among those who worked closely with Augustus, two figures stand out because of the leading roles they played, Maecenas and Agrippa. Cassius Dio (52.1-40) describes a debate, after Actium, between these two counselors in Augustus' presence. What was to be done? Agrippa suggests re-establishing the Republic; Maecenas recommends thinking up a new regime, a monarchy in all but name. This dialogue is a creative reconstruction of the very real influence of these two counselors, their absolute loyalty to Augustus, and the complementary sides of his regime: an imperial ideology with a republican façade, backed by the support of the army.

1   Maecenas, who belonged to the equestrian order, which he never wanted to leave, was about 10 years older than Augustus, and came from Etruria (his maternal family had formerly reigned over the city of Arezzo). A wealthy aristocrat with refined tastes, he was a disciple of Epicurus and a patron of Virgil, Propertius, and Horace, whom he drew into the Augustan circle, with lasting effects for the history of Roman literature. But his service to Octavian–Augustus was above all as a diplomat (he negotiated the treaties of Brundisium and Tarentum) and as a kind of informal minister of the interior.

Plate 8.4 Marble sarcophagus relief depicting a marriage ceremony. The couple clasp right hands, while the groom holds the marriage contract. Between them stands the matron of honor (*pronuba*), whose duty is to guide the bride to the groom. 160–180 CE. British Museum. ©The Trustees of the British Museum.

The active and very well-informed intelligence he received from friends and associates enabled him to thwart conspiracies and ensure Augustus' order. Nevertheless, during his last years (he died in 8 BCE) he appears to have retired from Augustus' circle or to have fallen from his favor.

2   Agrippa, born in 64 in an obscure family, was with Octavian at Apollonia when he received the news of Caesar's assassination. From then on his destiny merged with that of the future emperor, on whose behalf he helped win the war of Perusia and the victories at Naulochus and Actium. Long viewed by history mainly in light of his military activities, he has emerged from recent studies with a richer and more rounded personality. A faithful supporter, a clever strategist, a great builder, a peacemaker as well as an administrator, a public benefactor, the author of an autobiography and some technical works

Genealogy 8.1   Augustus and his family

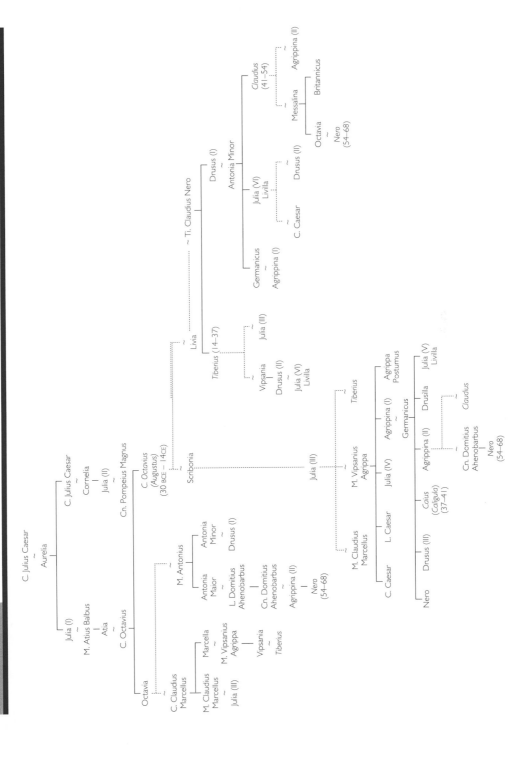

From J. Le Gall and M. Le Glay, *L'Empire romain*, pp. 56–7

– this multi-talented soldier devoted all his energies to the glory of Rome and its Empire, the emperor, and the dynasty. His devotion and the solid trust shown him by Augustus marked him out, on the death of the heir presumptive Marcellus, as the new husband for Julia, whom he married in 21. Five children were born of this union, including Gaius and Lucius Caesar. From 18 on, possessing tribunician power and proconsular *imperium*, he became Augustus' co-regent and colleague. His powers were renewed in 13, but he died the following year on his return from a campaign in Pannonia.

8.3 | A Hierarchy of Offices

The creator of a new regime hallowed by the traditional forms it claimed to have restored, Augustus also aimed at a return to traditional mores, the strengthening of social cohesion, and the re-establishing of state service as a high ideal. The desire to recover the moral order was possibly combined with a concern to bolster the numbers of the established population. To accomplish his ethical, social, and demographical reforms Augustus used legislation.

A series of laws in 18 BCE and 9 CE denounced bachelorhood and adultery (particularly female adultery) with freeborn citizens, and gave advantages to fathers of families. Similarly, the two forms of social mobility most likely to alter the established order, the emancipation of slaves and the granting of citizenship to foreigners, were restricted and controlled, with a new social status created to capture that class of slaves manumitted outside these measures, the Junian Latins. These last two sets of arrangements meant that under the Empire Roman society come to be structured, on the legal plane, as follows:

- the two *ordines* (the senatorial and equestrian orders);
- the Roman citizens of Rome, Italy, and the provinces;
- the Latins;
- the Junian Latins;
- foreigners (*peregrini*);
- the *dediticii* (free men who could never become citizens);
- slaves.

Augustus paid particular attention to the two top groups, the senatorial and equestrian orders. He refined them, set out clear conditions of entry, and worked on their development.

The Senate and the outline of a senatorial order

In the republican era there was no such thing as a senatorial order. The only condition demanded of members of the Senate was the possession of capital equivalent to the equestrian property qualification (400,000 sesterces). The son

Plate 8.5 Pont du Gard, near Nîmes, France. About 275 meters long and almost 50 meters high, it was built in the time of Augustus. Water was carried above the top tier. C. M. Dixon

of a senator was an equestrian. He himself became a senator, if he so desired, on the day he began his first magistracy, the quaestorship. He then returned his public horse to the state. In the case of a "new senator," that is, a senator not of the senatorial class but with at least an equestrian fortune if not an equestrian himself, entry to the Senate again coincided with his entry into the duties of the quaestorship. Beneath their toga, the members of the Senate wore on their tunic a broad band of purple, the laticlave. In the years after Caesar's death, the sons of senators and equestrians improperly used the laticlave to signal their ambitions. Furthermore the number of senators had increased. Augustus inherited this situation and reformed it gradually, combining the influences of the past and his own innovations. However, compromises, contradictions, and ambiguities were not completely eradicated.

Wearing the laticlave In 18 BCE, after his reduction of the Senate's numbers to 600, Augustus forbade the sons of equestrians to wear the laticlave, creating for them the angusticlave (a narrow band of purple). The use of the laticlave was thus reserved exclusively for the descendants of senators: According to Suetonius (*Augustus* 38), he allowed the sons of senators to wear the laticlave and attend meetings of the Senate immediately after they had received the toga of manhood, and he did this in order to familiarize them more rapidly with public affairs. In the emperor's eyes, senators' sons were thus the next generation of senators. However, although they were members of the senatorial order, these young men remained equestrians. The future emperor Claudius, for example, continued to belong to the equestrian order until 37 CE, when Caligula appointed him as his colleague in the consulship and made him a senator. In 18 BCE, the *ordo senatorius* was thus as yet only an outline of what it later became, its single mark being the wearing of the laticlave, which only the senators and their descendants, from the age of 17, were authorized to do.

The institution of a senatorial property qualification Between 18 and 13 BCE, a senatorial property qualification was fixed. It was now necessary for the sons of senators to have a capital of 1,000,000 sesterces to seek a quaestorship, in order to avoid corruption. For the same reason, if a man who was already a senator fell short of the required amount, he had to give up his senatorial office – unless the emperor made up the deficit. This was a new means of controlling the budding *ordo*, in addition to the fact that it did not contain all possible candidates to the Senate. Thus the senatorial order effectively lacked the power and security that such a monopoly would have offered. But the creation of a different and higher rating to that of the equestrian order raised a fresh barrier between equestrians and senators. And the inner coherence of the two orders differed considerably, to the advantage of the new one, for the descendants of senators tended to form a better-defined social group.

The ius honorum In order to be able to enter the Senate, those who were not the sons of senators also had to possess, in addition to the property qualification, a right of eligibility (*ius honorum*), that is, the right to stand as a candidate for the first magistracy. It appears that this right was granted to all the Roman citizens of Italy and the Latin colonies, and that it was denied to non-equestrian provincials and to citizens of Roman colonies and Roman *municipia* or free towns.

The Senate As under the Republic, admission to the Senate was by way of the quaestorship, but it was a process now largely subject to the will of the emperor. The terms on which the Senate functioned mostly remained the same as a century earlier. Augustus' reform in 9 BCE involved two sittings a month on fixed dates (with the possibility of meeting outside those days) and the necessity of a quorum for all senatorial decrees, which sometimes became law. Augustus aimed at confirming the traditional primacy that the Senate had possessed in republican society. He favored largely the exercise of senatorial initiative, within the bounds of his own authority. The Senate was the constitutional body that confirmed the powers of the emperor, providing them with the formal seal of legitimacy. It gained the right to set itself up as a tribunal to try its own members, retained the administration of certain provinces, and participated in the emperor's *consilium* (15 senators chosen by lot). Certain administrative posts (the prefect-ship of Rome, supervision of water, etc.) were also confined to senators. Although the republican traditions continued apparently uninterrupted, in reality the Senate was politically weak. It lost control of foreign and military policy and a large part of fiscal policy (around 12 BCE it was deprived of its right to strike coinage), and Augustus was consulted for help by the senators on several occasions. Members of the Senate wavered between submission to the emperor and a sterile opposition of failed plots. Nevertheless, by a paradox that became more marked as time went on, "the Senate continued to be recognized as the symbol of the *res publica*" (R. J. A. Talbert), and its prestige remained considerable.

Magistrates and assemblies

Regular elections for the magistracies were re-established in 28 or 27 BCE. Though there was a shortage of candidates for the minor posts (quaestor, tribune, aedile), the higher offices (praetor, consul) were much sought after. This was because they gave an entry, in effect, to the important offices in the admin-istration of the Empire. The number of praetorships increased (to 12), and from 5 CE on, the use of substitute consuls (*consules suffecti*) became normal, though it was the *consules ordinarii* by whose names years were recorded in the *fasti*.

Though he seemed to have restored the freedom of elections, Augustus in fact controlled the pool of magistrates by means of two procedures: the *nominatio*, his acceptance of the candidates' declaration of candidacy for the various offices, and the *commendatio*, his recommendation of specific candidates for these offices. Augustus' effective control of elections thus weakened the primary electoral bodies.

The *comitia* were therefore not reinvigorated by this reinstitution of regular elections, and the centuriate assembly in particular suffered a further substantial reduction in its political role after 5 CE, when a complex system of 10 mixed "centuries" (senators and equestrians) was instituted to take part in a *destinatio* (appointment) of praetors and consuls prior to the decision of the full *comitia*. In 5 CE, those mixed centuries were named after the dead grandsons of Augustus, Gaius and Lucius Caesar. In 19 CE, these voters were reorganized into 15 centu-ries. These were named after the deceased Germanicus, adopted son of Tiberius, Rome's second emperor (see the *Tabula Hebana* of 19 CE, more on which in chapter 9).

Thus Augustus' initiatives in this field hastened the decline of the *comitia*, which lost all judicial competence, and also deprived the traditional magistracies of much of their political and constitutional substance. The titles remained, however, marking the stages in the career progress of a senator (*cursus honorum*), the structure of which gradually developed under the early Empire.

Box 8.1 Simplified plan of a senatorial *cursus* under the early empire

Laticlave military tribunate (starting with the Flavians, second office).
Vigintivirate: 20 posts (in decreasing order) (starting with the Flavians, first office):

- *Triumvir auro argento aere flando feriundo* (triumvir responsible for the melting and stamping of bronze, silver, and gold)
- *Decemvir stlitibus iudicandis* (decemvir responsible for trying lawsuits)
- *Quattuorvir viarum curandarum* (quattuorvir responsible for road maintenance)
- *Triumvir capitalis* (triumvir responsible for public prisons and executions).
  (The post occupied often determined the course of the later career.)

Quaestorship: 20 posts, minimum age 25 years.
  In Rome and the provinces (responsible for finances in a senatorial province).
  Quaestorian function: legate of the proconsul in a senatorial province.

Tribunate of the *plebs* (10 posts) or aedile (6 posts).
  Patricians were exempt, hence a more rapid career.

Praetorship: from 10 to 18 posts, minimum age 30 years.
  Praetorian functions:

- legate of a legion
- proconsul of a praetorian senatorial province
- legate of a praetorian imperial province
- prefect of the treasury of Saturn, etc.

Consulship: minimum age 33 years. The first consulship was often as a *suffectus* or deputy consul.
  Consular functions:

- curator of aqueducts, the Tiber, etc.
- legate of a consular imperial province
- proconsul of a consular senatorial province (Asia or Africa)
- prefect of Rome (generally after the second consulship).

The equestrian order

There were several points in common between the equestrian *ordo* of the republican era and that organized by Augustus: Roman citizenship was a prerequisite; the property qualification of 400,000 sesterces was retained; the annual procession on July 15 was revived; appointments were made on the basis of one's "worthiness" to receive the title of equestrian, awarded now by the emperor acting in the role of censor. Being an equestrian brought privileges: the right to wear a tunic with a narrow purple band (angusticlave), a gold ring, reserved seats at public spectacles. These equestrian privileges were not hereditary: except for the sons of senators, who wore the laticlave, one was not born an equestrian but became one. The equestrians thus formed a group which, by its nature, was more open than that of the senators. The geographic or social origin of the new equestrian mattered little; what mattered most were his merits and his capacity to serve the state. Through his restructuring of the equestrian *ordo*, Augustus forged a body of active supporters, ready to uphold the new regime. Equestrians brought over to his side provincial notables and the most enterprising elements from the *municipia*, and formed an elite of diligent officials who undertook the bureaucratic administration of the Empire.

Of course, not all equestrians (perhaps between 10,000 and 15,000 men in all) entered the emperor's service, since many chose to forego the obligations and pressures of official appointments. These went on living on their lands or by their commercial enterprises, enjoying their wealth and social status. Inscriptions document their role as "patrons" of their communities. The careers of those who became administrators in the new regime are much better known. Their *cursus* fell into shape gradually and continued to develop in diverse ways with changing circumstances. Their initial administrative function in the civil sphere was essentially financial, involving mainly the management of Augustus' possessions or those of the imperial family. The former senior officers or equestrians to whom he seems to have entrusted this task carried the title of *procurator* (agent or manager). This term was retained as their title even when their business in civil administration became increasingly diverse and of much wider scope. A distinction was made depending on the provinces in which these men worked: in the imperial provinces they were increasingly regarded as state officials; in the senatorial provinces they remained the emperor's private employees, and kept an eye on the senatorial administration. The number of these procurators was initially limited (fewer than 30 are known to us from the Augustan era). Subsequent emperors developed the imperial civil administration set up by Augustus, in both numbers and organization.

The emperor similarly opened up career prospects for equestrians by devising posts reserved for them:

- Legion commands in Egypt; war fleet commands.
- Provincial governorships, e.g. in the Maritime Alps and Sardinia, though without the *imperium* or the right to impose the death penalty (*ius gladii*).
- Administrative posts in Egypt, which no senator had the right to travel to without imperial permission: the prefectship of Egypt (from 30 BCE), then the summit of the equestrian career; and various posts replacing those of officials of the Ptolemaic monarchy, while keeping their titles (*idiologus*, *epistrategus*).
- Two posts of praetorian prefect (*praefectus praetorio*), created in 2 BCE for the command of the praetorian cohorts.
- The post of prefect of the *annona* or grain supply (*praefectus annonae*), created at the end of the reign (about 8 CE) for the securing of the provisioning

of Rome. Throughout the late Republic Rome's grain supplies had been precarious, and often became the tool of political struggles. In 22 BCE, Augustus took charge personally and later appointed former praetors and consuls to secure them. With the creation of this prefectship, an equestrian assumed that responsibility.

- The post of prefect of the *vigiles* or watch (*praefectus vigilum*). Republican Rome had had neither firemen nor a police force. A fire-fighting corps of 600 slaves was set up in 23 BCE, commanded by aediles. In 6 CE, they were replaced by seven cohorts of *vigiles*, all freedmen, under the command of this prefect.

Thus a pool of candidates was gradually formed to fill the growing range of imperial offices. These included the military posts in which they began their careers, and those connected with the administration of justice and finances (tax farming and companies of tax collectors, though, did not disappear). In sum, Augustus' new equestrian order was a development of the old one, with elements necessary for the formation of a great body of state employees responsible to the emperor. At first its members were in competition with the traditional senatorial administration, but they gradually replaced it and became incorporated into the first order of society.

8.4 | The Army and its Conquests

The army

Augustus took particular care of the army, and with good reason. His very regime was the result of military victory, proclaiming him the champion of peace on the domestic and foreign fronts. The *princeps* could not overlook that body of men on whose loyalty and quality his system depended. Moreover, Augustus himself was personally identified with the army. The soldiers swore to him alone the oath (*sacramentum*) which, under the Republic, had bound the soldier to his general. It was he who chose the legions' legates and the governors with troops at their disposal (with the exception of the proconsul of Africa). Every victory and triumph belonged to him alone, as we saw in his suppression of the challenge posed by the younger Crassus' claim to the *spolia opima*. Augustus' legates achieved success only on his behalf, and all campaigns were fought in his name. On the other hand, his ubiquitous involvement as well as his own distaste for battle meant that he was less personally involved in the field. He was more at ease in ensuring that discipline was observed than in directing operations himself. He relied instead on the skilled generals he surrounded himself with, some of whom came from the imperial family itself (Agrippa, Tiberius, Drusus). Augustus' military policy, traditionalist in some ways, innovatory in others, may be roughly summarized under four headings.

sacramentum:
Solemn oath taken by the conscript on his enrolment. It bound the soldier to the state and his superiors and rendered "accursed" anyone who broke it.

Action on behalf of veterans

In the wake of Actium, troop numbers far exceeded both the requirements and the means of the Empire. Large reductions were necessary, as was a financial settlement that would keep the newly discharged soldiers satisfied and loyal to their emperor. In several stages, 300,000 men were returned to civilian life. Until 13 BCE, they generally received land in a colony, settled principally in Italy, in the Iberian peninsula, or in southern Gaul; after that date, veterans received a sum of money. In 6 CE, a special fund was created for veterans, the *aerarium militare*. It provided a retirement pension to a soldier who left the service with an honorable discharge (*honesta missio*). This amount was 3,000 denarii for a legionary, the equivalent of 13 years' wages. Its funds came from two new taxes: 5 percent paid by Roman citizens on inheritances and legacies (called the "twentieth," *vicesima hereditatum*), and 1 percent on sales by auction (called the "hundredth," *centesima rerum venalium*).

A permanent army

Although Augustus did not abolish the principle of obligatory military service for all qualified citizens (there were levies in 6 and 9 CE), voluntary enlistment sufficed to provide the 6,000 recruits to the legions needed each year. The army became a professional body. Length of service reached or exceeded 20 years for legionaries, whose basic pay was 225 denarii a year. The legions included provincials who were Roman citizens, but most recruits were Italian. A standing legionary army was thus eventually formed. These legions each received a number and a name (for example, the Third Augusta, stationed at the time at Haidra, modern Tunisia), and were supported by auxiliary units.

Legions and auxiliary units

The distinction between legion and auxiliary unit as regards recruitment, command, and distribution of missions already existed prior to Augustus but became more precise under him.

The auxiliary corps as a whole equaled the legions in numbers of men, a total of nearly 250,000. The auxiliary units were generally given names corresponding to the tribe or region they were raised from. For instance, the *ala Thracum* was a cavalry squadron of the Thracians (the cavalry flanked both sides of the legion like wings, *alae*). When released from service, an auxiliary could have Roman citizenship; his son would therefore be able to enlist in a legion.

Allocation of troops

Here again Augustus introduced innovations. He gathered around him what was in effect the only garrison on the Italian peninsula, and set up a new strategic

Box 8.2 Legions and auxiliary units

	Legion	Auxiliary unit
Numbers/ranks	5,000 foot soldiers 120 horsemen	Generally 480 men Horsemen: *alae* (wings) Foot soldiers: cohorts Foot + horse: mixed cohorts
Organization	10 cohorts (1 cohort = 6 centuries, except the 1st cohort, which comprised 5 centuries with double numbers)	Cohort divided into centuries *Ala* divided into squadrons
Legal status	Roman citizens, may not marry	Foreigners except for command (and exceptions)
Staff	1 legate (prefect in Egypt) 1 laticlave tribune 1 camp prefect 5 angusticlave tribunes 59 centurions, of whom one is a *primipilus* (chief)	1 prefect or 1 tribune (equestrian or senatorial rank) Plus centurions, and decurions (for the horsemen)
Length of service	20–5 years	25 years minimum
Wage	225 denarii p.a.	75 denarii p.a.

allocation of his forces in the provinces. By the end of his reign, Augustus relied on various bodies of troops in Rome.

1   There were nine praetorian cohorts, formed in 27 or 26 BCE, to be the emperor's escort. The praetorians served for 16 years, earned a wage of 750 denarii a year, and received on their discharge an award of 5,000 denarii. These cohorts were mostly garrisoned not in Rome but in the cities of Latium. Under Tiberius, the praetorians concentrated in Rome itself, and in subsequent decades they played a decisive role in imperial succession.

2   There were three urban cohorts, created in around 13 CE. They had the job of keeping order in the capital and were under the orders of its prefect. Their activities were not limited to simple daytime policing operations, however; if necessary they could be transformed into combat troops.

3   There were 500 Germani who formed Augustus' personal bodyguard.

By the end of his reign, these various bodies comprised a sort of city garrison, even if its barracks were not all within the city walls.

By that time too, the legions and auxiliary corps, distributed among the various provinces, were to be found only in the imperial provinces (with the exception of those forces in Africa). When the general Quinctilius Varus lost three legions, and his life, to the Germanic leader Arminius in the battle of the Teutoburg forest (9 CE), the total number of legions was reduced to 25.

Box 8.3 Allocation of the legions at the time of Augustus' death

Syria	4	Iberian peninsula	3	Pannonia	3
Egypt	2	Moesia	2	Upper Germania	4
Africa	1	Dalmatia	2	Lower Germania	4

The fleet

After Actium the Mediterranean had practically become a Roman lake, but Augustus nevertheless took steps to ensure safety of sea passages. Two ports, Misenum and Ravenna, controlled, respectively, the western and eastern divisions of this inland sea. Two permanent fleets were created (a novelty), and placed under the command of a prefect of equestrian rank. Besides performing their policing function, these fleets provided a pool of men, ensured the logistics of military operations, and transported troops and even the emperor himself. In addition, local maritime fleets and river flotillas were gradually formed.

This deployment of forces served the double purpose of ensuring peace and order in acquired territories, and expanding Roman conquests.

Conquests and peacemaking operations

Africa and Egypt

29–27 BCE   The first prefect of Egypt, C. Cornelius Gallus, suppressed a rebellion in the south and concluded an agreement with the Ethiopians of Nubia: the First Cataract (waterfall-type formation) of the Nile was to be the frontier, and the Ethiopians recognized the Roman protectorate.

25 BCE   Juba II was made king of Mauretania and part of Numidia. Until his death in 23 CE he proved a reliable and loyal ally.

25–24 BCE   A prefect of Egypt, Aelius Gallus, organized an expedition to southern Arabia (modern Yemen).

22 BCE   Following a new raid by the Ethiopians, a military zone, the *Dodekaschoenos* ("the twelve leagues"), was organized south of the First Cataract. It gave Egypt 250 years of peace.

21–20 BCE   In a raid against the Garamantes (of modern Fezzan), L. Cornelius Balbus reached their capital. His aim was to establish the security of the desert.

1–6 CE (or between 6 BCE and 9 CE)   Revolts of the nomadic and semi-nomadic Berber tribes (Nasamones, Musulamii, Gaetuli) necessitated a large-scale military action.

Plate 8.6 Roman warship, equipped with ram and prophylactic eye (the eye of Osiris). Mosaic from Sousse, Tunisia, late second century CE. Sousse Museum. C. M. Dixon

The East

25 BCE Galatia was annexed.

20 BCE After negotiations with Augustus, the Parthian king Phraates IV returned to Rome the military standards taken from Crassus and Antony. This scene was to become emblematic of the peace and stability guaranteed under the new regime. It is illustrated on the breastplate of the statue of Augustus (possibly posthumous) found at the villa of Livia at Prima Porta, near Rome. In the same year, Tiberius crowned Tigranes II king of Armenia. A client kingdom was thus restored in a disturbed and strategically vital region.

2 BCE–4 CE Following the death of Tigranes (in 6 BCE), Armenia went through a new period of turmoil. A number of diplomatic and military offensives were launched. While returning from a campaign there, Augustus' grandson Gaius Caesar (the son of Agrippa and Augustus' daughter Julia) died from his wounds on February 21, 4 CE.

6 CE Judaea and Samaria were placed under a prefect resident in Caesarea and responsible to the legate of Syria.

The West

29–19 BCE Military campaigns were fought on the Iberian peninsula, especially against the Cantabri and Astures (Spanish campaigns). Augustus was there

Plate 8.7   Marble statue of Augustus at Prima Porta. Augustus' posture and gesture suggest the act of a formal address to the army (*adlocutio*), emphasizing his power and authority over the military. The dolphin-riding infant at his side is Cupid, half-brother of Aeneas, ancestor of the Julian family. Augustus' chest-plate features the Parthian king Phraates returning to a Roman soldier (or possibly Mars) the legionary standards captured from Crassus and Antony in 20 BCE. 15 CE, possibly a replica of a bronze original, ordered by Augustus in 20 BCE. Vatican Museums. Alinari Archives-Anderson Archive, Florence

from 27 to 25. It was effectively his last military command. The fighting was hard, and despite the foundation of 21 new military colonies (for instance, Emerita Augusta), the presence of three legions was necessary to ensure peace and order.

12–9 BCE   Perhaps with the desire to push back the Empire's frontiers as far as the Elbe and establish communications between the Rhine and the Danube, Drusus, Augustus' stepson by Livia, invaded Germania and gained control of the North Sea coast. Defeating various local tribes (the Chatti, Suebi, Marcomanni, and Cherusci) he reached as far as the Elbe, which, however, he did not cross. On his return he died as the result of a riding accident.

9–7 BCE   Tiberius continued Drusus' campaigns, going beyond the Elbe as far as Brandenburg.

4–6 CE   Tiberius campaigned against the Marcomanni. In 6 CE, a revolt on the Danube forced him to leave this front.

9 CE   The government of P. Quinctilius Varus provoked a rebellion in the territories occupied by the Romans in Germania. The Germani under Arminius defeated Varus, annihilating three legions and nine auxiliary corps in the Teutoburg forest. As a result, the dream of a great Roman Germania crumbled. Even though in his *Res Gestae* Augustus refused to admit the abandonment of these plans, henceforward the Romans hardly advanced beyond the Rhine.

9–12 CE   Returning from Pannonia, Tiberius restored Roman authority over the Rhine by expeditions into Germania.

The Danubian frontier

29–28 BCE   Having repulsed an invasion of the Bastarnae and Getae, M. Licinius Crassus, the proconsul of Macedonia, subdued Moesia and occupied the regions north of the protected kingdom of Thrace. Although no administrative organization followed, the Romans now controlled the lower Danube. This acquisition remained to be consolidated.

15 BCE   In a combined operation, Tiberius, coming from Gaul, and Drusus, coming from Cisalpine Gaul, caught the Raeti in a pincer movement. They thus extended the Roman frontier to the upper Danube. The province of Raetia was created. The linking of this new province to the territories of Moesia to the south-east by way of Noricum and Pannonia was then embarked upon. Noricum was annexed in this same year and transformed into a province.

12–9 BCE   Tiberius subdued Pannonia.

9–6 BCE   The province of the Maritime Alps was created and the Cottian Alps submitted; the latter's king, Cottius, took the title of prefect on behalf of Rome. A trophy erected at La Turbie, above Monaco, mentions the names of the 45 Alpine peoples conquered by Augustus.

6 CE (date uncertain)   The province of Moesia was created.

6–9 CE   Pannonia and Dalmatia, in the province of Illyricum, rebelled, a violent revolt that threatened Italy. Five legions were sent from the East. The area was reconquered by Tiberius, and Illyricum was reformed into the provinces later known as Pannonia and Dalmatia.

The Empire left by Augustus on his death was very similar to that of the third century CE. Later emperors made rearrangements and some further conquests, but the bulk of Roman territories was already in place by 14 CE.

8.5 | The Administration of the Empire

For all its constitutional flexibility, military success, and political inventiveness, the new regime in Rome ultimately depended on its ability to control and administer the immense territories of the Empire, inhabited by approximately 50 million people. The façade of republican tradition which concealed its monarchical nature enabled Augustus to draw on the sense of civic duty and respect for the state that imbued the *mos maiorum*. His restructuring of the senatorial and equestrian orders, and the subsequent emulation between the two, provided the human resources, power dynamics, and incentives necessary for his administration. The universal desire for peace, stability, and material gain facilitated his task. The administrative work of the new regime was furthered by the fact that Augustus' administrators did not pressure the conquered regions into uniformity in their outlooks and behaviors. Indifferent to (rather than respectful of) indigenous traditions, Augustan governors also realized that a strict enforcement of conformity to Roman social structures might pressure provincials into undesirable reactions. Thus they settled themselves into administrative and social organizations that predated their own, which they then proceeded to exploit and mold to Roman interests. Their conviction that they served a model civilization, which they knew was imperfect but believed to be the best possible, found a receptive audience among the local elites, who were swiftly won over to this new way of life and coveted Roman citizenship. Yet the somewhat idealized and oversimplified picture outlined here must not obscure the administration's numerical weakness (a few dozen men to a province), its scanty resources, or its brutalities. We shall look at three administrative levels: those in Rome, Italy, and the provinces.

Rome

Augustus transformed Rome in three areas to better mold it as the backbone and showcase of the Empire, administratively conducive to the work of *census*-taking and the holding of elections, but also in keeping with the majesty of the new regime.

Administrative organization

The administrative structures of the capital had become antiquated, hardly suiting the city which had become the most heavily populated conurbation in the ancient world. Augustus altered them profoundly and adapted them to the new realities.

In 7 BCE, he divided the urban territory into 14 districts (*regiones*), each in the charge of a magistrate chosen by lot from the praetors, tribunes of the *plebs*, and aediles. These districts were themselves divided (in total) into 265 quarters (*vici*). At the head of each *vicus* there were leaders (*vicomagistri*), often freedmen, entrusted with religious and administrative functions. The whole of the capital's administration came under a prefect of the city (*praefectus urbi*) of senatorial rank, an old institution from the republican era made permanent by the emperor. This prefect was assisted by other senators (with the title of *curator*) who supervised the aqueducts, public works and places, sacred buildings, the bed and banks of the Tiber, and the streets. And the urban cohorts, created near the end of Augustus' reign, were placed under his command. Similarly, as we have seen, Augustus created a prefect of the grain supply (*annona*), of equestrian rank, to solve the problems of provisioning, and set up cohorts of watchmen to combat fires and conduct nocturnal policing.

Embellishment by monuments and new building works

Through the restoration and completion of monuments that had been left damaged or uncompleted by neglect or civil war, and through the creation of new works symbolizing the grandeur of the regime and celebrating the *Pax Augusta*, Augustus aimed to make Rome the most beautiful city in the world. The architectural and artistic imagery of Augustus' multiple public projects celebrated the new regime. This common thread runs from architectural theory (Vitruvius' *Treatise on Architecture*) down to the details of town planning (Augustus was the first to regulate by law the height of private buildings). Furthermore, the emperor's private domain was merged with public space: grounds belonging to him or his family were built on and given to the Roman people, and, conversely, areas that harked back to common history, like the Palatine, were annexed to the imperial *domus*. Urban spaces became the setting for the festivals of the new regime. Monuments celebrated visually the new order of things that Augustan poetry glorified in words, providing all with a material imagery of imperial ideology. Four areas of the capital received Augustus' special attention: the Roman Forum, the Forum of Augustus, the Campus Martius, and the Palatine.

Augustus' physical transformations of the city of Rome, though in many respects revolutionary, respected and even accented existing traditions. He had the towers and gates of the Servian wall restored, and did not have the *pomoerium* moved. The city remained within its traditional physical boundaries, even though the administrative boundaries now extended far beyond them.

The political and administrative capital

Augustus also began to sketch the outlines of those governmental and administrative arrangements that would later constitute the formal machinery of the central government of the Empire. Nothing was crystallized yet; but the following may be distinguished:

- An emperor's council (*consilium principis*) was formed in 27 BCE. It consisted of the consuls in office, a magistrate from each of the other boards or colleges of magistrates, 15 senators chosen by lot, and friends of the emperor. It was a way of associating the Senate with imperial decisions. The quick rotation of its members (senators stayed for six months, the other members for a year) enabled the circulation of fresh perspectives, rewarded loyal associates, and prevented the formation of dangerous alliances. In 13 CE, it was reorganized with a stronger imperial presence: 20 ordinary members were appointed by Augustus for a year, but Tiberius got a permanent seat on it. There was also a more informal imperial *consilium* that was summoned from time to time to assist the emperor in judicial or administrative matters. This unofficial *consilium*, rather than the regular senatorial *consilium*, foreshadowed the imperial privy councils of later years, such as the one formed by Tiberius.

- Augustus accomplished major road projects, to create easy access to and from Rome, and to set it squarely in the center of the Empire. He restored the existing road system to good working order, created numerous other road networks (such as the one which, centered on Lyons, served the three Gauls), and organized a postal service for the efficient circulation of official messages, the *cursus publicus*.

- Augustus was the first to institute these different "departments of state." Yet the Empire was still managed like a private business. The offices that served it were those of the imperial household, entrusted to its freedmen and slaves, and were as yet not well defined as regards their respective duties. Nevertheless, by the end of Augustus' reign a petitions office (*a libellis*), an official correspondence office (*ab epistulis*), a legal department (*a cognitionibus*), and a department which prepared papers and reports (*a studiis*) all operated in some form or other.

Italy

Italy, inhabited by between 5 million and 8 million people, enjoyed a special status: its free men were all Roman citizens; they paid no land tax; and, even though it was theoretically under the control of the Senate, its 470 or so *municipia* were all autonomous. Augustus divided it into 11 regions, no doubt for fiscal purposes, but also so that everyone could vote in his place of origin (until then it had been necessary to come to Rome to take part in the elections of the state's magistrates). For all that, Augustus scarcely ever intervened in its administration.

The provinces

As we saw, the settlement of 27 BCE between the Senate and Augustus gave rise to a distinction between senatorial and imperial provinces.

Senatorial provinces The governors of these provinces, who bore the title of proconsul (as under the Republic), and were assisted in financial matters by quaestors, were chosen by the Senate from among former consuls (for Asia and Africa) or former praetors (for Achaea, Bithynia, Crete–Cyrenaica, Macedonia, Sicily, southern Gaul, Cyprus, and Baetica). But by a law of Pompey's, which Augustus revived, a magistrate had to have been out of office for at least five years before seeking one of these provincial posts, and it could be held only for a year.

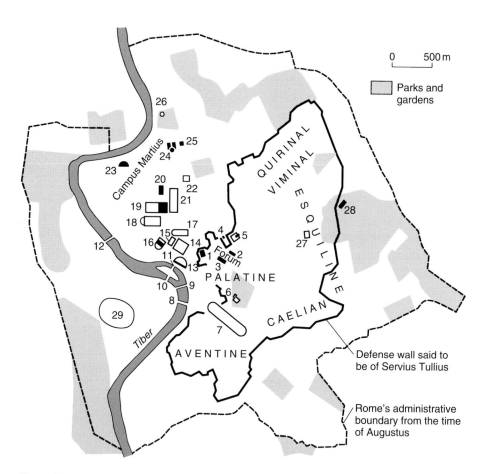

Figure 8.1   Rome in the Augustan period (from J.-P. Martin, *La Rome ancienne*, PUF, 1973)
1 Temple of Jupiter Capitolinus 2 Basilica Aemilia 3 Basilica Iulia 4 Forum of Caesar 5 Forum of Augustus 6 Temple of Apollo 7 Circus Maximus 8 Sublician bridge 9 Aemilian bridge 10 Cestian bridge 11 Fabrician bridge 12 Bridge of Agrippa 13 Theater of Marcellus 14 Portico of Octavia 15 Portico of Philip 16 Theater of Balbus 17 Circus Flaminius 18 Theater and portico of Pompey 19 Baths of Agrippa 20 Pantheon 21 Saepta Iulia 22 Portico of the Argonauts 23 Amphitheater of Statilius Taurus 24 Horologium of Augustus 25 Altar of Peace 26 Mausoleum of Augustus 27 Portico of Livia 28 Market of Livia 29 Naumachia of Augustus

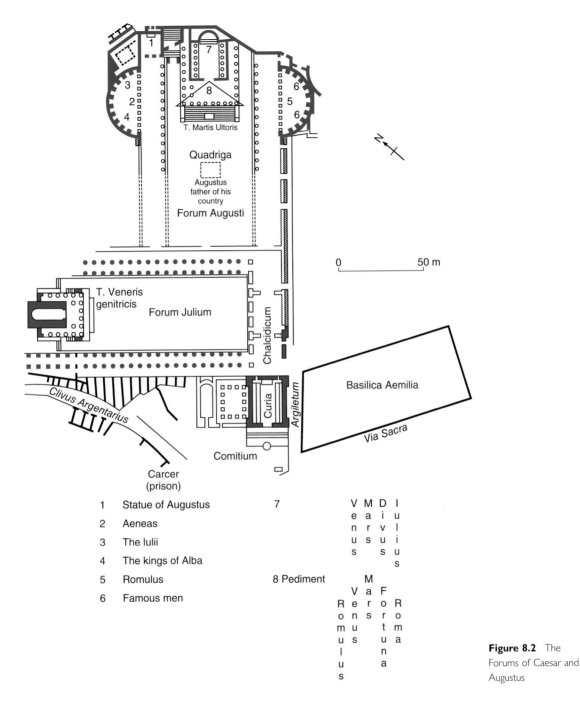

1	Statue of Augustus
2	Aeneas
3	The Iulii
4	The kings of Alba
5	Romulus
6	Famous men

Figure 8.2 The Forums of Caesar and Augustus

Imperial provinces The governors of the imperial provinces were chosen by the emperor, and whether they were former consuls or former praetors they bore the title of propraetorian legate of Augustus (*legatus Augusti pro praetore*). Provinces with more than one legion were governed by a former consul. The

Box 8.4 Imperial provinces

Consular	Praetorian	Equestrian
Tarraconensis	Lusitania	Raetia
Syria	Aquitania	Maritime Alps
Dalmatia	Belgica	Noricum
Pannonia	Lugdunensis	Judaea
Moesia	Galatia	Sardinia–Corsica
Military districts of Upper and Lower Germania		

length of a propraetorian legate's mandate depended on the will of the emperor. And he was accompanied by a procurator of equestrian rank who managed his finances, looked after the levying of taxes, and controlled the imperial assets (domains, salt works, mines, and quarries). Certain recent imperial provinces did not have a legion, but simply auxiliary troops. They were then governed by a prefect of equestrian rank.

Egypt The status of this province was special. Augustus proudly proclaimed that he had added Egypt to the *imperium* of the Roman people (*Res Gestae* 27). But in practice it was the property of the emperor, successor of the Ptolemies, who ruled through an equestrian prefect as his representative. Its capital city Alexandria, the commercial and cultural center of the Hellenistic world, led an active, and often turbulent, life separate from that of the province itself. The Latin formula *Alexandraea ad Aegyptum* ("Alexandria beside Egypt"), which is attested in inscriptions and papyri, seems to indicate an understanding of Alexandria as a special, if not independent, place in the province. Strabo provides an extensive description of the geography and history of Alexandria from ancient times to its transformation into a Roman province (*Geography* 17.1).

This general organization of the Empire may appear somewhat rigid but was in fact flexible and adaptable to changing circumstances. For that there were several reasons. First of all, the administrative status of a province was never definitive. If it was deemed necessary, an imperial province could become senatorial (as happened with Baetica between 16 and 13 BCE) or a senatorial province imperial (Illyricum in 11 BCE). Second, the boundaries of an existing province were not set in stone. Illyricum, for example, as we have seen, was split into two provinces in 9 CE, becoming Dalmatia and Pannonia. Similarly the organization of the Alpine provinces changed at different times.

Moreover, the overall organization of the Empire into types of provinces did not fix the scope of imperial action or set up inviolable legal and administrative boundaries. The same laws, for example, could be applied to both imperial and senatorial provinces. In the time of Augustus, imperial instructions (*mandata*) and imperial edicts, like the one in 12 BCE allowing the Jews to send money to Jerusalem, were addressed to all provinces. A marble inscription found in Cyrene documents a series of edicts regarding various judicial processes in this senatorial province. These include both personal mandates by Augustus (e.g. the third edict, regarding Greeks with Roman citizenship) and a senatorial decree (the fifth edict, also known as *senatus consultum Calvisianum*) establishing a new procedure for the trial of provincial governors charged with extortion (4 BCE). The Cyrene edicts clearly exemplify the imperial intervention in the local organization of a senatorial province.

Specifically in the matter of penal justice, the emperor's power was above that of all the governors, including those of the senatorial provinces. The emperor's intervention in the judicial matters of a province rendered its governor, even temporarily, a lower court judge. Ultimately, both imperial and senatorial governors were indirect representatives of the emperor, receiving a salary disbursed by him. Finally, the financial districts for the direct and indirect taxes that had to be paid by provincials did not always fall within the boundaries of a single province.

Leaving behind their overall organization and looking more closely at the arrangements within individual provinces, any impression of rigidity or uniformity is further dispelled. Within these provinces there existed a great variety of administrative and social frameworks: some dated from a period before Roman rule, while others were introduced by it. The eradication, preservation, or modification of any particular framework depended on factors such as the extent of Roman settlement, the density of towns, etc. In fact, each province or group of provinces was a special case: in the provinces of the Gauls, for example, the old tribal territories of the Gaulish peoples survived, somewhat altered, as the basis of the provincial administration, under the name of *civitates*. There were 60 such "cities" for the three Gauls, about 20 for Narbonensis – with their subdivisions of *pagi* and *vici*. Lusitania, on the other hand, like Baetica and Dalmatia, had imposed on it, for judicial purposes, an entirely different division into **conventus**.

pagus: The smallest recognized territorial unit, often subordinate to an urban community (*oppidum, municipium*).

If we looked even more closely at the urban centers within each province, we would see that each city was a special case with different privileges and obligations. In a way, the Empire was fundamentally a mosaic of cities.

conventus: A district of a province in which citizens assembled, and where the governor administered justice.

8.6 | Augustus: Showman and Gamesmaster of Rome

Augustus played a pivotal role in Rome's successful transition from Republic to Principate, and the durability of Rome's culture (*Romanitas*), society, and Empire can be traced back to his long rule, which included a very conscious and successful policy on games and spectacles. Suetonius (*Augustus* 43) says that Augustus "surpassed all his predecessors in the frequency, variety and magnificence of his public shows." In this, as in other respects, he was indebted to Caesar, but he was more thorough, more patient, more image conscious, and more in tune with the Roman people as a whole. According to Cassius Dio (52.30), Maecenas advised Augustus to "adorn this capital with utter disregard of expense and make it magnificent with festivals of every kind." Profoundly aware of the political potential of shows and of his own role-playing in public, Augustus established for future emperors a model of how to finance, produce, control, and preside at games.

Augustus' personal attention to games

Augustus' attention to games is indicated by their prominence in the *Res Gestae*, an account of his accomplishments written by himself and publicly displayed after his death (as we have seen in chapter 7). Depicting his actions and motives as he wanted them to be remembered, he presents himself in the *Res Gestae* as the ideal emperor in his relationship to the people and Empire; and conspicuous within that profile is his policy on entertainment (sections 22–3). By selection, omission, and "spin," he embellished his personal history, but the document is rich with reliable statistical information. Augustus obviously kept detailed records and people would have known if he misrepresented numbers and details.

At eight gladiatorial games given by Augustus (in his own name or the names of his sons or grandsons) about 10,000 men took part in combats. Three times (in his name or that of his grandson) he presented shows of athletes gathered from about the Empire. He also presented 27 shows (in the theaters or circus) in his own name or for other magistrates. With Agrippa, he presented the Secular Games in 17 BCE; and in 2 BCE he introduced the Games of Mars, which the consuls were obliged to produce annually thereafter. He also gave 26 beast shows (in his name or that of sons and grandsons) in the Circus, Forum, or amphitheater, and in these 3,500 animals were killed.

Suggesting Augustus' conduct as a model *triumphator*, who fulfilled vows and conducted proper rituals, the *Res Gestae* (4) declares that Augustus had two ovations and three triumphs and that he was hailed as *imperator* 21 times. His three triumphs, for successes in Dalmatia, at Actium, and in Egypt, were held over three days in August, 29 BCE. The battle of Actium was really part of a civil war, and therefore unworthy of a triumph, but Augustus had presented it as proper foreign war against Cleopatra, and the triumph went unopposed. As he points out, he later declined three more triumphs offered by the Senate, probably, as the *Res Gestae* suggests, not wanting to accept excessive honors – a mistake made by Caesar.

Overall, the *Res Gestae* shows that the provision of games was an effective way for Augustus to demonstrate his generosity to the people, his piety to the gods, and his devotion to his family. His spectacles also reveal his breadth of vision: his respect for tradition but openness to effective innovation, his syncretic view of the Empire, and his agenda of accommodating – within a structure – the different elements and interests of the people that he ruled. In his games policy and his administration overall, the Augustan "restoration" was a combination of new and traditional elements.

Secular Games

In 17 BCE Augustus put on the Secular Games. This elaborate festival supposedly was ordered by the Sibylline oracle to celebrate a new era, but Augustus clearly designed and artificially timed it to correspond to his Julian morality laws and his adoption of his grandsons Gaius and Lucius. According to the senatorial decree and to a special poem, the *Secular Hymn*, written by Horace and sung by a chorus of 54 boys and girls, the three-day festival included sacrifices and prayers by Augustus and Agrippa, as well as theatrical performances, chariot races, animal hunts, and more. The festival was to thank the gods Apollo and Diana, but the message was that Augustus was founding a grand new age of peace, prosperity, fertility, piety, and virtue for Rome.

Locations and facilities

A major source on the games of Augustus and his successors, Suetonius (*Augustus* 43–5), reveals Augustus' attention to the topography of shows at Rome. He says Augustus put on theatrical shows at numerous locations all over the city, and that he held gladiatorial combats in the Forum, the amphitheater, and also in the Circus and Saepta (a traditional gathering site in the Campus Martius). The athletic contests took place in the Campus Martius, and the sea fight was on the artificial lake built near the Tiber. Suetonius suggests that so many people attended these shows that Augustus felt the need to station guards throughout the city to prevent the looting of deserted homes.

Also indicative of Augustus' attention to the place of shows in the city life of Rome was the fact that his building projects included performance places. While embellishing Rome with impressive buildings for games, such projects also provided jobs for the underemployed urban poor. Around 30–28 BCE he built the *pulvinar* (ostensibly a sacral shrine but also an imperial box) in the Circus Maximus, and he added an Egyptian obelisk to the barrier in the racetrack. The portico of the Circus Flaminius was built in 33 BCE, and the theater of Marcellus, his son-in-law, was completed in 11 BCE. Augustus also had Agrippa renovate the Saepta for beast and gladiator combats. According to the *Res Gestae*, in 2 BCE Augustus arranged a mock naval battle (a naumachy) at a specially dug basin, (about 548 by 365 meters, across the Tiber. Thirty warships, and smaller vessels as well, and about 3,000 men (not including the rowers) fought in the battle. This naumachy, which took place on the right bank of the Tiber, supposedly re-enacted the battle of Salamis with Athenians against Persians. Although this particular basin was later filled in, later emperors built others and continued to stage sea battles.

Interestingly, Rome's first permanent, stone amphitheater was built in the Campus Martius by Statilius Taurus, a general at the battle of Actium. Perhaps even Augustus balked at building such an expensive facility, or perhaps Taurus' ties and loyalty to Augustus were sufficiently flattering. Built in 30 or 29 BCE, Taurus' amphitheater was the first major building in Rome to be dedicated after Actium, and it was completed in time for Octavian's triple triumph of 29.

Seating and social order Suetonius (*Augustus* 44) shows that the first emperor was attentive to proper seating arrangements – hierarchic by social status – and to decorous behavior in the stands at shows. Augustus arranged, by senatorial decree, that the first row of seats at any spectacle was for senators only, and he detailed regulations assigning seating arrangements for provincials, soldiers, boys, and other groups. He prohibited women from watching gladiators except from the highest section of seats, not allowing them to sit among the men as they had earlier. The Vestals, however, were exceptions to this, with seats at the lower level. Perhaps because of the customary nudity of Greek athletes, Augustus excluded women from viewing athletic contests, scheduling a boxing match, for example, early in the morning and not allowing women to arrive until it was over.

Elite performers, novelties, and oddities

As he had with Caesar, Suetonius takes particular note of Augustus' efforts to include free, non-professional, and even elite Romans in public performances. Suetonius says that Augustus had young noblemen hunt beasts, and that he often put on performances of the Game of Troy, a military ride by youths, which he favored as a traditional and worthy display by young nobles. Contrary to Roman values and perhaps with a mind to Greek customs (i.e. participatory athletics and ephebic or cadet training in equestrian and gymnastic events), Augustus seems to have been inclined to have Romans of status, both youthful and mature, perform in games; but the conservatives in the Senate were not so open-minded. Suetonius says that Augustus put Romans of the equestrian class in his theatrical and gladiatorial productions, but he stopped doing so when the Senate decreed that it was forbidden.

Augustus even responded to a popular interest in exotic animals and human curiosities by exerting personal control over the presentation of such creatures. Suetonius (*Augustus* 43) notes that Augustus showed a dwarf (of noble lineage, who was under 60 cm tall and supposedly weighed only 7.7 kg); presented the first Parthian captives seen at Rome "as a display" at a gladiatorial show, parading them through the arena and into the stands; and staged ad hoc exhibitions outside of games, for example of a rhinoceros, a tiger, and a huge snake.

Greek entertainments

Thorough and insightful, and perhaps assisted by Maecenas, Augustus had a culturally inclusive policy on spectacles. As Suetonius concludes (*Augustus* 45), Augustus endorsed by his interest "all types of performers" in the public spectacles. He was a boxing enthusiast: he liked to watch Latin boxers, even if they were not professionals, and he would match them against Greek fighters. He maintained and increased the privileges of Greek athletes, who were organized in professional guilds by the first century BCE. Not only did he arrange for athletes to perform three times at Rome, he created Greek-style contests, modeled on the Sacred Crown Games of Greece, both in Italy and in Greece. In 28/27 BCE Augustus created Actian Games at Rome and at Nicopolis (held every four years, and added to the Greek Periodos or circuit of Crown Games); and in 2 CE the Augustalia Games (with athletic and musical contests) began at Rome and Naples to honor Augustus. Such actions were consistent with his broad patronage of classical Greek culture to flatter his image and to aid imperial unification.

Personal example: Augustus as showman

Like a modern politician, Augustus was careful to present himself as an attentive fan, and in this he showed himself to be more sensitive to the average Roman than had the brilliant but aloof Julius Caesar. Suetonius remarks that Augustus would not let ill-health or dangers prevent him from appearing at shows: he had to be carried on a litter once, once his chair collapsed, and once he purposely sat in a certain section of seats to show spectators that it was safe. Augustus watched the chariot races from the homes of associates overlooking the racetrack, or at other times from his imperial box in the stands. Sometimes Livia and children of the family joined him. When he had to be absent, he excused himself and sent people to represent him. When he attended shows, Augustus made a point of a watching intently and carefully, perhaps because Caesar had been criticized for doing paperwork at shows, or because, as he admitted, he personally enjoyed and was sincerely interested in the events. Sometimes Augustus went beyond spectating in the stands to more overt participation as a patron and prize-giver. Suetonius says that he gave special prizes and gifts, paid for by himself, at other people's shows; and at Greek-style performances (possibly of athletes or theatrical performers) he always gave an appropriate present to each performer.

Arena reforms and regulations: Augustus the ringmaster

Augustus wisely monopolized the symbolic value of arena spectacles for the Principate. A diligent, patient administrator with a talent for performances, he overhauled what had been a rather unsystematic and dangerously volatile system of producing combats. While traditional festivals (*ludi*) were provided by the state, arena games (*munera*) traditionally were the personal gift of the producer; but Augustus used *munera* as another device conjoining his personal patronage as the "father of the country" to the staging of official state performances. Augustus, the great organizer, institutionalized and centralized *munera* on an official basis with legislation, and he laid the foundation for an imperial games administration. Wanting to control the giving of *munera*, in 22 BCE Augustus limited the praetors to two shows while in office, with a maximum of 120 gladiators. In effect, the astute Augustus was monopolizing the political value of producing gladiatorial combats, limiting to the imperial family the right to stage legitimized violence in Rome, and demonstrating the hierarchy of the *princeps* above magistrates.

Perhaps inspired by Caesar's attempts to save and accumulate gladiators, Augustus forbade the holding of gladiatorial combats "without reprieve" (*sine missione*). This phrase probably referred to contests in which the victor killed his opponent without presenting a choice. By demanding that life-or-death decisions were made, Augustus ensured quality combats for the spectators and guaranteed the possibility of reprieve or quarter for the combatants. Endorsing the elevation of these performers, he was managing resources wisely. Although he demanded strict discipline in wrestling and gladiatorial combats, he fully understood how valuable talented and popular performers were to his reign.

It was probably under Augustus that the shows in the arena settled into a tripartite routine, termed **munera legitima** – proper or regular shows. In the morning, about 9 o'clock, there were *matutina*, beast shows with hunting or fighting of beasts by trained, well-equipped hunters. By mid-afternoon spectators convened to watch the proper gladiatorial combats. Before that, however, at lunchtime, spectators might be absent or they might watch the *meridiani*, the "lunchtime shows," which included public executions of criminals in increasingly brutal and elaborate ways (see also chapter 11, "Beast hunts and executions").

For his own ambition but also for the stability of Rome in the crucial transition from Republic to Empire, Augustus institutionalized and centralized *munera* on an official basis, articulating a message of control but also one of imperial patronage and attentiveness. It seems quite possible that Augustus crafted an efficient Empire-wide administrative system for gladiatorial combats, using procurators. He perhaps even began the system of imperial gladiatorial training schools. With his various reforms and actions, the reign of Augustus saw gladiatorial combats mature fully into professional and spectacular sporting entertainments. In terms of the standardization of rules, equipment, procedures, and facilities through some centralized authority, Augustus can be said to have institutionalized gladiatorial combats as a national (and imperial) Roman sport – a brutal blood sport, yes, but a professional spectator sport nonetheless.

The *Res Gestae* and Suetonius concentrate on spectacles at Rome, but other sources, notably inscriptions and archaeology, show that Roman entertainments were spreading throughout the Empire under Augustus and later emperors. Gladiatorial combat, which had become emblematic of Roman culture, was in particular widely emulated. Under Augustus, amphitheater shows were established even in the Greek East by provincial elites trying to proclaim their Romanness. Games and shows were a form of cultural imperialism that reinforced a general process of Romanization throughout the provinces. Some of the events, especially beast and gladiatorial shows, were held annually in association with the emperor cult. In fact, it was a responsibility of the provincial high priests of that cult, tactfully and widely dispersed by Augustus, to put on such shows at their own expense. Moreover, prominent local provincials voluntarily funded and produced shows or built facilities for shows as benefactions to their communities. By such acts they demonstrated their wealth and character locally, but they also sent a message to Rome that they were culturally suited for promotion and favors.

munera legitima: Proper or regular shows in a tripartite format: *matutina*, beast shows with hunting or fighting of beasts; *meridiani*, "lunchtime shows" with public executions of criminals; gladiatorial combats in the afternoon.

Conclusion: Augustus as gamesmaster

Augustus utilized an expanded repertoire of games and festivals to distribute largesse (food and entertainment) in a generous and public manner, and personally to dictate and demonstrate proper behavior for citizens as spectators and for emperors as patrons at spectacles. Throughout, he kept firm control and supervision over practices, especially violent games, and he reminded future generations of his policies and generosity in the *Res Gestae*. By the end of Augustus' long reign, there was no turning back in terms of politics or spectacles. The Romans expected future emperors to provide entertainment at Rome, and the association between spectacles and Roman culture spread to the fringes of the Empire. Romanization went beyond law and Latin to include leisure and games. Augustus' system of spectacles continued under the Julio-Claudians and Flavians and remained intimately tied to the imperial regime. The bureaucracy and the facilities used expanded into elaborate imperial schools and the Flavian Amphitheater.

As suggested in his supposed deathbed remark about "playing his role in the mime of life" (Suetonius, *Augustus* 99), Augustus knew that he was *the* public figure of Rome, both at work and at leisure. The emperor's role was to provide imperial patronage and generosity as a producer of games. His personal attendance and attentiveness, with propriety and without personal participation as a performer, were crucial.

Later Romans evaluated emperors and accorded them popularity by comparison with the model of Augustus in all aspects, including their policies and actions concerning popular entertainments. Suetonius, writing later with several emperors for comparison, included treatments of emperors' games policies as reflections of the pros and cons of their personalities and their reigns. Augustus' policy was conscious and effective: later emperors emulated his balanced generosity and control or they suffered criticism. Magnificent, properly held games were a necessary if not sufficient condition for the popularity of emperors.

8.7 | Religious Policy

As with all his imperial projects, Augustus' religious policy was a combination of traditionalism and innovations, the most important of which was the foundation of an imperial cult. It is difficult, and perhaps irrelevant, to establish such a private issue as Augustus' "real" religious beliefs. Our sources stress his superstitious nature: he disregarded no dream, considered every **prodigy** and auspice infallible, and considered it a bad omen if he put his right foot into his left shoe in the morning (Suetonius, *Augustus* 92). Yet what strikes modern sensibilities as credulous is hardly unique in a world that blended religion, ritual, and superstition as seamlessly as the Romans did. Regardless of the sincerity of his elusive personal beliefs, Augustus exploited rituals and the religious occasions to his ends. For example, he banned Egyptian cults within the *pomoerium* in 28 BCE

prodigy:
Spontaneous and unusual manifestation of the divine will, for example rain of blood or ashes, lightning in a clear sky, etc. Gave rise to an expiatory ceremony.

after the conflict with Antony and Cleopatra, yet terra-cotta plaques showing Isis between two sphinxes were found in the temple of Apollo Palatine, which abutted on his residence.

A work of restoration and renewal

- *Restoration.* In order to elevate the dignity of the priesthoods, Augustus assumed the principal ones himself. We know from the *Res Gestae* (7) that he was *pontifex maximus*, augur, quindecimvir in charge of sacred ceremonies, *septemvir epulonum*, and one of the Arval Brethren, the Titian Brethren, and the *fetiales*. He restored 82 temples (*Res Gestae* 20), and renewed rites that had fallen into disuse.

- *Renewal.* He associated his various secular reforms and policies with the deities that matched the tasks; for instance, grain distributions were linked with the cults of Ops and Ceres. In addition, he attached favor and importance to certain gods and goddesses personally connected to him: Venus Genetrix was the matron of the Julian family, and we have already seen how Caesar touted his relationship with this goddess; Apollo had ensured the victory at Actium; Augustus had avenged the death of his adopted father with the help of Mars the Avenger (Mars Ultor). Augustus dedicated temples to these and other gods, exploiting the physical and symbolical proximity of these public spaces to his own private home on the Palatine. The poet Ovid suggests a plausible senatorial and popular response to these practices. Celebrating the dedication of a shrine to the goddess Vesta on the Palatine, he says "Vesta has been received into the house of her relative, thus have the just senators decreed. Apollo holds a part of the house; another part has been given to Vesta; Augustus, third in line, occupies what remains from those two . . . a single abode houses three eternal gods" (*Fasti* 4.949-54).

Moreover, through his attention to the founding of an imperial cult, Augustus subtly promoted the idea of his divinity throughout his long rule.

The founding of the imperial cult

Its origins

The various arguments concerning the sources of the imperial cult run the risk of reducing to a single explanation this complex phenomenon. Three main hypotheses have been proposed regarding its origins:

1 *Eastern origins.* In the Hellenistic world, kings and heroes had received divine honors. The most obvious model for Rome was Alexander: called "the new Hercules" (*neos Herakles*) in his lifetime, he was the object of a cult after his death. In the East, Greek cities had paid such divine honors to Romans such

| Chronology 8.2 | Establishment of the imperial cult | | |

BCE	Western provinces	Rome and Italy	East
32	The western provinces and Italy swear an oath of loyalty to Octavian.		
30		Honors to Octavian awarded by the Senate: ■ his name in the Salian chant; ■ libation to his *genius* at banquets.	Octavian as Pharaoh (Dendera). Many Greek cities begin a new era with Actium and take the name of *Caesarea*.
29			In response to requests from Greek cities, Octavian agrees that: ■ Roman citizens who live there will worship the Goddess Rome (Dea Roma) and the deified Caesar; ■ the Greeks will worship Octavian and Rome (Pergamum, Nicomedia, Ephesus, Nicaea).
28		Temple of Apollo on the Palatine; in its portico a statue of Octavian.	
27		"Augustus".	
26	Altar at Tarragona (or 25).		At Mytilene, a temple and priests consecrated to Augustus.
25		Augustus refuses to have Agrippa's Pantheon dedicated to him.	
23		In Horace's *Odes*, Augustus appears as a god descended to Earth.	
19	Three altars to Augustus at Noega (*numen* or *nomen?*): Arae Sestianae.	The altar of Fortuna Redux is erected at Porta Capena in honor of Augustus' return.	In Samos, a monument to Dea Roma and Augustus is built.
15	Altar to Augustus at Merida.		
12	Pledge by Drusus of an altar at Lugdunum (Lyons) to Rome and Augustus; consecrated 10 BCE.	*Pontifex maximus.* Association of the *Lares Compitales* and the *Genius Augusti.* Oath by the *genius* of Augustus; sacrifice to his *genius*; *Lares Augusti.*	
9	Altar of the Ubians (between 9 BCE and 9 CE).	Dedication of the Ara Pacis Augustae.	Reform of the calendar in Asia. It begins on the day of Augustus' birth.

BCE	Western provinces	Rome and Italy	East
8		Regular festivals for the anniversary of Augustus' birth. The month of *Sextilis* is renamed *Augustus*.	
6	In Baetica, Augustus is named *pater patriae*.		
3			Oath of the Paphlagonians to Augustus, his sons, his descendants, "By Jupiter ... and by Augustus." Imperial temples and altars of Augustus reported. Distinction between Greeks and Romans has disappeared.
2	Altar erected on the Elbe.	Dedication of the Forum of Augustus (Mars Ultor). From this date, development of the cult in Italy: ■ temple to Augustus and Rome, at Pola and Tarracina; ■ temple to his *genius* at Pompeii; ■ evidence of *flamines Augustales* in various cities.	
CE			
1	?Altar of the *gens Augusta* in Carthage.		In Caria, mention of a priest of Dea Roma and Augustus.
9		First public altar to the *numen* of Augustus.	
11–13	Altar of Narbonne to the *numen* of Augustus.		
14		Death of Augustus. Augustus deified by the Senate (apotheosis). A temple is vowed to him; dedicated in 37.	
15	Temple to Augustus at Tarragona.	At Nola, the house where he died is turned into a temple; at Bovillae, the place of origin of the *gens Augusta*, a sanctuary.	

as Flamininus, Mucius Scaevola, Lucullus, and of course Caesar. L. Munatius Plancus had proposed the title "Augustus" to Octavian after his return from the court of Alexandria, where he was probably inspired by the theocratic ambiance of Egypt's rulers. The beginnings of the imperial cult can be traced to attitudes and practices prevalent in the eastern part of the Empire.

2 *Roman national origins.* Roman legend and history were not unfamiliar with the concept of a deified ruler. Beginning with Romulus, kings had become gods. The Italian and foreign wars of the early Republic had produced quasi-mythical *imperatores*, exemplifying supernatural accomplishments of divine inspiration. Within the collective memory of Augustus' subjects, Caesar stood out as an exceptional individual who became divine. Natural phenomena (real or invented) also affected popular belief: the awe inspired by "Caesar's comet," observed a few days after his death, exemplifies the blending of religion and superstition that Augustus used to his benefit. As son of the deified Caesar (*divi filius*) Augustus could claim that he was descended directly from a goddess, Venus. From Caesar too he had the useful example of an oath sworn by the *genius* of the dictator (44 BCE), a divine privilege.

3 *Indigenous origins*, in particular Iberian. On January 16, 27 BCE, in the course of an extraordinary meeting of the Senate, a tribune of the *plebs* vowed himself to Augustus after the fashion of the Iberians and exhorted his compatriots to do the same. It was in the Iberian peninsula that the first municipal altar in the West in honor of Augustus was erected.

The establishment of an imperial cult

In seeking to understand how and why the imperial cult was established, we must also take into account local initiatives in the various provinces, following the chronology of its manifestations in the various parts of the Empire. From this chronology a few conclusions may be extracted.

- The initiatives taken were extremely varied. They came from towns and communities (Tarragona, Narbonne, the towns in the East); from members of the imperial family (e.g. Drusus), who acted, no doubt, with the emperor's consent; from legions (the three legions of Asturia and Cantabria with the three altars of the legate Sestius); and from individuals, often freedmen, who wished to participate in imperial cult (e.g. the altar of the *gens Augusta* in Carthage).

- The attitudes of the participants were influenced by factors such as their specific province, their proximity to urban centers, or their social group: there was a great difference between the religious perspectives of populations such as Roman senators, Athenian Greeks, Carian or Egyptian farmers. Consequently the forms of the imperial cult varied: different regions and individuals placed divergent emphasis on issues such as the association between the Goddess Rome and Augustus, his *genius*, his **numen**, the person of Augustus

numen: A divinity's power of decision; often meant the divinity himself or herself.

himself, or the soteriological aspect of his birth date. The less a region was Romanized, the more prominent the expressions of his cult.

- In the East, this type of worship eventually became commonplace. The western provinces followed, including Italy. Whatever form it took, imperial cult became a unifying agent surpassing regional differences, and the Empire as a whole regarded Augustus as its savior. The initial distinction made between a cult for Roman citizens and a cult for natives also dwindled, acting as another means for the disparate communities of the Empire to come together.

- Organized around various local altars, imperial cult is not to be confused with the modern concept of "state religion." The imperial house permitted or encouraged these demonstrations of adoration and loyalty, receiving the enthusiastic response and initiative of individuals and communities. Municipal worship, which was voluntary, provided opportunities for social activity and often ensured privileges from Rome (e.g. tax relief). In a few instances, however, Augustus played a more decisive and visible role in the establishment of imperial cult. The altar of the three Gauls, situated at the confluence of the Saône and the Rhône, and the altar of the Ubians on the Rhine (the future Cologne was created around it), are two such examples. In these two cases, political and religious institutions were set up following the emperor's wishes, in a regional framework with a hierarchical priesthood, a dedicated group of buildings, a special territorial status, and regular festivals. This organization was perhaps modeled on that of the East, where special provincial pontiffs (the Asiarch, the Bithyniarch) were elected for one year by an assembly of the delegates from cities in the province to supervise public games and religious rites associated with the cult. This formula, limited under Augustus' reign, was systematized and extended by his successors.

8.8 | The Succession

In order to secure the survival and development of his political, social, administrative, and religious achievements, Augustus had to secure his succession. This required primarily the transmission of what might seem not transmittable, a power that lay largely in the prestige, the authority, and the personal qualities of Augustus himself. This bequeathing of *auctoritas* had to be achieved within the narrow margins of the constitutional artifice which Augustus had exploited so advantageously throughout his reign. To appoint a successor publicly was to admit the reality of a monarchy and to found a dynasty, something that he had refused to acknowledge in all his actions. Yet to leave succession to chance, allowing free rein to the ambitions of individuals and clans, or to the negligible force of old republican institutions, would be to reopen the way to civil war. Augustus' dilemma was all the more difficult because he had no son of his own, and because he could not broach openly the matter of succession to the Senate and the people of Rome. Instead he favored a system of associating his preferred successor with his government through a marriage or adoption, thus indicating conspicuously where his own choice lay. Through this indirect designation of an heir, Augustus provided a semblance of legality and respect for the constitutional forms.

His first choice was the son of his sister Octavia, M. Claudius Marcellus. Born in 42 BCE, he was elevated at an early age to the pontificate. He was married in 25 BCE to Augustus' daughter Julia, and received an aedileship in 23 BCE, ahead of the normal age. But Marcellus died that same year, and his ashes were laid in the future tomb of Augustus on the Campus Martius. As Virgil indicates (*Aeneid* 6.860–86), Marcellus' death was considered a tremendous misfortune for the imperial house and the future of the Principate. Cautious or mistrustful, Augustus had also accelerated the career of his stepson Tiberius Claudius Nero (the future Tiberius), born in 42 BCE like Marcellus. However, when Marcellus died, it was not Tiberius who was approached but Agrippa, to whom Augustus remarried Julia in 21 BCE. Their two sons Gaius and Lucius were born in 20 and 17 BCE. On the birth of Lucius, the two boys were adopted by Augustus, becoming Gaius and Lucius Caesar. They could succeed, together or Gaius alone, either their adoptive father or their natural father, who had become co-regent in 18. In 12, Agrippa died. Augustus forced Tiberius to divorce Vipsania, Agrippa's daughter, in order to marry Julia (in 11). Honors and offices were heaped on the new son-in-law. But in 6 BCE, when he received tribunician power (as Agrippa had formerly) for five years, Tiberius asked for leave and voluntarily took himself off into exile in Rhodes, where he lived as a private citizen.

In 5 BCE, bypassing the rules regarding the entry age for the consulship, Gaius was appointed consul (but for five years later), and the Roman equestrians proclaimed him "the first among the youth" (*princeps iuventutis*), a title which came to denote the probable successor to the throne. Three years later, in 2 BCE, Lucius received the same honors. The two brothers were given commands, and took part in the imperial council, doing their apprenticeship in government. But their education in office was never completed. Both died on official missions to Spain and Armenia respectively, Lucius in 2 and Gaius in 4 CE, again disturbing Augustus' hopes for a seamless transition of his power. Speculation about the causes of their deaths and the future of succession must have been widespread, as Tacitus indicates (*Annals* 1.3). A temple at Nemausus, in southern France, known today as the Maison Carrée at Nîmes, preserves the honors paid to the two brothers and reflects the anxiety following their death: the reconstruction of an inscriptional text (from the holes that attached the bronze letters into the stonework) reveals that the temple, built by Agrippa, was later dedicated to the memory of Gaius and Lucius in their titles as sons of Augustus, princes of youth, consul, and consul designate.

After the death of Gaius and Lucius, Augustus' options for a successor were limited. He turned once again to Tiberius, adopting him in 4 CE, but at the same time he adopted Agrippa Postumus, the last surviving son of Agrippa and Julia,

princeps iuventutis: Leader of the equestrian order. Under the emperors, the probable successor to the throne (i.e. the crown prince).

Plate 8.8 Maison Carrée, Nîmes, France: one of the best-preserved temples throughout the Roman Empire. 19–16 BCE. istockphoto.com

born in 12 BCE after his father's death. Moreover, to add to his pool of candidates, he ordered Tiberius to adopt Germanicus, the son of Tiberius' brother Drusus. Tiberius was again vested with tribunician power. Agrippa Postumus on the other hand was subsequently repudiated, and following the death of Augustus he was murdered in exile under mysterious circumstances (Tacitus, *Annals* 1.6). In 13 CE, Tiberius received powers equal to those of Augustus. Even if the choice of Tiberius were a desperate solution, Augustus finally secured imperial succession, at least for the immediate future.

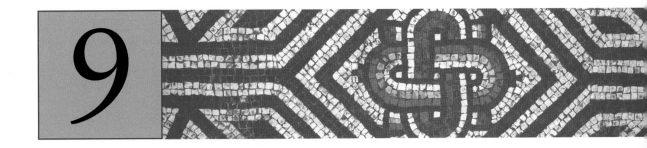

9

THE JULIO-CLAUDIANS

The System under Stress: 14–68 CE

By the time of Augustus' death, the one-man rule was generally acknowledged as necessary, and few questioned the legitimacy of the Principate. Even among those who supported the Republic in principle, hardly anyone proposed its re-establishment. Besides, the collective memory of the late Republic was fading away. "Internally, all was calm, the names of the magistracies were unchanged; the youngest men had been born after the victory of Actium, and even the majority of older men had been born in the middle of the civil wars; how many people were left who had seen the Republic?" wondered Tacitus (*Annals* 1.3). Dominated by the memory of Augustus, the political life of the Julio-Claudians was largely a matter of how senatorial and public opinion perceived them as compared to him. The personality of each emperor that followed Augustus became the most decisive element, in the verdict of ancient authors. In historical narratives about the Julio-Claudians common motifs can be discerned such as the influence of those closest to each emperor (family, counselors, freedmen), his relations with the Senate, and his popularity with the people. The emperor's relations with the various provincial armies and his interest in the administration and the provinces were also factors that determined his image in posterity as a "good" or "bad" emperor.

9.1 Four Personalities: Tiberius, Gaius (Caligula), Claudius, Nero

Tiberius: 14–37 CE

Senatorial historiography presents this second Caesar as a bad ruler, even a tyrant, who imparted an autocratic form to Augustus' subtle monarchy. It is clear, however, that the Empire suffered hardly at all from the moods of the emperor. Tiberius came to power at the age of 55. His merits were indisputable: he appears to have been one of the most capable and experienced men of his time, having already demonstrated his competence in all fields – military, administrative, and diplomatic. He was also a cultivated man: an excellent orator, a Hellenist, passionately interested in astrology, lacking in neither intelligence nor character. Yet, paradoxically, this man of duty, republican by conviction, the scrupulous heir of Augustus, never succeeded in becoming popular with the Senate or the people, inspiring on the whole fear rather than popularity. Perhaps Tiberius was unsure of himself and awkward rather than hypocritical as it seemed, hurt by having been the perpetual second runner in the race for the succession, irritated by the senators' lack of spirit, and reluctant to accept the constraints of public life. In any event, he is regarded by our sources as misanthropic, curt, and perpetually suspicious of potential rivals and imminent plots. Tacitus, a senator himself under the emperor Trajan, presents Tiberius' first dealings with the Senate in vivid episodes rife with mutual mistrust, double-bluffing, and evasive statements from both parts (*Annals* 1.11–12).

The principal events of his reign

Assuming power Augustus' will designated Tiberius and Livia as his principal heirs. The execution of the exiled Agrippa Postumus eliminated a challenge to Tiberius by a blood descendant of Augustus. The Senate, the magistrates, the army, and the people swore an oath of loyalty to the new emperor. Imitating Augustus' political gesture in the settlement of 27 BCE, Tiberius at first refused the duties offered to him before ultimately accepting them. After the official investiture, an enabling law was voted by the people, the *lex de imperio* (this would increasingly become a simple formality at the start of each reign). Two mutinies in the legions stationed on the Rhine and Danube were indirectly connected with the change of emperor. Tiberius, who stayed in Rome, had both of them suppressed through the agency of his natural and adopted sons, Drusus and Germanicus. Narratives of his reign distinguish among three general phases.

15–23 During these years, the regime was fairly moderate, but not without conflict. An alleged conspiracy against the emperor by M. Scribonius Drusus Libo resulted in the first treason trial, conducted by the Senate (16 CE). Tacitus provides an extensive narrative of Libo's conspiracy and trial (*Annals* 2.27–32), in order, as he says, to illustrate an evil that dominated later political life. External problems involved the revolts of Tacfarinas, a former auxiliary soldier, in Africa (17–24), and the revolt of the Gallic Treveri and Aedui, who had sunk into heavy debt (21). This rebellion was led by two local noblemen, Iulius Florus and Iulius Sacrovir. The expeditions in Germania (15–16), led by Tiberius' adoptive son Germanicus, were inconclusive and costly. Germanicus' return to the Teutoburg forest and his burial of the remains of Varus' legionaries, as well as his popularity in Rome, seem to have caused friction between him and the emperor. Livia might have played a role in this tension, since she was actively involved in Tiberius' decisions (she lived until 29). When Germanicus died in Syria in 19, general opinion suspected that the former governor of Syria, Gn. Calpurnius Piso, had poisoned him on the instructions of Tiberius in order to keep the succession for the emperor's son Drusus. The Senate voted Germanicus extraordinary funerary honors (see Tacitus, *Annals* 2.83), and, presided over by Tiberius, it conducted an investigation on Piso's involvement upon his return to Rome (20).

For a long time, Tacitus' *Annals* (3.10–19) was our most authoritative source on the events surrounding Piso's trial, his sudden suicide before the senatorial verdict, and Tiberius' role in the proceedings. Inscriptional evidence from Spain, however, has shed more light on these events. A bronze tablet documents the Senate's verdict, which takes as given Piso's involvement in Germanicus' death. The inscription also contains the Senate's address to the gods, the emperor, individual members of the imperial family, the equestrians, the people, and the soldiers, affording us with an excellent view of its status in relation to each of these agents in Tiberius' reign. This document, known as *Senatus Consultum de Pisone Patre* (abbreviated as *SCPP*), is complemented by two more discoveries, the inscriptions known as *Tabula Hebana* and *Tabula Siarensis* (also from Spain), parts of which record the funerary honors decreed to Germanicus by the Senate. These three inscriptions surrounding the death of Germanicus yield invaluable insights into the Senate's self-presentation and tentative relationship with Tiberius and various members of the imperial family. Additionally, they provide the rare opportunity to compare directly the official version of these events with their historical and rhetorical interpretation by Tacitus.

23–31 This period was dominated by Sejanus, who rose from his post as commander of the praetorian guard (15 CE) to a position of unprecedented influence with Tiberius. The son of an equestrian and himself an equestrian, he had family links with prefects of Egypt and with consuls. As praetorian prefect, he brought together into a common camp all the urban cohorts, which were previously dispersed throughout the city. His control of a concentrated military force, his social network and clientele, and his cleverly diplomatic dealings with Tiberius enabled him to become practically the emperor's second in command. Tiberius was so attached to Sejanus that he referred to him publicly as the "partner" of his labors. As a result of his growing influence over the emperor, the Senate accorded Sejanus honors that exceeded those due to his rank and office, and a court formed around him. The death of Drusus in 23 may even have given him hopes of one day becoming emperor himself. He asked to marry Drusus' widow, Livilla, a request that Tiberius refused (25). Sejanus' influence in Rome increased further when Tiberius, encouraged by his advice (given, perhaps, so that he might have a freer hand in the capital), retired to Campania in 26. The emperor shut himself away on the island of Capri, which he virtually never left again. In 30, Sejanus was appointed consul for the following year with Tiberius as his colleague – an exceptional honor for Sejanus. But then, in that following year, Tiberius, from Capri, brought about his downfall. Perhaps he feared Sejanus' ultimate ambitions or he was spurred to action by a group of nobles loyal to Germanicus, which was being persecuted by Sejanus. The affair remains relatively obscure, since a large section in Tacitus' *Annals* dealing with the fall of Sejanus has been lost. Suetonius (*Tiberius* 61) reports that Tiberius claimed in his autobiography that he punished Sejanus for plotting against the children of Germanicus. According to Cassius Dio (58.4), Tiberius realized that Sejanus could be proclaimed emperor at any given moment since he essentially controlled the Senate and the praetorian guard. In sum, it appears that in October 31, following Tiberius' covert undermining of Sejanus and, finally, his open denunciation of him in the Senate through a letter, Sejanus was arrested and summarily executed. A witch-hunt followed, including the execution of Sejanus' supporters and his young children.

31–37 From Capri, Tiberius continued to govern with the same attention to political affairs that he had shown before he retired there. In particular, he encouraged the practices of informers (*delatores*), "a class of people invented for the destruction of the state" (Tacitus, *Annals* 4.30). The informers prosecuted various individuals under the law of treason (*lex maiestatis*), and directed their trial by the Senate. If found guilty, the defendants were punished by death or exile and their fortunes were confiscated. Bitter and cynical, the emperor nevertheless also continued to give careful consideration to the larger concerns of the state – he halted a financial crisis and neutralized the Parthian danger.

Tiberius died in March 37 at Misenum without having prepared for his succession. It seems that he was hesitating between his own grandson and his great-nephew, the grandson of his brother Drusus, Gaius Julius Caesar Germanicus, better known as Caligula (who was rumored to have finished off the dying man).

Our modern assessment of Tiberius' reign is inevitably influenced by the magisterial narrative of Tacitus, and, to a lesser extent, those of Suetonius and Cassius Dio. However, we need to mention here an important counter-narrative to these perspectives. This is a two-volume compendium known as *History of Rome*, written by Velleius Paterculus. Velleius' life and career spans the reigns of both Augustus and Tiberius. He served as a military tribune in Thrace, Macedonia, Greece, and Asia Minor; later, from 4 to 13 CE, he was a cavalry officer and *legatus* under Tiberius, in Germany and Pannonia. He was quaestor in 7 CE, and praetor in 15. His (now fragmentary) narrative covers the time from the fall of Troy to 29 CE. This work is dedicated to M. Vinicius, consul in 30 CE, whom Velleius also addresses directly throughout his narrative. Velleius disappears from the record in 30, and it has been speculated that he was among the friends of Sejanus who were put to death in the aftermath of his downfall.

Neglected for a long time by many modern critics, Velleius Paterculus' short history is the earliest and most extensive narrative of a post-Augustan historian surveying the history of the Republic within the rise of the Principate. Having experienced the devastation of civil wars through the living memories of his elder contemporaries, Velleius understands the Principate as a natural evolution from the crumbling Republic rather than as the sudden and unwelcome enforcement of a monarchy. In this vein, Paterculus highly praises Tiberius, especially his military accomplishments in Germany. These he peppers with various anecdotes to which he was himself a witness. Once, Paterculus tells us, Tiberius' army was camped on the shores of the Elbe right across the barbarian line. An elderly man crossed the river in a small boat, and requested permission to see the emperor. Asked to state his mission, he said that he simply wanted to see and touch a god, and, once he had been allowed to do so, he returned to his boat and crossed over to his people (*History of Rome* 2.107).

It is easy to see why Velleius' effusive praise of his emperor has led many to consider his work an unreliable source for Tiberius. On the other hand, Velleius' counter-perspective to the much later accounts of Tacitus, Suetonius, and Cassius Dio demands our attention. Velleius saw continuity between the Republic and Augustus' Principate, if not the urgent need for the latter to stabilize the former. More importantly, unlike the three later authors, his perspective on monarchy is not blurred by the abuses of Caligula and Nero, or by the civil wars that followed Nero's death. Perhaps a more balanced appraisal of Tiberius can emerge once we canonize Velleius among our sources for Tiberius' rule.

Gaius (Caligula): 37–41 CE

We do not know much about the background of Caligula's accession. It seems that the praetorian prefect who succeeded Sejanus, a man named Naevius Sutorius Macro, promoted him to Tiberius. The Senate and the people of Rome joyfully welcomed the man whom the crowd acclaimed with cries of "our baby" and "our star" (Suetonius, *Gaius* 13). The funeral rites of Tiberius, whose ashes were taken to the mausoleum without deification, were carried out without incident. His will had already been nullified to give maximum powers to the new emperor, on whom the right of command over the armies and imperial provinces was conferred. Soldiers and civilians swore the oath of loyalty. An inscription from Aritium in Lusitania preserves the oath to Caligula administered to the Aritienses by the provincial legate in May 37 CE. Two parallel testimonies from Umbria and from a small town in the Troad (in modern Turkey) indicate the enthusiasm that pervaded the entire Empire at Caligula's assumption of the throne. The reasons for his initial popularity included his youth (25 years old on his accession), the popularity of his father, Germanicus, the length of Tiberius' reign (23 years), his childhood in the legionaries' camps, which earned him the nickname Caligula ("Little Boots"), the misfortunes of his family, victims of Tiberius and Sejanus, his relationship to Augustus and Antony, and his devotion to his family. His 2.7 billion sesterces, left to him by Tiberius, also added to his capital of popularity.

However, less than four years later, on January 24, 41 CE, the emperor was assassinated by a conspiracy of praetorian officers and imperial freedmen. No one seems to have been particularly perturbed: our sources mention neither outrage nor regrets. How had adulation turned to indifference in such a short time? Our sources paint such a bleak portrait of Caligula that their value is questionable. Speculation surrounds the question of his eccentricity. Already in antiquity, some suspected the presence of a mental illness (Suetonius, *Gaius* 51). Incidents such as his alleged appointment of his horse into a priesthood (Cassius Dio, 59.28) seem to point in that direction.

His foreign policy also seems incoherent, even grotesque if one thinks of his aborted attempt to land in Britain. Suetonius tells a tale that is hard to believe: drawing up his battle line on the shore of the English Channel, the emperor suddenly ordered his soldiers to collect sea-shells, proclaiming them "spoils from the ocean, owed to the Capitol and the Palatine" (*Gaius* 46). This strange anecdote might be genuine, or perhaps it conceals the clever ruse of an emperor faced with an ill-prepared expedition.

Some historians think that Caligula contemplated the revolutionary introduction into Rome of the Egyptian cults of Isis and Serapis; for others the indications that he did are not convincing. We know that Caligula emptied the treasury's coffers, annexed Mauretania, remained in control of the governmental and administrative machinery, and demanded that the Jewish people install his statue in the Holy of Holies in the Temple at Jerusalem. He certainly remains an enigmatic persona, an incarnation of imperial cruelty and moral bankruptcy in popular imagination. The mystery that surrounds him allows for alternative and creative interpretations. In his play *Caligula*, the author and philosopher Albert Camus (1913–1960) envisaged him as representing the systematic and insolent rejection of the falsehoods and hypocrisies of the system set up by Augustus.

Claudius: 41–54 CE

An involuntary emperor

After Caligula's assassination, while the Senate was discussing the possibility of restoring the Republic, the praetorians were scouring the palace for a member of the Julio-Claudian family. According to Suetonius (*Claudius* 10) "a soldier searching hither and thither having chanced to see his feet (he had hidden in the folds of a hanging placed in front of a door), was curious to discover who it could be, recognized him, dragged him from his hiding-place and as the terrified Claudius threw himself at his feet, hailed him as emperor." Behind this anecdote lie three truths: Claudius had no desire to become emperor; he was the first emperor to be invested by the praetorians; and, through fear, he was also the first emperor to try to secure their loyalty by promising them a sum of money (*donativum*) – 15,000 sesterces each. The political influence of the praetorians, which Sejanus had set in motion, would continue to build up and manifest itself in the succession of future emperors.

The man

Claudius, the son of Tiberius' brother Drusus, was born in Lyons in 10 BCE. He was thus the nephew of Tiberius, the uncle of Caligula, and the younger brother of Germanicus. Physically weak, and with a speech impediment, he seems to have been underestimated in the imperial house. Suetonius (*Claudius* 3) claims that his mother Antonia referred to him as "a caricature of a man, an abortion merely sketched by nature," sentiments shared by his grandmother Livia and his sister Livilla. Since his very intelligence was doubted, Claudius was considered the last possible candidate for important offices, let alone for governing the Empire. Naturally, his career moved very slowly. He remained an equestrian until Caligula took him on as his colleague in the consulship in 37. Living on the sidelines allowed him to develop his interest in philology (he later invented three new letters for the Roman alphabet) and for history (he wrote a history of Rome in over 40 volumes, one of Etruria in 20, and one of Carthage in eight, the last two works in Greek). This erudite emperor, who spent much of his time in his study with the freedmen who worked there, was ridiculed by Roman authors. In his satire *The Apocolocynthosis of the Divine Claudius* Seneca mocked the emperor's

apotheosis: Ceremony whereby a mortal was admitted to the number of the gods (*divus*). It was customary under the Empire, decided by the Senate as the prerogative of "good" emperors. "Bad" emperors (those who had persecuted the Senate) were subjected to the condemnation of their memory (*damnatio memoriae*); their names were struck off inscriptions and their enactments canceled.

apotheosis as a transformation into a pumpkin. Other sources portray him as a drunkard, the plaything of his freedmen (Callistus, Pallas, Polybius, and Narcissus) and his wives (he had four, two of whom have their place in history, one for her doubtless exaggerated escapades, Messalina, and the other for her political acumen, Agrippina, Nero's mother).

Modern historians, however, have re-evaluated Claudius' achievements on both the domestic and the foreign fronts. A lot of his work on the domestic front went toward remedying the damage done by Caligula (Cassius Dio, 60.5). Claudius also reorganized the central administration of the Empire into various departments attending to different administrative tasks. He undertook all kinds of construction and public works (the draining of Lake Fucinus, the building of aqueducts, the port of Ostia, and road systems). He looked favorably on the promotion of provincials. In 48 CE the Senate debated the claim of chieftains from northern and central Gaul to become senators. Tacitus creatively reconstructs Claudius' speech to the senators (*Annals* 11.23–5) urging them to accept these foreigners on the basis of Rome's cosmopolitan history and melting-pot culture. A bronze tablet found in Lyons preserves the transcript of Claudius' actual speech on this matter. Known as the Lyons Tablet, this document differs in tone and detail from Tacitus' version, but it still corresponds to the gist of his account. Like the *SCPP*, the *Tabula Siarensis*, and the *Tabula Hebana*, the Lyons Tablet provides the opportunity to compare the official version of an event with its interpretation by Tacitus, our most important source on the Julio-Claudians.

Claudius' other imperial accomplishments include his judiciary concerns, his revival of Augustus' religious policy, his interest in the provisioning of Rome, and his foundation of numerous colonies (e.g. Cologne). He took on the censorship in 47 and 48 CE (there had been no censor since 22 BCE) and exercised it scrupulously. He also engaged in a varied and, generally speaking, inspired legislative activity. In sum, Claudius combined a traditionalist outlook with innovatory, and even revolutionary, policies.

Chronology 9.1	**Principal Events of Claudius' Reign**

41   Caligula's murderers are punished. Dynastic policy is affirmed (Livia awarded apotheosis). Claudius rejects the title *Imperator*.

Free practice of the Jewish religion is confirmed; order is restored in Alexandria, with its large Jewish population, following disturbances there brought on by Caligula's anti-Jewish policy.

42   Mauretania is organized into two procuratorial provinces, Caesariensis and Tingitana.

43   The conquest of Britain is begun (imperial cult at Camulodunum, modern Colchester). Lycia, free since 168 BCE, becomes, in conjunction with Pamphylia, a new imperial province of praetorian rank. The whole of Anatolia is henceforward integrated into the Empire.

The Druidic religion is abolished.

44   Judaea once more becomes a Roman province.

The Senate's treasury (*aerarium Saturni*) is taken from the control of the two **praetores aerarii** and returned to that of two quaestors who are to be chosen by the emperor. In other words, the **aerarium** comes under imperial control.

46   Thrace becomes a procuratorial province.

47   Claudius holds the censorship.

Cn. Domitius Corbulo is in Frisia and Germania (Rhine–Meuse canal).

48   Claudius makes speech on the admission of Gallic nobles in the Senate.

Messalina's mock (?) wedding to the consul C. Silius takes place, and her execution after the machinations of Claudius' freedman Narcissus.

49   Claudius marries his niece Agrippina.

Seneca, recalled from exile, is appointed tutor to Nero, the son of Agrippina.

The *pomoerium* is extended by Claudius.

The deposed king of the Crimean Bosphorus, Mithridates, seizes control of the kingdom from his brother Cotys. Eventually, with the help of Julius Aquila, Cotys defeats Mithridates. He is sent to Rome, where Claudius accepts him as hostage.

50   Nero is adopted by Claudius; he thus moves ahead of Britannicus, the emperor's own son by Messalina.

51   The Parthian king Vologeses accedes to the throne. From then on, Rome again senses danger from the Parthians. This feeling is heightened by the intervention of Vologeses in the allied kingdom of Armenia.

54   October 13: Claudius dies, perhaps poisoned by Agrippina. He seems to have placed Britannicus side by side with Nero to succeed him. The Senate decrees Claudius' deification; Agrippina becomes the priestess of the Divine Claudius, as Livia had been of the Divine Augustus.

Plate 9.1 Roman circus, lion killing man, first century CE. Ancient Art & Architecture Collection

Nero: 54–68 CE

The son of Agrippina

When Nero succeeded Claudius, he was nearly 17 years old, the youngest of the Julio-Claudians to assume the throne. The manner in which his accession took place reveals careful preparation. Claudius' death was kept secret. Britannicus, Claudius' son by Messalina, was detained while Nero presented himself to the praetorians, accompanied by their prefect, Afranius Burrus. In return for the promise of a *donativum*, they acclaimed him emperor. In the afternoon, Nero went before the Senate, and there read out a speech prepared by Seneca in which he took up the Augustan theme of government shared equitably between the emperor and the Senate. Thus, within the space of a few hours after the death of Claudius and without any resistance, Nero outstripped those supporting Britannicus and became emperor. Behind this seamless transition of power many saw the presence and intrigues of his mother Agrippina, one of Caligula's sisters. But Nero's way was also eased by his resonant and inclusive ancestry, or at least, emphasis was placed on its most favorable parts to justify his claim. Through his mother and father (Cn. Domitius Ahenobarbus), Nero was descended from both the Divine Augustus and Antony. And as the adopted son of Claudius, he thus united in his person the two branches of the imperial family, the Julii and the

Claudii. According to Suetonius (*Nero* 6) Nero's birth, on December 15, 37, at Antium, was surrounded by both positive and ominous presages. These super-natural phenomena (a staple of Greco-Roman biographies of important men) summarize the ambiguity of Nero's personality, which is inextricably linked with his reign. Although it began under favorable auspices and popular acclaim, his political program quickly became a blend of aesthetic ideals and cruel practices. From his marvelous "golden house" (Domus Aurea), to the persecution of Christians, to fiddling while Rome was burning, these famous "Neroisms" have left an indelible mark on the popular conceptualization of Nero and of Roman emperors in general.

The emperor's personality

Two pictures of Nero emerge from our sources, more supplementary than con-trasting. The literary evidence is damning, portraying Nero as an emperor-tyrant in the tradition of Caligula. For these writers, Nero was "the enemy of the human race" (Pliny the Elder), a monster who killed his half-brother, practiced incest with his mother before having her killed, eliminated his wife and his tutor, had himself married to one of his freedmen, was a bad actor, played at being a chari-oteer, and set fire to the capital, not to mention other crimes and excesses. Jewish and Christian writers were even more damning: Nero became an apocalyptic figure, the Beast of the Revelation, the Antichrist. A parallel image is that of the autocrat as artist, his enterprises those of a cultural revolutionary aiming to make the Romans accept a very different mental outlook and scale of values from those they had known until then. The archaeological evidence reveals a lover of paint-ing and sculpture, singing, and music, who enjoyed architectural boldness. He dreamt of renaming Rome "Neropolis" (Suetonius, *Nero* 55) and possibly model-ing it on Alexandria. After the great fire of Rome, "in the ruins of his country," as Tacitus says (*Annals* 15.42), Nero built an exquisite palace, the Domus Aurea. This was conceived as a self-contained, miniature version of the natural world, complete with ponds, flora, wildlife, and Nero's colossal statue (Suetonius, *Nero* 31; Martial, *On the Spectacles* 2).

The character of Nero seems to have been a mixture of opposites, to be traced between the extremes of condemnation and contempt heaped on him by our sources. He was certainly fascinated by Greece and the ways of the East but maintained several Roman traditions. He was undeniably cultured, an amateur musician who took his lyrical pursuits very seriously, and a poet whose work, Tacitus tells us, was not to be laughed at. He was neither the greatest artist of his time, as he liked to believe, nor completely talentless. When he eliminated Agrippina and Seneca, his tutor, he sought to give an artistic turn to political practice by subjecting it to his interest in spectacles and entertainment. Certainly, since the days of the Republic, political savvy dictated the use of spectacles and entertainment for ensuring popular support in Rome. Augustus himself exploited brilliantly for his popularity the political capital of games, festivals, chariot races,

Plate 9.2 Fresco from one the five dining rooms (*triclinia*) of a villa in Moregine, south of Pompeii. Here Apollo with lyre is leading the muses around him (not shown). The close resemblance of Apollo's features to those of Nero has led some critics to identify the villa as a luxury inn or a vacation residency built especially for the emperor. c.64 CE. The VRoma Project (www.vroma.org)

and other public entertainments. But Nero took this concept to a new level by inserting himself into the spectacles not merely as a spectator, like his predecessors, but as a performer. Moreover, his frequently cruel and punitive imposition of his artistic aesthetics on his subjects turned them into compliant yet resentful collaborators in his escapism. The universal discontent that followed is clearly linked to his loss of the throne and his suicide in 68 CE. A performer until his last moment, Nero died supposedly exclaiming "What an artist dies in me!" (Suetonius, *Nero* 49). His deliberate confusion between performance and politics makes his reign difficult to assess.

His reign

The notion of clear-cut turning-points in the ever deteriorating career of a "bad" emperor begins with Roman authors. The narratives of Tiberius' reign, for example, are constructed along these lines. Similarly, in the case of Nero, the

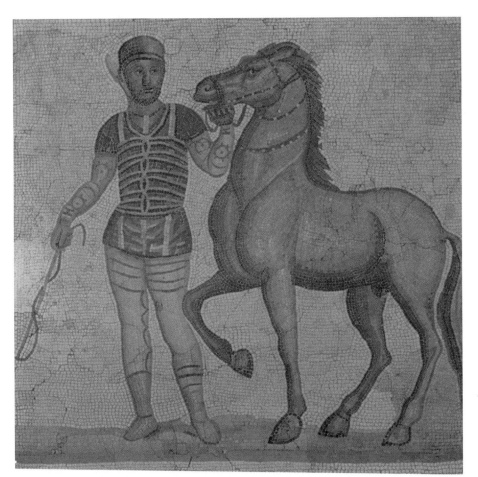

Plate 9.3 Mosaic of a charioteer wearing the colors of his sponsor and a leather helmet for protection. National Archaeological Museum, Rome. C. M. Dixon

54   The advisers of the new emperor are Seneca the philosopher, Burrus the prefect of the praetorian guard, and
         Agrippina for foreign policy.
       War starts in Armenia against the Parthians.
55   Britannicus is murdered.
       There is a reaction against the policies of Claudius.
       Corbulo is sent in the East against the Parthians. Talks are held with the latter.
58   The Senate rejects a fiscal reform proposed by Nero.
       Corbulo drives the Parthians out of Armenia.
59   Agrippina is murdered.
       Nero's reform of values begins: he introduces games called the *Iuvenalia* and creates the *Iuvenes Augustiani*, a
         select body of youths.
       Tigranes V is installed as Rome's new vassal king of Armenia.
       The Alpine kingdom of Cottius is annexed (perhaps as early as 58), and transformed into a procuratorial imperial province.
60   The first Neronia (quinquennial games) are held, which included musical, gymnastics, and equestrian competitions
         and were inspired by Greek traditions such as the Olympic Games.
       Baths and a gymnasium are inaugurated.
61   Boudicca (Boadicea) rebels in Britain; Colchester and London are destroyed, but she is eventually defeated and
         commits suicide by poison.
       War breaks out between the Parthian Vologeses I and Tigranes, the king of Armenia supported by the Romans.
62   Burrus dies; Tigellinus, the emperor's henchman, becomes praetorian prefect.
       Seneca gradually withdraws from the court.
       Treason trials are revived in the Senate.
63   There are successful initiatives by Corbulo on the eastern front. The Romans recognize Tiridates, the protégé of
         Vologeses, as king of Armenia, who offers in return a great show of compliance to Nero. The Parthian war ends.
       The rebellion in Britain ends.
64   For the first time Nero appears on a public stage, in Naples.
       July: Rome burns; a new city is planned; the construction of the Domus Aurea begins. Christians are blamed for
         the fire and punished in various spectacles organized by Nero.
       The kingdom of Pontus is annexed.
65   A conspiracy against Nero by G. Calpurnius Piso fails; Piso, Seneca, Lucan, Petronius, and others involved commit
         suicide.
66   Tiridates arrives in Rome, where he is crowned king of Armenia and hails Nero as the god Sol.
       The colossus of Nero is constructed and set up in the entrance to the Domus Aurea.
       The doors of the temple of Janus are closed and universal peace is proclaimed.
       Nero leaves for Greece.
       There is a rising of the Jews in Judaea – the start of the Jewish War.
67   Nero enters an athletic contest in Greece.
       The digging of the Corinth canal is started. Greece is proclaimed "liberated." At the end of the year, Nero returns to Italy.
       Corbulo commits suicide.
       Vespasian is appointed commander of the war in Judaea.
68   February: contact is made between Vindex, legate of Lugdunensis, and other governors, such as Galba, legate of
         Tarraconensis, with the aim of overthrowing the emperor.
       March: Nero has an artistic triumph in Rome; Vindex leads an uprising in Gaul.
       April: Galba rebels.
       May: Vindex is crushed at Besançon by the loyalist troops of Verginius Rufus, governor of Upper Germany.
       There is a rising in Africa led by the legate Clodius Macer; Otho, legate of Lusitania, and Caecina, quaestor of Baetica,
         give support to Galba; in Rome, the praetorians also declare their backing for Galba; the regime collapses.
       On June 9, declared a public enemy by the Senate, deserted by all but four servants, Nero kills himself shortly
         before being arrested. He is 30 years old. Galba enters Rome later that year, but is murdered in January of 69
         CE. A year-long civil war begins.

first five years of his rule (54–59) are generally viewed as a period of political prosperity that was terminated in March 59 by his murder of Agrippina. Another political turning-point could be traced in the years 61 or 62, when Nero's attitude to the senatorial aristocracy hardened. However, the disintegration of Nero's reign is rather subtle and gradual, its components reflecting his personality and the power struggles around him already at his succession. Certainly Agrippina's death seems to have been an important shift in terms of his independence, and our sources unequivocally condemn Nero for matricide. After his mother's demise Nero openly intensified and imposed his artistic ambitions in Rome, offering games, festivals, luxury, and indulgence, instead of institutions that he considered dull and uninteresting: martial contests, stern traditions, self-restraint, and security.

9.2 | The Institutions and Innovations of the Julio-Claudians

It is difficult to judge which of Augustus' institutions the Julio-Claudians preserved and which they innovated in. The new regime seemed to have been fully formed down to the last detail by the time of Augustus' death, with his heirs needing only to maintain their heritage. However, the Julio-Claudians were not mere followers. They introduced innovations, frequently deepening and consolidating Augustus' hallowed achievements. Regardless of their individual personalities, the Julio-Claudians strived to define themselves in relation to Augustus, whether they imitated or opposed his actions. Tiberius asserted that he regarded everything that Augustus did or said as the law. His successor, Caligula, thought otherwise. According to Suetonius (*Gaius* 23), "he proclaimed that his [own] mother was the fruit of an incestuous act committed by Augustus with his daughter Julia; and not content with thus sullying the memory of Augustus, on the pretext that the victories of Actium and Sicily had been disastrous and lethal for the Roman people, he forbade their celebration by traditional festivals."

Following, as it were, the practices of the Julio-Claudians themselves, we shall therefore look at their achievements in relation to those of Augustus. These can be delineated, if oversimplified, in terms of constants and developments, and then in terms of innovations and shifts.

Constants and developments

Power and the dynastic idea

As we saw, Augustus exploited his relationship to the deified Caesar, and throughout his reign he tried to associate members of his family with the government of the Empire. The dynastic principle was thus already in place, but it had not yet emerged as an acknowledged principle by which a claim to power could be justified. This development came under the Julio-Claudians. With the exception of Tiberius, all the Julio-Claudians were of the blood of the Julii (a line that ended with Nero), evidence that dynastic heredity became more important than imperial "talent," or even adoption. It was because he did not possess that blood that Tiberius ostentatiously displayed his loyalty to his adoptive father: like Augustus he initially refused the power that was offered to him, similarly affected a "democratic" simplicity, and claimed solemnly that "only Augustus' mind was capable of shouldering the great weight of the Empire" (Tacitus, *Annals* 1.11). Tiberius' effort to connect with the Julian side of his family and to celebrate the idea of dynasty is indicated also by non-literary sources. A sardonyx cameo known today as the Great Cameo of France (plate 8.1 above) raises some interesting issues of imperial ideology. Provided that the interpretations are correct, the cameo depicts the living members of the imperial family (in the middle), the deceased members (in the upper part), and vanquished enemies (in the lower part). In the center are Tiberius and his mother Livia facing each other. Starting from them and radiating outwards, the imperial family is arranged as on a genealogical tree. Names and dates are still arguable, but there is no doubt that it is a glorification of the *gens Augusta*. Less intricate onyx cameos such as the Gemma Augustea (depicting the deification of Augustus) and the Blacas Onyx Cameo (featuring Tiberius' military victories and Augustus as Jupiter) also celebrate the Julio-Claudian spirit, and the legitimacy and authority of the imperial family.

Unlike Tiberius, his successors Caligula, Claudius, and Nero belonged directly to the Julian side of the dynasty. They based their legitimacy on their relationship – grandson, son, and great-grandson – to Antonia minor, the younger daughter of Antony and Augustus' sister, Octavia. All three successors clearly affirmed their dynastic policy. Caligula laid the ashes of his mother and brother in Augustus' mausoleum, bestowed the title of *Augusta* on his grandmother Antonia, included his three sisters in his rule, and honored his uncle Claudius by appointing him as his colleague in the consulship. Claudius married his cousin Messalina, and then his niece Agrippina, in order to monopolize the bloodline of Augustus. The study of imperial coinage is particularly instructive in matters of dynastic ideology. At the start of Nero's reign Agrippina appeared on coinage with the new title *Augusta mater Augusti*, "Augusta mother of Augustus" (she had been *Augusta* since 50). Nero's first wife, Octavia, was presented only as the wife of *Augustus* Nero, while his second, Poppaea, was officially proclaimed *Augusta* in her own right. Ingeniously exploited by Augustus, public media such as coinage, art, and architecture continued to implant the dynastic idea in the collective consciousness under the Julio-Claudians.

Relations with the Senate

Augustus had ensured that the Senate should preserve a semblance of liberty and power while in fact it was he who possessed the ultimate power to make decisions. His successors all pursued this line of collaboration with the Senate, at least initially. As the Julio-Claudians established their hereditary dynasty and entrenched the imperial idea, the monarchical model became more obvious, causing strain in their relationship with the Senate.

Tiberius received his powers from the Senate and he waited until it confirmed them and awarded him *auctoritas*. His respect for what was in fact a simple formality (he had already obtained the army's oath) revealed his desire to see the Senate participate in government. Yet the power imbalance between Senate and emperor explicably caused confusion among the senators, who could not be certain about the degree of autonomy and participation that Tiberius desired from them. Several of his gestures to the Senate seemed encouraging. He declined the titles of *Imperator* and *Pater Patriae* that the Senate proposed for him, keeping only that of *Augustus*. He showed courtesy to the senators both individually and as a body. They were consulted on numerous points (taxes; buildings; the distribution, levies, and disbanding of troops). And he occasionally allowed them decisions that went against his own views: "A good and helpful ruler," he said to the senators, "should be at the service of the Senate and all citizens" (Suetonius, *Tiberius* 29). In three fields (legislative, electoral, and judicial), he even strengthened the prerogatives of the Senate. It voted laws in the form of senatorial decrees, one of which laid down for the first time rules concerning private law; it gained the right to elect magistrates, a right hitherto reserved for the people; and it developed its role as a high court of justice, where the emperor intervened only in order to mitigate punishments.

This cooperation ceased around the thirties. Either Tiberius, disappointed by the hesitant behavior of the senators, gave up listening to their opinions, or, in the face of the emperor's growing suspicions, the Senate (through weakness or fear) gave itself over to treason trials, decimating itself in the process. According to Tacitus (*Annals* 3.65), every time he left the Senate the exasperated Tiberius used to cry out in Greek "men ready for slavery!"

A similar development is traced by our sources in the relations between Caligula and the Senate: good to start with, and then quickly deteriorating. By having admitted a few Italian equestrians into the Senate, Caligula did not upset its composition at this time. He has been considered the real creator of the *ordo senatorius* in its full sense, inasmuch as in 38 he had instituted the practice of granting the laticlave (the wearing of which had been confined by Augustus to senators and their descendants) to selected equestrians or notables of Italian or provincial towns, provided they met the property qualification and citizenship conditions. He therefore made it necessary to distinguish the senatorial order (2,000 or 3,000 individuals), to which the laticlave was the symbol of belonging, from the senatorial class itself (comprising the senators and their descendants). This grant of the laticlave, which came to be awarded at any time during an emperor's reign, effectively enabled the man who had it to join the senatorial order, usually before the age of 25. More importantly, if the man awarded this honor severed all links with the equestrian order he previously belonged to, the laticlave provided him with access to the quaestorship, that is, access to the Senate itself. One important consequence of Caligula's policy was that the careers of young members of the senatorial order and those of young equestrians would in the future be quite distinct.

It appears that relations between Caligula and the Senate were strained following his authoritarian replacement of the two consuls on September 2, 39. Beginning at this time, it is possible to speak of Caligula's open attempt at imperial absolutism. On the other hand, the idea of a precisely dated turn for the worse is found in the accounts of the reigns of nearly all the emperors denigrated in historical and biographical narratives.

The policy of Claudius toward the Senate was both conciliatory and authoritarian. There was an undeniable return to Augustan practices, with the recruitment of 42 CE. This involved the resignation of those senators who no longer reached the required property qualification, and their replacement by equestrians. The office of the censorship was revived, which Claudius himself held for 18 months in 47–48. Claudius' advisory speech on the admission of Gallic nobles into the Senate (surviving, as we saw, in Tacitus' *Annals* and the Lyons Tablet) also speaks to his desire to develop a respectful working relationship with this body and to encourage senatorial initiative.

Conversely, it is also clear that Claudius wanted to have a degree of direct control over the Senate. This more authoritarian side to his policy was probably due to practical and administrative concerns rather than the whims of his freedmen, as suggested by hostile narratives. He removed the Senate's right to grant leave to individual members, appropriating it for himself, and he appointed the quaestors in charge of the Senate's treasury (*aerarium Saturni*). But mainly, he used his censorial authority, by which the senatorial roll (*album sanatorium*) was produced, to modify the composition of the Senate. This method of recruitment (*adlectio*) involved the direct appointment of a "new man" to the Senate by classifying him in the *album* above the entry magistracy, from which he was exempted. Under Claudius, we know of three *adlecti* among the tribunes of the *plebs*. Similarly, the emperor strictly separated the obligations of future senators and those of equestrians by setting out precisely the military duties that a young equestrian had to fulfill: command of a cohort, command of an *ala*, legionary tribunate.

Nero's relations with the Senate follow the same pattern of collaboration at the start of the reign, mistrust and discord later on. Until 62, the emperor showed favor to the senators, financially helping them to hold games or to keep their property qualification. For its part, the Senate intervened in institutional and social matters, and concerned itself with maintaining order in Italy (as in the case of a brawl between Pompeians and Nucerians in the amphitheater of Pompeii, in 59 CE). The Senate's refusal in 58 to accept the fiscal reform proposed by the emperor signaled the start of a change in attitude. In 62, the first treason trial took place, when the praetor Antistius Sosianus was prosecuted for writing satirical poems about Nero and reading them in the Senate. His defense from the death penalty by the eminent senator and Stoic philosopher Thrasea Paetus aroused

Nero's discontent, marking his growing conflict with the Senate. From then on the authority of the *patres* was weakened as Nero eliminated or disregarded the great senatorial dynasties. His developing unease about his authority is indicated by his use of the title *Imperator*. Like his predecessors, Nero had refused it as a title at the start of his reign. In 66, however, *Imperator* appeared in inscriptions. It made Nero the equal of Augustus.

Foreign policy

Narrating the recommendations on matters of foreign policy made by Augustus in his legacy to Tiberius, Cassius Dio (56.33) says that Augustus was of the opinion that they should be content with the present boundaries of the Empire and not in any way seek to extend them; for if they did, he claimed, it would be difficult to keep what was gained, and there would be a risk of losing what they already possessed. The few defeats that Rome had experienced in his time, especially Varus' disaster in Teutoburg, had demonstrated that there were limits to the enterprise of expansion. This particular disaster weighed heavily with Augustus, who often lamented Varus' loss of three entire legions (Suetonius, *Augustus* 23). Augustus' conservative foreign policy was tripartite: a consolidating rather than expansive military presence at the frontiers, active diplomacy, and the system of client kingdoms. Those three lines were followed in different degrees by the Julio-Claudians. The most faithful was Tiberius: expeditions to intimidate the Germani but not to conquer, clever diplomacy in the East, and a solid network of client states along the Danube. Caligula may have had plans for a great expansionist policy in the West, but the brevity of his reign and the meager evidence make it hard to tell with any certainty. Claudius and Nero partly distanced themselves from the Augustan warning. A sizeable departure on Claudius' part was the conquest of Britain. Nero was forced by circumstances to intervene in the East, envisaging at first the pursuit there of an active expansion before settling for what could be called "semi-expansionism." In the West, apart from his annexation of client kingdoms (one of the causes of Boudicca's rebellion), what he did accorded with Augustus' policy.

Opposition to the imperial regime

Enduring opposition, from the reign of Augustus to that of Nero, came from within two groups: the provincials and the aristocracy of Rome. This conflict took a different form depending on factors such as the geographical proximity to the capital or the social status of the dissenters.

The lower classes of Rome, whose everyday lives had been affected little by the Principate (and, in many cases, had been improved), were less prone to rebel, unless provoked by a specific incident. Survival anxiety was obviously a major motivation: the unreliable grain supply from overseas often became the cause of popular discontent. Suetonius (*Nero* 45) reports that, in 68, at a time of famine

Plate 9.4 Cavalry-man's tombstone from Gloucester, first century CE. It reads: "Rufus Sita, cavalry-man of the 6th Thracian cohort, lived 40 years, served 22. Erected by his testamentary heirs …" © Gloucester City Museum and Art Gallery

in Rome, a ship arrived from Alexandria bearing sand for use in wrestling matches. This incident added fuel to the growing resentment against Nero, and encouraged hopeful conversations about Vindex.

The fates of various imperial family members were another motivation for popular reactions in the capital. The death of Germanicus, for example, occasioned a major outpouring of national mourning, from Brundisium, where the Elder Agrippina landed with his ashes, to Rome itself. As we have seen, public spaces such as the circus or the theater were important platforms for expressions of popular acclaim or protest. Suetonius' biographies are filled with such "spectacular" anecdotes, describing the emperor's interaction with his people in the context of a public spectacle. Once, when Augustus was sitting at the theater, an actor spoke the phrase "O good and just master!" The line aroused the crowd's enthusiasm, but Augustus immediately discouraged their effusive flattery (*Augustus* 53). Conversely, under Nero, an actor accompanied the words "death guides your steps" with a telling gesture toward the senatorial seats (*Nero* 39), a message that was certainly not lost on his audience. Such incidents indicate the political importance of public spaces and occasions in Rome, as well as how attuned the Roman public was to the contemporary resonance of drama and farce.

The provincials In the Empire as a whole during this period, revolts and risings were ultimately few and local. These rebellions never posed a serious threat to Rome itself, but only to the local authorities. Moreover, since the situations were different, the seriousness of the disturbances and the Roman intervention varied considerably. Nevertheless, the nature of this opposition remained the same. What was disputed was not the imperial system itself but rather the Roman presence, which was constantly and forcefully underscored by the burden of taxation, the often idealized memories of an independent, pre-Roman period, and the difficulties of adapting to a bureaucratic administration (taxes, censuses, land surveys, etc.).

The aristocracy Opposition was keenest among the great senatorial families. The Empire had after all been built against them. It was thus within the bosom of the aristocracy that plots and conspiracies were hatched, above all if those families were close to the government. Scions of the Junii Silani, the Silii, the Scribonii Libones, the Calpurnii Pisones, and the Annii were the ones to be found from reign to reign in the opposition lists until the extinction of the family by assassination or suicide. An enduring influence on this opposition was the philosophical school of Stoicism. Curiously, it found in this not a political argument

Chronology 9.3	**Revolts and internal risings under the Julio-Claudians**	
17–24	Tacfarinas	Africa
21	Risings	Thrace
	Florus and Sacrovir	Gauls
25	Risings	Thrace
36	Revolt of the Cities	Cappadocia
39–40	Disturbances	Judaea
42	Insurrection	Mauretania
52	Disturbances	Judaea
61	Boudicca's revolt	Britain
66	General rising	Judaea
68	Vindex's revolt	Gauls

(since Stoicism would rather have been favorable to the monarchy) but a moral code. Nevertheless, the doctrine produced its own lineage of opponents: Caecina Paetus and Arria in 42; their daughter Arria and her husband Thrasea Paetus under Nero; then *their* daughter and her husband Helvidius Priscus under Vespasian. Throughout this period, the Roman aristocracy produced a constant stream of opponents, the nature of whose opposition varied little from reign to reign. There was no real will for change; the imperial system as such was not in question, and discontent focused not on institutional problems but on specific people, with opponents blaming the emperor, his vices, his entourage, his colleagues, and his freedmen.

Innovations and shifts

Strengthening the role of the military

On the death of Augustus, Tiberius knew that the true source of imperial power rested with the army, and its constitutional mantle with the Senate. He gave orders to the praetorian cohorts and wrote to the provincial armies "as if he already held the Principate," notes Tacitus, adding: "He never showed any hesitation except when it was his turn to speak in the Senate" (*Annals* 1.7). During his reign Sejanus reinforced the praetorian cohorts, by adding to them the urban cohorts, and then installed them in the "camp of the praetorians" (*castra praetoria*), just north-east of Rome. Sejanus was also the first praetorian prefect who gained prestige and political influence with the emperor. His successor, Sutorius Macro, expanded the responsibilities and power of the office, promoting Caligula's career with Tiberius and his accession after his death. But the support of the praetorian guard was not always guaranteed.

In January 41 the tribunes and centurions of the praetorian cohorts rebelled, slaughtering Caligula and hailing Claudius as emperor. He was taken to the camp of the praetorians, an act which became a ritual at the start of each reign. Together with the imperial palace on the Palatine and the Curia, the Castra was henceforth one of the supremely important spaces in Roman political life. Again, it was a praetorian cohort that acknowledged Nero after Claudius' death and carried him in a litter to the camp, where, as Claudius had, he granted a reward to each praetorian (*donativum*). And it was the rising of the armies of the provinces, followed by the treason of the praetorian prefect Nymphidius Sabinus, that brought about Nero's flight and suicide. In subsequent decades, praetorian prefects, the praetorian guard, and even the provincial armies (after Nero) would play increasingly important roles in imperial succession. The entry of the army onto the political scene as a separate player and even a "king-maker" was one of the most important new elements in the transformations of the first century.

Overall, however, the army remained loyal to the Julio-Claudian house. The only emperor among them to have lost its respect was Nero. A tribune of a praetorian cohort, implicated in Piso's conspiracy, revealed the reasons why before he was put to death. When Nero asked him why he had forgotten his military oath, he replied "I hated you! No soldier could have been more loyal to you as long as you deserved to be liked. I began to hate you when you proved to be the murderer of your mother and your wife and became a charioteer, a ham actor and an arsonist" (Tacitus, *Annals* 15.67).

Extension of the imperial cult

The imperial cult under Augustus involved the worship of the deified Caesar and of the living Augustus, not directly, but through his *genius* or *numen*. These two aspects of the cult continued to thrive under the Julio-Claudians and they were strengthened by the apotheosis of Augustus (decreed by the Senate), the innovations of Caligula and Nero, and the development of a dynastic awareness. Imperial cult was culturally extended and further entrenched in society, becoming in effect a new religion, more official and structured than before.

The dead emperors After Augustus, Claudius alone among the Julio-Claudians attained the rank of god. Nevertheless, the honors that Tiberius awarded the Divine Augustus served as a model for his successors. These honors were as follows:

- The ritual of apotheosis, begun for Augustus, reached its peak in the second half of the second century but all along kept the same sequence of events. First, the body (later, a wax effigy) was placed on a high pyre erected on the Campus Martius. Then, after the priests had consecrated the site, the various bodies of society walked in procession around it, and an eagle was released from the pyre, supposedly bearing away the emperor's soul. After the cremation, the ashes were collected (by Livia in the case of Augustus) to be placed in the tomb (in later times, the body itself was placed there). The same person could be honored as both a divinity and a dead human being, a concept that delighted a few skeptical minds in Rome. The emperor Vespasian is supposed to have quipped on his deathbed "alas, I think I am becoming a god" (Suetonius, *Vespasian* 23).
- A temple to the Divine Augustus was begun in the Forum, south of the Basilica Julia (it was inaugurated in 37, under Caligula), and priests were pledged to him: a *flamen augustalis* (the first was Germanicus) and a college of *sodales augustales* recruited from members of the imperial family and the greatest Roman families (this college is not to be confused with the **seviri augustales**, who were already, under Augustus, in charge of the imperial cult in the towns of Italy). These were the elements of an official state cult and were features of virtually every Roman deification.
- Similarly, a domestic cult of Augustus grew up. It was born within the imperial family, with Livia as its priestess, and was then taken up by the great families of Rome.

seviri augustales (priests of Augustus): Associations of six people, generally freedmen, formed to celebrate imperial worship at municipal level. See **flamines**.

On the death of each important member of the imperial family (except for Livia), an upsurge of the imperial cult occurred: for instance, on the death of Germanicus in 19, and on the death of Caligula's sister Drusilla, deified in 38.

The cult of living emperors The temperament, personal beliefs, and policy of each emperor tailored the form of the honors rendered to him, and influenced the form of those that he accepted.

Tiberius, with a few exceptions in the East (for example, at Claros in Asia), always refused the divine honors offered to him. Two testimonies are particularly eloquent regarding his attitude. A letter from Tiberius to the ephors of Gythium in the Peloponnese (preserved in two stone inscriptions found there) relates his response to their request to bestow divine honors on Augustus, Livia, and himself. Tiberius gave his consent for Augustus (who had died recently – the inscriptions date between 14 and 19 CE), reserved his reply for Livia, and refused for himself. Similarly, in a speech delivered to the Senate in 25, in response to a petition from the provincials of Baetica who wished to erect a temple in his honor, he declared that he was a mortal and above all desired temples and statues in the hearts of men (Tacitus, *Annals* 4.38). However, starting from his denunciation of Sejanus, an ideological development formed promoting the notion of the emperor's divine assistance against harm. On coins and in official inscriptions, a deified Providentia was associated with Tiberius. As a personified concept, Providentia expressed the strength of imperial power protected by the gods. By suppressing Sejanus and his supporters, Tiberius claimed that the divine and imperial orders were in accord.

The short reign of Caligula poses a difficult problem. For some, he was the first emperor to want to impose a theological and theocratic conception of government. He is said to have appeared dressed as Bacchus, Apollo, and even Jupiter. Moreover, in 40, he ordered a statue of himself in the guise of Jupiter to be installed in the Temple at Jerusalem. To those who do not dispute these facts but explain them as imperial eccentricities or as imitation of Egyptian models, it seems that Caligula would not have tried to institute an eastern-style despotism and impose his worship on the Romans during his lifetime. Perhaps Caligula's personal flamboyance and practices fed the libels and slanderous anecdotes that are so common in imperial biographies.

Claudius, infatuated with religious sciences (he reorganized the *haruspices* and the worship of Cybele, and persecuted the Druids), shared the attitude of Tiberius but also resumed the provincial and western religious policy of Augustus. Following the conquest of Britain in 43, a temple and altar in front of it were dedicated to Claudius in the captured royal capital, Camulodunum (Colchester). In fact, beginning with Claudius, Roman Britain has produced a wealth of inscriptional evidence that illuminates cultic practices among the legionaries and auxiliary units.

Nero's religious policies must be contextualized by his relentlessly denigrated portrait in our sources. On the one hand, he seemed indifferent to traditional Roman religion; on the other, he consulted astrologers, resorted to magical practices, and turned to eastern cults. He also made use of the opportunities of the imperial cult, gathering and encouraging divine associations to himself. Although inscriptions ascribe to him the prerogatives of a Hercules, a Mars, a Jupiter, he was primarily, and from the start of his reign, associated with Apollo. His choice makes much sense considering Augustus' association with Apollo, as well as Nero's own predilection for lyre-playing and singing. Historians are divided on whether Nero's cultic excesses marked a new and individualized form of imperial worship. Was he aiming to establish some sort of absolute monarchy underpinned by a sun-god theology? The colossal statue of Nero as Helios, the construction of the park of the Domus Aurea, the dissemination of mythology relating to his birth, the issues of coins on which he wears a radiant crown, symbol of the Sun, and the numerous inscriptions which make him out to be a new Apollo seem to suggest so. His emulation of eastern (Greek, Egyptian) models and practices certainly inspired a lot of his extravagant practices. On the other hand, perhaps these were personal whims rather than an organized agenda to institutionalize eastern models of imperial worship in the West.

For the sake of convenience we have made a distinction between the cults of the dead and living emperors, which were often complementary. Veneration for the dead emperors strengthened the authority of the living ones as potentially "deifiable." The association of the dead and the living in the imperial family appears in visual media such as the Great Cameo of France, in a sanctuary at the gates of Rome, with the first appearance, under Tiberius, of the concept of the divine house (*domus divina*) embracing the dead and the living in the same community, and in the sumptuous Sebasteion of Aphrodisias in Caria.

A "spiritual revolution"?

The imperial cult and the Christian faith were born at much the same time, as part of the "spiritual revolution" in the Mediterranean world. The great Italian historian Santo Mazzarino (1916–1987) parallels what he calls rhetorically the "gospel of Augustus" to that of Jesus in order to underline the soteriological expectations that pervaded the ancient world in the early first century CE. There was indeed some incipient tension between Christianity and the imperial cult, but not a direct confrontation at this time.

Jesus Near the end of Tiberius' reign a man named Jesus was put to death by crucifixion in Jerusalem. Those whom he had drawn to him, the disciples, members of the Jewish community, were disoriented after his death. The prefect of the province of Judaea, Pontius Pilate, whose existence is attested by an inscription, very probably submitted a report on the matter to the emperor, but it appears that no echo of this local news reached wider circles in Rome.

The case of the Jews The Jews were the only people in the Empire whose beliefs were completely alien to the ideology of the imperial cult. To take part in an act

(a)

(b)

Plate 9.5 Imperial reliefs from the Sebasteion of Aphrodisias: **(a)** Claudius with Agrippina and a personification of the Roman Senate or people, and **(b)** Agrippina crowning Nero. 20–60 CE. Photos: Courtesy of New York University Excavations at Aphrodisias

of worship purely as part of the imperial cult (or any other pagan cult) was blasphemy for a Jew. Death was preferable. This exclusive faith was not confined to Palestine; the Jews of the diaspora, scattered throughout the Mediterranean basin, also retained the faith of their ancestors. To serve the singular needs of this self-contained community, whose monotheism, dietary prohibitions, and other rites and customs (such as circumcision) also tended to single them out from the other inhabitants of the Empire, a series of privileges had been obtained from the Roman authorities, mainly in the religious domain. Under the Empire, the council of the Sanhedrin (their supreme court of justice, presided over by the high priest, vested with authority to deal with all cases coming under Mosaic law) and their religious organization were secure. For the purposes of the imperial cult, they were required to offer a daily sacrifice to their God for the emperor (a compromise that Caligula challenged). But even though for Rome the Jewish religion was permitted and legally recognized, a Jew, even if a Roman citizen, had great difficulty in obtaining a magistrate's office or holding an imperial post. This unusual status within the Empire was compounded by a special politico-religious situation which divided the Jewish people into several sects or parties

Box 9.1 Four great Jewish sects

Parties/sects	Social situation	Religious nature	Attitude to Rome
Sadducees	Great priestly families	Bound to the letter of the Torah; importance of priests and Temple	Fairly definite collaboration; divided in 66/67, some for revolt, others for conciliation
Pharisees	Less homogeneous recruitment: lower classes and comfortably off	Written and oral tradition; study of Scriptures; importance of rabbis and schools	Reserve; cautious participation but dissociated themselves from opponents
Essenes	Known from the Dead Sea scrolls; lived in communities far from Jerusalem	Eschatological glorification that must end in the victory of Good over Evil	Hostility; participation in revolt of 66
Zealots	Of the people	Same doctrine as Pharisees, but awaited a Messiah to liberate them from Roman domination	Active hostility; preached rebellion in 66

according to the positions they adopted with regard to the Law, the Temple, and the priesthood. Flavius Josephus defines four great Jewish sects, which are schematized as shown in box 9.1.

On the fringes of official Judaism there was an intense religious ferment. Numerous prophetic and popular movements cultivated a constant disorder, increasingly marked by its fundamentally anti-Roman nature.

Jesus and his disciples Jesus seems to have rejected these divisions, and to have kept aloof from both the Zealots and the Sadducees. The Sadducees attempted to have him condemned by the Roman governor by making the Sanhedrin treat him as an agitator, imparting an immediate political dimension to his messianic claims. Hence the trial conducted by the Roman authorities and the *titulus* "King of the Jews" affixed to the cross. For the Romans, the founder of the new religion thus appeared as a rebel, a troublemaker, in short a "zealot." Jesus had continually stated that his kingdom was not of this world, and that those things that were Caesar's should be rendered unto Caesar (in other words, that taxes should be paid). However, in its very message of political and civic compliance, Christianity argued for a social aloofness that was at odds with Roman society, and was thus suspect or disturbing in Roman eyes.

Jews and Christians The great innovation of the early Christian communities was to have extended their proselytizing to the Jews of the diaspora, and then to the pagans. The internal conflicts that arose over the accommodations involved in this converting of the pagan world may be simplified as the conflict between the Judeo-Christian Peter and the apostle of the Gentiles, Paul. The victory of the Pauline tendency meant that the Christian communities gradually cut themselves off from the Jewish colonies of the diaspora, the largest of which was in Rome (30,000–50,000 members), while in Jerusalem they dissociated themselves from the Jews at the time of the great Jewish revolt (66–70 CE). But when they broke their links with Judaism, the Christians were no longer covered by the official privileges conferred by Rome on the Jewish people. Even though in its monotheism and rejection of any concession to the imperial cult it was the direct heir of Judaism, the new Christian religion, unlike Judaism, was ardently preached and aimed at universalism. Once it severed its ties with the Jewish state and people, it lost that protection and instead became illegal and illicit.

Christianity and the Roman state   Following Jesus' precept "Give onto Caesar what is Caesar's," Christians did not challenge directly the Roman state: a Christian had to obey the emperor and his officials, respect the existing social order, including the position within it of Christian slaves, and trust in imperial justice (as did Paul, who as a Roman citizen appealed to the imperial tribunal). This compliance was not part of a Christian "strategy," but of profound belief. It was believed that the kingdom of God was yet to come, and would be signaled by the return of Jesus and the resurrection of the dead. This expectation of the Second Coming was a passionate experience, and the event was regarded as imminent. Consequently, the temporal world took second place. According to Paul, the Christian city lay in the heavens. Such an affirmation was perceived as extreme political dissent in the ancient world, where the bond and loyalty of a citizen to his state was paramount. However, early in the first century CE, the Roman state took little interest in the Christians. They were initially confused with the Jews, as in the first allusion to Christianity we have in a non-Christian document. Suetonius (*Claudius* 25) notes "Claudius expelled from Rome the Jews who were constantly agitating under the influence of *Chrestus*." Much debated, Suetonius' statement seems to refer to an agitation that resulted from Christian preaching among the Jewish colony in Rome in 49 or 50. Less than two decades later, a clear distinction between Jews and Christians is evident. Again Suetonius (*Nero* 16) relates that, after the great fire of Rome in 64, "Christians were put to the torture, a kind of people addicted to a new and harmful superstition." Tacitus, who devotes an extensive narrative to the fire of Rome, corroborates Suetonius' bias, suggesting that the reason the Christians became easy scapegoats for the fire was because the public loathed them (*Annals* 15.44). There was no law to punish adherence to the Christian faith, and it would be anachronistic to talk about a persecution, in the strict sense, under Nero. But his brutally inventive punishments of Christians initiated a long period of insecurity for Jesus' followers.

9.3 | Development of the Administration

Augustus had organized an efficient administrative apparatus, centered on Rome and adapted to the scale of the Roman world. Its ability to administer the vast regions under Roman control depended on its flexibility, adaptability, and capacity for transmitting orders and gathering knowledge of the resources of the Empire. That it was capable of keeping the emperor supplied with overall information can be seen from an account of the entire Empire that Augustus left on his death (Suetonius, *Augustus* 101). This document, providing a complete list of military resources and dispositions, diplomatic and administrative obligations, and indicating as well the treasury's reserves and state revenues, was read in the Senate immediately after Augustus' funeral, at Tiberius' instigation. Augustus' administrative apparatus was developed under the Julio-Claudians, with a concomitant increase in the power of the state. The growth of the imperial departments could be seen in the urban geography of Rome, where many of the state officials were to be found (yet their number was still small by modern standards). It was especially visible in the extension of the palace area on the Palatine. From the residence of Augustus and his family and staff, confined to the north-west quarter, it expanded through successive stages to occupy the entire hill, which became a sort of imperial city (see next chapter, figure 10.1).

Central administration

The changes that transformed the administrative apparatus left by Augustus into a true central administration were essentially the work of Tiberius and, chiefly, Claudius.

Tiberius Under Tiberius, the emperor's council as it had functioned under Augustus disappeared, and was replaced by a circle of "companions" or "attendants" (*comites*) more informal than the old senatorial *consilium* but apparently more efficient. Moreover, Tiberius filled in some of the outlines of the central administration sketched by Augustus, keeping watch over the way the various services worked, and making improvements by placing men of consular rank at the head of some of them and by increasing the number of technical posts.

Claudius Claudius was the true organizer of the central administration. He entrusted various departments to his freedmen and elevated them with various honors. This was considered by some as evidence of his meekness (Suetonius, *Claudius* 28). Thanks to his freedmen, however, administrative departments became more like modern state ministries, rendering the emperor independent of the Senate and the equestrians. We know of four freedmen who held great influence with Claudius and were in charge of different departments.

1   Narcissus became the private secretary in charge of imperial correspondence (*ab epistulis*).

2   Pallas became secretary of finances (*a rationibus*), which were divided between several departments but which Claudius began to dominate by the creation of a central fund, the *fiscus Caesaris*. Surpluses from provincial revenues were channeled into it. Moreover, the free distributions of grain, formerly funded by the Senate's finances, were henceforth the responsibility of this *fiscus Caesaris*.

3   Callistus was in charge of the bureau *a libellis*, receiving and replying to requests and petitions addressed to the emperor. In fact, he was a sort of minister of justice.

4   Polybius was responsible for the bureau *a studiis*, which carried out various inquiries and compiled records and files.

These departmental heads were helped by assistants, the *adiutores* (slaves or freedmen), aided by numerous other employees (*scrinarii*).

This careful and efficient administrative organization runs contrary to what Tacitus, Suetonius, and Cassius Dio variously claim: that Claudius had little initiative of his own and that he was essentially the plaything of his freedmen. The status, wealth, and influence of Claudius' freedmen continued to shock senatorial authors decades later. Tacitus, narrating the events surrounding Messalina's death, observes pithily on the decisive influence of Narcissus that "everything was obeying the freedman" (*Annals* 11.35). Similarly, Pliny the Younger vents his irritation to a friend, in a long letter describing the extraordinary honors and wealth granted to Pallas by the Senate (*Letters* 8.6).

Provincial administration

Under the Julio-Claudians, there were few fundamental changes to the Augustan organization of the provinces; the changes were mainly alterations and rearrangements due to annexations or conquests. (With one exception, Lycia–Pamphylia, the new provinces increased the domain of the imperial provinces.) An improvement in provincial administration was noticeable. Governors were generally controlled by provincial assemblies, such as the assembly of the three Gauls. And the number of known procurators' posts doubled: 23 under Augustus, 25 under Tiberius, 27 under Caligula, 38 under Claudius, and 46 under Nero. Here again, Tiberius and Claudius instigated important developments.

Tiberius attempted to create a more just administration. During his reign, several governors were sentenced for misappropriation of public funds and abuse of power. He was aware of the cost of crushing provinces under the burden of heavy taxes: "A good shepherd," he said, "shears his sheep; he does not flay them" (Suetonius, *Tiberius* 32). He also kept the governors he valued in their posts for long periods: C. Poppaeus Sabinus stayed as governor of Moesia for 24 years. Tiberius' concern for provincials was further revealed by the financial aid he gave at times of disaster and by his reforms of customs districts.

As we saw, Claudius (himself born in Lyons) paid attention to the interests of the provinces. In the context of his general disparagement, he was satirized for "deciding to see every Greek, Spaniard, Gaul, and Briton in a toga" (Seneca, *Apolocynthosis* 3). His provincial policy had four principal aspects:

1 Colonies were founded and *municipia* created on a regular basis and a vast scale, linking his policy to those of Caesar and Augustus. Favored regions were Britain, Germania, Mauretania, Pannonia, Dalmatia, Thrace, Cappadocia, and Syria.
2 There was a generous policy of naturalization, the extent of which is shown in several documents: full rights for the Alpine peoples, and for the provincial elites; a request for the right to enter the Senate for notables of the three Gauls who already had full Roman citizenship; individual grants of citizenship for easterners; the naturalization of auxiliaries after they had served out their term. Citizenship, however, was not extended indiscriminately: it was removed from provincials who did not know Latin, and those who were found to have wrongfully assumed full rights were executed.
3 The powers of imperial procurators, in both senatorial and imperial provinces, were reinforced.
4 There was a policy of major public works (roads, aqueducts).

The Julio-Claudians' experiments with the Augustan system produced satisfactory results in every field. It was a period rich in innovations, trials, errors, and corrections; and one that brought decisive changes on the administrative level. It witnessed the apogee of Italy in relation to the provinces and contained the seeds of future developments: the strength of the army, the conflict with Christianity, and the expansion of the provinces. At its end the vexed question of the succession emerged afresh. But the Republic had been laid to rest. It survived as an idealized and almost legendary past, but no one challenged the necessity and efficiency of the Empire. Still, soon after Nero's death, the Civil Wars of the late Republic began to haunt the Romans as precedents of contemporary events. The year 69 CE, often referred to as the "year of the four emperors," was in many ways a compressed replay of the last century of the Republic.

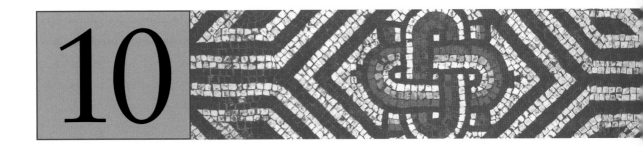

10

THE FLAVIANS

Consolidating the Imperial Order: 68–96 CE

The death of Nero opened a period of crisis lasting almost two years. It was serious not only because of its geographical extent, affecting Rome, Italy, Gaul, the Germanies, Spain, Africa, Syria, Judaea, and Egypt, but also because of what was at stake, because of the forces engaged, and because of its possible consequences. The civil war that followed among four imperial pretenders laid bare the contradictions and ambiguities of the system set up by Augustus. In many respects it closely resembled the republican Civil Wars, whose memory was still strong in people's minds, more than any other episode in the history of the Empire. Certainly, the field of battle was on an Empire-wide scale, but the conflict was motivated by ambitions similar to those that had driven Marius, Sulla, Caesar, Pompey, Octavian, and Antony. The political power, and potential threat, of legions became clear at this time. As Tacitus (*Histories* 1.4) observes, "the secret of the Empire was laid bare: an emperor could be created elsewhere than in Rome." The governors and legions who participated in this civil war were Roman citizens, almost all Italian, while the provincials waited for the outcome. One of the results of this war was that it obliterated the idea of the Principate ruled by a long-established Roman family (such as the Julii or the Claudii). The family which re-established peace and a dynasty, as Augustus had done, was that of the Flavii, who belonged to the Italian municipal gentry. The provincials remained on the outside for the time being, but it was clear that the Romans' exclusive right to the throne had been broken.

In order to get a better grasp of the possible interpretations of this complex crisis, we first need to turn to the four imperial contenders and the events surrounding their conflicts throughout 69.

10.1 | Events and Contenders

Galba: June 68–January 69 CE

Born in 3 BCE, the scion of an old patrician family, Sulpicius Galba had been held in esteem by all the emperors and had had the classic and in his case brilliant career of a loyal and highly regarded senator. In 68, having been proconsul of Africa under Claudius, he was the governor of Tarraconensis, an elderly, rigid, and stern figure – the antithesis of Nero. Informed that Nero wanted to have him assassinated and having been invited by Vindex, the governor of Gallia Lugdunensis, to be the new emperor, he too rebelled. After the death of Vindex, he headed the revolt against Nero, while remaining in Spain. There he received news of the death of Nero and his own acclamation as emperor by the praetorians and the Senate. In October he arrived in Rome, where he committed one political blunder after another. In order to restore the finances, he refused to give the promised *donativum* to the praetorians, allegedly claiming "I do not buy my soldiers, I choose them" (Tacitus, *Histories* 1.5). This noble sentiment was belied by the fact that he did grant benefits to his supporters among the Gauls. Moreover, Galba executed Nero's associates and massacred Nero's troops in Rome. He took action against those accused of treason, merely on the evidence of informers and without going through the Senate. He left matters to his own associates: Titus Vinius, commander of one legion in Spain under Galba, was chosen by him as his colleague in the consulship for 69. Cornelius Laco became head of the praetorian guard after the suicide of C. Ophonius Tigellinus, Nero's praetorian prefect. Icelus, Galba's freedman, had been elevated by him to equestrian status, an indulgence reminiscent of Claudius. Because of their influence on Galba, these three were mockingly called "the pedagogues" (Suetonius, *Galba* 14). They antagonized each other in striving for influence with Galba, a conflict that contributed greatly to his unfortunate decisions and eventual downfall.

In under six months Galba alienated almost all classes in Rome: the praetorians, the Senate, and the people. While he presented himself as the exact opposite of Nero, he fell foul of those who actually missed Nero's flamboyant popularity and indulgence. Galba showed the same tactlessness and short-sightedness in his treatment of the army. Whatever his motives were for recalling to Rome Verginius Rufus, the prominent legate of Upper Germania who had defeated Vindex, his recall caused great resentment among the German legions, who felt slighted that their commander was being held hostage in Rome. Galba made his position even more vulnerable by sending the only legion loyal to him to Pannonia. He thus had no one to help him when the legate of Lower Germania, Aulus Vitellius, was proclaimed emperor by his troops on January 2, 69. Galba responded to the crisis merely by adopting L. Calpurnius Piso and designating him as his successor on January 10. Tacitus relates a speech by the emperor in which he attempts to justify his setting of a precedent for adoption outside the imperial family

(*Histories* 1.15–16). There Tacitus creatively summarizes Galba's idealistic sentiments about the Republic, points out his willful ignorance of legionary power and praetorian *realpolitik*, and shows him as a victim of his obsolete political mores and his high standards on military ethics. Five days later the praetorians killed Galba and Piso and hailed M. Salvius Otho as emperor.

Otho: January 15–April 14, 69 CE

Born in 32 CE, a patrician but of a recently ennobled family, Otho had been appointed by Nero as governor of Lusitania in 58. His close relationship with Nero is not disputed, although its details are unclear. According to some traditions, he had kept Nero's lover Poppaea under his protection in a sham marriage, until Nero could get rid of Octavia and marry her instead. Alternative versions claim that Otho and Poppaea were actually married but Nero took Poppaea away and sent Otho to Lusitania to keep him away from her. Whatever the reasons behind his appointment, Otho stayed in Lusitania for 10 years, and was the first to support Galba, whom he hoped to succeed. Suetonius both disparages Otho as an indulgent playboy and states that he governed Lusitania with effectiveness and moderation.

On the evening of January 15, directly after Galba's assassination in the Forum, the Senate awarded Otho tribunician power, the name of Augustus, and all the imperial honors. The legions of the Danube, the East, Egypt, and Africa soon all gave him their backing. Otho astutely rallied the praetorians to his cause by a *donativum*, and the people by reinstating the memory of Nero. He undeniably enjoyed a measure of popularity.

In February, Vitellius' troops invaded Italy. Against his 60,000 men, Otho could range, immediately, only a much smaller force. He nevertheless set out without waiting for the legions from the Danube. He sought a decisive battle before he could fight on equal terms, leading to his army's defeat, in his absence, at Bedriacum in northern Italy, near Cremona, on April 14. Despairing after the battle, or hoping to end the civil war, he committed suicide on the same day. Consonant with Roman ideals about a dignified exit, Otho's suicide certainly puzzled his severest critics and even earned him some respect. As Plutarch says, "when he was gone, those who applauded his death were no fewer or less illustrious than those who blamed his life" (*Life of Otho* 18).

Vitellius: April 15–December 20, 69 CE

Born in 15, Vitellius had been consul, and proconsul of Africa, before being appointed by Galba to head the army of the Rhine. Having been hailed as *imperator* by his soldiers while Galba was in power, he happened to be in Lyons when his lieutenants informed him of the victory at Bedriacum and Otho's suicide. By April 19, the Senate had recognized him as emperor, and Vitellius promoted himself as the avenger of Galba. Without hurrying himself he took the road for

Rome, his troops looting and pillaging the countryside on their way. He sent the Othonian legions back to the provinces and dismissed the praetorians, whom he replaced with his own soldiers. And at the beginning of July he entered Rome with a force of 60,000 men. This tremendous influx of soldiers in the close urban quarters of Rome soon caused troubles, ranging from insanitary conditions to uncontrolled brawls with civilians. Vitellius settled in Nero's Golden House and did very little to control his troops and establish order.

Vespasian

Meanwhile in the East, the legate of Syria, Licinius Mucianus, and the prefect of Egypt, Tiberius Alexander, in charge of Rome's all-important grain supply, conferred with the commander of the troops in Judaea, T. Flavius Vespasianus (Vespasian) making their own bid for the throne. They ensured the support of the Danubian troops, those of client kingdoms, and that of the governors of other provinces, and in Alexandria on July 1, 69, the legions under the prefect of Egypt acclaimed Vespasian emperor. The legions of Egypt, Judaea, Syria, and the Danube rallied to him. Vespasian himself secured control of Rome's grain supplies at Alexandria, while his son Titus took his place in conducting the war against the Jews. In the autumn of 69, Flavian troops entered the north of Italy. And on October 24, Vitellius' forces were crushed at Cremona. Spain, Gaul, and Britain joined Vespasian.

In Rome, chaos ensued due to Vitellius' indecision and his failed negotiations with Flavius Sabinus, city prefect and Vespasian's brother. The praetorians and the people stood behind Vitellius and opposed any agreement with Vespasian or his supporters. On December 18, Rome became the stage for a battle waged between the two sides. The Capitol, to which Vespasian's supporters had withdrawn, was burnt and Sabinus was killed by the crowd. Domitian, Vespasian's other son, managed to escape disguised as a devotee of Isis (Suetonius, *Domitian* 1; Tacitus, *Histories* 3.74). On December 20, the armies of the Danube made an assault on the capital. Vitellius was killed, and the Senate acknowledged Vespasian as emperor. He wisely waited until peace had been re-established in Rome before leaving Alexandria. The task waiting for him in Rome was formidable: he had to rebuild and restore Augustus' accomplishments, both the material and the institutional ones.

10.2 | Interpretations

There are many possible interpretations for the crisis of the "long year 69." One perspective on the war is to interpret it as the expression of social antagonisms between upper and lower classes, both civilian and military. Vitellius can be seen as representing the lower classes and Vespasian standing for the upper ranks.

However, the reasons and motivations behind the war are multiple and overlapping. Certain factors are clear:

- It was not a constitutional crisis – no one dreamed of re-establishing the Republic. It stemmed from the failure of Nero to generate authority and respect, and his lack of an heir to claim the throne after his suicide.
- The memory of Nero continued to divide political life. Behind the differences in attitude to his memory it is possible to see an opposition between two conceptions of government: one popular and monarchic, with Otho and Vitellius; the other more senatorial, with Galba and, to a certain extent, Vespasian.
- The role of the praetorians was effaced by that of the armies from the provinces, among whom we must make the distinction between legionary and auxiliary troops. Furthermore, each great corps of the army had its own quite distinct character, traditions, and loyalties (e.g. the Rhine army was very different from the Syrian army), provoking rivalries between them. Even though organization, chain of command, and recruitment were practically the same for all the legions, a higher number of local soldiers dominated those stationed in the East.

At the end of 69, the Empire was still suffering the effects of the year-long civil war. In Tacitus' words, "the death of Vitellius meant the end of the war rather than the beginning of peace" (*Histories* 4.1). And, indeed, various difficulties suggested the possibility of a relapse into a state of chaos. The emperor was not in Rome. The Capitol, the most sacred sanctuary, lay in ruins. The war against the Jews was dragging on, the provinces were in a state of agitation, and nations were in rebellion or making agreements with the barbarians. Bands of riotous veterans and deserters from routed armies roamed the countryside, and even the victorious armies were disturbed and divided. Administrative problems accumulated because of unsettled and contradictory appointments, adding to the bitterness and resentment of the defeated. Therefore it is an extraordinary feat that, within two years, Vespasian had restored this situation and inaugurated the second imperial dynasty of Rome, that of the Flavians.

10.3 | The Flavian Dynasty

Vespasian: 69–79 CE

Vespasian was 60 years old when he became emperor. He came from a family of municipal notables (his father belonged to the equestrian order) in the Sabine region of Rieti, and had begun his career in the equestrian order. Having received the laticlave in 35 or 36, he was a praetor under Caligula, legionary legate during the conquest of Britain, in which he took part, consul in 51, and proconsul of Africa in 61 – a solid career without any dazzling or potentially threatening highlights. His elder brother, by contrast, pursued an impressive senatorial career, leading him as far as the prefectship of Rome. Vespasian had, however, given proof of his skill and energy, so that when a vigorous leader was being sought at the time of the Jewish revolt in 66, Nero appointed him. Biographical traditions seek to foreshadow retroactively Vespasian's imperial potential. His fate is marked by omens and prophecies long before 69 (Suetonius, *Vespasian* 5), and even by his performance of miracles while in Alexandria (Tacitus, *Histories* 4.81). Even the less bright sides of his background seem to conspire for his future success. Suetonius remarks that Nero chose Vespasian to lead the Jewish war because "there seemed little to fear from him, seeing the obscurity of his birth and name" (*Vespasian* 4).

With the modesty, realism, and caution characteristic of many Roman military men, Vespasian restored successfully various administrative and financial matters. Concerned with his succession, he groomed his older son Titus for the throne as early as 69.

Titus: 79–81 CE

Born in 39 CE, Titus was raised at court with Claudius' son Britannicus. His career brought him military postings in Germania, Britain, and then Judaea at

Genealogy 10.1   The Flavians

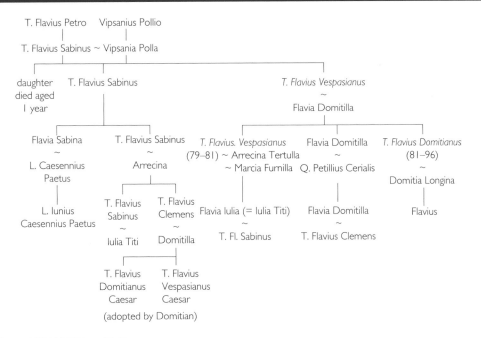

From G. Townend, *JRS*, LI (1961), pp. 54–62

his father's side. During 69, he acted as an intermediary between Vespasian and the associates of his uprising, including the Jewish princess Berenice, with whom he had a liaison. When his father went to Alexandria, he assumed leadership of the troops that remained in Judaea and finished the war with the sack of Jerusalem. His intention of succeeding his father was both expected and welcome. In fact the collective support of Vespasian was partly due to the fact that his two sons could ensure the succession without his resorting to adoption outside his family. Given the outbreak of civil war after Nero's death, and Galba's unpopular adoption of Piso, the promise of a seamless transition of imperial power must have been a powerful incentive for soldiers and civilians in favor of Vespasian.

Unsurprisingly then, even before his assumption of the throne, Titus became Vespasian's partner and his designated heir. In 69, he was named *Caesar* and *princeps iuventutis*. Father and son together assumed the consulship in 70, 72, 74, 75, 76, 77, and 79; and in 73–74, they both held the censorship. Titus was included in the tribunician and proconsular powers of the emperor. More importantly, although he was a senator, he became the sole commander of Vespasian's praetorian guard from 71. He thus became his father's guardian, an astute choice on Vespasian's part given the increasing power of praetorian prefects from Sejanus onwards.

Titus' brief rule did not allow much scope for blame in his biographies. Suetonius says that Titus was the love and delight of the entire human race, either because of his natural disposition or because of his popularity and good will throughout his time as emperor (*Titus* 1). One of the most notable events of his reign was the eruption of Vesuvius in 79. According to Suetonius and Cassius Dio, Titus provided immediate relief to the victims and sent two ex-consuls to Campania to supervise its restoration. Only traces of criticism remain, in accounts of Berenice's visit to Rome, Titus' lavish parties, and his assimilation to Nero. Undoubtedly the positive aspects of his reign were embellished in order to make Domitian's later "reign of terror" stand out more sharply.

Domitian's early career: until 81 CE

Vespasian's second son, Domitian, was born in 51. According to Suetonius (*Domitian* 1) he spent his early years "in poverty and infamy," qualities no doubt foreshadowing his later portrait as an abusive and cruel emperor, a sort of "bald Nero" (Juvenal, *Satire* 4.38). In December 69, he survived the burning of the Capitol, and, after Vitellius' death, he represented the imperial family in Rome, while his father and brother were still in the East. He was named *Caesar* and *princeps iuventutis*, and for 70 received the praetorship with the consular *imperium*. He then wished to govern, in his father's absence, and was outraged when he was given a mentor. This was the former legate of Syria, C. Licinius Mucianus, who was among the first instigators of Vespasian's uprising. Suetonius describes a classic sibling rivalry between Titus and Domitian; Cassius Dio (67.2) says that Domitian even forbade the practice of castration as an insult to the memory of the dead Titus, who had been fond of eunuchs. Although Domitian was kept away from real power under Vespasian and Titus and excluded from military expeditions, he was a member of all the major religious colleges. His name also accompanied those of Vespasian and Titus on public monuments, as well as on their triumph over the Jewish War. He became consul six times during his father's reign though only once as regular consul, at Titus' request. Domitian considered that his family had acted unfairly to him, and, although associated with the government, he remained apart and was even involved in conspiracies, both open and secret ones. His early career is overshadowed by the restoration of peace throughout the Empire after the civil war of 69. This was the task of Mucianus in the West, and Vespasian and Titus in the East.

Restoring peace

Restoration in the West

Mucianus first re-established order in Rome itself. There were no reprisals against the vanquished troops; and the victorious troops were sent back to their provinces. A commission was set up to return goods stolen during the war. On Vespasian's orders, Mucianus embarked upon the reconstruction of the temple of Jupiter Capitolinus, and its rededication took place on June 21, 70. In the West, the only trouble to persist was the revolt of the Batavians (69-70). This was a Germanic tribe, originally part of the Chatti, inhabiting the area among the diverging mouths of the Rhine, in the modern-day Netherlands. Resentful of the Romans' aggressive recruiting of auxiliaries from their communities, and taking advantage of Rome's civil war, they revolted at the instigation of a romanized Batavian noble, G. Iulius Civilis. Early in 70, various Gaulish tribes (the Lingones and Treveri in particular) joined Civilis and proclaimed an "Empire of the Gauls." Relying on the support of the auxiliary troops, reinforced by Germani from across the Rhine, and taking the opportunity of the legions' confusion in the civil war, they took Xanten, Mainz, Bonn, and Cologne. But the motivations and goals of these ethnically diverse armies were not the same. Tacitus creatively summarizes their differences, relating that their leaders exhorted them to battle "appealing to the Gauls in the name of liberty, to the Batavians in the name of glory, and to the Germani for loot" (Tacitus, *Histories* 4.78). Worried about the alliance with the Germani, the Council of the Gauls (Lugdunensis, Belgica, and Aquitania), met in Remi (Reims) to establish a common position. They chose to abandon the war and to remain loyal to Rome, fearing the reprisals of the eight legions deployed against them. The fragmentation of the rebels, combined with the energetic campaign of Q. Petillius Cerialis, appointed by Mucianus himself, established order on the Rhine frontier before the end of 70.

Restoration in the East

The main Roman concern in the East was the Jewish War. This had started with the Jews' Great Revolt in Jerusalem in 66, following the abuses of the Roman procurator Gessius Florus. The army commanded by Vespasian in Judaea numbered about 60,000 men. At the beginning of the summer of 68, the insurgents controlled only Jerusalem and its region as far as the west shore of the Dead Sea. Then came the death of Nero, the civil wars, and Vespasian's departure for Egypt. Roman operations were suspended. They resumed in the spring of 70 under the leadership of Titus. He had at his disposal four legions, auxiliary corps, and men levied from the garrisons of the Euphrates and Egypt. His siege of Jerusalem lasted five months. The Temple fell on August 30, then the lower town, and finally the upper town on September 25. The entire place was pillaged and set on fire. Elsewhere, several strongholds still held out. The complex of palaces and fortifications in Masada, the rebels' last bastion, was taken in 73. Josephus describes the dramatic moments on the eve of the Romans' final push up the Masada plateau, and the silence that greeted them on the next day after the mass suicide of the Jews (*Jewish War* 7.402–6). The consequences of the war were profound. Judaea became a praetorian province, its population diminished by a third, and a new diaspora took place. The Sanhedrin vanished. The Temple building was destroyed and the liturgy of the Temple was abolished. The construction of a new place of worship was prohibited. And the didrachm (the tax the Jews paid to the Temple) was henceforth to be paid to a new fund, the *fiscus Judaicus*, to the profit of the temple of Jupiter Capitolinus.

When Vespasian left Alexandria for Rome in September 70, peace had been virtually re-established in the East. The following year, together with Titus, he celebrated a triumph over the Jews. On the arch of Titus in the Roman Forum, pictures of that triumph may still be seen: on one side, Titus in triumph on his chariot; on the other, the procession carrying Jewish spoils: the seven-branched candelabrum (menorah), the shew-bread table, incense vessels, and the silver trumpets of the Temple which called the Jews to Rosh Hashanah.

Restoring confidence

Once peace was restored it had to be preserved. Vespasian set out to re-establish imperial authority, to unite the inhabitants of the Empire, to obliterate the memory of Nero and of the terrible previous year, and to construct his own imperial image. He also had to reconcile the different parts of the Empire with one another, stabilize the provinces, and strengthen their administration. Lastly, there was a need to ensure the security of the Empire as a whole, by consolidating its boundaries.

Re-establishing the authority and prestige of the imperial office

Establishing the present   As we saw above, Vespasian was acclaimed emperor by the legions under the prefect of Egypt on July 1, 69, at Alexandria. This "provincial" and rather informal accession elevated to the throne a competent general who did not even originate from the capital and was a plebeian to boot. As Suetonius says, "Vespasian lacked prestige and a kind of majesty, because of

Plate 10.1
Triumphal arch of
Titus, erected by
Domitian after his
brother's death to
celebrate the capture
of Jerusalem in 70 CE.
The arch stands on
the Via Sacra as it
leads into the Roman
Forum. This famous
panel depicts the
triumphal procession
with the treasures
from the Second
Temple in Jerusalem.
Joseph Calev/
shutterstock.co.uk

his unexpected and still recent elevation" (*Vespasian* 7). As we also saw above, a biographical tradition emerged (both contemporary to and later than his reign) which vested him with supernatural qualities, divine premonitions, and miraculous achievements that explained deterministically his accession. Tales about his healing of a blind man and a crippled man in Alexandria, his visit to the temple of Serapis, and an inspired discovery of a cache of ancient vases in Arcadia that displayed his portrait are examples of the mythology surrounding his career before and during 69.

Vespasian had achieved the only successful *coup d'état* in 69, and his imperial power rested on an even less constitutional foundation than that of the Julio-Claudians. After the death of Vitellius, at the end of December, the Senate decreed to Vespasian all the imperial powers (Tacitus, *Histories* 4.3). This was at the end of December, six months after his proclamation by the troops in Alexandria. Traditionally, the date of the senatorial investiture of an emperor was the official birth date (*dies imperii* or *dies principatus*) of his reign. Vespasian, however, flouted protocol, deciding that his *dies imperii* was the day when the army had proclaimed him, on July 1, 69. This is suggested by the latter part of the Senate's legislative action, which survives in a bronze inscription known today as *lex de imperio Vespasiani* ("law regulating Vespasian's authority"). Clause VIII in this inscription confers on Vespasian retroactively all imperial authority, stating "whatever before the passage of this law has been done, executed, decreed, ordered by Emperor Caesar Vespasian Augustus or by anyone at his order or mandate, these things shall be legal and valid, just as if they had been done by the order of the people or of the plebs." Seven other known clauses enumerate the laws relating to the *imperium* and the tribunician power. This inscription is one of most important sources for Vespasian's reign.

In addition, the *lex de imperio Vespasiani* provides important information for the development of the institution of the Principate and a poignant contrast with Octavian's gradual constitutional development into Augustus as documented in his *Res Gestae*. Up until the time of Vespasian, the conferment of titles and powers had been distributed throughout an emperor's life. Here, all the powers are accorded *en masse*, with details and new features that emphasize the absolutist aspect of the imperial office. At the same time, the imperial title is fixed in its canonical form: *Imp(erator) Caesar Vespasianus Aug(ustus)*. The first term is abbreviated, like a *praenomen*; the second links the emperor to the founders of the regime; the third, his personal name, identifies the emperor; the fourth transmits to the title-holder the religious aura of the first Augustus. But unlike Augustus' powers, which relied primarily on that aura and on the implicit senatorial collusion with the idea of the *princeps* as the first among equals, the *lex de imperio Vespasiani* codifies and institutionalizes the emperor's supremacy as well as his explicit control over senatorial decisions.

Connecting with the past The civil wars that preceded Vespasian's accession recalled the circumstances of Augustus' assumption of imperial power. A chronological coincidence accentuated the parallel: 100 years had passed since Augustus' victory at Actium. Resonating with ancient fatalistic sensibilities, the ideological potential of this coincidence was heavily exploited by the Flavians. Several monetary issues of 70–71 consciously imitated Augustan coinage: while Augustus had been given the title *Vindex* (champion) of liberty and the Roman people, Vespasian was portrayed as the *Adsertor* (protector) of public liberty. Like Augustus at the beginning of his Principate, Vespasian occupied the consulship on an almost permanent basis. And just as Augustus had raised an altar to Peace (Ara Pacis), so Vespasian in 71 began a temple to Peace (Templum Pacis), celebrating his victory over the Jews, with its façade facing the Forum of Augustus. This temple, dedicated in 75, was considered among the most magnificent structures in Rome (Pliny the Elder, *Natural History* 36.102).

Indeed, throughout the Flavian period, Augustan imagery was exploited and reinvented to celebrate Vespasian's restoration of a new order. Vespasian's emulation of Augustus' model and authority was foreshadowed in the *lex de Imperio Vespasiani*. It was further enriched by acts and measures that allowed Vespasian to appear as the heir of the "good" Julio-Claudians, Tiberius and Claudius. Claudius was highly honored, especially since Titus had been raised at his court. Just as Claudius had done, Vespasian assumed the censorship and extended the *pomoerium* (a measure not without fiscal repercussions). He also finished the temple to Claudius on the Caelian hill. Construction on this project had stopped when Nero used the platform intended to support the temple as the foundation of a garden grotto (*nymphaeum*) for his Golden House. By completing and rededicating the original temple to the Divine Claudius, Vespasian made a public gesture of distancing himself from Nero. His anti-Neronian policy was further revealed in the dismantling of the Domus Aurea. Its baths were rearranged to become those of Titus, and its drained lake made way for a gigantic amphitheater, the now famous Colosseum. Vespasian thus could claim that he handed Rome back to the Romans, and he celebrated this revived Rome in his coinage. After his restoration of the city from the ravages of the past, the emperor turned to the safeguarding of its future.

Preparing for the future With great self-assurance, Vespasian "dared to tell the Senate that his sons would succeed him or he would have no successor at all" (Suetonius, *Vespasian* 25). We have seen how, at the end of 69, his two sons were both named *Caesar* and *princeps iuventutis*. This dynastic policy extended to other members of the *domus divina*. The daughter of Vespasian, and later Titus' daughter, received the title *Augusta*. Domitian erected a temple to the Flavian family (*templum gentis Flaviae*) on the site of Vespasian's original house on the Quirinal, in which he himself was born. After his murder, it was there that his ashes were secretly placed, suggesting perhaps that Domitian had intended the *templum* as the family mausoleum. The priestly college of the *sodales Flaviales* was established, modeled closely on the *sodales Augustales*, to render worship to the deified members of the family.

The better to entrench this restored power, Vespasian made use of the imperial cult, which he developed and organized on the provincial level, at least in the West. Before Vespasian, the imperial cult had not gone beyond the municipal level in the provinces of Baetica, proconsular Africa, and southern Gaul. In each of these, he instituted a chief priest (*flamen*) at the head of the provincial *concilium*, whose duty was to celebrate the official cult of the emperor by sacrifices and games. Vespasian's final quip about becoming a god implies both existential humor and genuine concern about the after-life of his cult. However, Vespasian and his sons also departed from Augustus' policies. Whereas Augustus had suppressed the Egyptian cults, Vespasian linked them with the destiny of his family. This is an explicable choice, given the role of Egypt in Vespasian's accession and even in Domitian's divine protection by Isis during his escape from the Capitol. In fact, on the eve of their Jewish triumph, Vespasian and Titus spent the night in the temple of Isis on the Campus Martius (Josephus, *Jewish War* 7.123). This temple was represented on the reverse of coins in 71, and was rebuilt by Domitian after its destruction in the great fire of 80, which destroyed the Capitol and Agrippa's original Pantheon, among other landmarks of the city.

Plate 10.2 Interior of the Colosseum, Rome, dedicated in 80 CE. The floor (*arena*) has been excavated to reveal the vaulted subterranean structures. C. M. Dixon

Reinforcing the Empire

Vespasian attempted to strengthen the basis of the Empire by remedying provincial administration.

Provincial reorganization Like Tiberius, Vespasian was very familiar with many provinces long before his accession. He had spent time in Thrace, Crete–Cyrenaica, Gaul, the Germanies, Britain, Africa, Syria, Judaea, Egypt, Greece, and Asia. His structural, constitutional, and administrative modifications to the organization of the provinces aimed to increase the Empire's security and improve its tax system:

72   The Commagene region was annexed and joined to Syria.

Armenia Minor was annexed and incorporated with Cappadocia, which, joined to Galatia, became a consular (imperial) province with two legions.

In the south of Anatolia, the praetorian imperial province of Cilicia was created.

The province of Lycia–Pamphylia was reconstituted (date uncertain).

77   Rhodes, Samos, and Byzantium lost their liberty. The first two were attached
     to Asia; the last to Bithynia.

Financial reorganization Suetonius comments that the only fault of Vespasian
was his greed (*Vespasian* 16), but this criticism actually suggests the emperor's
rigorous attention to fiscal policies. He increased revenues by canceling the tax
exemptions granted by Nero and Galba, together with the franchises enjoyed by
certain free cities; he also increased taxes in the provinces; he created a *fiscus
Alexandrinus*, a *fiscus Asiaticus*, and a *fiscus Judaicus*. He instituted new
taxes in Rome; when Titus objected to the toll on the city's urinals, the emperor
made the clever repartee that he did not find the smell of those coins offensive
(Suetonius, *Vespasian* 23). He continued to collect in peacetime the exceptional
taxes levied in wartime, and even tried to launch a state loan. On the other hand,
following Augustus' generous policy on public works, he spent freely on such
projects both in Rome (rebuilding of the Capitol, construction of the Colosseum,
temple of Peace, granaries, etc.) and throughout the Empire (numerous road-
building enterprises). He helped senators to meet the senatorial property qualification, paid an allowance to impoverished former consuls, and gave aid to towns
destroyed by fires or earthquakes. He was also the first emperor to endow academic chairs. He established two in Rome (one for Greek and one for Latin
rhetoric), funding them from the imperial revenues. Furthermore, to simplify the
financial departments, he incorporated the wealth of the Julio-Claudians with
that of the crown (*patrimonium*).

Economic reorganization During 69, lands in many areas had been fraudu-
lently seized by private owners, as it had happened during the Civil Wars of the
late Republic. Vespasian organized land surveys to establish the status of these
lands, to determine who the owners were, and to quantify the total land taxable
for each owner. Inscriptions of these surveys discovered in Italy and many provinces (for example, the inscriptions from modern Orange, in Gaul) show that this
massive and lengthy task was realized throughout the Empire. As we know from
accounts of land surveys, Vespasian also turned to public lands that were not
delimited and "centuriated" (*agri centuriati*, from the word *centuria*, the basic
Roman plot unit). He put up for sale or rent these unmeasured and unassigned
lands (known as *subsiciva*). In northern Italy he paid subsidies to revive agricultural life, while in the provinces he regularized the administration of imperial
estates and state-owned land. A series of agrarian inscriptions found in the
Bagradas valley of Tunisia mentions extensively a Flavian *lex Manciana*, which
regulated land tenure by the local population.

Watching over the Empire's safety

Vespasian's success had been largely due to his support by provincial legions and
to the disgruntlement of the soldiers disbanded by Vitellius after Bedriacum. As

a soldier, Vespasian knew that he had to secure the military safety of the Empire. Once he had restored discipline to the army by regrouping the legions and reducing the number of the praetorian cohorts, he strengthened the fleets (mainly those in the East) and reorganized the provinces in light of strategic concerns. Then he set about consolidating the limits of the Empire, either by means of expeditions and peacemaking operations, or by fortifying the frontiers.

Expeditions and peacemaking operations
- Africa: there was an expedition against the Garamantes, who had come from Fezzan to harass the towns of Tripolitania.
- Britain: three great legates (Q. Petilius Cerialis, Sex. Julius Frontinus, and Cn. Julius Agricola, the father-in-law of Tacitus) resumed a forward policy toward Wales and the north of England, bringing both under control, and then continuing northward. Agricola was sent to Britain in 78, and by 81 had progressed as far north as the line of the Forth–Clyde isthmus. If it were not for Tacitus' biography of Agricola, we would know very little about his career in Britain (he is mentioned by Cassius Dio, 66.20, and in the Verulamium Forum inscription dating to 79). Tacitus' biography is an invaluable source for Agricola's career, for the later years of Domitian's reign, and for Roman ethnographical perceptions of Britain.
- Germania: the weakest point on the frontier was the angle formed by the valley of the Upper Rhine and the upper course of the Danube; from 73 onwards, a series of actions resulted in a cautious advance: the Black Forest was occupied. Another monograph by Tacitus, *Germania*, provides a detailed, and highly idealized, ethnographical portrait of German tribes.
- The East: the Parthian king Vologeses had offered 40,000 cavalry to Vespasian while the civil war was still going on, but his offer had been turned down. In 75, Vespasian again rejected the king's appeal to assist the Parthians, who were at war with the Scythian Alani. Vologeses, in revenge, attacked the Roman province of Syria but was repulsed, and died soon afterwards.

Fortifying the frontiers With the systematic installation of the legions along the frontiers (except the legions of Jerusalem, Alexandria, Tarraconensis, and Dalmatia), a solid line of defense was gradually set up at each frontier, comprising a road network, and a series of fortifications between which the legions could move. This system allowed Rome to have in-depth defense along a tract of ground stretching around the boundaries of the Empire. This type of defense system gradually acquired the name *limes* (this meaning of the word is attested for the first time by Tacitus in 98). The defensive imperative in the face of possible invasions or incursions by organized forces is understandable. The fortified zone could also keep surveillance on nomads, filter barbarian groups, and even supervise trade between the Roman world and the world beyond. However, one must not imagine the *limes* as impermeable or fully manned along its periphery. Once that strip of ground had been passed, a potential enemy would be well inside a province, with no troops ahead.

- Africa: Vespasian and Titus set up a *limes* intended to provide better control of the line of the Aurès mountains (on the north-western border of Tunisia with Algeria). The camp of the Third Augusta was transferred from Haidra to Tebessa, farther west, with a detachment at Lambaesis. Moreover, auxiliary units were installed to the west and south of the Aurès.
- Britain: a series of forts and fortresses marked the progress of the legions westward and northward; in particular, there were two legionary camps at York and Chester.
- Germania: in Lower Germania the *limes* rested on the old legionary camps at Xanten, Bonn, and Neuss and the new camp at Nijmegen; in Upper Germania, on those of Mainz, Strasbourg, and Vindonissa. Under Vespasian, these camps and the fortresses that accompanied them were restored, and wooden structures were replaced by stone walls. Vespasian also established new forts on the right bank of the Upper Rhine (for example, Heidelberg), and founded a settlement, perhaps in 73, to keep watch on a road that connected the Rhine and the Danube through the Black Forest. The Latin name of this settlement, Arae Flaviae (modern Rottweil), suggests the presence of an altar and hence of imperial cult. Another route was established farther north, linking Mainz with Augsburg, the capital of Raetia.
- The Danube: Vespasian, and then Domitian, reorganized the Danubian fleet, created auxiliary camps, and considerably strengthened the Danubian frontier.
- The East: client kingdoms no longer existed here. The Euphrates became the eastern frontier of the Empire. With the creation of Greater Cappadocia, Rome possessed a solid line of defense stretching from the Black Sea to the Arabian desert, connected internally and with the rest of the Empire by a well-protected and well-constructed system of strategic routes, and manned by the six legions permanently posted there as well as numerous auxiliary units.

As we have seen, Vespasian was celebrated as the restorer and champion (*adsertor, conservator*) of freedom and the state. Both he and Titus were deified soon after their deaths, evidence of their popularity and sound administration. By contrast, upon his assassination Domitian received not a deification but a *damnatio memoriae*, the permanent erasure of his name from all public records and monuments. Our sources almost unanimously condemn Domitian's rule as a reign of terror, and the restoration of his name has been a long and difficult task.

10.4 | Domitian and Tyranny: 81–96 CE

Domitian assumed the throne after Titus' mysterious death in 81. Our sources suggest that Domitian murdered Titus, or at least that he was callous toward his brother's illness (Suetonius, *Domitian* 2). His indifference perhaps reflects the pressures of imperial expediency: as Titus lay dying, Domitian left him to go to the praetorians' camp, where he had himself hailed emperor and distributed a *donativum* (Cassius Dio, 66.26). The next day, September 14, 81, the Senate conferred full imperial powers upon him. At the age of nearly 30, the new emperor had no time to lose. Since the accession of his father, and even more since that of his brother, he had been associated with honors but kept away from government. And he fully intended to rule.

His reign lasted 15 years. On September 18, 96, he was stabbed to death. The conspiracy included his wife, Domitia, the two praetorian prefects, members of the palace, and a few senators. One of these senators, M. Cocceius Nerva, had been designated in advance as the new emperor. Domitian's *damnatio memoriae* was followed by a scathing denigration from diverse authors (Pliny, Tacitus, Juvenal, Cassius Dio), who portray him as a cruel tyrant. The senatorial authors Pliny and Tacitus began their successful careers under Domitian, a fact that they both admit in their writings, with varying degrees of comfort. The poet Juvenal provides a deeply satirical portrait of the emperor and his council (*Satire* 4), while, in other authors, the line between eulogy, humor, and satire is less discernible (Statius, *Silvae* 1.1; Martial, *Epigrams* 9.1). In the end, the most balanced judgment lies with Suetonius. He presents Domitian's qualities as a ruler, his attention to the conduct of his magistrates and provincial governors, and his innovations, as well as his personal flaws that led him from being a lenient and generous emperor to becoming increasingly cruel and paranoid. Suetonius also discusses senatorial opposition to Domitian, a theme explored too by Tacitus in his *Agricola*.

A few highlights of Domitian's deteriorating reign may be picked out from our sources. The years between 81 and 89 were relatively quiet. Conspiracies by political factions in 83 and 87 met with a brutal response from the emperor, but nothing major occurred. Then, in 89, the legate of Upper Germania, L. Antonius Saturninus, rebelled, having himself proclaimed emperor and bringing with him two legions and some Germani. This rebellion too was put down. Lastly, after a hesitant effort at rapprochement with the Senate, Domitian engaged in a trial of strength with it at the end of 93, leading to a bloody persecution of senators, the expulsion of philosophers from Rome and Italy, and proceedings against Jews and Christians. Even the imperial family was not spared. Domitia, feeling threatened, encouraged the decisive plot.

In all, there were perhaps fewer death sentences than has often been thought (probably about 20, over half of which resulted from treason trials) and only three years of tyranny. Perhaps it is these last dramatic years that filter the perspective of authors reflecting summarily on Domitian's entire reign. In the beginning of the *Agricola*, Tacitus says that for 15 whole years, the most energetic citizens fell victims to Domitian's cruelty, while the survivors grew old and reached the end of their lives in silence (*Agricola* 3). However, a more moderate view of Domitian emerges once we look more closely at his policies, which, for the most part continued those of his two predecessors.

The emperor of continuity

The institutional field

Domitian amassed consulships (17 in all, 10 of which were during his reign). In 85, he had himself granted censorial powers, altered to censorship in perpetuity the following year. He was acclaimed *imperator* 22 times, and he celebrated triumphs for his victories over the Chatti and the Dacians.

Building activity

Besides restoring the areas of the Capitol and the Campus Martius that had been damaged or destroyed by the fire of 80, he completed the building works begun in the two preceding reigns: the Flavian amphitheater (the Colosseum, which he complemented with a school of gladiators, the Ludus Magnus), the baths of Titus, and the temple of the Divine Vespasian at the foot of the Capitol. Moreover, he developed further this Flavian policy of public building works, undertaking, notably, the arch of Titus, the temple of the *gens Flavia* on the Quirinal, the Campus Martius stadium (the present-day Piazza Navona follows its shape), and a modest forum which became the main thoroughfare between the Subura, the Forum Romanum, and the other imperial forums. Because of its location it was named Forum Transitorium, but after its formal inauguration by emperor Nerva it became known as Forum Nervae (Suetonius, *Domitian* 5). Domitian also completed the imperial Domus Flavia ("Palace of the Flavians"), occupying the entire central part of the Palatine.

Administration of the provinces

According to Suetonius (*Domitian* 8), the emperor "put so much zeal into suppressing the intrigues of provincial governors that they were never again more impartial or just, whereas after him we have seen many of them accused of all kinds of crimes." The epigraphic record concurs with this positive assessment. An inscription from Baetica relates information about a local governor accused of embezzlement, who was sentenced to pay damages to the wronged provincials. The application of this apparently unusual surveillance was perhaps one of the causes of the antagonism between the Senate and the emperor. A number of other testimonies to Domitian's intervention in the life of the provinces form a similar picture. He actively pursued the renewal of land surveys and settled the issue of unallocated public land (*subsiciva*) to the satisfaction of the cities. He also advanced many detailed measures to improve the well-being of the provincials, as well as measures that may have been intended to strike a balance in the production of certain crops at Empire level. A stone inscription from Pisidian Antioch (dating to 93) records an edict about the measures taken by a governor to ensure the supply of cheap grain to the inhabitants. Edicts on viticulture (dating to about the same time) seem to have aimed at reducing the number of

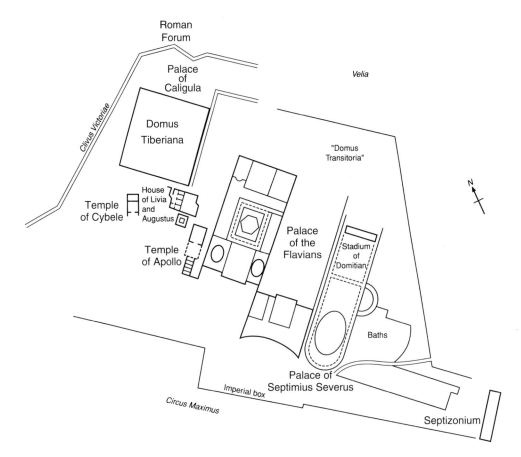

Figure 10.1 The imperial palaces

vineyards in order both to increase grain production in Italy and the provinces, and to defend the income and value of lands belonging to the great owners. Lastly, inscriptional evidence also suggests that it was perhaps Domitian who was responsible for the creation of the post of city curator, an official of the central government appointed to help with the problems of provincial cities.

Frontier safety

Britain Agricola continued his advance northward. He occupied a large part of Scotland, and, in 83, built a legionary camp known as Inchtuthil (on the river Tay). He then proceeded to defeat the inhabitants of the Highlands under the Caledonian noble Calgacus, in the battle of Mount Graupius. Agricola also succeeded in taking his fleet round the north coast of Scotland. In 84, Agricola was recalled by Domitian back to Rome. Roman order was established in Britain, but Scotland remained outside the Empire.

The Germanies A Germanic people, the Chatti, living in the region of the Taunus mountains, threatened and harassed the Roman settlements of the Rhine valley and Vetteravia (Wetterau). Domitian launched a powerful campaign against them, led in 83 by the emperor himself and completed by peacemaking negotiations. A second campaign in the region of Upper Germania, in 89, followed the revolt of Saturninus. These two German campaigns had several consequences: the Chatti were repulsed and driven from the Rhine valley; Lower and Upper Germania were formally established as provinces; the territory controlled by Rome on the right bank of the Rhine was increased southward and eastward into a triangle between the Main and the sources of the Danube and the Rhine. This area, which Tacitus (*Germania* 29) calls the Agri Decumates ("Ten Lands," still a mysterious term), became a part of Upper Germania. Thus the *limes* of this region formed an almost continuous defense line, securing the links between the Rhine and the Danube.

The Danube In these regions the Julio-Claudians had made use of diplomacy rather than armed force. But the appearance on the scene of an organized Dacian nation, and of the Sarmatians, nomadic peoples from the borders of Europe and Asia, with their mixed populations, altered the geopolitical situation along the river. In 85, the Dacians crossed the Danube, invaded Moesia, and killed its governor. An initial Roman expedition (85–86) ended in a defeat in which a praetorian prefect died. Others followed (87–88), and an important victory (88) resulted in a compromise peace (89). Meanwhile, Moesia had been divided into two provinces, Upper Moesia (four legions) and Lower Moesia (two legions). The Dacian peace, however, did not stop Roman operations on the Danube. Domitian fortified the Danubian frontier and returned to Rome in late 89 to celebrate a double triumph over the Chatti and Dacians that included lavish games. From 89 to 92 his legions moved into Pannonia, against the Quadi and the Marcomanni, to take revenge for their refusal to assist in the Dacian wars. Domitian's inconclusive campaign on the Dacian front, his financial settlement with Decebalus, and the fact that he nevertheless celebrated a triumph were later subjected to intense criticism (Pliny, *Panegyric* 16; Cassius Dio 67.7).

The East There was little change here. Domitian strengthened the defense systems, and a Roman expedition reached as far as the eastern end of the Caucasus. A rock inscription found at the shores of the Caspian Sea (Baku region), dating to 75, documents a dedication to Domitian by a centurion of the Twelfth Fulminata named Lucius Julius Maximus.

Domitian's innovations

Absolutism

According to Suetonius (*Domitian* 13), Domitian was the first emperor to establish the address to himself as "lord and god" (*dominus et deus*), beginning his public letters with the formula "Our lord and god commands the following." This double title was not official (like, for example, *imperator*) but it nevertheless codified the emperor's wish to be no longer merely the first citizen but an absolute monarch, in the eastern style. His massive marble statue outside his temple in Ephesus was the center of the imperial cult in Asia Minor. He also introduced various eastern rites at his court (the kissing of feet, for example). He avoided any display of familiarity with his subjects and invested his person with a sacred character. These tendencies are suggested by the extraordinary grandeur of the imperial palace (see Martial's praise, *Epigrams* 7.56, 8.36), his constant wearing of the triumphal purple, the divine qualities attributed to him by his poets, the placing of his equestrian statue in the center of the Forum, and the setting of his

Plate 10.3 Colossal cult statue of Domitian. It stood outside his temple in Ephesus and was destroyed after his assassination, during his general *damnatio memoriae*. 81–96 CE. akg-images/Erich Lessing

own statues in the temple of Jupiter Capitolinus. A century later, such imperial practices were common, but at the time they offended most senators.

Military policy

For the first time since Augustus, the pay of the praetorians, legionaries, and auxiliaries was increased by a considerable amount (about a third) under Domitian. The legions and praetorians were consequently favorable to him. As we will see below, the praetorians' desire to avenge Domitian's death resulted in a brief crisis with his successor, M. Cocceius Nerva, in 97.

Administrative policy

Domitian began the practice of replacing freedmen in the central administration with equestrians. Thus, the management of the departments of imperial correspondence (*ab epistulis*) and taxation on inheritances (*a patrimonio*) was transferred to the equestrians. Furthermore, senior officials were provided with an assistant of equestrian rank, who would at the same time keep an eye on them.

10.5 | A Developing Municipal Life and a Changing Society

The supplanting of a dynasty of Roman aristocrats by a family of Italian municipal notables was in itself a social revolution, a sign of the socio-political transformations that had been precipitated by the Augustan revolution. The Flavian era ushered in a model of urban and municipal life, which in turn brought profound social changes.

Although the situation varied from one province to another, and sometimes from one region within a province to another, we can draw a rough distinction between urban life in the eastern and the western parts of the Empire. In the West, Rome was the major urban and cultural center, followed by a few cities of Greek or Punic origin. Conversely, in the East, city planning, organization, and traditions antedated Rome by several centuries, and were therefore more structured and varied than in the West. We will draw here a general sketch of municipal life in the Empire, including aspects of both its urbanization and its Romanization. But we should bear in mind that life in each city varied according to its geographical and ethnographical makeup and that, in many respects, the Empire was a patchwork of cities, many of which remain unknown to us.

The status of the cities

With the exception again of Egypt, the inhabitants of the Empire lived in areas belonging to one of three juristically defined types of communities: peregrine cities, *municipia*, and colonies.

Peregrine ("foreign") cities

These were communities and their territories as they had existed before Roman rule, or as the Romans had remodeled them after conquest but without granting them Roman or Latin rights. These cities preserved their own laws, and their inhabitants remained *peregrini*, although groups of Roman citizens, of course, lived there. At the start of the Empire, these represented the majority of provincial cities and were divided into three categories according to their status with regard to Rome.

- Stipendiary cities: these were the most numerous. They were subject to Rome and paid a tribute (*stipendium*). In theory, the provincial governor had legal control over all their affairs.
- Free cities: these were theoretically autonomous and juristically outside the provinces. Their rights were conceded by a unilateral act of Rome. Some, though that became increasingly rare, were exempt from paying tribute.
- Federated free cities: these were a minority of free cities which had signed a treaty with Rome putting them on an equal footing with it.

The municipia

A *municipium* was a city that developed from a pre-existing community of *peregrini* (and might even retain some of its institutions) through a grant by Rome to that community of either Roman or Latin rights. The distinction between these two classes of provincial *municipia*, Roman and Latin, resulted from the historical conditions under which the rights had been granted. At first, as at the time of the organization of Italy after its conquest, Rome had granted Roman rights to *municipia* situated in the provinces. Thus Italica, in Baetica, founded in 206 BCE and peopled by ex-soldiers, became under Caesar a *municipium* with Roman rights. The last known *municipium* of Roman citizens was Volubilis in northern Africa, which was awarded that rank by Claudius in 47. Starting with Claudius (or perhaps Vespasian), there were no further creations of *municipia* with Roman rights (although the early ones did not disappear), and the provincial communities that newly became *municipia* were all initially granted Latin rights. In these *municipia* with Latin rights, municipal office gave access to Roman citizenship. Thus, from the Roman viewpoint, there were two sorts of inhabitants of *municipia* with Latin rights: first, there were those who moved beyond their local citizenship and became full-blown Roman citizens because of the office they had held, or individually through the emperor's generosity. The others were those who, while remaining *peregrini*, benefited from the advantages of Latin rights (which are still nebulous to us).

The colonies

Unlike the creation of a *municipium*, the founding of a colony was the creation of a new town, with the introduction of colonists (*deductio*) into lands seized from conquered cities or peoples. It was most frequently created on a previously uninhabited area. If not, then it had to be religiously and legally severed from the earlier settlement. The colony adopted full Roman rights; and if it also received the privilege of Italic rights (*ius Italicum*), it was considered Italian soil, and was thus exempt from land tax. In southern Gaul (Nîmes), however, there still existed a particular type of colony with Latin rights, where, as in Latin *municipia*, the majority of inhabitants were *peregrini*.

In this way a hierarchy was established and there was emulation between cities for tax benefits and other imperial benefactions. The peregrine cities aspired to become *municipia* with Latin rights, and the *municipia* with Latin rights aspired to obtain Roman rights. They also increasingly asked for the title of honorary colony, that is, a colony that had not been ritually founded, and without a settlement of colonists. We do have some evidence for the change of status of various communities. Vespasian changed the status of Leptis Magna (c.73–74) from free peregrine city to Latin *municipium*. Moreover, by granting Latin rights to all the communities of Spain at the beginning of the seventies, Vespasian may have forged the link between *municipium* and Latin rights. Employing general municipal constitutions, which each city personalized, native Spanish cities were allowed to claim the status of Latin *municipium*. Fragments of municipal laws from several cities of Spain (Salpensa, Malaca, Irni) from Domitian's reign provide a wealth of information about local justice, collection of taxes, public activities, and the relationship of these communities with the emperor and the governor of the province. Despite the inscriptional record, however, we do not know whether there was an automatic connection between the granting of Latin rights and the move to a form of municipal organization.

The cities were also sometimes subdivided into districts of various kinds, each fairly autonomous, such as the *pagi*, *vici*, *castella*, and the *oppida* in the West (these names varied according to the province). Moreover, there were judiciary districts wider than the city, like the *conventus*, which grouped several cities together and which, under the Flavians, were extended to cover the whole of the Iberian peninsula.

Municipal institutions

Generally speaking, there was no intermediate administrative level between city and province. For the majority of the Empire's inhabitants, the city was the backbone of life, personal, social, and political. These basic cells organized their own local administration: they levied the greater part of the taxes that were then passed on to the provincial collector, attended to the structure and maintenance of their buildings, and administered justice at the lower court level. Their institutional machinery, and the men who ensured that it functioned well, provided this municipal autonomy with resilience and efficiency.

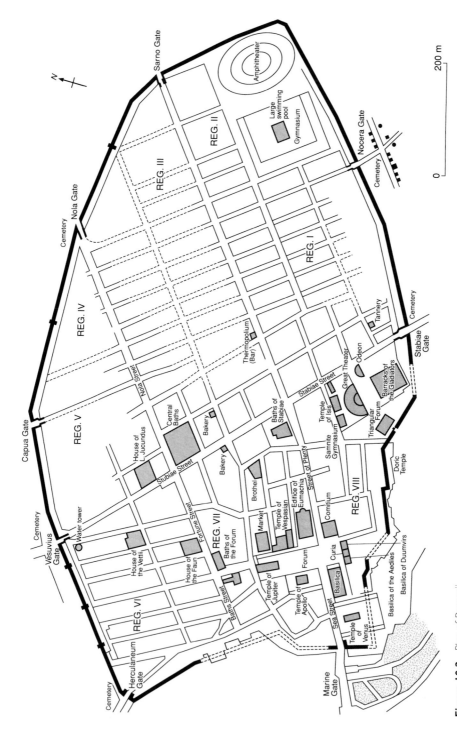

Figure 10.2 Plan of Pompeii

Municipal institutions depended on the status of the city. Peregrine cities kept their native magistracies and particular laws. Thus, Athens maintained its institutions, its archons, its calendar, and its festivals; only the military magistracies disappeared or were altered. The *strategos*, the most important officer in fifth-century Athens and with a prestigious military pedigree, now had the task of supervising grain supplies. Local magistrates (like the Punic *suffetes* or Celtic *vergobrets*) survived, either under their own titles or Latinized (as praetors or *magistri*). The indigenous cities, and more especially those of the West (which were more recent and therefore less resistant to change), seemed to follow the model of the *municipium* or the colony.

The institutions of the *municipia* and colonies were modeled on those of Rome. The civic body (*populus*) was defined as a *respublica*. Citizens were divided into *curiae*, which assembled in the *comitia* to elect the city magistrates. A bronze tablet found in Malaca, Baetica (dating between 82 and 84), describes in detail the voting procedures for the community and the conditions for eligibility for the various offices (*lex Malacitana*). In order to be a candidate, a man had to be free and a local citizen, to meet a property qualification (which varied according to the wealth of the city), and to be at least 25 years old. Furthermore, for certain posts, financial pledges were required, since there was a personal responsibility in management. The whole range of municipal offices, each tenable for one year, without any compensation, formed a municipal *cursus honorum* of three stages, each of two posts: first, those of the two quaestors, who looked after financial matters; second, those of the two aediles, who regulated and controlled food supplies, the markets, buildings, roads, etc.; and, lastly, those of the *duumviri*, the two supreme magistrates, who were in charge of justice and responsible for conducting a *census* of the population every five years.

To assist these magistrates, there was a local Senate, the size of which varied according to the importance of the city. Its members, the decurions, were recruited from the former magistrates and wealthy notables, and though formally making up an advisory body, were in reality in charge of all the municipal departments. In their decrees, the decurions decided on issues of infrastructure, public buildings and monuments, festivals and celebrations, and embassies to the province governor or to Rome. They also elected the city priest in charge of the imperial cult. Furthermore, they were responsible for the collection of the imperial taxes, and, in the event of a shortfall, they had to make up the deficit from their personal funds. Frequently interconnected by marriage, these local dignitaries formed a pool from which the emperors could draw new members of the equestrian order.

10.6 | Social Changes

The most profound social change of the Flavian era was the rise of the provincials. They moved into the political limelight, which had been dominated by the Italians (these, in turn, now took a place at the very head of the Empire). The emergence of the provincials at this time is due to three factors. First, the peace and the stability ensured by the Flavians allowed the provinces to acquire an economic and cultural strength superior to that of Italy, which had been ravaged by the civil war and its own weary economy. Second, the accelerated Romanization of the western provinces (which for historical, geographical, and political reasons had been favored since Actium) now became evidently prominent. In fact, at the end of the first century CE, the western part of the Empire was thriving more than the East. Third, the Flavians' conscious fostering of the provinces (granting of Latin rights to the provinces of Hispania, more frequent recourse to the *adlectio*, a policy of winning over the Gauls, the setting up of urban centers in Germania and in Africa) and the granting of favors of every kind in the East abetted all the other advantages accruing to the provincials. Here are a few examples illustrating the rise of the provincials and the provinces during the Flavian era:

The political field The proportion of provincials in the Senate increased notably until, under Domitian, it comprised almost a third of its members. Of these known provincials, most originated from the Iberian peninsula or southern Gaul, although over a third were eastern in origin.

The military field The situation here parallels that of the Senate, but it is even more marked. From the time of Vespasian (although not because of any specific imperial policy) the number of legionaries recruited in Italy began to diminish. Correspondingly, the number of non-Italians went up. In the western part of the Empire, they came from the richest and most Romanized senatorial provinces – southern Gaul, Baetica, Africa, and Macedonia – and even from the imperial provinces where regional recruitment was beginning to develop. In the eastern part, recruitment was mostly regional. Only the praetorian and urban cohorts continued to be composed principally of Italians.

The economic field The decline of Italy from its position of economic pre-eminence is illustrated by the abandonment of Pompeii, Herculaneum, and Stabiae. Despite lying in the traditionally fertile and wealthy region of Campania, these towns never recovered from their destruction after the eruption of Vesuvius in 79. In this respect, the case of the wine trade between southern Gaul and Italy tells a story. Before the first century CE, the flow of trade was largely from Italy to Gaul. The first evidence of Gaulish wine imported into Italy is datable to the first half of the first century CE. Beginning with Augustus' later years, the boom in vineyards in the south of Gaul, and the appearance in Narbonensis of a few amphora workshops, reduced imports of Italian and Spanish wine into Gaul. Eventually the trade circuit was fully reversed, as the archaeological record indicates: at the praetorian quarters at Ostia no Gaulish amphorae were found in the Claudian level of the deposit; but they form 40 percent of the wine amphorae of the Flavian level (against less than 30 percent from Italy and less than 15 percent from Spain).

The religious field In this area, the emergence of the provinces is less measurable, but it is evident in the popularity of eastern cults in Rome. Rome's adoption of foreign cults is not, of course, particular to the Flavian period. Nevertheless, the lively presence of eastern cults was marked at this time. Vespasian's connection with Egypt was certainly one factor in this: in the Domus Flavia on the Palatine, for example, a chapel of Egyptian worship housed the imperial devotions. Under the Flavians the first bull sacrifices to Mithras appeared in Rome. On the other hand, converts to Judaism, or, less probably, Christianity, within the imperial family were exposed and persecuted by Domitian in 95.

The intellectual field The province of Spain yielded the author Columella, whose manual on farming is one of the few works we have on the topic; Quintilian, whose textbook on rhetoric provides us with information on Roman literary history and criticism; and Martial, whose epigrams are a rich source of Roman social mores. The Greek Plutarch wrote parallel biographies of Greek and Roman men, as well as philosophical essays on morality. The stoic philosopher Epictetus from Phrygia also belongs to this time, as does the early work of Tacitus (whose *Germania* is traditionally dated to 98). As we will see below, in the next century this provincial eminence developed into further political power and a successful claim to the throne.

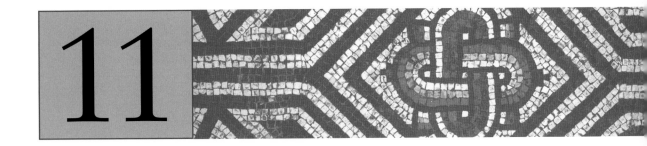

11

THE ANTONINE
EMPIRE: 96–192 CE

In the eyes of its contemporaries, it was a golden age, hailed as such by several issues of coinage. Never had the ancient world known its like. "The Universe has become a single city," exclaimed Aelius Aristides, a Greek-speaking rhetor writing around the middle of the second century. He added, "The whole world is in festive mood. It has abandoned its weapons of war to give itself up to the joy of living." His *Eulogy of Rome* sings the praises of this coherent Empire with its perfect administration, which, like a freshly polished wineglass, emits a single note, and which unanimously obeys the "supreme governor, provider of all things." Appian, his contemporary, a Greek from Alexandria, reflecting on the consequences of the Roman policy of conquest, affirms that "the Capital was rendered far more beautiful, incomes were considerably increased, and a sure and lasting peace instituted to create permanent happiness." Some years later, an emperor who wanted to prove himself the emperor of peace, Marcus Aurelius, became the emperor of war. In his own words, he hunted the Sarmatians as a spider hunts flies. The subject of war, which had disappeared from artistic production for half a century, now became topical again. But there are great differences to be seen on two monuments of the same kind but separated by this period, the columns of Trajan and Marcus Aurelius. While Trajan's column glorifies an offensive battle, that of Marcus Aurelius represents a defensive one. These two structures represent both different challenges to the empire, and changing attitudes toward the Roman army and war in general.

11.1 | Italo-Provincial Emperors

The dynasty of the Antonines was formed primarily through sequential adoptions, and the term "Antonine" emerged retrospectively using the name of the fourth emperor. It started with Domitian's successor, Nerva, continued with Trajan, Hadrian, Antoninus, and Marcus Aurelius, and concluded with Aurelius' natural son, Commodus. In terms of their "national" origins, the Antonines could be considered in terms of a Spanish dynasty (Nerva, Trajan, Hadrian) and a Narbonensian dynasty (Antoninus, Marcus Aurelius, Commodus). Trajan's and Hadrian's personalities dominate our perception of their reigns, but the second century CE is mostly defined by collective and quiet shifts, whether they were signs of prosperity or causes of trouble.

Nerva: 96–98 CE

Even before Domitian's assassination, Nerva had been designated to succeed him. There was no power vacuum: on the eve of the murder the Senate confirmed the conspirators' choice. It was a choice without risk; Nerva was reassuring. The childless descendant of the republican family of the *Cocceii Nervae* from Narnia, Nerva was already 70 years old but seemed in good health. A prudent career had allowed him to win the respect of a succession of emperors and the esteem of the Senate. Nerva skillfully and firmly contained the senatorial reaction against himself (like many senators, he had supported, or collaborated with, Domitian), he restrained the grumblings of the praetorians who were partial to Domitian, he quelled a military uprising in Upper Germania, and he restored to their owners several properties that had been confiscated by Domitian. He gave various allotments to the urban poor in Rome and even designated Domitian's palace on the Palatine as a public space (Pliny, *Panegyric* 47). Authors are unanimous in their praise of his short reign. Tacitus (*Agricola* 3) claims that Nerva reunited two previously incompatible things: the Principate and liberty. Similar concepts are advertised on Nerva's coinage.

Yet not everyone was content. In 98 the fragility of Nerva's position was exposed when the praetorians, led by their prefect Casperius Aelianus, blockaded the emperor in his palace, demanding that he avenge Domitian's death. In many ways this mutiny recalled the praetorian uprising against Galba in 69: it exposed again both the importance of an ensured succession, and the increasing power of the army to "usher emperors in and out, just like actors on the stage" (Plutarch, *Galba* 1). Nerva neutralized this double threat by a clever maneuver: on October 28, 97, in a ceremony at the Capitol, he announced that he was adopting the legate of Upper Germania, M. Ulpius Traianus (Trajan). The Senate immediately conferred the title of *Caesar* on Trajan *in absentia* and awarded him tribunician power, proconsular *imperium*, and the *cognomen* of Augustus. It is uncertain whether Trajan knew beforehand about his adoption; at Nerva's request

Plate 11.1   Detail of Trajan's column, Rome, showing the building of a fort. The column was erected in 113 CE. C. M. Dixon

he remained on the Rhine. Three months later Nerva died (January 27, 98), and the news of his death was soon after announced to Trajan in Cologne by P. Aelius Hadrianus (Hadrian), Trajan's great-nephew.

Nerva had been a sensible, clear-sighted, and realistic interim emperor. He had chosen his successor by adoption, his selection based not on kinship (though he had some eligible relatives) but on merit, capabilities, and popularity. It was Galba who had created this precedent with the adoption of the short-lived Piso Licinianus, but, unlike Galba, Nerva had selected an experienced military man who met with a consensus in Rome, thus avoiding a replay of the civil wars in 69. Some consider this edifying story of Nerva's wise adoption as suspect, assuming that the choice of Trajan was imposed on Nerva by a group of soldiers and Spaniards. But even if that were so, it was a clever appointment. Trajan had the military prestige to bring the praetorians to heel, and enough connections to obtain the backing of the different armies. As a provincial, the provinces and world of the *municipia* would support him. As the son of a senator, and a traditionalist by nature, he would not clash with the Senate. Trajan seemed to meet with unanimous approval.

Plate 11.2 Food shop, Ostia, c. second century CE. C. M. Dixon

Trajan: 98–117 CE

Early career

Trajan was born in around 53 at Italica in Baetica, the oldest Roman foundation on the Iberian peninsula, to a family of local nobles. His father (referred to as Traianus pater) had had a brilliant career under Vespasian, crowned by the pro-consulship of Asia in 79–80. Trajan's career, which developed entirely under the Flavians, was marked by a predilection for military posts. Thus, for example, he remained a legionary tribune for 10 years instead of the customary one year; and throughout his *cursus*, he showed his loyalty to the ruling emperor (in 89, he fought Saturninus' rebellion), winning at the same time a reputation as an army leader.

The man

Our sources are unanimously positive on Trajan, presenting him as military man of action, with simple tastes and pastimes such as mountaineering and hunting. Cassius Dio (68.7; see also 68.21) comments uncomfortably on the emperor's excessive drinking and pederasty, adding that, nevertheless, he remained within the bounds of dignity and never harmed anyone with his practices. In the tenth book of his *Letters*, Pliny preserves a series of his epistolary exchanges with Trajan, written while Pliny was serving as governor of Bithynia. The replies to Pliny's queries about various administrative matters bear the stamp of common sense, efficiency, and respect for law and justice. A man of experience and action,

Chronology 11.1	Principal events of Trajan's reign		
Date	**Internal politics**	**External politics**	**Civilization**
99	Trajan's arrival in Rome (between spring and autumn). Distribution of a *congiarium* to the people.	*En route* for Rome, he consolidates the frontiers of the Rhine and Upper Danube.	
100	Trajan's third consulship. Trials of provincial governors.		Foundation of Timgad. Pliny the Younger: *Panegyric of Trajan*.
101	Trajan's fourth consulship. Extension of the *alimenta* (tables of Veleia, and Beneventum) (around 101).	First Dacian War.	
102	Triumph of Trajan: surname of *Dacicus*, second *congiarium*.	End of the First Dacian War.	Commencement of the laying-out of the port of Ostia.
103	Trajan's fifth consulship. Division of Pannonia into Upper and Lower Pannonia (between 103 and 106).		
105		Second Dacian War.	Bridge over the Danube at Dobreta (Turnu Severin).
106		Capture of Sarmizegethusa, suicide of Decebalus, capture of 50,000 Dacians, vast booty (Dacian gold). Annexation of Arabia, which becomes a province (roughly present-day Jordan).	Bridge of Alcantara. Construction of a road between Damascus and Eilat. Roman fleet in the Red Sea.
107	(before 107) Law obliging senators to invest one third of their wealth in Italy.	Dacia, Roman province.	Beginning of major public works in Rome.

Date	Internal politics	External politics	Civilization
	123 days of festival and games to celebrate the second Dacian triumph. Third *congiarium*.	Indian embassy to Rome.	*Via Traiana* Beneventum–Brindisi. Trophy of Adamklissi. Trajan's Baths: Aqua Traiana. Tacitus, *Histories*.
c.110		Break with the Parthians over succession to the throne of Armenia.	
111			Pliny legate in Bithynia.
112	Trajan's sixth consulship. His father and sister are deified.		Pliny's letter on the Christians to Trajan. Dedication of the Forum of Trajan. The ancient Red Sea–Nile canal is restored.
113			Dedication of Trajan's Column.
114	Thrace becomes a praetorian province for strategic reasons. Title of *Optimus* for Trajan.	Start of war with the Parthians. Invasion of Armenia, which, annexed to Armenia Minor and Cappadocia, becomes a Roman province. Campaign in northern Mesopotamia, capture of Nisibis.	Dedication of the Arch of Beneventum.
115	Jewish rebellion in Cyrenaica, Egypt, Judaea, and Mesopotamia.	Temporary occupation of Dura-Europus on the Euphrates.	
116	Trajan receives the title *Parthicus Maximus*, which he retains even after his death.	Invasion of Adiabene, a district of Babylonia across the Euphrates. Capture of Seleuceia, Ctesiphon, and Babylon; Trajan reaches the Persian Gulf. He contemplates a province of Assyria and one of Mesopotamia.	
117	End of the Jewish revolt. Hadrian, governor of Syria. Trajan dies at Selinus *en route* for Rome, on August 9. His ashes, carried to Rome, laid in the base of Trajan's Column.	Parthian counter-offensive. Victory of Trajan, who has to give up the idea of a Roman settlement in Assyria and Lower Mesopotamia.	Tacitus, *Annals*.

| Genealogy 11.1 | Trajan and Hadrian |

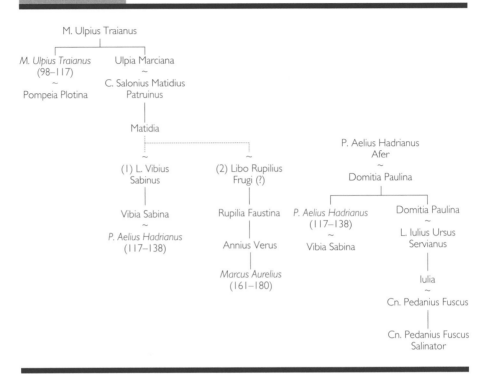

he led a simple life, was affable in his manner, and made rapid and clear-sighted decisions. He also knew the value of the gesture that strikes the imagination and consolidates popularity, such as his solemn entry (*adventus*) into Rome, on foot and without a bodyguard, and his swimming in the Euphrates, when he was over the age of 60. Deferential to the senators and magistrates and courteous to those under his administration, he nevertheless agreed, in 114, to be known as Optimus ("the Best"), a title he shared with Jupiter. For, despite his modest self-representation, Trajan did not yield any of the essence of his imperial power.

Trajan's conquests

The three cases (Dacia, Arabia, and Mesopotamia) were different.

1   The causes of the Dacian wars are obscure. The Dacian danger had existed since Domitian. Possibly Decebalus, the Dacian king, tried to create an anti-Roman coalition. The alliances he concluded with other barbarian peoples, and perhaps with the Parthians, would lead one to suppose so. It does not

Plate 11.3   Nabataean rock-hewn temple, 40 meters high, Petra (modern El Deir – the Monastery), Jordan. First century CE. C. M. Dixon

appear that Trajan's principal aim was to alter the Danubian frontier and collect as his prize the gold mines of Dacia ("You do not fear war, nor do you provoke it," claims Pliny in his *Panegyric*, 16). Fear of the barbarians, a feeling of insecurity, and perhaps a desire for military glory seem to have been the motives for the initial Dacian expedition.

2 The kingdom of the Nabataeans threatened the sole direct land link between Egypt and Judaea, by way of Gaza. Moreover, it imposed a tax on Roman traders on their way to the Red Sea. Here, then, the motive was strategic (to do away with the need to rely on the Gaza corridor), but mainly economic and political.

3 Three kinds of explanation have been proposed for the Parthian wars. For the ancients, it was a matter of Trajan's personal ambition, his desire to equal the exploits of Alexander and take up on his own account the dreams of Caesar and Antony. Strategic considerations were also significant: consolidating that frontier, and creating a protective buffer zone beyond the Euphrates as a safeguard for Syria. Lastly, economic reasons have been suggested among Trajan's motivations, related to the control of eastern trade routes and large-scale commerce with the Far East.

The exercise of power

"Here is something that I hear for the first time, that I learn for the first time, that the emperor is not above the law, but that the law is above the emperor," Pliny declares in his panegyric for Trajan. It is from the time of Trajan and his government that some modern historians begin to speak of a more liberal Empire, guided by a sort of official Stoicism. One may wonder, however, whether these historians may not have fallen into the verbal trap of arguing in nineteenth-century terms such as "liberal" about a period in which those terms have little or no real application. Thus they may have overlooked the fact that the second-century emperors (including Trajan) in fact possessed more power than first-century emperors, because the very success of the monarchical regime set up by Augustus met with less opposition. We may judge the exercise of this power in four areas.

Ideology The *Panegyric of Trajan*, a speech of thanks delivered by Pliny, and the *Discourses on Royalty* by Dio of Prusa (later known as Chrysostomos, "Golden Mouth") set out, in fairly similar terms, the major features of the ideal ruler. This ideal emperor-king is chosen by divine providence and acts in harmony with the supreme god. He governs, in Pliny's view of the emperor, in accordance with the political principles of the Senate, and his life is devoted to fulfilling the duties of his office. Father and benefactor to his subjects, he leads free men and not slaves. And his friends as well as the nobility must participate in the administration of the state. This formulation of general (and also Stoic) standards may reflect a victory of the cultivated classes in the Empire, for whom the accomplished *homo Romanus* had become the inhabitant of the *orbis Romanus*. And in many aspects, the exercise of power by the soldier-king embodied by Trajan matches this model. His virtues in the exercise of political power and his successes in military command suggested to his contemporaries a victorious *numen* shining in him and forming the basis of his authority over theworld.

Echoing Pliny and Dio, the "Jovian" theory of the government instituted by Trajan goes a step further. Inspired by the example of Domitian, but nevertheless setting aside all idea of deifying the living emperor, it claims that, with Trajan, the emperor became the agent on earth of Jupiter, vested with his power and charged with governing all peoples in his name, as the Empire enveloped the whole inhabited world. On the attic of the arch of Beneventum, on the town side, Jupiter welcomes Trajan, to whom he proffers his thunderbolt.

Relations with the Senate Trajan exercised both courtesy and control in the Senate, expressed by many attentions on his part (his presence at sittings, his choice of consuls, his allowing the election of magistrates by the Senate, etc.). He emphasized provincial entries into the assembly, so that under him about 45 percent of the senators were provincials. His censorial powers were tacitly acknowledged, and in exceptional circumstances he interfered in senatorial provinces (e.g. by sending Pliny to Bithynia–Pontus).

Plate 11.4 Roman brick architecture at Trajan's markets, Rome, constructed c.100–112 CE. C. M. Dixon

Administration The prominence given to the emperor's friends and to his council, which was still informal, was one of the main features of Trajan's administration. Among his "friends" were several groups: the "marshals," the Spaniards, the intellectuals, and the technicians. They had in common an administrative ability, and a loyalty to Trajan that brought some of them to their death at the start of the following reign. A second feature of his administration was the development of the governmental machinery to the benefit of the equestrians, whose *cursus* was already established before Trajan. Thus, the number of known equestrian procurators went up from 64 under Domitian to 84 under Trajan. Except for the department *a libellis et censibus*, the great central offices were now all run by equestrians.

Finances The tense financial situation that had marked Domitian's reign continued, despite the acquisition of the booty from the Dacian wars and the gold mines of that country. At the start of Trajan's reign, outstanding debts to the state and the coronation gold exacted from the provinces on the accession of a new emperor could be remitted, to popular acclaim. But construction work, a larger administration, military expeditions, and soldiers were very expensive.

All in all, there were few novelties in the field of financial administration. The changes that occurred were more in the nature of developments, alterations, and rearrangements, though there were a few innovations: a tax of 5 percent on inheritances by officials, and the end of farming the *portorium* (customs), now entrusted to *conductores*, who retained either a percentage or a fixed sum.

Trajan's reign left a dazzling memory. To emperors of late antiquity, the wish was expressed that they should be more fortunate than Augustus and better than Trajan. This renown resulted from his last great conquests, from the monuments and embellishments of the capital and the Empire, from his affable imperial style, and from his efficient government. But, paradoxically, Trajan, who prepared his campaigns so meticulously and ran his administration with such precision, did not make early provisions for his succession. That seems to have been left largely to the circumstances at the time.

Hadrian: 117–138 CE

The accession

On August 8, 117, did Trajan on his deathbed in Selinus, Cilicia, designate Hadrian his successor, as the official version would have us believe? The early authors doubted it. And it is true that the circumstances are elusive. The letter announcing the adoption to the Senate was signed by Plotina, Trajan's wife; on August 9, at Antioch, Hadrian learned of his adoption, and on the 11th it was announced that Trajan had died. The army immediately acclaimed Hadrian emperor, and he wrote to the Senate assuring it of his respect and asking it to confirm the imperial titles. This was done. So what actually happened? Was there some help from Plotina and the praetorian prefect, who was known to support Hadrian? Was the throne granted to him because he was Trajan's only male relative, his great-nephew, and the husband of his great-niece? Was his accession the recognition of the *de facto* power that Trajan had given him by entrusting him with the key region of Syria? Was it the culmination of a career spent at Trajan's side since the First Dacian War? None of these arguments taken in isolation is convincing. But taken as a whole they suggest Trajan's intentions for his succession. Hadrian's career seems to have been encouraged throughout by Trajan.

Early career

Like Trajan, Hadrian belonged to a family of Italians who had emigrated to Spain. His date of birth is certain (January 24, 76) but not his place of birth:

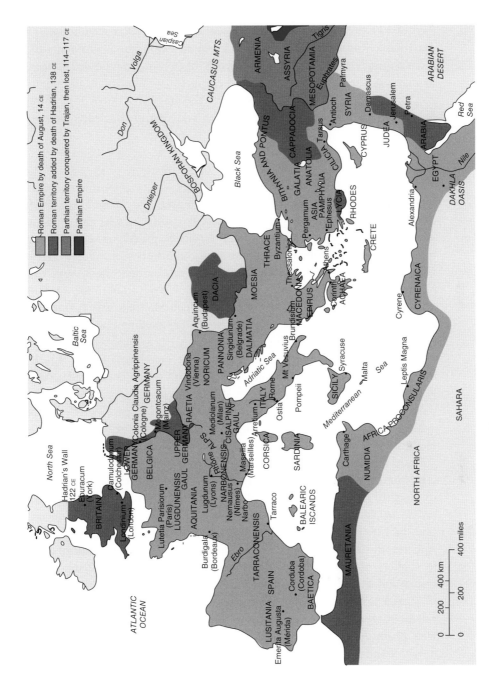

Roman Empire by death of August, 14 CE
Roman territory added by death of Hadrian, 138 CE
Parthian territory conquered by Trajan, then lost, 114–117 CE
Parthian Empire

BRITAIN
Eburacum (York)
Hadrian's Wall 122 CE
Camulodunum (Colchester)
Londinium (London)
GERMANY
LOWER GERMANY
Colonia Claudia Agrippinensis (Cologne)
BELGICA
UPPER GERMANY
Mogontcacum (Mainz)
RAETIA
Vindobona (Vienna)
NORICUM
Aquincum (Budapest)
PANNONIA
Singidunum (Belgrade)
DALMATIA
DACIA
MOESIA
THRACE
Byzantium
BITHYNIA AND PONTUS
ARMENIA
ASSYRIA
MESOPOTAMIA
Euphrates
Tigris
Palmyra
Damascus
CAPPADOCIA
GALATIA
ANATOLIA
Pergamum
ASIA
PAMPHYLIA
Ephesus
LYCIA
CILICIA
Tarsus
Antioch
SYRIA
CYPRUS
JUDEA
Jerusalem
Petra
ARABIA
EGYPT
DAKHLA OASIS
Nile
Red Sea
ARABIAN DESERT
Alexandria
RHODES
CRETE
Athens
ACHAEA
Corinth
EPIRUS
MACEDONIA
Thessalonica
Brundisium
Adriatic Sea
ITALY
Arretium
Rome
Ostia
Pompeii
Mt Vesuvius
CISALPINE
Mediolanum (Milan)
Rhone Alps
GAUL
NARBONENSIS
Nemausus (Nimes)
Narbo
Massilia (Marseilles)
LUGDUNENSIS
Lugdunum (Lyons)
AQUITANIA
Lutetia Parisiorum (Paris)
Burdigala (Bordeaux)
TARRACONENSIS
Tarraco
Ebro
SPAIN
LUSITANIA
Emerita Augusta (Mérida)
BAETICA
Corduba (Cordoba)
BALEARIC ISLANDS
CORSICA
SARDINIA
SICILY
Syracuse
Malta
Mediterranean Sea
Leptis Magna
Cyrene
CYRENAICA
AFRICA PROCONSULARIS
Carthage
NUMIDIA
MAURETANIA
NORTH AFRICA
SAHARA
North Sea
Baltic Sea
ATLANTIC OCEAN
BOSPORAN KINGDOM
CAUCASUS MTS.
Caspian Sea
Black Sea
Volga
Don
Dnieper

0   200   400 km
0   200   400 miles

Map 11.1 The extent of the Empire under Augustus, Trajan and Hadrian

perhaps Italica but more probably Rome. His career was that of a senator, with numerous honorific posts. In 108, he was appointed *consul suffectus* at the age of 32 – not the usual age, but not exceptional for one so close to the emperor. And in 111 (or 112) he was elected archon in Athens, a rare honor. The most remarkable feature of his *cursus* was his almost continuous proximity to Trajan. He was hardly ever away from the center of power. He followed Trajan to Germania, was imperial quaestor while the emperor was in Rome, accompanied him to Dacia and then to the East. And like the emperor's councilors, though they were older and had more experience, he was one of the senior administrative staff.

The man

Hadrian's personality (popularized in the novel *The Memoirs of Hadrian* by Marguerite Yourcenar) divides historians. For some he was an inquisitive intellectual, rebelling against authority and tradition, practicing several forms of art though rather as a dabbler, an admirer of the beauties of nature, but as a man vain, cruel, and obstinate. In contrast with this extreme view, numerous other judgments range from an almost unconditional admiration to the adoption of an ancient author's definition, according to which Hadrian was *varius, multiplex, multiformis*. It is difficult to encapsulate his personality in a single definition. A good example of a work of his that may be seen as an expression of his personality but is difficult to interpret is his palace at Tivoli near Rome, which he had built in two stages (118–125 and 125–133) and which comprised a dozen or so great complexes numbering about 30 buildings. Interpretations of the Tivoli palace differ widely, but they fall into three general categories: the collections of a dilettante and souvenirs of a traveler; a sort of résumé of the Empire over which Hadrian reigned; or an instrument of imperial deification.

Hadrian's personality confounded even his contemporaries, who did not appreciate him greatly. We can extrapolate from our sources that he was characterized by physical strength, a vast if slightly pedantic culture, a good knowledge of the provinces, and a solid military background. During a tour of provincial inspection, in 128, he observed the training maneuvers of a detachment of the Third Augusta, the legion stationed in Lambaesis (modern Algeria). Five of his speeches to soldiers of different ranks have survived, albeit fragmented, praising their tactics and skills (known as Lambaesis inscriptions).

According to our sources, Hadrian's tastes were simple, which by no means ruled out refinement in certain areas. He had a liking for taking part in debates with professionals, and immersed himself in intellectual disciplines (geometry, music, architecture, etc.). He liked to hunt, and indeed his hunting assumed a symbolic value, as the manifestation of his imperial *virtus*. His enjoyment of traveling led him to travel almost as a tourist (climbing to the summit of Etna, making a detour in order to visit a monument). His admiration of Greece earned him the nickname Graeculus from the Romans. His spiritual concerns took

several forms. Besides the usual interest in astrology and respect for traditional religion, he showed great enthusiasm for Greek cults (in particular that of Demeter at Eleusis, and Asclepius at Pergamum), as well as Egyptian cults. In fact Egyptian influences seem to have led him to institute a new cult, that of Antinous. This was a young slave and lover of the emperor who was drowned in the Nile under mysterious circumstances (Cassius Dio says that despite

Hadrian's claims about Antinous' accidental death, he himself killed the young man in some sort of sacrifice; 69.11). Afterwards, at the instigation of Hadrian, Antinous was worshiped as a god.

The exercise of power

A more marked authoritarianism Although Hadrian may not perhaps have been responsible for the murder at the start of his reign of the four ex-consuls, Trajan's supporters, his rule was nevertheless marked by a tightening of control. This can be seen in the codification of the social hierarchy that he initiated, with the intention of rationalizing and moralizing social relations; in the attempt to lighten the workload of Roman magistrates by dividing Italy into four judiciary districts, each entrusted to a *consularis*; and in his strained relations with the Senate (which decreed his apotheosis only on the orders of his successor).

His journeys Hadrian spent a dozen of the 21 years of his reign traveling throughout the Empire, accompanied, apparently, by part of his council. These

Plate 11.6 Hadrian's Mausoleum (known better under its medieval name, Castel Sant'Angelo), erected on the right side of the Tiber between 134 and 139 CE. Here it is seen from the Pons Aelius, also constructed at that time. istockphoto.com

| Chronology 11.2 | **Principal events of Hadrian's reign** | |

Date	Internal and external politics	Hadrian's journeys (sp = spring, s = summer, a = autumn, w = winter)	Civilization
117	Disturbances in the provinces (Mauretania, Britain, Danube). Abandonment of Trajan's eastern conquests.	s: Antioch. a: departure from Syria: Tyane, Ankara. w: Nicomedia or Byzantium.	115–120 Beginning (at the latest) of the construction of the new camp at Lambaesis.
118	Hadrian's second consulship. Troubles caused by the Roxolani on the Danube. "Conspiracy of the four ex-consuls," all four executed by the Senate, an act perhaps inspired by Hadrian.	w/sp: Moesia. sp: Pannonia. July 9: Rome.	Start of work on the villa at Tivoli, and rebuilding the Pantheon.
119	Hadrian's third consulship.		
120	Creation of four judiciary districts of Italy, entrusted to former consuls (the *quatuorvir consulares*). Dacia is divided into two provinces, Upper and Lower. Then, in c. 123, the former is subdivided into two with the creation of Dacia Porolissensis.		Suetonius, *The Lives of the Caesars*.
121	Reinforcement of the Rhine and Danube *limites*.	May–August: departure from Rome for Gaul. w?: in Lyon.	
122	Beginning of Hadrian's Wall. Death of Plotina.	sp: Upper Germania, Raetia, Noricum, Lower Germania. s: Britain. a: return via the three Gauls and Narbonensis (Nîmes, Avignon, Apt). w: Tarragona.	
123	Restoration of the sanctuary of Augustus at Tarragona. Peace with the Parthians.	w: Tarragona. w: Mauretania? (or 128). s: departure for Syria. s?: on the Euphrates. s/a: inspection along the *limes* of the Euphrates, in Cappadocia. w: return to Bithynia.	
124		sp/s: visit to Asia (Pergamum, Ephesus). a: Rhodes, Eleusis. w: Athens and journey through the Peloponnese.	
125		w/sp: journey in central Greece (Delphi).	

Date	Internal and external politics	Hadrian's journeys (sp = spring, s = summer, a = autumn, w = winter)	Civilization
126		March: initiation at Eleusis.	
127		s: return to Rome via Sicily (Etna); Rome/Tivoli; journeys in Italy.	
128	July, speech to the army of Africa.	s: Sicily, Africa, ?Mauretania (or 123). s: Rome. a/w: Athens, Eleusis.	
129	Large-scale building works in Athens.	w: Athens. sp: Ephesus. sp/s: Asia, Phrygia, Cappadocia, Cilicia. a/w: Antioch.	
130	Jerusalem becomes *colonia Aelia Capitolina*.	w: Antioch. sp: Palmyra, Arabia, Judaea. s: Alexandria, trip on the Nile. a: Thebes (colossi of Memnon), return to Alexandria.	?Start of work on Hadrian's Mausoleum. Death of Antinous and founding of Antinoöpolis (October 30).
131	Edict of the Praetor given definitive form.	sp: departure from Alexandria, coastal journey along the coasts of Syria and Asia. s/a: ?Thrace, Media, Dacia, Macedonia. w: Athens.	Inauguration of the Olympieion (Athens).
132	Jewish revolt in Judaea known as that of Bar Kochba. The cause was the plan to build a Roman town at Jerusalem, now *colonia Aelia Capitolina*.	Return to Rome. (The journey to Judaea is not certain.) Tivoli.	
134	Recapture of Jerusalem.		Inauguration of the Aelius bridge (present-day Sant'Angelo in Rome). Dedication of the temple of Rome and Venus (Rome).
135	End of the Jewish revolt. Judaea becomes the consular province of Syria–Palestine.		
136	Start of Hadrian's illness. Problem of the succession: adoption of L. Ceionius Commodus, who becomes L. Aelius Caesar.		
138	L. Aelius Caesar dies (January 1). Adoption of T. Aurelius Antoninus (the future Antoninus Pius), who himself has to adopt L. Verus and M. Annius Verus (the future Marcus Aurelius).		

journeys enabled Hadrian to make sure of the frontiers and see to their reorganization, and, as we saw in Lambaesis, to check on the morale of his troops, their loyalty, discipline, and capabilities (under his reign, Disciplina became a personified figure that was worshiped). By journeying through the provinces he could also assess the management of the governors. Additionally, it was an opportunity for him to meet provincials, take stock of the condition and needs of cities, and help them by, for example, providing material aid in the form of financial benefits or construction works, appointing *curatores* to supervise their affairs, or granting them the status of colony. Under him, the political integration of Greek-speaking elites was fully achieved.

Change of strategy Trajan's conquests were too widely spread to be held with any success in an Empire whose reserves in terms of manpower were virtually the same as in the Augustan era. So, in the East, Hadrian completed the strategic withdrawal begun at the very end of Trajan's reign, and the new provinces of Armenia, Assyria, and Mesopotamia were abandoned as early as the end of 117. Elsewhere, Hadrian pursued a policy of consolidation that would enable the Empire to defend itself.

Imposing legislation This was in the domain of civil law in particular. The Edict of the Praetor had been the principal source of private law. In theory, this catalogue of all the actions open to litigants, as formulated by the *praetor urbanus*, was applied only during the year of office of the magistrate who made it public on taking up his post. It was then renewed by his successor, so that it comprised of a substantial body of rules in flux. Hadrian appointed a jurist to give it a definitive form. This "perpetual" edict would remain the basis for the taking of legal action by private citizens until the sixth century. Hadrian's legislative acts embraced all sectors of society. They concerned soldiers, criminals, and slaves, but also re-established the wearing of the toga, denied full rights of citizenship to children of a union between a Roman and a foreign woman, and fixed numerous economic regulations in the imperial domains.

A masterful administration Under Hadrian, the imperial council became a permanent organ of central government, with jurists, senators, and equestrians. The jurists were divided into two categories according to their remuneration. Under Hadrian too, the equestrians, whose *cursus* was now established, completed their run of administrative conquests. They supervised all the great offices of the imperial bureaucracy, and obtained new financial posts (such as that of the *advocatus fisci*, an official charged with representing the interests of the tax administration in lawsuits). With 104 known equestrian officials, organized in a hierarchy that permitted military and civil advancement, the administrative machine worked well. The number of posts was not very high. This efficiency was a direct result of the peace and stability provided by the imperial regime.

Plate 11.7
Gateway to the
Roman fort at
Chester on Hadrian's
Wall. Mark
Boulton/Alamy

Hadrian's arrangement for his succession still arouses the curiosity and exercises the ingenuity of historians. Following the death of L. Aelius Caesar, his first choice, he adopted T. Aurelius Fulvius Antoninus Boionius Arrius, who in his turn had to adopt a child aged seven, L. Verus, and a young man of not yet 17, M. Annius Verus (the future Marcus Aurelius), his nephew by marriage. From that time (February 25, 138) Hadrian, increasingly ill, handed over the office of imperial power to the one who would replace him. He died at Baiae on July 10, 138.

Antoninus Pius: 138–161 CE

Stability, prosperity, happiness, harmony: these are the words constantly used to praise the reign of the man who gave his name to the dynasty. Yet this reign, which marked the apogee of the Empire, may seem insipid and lacking in artistic imagination – rather like the image of the man himself, of whom little is really known. He was born in 86 at Lanuvium in Latium, but part of his family originated from Nîmes. It was an illustrious family: one grandfather had been prefect of Rome, the other proconsul of Asia. With brickfields in the Roman region and vast properties in Italy, Antoninus was one of the wealthiest senators in the mid-second century, and his fortune had been further increased by marriage. We know next to nothing of his *cursus* before he became emperor, except for his consulship in 120, his appointment as one of the four *consulares* of Italy, his proconsulship of Asia (133–136), and his membership of the imperial council.

The sources never run short of eulogies on his qualities as a man. What we know of him and his tastes (simple and rustic) is all in the same vein. The idealized portrait of him at the helm of state by Marcus Aurelius (*Meditations* 1.16) reveals no flaw: the statesman appears to be as one with the private man. All seem to have subscribed to the recommendations Marcus Aurelius set for himself: "In all things act as a disciple of Antoninus: look at his efforts to suit his actions to reason, his equitableness in all things, his piety, his gentleness, his scorn for empty reputation, his desire to grasp reality . . . May your last hour find you with a conscience as pure as his" (*Meditations* 6.30). Antoninus died on his Lorium estate on March 7, 161. It is said that one of his last utterances was the watchword given to the tribune of his praetorian guard: "Aequanimitas" (equanimity).

There were few outstanding events in his long and peaceful reign, during which (in 148) he celebrated the 900th anniversary of Rome's founding. No senator was put to death, the state's reserves increased, the various parts of the administrative machinery functioned smoothly (although the four consular governorships of Italy, an unpopular creation from the start, were abolished), eastern cults made headway (the first **taurobolium** known in the West, at Lyons, is dated to 160)

taurobolium: Sacrifice of a bull, followed by a "baptism" accomplished by sprinkling the blood in a trench. Practiced in the worship of Cybele.

but were linked with the imperial cult, the rise of the jurists continued, and the provinces grew richer. There were some dark patches, however.

- In Britain, between 141 and 143, a new wall was built, between the Clyde estuary and the Firth of Forth, and thus farther north than Hadrian's Wall. Why this further outpost of the Empire? Was there a rising of the Brigantes? A revolt by the inhabitants of the lowlands? A strategic review? We do not know. But around 154–155 the coinage celebrated a fresh subjection of Britain. At the same date or soon after, Antoninus' Wall was abandoned, but it was repaired about 158, before being gradually abandoned once more from 159 on.
- In Egypt, around 142–144, a peasant revolt broke out, probably economic in origin.
- Disturbances in Mauretania around 145 required reinforcements to be brought from the Rhine and Danube frontiers.
- Military expeditions were organized in Dacia in around 156–157.

None of these threats was particularly serious: a few small risings broke out around the Empire and were easily controlled. But what would happen if graver threats occurred simultaneously at several points on the *limes*? The next emperor, Marcus Aurelius, did not foresee the potential danger.

Genealogy 11.2	The Antonines

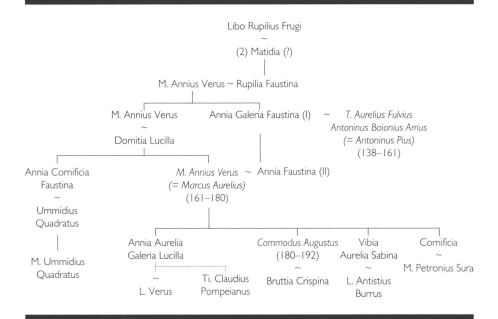

Marcus Aurelius: 161–180 CE

> Now, that unto everyone is most profitable which is according to his own constitu-
> tion and nature; and it is my nature to be rational in my actions and sociably and
> kindly disposed toward my fellow members of a city and commonwealth; as an
> Antonine, my city and my country is Rome; and speaking as a man, the whole
> world. Those things that are expedient and profitable to these cities are the only
> things that are good and expedient for me.

There can be nothing more unequivocal than these declarations from the *Meditations* (6.39). Everyone must submit to the guidance of his conscience; everyone
must carry out his duty as his conscience teaches him. And when one is a Roman
and an Antonine, one owes it to oneself to be a good Roman and a good Antonine. For Marcus Aurelius, to be emperor was first and foremost a duty. It was
also, in the unlikely event that world order no longer existed, up to him to persist,
to put the world in order: "If God exists, then all is well; or if all things go by
chance and fortune, yet mayest thou use thine own providence in those things
that concern thee properly, and then art thou well" (*Meditations* 9.26). This sense

of duty and concern to maintain order seem to have been the determining factors in the deeds of Marcus Aurelius.

His early life

He was born in Rome in April 121 and named M. Annius Verus. His family, which had consuls on both sides, came from Baetica (on his father's side) and was related to the family of both Trajan and Hadrian. Three features of his childhood and upbringing should be noted.

1 Hadrian noticed him very early on and granted him distinctions that were exceptional for his age: at six he became an equestrian, and at seven he entered the brotherhood of the Salians. Then at 15 he was betrothed to the daughter of Hadrian's short-lived intended successor, L. Aelius Caesar. Lastly, in 138, he was adopted by Antoninus. Henceforward, he was known as M. Aelius Aurelius Verus. At the age of nearly 17 he knew that he was to be the head of state.

2 From his infancy he was brought up as a ruler. One of 19 tutors, M. Cornelius Fronto, who taught him Latin rhetoric, remained in the emperor's service until his death, in around 166. Between teacher and pupil a correspondence was kept up that has come down to us. The pupil was of a rare seriousness. At 14 he chose to adhere to the principles of Stoicism, and all his life he remained loyal to its moral code, practicing spiritual exercises which he consigned to a collection of notebooks traditionally called the *Meditations*. Written in Greek, these notebooks are the last great testimony of ancient Stoicism.

3 During Antoninus' reign, Marcus pursued an accelerated *cursus*, becoming quaestor in 139 and then serving as consul with Pius in 140, shortly before his nineteenth birthday. He stayed in the emperor's entourage, marrying Antoninus' daughter Faustina in 145, by whom he had 14 children. In 147 he received tribunician power and the proconsular *imperium*.

Rarely had an emperor been so well prepared in the theory of government. What he lacked was practical experience: he had had no military command, had made no tour of the provinces, and had no acquaintance with provincial administration. Frail in health, Marcus Aurelius wore himself out in the task of government, which he tackled with good will and conscientious vigor. The man who dreamed only of books was forced to spend the greater part of his life among soldiers, spending 17 out of the 19 years of his reign on campaign.

Lucius Verus

In 138, together with Marcus Aurelius, Antoninus had had to adopt a child of seven, L. Ceionius Commodus, son of the dead L. Aelius Caesar. He had studied

(a)

(b)

Plate 11.9 (a) Replica statue of Marcus Aurelius, outside the Capitoline Museums in Rome. The original bronze (dated to 175 CE) occupies the center of a large circular gallery inside the museum. Danilo Ascione/shutterstock.co.uk **(b)** Arch of Marcus Aurelius in the Phoenician city of Oea (Tripoli), Libya. The arch was built in 165 CE, to celebrate the victories of Lucius Verus, Aurelius' brother, in Parthia and Armenia. The north-west face, shown here, is the best preserved. On the top right, the chariot of a personified Roma is drawn by sphinxes. © Roger Wood/CORBIS

under the same teachers as Marcus Aurelius, but he was the complete opposite of the philosopher-emperor. Perhaps he was not merely the jolly fellow so often described, but of the two (adoptive) brothers Antoninus preferred the elder, who was also his nephew by marriage. So Ceionius Commodus stayed in the background and did not become *Caesar*.

On his accession, Marcus Aurelius got the Senate to agree that his brother should be associated with him with the same titles, except that of *pontifex maximus*, which could not be shared. This was an original arrangement: for the first time a collegial administration was at the head of the Empire. Commodus became Imperator Caesar Lucius Aurelius Verus Augustus, better known as Lucius Verus. Theoretically, then, the brothers had much the same powers, but in fact Marcus Aurelius always kept an advantage unchallenged by Verus. Although he was not a hindrance to Marcus Aurelius, neither was he a great support. However, the philosophical emperor allowed Verus to marry his (Marcus Aurelius') daughter Lucilla in 164. It was necessary to produce solid evidence of the harmony between the two emperors, celebrated by an issue of coinage in 168.

Continuing wars

Since 117, the Empire had lived in almost total peace, but in 161, war returned, brutally and on all fronts. In Britain it was mere unrest, in Raetia and Upper Germania an incursion by the Chatti. But the main event at the beginning of the reign was in the East.

War against the Parthians: 161–166 Vologeses III, king of the Parthians, launched a double offensive against Armenia and Syria. The legions were beaten, and one was massacred at Elegeia. In response, three legions were transferred from the Rhine and the Danube to the East under the command of L. Verus, who installed himself at Antioch and entrusted the direction of operations to some remarkable generals, such as Avidius Cassius, a Syrian. In 163, Armenia was reconquered and the Parthians were driven out of Syria. In 165, Avidius Cassius invaded Mesopotamia and set up a Roman protectorate there, penetrating as far as Media. In 166, a peace treaty was concluded with the Parthians, and Dura-Europus was reoccupied. This brought two consequences: in the East, a great military command including Egypt was entrusted to Avidius Cassius; and from the East, the army brought back the plague to the West. It ravaged the Empire for 15 years.

Meanwhile, in the same year, 166, Marcus Aurelius raised two legions which he installed in northern Italy. For a new danger threatened, this time on the Danube, where the provinces were reorganized and put in the hands of experienced generals. In 168, after Verus' return, Marcus Aurelius announced to the

Senate that the two emperors would have to leave Rome in order to settle matters on the Danube.

The Danubian Wars The various episodes of these wars are not well known, and their chronology is far from certain. However, it is clear that they originated with the slow movements of the Germanic peoples. Probably because of over-population, the Germani from Scandinavia (Gepidi in the second century, Goths before them) had begun to move southward, crowding out of central and eastern Europe the eastern Germani (Burgundii, Vandals, Semnones). They in their turn pushed against the western Germani (Marcomanni, Quadi, Suevi) and the Sarmatian Iazyges. Confined in an inner Germania reduced in size by the advance of the imperial frontier, both groups saw only one solution: to negotiate or force their way into the Empire. Several wars ensued, which may be broadly grouped in two series. They are separated by a precarious interval between the spring of 175 and the autumn of 177.

The second Germanic war: 177–180 Even less is known about this second series of operations along the Danube. Everything started up again: guerrilla warfare, banditry, insecurity. The situation deteriorated so much that the presence of the emperors became necessary (from January 1, 177, Marcus Aurelius' son Commodus was co-emperor). They left Rome in August 178 with an impressive staff. The following year a victory was achieved, probably over the Quadi. The barbarians seemed to be wearing themselves out. The Iazyges remained calm and even found advantages by joining Rome's side; similar overtures were extended to the Marcomanni. Meanwhile, the Quadi were contemplating emigrating northwards. Thus, in the spring of 180, the creation of two new provinces beyond the Danube did not appear quite so utopian. But on March 17, 180, two days before the opening of the new military campaign, Marcus Aurelius died on the Danube, at Vindobona (Vienna). He was almost 59.

We must assess the importance of these wars. Militarily, the breaches of the Empire's defenses, though serious, were less catastrophic than was then believed. Yet these threatening barbarian invasions, the terrible plague, and the endless wars were such a decisive time in Rome's history that many historians see the Empire's crisis as beginning with the reign of Marcus Aurelius. Without entering a debate that turns on one's approach to the philosophy of history, we can agree that the government had lost impetus, and that there was widespread anxiety. In its most elementary form it showed itself in the persecution of the Christians, who were held responsible for the gods' anger. This same anxiety may be traced also in art, for instance, in the sarcophagus of Portonaccio (dating from 190, slightly later therefore), which represents a battle against the barbarians. The artist depicts a seething mass of tangled combatants framed by the

Chronology 11.3	**The first Germanic wars (167–175)** CE

167   The plague devastated and terrified Rome, where old purificatory religious ceremonies occupied the emperors. The Langobardi invaded Pannonia, and the Iazyges attacked the Dacian gold mines. The situation was restored, but not decisively.

168   The Marcomanni and other peoples created trouble on the Danubian frontier. The emperors went to Aquileia and negotiated with the tribes, who desired peace. There was an inspection of the Pannonian *limes* (Marcus' first journey outside Italy), and the *praetentura Italiae et Alpium* (advanced defense line of Italy and the Alps) was set up, a military zone north of Aquileia, where the emperors stopped, until the ubiquitous plague forced them to leave this port.

169   Lucius Verus died. Marcus Aurelius returned to Rome for the funeral and apotheosis. He was intent on preparing a large campaign and subduing permanently the troublesome regions to the north of the Danube, but at the same time he was faced with a financial crisis. So he took urgent and perhaps unwise measures to secure the means he required (raising troops that included brigands and slaves, auctioning the imperial tableware). By the autumn, he was once again on the Danube.

170   In the spring, there was a strong Roman offensive across the Danube. It was a disaster. Northern Italy was probably invaded by the Quadi and Marcomanni, who may have thrust as far as Aquileia, while the Costoboci (perhaps from the north of Dacia) invaded Macedonia and, raiding rapidly southwards, reached as far as Eleusis. Backed by excellent generals (Pertinax and the emperor's new son-in-law Pompeianus), Marcus Aurelius repulsed the invaders. A new great command was established in the three provinces of Dacia (Tres Daciae) and Upper Moesia.

171   Marcus Aurelius was now at Carnuntum in Pannonia. Realizing that the Marcomanni were the main danger, he drove out the last invaders, made peace with the Quadi, and organized a large-scale expedition against the Marcomanni. Barbarians were settled in regions depopulated by war and plague.

172   The Romans entered Marcomanni territory, won a victory, and then attacked the Quadi. During this campaign, lightning and rain helped the Romans (recorded as supernatural phenomena in the panel of the "rain miracle" on Aurelius' column, and on coinage). A treaty was agreed with the Marcomanni: they were forbidden to form alliances amongst themselves, and they promised to trade under Roman control, to hand over spoils and hostages, and to keep at least 5 miles from the Danube. (There was also a rebellion in Egypt of the *boukoloi*, herdsmen of the Delta, as well as incursions of the Moors into Baetica and disturbances in Armenia.)

173   There was a succession of small engagements. Marcus Aurelius stayed at Carnuntum.

174   A new war was waged against the Quadi and a campaign against the Iazyges, who were defeated in a savage war.

175   A fresh assault was made on the Sarmatians. Marcus Aurelius seemed determined to create new provinces out of these regions. However, when he learned that the governor of Syria, Avidius Cassius, had proclaimed himself emperor and that the eastern provinces had rallied to the usurper, a peace was arranged with the Iazyges.

great figures of the barbarian princes who had been taken prisoner; exhausted, emaciated, and marked by grief and humiliation, they can be seen as born of a new awareness of human frailty. A similar reading can be applied to the deep reliefs of Aurelius' column, which was completed posthumously, to celebrate the emperor's Danubian wars. Although it was clearly modeled on Trajan's column, the orderly and almost peaceful figures populating the Dacian campaigns have been replaced by tangled and suffering bodies. Beginning with Aurelius, it seems that the vulnerability of its frontiers drove home for Rome the sufferings of war.

The exercise of power

If war was the major preoccupation of Marcus Aurelius' government, the running of the Empire was by no means neglected. The tenor was conservative, but with some innovations.

The overall running of affairs was inspired by the example of Antoninus, the model for Marcus Aurelius, or governed by the functional development of the imperial administration's major offices. Relations with the Senate were good, in spite of the reinstatement of the *consulares* of Italy under the title of *iuridici*, chosen from former praetors. There was a further increase in officials of equestrian rank (there were now 125 known procuratorial posts, the chief one with an annual salary of 300,000 sesterces). The position of the imperial council was confirmed. There were measures to limit fraudulent claims to Roman citizenship and to resolve fiscal problems. Talented men were promoted, these frequently of modest social origin (Pertinax, Pescennius Niger) or from the provinces (Pompeianus, Severus). And there was a further extension of imperial legislation (over 300 known laws, half of which concern women, children, and slaves).

Out of respect for Hadrian's intentions, Marcus Aurelius had associated Lucius Verus with the government of the Empire. This experiment in collegiality was repeated: on January 1, 177, Marcus Aurelius' son Lucius Aelius Aurelius, born in 161 and Caesar since 166, became Augustus, with the same powers and the same subordination as Lucius Verus had had (he was not *pontifex maximus*). The succession was secure. This innovation of the unequal sharing of supreme power was accompanied by a trial delegation of powers. The most obvious instance is that of Avidius Cassius, who received supreme command over all the provinces in the East. The risk of usurpation that this carried manifested itself in April 175, when Avidius Cassius proclaimed himself emperor. In this case, the army remained loyal and there was no civil war. Despite the military advantages in creating great positions of command, the political drawbacks were obvious.

In the preceding reigns there had been some Christian martyrs. Their renown, however, did not approach that of those in Marcus Aurelius' reign (the most celebrated being the apologist Justin in Rome, and the group from Lyons and Vienne in 177) or those at the start of Commodus' reign (such as the first African martyrs at Scillium in Numidia in July 180). This increase can be variously explained. Since the edicts on the Christians of Trajan and Hadrian, imperial policy toward them had not varied. Theoretically, a governor had to punish any Christian who was denounced eponymously, who proved to be such, and who persisted in his faith. In practice, as the initiative never came from the public authorities, Christians were not generally persecuted or systematically sought out. Each affair was a special case that depended on the state of relations between Christians and non-Christians at that particular place and time and on the attitude of the governor. Like other pagan intellectuals (for example, Celsus, whose *True Account* was written in about 178), Marcus Aurelius felt no sympathy for Christians. He blamed them for their obstinacy in exposing themselves to death and, far from seeing it as an act of courage, condemned it as fanaticism. Nevertheless, he had no desire for confrontation with the Christians because of their beliefs; what occurred was merely the application of the law currently in force. The main causes of these martyrdoms are to be sought elsewhere. There were three.

1   The spread of the new religion. It reached the western provinces and penetrated intellectual and military circles. In expanding, the church encountered its first heresies, such as Montanism in Phrygia and Rome, which glorified and encouraged the thirst for martyrdom during the 170s.
2   Popular hatred. Not very well known, living apart, the Christians of this anguished period were used as scapegoats for every political and social ill.
3   The Christians' refusal to recognize the gods of the Empire and the divinity of the emperor, which automatically placed them among the subversive elements of society, since their loyalty thus seemed conditional.

Commodus: 180–192 CE

The succession

For the first time an emperor had been born to the purple. Commodus' education had been meticulous, he had been prepared for his office, and, since 177, he had been co-emperor. On the death of his father, he became sole emperor without any opposition: whatever the new emperor's defects, he was Marcus Aurelius' only surviving son. Historians have argued over whether Marcus Aurelius made the best choice, but the question is pointless, since he could hardly have hesitated to choose the son of the man placed by the gods at the head of the Empire.

The chief events of his reign

180   Influenced by some of his father's friends, Commodus stayed on the Danube, negotiated a victorious peace with the Quadi and Marcomanni, and then returned to Rome in October.
182   A plot by Lucilla, Commodus' sister, with the help of certain senators, almost succeeded. From then on, Commodus distrusted the Senate and lived

in fear of assassination. He inaugurated a reign of terror, had friends of Marcus Aurelius executed, and let others govern on his behalf in order to give himself over to debauchery.

182–185   The prefect of the praetorian guard, Tigidius Perennis, became influential. Competent in military matters, he kept an attentive eye on the frontiers, but he also engaged in personal politics; he apparently favored the equestrians over the senators and even tried to elevate his son to the purple. He was murdered by the soldiers.

185–189   Government was under the chamberlain Cleander, a former slave promoted to the rank of equestrian. While Commodus took no interest in anything but chariot races and gladiatorial fights, Cleander sold offices, debased the Senate and the magistracies, had important people killed, and had himself appointed praetorian prefect in 189. He was executed on the orders of Commodus, who wished to pacify the starving and rebellious Roman crowd (end of 189 or the spring of 190).

190–192   Conspiracies real or imagined, murders, favorites, concubines (especially Marcia), and intrigues formed the political fabric of these years. Commodus increasingly revealed signs of a religious obsession whose first symptoms had appeared early in his reign. He claimed to be Hercules, refounded the city of Rome as the *colonia Commodiana*, and gave legions, fleets, the city of Carthage, and the months of the year names that he claimed as his titles, such as *Exsuperatorius* ("he who prevails over all"), a title reflecting the influence of eastern astrology and Greek theological thought. Posing as the first among the gladiators, he insisted that the ritual procession of January 1, 193, should be transformed into a gladiatorial procession, after which (although this is disputed) various people were to be put to death. Three of his intended victims, including Marcia, stole a march on Commodus–Hercules, poisoning and strangling him on December 31, 192. Cassius Dio (73.18) assured his readers that all of Commodus' spectacular eccentricities were true, since he himself as a senator had been a witness to the emperor's public conduct.

The exercise of power

The madness of Commodus had significant repercussions only in the capital; the Empire suffered hardly at all. The administrative machine worked by itself; the imperial council and central offices took decisions and the emperor added his signature. There was one modification, however: the post of praetorian prefect became the most elevated, its holder a sort of vice-emperor who directed the imperial council. Troubles in Britain were reported, and the frontier was withdrawn to Hadrian's Wall; likewise, there was disorder in Gaul, caused by bands of deserters led by a certain Maternus. The supposed economic crisis of the time is now often regarded as beginning about a decade later. In fact, the reign of

Commodus is not very well known. The sources in general merely list him among the bad emperors – yet his successor, Septimius Severus, insisted on declaring himself a brother to Commodus.

With the death of Commodus a dynasty and an era came to an end. A period of crisis began, the most serious since the year of the four emperors. Before we resume this narrative in the following chapter (section 12.1), we now need to turn to the several geopolitical, social, and cultural features of the Antonine period: the status of Italy and the provinces, the process of their Romanization, the Mediterranean economy, the army, and, finally, the political and cultural expansion of spectacles and entertainment in Rome.

11.2 | Italy in Decline, the Provinces Expanding

By giving a new administrative structure to the provinces and Italy, Augustus had changed the traditional relations between the peninsula and its conquests. Until that time the provinces had been exploited for the benefit of the victors. Starting with the Julio-Claudians, the new status of the provinces allowed them to develop in their own way, almost on an equal footing with Italy. But the consequences of this change – the relative decline of Italy and an uneven but general expansion of the provincial world – did not begin to show until the time of the Flavians. Under the Antonines, this provincial advantage was obvious, and it is reflected in the geographical origin of the imperial families.

Italy

Italy was distinct from the provinces, and occupied a privileged position that had ensured its prosperity in the first century. Peopled entirely by Roman citizens (among its free inhabitants), divided since the time of Augustus into 11 regions, administered by the Senate and senatorial magistrates, and benefiting from a privilege that exempted it from land tax (*tributum*), Italy also maintained an active municipal life. After all, this is where the Flavian dynasty had emerged from. However, in the second half of the century, Italy began to show signs of a decline, which became more marked in the second century.

Signs of decline

Administration and law The features of the peninsula in the domain of administration and law that had made it entirely distinct from the provinces became imperceptibly blurred, more for technical reasons than by political will. To ensure better administration and better justice, Hadrian created four judiciary districts entrusted to former consuls. The measure was so unpopular that his successor revoked it, before Marcus Aurelius re-established it in a weaker form with the *iuridici*, former praetors and all Italian. Similarly, for trials beyond the competence of municipal magistrates, it was the praetor, the prefect of the capital (in a radius of 100 miles around Rome), or the praetorian prefect who stepped in. Since the reign of Marcus Aurelius, the praetorian prefect had also been responsible for maintaining order in the peninsula. Lastly, the maintenance of roads and riparian lands was supervised by senators or equestrians.

Politics Under Trajan, around 45 percent of the senators were provincials, and under Commodus around 60 percent. In the pressure groups that formed within the Senate, the Italians had little influence, except under Antoninus.

Military domain Until the time of Marcus Aurelius there had been no great troop concentrations in Italy, apart from those stationed in Rome and the ports of the praetorian fleets. The barbarian threat on the Danubian frontier compelled troops to be stationed in the northern part of the peninsula, though not permanently. Second, Italians virtually disappeared from the legions. Starting from Hadrian's time, the movement was very clear, and was to be found at all levels of the military hierarchy. Among the rank-and-file legionaries, Italians became rare (the ones remaining often came from Cisalpine Gaul), and among centurions and those of the rank of *primipilus* (the senior centurion of each legion and commander of its first cohort), Italians were henceforth the minority. Explicably, Italians who joined the military preferred the Rome garrison.

The economy The economic decline of Italy during this period, known to the ancients and given varying interpretations in modern times, took different forms according to the region, economic sector, and type of property. It was noticeable as early as the beginning of the second century and was accompanied by the problem of a workforce that had become scarce, expensive, and, according to Pliny, lacking in ability or, as modern historians suggest, not properly used. Generally speaking, those regions of Italy with products in competition with those of the provinces (pottery in the case of Etruria, wine and oil in that of Campania) suffered a decline, while those which preserved a local market (Latium and Rome, for instance) or made gains (such as Cisalpine Gaul with the development of Aquileia and its region) maintained their activities without interruption. Hence, the picture of the Italian economic decline is a fragmented one, since local conditions played a determining role: the Apennine territories, which lived somewhat apart, the rural areas in the south, and those of Campania appear to have been the most affected. In nearly all the regions where the decline was apparent (in Etruria, for example), there was a perceptible retreat into self-sufficiency or economic stagnation rather than a brutal collapse. With the expansion of interprovincial trade, Italy no longer played the role of middleman that it had once enjoyed. It no longer had anything to sell to the East, and had precious little to offer the West.

Box 11.1   Rome under the Antonines

The fabric of the city of Rome, with its rich monumental inheritance, was renovated by the building works of the first Antonines (chiefly Trajan and Hadrian). The political, intellectual, artistic, and chief consumer center of the Empire, it was a cosmopolitan city of around a million people, with a hierarchized social stratification that reflected imperial society (slaves, freedmen, *peregrini, humiliores, honestiores*). Built without any overall plan, and with construction work permanently going on, it juxtaposed private houses of one or a few storeys (*domus*) and multi-storey apartment blocks (*insulae*), residential quarters and working-class quarters. The city was an interlacing of narrow, cluttered, twisting streets (about 85 km), public and private buildings, open squares and gardens. Despite the spectacles provided by this leisure capital, despite the abundance of water and a more or less satisfactory drainage system (for surface water), and despite the "lungs" provided by the Tiber, life seems to have been hard for the common people and turbulent for the great, but everyone was proud to live in this city *par excellence*, the center of power, where everything converged – men, products, religions.

The intellectual field A recess in intellectual activity and creativity became increasingly evident in Italian circles during the century. Authors compiled, summarized, and began to repeat the ideas of former times. There are some memorable names, though in some instances they still belonged to the first century, by virtue of their education: Tacitus, Pliny, Suetonius, Juvenal, Aulus Gellius. But it is significant that Marcus Aurelius wrote his *Meditations* in Greek, the language of philosophy certainly, but also of intellectual renewal. The only area that continued to advance was the law, in which field Roman jurists, despite tough competition from the Greek schools, still preserved their supremacy. In particular, manuals of jurisprudence were written, such as the *Institutes* of Gaius (perhaps a Greek).

A relative decline

The image of an Italian decline needs to be modified in a number of ways. First, it took place over a long period of time, though generally it was more perceptible at the end of the second century than at its start. Second, since the wealth of the regions was not identical to begin with, a region in crisis like the developed Campania could still be richer than one that had always been neglected. Third, certain economic sectors (brickworks, metal industries, luxury crafts, grain growing, and wool weaving) maintained their position or even advanced. Building activity and municipal benefaction in the cities showed no signs of faltering up to the reign of Marcus Aurelius and even beyond. Furthermore, one must take into account Italy's amenities (roads, monuments, baths, standard of living, etc.), which were more complete and more established than those of the provinces and required maintenance (generally carried out) rather than addition. Last, we should not overlook the importance of the prestige of the land and history of Italy, with the Latin language learnt in the provinces, and with the presence in Italy of the center of political decision-making. For all the factors leading to

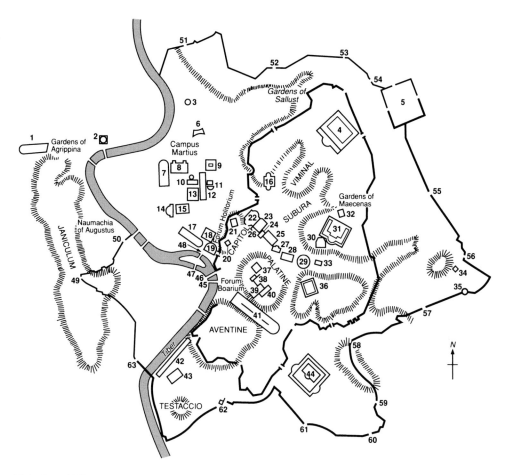

Figure 11.1 Imperial Rome

1 Circus of Caligula 2 Mausoleum of Hadrian 3 Mausoleum of Augustus 4 Baths of Diocletian 5 Camp of the Praetorians
6 Horologium of Augustus 7 Stadium of Domitian 8 Baths of Nero 9 Temple of the Divine Hadrian 10 Pantheon 11 Temple
of Isis 12 Saepta Iulia 13 Baths of Agrippa 14 Theater of Pompey 15 Portico of Pompey 16 Baths of Constantine 17 Circus
Flaminius 18 Portico of Octavia 19 Theater of Marcellus 20 Temple of Jupiter Optimus Maximus 21 Arx 22 Forum of Trajan
23 Forum of Augustus 24 Forum of Nerva 25 Forum of Peace 26 Forum of Caesar 27 Basilica of Constantine 28 Temple of
Venus and Rome 29 Flavian amphitheater (Colosseum) 30 Baths of Titus 31 Baths of Trajan 32 Portico of Livia 33 Ludus
Magnus 34 Baths of Helena 35 Amphitheater Castrense 36 Temple of the Divine Claudius 37 Palace of Tiberius 38 Palace of
the Flavians 39 Palace of Augustus 40 Stadium 41 Circus Maximus 42 Portico of Aemilia 43 Warehouses of Galba 44 Baths
of Caracalla 45 Sublician bridge 46 Aemilian bridge 47 Cestian bridge 48 Fabrician bridge 49 Porta Aurelia 50 Porta
Septimiana 51 Porta Flaminia 52 Porta Pinciana 53 Porta Salaria 54 Porta Nomentana 55 Porta Tiburtina 56 Porta
Praenestina 57 Porta Asinaria 58 Porta Metronia 59 Porta Latina 60 Porta Appia 61 Porta Ardeatina 62 Porta Ostiensis
63 Porta Portuensis

decline, there remained stimulating factors in Italian economic life: the influence
of the capital and its satellites, the ports, and numerous towns. By way of Cisalpine Gaul, Italy was linked with a market that, in the second half of the century,
began to escape the pull of the Mediterranean and to turn toward continental

Europe. Moreover, the Antonines, except for Hadrian, always paid great attention to the position of Italy, which they wanted to support.

In this respect, Trajan's policy was significant, even if it is hard to discern the results. The price of land had gone down. By obliging senators to invest one third of their wealth in Italian land, the emperor sought to increase the value of properties in Italy. Working in the same direction, he developed one of Nerva's creations, the *alimenta*. These were permanent loans at around 5 percent granted by the imperial tax administration to Italian land-owners. Interest was collected by the public administrations of cities, which distributed it to poor children (first boys, then girls). It has been suggested that it was a sort of land bank intended to encourage farmers to develop their lands. Perhaps it is more realistic to see the *alimenta* as a work of public assistance and relief, perhaps meant to combat population decline, with the ultimate aim of ensuring the military recruitment of Italians. At all events, the imperial initiative led to other, similar private foundations.

The western or Latin Empire

Since Actium, on the psychological level, and since the dual chancellery (Latin and Greek) instituted by Claudius, on the administrative level, one may legitimately make a distinction between two sides: the West, where Latin was the sole official language, and the East, where Greek competed with it.

Roughly speaking, the boundaries were administrative: south of the Mediterranean the dividing line coincided with the frontier between proconsular Africa and Cyrenaica; to the north, the northern frontiers of Macedonia and Thrace, although the Moesias, Latin-speaking (above all, the army), also spoke Greek. It was possible to get on in the world without speaking Greek (although Romans of the cultivated classes were bilingual); it was less possible to do so without a knowledge of Latin.

In the second century, the western provinces reaped the benefits of the Flavian initiatives and the peace guaranteed by the Empire. For all of them, the Antonine era was, to varying degrees, a period of great prosperity. It is true that during the last quarter of the century there were signs of a developing climate of uncertainty – for instance, those caches of coins that archaeology has revealed in Gaul, hoarded in the reign of Commodus. Nevertheless, the West's political supremacy, only marginally disturbed by Avidius Cassius' bid for power in the East, was undeniable. It was accompanied by great administrative stability: with the exception of Dacia, and some alterations of status linked with problems of security (under Marcus Aurelius, Baetica was for a time an imperial province, and Noricum and Raetia, from being procuratorian, became praetorian provinces), the western provinces retained the same administrative status as in the preceding century.

These provinces enjoyed unprecedented economic success, which showed itself in the expansion of cultivated land in rural areas and the embellishment and expansion of towns (Lyons, for example). Other cities often found themselves cramped within their original boundaries, like Cuicul (Djemila), in Africa, a colony founded under Nerva, which was already overflowing its early walls. The western provinces also now possessed an intellectual life. Africa, (with Florus, Fronto, Apuleius, and Tertullian, one of the leading Christian writers in Latin) took over from Italy as the main source of Latin literature. Finally, throughout the West, and apparently more there than in the East, local elites obtained Roman citizenship, either by personal promotion (auxiliaries, magistrates, and even decurions since Hadrian) or by collective advancement (honorary colonies). It was bestowed without necessarily supplanting the traditional or customary rights of the local community: an inscription recovered from Banasa (modern Morocco) shows that in 177 the chief of the Zegrenses tribe in Mauretania Tingitana both obtained full citizenship rights and retained the traditional right of his tribe.

The islands

Sicily, a senatorial province, remained a land of large cereal-producing estates (especially imperial ones). Since the time of Augustus, its inhabitants had benefited from Latin rights, and the exploitation of republican times had ceased. There was a strong Romanization, but Apuleius indicates that people there still spoke Greek and Siculian alongside Latin. The three main towns were Syracuse, the capital, Catana, and Tauromenium (Taormina), which, with its famous theater, dates as we know it from the Antonines.

Sardinia was generally administered by the Senate, and Corsica by an equestrian procurator. Each in its own rhythm, these two islands participated in western expansion. In both cases, urbanized coastal regions (Olbia, Cagliari, and Porto Torres in Sardinia; Aleria and the east coast of Corsica) contrasted with a hinterland where life carried on traditionally, as it had in the previous centuries. Sardinia exported metals and grain; Corsica made the most of its resources of coniferous trees and tar.

The Iberian peninsula

The Iberian peninsula comprised three provinces, one senatorial (Baetica), the other two imperial (Tarraconensis, where the Seventh Gemina was stationed, and Lusitania), each divided into *conventus*. By the start of the second century, it had undergone three waves of Romanization (the Second Punic War, Caesar and Augustus, the Flavians), and was now considered as one of the leading provincial areas, having given the Empire not only great writers but also the first non-Italian emperor. It was fortunate enough to possess some significant advantages. It was the only large portion of the Empire remote from a dangerous frontier. Its rivers were accessible far into the interior, its plains were fertile, its mountains contained minerals, and its coastal waters teemed with fish. Its traditional civilizations were also mixed with Phoenician, Greek, and Punic influences. It exported grain, excellent olive oil, and wine, and its flocks were plentiful. Workshops producing garum (a thick sauce prepared from pickled fish) dotted the southern coasts. Mining territories, with special procurators, were formed in the north-west, the south-west, and Baetica. And the numerous towns in the south and in the valley of the Ebro rivaled the three capitals, Cordoba, Mérida, and Tarragona, not to mention Italica, which neither Trajan nor Hadrian neglected.

The Alpine provinces

These were procuratorian and followed the same pattern as each other. There were few novelties, but rather a consolidation of the features of the preceding century: a mountain economy (wood, honey, cooperage, cheeses, tolls on the mountain passes).

The three Gauls: Lugdunensis, Aquitania, Belgica

These comprised about 60 "cities" which gathered once a year, in a sort of federal district at Condat on the slopes of the Croix-Rousse between the Rhône and Saône facing the colony of Lyons, to celebrate the cult of Rome and Augustus, and to deliberate in a Council of the Gauls. In this sense, they indisputably formed a political and territorial entity. Within this, the presence of the Roman army was felt more and more the closer one was to the Rhine, especially through its influence on economic production – thus, cereals and wool produced by the villages of the north (modern Artois and Picardy) were funneled to the legions of the Rhine. In the second century, the three Gauls enjoyed material prosperity, based on their varied agricultural produce (grain, wood, abundant livestock, wines, textiles), advanced techniques (scythes, "harvesters," marling), sound craftsmanship (pottery, textiles, metalwork), a road network improved by Antoninus, navigable rivers, and active traders (such as the merchants of Lyons and Trier). This material prosperity was enhanced by the urban development in several towns, particularly Lyons, which the Antonines showered with favors; then came Trier, Bordeaux (which, during the second century, became the capital of Aquitania), Autun, Reims, followed by the large towns of Metz, Poitiers, Limoges, and Lutetia. In the south-west, the center, the west, and the north, where towns were very sparse, there were immense empty spaces. This urban disposition was to a great extent the model for the present-day network of towns and cities in this area.

There is no doubt that the three Gauls were among the richest provinces in the Empire and, because of the diversity and complementary nature of their resources, they were most prepared to live independently. Yet their loyalty to the regime was total. Farmers, traders, artisans, urban notables, and native chiefs were committed to the peace that secured their incomes, protected them from the Germani, and ensured their social position. Paradoxically, therefore, very few Gallo-Romans, originating from these regions, are known to have had the desire to play a political role in the capital. A municipal or guild setting seems to have attracted them much more.

Plate 11.10
Butcher's shop. Relief from Dresden. C. M. Dixon

The two Germanies

These two military provinces formed the shield for the Gauls. Lower Germania, to the north, extended east only to the banks of the Rhine and IJssel, with Cologne as its capital. Upper Germania overflowed into Switzerland, Burgundy, and Franche-Comté on the left bank of the Rhine, on which bank its capital (Mainz) lay, and covered to the east the Taunus mountains region and the Agri Decumates. In these provinces, the army left its mark everywhere: towns arose from the legionary camps, permanent or temporary; forts and fortresses gave birth to little villages; tanneries, brickfields, farms, and every kind of craftwork all served the army; political life was linked with loyalty to the generals. At the end of the second century, it was no longer a Roman army in the Germanies, but the Roman army *of* the Germanies. Trade with independent Germani and contacts with the Danubian provinces and Britain all played a part in the area's development.

Britain

This province contained three colonies (Colchester, Lincoln, Gloucester), some 20 "cities," *municipia* (including London, where the governor resided), and three legions. In relation to the size and population of the province, these legions rendered Britain the largest garrison in the Empire. In reality, two Britains were living side by side: in the south, a country Romanized by veterans, with villas and a few centers of Roman urban life; in the north, a military zone. There were also mines, mainly of silver and iron, and there was extensive trade with the Rhineland by way of Boulogne, the British imports through which in the second century eclipsed those of products from southern Gaul and Italy. Like the three Gauls, Britain began to depend on its own economic development.

Dalmatia

The territory of Dalmatia was broadly the same as that of the former Yugoslavia. Since the Flavians, there had been no troops stationed there on a permanent basis, but it remained a consular imperial province. The governor resided at Salonae, which blossomed around the mid-second century, at which time it possessed some 60,000 inhabitants, an amphitheater, and baths. In the last quarter of the century, a new equilibrium emerged. Until then, the coast, which had been colonized early on and was thoroughly Romanized, had been the wealthiest region. At this time, however, it appears to have entered a period of stagnation, to the advantage of the interior, a reservoir for army recruits, which rose to prosperity.

The Danubian provinces

Lying along the banks of the river, these provinces were crisscrossed by military flotillas. There was one province on the left bank, Dacia. All the others lay on the right bank.

Dacia The administrative status and internal arrangement of Dacia changed several times until, under Marcus Aurelius, it was organized in three sectors, each supervised by a procurator, under a single governor of consular rank. Heavy colonization began in the reign of Trajan. Civilians and ex-soldiers from all over the Roman world settled there. The Dacians were attracted by Roman civilization and Dacia was Romanized rapidly and in depth. The former capital, Sarmizegethusa, became a Roman colony between 108 and 110. But the governor resided in another large town, Apulum. The province had the advantages of a good road network and mines, but these mines yielded less than had been hoped.

Raetia Snugly fitted in between the Agri Decumates to the north, Upper Germania to the west, and Italy to the south, Raetia, a poor and barely Romanized imperial province, became praetorian in status under Marcus Aurelius. It had two towns of importance: the capital Augsburg, a Roman foundation that enjoyed its greatest prosperity in the second century, and Regensburg, where the legion commanded by the legate was stationed.

Noricum The administrative development of Noricum paralleled Raetia's. But this province was richer (iron mines, chiefly exploited in the second century, and earlier Romanization) and it carried more strategic weight because of its position as a communications center: its capital, Virunum, and the town of Celeia (Celje, in Slovenia) were the junctions commanding the roads to the Danube and Aquileia.

The Pannonias Emerging under Augustus from the fragmentation of Illyricum, Pannonia was divided by Trajan: to the west, with its northern frontier resting on the Danube, Upper Pannonia (capital, Carnuntum, 40 km east of Vienna); to the east, Lower Pannonia, bound by the river, whose line it followed (capital, Aquincum, Budapest). In the center of the Danubian *limes*, these two provinces (four legions in the second century) occupied a vital position, and would constantly grow from the time of the Severi. But it was in the second century that their nature was established. It involved four elements:

1 Romanization was early, with strong urban development under the Flavians (Siscia/Sisak and Sirmium, two colonies that enclosed the River Sava) and under the first Antonines (Carnuntum and Aquincum became *municipia*; Poetovio and Mursa, colonies that kept watch on a more northerly line than that of the Sava, the Drava). As early as in Trajan's time, each of these provinces had a *concilium*.
2 The integration of the indigenous peoples was successful. They adhered to the municipal system, and many of them served in the army. At the beginning of Trajan's reign some Pannonians reached praetorian rank.
3 There were few large landed estates, but very many small and medium-sized properties belonging to veterans and native free farmers. Both were influenced by the presence of the armies and maintained a particular outlook, little removed from that of the "soldier-farmer."
4 Trade, which was in the hands of foreigners, was lively. There was the old north–south amber route as well as the new Danube route, with many traders from Cologne and Trier, and with outlets from the eastern provinces via Sirmium.

The Moesias Created by Domitian, the two consular provinces of Moesia straddled the Latin and Greek worlds. To the east, Lower Moesia opened on to the Black Sea, where Greek towns preserved their autonomy (Tomi, Callatis); to the west, Upper Moesia adjoined Lower Pannonia. Under the protection of the omnipresent army, a basically agricultural economy developed under the Antonines. The primary function of the towns was military, whether it was Viminacium (a *municipium* under Hadrian), Trajan's headquarters at the time of the First Dacian War, or Oescus, also on the Danube, a colony under Trajan and former legionary base.

The eastern or Greek Empire

Compared with the West, the East gave the appearance of being a more unified entity. The reality was different: the ethnic and cultural diversity was perhaps even greater. Like the western provinces, those of the East enjoyed significant prosperity in the second century, but the equality of achievement of the two parts of the Empire in the middle of the century actually masked an unequal strength. The western provinces reached their peak at this time, and this achievement was not prolonged much beyond the end of the century, except in Africa. Those in the East, despite a few bad patches, maintained their economic expansion, extended their intellectual pre-eminence, and, in the following century, became the vital center of the Empire. So the province-by-province study of the East will be integrated into the picture of the Empire in 235 (see below, chapter 13).

The reasons for prosperity

The overall expansion of the East to the detriment of the West can be discerned in the second half of the Antonine century. But the reasons for it trace further back. Before we come to these, we must first note that those eastern lands were all countries with ancient civilizations and had never stopped being rich, so great was the capital that still lay in the memory, knowledge, and experience of men in every area (technical, commercial, social, political, economic, and spiritual). It was just that piracy and brigandage, conquest and pillage, civil war and destruction had all weakened and divided these regions, bringing some decline.

The first reason, or cause of this prosperity, was the restoration of confidence following the annexations and alterations of the first century CE. At the dawn of the Antonine century these events, together with the various expeditions to the frontiers and outside the Empire, brought about an almost complete internal peace and stability (with the exception of the Jewish revolts, and endemic but feeble brigandage in Roman Egypt, Thrace, and the north-east of Cappadocia), and the disappearance of all the client states west of the Euphrates (the last being the Nabataean kingdom, annexed in 106). Also a more honest and careful administration emerged (as indicated by the correspondence between Trajan and Pliny), and an increase in wealth due to the presence of the troops – all results likely to restore confidence throughout the whole of the East. But there were too the particular local effects on commerce. In Syria, for example, more intense and profitable commercial relations with the Parthian Empire resumed in the wake of Trajan's Parthian expeditions.

The second cause of eastern expansion in the second century was the creation by Rome of a policy adapted to the East that encouraged the reinvigoration of its intensely urban life. The extent of the East's urbanization was remarkable not only in terms of the number of towns and cities to be found there, and of their size (in the Augustan era, Alexandria had over 600,000 inhabitants and Antioch around 300,000, and many in Asia Minor over 50,000), but also in terms of the importance they had achieved, culturally and historically. The city and the town lay at the very heart of the history of the East, where for centuries they had fulfilled administrative, economic, and religious functions. Although these diverse towns had entered a period of decline (of the 53 towns known in Boeotia in classical times, 10 had disappeared by the end of the republican era), the peace and stability brought by the Empire had checked it, although not everywhere (in Boeotia only 32 remained in the second century). Under Augustus, several eastern cities set about honoring the emperor with monumental buildings, in order to obtain from him advantages that would allow them to outstrip a rival. It then became clear that, confronted with these numerous, heavily populated towns, often haughtily proud of their past, yet also anxious to gain Roman favors and preserve their privileges, Rome could not conduct a policy comparable to the one it had used in the West.

There are too many missing parts for us to know all the aspects of the policy that Rome adopted in the East. It seems to have manifested itself in two complementary ways. First, Rome exercised tolerance of the institutions that had pre-existed Roman government, as long as they supported it. Second, it presented a model state – its own – which could be adjusted to suit different places and circumstances to achieve its full effect. A clear (if extreme) example of the first case was that of Egypt. Apart from the introduction of a few high officials and a poll tax (payable by all, except Greeks and Romans, between the ages of 14 and 60), as well as a modification of the status of lands and the creation under Hadrian of the Greek city of Antinoöpolis, there were no basic changes in the institutions of the Ptolemaic period. Similarly, in the Hauran valley, in the south-western region of modern-day Syria, where Rome could not rely on a network of cities but where numerous rural communities existed, doing a fairly adequate job of self-administration, Rome encouraged these villages to provide themselves with more-structured institutions, and granted the largest of them the privileged rank of *metrokomia* (mother-village). Again, it is revealing that the number of free and autonomous cities (e.g. Laodicea under Hadrian) was far higher in the East than in the West.

An example of the second type of case is Patras, whose resettlement took place through a combination of Greek populations founded as a Roman colony, whereas farther west and north, in Nicopolis, the foundation established by Octavian after Actium had been created not as a colony but as a "Greek city." In interior Anatolia, tribal communities formed themselves into a new city, and Anatolian towns that in earlier times had preserved their status of sacerdotal state became ordinary *poleis* during the first century (Hierapolis in Phrygia). In Pisidia, the veterans of the Augustan colonies were rapidly absorbed by the native milieu, and in the Biqa' valley, indigenous and Roman colonial communities (there was a *pagus Augustus*) closely adjusted their lives to one another to their mutual benefit.

The final factor that gives us a better understanding of the East's expansion in the second century is the attitude of the emperors. As we have seen, once the war with Antony was over, Augustus took care to repair the disastrous consequences of the Civil Wars and to restore friendly relations with Greece and the East. He was drawn along that path by the rapidity with which the eastern cities had greeted his victory and the eagerness with which they promoted the imperial cult (the first sanctuaries of Rome and Augustus were set up at Nicomedia and Pergamum). His attention to eastern provinces (aid for Corinth, for Paphos when it was devastated by an earthquake, for Athens, etc.) was met by evidence of loyalty and enthusiasm on their part (temples, towns that changed their name, etc.). This double movement continued and spread during the first century CE. Claudius took a special interest in Apamea, which renamed itself Claudia Apamea in his honor. And in 77, Corinth, ravaged by an earthquake, was treated with great generosity by Vespasian, in whose honor it changed its name to the colony of Julia Flavia Augusta Corinthiensis. This change might have seemed no more than a simple form of adulation had it not been accompanied by an architectural reorganization of the town center, henceforth dominated by buildings connected with the imperial cult. The East increasingly asserted its Roman nature.

Since it had been building up for a century, the prosperity of the eastern part of the Empire perhaps rested on foundations that were firmer than those of the western part, or at least on foundations that lay more outside Roman tradition. The signs of its prosperity are evident in all sectors of social activity.

The signs of prosperity

Proliferation of public buildings The construction of public buildings was carried out swiftly and on a large scale, with occasional disasters (e.g. the collapse of the theater in Nicaea). The overlapping motives behind these constructions were social, economic, aesthetic, celebratory, and functional. What precipitated the construction varied: significant occasions include the visit of an emperor (from Athens to Jerash in Jordan, from Ephesus to Pergamum, new buildings marked out the journeys of Hadrian), benefactions by rich notables (Herodes Atticus in Athens and Corinth, Vedius Antonius at Ephesus, Maleus Agrippa at Palmyra), competition between towns (Nicomedia and Nicaea, Prusa and Apamea), and reconstructions after earthquakes. The range of edifices constructed was accordingly extremely wide. Three new features should be noted. First, in the second century, the imitation of Roman buildings and architectural forms (baths, triumphal arches, amphitheaters, drains and aqueducts, covered markets) intensified. Second, there was an evident taste for gigantic proportions, expressed in imposing colonnaded avenues, and in colossal constructions often connected with the imperial ideology. Last, a composite but harmonious art was developed and employed in these works, in which, to varying degrees, three influences may be distinguished – Hellenistic, Roman, and indigenous (see Ephesus, Aizanoi, and Baalbek). One point remains open: was this proliferation of constructions necessarily a sign of economic growth? It seems not, but one must qualify according to the cities and their regions.

True economic wealth Although some regions merely struggled to get by (Boeotia, eastern Anatolia), the dominant impression of the East during the Antonine period is one of undeniable prosperity, even opulence, in the agricultural, artisanal, "industrial," and commercial sectors, with the long-distance trade with China and India exclusively eastern and going via Petra, Palmyra, or Alexandria (depending on routes and products). In the commercial sector, the

Plate 11.11 Odeon of Herodes Atticus. This stone theater on the south slope of the Acropolis in Athens was built in 161 CE by Herodes Atticus in memory of his wife Regilla. With a capacity of 5,000, it was used primarily for music concerts. The Odeon was one of Atticus' many public projects in Athens aiming to revive the classical grandeur of the city. Hervé Champollion/akg-images

Syrians in particular were very successful. They dominated small- and large-scale commerce, and were found all over the Empire, from Cadiz to Cologne, Ostia to Lyons. In Lyons, the funerary inscription of a merchant from Laodicea specifies that he had come to bring to "the Celts and the lands of the West all that God had chosen to give to the lands of the East, fruitful in all produce."

Intellectual renaissance In the second half of the Antonine century, the East flourished in all areas of intellectual life. Among these were history, with Philo of Byblos, Plutarch of Chaeronea, Arrian of Nicomedia, Appian of Alexandria (and Pausanias, the traveler), and rhetoric, with Herodes Atticus, Dio Chrysostom, Aelius Aristides, Lucian of Samosata, and Maximus of Tyre. The easterners were equally masters in medicine, with Galen; in astronomy, with Ptolemy; and as novelists, with Longus of Lesbos and Philostratus of Athens. Trajan chose as his master architect a Syrian, Apollodorus of Damascus, who built for him a stone bridge over the Danube and his Forum in Rome. Even the field of law, until then the unquestioned domain of the Latin West, was now challenged by eastern schools, such as that of Beirut.

A new feeling: being a Greek-speaking Roman While in the first century certain Greek writers had still scornfully surveyed the Roman barbarians from the West and cultivated the memory of the past, that attitude disappeared in the second century. In no way did it mean abandoning one's city of origin, but the feeling of belonging to the *orbis Romanus*, the Roman world, was much stronger. Aelius Aristides, a Mysian, proclaimed it in his *Eulogy of Rome*: there are no longer any but Romans who speak Latin and Romans who speak Greek. This was not rhetorical flattery, but simply a common-sense observation. Syrian villages built Roman baths, and there are records of over 350 monuments connected with gladiatorial fights and animal fights (*venationes*) in the eastern world: leisure activities and games took their inspiration from the Roman model. Moreover, it was no longer inconceivable that the emperor should be an easterner: in 193, it was proposed to Ti. Claudius Pompeianus, who was one of Marcus Aurelius' sons-in-law, but also the son of an equestrian of Antioch, that he should be emperor. He refused on account of his old age and near blindness. But this peaceful invitation contrasted with the unsuccessful attempt at usurpation by Avidius Cassius (another Syrian) that had occurred some years previously. In fact the possibility of an eastern emperor became a reality in the next few decades.

11.3 | Romanization

Historians and archaeologists have long debated the nature and extent of the Romanization of the provinces of the Empire. But there is little agreement about how Romanization is to be recognized, or even about what it really means. The process is usually understood to describe the adoption or the imitation of Roman ways of thought, behavior, construction, or manufacture. Inexact characterization may be unavoidable: few sources record provincial sentiment, especially outside the literate and mostly urban, native elites, who wanted to advertise their connection to the governing power, and for whom Roman material culture represented a means of maintaining or enhancing the prestige of their own positions.

Being a Roman, it has been said, was largely a matter of law, not of culture. It is reasonably clear also that Roman cultural attributes were modified over time, in ways that are now difficult to identify, as more provincials were admitted to the Roman citizenship, and even to the inner circles of the ruling elite. The end-product will have been a cultural mixture whose constituents it is now difficult to distinguish. At the same time, it cannot be denied that there *was* an identifiable Roman cultural matrix, at least through the first and part of the second centuries CE, defined, at least in part, by language and custom, perhaps also by artifacts and architectural forms.

In some ways, at least, Romanization can be readily identified in the material record, in deposits of Roman-made dinnerware beyond the Rhine, for example, or in badly written Latin inscriptions at the edges of the Empire. The adoption of Roman architectural forms can also serve as an index of Romanization. In Britain, for example, it was the influence of Roman styles and methods of construction that led to the building of heated homes, of rectangular timber and clay buildings that functioned both as house and as shop, and of Roman-style villas in the countryside. In many parts of the Empire, towns came to be equipped with Roman-style public buildings, including forums, baths, temples, theaters, and amphitheaters. The substitution of Roman for native names, or their translation into Latin, is another indication of Romanization, especially in those areas where the practice seems to have been fairly common, like north Africa (where "Muthun," for example, was replaced by "Donatus"). Likewise, the adoption of Roman religious practices is evidence of the assimilation of ideas that were, at least at some level, culturally specific. The cult of the Capitoline triad (Jupiter, Juno, and Minerva), the emperors, and the city of Rome is attested even at a place as remote as Mena'a (Algeria), in the heart of the Aurès mountains. In many places, local gods were Romanized (or partly so): in north Africa, for example, Shadrapa came to be identified with Bacchus, Melqart with Hercules. There is, however, good evidence also of a continuing attachment to indigenous beliefs. So Saturn, a fairly transparent disguise for the Punic god Baal, seems to have been enormously popular in north Africa, especially among soldiers and the rural poor. And native (perhaps ethnic) gods like the dii Mauri, dii Magifae, and dii Macni continued to be worshiped well into the period of Roman rule.

Roman or Roman-style goods are found in every part of the Empire, and beyond, like the imported Roman-style pottery called terra sigillata that has been recovered on the German frontier, and which suggests the use of individual sets of dishes in a region where it had been local (La Tène) custom to share drinking vessels and other items of tableware. The adoption of Latin, especially as a spoken language, or of Roman dress is probably even better evidence of the desire to assimilate Roman patterns of behavior. It is a tendency that is exemplified by the wealthy Carthaginians who took to wearing togas or to fixing their hair in the styles favored by the women of the imperial family. The Punic script seems to have disappeared from north African cities by about the end of the second century CE. It is worth noting, however, that a bastardized version of the language (generally called "neo-Punic") continued to be spoken in the countryside.

The last example is intended to be a cautionary one. It is obvious that there was some Romanization in each of the provinces. The real question is, how much? Unfortunately, there are serious methodological obstacles to measuring the extent of Romanization, or its practical effect. For one thing, there is almost no evidence to describe the intentions or aspirations of the Romanized. And what little there is deals almost exclusively with the wealthy, mainly urban, provincial elites, who are likely to have absorbed Roman cultural attributes most readily, if for no other reason than that they possessed a greater capacity to acquire the products of Roman material culture. It cannot be taken for granted either that provincials will have adopted as many characteristics of Roman culture as they could afford. What was it, after all, about Roman culture that was inherently desirable? According to the historian Ramsay MacMullen, the answer is "hot baths, central heating, softer beds, and the pleasures of wine." Nor can it be said that Roman habits were adopted because they were self-evidently superior to the indigenous. A Roman-style name and clothes, at least a rudimentary knowledge of Latin – these were among the prerequisites for advancement, in army life or in the bureaucracy. It was Tacitus' understanding that Britons who adopted Roman ways did so because they were eager to be promoted (*Agricola* 21). Were Roman goods used because they were thought to be culturally superior or prestigious (insofar as they were symbolic of the ruling power), or simply because they were cheaper or better made? In any event, it would be wrong to assume that Roman artifacts turned provincials into Romans: driving a Japanese-made car does not make one Japanese.

It is not unlikely either that the gaps in the historical record conceal a complex cultural reality, according to which the typical response to Roman conquest and occupation may be located at some (indefinable) point along a continuum bounded by the extremes of those who eagerly embraced Roman values and those who rejected them. Put another way, it is difficult to identify those who were, in varying degrees, partially Romanized. It might even be supposed that there existed a second world beneath the one described in our sources, a world that was wholly un-Roman in nature.

All this is not to deny either that Romanization occurred, and on a large scale, or that it had a significant impact on the cultural life of the provinces, especially in the western half of the Empire. It is, rather, to argue against assuming that the mass of ordinary provincials were affected in ways that were either profound or lasting. In Gaul, Spain, and parts of north Africa, cultural patterns *were* transformed, but mainly, it seems, among the wealthy, urban elites. The rhythms of rural life went on probably much as they always had. But it is hard to know for sure. In the present state of the evidence, it is almost impossible to reconstruct much of the human experience of Roman imperialism. In the end, what is reasonably clear is that the extent and the effect of Romanization varied considerably over time, and from one region to the next. It could even be said that, in reference to certain places, at certain times, the very term "Romanization" is inappropriate, insofar as it implies a unilateral absorption of Roman culture. In the early part of the third century CE, for example, it might be more accurate to talk of the "Africanization" of Roman civilization.

11.4 | A Mediterranean Economy

Economic thinking existed among the Romans, but its reasoning was not the same as our own. In Rome, economic thinking was part of an all-encompassing set of beliefs and thoughts whose heart was the state, and it was the moral equilibrium of the state that mattered. There would always be confusion between morality and economy. Thus, the wealth brought by trade could be regarded at the same time as an economic resource, a sign of political domination, and a source of moral corruption.

That said, economic history itself has made enormous strides in the space of a few years. Though it is not possible to have an overview of the whole Empire (economic studies are most frequently regional), one may nevertheless assemble enough information to look at the major economic sectors. There is no question here of our presenting the results in their entirety. Rather, we shall give a few broad indications, both specific and general, concerning economic life in those sectors in the second century of the Empire.

Before we do so, we should recall that the conditions were extremely favorable to economic development. There was peace, a network of roads that were continually maintained and improved, a spread of rivers that allowed access to the interior from the Mediterranean, the sea itself, which had become safer (though it was not much frequented between November and March), and ports that were constantly being developed (Ostia, Carthage, Alexandria, Leptis Magna, Seleucia of Pieria, etc.). There was the very extent of the Empire, offering a huge range of varied and complementary resources, and there were vast centers of consumption (Rome, the large towns, the frontier zones). There was the continuing evolution of a society which consumed more and more, together with an almost stable currency (despite a weakening under Marcus Aurelius), and a population increase that encouraged the opening up of new lands. All in all, it was an era of such obvious economic prosperity that its material effects impressed even a Christian writer of anti-establishment temperament: "We note with certainty," Tertullian wrote in around 210,

> that the world daily grows better cultivated and better supplied with everything than it used to be. Everything is accessible, everything is known, everything is used; delightful rural domains have forced famous deserts to retreat, furrows have tamed the forests, herds have put wild animals to flight; stretches of sand have been sown with seed, roads are opened through the rocks, marshlands are drained, there are now as many towns as there once were houses . . . Everywhere there are dwellings, peoples, cities, life. (*A Treatise on the Soul* 30)

Agricultural life

The foremost economic activity was agriculture, and the foremost source of wealth was land. Of the Empire's 50–60 million inhabitants, at least 90 percent made their living from the land. An aristocrat's resources and social standing were measured in land property: one rich in land was considered an upright, worthy man. Moreover, the emperor was the chief land-owner. No more perfect

Plate 11.12 Mosaic in the Square of the Corporations at Ostia, depicting a lighthouse, a dolphin, and two ships with large steering oars. Second to third century CE. C. M. Dixon

happiness in the world could be imagined than a peasant's life. The good peasant lives far from towns, says Dio Chrysostom in the *Euboicus*. Pliny also waxes poetic about the solitude of the forests, and his villas and farms in the countryside.

Rome's imprints

With the expansion of centuriation outside Italy and the appearance in the provinces of a type of farmhouse built in stone, the *villa*, Rome's presence there could be seen in material form in the rural landscape. Centuriation was the dividing of land into regular plots (*centuriae*) on a grid based in theory on north–south and east–west lines. With both a fiscal and land demarcation purpose, these "centuries" were introduced throughout the Empire following the same system. In contrast, the *villa* could be flexibly adapted to local traditions, different climates, and the area of its land, the *fundus*. Whether it emerged from the influence of the conqueror or demonstrated a Romanization of those who had been conquered, this sign of Roman colonization, generally constructed on a symmetrical plan and built on a carefully selected site, most often comprised two parts: the dwelling of the master or his representative (*pars urbana*) and farm buildings (*pars rustica*). Nearby there is often evidence of the presence of indigenous inhabitants, sometimes scattered, sometimes grouped together. From Tunisia to the London basin, from Picardy to the Hungarian plains, aerial photography has enabled us to discover thousands of such villas.

Plate 11.13 Roman matron and her servant bathing a baby. Detail of a sarcophagus, second century CE. Capitoline Museum, Rome. C. M. Dixon

Movements during the century

Four major developments became evident in agricultural life during the second century, apart from its growing prosperity. First, the huge estate (*latifundium*) was replaced by small and medium-sized holdings within the framework of large-scale property. The sharecropper colonist thus appeared, and we can follow the development of this kind of colony thanks to Pliny's letters and three inscriptions from Tunisia (inscriptions of Henchir Mettich, Ain Djemala, and Souk el Khemis). Second, an expansion of cultivated areas is evident – for example, in North Africa, the Agri Decumates, Dacia, and the Fens in England. Third, alongside large-scale farming devoted mainly to the growing of cereals, which was in decline, an intensive and more dynamic type of farming was found, diverse in its products and activities but centered on a principal crop (vineyards, orchards, olive groves) and livestock breeding. Last, the second century seems to have been one of agricultural science. The great land-owners read treatises by agronomists, aspired to the commercialization of their surpluses, and sometimes specialized their products. Land was considered seriously as an investment in its own right rather than merely as a sign of social status.

Ways of working the land

The ways of working the land depended on the size of the property. In charge of the vast imperial domains (*saltus*) which went beyond the territory of the cities were procurators, either one or two (equestrian) procurators per province for the imperial possessions in that province, or one procurator (freedman) per great domain. The procurator was assisted by a *conductor* (farmer general), who leased out land to colonists, the real farmers, who paid rent and were obliged to supply a certain amount of free labor. The domain itself was divided into four parts: one part was cultivated for the procurator, another by the colonists for themselves, the third comprised pasture lands, and the fourth was land left fallow. The organization was the same for a large private estate, but the procurator was replaced by a steward (*villicus*). At the other end of the scale, the small freeholding was directly worked by the owner (veteran, native inhabitant), with or without the help of slaves. Between these two types of holding was a whole range of others combining the various different elements, and involving also the use of day-laborers.

Provincial variety

The provinces varied enormously in how prevalent the various types of ways of working the land were within their regions and in the precise form that they took. These were matters linked to the status of the lands (in Syria, towns and temples owned huge properties which they administered themselves, and agricultural slavery was little developed), to native traditions (small and medium-sized properties seem to have predominated in western Gaul, Asia, Pannonia, etc.), and to the vicissitudes of history (settlements of colonists and veterans, confiscation of lands by the emperor).

Industry and commerce

Industry

Industrial production grew without technical progress: improvements were made on what already existed. As it increased, this production diversified and, above all, tended to become less concentrated, in most cases in keeping with the size of the province. Domestic industry (the manufacture of products in a domestic setting) maintained its strength. Such was the case in rural areas, where people spun, forged metal, wove, etc. Urban crafts were also vigorously developed. On the other hand, a relatively heavy, though still in modern terms modest, concentration is noticeable in the case of certain activities which were created around a heavy or very localized raw material (mines, quarries), or which were involved in the mass production of one model (lamps, crockery) or required a high degree of skill (glassmaking). Let us look more closely at two areas of production: mines and manufacturing industries.

Mines and quarries (in Latin a single word, *metalla*) were spread throughout the Empire and were worked intensively in the second century. Since the first century CE, the largest deposits had belonged to the state or to the emperor personally. Depending on the region and the mine, they could either be exploited directly by the government or be leased to individuals or companies. One equestrian procurator per province supervised the mines, which were sometimes divided into sectors, each entrusted to a subordinate procurator (freedman). These mining districts had special status, known to us through inscriptions (the bronze tables of Vipasca in Portugal): they stood outside municipal jurisdiction and were directly administered by imperial officials. Though there were miners who were free men, the majority were slaves and convicts. But these two sources of labor were inadequate for the demand and working conditions and tools did not improve. Thus labor for the mines became increasingly scarce.

Manufacturing industries may be placed in two categories: common and specialized. In the first group belong textile production (wool, linen), dyeing, shoemaking, furniture-making, building trades, etc. In the second are luxury industries (cotton, goldsmithing, silk, perfumes, glassware, papyrus paper, parchment), almost all of their products originating from Asia, Syria, and Egypt; food industries (garum, oils), essentially situated in a relatively few geographically extensive "production areas"; metalwork, relatively scattered, because there were countless small deposits of iron and copper; and lastly pottery, which made the fortune of Gaulish craftsmen gathered together in large centers, first in workshops in the south of Gaul (Montans, La Graufesenque, Banassac) from 30 BCE to 120 CE for their greatest output, then in workshops in central Gaul, which had a period of industrial production from Vespasian to Commodus (Lezoux), and lastly in workshops in the east of Gaul which opened at the end of the first century CE and in some cases survived until the third century (Mittelbronn, La Madeleine, Rheinzabern).

Commerce

Trade was the Empire's second source of wealth. Ancient routes brought into use again, powerful infrastructures, general peace, and the existence of numerous products all favored a great expansion in trade. Since the middle of the first century CE, Italian merchants had lost control of the Empire's trade to easterners (Jews, Egyptians, Syrians), both within the Empire and beyond the frontiers.

Internal trade A Mediterranean world with a few Atlantic and continental links, the Empire could meet all its needs with the exception of exotic products. Trade occurred on three levels. First, there was local, regional trade, a permanent retail trade, existing in every city, but about which very little is known. Then came inter-regional trade centered on the large ports (Carthage, Narbonne) and towns situated at communications junctions (Lyons, London). Last, there was "centralized" trade that converged on Rome, with four maritime routes of prime

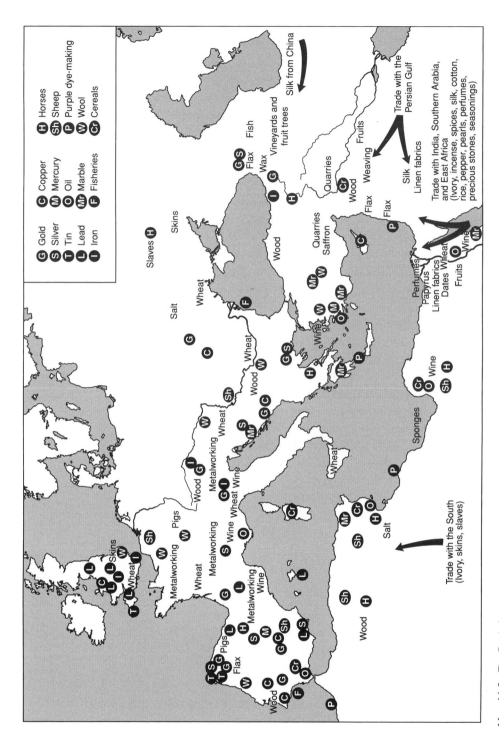

Map 11.2 The Empire's resources

importance: Alexandria–Rome, Carthage–Rome, southern Gaul–Rome, and Iberian peninsula–Rome. One may then understand the fundamental position occupied by certain ports, like Alexandria, the largest exporting port in the Roman world. In the second century, a new circuit began, abandoning the Mediterranean to follow the Rhine and the Danube, thus putting Britain in contact with the Black Sea. Transported goods were surpluses produced by the provinces or imported from abroad. For Rome they obviously corresponded to its provisioning primarily in goods of the *annona* (grain, oil). Quantifying involves some guesswork, but an annual figure of about 190,000 tonnes of grain for Rome seems a reasonable estimate.

External trade This took four different directions:

1 Countries of northern Europe. Amber, slaves, hides, furs, and dried fish were bought there. Finished goods (gold and silver vessels, glassware, and pottery) were exported to them. The big frontier post was Carnuntum on the Danube, with Aquileia as its Mediterranean opposite number.
2 Countries north of the Black Sea. Traffic went by way of Olbia and Tanais and was mainly in horses, slaves, and jewels.
3 Countries of black Africa. A modest amount of traffic came via Nubia and the Nile Valley; the rest by way of the desert (Fezzan) and Leptis Magna, although we do now know the Saharan commercial routes.
4 Countries of the Far East and Southern Arabia. This was the supreme example of large-scale trade, which allowed the acquisition of incense from Arabia, silk from China, and pepper from India, with additional merchandise (precious stones, skins). Three routes were used, ending at Antioch and Alexandria, craft center, transit and export port, the only harbor complex that by its activity could supplant Ostia's.

This external trade was hardly two-way. Rome paid in gold. For a long time this was described as a "hemorrhage" of gold, but it is now known that such views were built on the Roman tradition of discourse against luxury, and that the 100 million sesterces involved did not put the Empire's economy in danger.

In the trading cities, mainly in the West, craftsmen, merchants, and shippers got together in guilds formed on the model of municipal *curiae*. These guilds also had a religious aim, promising their members proper funerals, and they played a considerable role in the lives of their cities, as did, for example, the guild of wine merchants in Lyons.

11.5 | The Army

With Augustus, a new army had been born – the imperial army. His successors had transformed this into a standing army with one principal mission, to defend

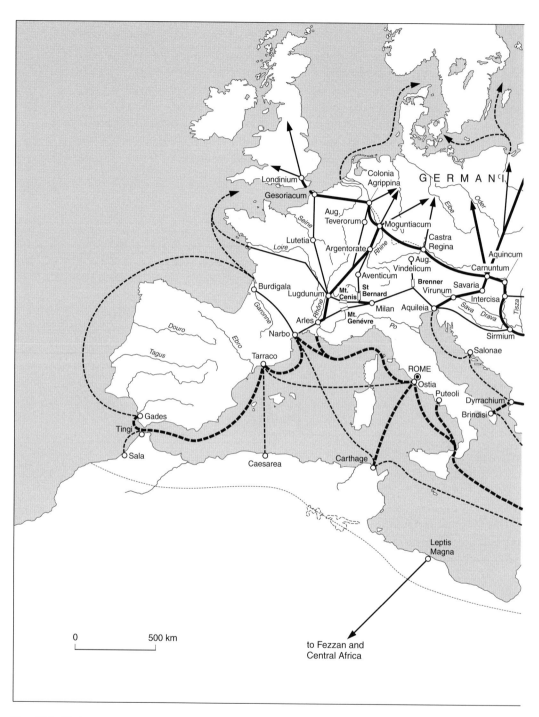

Map 11.3 Trade routes (from P. Petit, *La Paix romaine*, PUF, 1967)

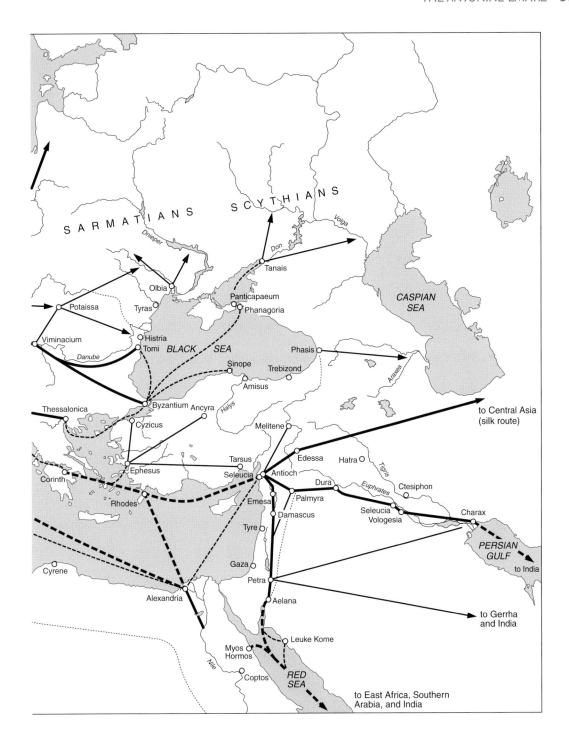

to Central Asia
(silk route)

to India

to Gerrha
and India

to East Africa, Southern
Arabia, and India

the Empire against any external aggression; a secondary function was to ensure order within the frontiers (keeping watch on roads, controlling nomads, preventing piracy, etc.), with subsidiary functions in administrative tasks, official mail, and public works.

Organization and recruitment

Organization

Rome's garrison

- Ten praetorian cohorts, basically made up of foot soldiers, were under the orders of the praetorian prefect. Each cohort comprised 500 men. They used a camp situated on the Viminal, to the north-east of the capital.
- There were three or four urban cohorts, each of 500 men. The term "urban" refers not so much to their mission as to their original garrison. In fact, even though they played a "policing" role in the capital, they were true military units (they took part in the Dacian campaigns) and gradually became indistinct from the praetorian cohorts, whose camp they shared.
- Seven cohorts of the watch were first of all firemen. However, these cohorts of 1,000 men, commanded by the prefect of the watch, became militarized during the second century.
- In addition, there were various corps whose task was to protect the emperor – his personal cavalry (*equites singulares Augusti*) and bodyguards – as well as special servicemen (looking after foreign residents, commissariat for the distribution of grain), and seamen.

The army of the provinces With the exception of the single urban cohorts set up under the Flavians in Lyons and Carthage, the army of the provinces consisted of legions and auxiliary units.

The legions There were 28 or 30 (according to the period), each of about 5,000 men, representing the elite of the provincial army. Composed of foot soldiers and 120 horsemen, each legion was organized in ten cohorts of three maniples or six centuries apiece, except for the first cohort, whose five centuries were double the size of the others. A legion was designated by a number and a name (e.g. the Third Augusta), and as its emblem and principal standard it had an "eagle" (*aquila*), which was an object of veneration and was in the charge of a standard-bearer (*aquilifer*). Each legion was commanded by a *legatus* of senatorial rank (except for legions stationed in Egypt), assisted by a laticlave tribune (also of senatorial rank), a camp prefect, and five angusticlave tribunes (equestrians). Subordinate to this headquarters staff, 59 centurions supervised the troopers, themselves hierarchized according to three criteria: fatigue duties (exempt or not), pay (from basic to triple), and merit gained from the exercise of an office. Each legion had its musicians (to transmit commands), its instructors, health officers, engineers, caterers, security officers, and administrative personnel.

The auxiliaries These troops had the task of assisting the legions, but could be used separately. Divided into corps of 500 or 1,000 men (theoretically), in total they may nearly have equaled the number of legionaries. There were three kinds of auxiliary corps. The first kind, the *alae*, were formed of horsemen, and the second, the cohorts, of foot soldiers (there were, however, also mixed cohorts, comprising infantry and horsemen). They were both commanded by an equestrian (prefect or tribune). The *numeri*, the third type of unit, were troops of indigenous and national soldiers who kept their ethnic character (language, uniform, weaponry) and were designated by the Romans according to their origins: the Moors, the Palmyrans, etc.

The navy There were two chief naval ports, Misenum and Ravenna, sheltering the two great praetorian fleets, which patrolled the western and eastern Mediterranean. Provincial squadrons ensured the Roman presence on peripheral seas and the great rivers (fleets of Britain, Germania, Pannonia, Moesia, Pontus, Syria, and Alexandria). In total, this was a large network of naval bases, with naval resources of around 250 vessels and 45,000 men. For a long time, the military usefulness of this navy was questioned by historians. However, it is now acknowledged that its military mission was of prime importance, and that its strength and technical standards commanded its enemies' respect. Besides performing a deterrent role, the imperial navy ensured army logistics, transported troops, horses, arms, and food supplies, fought on the rivers of the frontier defense line, took part in combined operations, and, at least in the second century, made all its men undergo training for fighting on land.

The *vexillationes* In exceptional circumstances (a mission, war, building works, etc.), legions, auxiliaries, and fleets dispatched fairly large detachments known as *vexillationes*, from the standard (*vexillum*) around which these soldiers were assembled.

Taking all its forces together, the Roman army in the middle of the second century could line up around 350,000 men, whose supreme leader was the emperor, the only one entitled to celebrate a triumph.

Recruitment

- The officers: they came from the senatorial or the equestrian order. Not specialized, men of peace as well as men of war, they regarded military activities as a temporary stop in their careers.

- The centurions: in the second century, the majority were provincials (chiefly from the western and Danubian provinces). Most frequently they were the sons of municipal notables, fully Romanized from the earliest times, who reached this grade without always going through the ranks. A minority were soldiers' sons.

- The legionaries: it was compulsory for them to be Roman citizens. Early in the second century, a uniform development began of regional recruitment gradually moving to local recruitment, through an intermediate phase when soldiers came from cities ever closer to the fortress. A good example of this local recruitment is the Third Augusta, which was stationed in Africa: in the first century CE its legionaries were already foreigners (Italians and Gauls); at the beginning of the second century Africans entered the legion, but still in smaller numbers than Bithynians, Danubians, and Syrians; by the end of the second century, however, the Africans predominated: these were at first from Mauretania, and later from Numidia, where the legion was stationed. As for the legionaries' social origins, it seems that they belonged to the elite of the lower plebeians, a choice reflecting the imperial policy of recruitment.

- The praetorians: at the beginning of the second century, 89 percent were Italian. This figure barely changed under the Antonines. To the extent that it did, Dalmatians and Pannonians were the ones who first entered the praetorian ranks.

- The auxiliaries: these might be either Roman citizens or *peregrini*. Between the reign of Hadrian and 170, the first were as numerous as the second, who received citizenship on completion of their service. Recruitment was spread both westward and eastward. Auxiliaries came chiefly from Tarraconensis, Belgica, Lugdunensis, Thrace, Pannonia, and Syria. It appears that, unlike the legions, there were auxiliary corps that did not gradually move toward local recruitment. This means that overall among the auxiliaries there was a balance between local and external recruitment. There were three reasons for this demographic spread: first, wherever they were stationed, the *numeri* were always barbarian troops; second, barbarian recruits were always, and prudently, sent far from their homeland (e.g. no Briton was garrisoned in Britain); third, certain specialized units always came from the same region (e.g. archers from Palmyra).

- The fleet: this included many non-citizens (*peregrini* for the most part), but the methods of their recruitment are uncertain. In general we know much less about Roman fleets, especially about river fleets throughout the Empire, than we do about the army. However, new archaeological and inscriptional materials, as well as the re-examination of relevant iconography (e.g. on tombstones and the mosaics from Ostia), have provided us with more information regarding harbor installations, the composition of the fleet, individual careers, and the fleet's economic activity and peacetime works (such as the manufacture of bricks and tiles).

To ensure that numbers in the whole imperial army were kept up, it was necessary to recruit at least 18,000 men a year (service was voluntary, although in theory the obligation to serve had never been abolished). This seems an easily achievable figure, yet the authorities sometimes had difficulty in assembling such a contingent. Besides the hardships of military life, the length of service perhaps discouraged potential recruits. This was 16 years for the praetorians, 25 for the auxiliaries, 26 for the sailors, and 20 years for the legionaries (in theory, but they served more; some stayed in the barracks even after their discharge).

Strategy, tactics, and training

When, under the Flavians, the legions were put back on the Rhine, the rudimentary winter camps, built of wood and earth, were replaced by camps built in stone. This change in building methods was perhaps the first evidence of a new strategy. The confident Empire of the Julio-Claudians was being succeeded by a more cautious Empire, defined by its strategy of defending the perimeters by setting up along them a permanent line of defense. There was no thought of further extending the frontiers, or at least none of operating beyond the range of fixed bases. After Trajan's expeditions, this concept of preventive defense was imposed along all the frontiers (*limes*), that is to say, 10,200 km including Dacia (9,600 without), plus 4,500 km of coastline.

Tactical aspects of frontier defense

The various fixed parts of the *limes* were initially conceived of as a way of countering minor threats (infiltrations, raids, etc.), and not as a way of providing total protection against large-scale attacks. The fixed parts served as points of departure for mobile forces setting out to intercept the attacks in advance or to cause them to be aborted. The battlefield thus lay beyond the frontier, rather than within it. These fixed defensive structures of the *limes* were:

- A physical barrier (wall, palisade, earthwork and ditch) following the "frontier" of the Empire, as in Britain (Hadrian's Wall in northern England and Antoninus' Wall in Scotland), Upper Germania, Raetia, Romania, and North Africa (the Fossatum Africae). But this was not continuous and was not a crucial part of the *limes*: the Empire never surrounded itself with a long continuous wall such as the Great Wall of China.
- Watchtowers and forts with outposts, which kept watch and gave warnings. The zone of external surveillance could extend as far as 80 km from the frontier.
- A system of visual communications (smoke, torches), which worked in two directions: along the frontier (even if there was no physically constructed line

of defense) and across the frontier, between the outposts and the interior fortresses.

- Military bases: guard posts, auxiliaries' forts, legionary camps, all situated, in general, well behind the lines.
- Roads, which formed an essential element of the system. Some were at right angles to the frontier, which they crossed; others were parallel to it. The denser the network, the greater the strategic importance.

These material parts of the *limes* were merely the framework of the system. It was fleshed out with the activities of patrols, diplomatic missions, trade, and constant troop movements, and involved local adaptations and the strategic use of natural topography such as rivers, mountains, or even the desert.

Strategic aspects of frontier defense

Rome's military forces were spread unevenly along the frontiers and were divided into provincial or regional armies (*exercitus*) which, in Hadrian's time, began to acquire a measure of autonomy. Each of these armies was organized around a nucleus of legions permanently stationed in a province, reinforced by auxiliaries, and sometimes by naval forces, which were also deployed around the perimeter of the Empire, except for the two central fleets.

Given the geographic configuration of the Empire, the delays in internal communications (Cologne was 66 days' march from Rome, Antioch 126), the considerable distances between the various sectors, and the fact that reserves were very limited, the choice of a policy of regional deployment was, it seems, inevitable. But it was also admirably suited to allowing adaptation to regional frontiers, chosen, it would seem, not solely for topographical and tactical reasons, but also for strategic purposes. Thus, at the end of the reign of Antoninus there were 28 legions.

Training

According to the Jewish writer Flavius Josephus, the Romans "do not wait until hostilities begin to give the men their first lesson in arms . . . they undergo continual training and never wait until the last moment to confront an unexpected danger." Even though Josephus spoke of his Roman experience under the Flavians, his remark was more topical than ever in the second century. Continuous and intensive training maintained the fighting potential of an army that had to stay in active duty for an indeterminate period during a time of almost total peace. The morale and proficiency of the troops were kept up by means of drills and peacetime projects such as road and aqueduct construction and maintenance. The attention given to the training and professional specialization of the soldier is evident in the technical terminology of the Lambaesis inscriptions, describing the tactical drills of the Third Augusta.

Box 11.2 Allocation of the legions under the Antonines

Britain	3 legions
Rhine	4 legions
Lower Germania	2 legions
Upper Germania	2 legions
Danube	10 legions
Upper Pannonia	3 legions
Lower Pannonia	1 legion
Upper Moesia	2 legions
Lower Moesia	3 legions
Dacia	1 legion
Orient	8 legions
Cappadocia	2 legions
Syria	3 legions
Judaea	2 legions
Arabia	1 legion
Egypt	1 legion
Africa	1 legion
Iberian peninsula	1 legion

(from E. Luttwak, *La Grande Stratégie de l'Empire romain*, Paris, 1987, p. 70)

Weaknesses

Numerical weakness This could be partly offset by high standards and good training, but even so could constitute a serious handicap, especially in long-lasting wars, given the difficulties in keeping up even existing numbers.

The financial burden Maintaining such an army was a heavy expense: it was the main charge on the state budget – between 40 and 50 percent. Estimates are only approximate, and are based on pay, but it is calculated that the cost of a legion was in the region of 2.25 million denarii annually. And the entire cost of the army, if the navy cost as much as, or slightly less than, the auxiliaries, would be somewhere between 140 million and 145 million denarii annually (other, lower estimates vary between 80 million and 90 million).

The system itself The Empire's military strength was first of all a diplomatic instrument: the threat of its use dissuaded potential enemies, who, in the second century, never produced a force likely to worry the legions. But beyond the frontiers it could take only a federation of tribes or another Empire to outface the *limes*, conceived as a deterrent to threats on a small scale: the extreme overstretching of the units did not allow the detachment of a large part from one front to be sent elsewhere. The system lacked flexibility. What would happen if organized frontier peoples attacked at the same time at two very distant points?

The army under the Antonines attained its objective: to ensure permanent security for the populations living within the Empire's frontiers. This was a main objective in the designs of the Empire itself: to create a new society in which the barbarians within the frontiers, increasingly integrated into the Roman world and increasingly cut off from the barbarians outside, would become heartfelt citizens of the Empire.

11.6 | Spectacles and the Roman Empire

Even after Superbowls and World Cups, the extent, diversity, frequency, and brutality of the Roman spectacles still amaze us. Since early Christians suffered persecution as victims of some of these shows, the Christian West has long been unable to be dispassionate about the games, especially those of the arena. Moderns have inherited a centuries-old bias that Roman entertainments were excessively popular, decadent, and dehumanizing. Despite the traditional condemnation of them, Roman spectacles have remained fascinating in modern times, leading artists, such as the nineteenth-century academic painter Jean-Léon Gérôme, to produce romantic and disturbing images of the racetracks and arenas of Rome. The film industry has also fully exploited the violent and brutal image of Roman entertainment. It has been too easy to be titillated and disgusted by Roman spectacles, to marvel that an empire so impressive and civilized in art, architecture, and law could be so vulgar and brutal in its entertainments.

A famous quotation from Juvenal (*Satire* 10.78–81) suggests that the Romans surrendered their freedom to autocracy in exchange for shows and state support: he said that the only things that the people cared about were "bread and circuses" (*panem et circenses*). With such ammunition, and with the moralistic agenda of presenting a warning lesson for today, it has been easy for moderns to see the free food and circuses as the "opiate of the masses," the means by which the mob was manipulated. However, Juvenal, like other ancient social critics speaking from an elitist, intellectual perspective, does not give a balanced or complete picture of the role of the games, the masses, or the emperor.

From satirical poems to imperial histories to Christian treatises, from inscribed decrees to law codes to epitaphs on tombstones, the volume and variety of textual evidence of Roman spectacles attest to their magnitude as a phenomenon, one whose chronological and geographical scope spans the whole history and territory of the Empire. It is essential that we also integrate archaeological evidence, most of which suggests pride in the games, for a fuller understanding of the events and practices. From household lamps, ceramics, and children's toys, to mosaics, statuettes, coins, works of fine art, and ruins of monumental facilities, physical evidence shows that spectacles played a major role in the festival calendar, the social life, and the public space of ancient Rome (and the Empire) for over a millennium.

The expansion of games and facilities

To suggest the scale of the phenomenon, some studies calculate the number of state-funded games days within the number of festival days per year; for example, 65 under Augustus and 93 under Claudius out of the 159 days of festivals in the early Empire, and 135 out of 230 under Marcus Aurelius. In the Calendar of Philocalus, of 354 CE, of 200 festival days 176 were show days: 102 theatrical, 64 circus, and only 10 gladiatorial or venatorial. Moreover, normal festival calendars, listing games offered on a regular basis, do not reflect the spontaneous and lavish games irregularly put on for triumphs, coming-of-age celebrations, birthdays, and anniversaries. While Rome continued to have many days of theatrical shows, mainly mimes and pantomimes, which were cheaper and easier to arrange, later ages have been more fascinated with the activities of the amphitheater and circus: the great chariot races, the gladiatorial combats, and the beast fights.

An entertainment industry

The grand (and to us sometimes gruesome) spectacles of the Empire largely were expanded, embellished versions of earlier forms of performances under the Republic, adapted even more for the comfort and entertainment of the spectators. Rome approached mass entertainment with the same talent for organization, the same imperial resources, and the same notions of social hierarchy and order that characterized other aspects of Roman civilization. It is not an overstatement to speak of Rome's entertainment industry, with stars, fans, and blockbuster shows. With energy and pride, Rome scoured the Empire for victims, built monumental facilities, orchestrated events, and immortalized the performances in art and literature. When resources permitted, emperors put on spectacles as impressively as they could, and the obligation on the leader and the appreciation by the people continued into the late Empire.

Spectacular facilities

That Roman spectacles were dominated by concern for the spectators, their access, view, comforts, and – above all – their entertainment, is well demonstrated by the development of spectacular facilities, most infamously the amphitheater. Monumental structures were expanded or built anew throughout Rome under the Empire. With capacities of around 150,000 at the Circus Maximus and 50,000 at the Colosseum, there can be no doubt that spectacular mass entertainment was a vital part of life at Rome. Moreover, with Rome as the model, games, spectacles, and the structures to house them spread to the provinces.

Games across the Empire

Beyond Rome itself, from London to Carthage to Constantinople, distinctively Roman shows and their facilities were compelling, concrete symbols of the power and the ideology of the Roman Empire. Spectacular public entertainments were indelibly associated with Roman culture and society. A city of over a million people, Rome controlled an Empire of perhaps 40 million to 60 million, holding it together not only by military might and a strong political system but also by the unifying force of Roman culture: *Romanitas*, which included games and shows as well as language and law. The spread of Roman entertainments, the activities involved and the facilities needed, followed the armies to provincial centers; when provincials embraced and adopted the practice, financing the facilities themselves, it was to show how suitably Roman they had become. Like the spread of soccer, cricket, or baseball in modern times, these games were markers of cultural imperialism. Even today, the ruins of their physical settings remind us of the extent and durability of the Empire.

Emperors and spectacles

The politicization of the games – the use of spectacles and largesse to gain popular support – was well established in the late Republic, and the careers of Julius Caesar and Augustus set the example for imperial history. The key figure at spectacles was the emperor himself. After Augustus, emperors dominated the blood sports in particular in Rome, organizing the shows and providing the resources for the arena. Emperors were prominent spectators in their special boxes in the stands at both the amphitheater and the circus; and the assembled crowd, feeling safe in their mass anonymity, used the opportunity to view the emperor and to comment on his rule. Wise emperors, understanding the dynamics of such political theater, attended to the opinions of the citizens at spectacles. They had absolute power but they still were expected to act with decorum and magnanimity.

Unfortunately, sensationalistic ancient sources, notably the imperial biographies of Suetonius, used accounts of emperors' games (and of emperors at and even in games) to indict the autocratic power held by emperors, sometimes depicting them as deranged sadists. Note, however, that examples of imperial abuses – mistreating workers or spectators, forcing viewers into the arena, and, above all, emperors themselves performing in the arena – are presented by critical authors as extraordinary outrages against the traditions and proper conduct of shows. Undoubtedly, as intended, most shows and most emperors pleased the people.

Spectators and fans

From the emperors who took pride in the productions, to the spectators, noble and lowly, who flocked to the shows, Romans of all classes attended, approved of, and enjoyed the games. Attentive and knowledgeable, some spectators, including some emperors, were true fans, or even fanatics, and some perhaps were sadists. People were drawn to spectacles for a multiplicity of reasons: by the allure of violence, by the exotic and erotic sights, by an appreciation of the skill and courage of some participants, or by the anticipation of the harsh but acceptable punishment of others. Some went for the crowd and the gambling as well as the violence, and many perhaps went simply to escape their deplorable living conditions. Romans of different stations and from different viewpoints found something redeeming or entertaining about the games, be it how well gladiators faced death, the skill and daring of charioteers, the opportunity to interact with the emperor, or the viewing of foreign peoples and animals. The performers themselves, from gladiators to charioteers, were often slaves who had little choice but to perform well, but the spectators came to appreciate them for their skills and bravery. Some Stoic and elitist authors criticized the excess and irrational passion of spectators at the games, but there was little humanitarian opposition to the violence or morality of the games themselves.

As social functions, spectacles were occasions, as Tertullian (*On the Spectacles* 25) said, for "seeing and being seen," for seeing performances of skill and courage, and for being seen as producers and patrons of games sitting at prominent vantage points, as citizens of status in seats of privilege, as citizen-spectators participating in and sanctioning the rules and rulers of Rome. There were a few incidents, such as the riots at the amphitheater at Pompeii between local fans and those from neighboring Nuceria, in 59 CE (see Tacitus, *Annals* 14.17). In 532 CE fans of the "Blue" and the "Green" chariot teams attacked each other in the Hippodrome (the Circus) in Constantinople; and in the so-called "Nika" riot emperor Justinian, who was attending the races, was attacked, and had to flee to the palace for safety. However, by and large, the huge and excited crowds at the Colosseum and Circus Maximus were essentially free of violence. There was no parallel to the hooliganism or riots of modern soccer games.

Emperors and triumphs

The great triumphs of the late Republic were associated with generals who aspired to lead the state, and Augustus himself held a triple triumph in 29 BCE. When Augustus established the emperorship, however, he curtailed the excess popularity of generals with the legions and the people. He and later emperors monopolized the privilege of triumphs for themselves and members of the imperial family. What had been in origin a religious thanksgiving to Jupiter and various individual generals became a ceremony emphasizing the emperor as supreme commander and conqueror. The actual generals might be granted special titles and privileges called triumphal ornaments, or the emperors might simply take credit for the military conquests of others. Some emperors (e.g. Caligula, Domitian) were criticized for staging unmerited triumphs with fake prisoners of war and spoils. Claudius was politically astute enough to present himself in a general's costume, in effect as a *triumphator*, when he staged a mock battle in the Campus Martius as a re-enactment of the defeat and surrender of the British kings. Even Nero staged a grandiose and presumably awkward triumphal entry into Rome in 68 CE in celebration of his non-military victories in Greece. Emperors, including Augustus, also tended to dedicate a monumental triumphal arch as a reminder of their achievements, the arch of Constantine near the Colosseum being the most famous example.

An imperial triumph   With first-hand knowledge, Josephus wrote a detailed account (*Jewish War* 7.121–57) of the joint triumph in Rome by the young and popular Titus and his father, the emperor Vespasian, after the fall of the Temple in Judaea in 70. On the day of the triumph, Josephus notes, the buildings of the city were mostly empty. As the throng of people converged, there was standing room only and barely enough space left for the procession to pass. Josephus marvels at the abundance of war booty, at the artworks and the rich costumes, and the movable painted stages – what we today might call floats – with tableaus and captives. Some 700 Jewish prisoners of war, selected for their physical impressiveness, were displayed in the procession. Among the spoils, Josephus takes special note of a heavy golden table and grand menorah (seven-branched candlestick) looted from the Temple. Corroborating the account, the triumphal arch erected to honor Titus after his premature death, which still stands in Rome today, bears reliefs with scenes of his Jewish triumph.

Josephus also adds a gruesome but telling detail. According to "time-honored custom," when the procession reached the temple of Jupiter it awaited news that the enemy leader was dead. The leader, Simon son of Gioras, was taken from the prisoners in the procession, beaten and dragged by a noose, and executed at the edge of the Forum. News of the death of the captured Jewish leader, representing the vanquishing of the threat to Rome, was met with widespread expressions of joy and satisfaction. Then officials performed sacrifices, made offerings, and said prayers. With the formalities over, feasting and festivities continued throughout the city in celebration of the army's victory and the renewed hope for future prosperity. Such callous celebration of the suffering and death of others seems disturbing to us, but we must remember that violence was part of the very fabric of Roman history and society.

Greek games: acceptance and patronage

As the Empire incorporated more and more Greeks and more Hellenistic territories, Greek athletics made inroads, but they never rivaled the chariot races and blood sports for popularity at Rome. The endorsement of Greek games in shows by Caesar and Augustus probably had a positive effect, but wider acceptance of Greek sport came later with the festivals and facilities established by Nero and Domitian: Nero created the Greek-style Neronia games in Rome in 60 CE and competed at Olympia in 67, and Domitian created the Capitolia Games in 86 and built the Stadium of Domitian. In time, philhellenic emperors like Hadrian came to patronize the Olympics, to sanction the establishment of more athletic festivals, and to finance the pensions of great athletic victors throughout the Empire. Inscribed records and depictions in art suggest that imperial patronage supported rather than corrupted Greek sport.

As the skills of Greek athletes became more admired, traditionalists like Tacitus (*Annals* 14.20) still feared that the exercises and immorality of the Greek gymnasium were a threat to the character of the youth and the military vigor of Rome. With the expansion of great bathing complexes, which came to include running tracks and exercise areas, more Romans practiced Greek sport for health and recreation; but, pragmatically, many still felt that the proper orientation of Roman physical education should be toward preparation for warfare.

Chariot racing and Rome

The most popular Roman spectator sport, the one that was held regularly (on over 60 days a year in the fourth century CE) and drew the biggest crowds, the one that existed from the beginning of Rome and persisted in the Byzantine Empire, was chariot racing. Like modern horse racing, Roman chariot racing had grand tracks, magnificent thoroughbreds from stud farms, excited fans, tight races, betting, and victory purses. However, as discussed earlier (see chapter 6, section 6.3, "Spectacles in the late Republic"), chariot racing at Rome had distinctive features, such as the factions and the special design of the Circus, and the Empire saw more even expansion and enthusiasm.

While the emperors came to monopolize the shows in the arena, the factions retained their private status and their influence long after the Republic. Perhaps the emperors were reluctant to interfere with the traditional arrangements, or perhaps they wanted to economize by renting the factions' valuable resources, rather than owning and maintaining them as they did with gladiators. However, like the amphitheater, the circus, as a surrogate assembly, offered the people a chance to see and interact with the emperor. Usually this interaction was positive, but imperial historians criticized enthusiasts, like Caligula, if they favored one color too much.

The imperial Circus Maximus

The Circus Maximus remained a fairly rudimentary facility until extensive rebuilding by Caesar and then Augustus. The basic form emerged under Caesar as an elongated oval track with tiered rows of seats on both sides and around the curved end. Augustus added an obelisk in the center of the central barrier, as well as a platform area (*pulvinar*) in the stands at one side, which housed a shrine (from which the gods might view the races), and also a royal box. Claudius redid the formerly wooden starting gates (*carceres*) in marble, and Nero made improvements, including adding seating for the equestrians. Domitian rebuilt the Circus when both sides of it were destroyed by fire (probably in 80 CE). It was Trajan's massive renovation that established the canonical form in elements, decoration, and mechanics, by 103 CE, when he rebuilt the *pulvinar* and replaced the wooden seating with a structure of brick-faced concrete. Overall the exterior was roughly 650 by 140 meters, with the arena inside roughly 580 by 79 meters. After Trajan's expansion, its capacity was about 150,000 or more, but not the 250,000 of some modern estimates.

Designed to maximize fairness and visibility, the Circus had a solid barrier, running down the middle of the track, which was decorated with water basins (hence the term *euripus*, channel), lap counters (in the form of eggs and dolphins), fountains, an obelisk, and images of gods. After an elaborate procession, chariots bolted from mechanically opened starting gates (*carceres*) and raced seven laps (of about 1,500 meters each) down and back around the barrier and conical turning posts (*metae*), which were substantial and dangerous.

Charioteers

Drivers came from humble social origins; probably most were slaves purchased and trained by a circus faction, or freedmen hired by it. Nevertheless, talented and successful charioteers could become wealthy and famous. Juvenal (*Satire* 7.243) complained that a charioteer could make more money in one race than a teacher made in a year. Apparently, drivers received a portion of the prize money given for victories, and in time they could purchase their freedom and, in effect, negotiate for themselves as free agents. It is also clear that charioteers like Diocles below changed factions at times, by their own negotiations or by being sold.

Inscriptions and literature testify to the careers and popularity of charioteers, and also to the dangerous nature of their sport. Funerary epitaphs lament their short lives and bad luck. According to Martial, Scorpus, who died at age 27 with 2,048 wins, was the toast of the town, and images of him were common about Rome in the late first century CE. Martial (*Epigrams* 10.74), lamenting his own meager earnings, complained that Scorpus could make 15 bags of gold for winning one race. Another famous charioteer, Diocles, originally from Spain, won 1,462 of the 4,257 races he entered during a 24-year career. He died at 42 in the mid-second century CE, and his epitaph carefully details his races, the tactics used, and the purses won (worth a career total of 35,863,120 sesterces).

A stirring account in Sidonius Apollinaris (*Poems* 23.323–424), from the fifth century CE, shows that there were few rules and some quite brutal tactics employed during races. Bumping among charioteers was permitted and common, and contact with the barrier or turning post would shatter chariots, which were lightly built for speed. "Shipwrecks" (*naufragia*) could involve numerous chariots and deaths of drivers and horses. Drivers had leather helmets and some protective wrappings for their legs and torsos, but they tied the reins around their waists to add force by leaning back. They had knives to cut themselves free in an emergency, but the risk of dragging, injury, or death was very high.

Spectators and seating

The factions or colors also applied to partisanship in the stands, and spectators were passionately devoted to their color or team, and its leading charioteer. Typical of other elitist critics of the masses as idle and fickle, wasting their time on ignoble interests, Pliny (*Letters* 9.6) mocked the enthusiasm of the circus crowd. He claimed to be amazed that, while he was interested in literature, thousands of people were drawn to the races. He suggested that it was not the speed or skill involved that they loved but rather the team colors, a bit of cloth, and that if the colors were switched in a race the fans would mindlessly shift their loyalties.

Pliny might well have admitted that the circus had many social attractions in addition to the races themselves. Although some seating was reserved for senators and equestrians by the early Empire, general seating was open to all. This provided an opportunity for the lower classes to leave their humble lodgings, to mix with others who shared their interests, and to view the emperor and other notables. Ovid highly recommended the narrow, crowded seating, in which males and females intermixed, as an opportune site for amorous overtures. Also, informal betting along team lines abounded in the stands.

Gladiators and Empire

The infamous arenas of Rome housed gladiatorial combats and animal hunts, and increasingly under the Empire there were also ritualized and even mythologized executions. In the early Empire, as we have seen on chapter 8, these blood sports were regularized into a tripartite format. Different events were held in sequence throughout the day: hunts in the morning, sometimes supplemented by executions with animals; lunchtime shows (*meridiani*), which came to feature staged and often aggravated executions; and gladiatorial combats in the afternoon. Even modest or local shows required extensive preparation, and the extravaganzas of the emperors could only be produced and afforded by a large, autocratic Empire. At Rome under the Empire, officials arranged and produced shows for the emperors, and each of four imperial gladiatorial schools had facilities for housing gladiators and a small arena for their training.

Gladiatorial equipment and combats

Studies of the various equipment and techniques of combat agree that gladiators were well-equipped professionals. Their elaborate armor was flashy but effective. Whatever the type of gladiator, the fighter's head, arms, and legs were well protected, but his torso, the main target, was usually bare, as if to symbolize his bravery.

In the early imperial period, the heavily armed Samnite, with helmet, sword, and probably a greave on his left leg, was replaced by the *Murmillo* and *Secutor*.

The *Murmillo*, bare-chested, with a heavily padded left leg with a short greave, wore a brimmed helmet with an angular crest in the shape of a fish. With a tall, oblong shield and sword, this gladiator was often set against the *Thraex* or the *Hoplomachus*. These two types shared some equipment (trousers, arm guards, pairs of high greaves), but the *Thraex* was distinguished by his small rectangular shield and curved sword. His helmet was like that of the *Hoplomachus* but with a curved crest and griffin. The *Hoplomachus* had a small round shield, thrusting lance, and dagger. The *Provocator*, a middleweight with a breastplate and straight sword, often fought another of his type.

The most glamorous type, the *Retiarius*, an introduction of the early imperial era, used a net, trident, and dagger. His protection was limited to an arm guard and a shoulder guard on the left side. The net fighter was famous for his lack of helmet and therefore the visibility of his face, while other gladiators under the Empire wore visored helmets. The *Secutor* was a specialized opponent routinely set against the *Retiarius*. He had the same equipment as the *Murmillo* except for his rounded helmet with small eyeholes and a rounded crest, so designed to avoid entanglement in the net.

A fictional but credible account in Pseudo-Quintillian tells of preparations in the arena. After a procession of glamorous gladiators, exotic beasts, and abject convicts, weapons were sharpened and inspected, and braziers were used to heat pokers, which were used, like whips, to motivate fighters and also to check that casualties were truly dead. Combatants were paired with a view to entertainment, usually by contrasting and therefore complementary styles, often by setting a net fighter against a heavily armed pursuer. The matching of opponents was important, for gladiators usually fought duels, one pair at a time, not mass fights. Gladiatorial combat has often been represented as indiscriminate slaughter and murderous mayhem. Rather, the combats were well orchestrated and controlled. The risks were real, but there were rules and referees.

Since fighters carried about 20 kg of equipment, combats only lasted a few (perhaps 10–15) minutes until one combatant, by injury or fatigue, was incapacitated or overly vulnerable. The attentive crowd, aware of his plight, then called out "he's done." If able, the defeated gladiator dropped his weapon and raised his finger in admission of defeat and as a plea for a positive decision about his fate – a reprieve from death. A referee with a staff would make sure that the victor awaited the decision. The loser's fate was up to the show's sponsor, since his property was at stake; but he would often defer to the crowd, which made its decision on the basis of the quality of the fight. As at a modern boxing match, some viewers perhaps came only for the violence, but most ancient Romans were knowledgeable and discerning consumers of gladiatorial combat.

Contrary to common opinion, the signal for death seems not to have been thumbs down but rather thumbs turned up toward the throat. The gesture for mercy or release apparently was two fingers pointed away or out. If the decision was death, the loser accepted the quick and efficient deathblow. In Roman terms, the defeated fighter died like a soldier, having retrieved a certain degree of dignity for his efforts. While the dead opponent was being removed, the victor accepted the applause of the crowd as he took a victory lap and collected his prizes, normally money and a palm frond. If he had completed three of his five years as a slave gladiator, he also earned the wooden sword (*rudis*), symbol of release from fighting (manumission came after five years).

Unlike hunted beasts or executed convicts, elite gladiators had a chance of survival. Gladiators did not fight as often as might be expected: usually only once per show, and perhaps only twice or a few times per year. Inscriptions, especially epitaphs, often refer to multiple draws or ties and even losses, so many fights must not have been to the death. While injuries were common, wounded gladiators were well tended by doctors. Clearly, many gladiators survived the arena to achieve freedom, and some even earned wealth and fame.

Owners invested time and training in gladiators, and they often sold or rented them. Such valuable resources were not to be squandered, unless for effect. An inscription from Minturnae of 249 CE says a sponsor gave a show with 11 bouts in which 11 gladiators died, as if this were unusually generous. Owners took precautions against the unwished-for death of valuable gladiators: in rental contracts of the second century BCE gladiators were worth 80 sesterces if they survived uninjured, but clauses stipulated extra payments if they were killed or maimed. Gladiators were such a costly commodity that Marcus Aurelius and Commodus decreed maximum prices and maximum expenditures for various levels of games in an effort to lessen the financial pressure on provincial producers of games.

Volunteers, dilettantes, and females

Veteran freedmen gladiators often contracted themselves out as free agents, temporarily surrendering their freedom for the sake of gain, or to pursue their career. Too much, however, has been made of volunteer or dilettante gladiators. Out of debt or obsession with the allure of the arena, some free citizens did contract themselves out as gladiators, but such participation by the elite as paid gladiators was repeatedly condemned. A senatorial edict of 19 CE prohibited relatives and connections of equestrians and senators from appearing on stage or in the arena. Proper Romans were not to display their skills and bodies for the entertainment and pleasure of others.

The erotic appeal of gladiators was like that of modern boxers and matadors, and references to gladiators as sex symbols are found in the silver Latin of Ovid, Juvenal, and Martial, as well as in graffiti at Pompeii. Tertullian and Juvenal claim that gladiators were attractive even to noble women, but Romans became upset if proper women actually fraternized with gladiators.

A grave discovered in the Southwark district of London of a Roman woman has been seen as that of a "gladiatrix" because of its location and artifacts (e.g. a lamp with an image of a gladiator), but it is more likely that she was a prostitute or gladiatorial consort. Female gladiators were not unknown, and a relief from

Halicarnassus from the first or second century CE commemorates the release of two female gladiators. However, female gladiators were exceptions and novelties, mostly associated with the games of Nero and Domitian, and in time the emperor Septimius Severus banned such public performances by women.

The Colosseum as a purpose-built amphitheater

Rome received its first stone amphitheater as a benefaction from Statilius Taurus, an associate of Augustus. After that amphitheater was destroyed, Nero built a wooden amphitheater in 57 CE, also in the Campus Martius, but it too was destroyed. Rome's most infamous venue for spectacles, the Flavian amphitheater was later known as the Colosseum because of the colossal (37 meters high) statue of Nero that stood nearby. When the Flavians came to power in 69 CE, they constructed a purpose-built facility, monumental and in stone, as a gift to the people. Begun by Vespasian, the construction continued under Titus, and a structure 188 by 156 meters in extent, 50 meters in height, surrounding an arena 86 meters by 54 meters, arose in central Rome near the Forum. A contemporary observer, Martial, penned a poem, *On the Spectacles*, praising the extravagant spectacles that Titus provided, which lasted 100 days and involved thousands of men and animals, when he dedicated the structure in 80 CE.

Often used as a metaphor for Rome's hierarchically ordered society, the Colosseum had seating in four tiered levels. The podium, a high platform directly above the arena, had special seats for the emperor, priests, Vestals, and senators. The level above was assigned to equestrians, the next to normal citizens, and the highest level was for women and slaves. Sub-chambers on two levels, added or enlarged by Domitian under the wooden floor of the arena, allowed beasts and fighters to emerge from trapdoors to appear suddenly and dramatically in the arena.

Beast hunts and executions

Associated mostly with triumphs and the circus under the Republic, under the Empire beast shows increasingly moved to the amphitheater. Shocking numbers of animal victims are recorded for extraordinary games: 9,000 in 80 CE in Titus' games to dedicate the Flavian amphitheater, and 11,000 in Trajan's games of 108–109. The numbers escalated as ambitious emperors put on lavish shows to bolster their popularity and their legitimacy in the emperorship.

The goal always was to put on a good show. As earlier, sometimes animals were hunted – increasingly artificially, given the circumstances, scenery, and lack of any chance of escape – by trained hunters with specialized weapons and equipment, sometimes assisted by hounds. Sometimes beasts were pitted against each other, as if to suggest hunts by predatory carnivores of herbivores (e.g. lions after deer). Sometimes odd pairings of animals, who would not naturally confront each other, such as a bull against a bear, or an elephant against a rhinoceros, were forced to fight by whips or firebrands, or by being chained together. As Martial wrote of Titus' games, even nature yielded to the will of the emperor.

From the early Empire on, various forms of ritualized public executions of criminals (and Christians later) were performed in an increasingly spectacular way in the arena. For a host of crimes Rome punished criminals of low status with aggravated punishments, which included exposure to wild beasts, crucifixion, and burning alive. The victim's lasting agony and death provided a terrifying and exemplary public spectacle.

"To the lions": exposure to beasts

While the objective of the morning hunts was to show that humans and Roman civilization could triumph over any threats from nature (or the territories symbolized by the exotic beasts), other morning shows used beasts to demonstrate Rome's ability to punish human beings. Exposure to beasts (*damnatio ad bestias*) became more widespread under the Empire as a penalty for slaves, foreign enemies, and free men guilty of heinous offences. Criminals were led into the arena almost or fully naked; and, without weapons and sometimes bound to posts or wheeled platforms, they were exposed to aggressive and ferocious beasts, which were forced toward the helpless victims by handlers with whips and fire.

Mass combats as executions

Lunchtime shows might include mass executions staged as combats. Not to be confused with gladiators who fought duels later in the afternoon, these hopeless, desperate, unskilled criminals were provided with weapons but not armor, and they were forced to fight each other to the death. Seneca's account leaves no doubt about the lack of artistry and the lack of escape: "now all the trifling is put aside and it is pure murder. . . . In the morning they throw men to the lions and the bears; at noon, they throw them to the spectators" (*Epistles* 1.7). Despite Seneca's indignation, such ritualized executions of pathetic victims, like the mass deaths in naumachies, rid Rome, a society not inclined to prisons and rehabilitation, of undesirables. These spectacles also presented an explicit lesson of deterrence for potential lawbreakers.

Fatal charades

Executions became even more spectacular and dramatic in what Kathleen Coleman calls "fatal charades," shows in which criminals were forced to play roles in mythological contexts. In such shows the victims usually were killed. For example, under Titus, a certain Laureolus, as the character Prometheus in a play, was crucified and mauled to death by a bear on stage in the amphitheater. As Martial said, myths and legends became real punishments in the arena.

Against the perspective of aggravated executions and fatal charades, the methods of execution of Christians in the persecutions seem less bizarre or extreme. Although special animosity or abuse possibly was involved, punishment of Christians was not unique, nor was it the most prominent or recurrent element in Roman spectacles.

The decline of violent spectacles

Amphitheaters and gladiatorial combat spread, flourished, and ultimately declined with the Empire. In the late Empire, arena games were opposed by clerics and prohibited by Christian emperors. Tertullian and many **Fathers of the Church** protested that all forms of public spectacles were rooted in idolatrous worship of the dead, and that any spectatorship by Christians would deny them salvation. By the mid-fourth century gladiators had largely died out in the East, but they persisted in the West for many years. After the monk Telemachus was killed by the crowd in Asia Minor for trying to stop games, the Christian emperor Honorius formally banned gladiatorial combats in 404.

In mundane terms, gladiatorial combat had been dependent on imperial power and munificence for centuries. As the most expensive and infrequent spectacles, they were vulnerable to the systems collapse of the western Empire. With a few exceptions they ended in the West with the demise of emperorship. Beast shows struggled with supply problems but continued on a reduced scale. In Byzantium in 499 Anastasias banned them for economic reasons, but they revived. The last beast shows to be referred to in Constantinople were in 573, and they were officially abolished in 681, only to revive again in sporadic animal acts and beast baitings in the Middle Ages.

> **Fathers (of the Church):** Post-classical designation of the many first–sixth-century theologians who developed the doctrine of the Church.

11.7 | Religious Life

In his discussion of various religions of the Empire, Ramsay MacMullen (*Paganism in the Roman Empire*) observes that it was a true melting-pot. "Even if you skim lightly through the Roman Empire, or however cursorily you look at its religious diversity, you cannot fail to be struck by the proliferation of beliefs." In his study, MacMullen refrains from analyzing the "constituent parts, [the] particular cults, their derivations and specific nature," in order to deal with the complete system and its exchanges. Doubtless he was right; but it is still necessary to know something of the essential features of its main components: traditional Roman religion, the imperial cult, and indigenous cults, some of which developed beyond their region of origin.

Traditional Roman religion

In his capacity as head of the Roman religion, *pontifex maximus*, Augustus restored and revived religious practices in Rome. Henceforth, the emperor was the sole master of both the sacred and the profane: the auspices of the magistrates were thus subordinate to the auspicial pre-eminence of the emperor. There was nothing new about Augustus' infiltration of a political agenda into religious practices such as augury and sacrifice. Far from impoverishing traditional religion, his modifications, and those of subsequent emperors, seem to have enriched it. Three general characteristics mark its development during the second century.

Continuity

For a long time, the traditional religion of the imperial era was considered virtually moribund. But now, a reinterpretation of the texts from a non-spiritual perspective, a better use of cultic documents such as inscriptions, and an analysis of the relations between religion and civic activities have led us to place greater emphasis on the durability, continuity, and vitality of that religion.

The ancient rites (those of the Salii and Luperci, for instance) were still scrupulously celebrated, and the proceedings of the Arval Brethren were still strictly recorded. Jupiter continued to be the most popular god in the pantheon, now in implicit association with imperial worship. The conduct of the devout pagan does not seem to have changed: according to Apuleius (*Florides* I) "Pious travelers, if they come across some sacred wood or holy place in the course of their journey, are in the habit of making a vow, offering a fruit or sitting down for a moment."

The role of the emperors

Until the time of Commodus, the Antonines regarded themselves as guardians of the state, safeguarding Rome's material and moral heritage by preserving the gods and rites whose existence affected that of Rome and the Empire, and the fundamental values of Greco-Latin civilization. Their action took various forms:

- Honoring the priesthoods. Following Augustan tradition, the emperor not only was *pontifex maximus*, but also held several priesthoods concurrently. Nerva, for example, belonged to the four great colleges (pontiffs, augurs, quindecimvirs in charge of sacrifices, *epulones*). Hadrian had the young Marcus Aurelius entered in the college of the Salians at the age of seven (a unique privilege); and Commodus, having just become *Caesar*, was also received into the four great colleges (in 175), as his father had been in 140. The emperor was indeed always admitted to those four colleges. Marcus Aurelius also revived the ancient rite of the fetial declaration of war.
- Controlling the priesthoods. Whether it was a matter of appointing someone to an individual priestly office, or of filling places in colleges or sodalities, the emperor, in fact if not in law, could appoint his own choice.

- Dedication to a particular god. Trajan, for example, was devoted to the Hercules of Gades (Cadiz), the Latin name for the Phoenician tutelary divinity Melqart. Rather than impose this foreign god on Rome, he preferred to make the Roman Hercules benefit from his fervor. Vows, medals, games, and his representation on the arch of Beneventum all demonstrate the particular favor accorded to Hercules during Trajan's reign.

- Honoring the whole range of traditional gods. Trajan's coinage reveals a great deal here. The images of Jupiter, Rome, Vesta, and Victory are the most frequent, followed by those of Apollo, Ceres, Diana, the Dioscuri, Flora, Hercules, Janus, Juno, Mars, Mercury, Minerva, Nemesis, Neptune, Quirinus, Saturn, the Sun, Venus, Vulcan, and even Aeneas. Personified abstractions such as Concordia, Libertas, Pietas, and Spes are also featured on his coins. The legends of archaic Rome were still held in honor under Hadrian and, even more so, Antoninus, who attached remarkable importance to the old cults of Latium and the deities of rural Italy.

- Building and restoring. In this area, Hadrian well deserves the title of champion of traditional religion. This claim rests on his restoration of celebrated Roman monuments such as the Pantheon and the temple of Venus and Rome, promoted now to the rank of official deity, Roma. He also renovated smaller temples, for example those in the town of Lanuvium, in particular that of Juno Sospita (the most venerable of all the Italian shrines to this goddess).

The century of virtus and pietas

It was not by chance that, even before Trajan made his entry into Rome (summer 99), the Senate issued an *as* showing Victory with a shield, modeled on the reverse of the coins struck under Augustus. The shield of Augustus was a potent symbol of the victor armed with virtue. It featured both *virtus* and *pietas*, virtues which were considerably promoted by the Antonines.

- *Virtus*, the foremost of the Augustan virtues, manifested itself especially in combat. Under Trajan, it eclipsed *fortuna* and *felicitas*. Henceforward, it was no longer these two which ensured victory, but rather the personal *virtus* of the emperor. With Hadrian, the idea of *virtus* was altered. The purely military aspect became less prominent, and *virtus* was tellingly revealed in the hunt: official imagery glorified the emperor's hunting exploits, likening them to bold displays of *virtus* on the field of battle. In a way reminiscent of Pliny's praise of Trajan's hunting (*Panegyric* 81), the eight medallions on the arch of Constantine with scenes from Hadrian's hunts suggest the symbolical capital of hunting as a testament to imperial *virtus*. (On the significance of imperial hunting, see also Dio Chrysostom, *Speeches on Kingship* 3.136. Although he does not mention Trajan by name, it is commonly agreed that the anonymous ideal king featured in this speech is Trajan himself.)

- *Pietas* was invoked as early as Nerva's time. Pliny had praised Trajan for his piety toward his family and the gods. But with Antoninus, *pietas* reached its zenith. Its imagery appeared in the first issues of coinage in his reign, and the emperor himself chose his *cognomen* of *Pius*, for he wanted to advertise and spread his innate virtue.
- *Pietas* became the ideal proposed by this ruler to his century and the fundamental principle of the regime.

Imperial religion

Created by Augustus and institutionalized by Vespasian, the imperial cult was simultaneously individual, municipal, provincial, and imperial, addressed to dead emperors and aiming to satisfy the living ones, whether or not they were associated with the goddess Rome in worship. In the second century, the imperial cult underwent a notable expansion. There were several contributory factors.

The Jovian theology of the Principate Early on, Augustus had discreetly associated himself with Jupiter. Trajan fostered a close association between himself, the first among the Romans, and the first among the gods. Pliny (*Panegyric* 23) relates that on the day of Trajan's *adventus* into Rome, the emperor was hailed by the crowds as *Imperator* on the Capitoline hill. There too stood a statue to Jupiter Imperator and the largest temple in Rome, dedicated to Jupiter Optimus Maximus. From that time on Jupiter was ever-present in Trajanic imperial ideology. He is represented on the arch of Beneventum delegating his powers to the emperor. Far from disappearing with Trajan, this idea was reinforced by his successors. An eagle proffers a scepter to Hadrian, Providentia lends her thunderbolt to Antoninus, and Jupiter himself helps Marcus Aurelius in his struggles against the barbarians. It is no surprise, therefore, to see numerous new temples dedicated to the Capitoline Triad in provincial towns between 150 and 170. Rather than representing a relative weakening of the imperial cult, this marked the complete assimilation of the deified emperors to Jupiter Optimus Maximus, the most popular, and political, of all the gods.

The cult of dead emperors In 183, out of the 16 deified persons officially honored by a cult, 12 were Antonines – the emperors Nerva, Trajan, Hadrian, Antoninus, and Lucius Verus, together with various sisters and wives. Whether deliberately or by a sort of natural development, the Domus Augusta occupied an increasingly eminent position in religious life. A temple was erected for nearly every deified member, and further sodalities (for Hadrian and Antoninus) were created.

The success of the provincial and municipal cult The imperial cult was successfully transplanted into various cities and provinces around the Empire. Cultic practices varied depending on the province, with the assemblies variously formed (*concilium*, *koinon*) and the districts often particular to the province (the three Gauls, the numerous reorganizations of Syria). The popularity of the emperors expressed at these assemblies seems to have been much the same everywhere.

A popular cult? For a long time, historians doubted the popularity of the imperial cult. It was thought that, because it was official, it could only be superficial. It now seems, on the contrary, that the "love of Augustus" was firmly entrenched in hearts and minds. The divine and quasi-divine attributes of the emperor's deeds were venerated, sacrifices were made for the emperor's health, and evidence shows that in both town and country, in both Italy and the provinces, this was more than mere affectation among the Empire's inhabitants.

Indigenous religions

Under this general term, we include all the religions in the Empire except Italian religions. To go into the subject in detail would necessitate a tour of the Empire, province by province, even region by region. And no overall view is really pertinent: these religions were rooted in a precise area, history, and society (though some journeyed far from home). The most we can do here is to present a few evolutionary features that some of them had in common.

Continuity

The second century, which has produced a greater number of documents, gives the illusion of a renaissance of indigenous cults even though there had been no decline in the first century. Perhaps a more fruitful venue of exploration is that of their Romanization. In a study of the north-west of the Iberian peninsula, it has been noted that Rome's religious policy allowed and facilitated the development of local religions insofar as they accepted a gradual assimilation with Roman deities; and this statement, with a few qualifications, could be applied to other provinces. For example, while the coming of the Romans to Gaul had been the death of the Druids' most authentic rites (human sacrifice, display of heads), as well as their clergy and lore, it was through representations and inscriptions drawn from contact with Roman polytheism that Celtic polytheism expressed itself. In Africa, despite all the apparent Romanization, Saturn, the simple Latin translation of Ba'al-Hammon, remained an African god to the very end. Rome did not seek to impose a form of religious life (with the exception of the prohibition of human sacrifice, banned in the first century). The cult of Rome and Augustus was no threat to indigenous cults and, in fact, the two were often associated.

Of course, the Romans had their reservations. The most obvious was the fear of Egypt, a tradition that can be traced back to the Greek historian Herodotus, and was kindled in Roman consciousness by the memory of Cleopatra and Antony's "orientalization." Romans scorned Egyptian gods with animal bodies, considering them both daunting and ridiculous. But they left anyone who wished to worship them free to do so. All in all, in this encounter of polytheisms, continuing indigenous religions trace an invisible frontier – that of the Romanization of souls.

Interpretatio Romana

In his *Germania*, Tacitus introduces a very important idea regarding the religious syncretism of the Empire: "Among the Naharvali [an independent Germanic people], a sacred wood is to be seen, the place of worship of a very ancient cult. Its lord is a priest dressed as a woman, but it is said that the gods of the place are Castor and Pollux, according to the Roman interpretation" (*Germania* 43). Tacitus' phrase "the Roman interpretation" reveals the way in which a foreign observer understands an unknown god by likening it to, or identifying it with, a god that he knows. So we see a dual phenomenon, of major importance in the history of indigenous religions. Working one way is the *interpretatio Romana*, which dresses a native god in Roman guise, or sees a native god as a Roman god in local or native guise. Caesar, to take an example from an earlier period, recounts that the Gauls are very religious people, worshiping above all Mercury and, after him, Apollo, Mars, Jupiter, and Minerva (*Gallic Wars* 6.17). Working the other way is the *interpretatio Gallica* in Gaul, *Africana* in Africa, or *Iberica* in Spain, for example, through which a Roman god comes to be assimilated and fused with Gaulish, African, or Iberian dieties. In fact, these two processes often occurred simultaneously. For example, in Gaul the name "Mars Vesontius" could designate:

- the Roman Mars honored in the town of Besançon;
- a great native god whom the Bisontini identified with Mars;
- a local native god likened to the Roman god.

If these examples are multiplied, one may understand both the richness and complexity of this phenomenon.

Established indigenous religions

This term covers the majority of the indigenous religions. It refers to non-Italian religions (Gallo-Roman, Iberico-Roman, etc.), evidence for which is to be found primarily in their places of origin. All preserved their native identity, which survived, more or less altered, in Roman guise. Two examples follow.

Gaul Over 400 sanctuaries are known, most frequently in the vicinity of a spring, a cave, or a cliff, or on a peak, in a mountain pass, or at a river crossing. These sanctuaries took various forms. Some, for example, were chapels (*fana*) with a gallery in which people could circulate; others were comprised of several buildings and received many pilgrims (e.g. see the stone and wooden images of pilgrims from the healing sanctuary at Fontes Sequanae, in modern Burgundy). Votives and offerings, which are being increasingly studied, reveal the indigenous nature of the worshipers. Only 4 percent of the Gaulish inscriptions addressed to native gods come from people whose names are not Gaulish. The divinities worshiped in these places are only partly known. They are represented in unusual poses (e.g. cross-legged) and are often accompanied by animals. Frequently linked to naturist cults, they were gods and goddesses of the waters, of the fruitful earth, livestock, and trade. For example, the typically Celtic Mother Goddesses, who bore a Latin name, the Matres (sometimes distinguished by a pertinent adjective of native origin), were mostly represented in a group of three, with a child and a horn of plenty.

Africa Here the case was very different. The native pantheon was dominated by a great god, whom the Romans assimilated with Saturn. Omnipotent, father of the gods, lord of the world, fauna and flora, protector of the dead, flanked by the sun and the moon, he was, despite his Roman name, in fact far removed from the Greco-Roman god who succeeded Janus. The African god's cult, his sanctuaries and their decoration, the sacrifices offered to him (especially the *molk* sacrifice, the bloody offering of the first-born, and its substitute, *molchomor*, the sacrifice of a bull or a ram), and the country folk background of his worshipers provide clear evidence of his indigenous nature. He seems to have been of Punico-Berber origin, the heir of Ba'al, who had resisted all attempts at Romanization. This makes it easier to explain his success in north-western Africa and his lack of success elsewhere.

Dynamic indigenous religions

These are those indigenous religions (a minority on the scale of the Empire but important nevertheless) that spread to Italy and Rome, and to nearly all the western provinces, from their native areas in the East. These "foreign" religions, as the Romans termed them, would be better termed religions of eastern origin or Greco-eastern religions, for their cults were not directly transposed from East to West, but were modified by contact with Greek religion and adapted to local conditions.

It has been noted that the dates when these religions appeared in Italy (and the same phenomenon is to be found in the provinces) are spread over several centuries, and that the political, social, and psychological circumstances of their arrivals were very different. For example, the cult of the Great Mother Cybele was said to have entered Rome during the Second Punic War to assist the Romans, while Isis, Horus, Serapis, and other mystery cults infiltrated Rome under less clear circumstances. The fact that we consider all these cults generally as "eastern" is an illusory perspective contrived by the fourth-century Christian author Firmicus Maternus. He first classified them as a distinct group, polemically opposed to the one true religion, Christianity. This tradition leads some historians to ignore the specific characteristics of these individual religions and classify them all in the same category as "mystery religions" offering spiritual solace and after-life assurances, but the picture is more complex and more interesting than that.

The reasons for the success of eastern cults in the West also divide historians. This success has traditionally been explained by the presence there of people who had adopted these cults in the East. These eastern devotees supposedly converted Romans and indigenous peoples in the West who thus found a spirituality lacking in their own religions. The presence of devotees from the East can be argued for from the nature of these cults. For these Greco-eastern religions, which formed small communities distinct from the city, involved a religious commitment – even an initiation – at the end of which the believer shared in a revelation. This commitment, which was not open to all, presupposes a spiritual and theological preparation organized by a specialized and sometimes learned clergy. Conversion was aided by ceremonies and festivals, made appealing and mystical by music and processions. These religions often encouraged individual morality, an idea that resonated with the spiritual quests of the times. This moral code stressed the merits of purification and the promise of immortality. In comparison with the less spiritual and more ritualistic Roman religion, which did not aim to address individual conscience, intelligence, or feelings, eastern religions succeeded in convincing people of their usefulness. This was especially so since a conversion did not have to exclude involvement with the traditional Roman rituals.

Some historians think that there were relatively few conversions: "under the follower of Isis in Ostia was hidden the man or woman from Alexandria or Antioch, or perhaps the descendant of a family originating from one of those towns. Similarly, the follower of Isis in Lyon concealed not a convert, but an immigrant" (Ramsay MacMullen). In that case, it is probable that the religious history of the West, more than it would seem at first glance, is closer to that of the East, the same calm reigning in both parts of the Empire. If so, it was slaves and their descendants who provided the mass of adherents of these cults. For example, in Campania, Etruria, and Apulia, three quarters of the signatories of inscriptions dedicated to Isis were slaves and freedmen; in Rome, the Veneto, and Sicily, they form three fifths. In all, nearly half the followers of Isis in Italy had non-Italian origins.

Nevertheless, it is undeniable that there were conversions. For instance, in Spain, Gaul, Africa, Mauretania, Germany, and even Britain, Isis went beyond the port districts and commercial towns frequented by Greco-Egyptians and reached the indigenous populations. Similarly, the cult of Cybele found fertile soil in Gaul, where over 60 altars for bull sacrifice have been found, more than in any other region of the Empire. Perhaps the indigenous worship of the Mother Goddesses had prepared the ground for the cult of the Great Mother Cybele. So we can steer a middle course in our interpretation: we can assume that the presence of eastern worshipers in Italy (Campania) and Romanized regions of the western provinces was followed by local diffusion of converted populations. We

Box 11.3 Principal eastern religions

Name of god/goddess	Origin	Appearance in Italy and development
Cybele and Attis	Asia Minor	204 BCE in Rome; development under Claudius; first mention of a *taurobolium* in 160 CE.
Isis and Serapis	Alexandria	Before 105 BCE in Pozzuoli; early first century BCE in Rome; expansion under Caligula and (mainly) the Flavians.
Dea Syria (Atagartis)	Hierapolis–Bambyke (Syria)	As early as the end of the second century BC in Sicily; first century BC in Italy.
Jupiter Heliopolitanus	Heliopolis–Baalbek (Lebanon)	Developed from the time of Augustus in the East (Baalbek a Roman colony; theological creation around 16 BCE); expansion in the West in the second century CE.
Jupiter Dolichenus	Doliche–Duluck (Turkey)	The type of god appeared in the first century CE; in the West under Hadrian; shrine in Rome in the middle of the second century.
Mithras	Iran	Under the Flavians, first epigraphic and literary attestations.

also need to make a distinction between their relative success, when we examine the influence of each cult. The worship of Isis, Cybele, and Mithras, for example, spread widely in the West. The Syrian gods, by contrast, remained marginal and were almost always honored only by migrants and foreign residents.

The spread of these various religions was advanced in a number of ways. A cult might be encouraged by the emperor, directly through personal belief or for political reasons, or indirectly through his entourage (wife, artists, slaves, and freedmen) and the court. Moreover, the adherents of these religions often linked their cults with the imperial cult, very often from civic solidarity – this was rare, however, among the devotees of Alexandrian cults. Imperial officials and soldiers, too, at all levels of their hierarchies, were important agents of diffusion. The soldiers reveal a marked preference for Mithras, Jupiter Dolichenus, and Jupiter Heliopolitanus. Leaving aside Rome and Ostia, the map of the spread of these three cults virtually matches that of the military zones. Civilians were also involved, since they were often connected by their activities to the service of the armies and the imperial machinery. Lastly there are the traders, who were nearly all eastern. Their gods traveled with them. They were present in the ports (Puteoli, Ostia, Carthage, Marseilles), along the rivers (the valleys of the Rhône, the Rhine, the Danube, the Guadalquivir, the Ebro), and along the land routes (Alpine passes, the Rhône–Rhine axis), in cosmopolitan and commercial towns, and at road junctions in general (Lyons, Poetovio, Trier).

All in all, the worshipers of these gods were continually on the move or cut off from their city of origin. They needed gods that could go outside the limits

Plate 11.14
Dancers in an erotic
revel, second century
CE. Ancient Art &
Architecture
Collection

of the city, were omnipresent, and represented little communities of comfort and
safety. Watching over individuals and in charge of the world, these eastern gods,
removed from their native lands, intimately present in the hearts of their devotees,
and endowed with limitless powers that transcended all the functions of the gods
in the classical pantheon, were truly in keeping with the cosmopolitan Empire.

12

THE AFRICAN AND SYRIAN EMPERORS: 193–235 CE

Just as the death of Nero in 68 was the end of the Julio-Claudians and ushered in a year of civil war, known as "the year of the four emperors," so the murder of Commodus (see chapter 11 above, section 11.1) ended the Antonine dynasty and launched a year of civil war, marked by short-lived reigns and attempted usurpations. The year 193 has justly been called "the year of five emperors" (Helvius Pertinax, Didius Julianus, Pescennius Niger, Clodius Albinus, and Septimius Severus), a modern title aligned with the Romans' own concept that civil war was a repetitive event within the grand narrative of their national destiny. In any event, the year ushered to the throne the first non-Italian family there: the Severans. This dynasty was founded by the African general Septimius Severus, and its nine-emperor rule extended from 193 to 235 CE. Although Septimius Severus successfully restored peace following the death of Commodus, his dynasty was disturbed by family conflicts and plots, political turmoil, and external threats, all eventually contributing to what is referred to today as the "crisis of the third century" (see below, chapter 13).

12.1 | The Crisis of 193–197 CE

On the very night of Commodus' murder (December 31, 192), conspirators persuaded the reluctant prefect of Rome, P. Helvius Pertinax, to accept the throne, took him to the praetorian camp, and then before the Senate. The praetorians acclaimed him *imperator* under pressure from the people and on the promise of a *donativum*; the senators did so in the flush of their deliverance from Commodus, for whose *damnatio memoriae* they at once voted, and from esteem for Pertinax, who received the imperial titles and, contrary to tradition, immediately assumed that of *pater patriae*. He was 66 years old. A native of Liguria and the son of a freedman, he had first followed an equestrian career before being admitted by Marcus Aurelius to the Senate among former praetors, and thanks to his qualities had eventually reached the peak of the senatorial career as prefect of the city. Worried by the condition of the imperial finances, attentive to the economic situation, and anxious about the barbarian threat, the new emperor was determined to apply measures that did not earn him popularity, especially with the praetorians (Herodian, 2.4). On March 28, a party of them broke into the imperial palace and, despite his courage, Pertinax was assassinated. He had ruled for just 87 days. In the words of Cassius Dio, the reason for his assassination was that "he did not realize, though a widely experienced man, that one cannot safely reform everything at once, and that the restoration of a state requires both time and wisdom" (74.10).

This abrupt mutiny, without any precise aim, had no political pretensions. Uncertain what to do about their crime, and since the Empire could not remain without an emperor, the praetorians let it be known that they would offer the post to the highest bidder. There were two competitors. For 5,000 sesterces per praetorian more than his rival (in all, 25,000 sesterces to each), the rich senator M. Didius Julianus won. Originating from Milan (where he was born in 133 or 137), and with family ties in Africa, he had pursued an exemplary senatorial career, culminating in the proconsulship of Africa (189–190). He was one of the most senior men of consular rank, and had both wide experience and good contacts. However, given a cold welcome by the Senate and jeered at by the people, Julianus, as emperor, could count on no one in Rome except the praetorians. Cassius Dio (74.12–13) describes vividly as an eye-witness the senators' fear on the night of Julianus' accession, as well as the popular protests that followed.

Julianus was even less supported in the provinces. At the end of April, he learned that military risings had occurred in Pannonia and Syria, and that L. Septimius Severus and C. Pescennius Niger, respectively, had been proclaimed emperor by their armies. At Julianus' insistence, the Senate declared the two men public enemies and offered an amnesty to their troops. Julianus attempted a reconciliation, asking the Senate to decree Severus and himself joint rulers. Yet he had already lost the support of the praetorians, who also feared the advent of Severus. The Senate voted for Julianus' execution after only 66 days of rule.

Meanwhile, in April 9, 193, at Carnuntum, the governor of Upper Pannonia, Septimius Severus, was hailed as emperor by his troops. The ultimate victor in this conflict would be Septimius Severus, who inaugurated the African dynasty of the Severans.

12.2 | Septimius Severus and his Sons

The African emperor: Septimius Severus: 193–211 CE

His early career

Septimius Severus was born in April 145 in Leptis Magna, Tripolitania. On his mother's side he was descended from Italian immigrants (the Fulvii) who had married natives with Roman citizenship; on his father's side, he came from a family of Libyco-Punic origin (Roman citizens since the first century). This had divided into two branches, one Italian, the other African, which had entered the senatorial order in the generation of Severus' father, though his father himself did not belong to it. There had been notable men on both sides. For example, his paternal grandfather had been both chief magistrate (*suffes*) and prefect of Leptis before becoming its first *duumvir* when the city became a colony under Trajan. Members of this ramified family helped one another. One of Severus' father's cousins, for example, arranged for him to receive the laticlave.

Around 164, Severus began a senatorial *cursus honorum* that led him to a consulship in 190 and the governorship of Upper Pannonia in 191. The highlights of his career during these years are the following:

- He received the training of a jurist and rhetor (as well as Punic, he spoke Latin and Greek) in Leptis, and then in Rome. Oddly enough, this emperor who did much for his soldiers did not serve as a military tribune and received an important command only when he became governor of Upper Pannonia and its three legions came under his orders. First and foremost, he was an energetic administrator.
- He knew the Empire well. In the emperor's service, he had been posted to Tarraconensis, Sardinia, Africa, Syria, Lugdunensis, and Sicily. He had also spent two years in Athens, in a kind of semi-exile (183–185).
- The year 180 stands out as important for his future. As a legate of a legion in Syria in this year, he became a friend of his superior, Pertinax, the future emperor, and at Emesa he met the Great Priest of the Sun, Julius Bassianus, and his daughters, Julia Domna and Julia Maesa (see genealogy 12.2 below). In 187, he married Julia Domna, by whom he had two sons, Bassianus (Caracalla), born in Lyons in 188, and Geta, born in Rome in 189.

Some further aspects of his character may be picked out. He had a strong affection for his family and city of origin, and a facility for building relationships

(a)

(b)

Plate 12.1 **(a)** Triumphal arch of Septimius Severus, erected in 203 CE to celebrate his victories over the Parthians. It spans the Via Sacra and leads to the ascent of the Capitoline Hill, the final destination of triumphal processions. akg-images/Bildarchiv Steffens
(b) Arch of Septimius Severus in Leptis Magna, built in 203–204 CE. Its four different façades depict military victories, triumphal processions, the imperial family, and personified virtues and deities such as Concordia and the patron deity (Tyche) of Leptis. shutterstock. co.uk

and making good use of them. His faith in astrology was deep, with astrological considerations often dictating his actions. According to one version, he married Julia Domna because her horoscope had predicted that she would be queen (*Augustan History*, *Severus* 3). He also possessed both religious curiosity (he was a devotee of Serapis and may have been initiated into the mysteries of Eleusis) and an interest in intellectual life and in antiquities.

The victor in the civil war

The conqueror of Didius Julianus Upon his proclamation by his legions, Severus presented himself as the avenger of Pertinax, whose name he adopted among his own names. From the beginning of the month, he had been in contact with the legates of the neighboring provinces, with the result that in the following days the 16 legions of the provinces of the Rhine and Danube rallied to his cause. Before he had begun marching on Rome to win over the city and the Senate, he learned that, in Antioch, Pescennius had also been declared emperor, dragging all the East and Egypt into this venture.

In May, Severus left Carnuntum for Rome and marched through Italy without meeting resistance. On June 1, he was at Interamna, about 80 km north of the

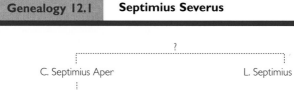

Genealogy 12.1   **Septimius Severus**

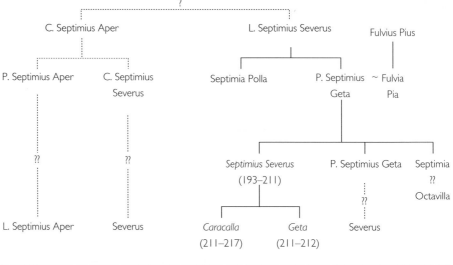

capital. The Senate acknowledged him as emperor and sent him a delegation. Julianus, abandoned, was killed the same day, and the praetorians guilty of the murder of Pertinax and putting the Empire up for sale were arrested. On June 9, having first dismissed the whole of the praetorian guard, Severus entered Rome at the head of his troops. To the Senate he promised not to put any senator to death without its consent, and set out to reorganize the Rome garrison, to arrange for the obsequies and apotheosis of Pertinax, and to supervise the provisioning of Rome. He could then turn his attention to Pescennius Niger, and in July 193 he duly left Rome for the East.

The conqueror of Pescennius Niger Born between 135 and 140, Pescennius rose to senatorial rank having followed an equestrian career. In 191–192, he was appointed legate of Syria. Popular both with the army and in Rome, he represented a formidable threat, with his nine legions, the support offered to him by Egypt (one of the two main sources of Rome's grain supply), and the proposed backing of the eastern monarchs and the Parthians. Furthermore, he had already taken the offensive in Thrace and captured Byzantium. Septimius Severus and his marshals laid siege to that town (which capitulated at the end of 195, after two years), and won victories at Cyzicus and Nicaea in late 193 and early 194. These two victories opened up Bithynia and Asia and brought Egypt and Arabia to the Severan side, as well as some Syrian towns (Tyre, Laodicea), which were immediately punished by Pescennius. Beaten again at Issus (April 194), Pescennius retreated to Antioch, which was overrun and captured by Severan troops. He then sought refuge near the Euphrates, possibly among the Parthians. During his flight he was captured and executed.

In under two years, Severus had re-established the unity of the Empire. But Syria, wealthy, well populated, and defended by three legions, remained inclined to support every imperial ambition. It was therefore divided for strategic purposes. The northern part, with two legions, received the name Syria-Coele ("Hollow Syria"), with Laodicea as its capital, which was also rewarded by being granted the title of colony with the *ius Italicum*, whereas Antioch, which had supported Niger, was punished by being given the status of a township in the territory of its rival (until 202). The southern half, with one legion, was called Syria-Phoenicia, with Emesa or Tyre as its capital (no one is sure which). Lastly, in order to punish peoples who had supported Niger, and to establish a more secure line of defense in the East than that of the Euphrates, Severus conducted two campaigns against the Osroëni, the Adiabeni, and the "Scenite" Arabs. He subsequently annexed the kingdom of Osroëne, with the exception of a small enclave around Edessa which he left to the sovereign, and turned it into a procuratorian province extending as far as Nisibis and the Tigris.

The conqueror of Clodius Albinus Decimus Clodius Albinus, who also came from a provincial family in North Africa, was commanding the British legions. Upon the murder of Pertinax, Albinus was proclaimed emperor by the legions in Britain and Hispania. Fearing Albinus' popularity, Severus appointed him as his intended successor (*Caesar*) while he busied himself with Pescennius Niger in the East. In order to foster Albinus' hopes and increase senatorial faith in him, Severus ordered coins to be struck with Albinus' image and issued him other imperial honors (Herodian, 2.15). Albinus remained ruler of much of the western part of the Empire, supported by his legions.

After Pescennius' defeat, Severus sent assassins to kill Albinus, who in the meantime had proclaimed himself sole emperor with the title *Augustus*. Albinus left Britain with his troops (it is not entirely clear whether this weakening of the Roman military presence there enabled the Caledonian tribes to invade), and, having reached Gaul, rallied almost all communities to his cause, won over Tarraconensis as well, and set up his headquarters in Lyons. Opposing him were the armies of the rest of the Empire.

At the beginning of 197, Severus took the initiative, advanced into Gaul from Upper Germania, and fought the decisive battle near Lyons. On February 19, the defeated Albinus killed himself. According to Cassius Dio (76.6-7), the Empire suffered a terrible blow, with countless soldiers killed in that battle. Lyons was pillaged and burnt, Albinus' provincial partisans were hunted down and executed, and, in Rome, 29 senators were put to death. The confiscations of property were so large that procurators were appointed to record and administer them. Septimius Severus was now sole master of the Empire.

Map 12.1 Senatorial and imperial provinces around 200 CE (from F. Jacques and J. Scheid, *Rome et l'intégration de l'Empire*, PUF, 1990)

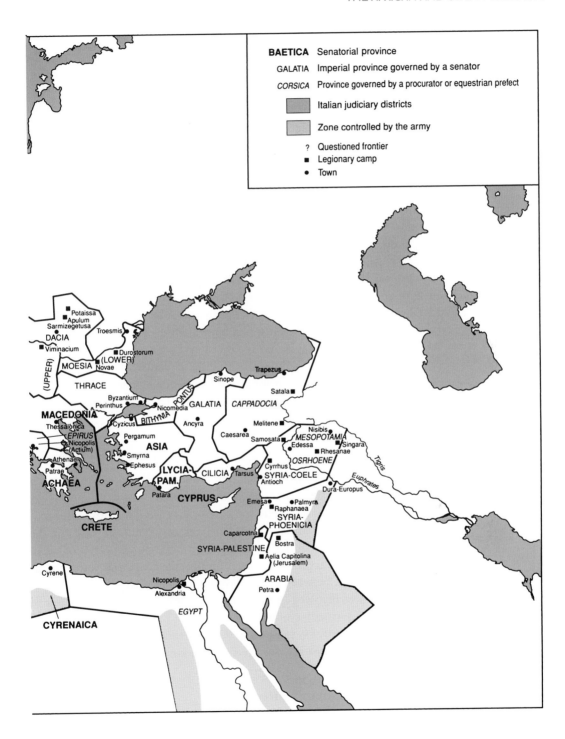

BAETICA   Senatorial province
GALATIA   Imperial province governed by a senator
CORSICA   Province governed by a procurator or equestrian prefect

Italian judiciary districts

Zone controlled by the army

?   Questioned frontier
■   Legionary camp
●   Town

The reasons for Severus' victory

- The African connection played its part, in strengthening ties and granting the support of certain commands. But Clodius Albinus, another African, might equally well have benefited from it.
- Severus' troops were greater in number and better trained than those of his rivals. (The Danubian legions henceforth also outstripped those of other regions, in particular those of the Germanies, in their strategic and political influence.) The military experience of Severus himself was, it seems, modest (according to Cassius Dio, the battle of Lyons was the first big engagement in which he had personally taken part), but he had been able to gather round him some remarkable marshals, the nucleus of a new aristocracy. His determination to be the sole ruler also motivated his efforts.
- Severus made excellent use of imperial propaganda through various media such as coinage, pamphlets, copies of imperial proclamations distributed to the troops and the populace, and the diffusion of prophecies and presages. The use of such means by rivals was not new; it traced back to the war of words, ideas, and imagery between Octavian and Antony.
- Severus outdid the others politically, first by presenting himself as the avenger of Pertinax, and then by playing on the divisions of his enemies. He also had a better appreciation of the scale of the Empire, made use of all the means at his disposal, and was able to inspire a sound team of administrators and generals. Cassius Dio says, and with good reason, that Severus was the most intelligent of all the pretenders to the throne.

Features of the war years

- The Senate, forced by various usurpers into sudden repudiations and much indecision, disappeared completely as a political force.
- The provincial armies, and no longer the praetorian guard, were the determining force in the choice of an emperor. This was especially the case for the soldiers of the Danubian frontier.
- The conflicts of these years took on the form of inter-provincial wars; and at regional level, rivalries between cities played a leading role.
- Among the provinces involved in these conflicts, three provinces or groups of provinces assumed particular importance: Britain, the Danubian provinces, and the East. They definitively signposted the new trade route (Rhine–Danube–Syria) that counterbalanced the Mediterranean axis (East–Rome–West).

The guarantor of the Empire's integrity

The Second Parthian War: 197–199 CE No sooner had Severus returned to Rome than he left again for Syria (June–July 197); for the Parthians had invaded Mesopotamia. Immediately on his arrival in Syria, he set out for that region. Crossing the Euphrates, he advanced toward Nisibis, where the Parthians abandoned their siege. In the autumn of 197, he occupied Babylon, which had long been deserted, captured Seleucia and then crossed the Tigris and took Ctesiphon, which was sacked. On January 28, 198 (exactly 100 years after Trajan's accession), like Trajan, he was proclaimed Parthicus Maximus. On the same day, his elder son, Caracalla, received the title of *Augustus* and his younger son, Geta, became *Caesar*. Returning from this Parthian expedition, Severus had a failure at Hatra, a stronghold and city used by caravans between the Tigris and Euphrates, which he still did not succeed in capturing at a second attempt (winter 198–199), although its king made an act of submission. Then, resuming his plan for reorganizing the eastern frontier, he created the new province of Mesopotamia, east of Osroëne, between Syria-Coele and the Tigris. Like Egypt, it was to be governed by a prefect of equestrian rank (residing at Nisibis). For strategic reasons, he also rearranged the provinces of Syria–Phoenicia and Arabia, after which he made stops in Palestine and Egypt.

Egypt: 199–200 CE In many respects, his journey through Egypt recalls Hadrian's, combining tourism, religious pilgrimage, and administrative inspection. In the administrative field, he made innovations, giving a municipal Senate to Alexandria and the main cities in Egypt, and for the first time allowing Egyptians to enter the Roman Senate.

In late 200 or early 201, Severus reached Syria once more. There, at Antioch on January 1, he assumed the ordinary consulship with Caracalla (it was the first time that two emperors were ordinary consuls simultaneously, and away from Rome). During this stay, he also reviewed and annulled the sanctions taken against the cities that had helped Niger. Then, by way of Asia Minor and the Danube, he returned to Rome (April or June 202), which he had left five years earlier. There he celebrated the 10 years of his reign, his Decennalia.

The African journey: 202–203 CE Known only from an allusion in a disputed document, the existence of this journey is not accepted by some historians. Those who do accept it as fact place it in 202 and early 203, using coinage, inscriptions, and archaeological testimony as evidence. Its route is largely hypothetical, but it would seem that during this journey Leptis Magna, Severus' birthplace, received the *ius Italicum* (the third city in Africa to obtain it, after Utica and Carthage), a number of indigenous cities in the north-east of Africa Proconsularis became *municipia*, and some existing *municipia* there became colonies. Perhaps at this time Numidia became an autonomous province, detached from Africa Proconsularis. Previously it had existed as a *de facto* province (before it did so in law), and its legate had civil, judicial, and religious powers in addition to his military command of the Third Augusta. However, other dates have been proposed for the change into the status of Numidia: 198 or 199 in the view of some, 206–208 in that of others, and no earlier than 221 in that of a third group. At all events, under Septimius Severus, military organization in Africa was brought to its peak.

His stay in Rome: 203–207/208 CE This would be the longest stay that Severus made in the capital. In June 203, the emperor was in Rome, probably for the dedication of the triumphal arch erected in his honor in the Roman Forum. In the following year, he presided at the Secular Games, which were being held two *saecula* (each of 110 years) after the games of Augustus. In the ceremonial hymn (*carmen saeculare*), prayers were offered to Hercules and Bacchus, the gods of Leptis Magna. People came to these games from all over the Empire to celebrate the end of one *saeculum* and the beginning of another. Caracalla and Geta, consuls for 205, inaugurated the happy and fruitful new age. In Rome, too, Severus suppressed, by murder (205), the ambitions of the praetorian prefect Plautianus, Caracalla's father-in-law. Severus also had the temple of Peace restored, began several new buildings, updated a marble map of the city (*forma urbis*), numerous fragments of which have survived, and wrote an autobiography, of which nothing remains.

> **carmen**: An incantatory formula, magical and usually in verse, uttered on a certain note and with a certain rhythm.

War in Britain: 208–211 CE In 207, the Maeatae (peoples who lived near Antoninus' Wall), reinforced by the Caledonians, rebelled, and the governor of Britain apparently appealed to the emperor. There is no knowing whether this revolt required the presence of Severus, or whether he was finding inactivity burdensome. By taking his two sons with him, he perhaps hoped to remove them from the luxuries of Rome and give them a military education. He may have thought that the army, in the inactivity of peacetime, would lapse into habitual idleness. Possibly, he wanted to achieve a victory over the still untamed northern barbarians. These are probably overlapping motives (Herodian, 3.14). Whatever the truth of the matter, Severus gladly seized the opportunity and placed himself at the head of an expedition to Britain (208), assembling a large army and fleet. Both made a great impression on the rebels, who sued for peace. Severus refused. He seems to have been resolved to complete the conquest of the island.

Textual sources are imprecise, but there appear to have been two campaigns, with the emperor setting up his headquarters in York (Eburacum). The first took place in 208–209. Starting from north-east of the Forth–Clyde line, Severus skirted the Grampians on the eastward side and ventured as far north as the Moray Firth, an itinerary marked out by the camps that have been discovered. A truce was concluded. Severus and his elder son assumed the title Britannicus, and Geta was promoted *Augustus* (209). There were thus now three emperors. During 210, disturbances began again. Severus, who was ill, entrusted Caracalla with the task of leading a punitive expedition. The winter of 210–211 was spent preparing the expedition.

Septimius Severus died on February 4, 211, at his York headquarters. Cassius Dio claims that the emperor left this advice to his sons: "Live in harmony, make the soldiers rich, and don't give a damn for anything else." And, touching the urn destined to receive his ashes, he is reported to have said: "You will contain a man whom the universe has been unable to contain." According to other traditions, however, his last words were somber, foreshadowing ominously the future of this dynasty and the Empire: "When I received the state, it was troubled on every side; I leave it at peace, even in Britain. An old man now, and with crippled feet, I leave to my two Antonini an empire which is strong, if they prove good, but feeble, if they prove bad" (*Augustan History, Severus* 23).

The exercise of power

Vitality, drive, activity – these words recur constantly in descriptions of the achievements of Severus, who, attuned to his era, brought about great changes in the way that imperial power was exercised. In doing so he promoted the military, dynastic, anti-senatorial, and absolutist aspects of the regime.

A military monarchy   Though he had not had much military training, his two years spent at the Danubian frontier (191–193) and the four years of civil war had made Severus familiar with camp life, and this, together with the experience and advice of his marshals, the information gleaned from the campaigns of Marcus Aurelius, and the knowledge that he owed the throne to the legions, had also made him aware of the weaknesses in the military machine. Severus considered it essential to improve a system that had become unsuited to the new defensive situation. Whether his various measures formed part of a coherent whole or were taken in response to specific problems is of little importance. His deep reforms altered the Roman army and steered it along new paths of development. Three areas were affected by his changes.

1   *The organization of the army*   In 193, Severus reorganized Rome's garrison. The praetorian cohorts were brought to a strength of 1,000 men (10,000 in total) and these were no longer recruited in Italy or even in the old Romanized provinces, but rather selected from the best of the provincial legions (Illyrians, Thracians). The numbers of each of the urban cohorts were tripled, from 500 men to 1,500, while the watch cohorts remained unchanged (seven cohorts of 1,000 men). Furthermore, between 193 and 197, Severus recruited from Parthia to raise three additional legions (bringing the number up to 33), all commanded by equestrians, and while two were stationed in Mesopotamia (the First and Third), the Second was based at Albano, near Rome. This means that, if we add to all these forces based in or near Rome the 1,000 *equites singulares Augusti* (the emperor's personal cavalry), charged with the ruler's close protection, Severus had at his disposal in the heart of Italy an army of 30,000 men (compared with 11,500 formerly). He thus had the means of forestalling any usurper's plans and of keeping an eye on Rome. Above all, he now possessed the massive reserve force necessary to defend Italy if barbarian elements crossed the frontier. Thus began the concept of a centralized campaign army (in Caracalla's reign, the praetorian guard and the Second Parthica were both put into combat).

Severus also allotted a considerable role to large expeditionary corps organized for a single expedition and composed of detachments (*vexillationes*) commanded by *duces* or *praepositi* appointed by the central government – strong detachments from Germania's four legions, for example, were employed in the Second Parthian War. Similarly, he seems to have stepped up the use of auxiliaries (such as the corps of Osroënian archers) alone, independently of the legions, and in large numbers. Although Severus was accused of deliberately barbarizing the Roman army, recent studies have shown that he did nothing of the kind. Italians never completely disappeared, especially among the centurions and officers of equestrian rank; what happened was that the most Romanized sources of troops were used less and less, and that senior officers began to rise from the ranks.

2   *The strategy on the frontiers*   The main objective of this strategy was, of course, to secure the Empire's defense. This required that the safeguarding of one sector be achieved without weakening another, even though resources were limited and the location and intensity of the dangers varied. Hence the series of measures taken by Severus intended to adapt the system more closely to the threats that were presently feared, in the East against the Parthians and on the Danube and Rhine against the Germani. Everywhere, there was a reinforcement of existing fortifications and communication systems (Africa, Rhine, Danube). Two new legions, the First and Third Parthica, were installed in the East (this front, with 11 legions, henceforth rivaled that of the Danube with its 12 legions). Administrative and territorial modifications were made. Regular expeditions were undertaken, and, as we have seen, considerable use was made of special corps of *vexillationes*, brought together as the need arose to strengthen a threatened sector. Lastly, in the same period, following a first-century development, regional recruitment seems to have become the rule – in Africa, for instance, among the soldiers of the Third Augusta, "foreigners" were in the minority, which had not been the case at the beginning of the century, and the Africans were predominant.

3   *Military life*   An improvement in the soldier's lot was an essential part of dealing with the continuing recruitment crisis. To make army life seem more attractive and so to encourage recruitment, Severus effected the deepest military reforms since the time of Augustus, bringing social, economic, and honorific benefits to soldiers, and a measure of "democratization" to the army: pay, which had not changed since Domitian's time, was increased; a military *annona* was organized (without creating a new tax – part of the old civilian *annona* was automatically diverted to the army); soldiers were permitted to live with their families outside the camp; and they were accorded the right to form colleges even during their years of service (until then only veterans had had this right); centurions were given direct access to the equestrian order (without, that is, having to go through the office of the *primipilus*); *principales* (non-commissioned officers or soldiers exempt from fatigue duties) were allowed to wear a gold ring, formerly, the distinctive right of equestrians; and veterans were given immunity from personal municipal charges.

A hereditary monarchy Severus had presented himself as the avenger of Pertinax, as much through opportunity (one of the three legions in Upper Pannonia had been commanded by Pertinax) as from conviction (he had been one of Pertinax's lieutenants). He delivered Pertinax's panegyric on the day of his apotheosis, thus formally marking his relationship with the deified emperor. This was the first step he took to legitimize his *coup d'état* and consecrate the founding of his power. He also established a connection with the Antonine dynasty, by means of a retroactive adoption. In 195, he declared himself the son of Marcus Aurelius and brother of Commodus. Henceforward, his portraits resemble those of his "ancestors," and inscriptions trace his genealogy back as far as Nerva, making him the latter's descendant to the fifth degree. It was then unthinkable that he should long remain the brother of a non-deified emperor, and, in 197, Commodus was duly deified. Securing thus the position of his family in the past, Severus also aimed to gain a place for it in the future. As we have seen, in 195 Caracalla was given the name Marcus Aurelius Antoninus, and in the same year was designated *Caesar*. In 198, he became *Augustus*, while Geta was raised to the rank of *Caesar*; and in 209, Geta in his turn became *Augustus*. There were then three *Augusti* at the same time, even if, in practice, they were not equal in rank.

This dynastic policy extended to the entire imperial family, the *domus divina*. As *Augusta*, Julia Domna was associated with government. Like the emperor, she was called Pia and Felix, but also "mother of the *Augusti*," "mother of the camps," and "mother of the Senate." With her two children, she accompanied Severus on all his expeditions, to the East as well as to Britain. The images and names of the imperial couple and their sons were on display everywhere, on coins, on monuments in Rome (the arch in the Roman Forum, the arch of the money-changers in the Forum Boarium) and in the Empire (the four-façaded arch of Leptis Magna), and even on the flaminical crown. Severus and his family emphasized the hereditary aspect of imperial power as the heirs of the Antonines, to whom reference was constantly made, and ushers of a new age, whose birth was marked by the Secular Games of 204.

Both branches of the family, African and eastern, reaped the benefits of imperial favor. The emperor's brother and the brother-in-law of the empress, for example, would not have had as much success as they did in their careers without such favor. But the most significant case is certainly that of C. Fulvius Plautianus. Originally from Leptis Magna, and connected by marriage with Severus' family, this equestrian became prefect of the praetorian guard in 197, and remained in the post until his death. His rise and fall are somewhat reminiscent of Sejanus' meteoric career under Tiberius. The emperor's trusted man, Plautianus supervised all the troops stationed in Italy, became consul with Severus in 203, and even had coins struck with his portrait. By marrying his daughter to Caracalla he entered deeply into the imperial family, just as Sejanus had attempted to do by asking Livilla's hand in marriage from Tiberius. Eventually Plautianus' excessive powers, and the suspicion that he was trying to overthrow the imperial family, unnerved Julia Domna and Caracalla, who arranged for his assassination in January 205 with the connivance of the emperor.

Severus' desire to restore the prestige of the Roman state steered the imperial cult in a more absolutist direction, giving new impetus to an institution that was showing signs of decline (in particular, the *seviri augustales*). The cult of the living emperors thus became more closely linked with that of their dead predecessors. Gold coins of 194 show Jupiter proffering the globe of the world to the emperor; Severus was not regarded as a living god, but he was frequently likened to a god (Jupiter, Helios) in the attitudes and attributes of his figure in his portraits. Together with the rest of the imperial family, he already belonged to the same world as the gods. He had his statue placed in the Augusteum at Ostia beside those of the divine emperors (and his relations by "adoption") Antoninus Pius, Marcus Aurelius, and Lucius Verus; and by giving his son Caracalla the exact *tria nomina* of Marcus Aurelius he conferred on him a kind of pre-deification. The qualifications "sacred" and "divine" began to be applied to everything pertaining to the emperor, added to the existing title *dominus*. Numerous dedications, to various gods, were made "in honor of the divine imperial family" (*in honorem domus divinae*).

Moreover, astrology, of which Severus was an ardent follower, became more closely linked with the imperial person. In the imperial palace on the Palatine, Severus held audience under a ceiling on which his personal horoscope was painted, thus attributing a cosmic sacredness to his power. In addition, a monumental freestanding entrance to the palace was inaugurated in 203, at the southeast corner of the Palatine hill. This structure, known as the Septizonium (*Augustan History, Severus* 19), was turned toward Africa. It featured a façade with niches where the seven planets were arranged around the monarch, represented as the Sun. In the previous century, an emperor's active promotion of his divinity and cult had been considered a sign of a tyrannical or deranged mind (e.g. Caligula, Nero). Now this imperial agenda was accepted by all. The contrast between the Principate (from Augustus and the Julio-Claudians to the Antonines) and the "Dominate" is slightly artificial, but it nevertheless reveals well how attitudes had changed and conformed.

An anti-senatorial monarchy From the first years of his reign, and above all after the senatorial purges that followed the defeat of Albinus, Severus' relations with the Senate were strained. This situation is perfectly symbolized by the position of his triumphal arch in the Roman Forum: facing the temple of Concordia, it stands between the Rostra and the Curia, both of which it dominates.

Although the Senate continued to enjoy great social and cultural prestige, it showed many signs of political enfeeblement: Severus' personal choices and regulations for the previously senatorial office of the city prefect signaled to the Senate the curtailing of its influence. Other such limitations followed, such as the massive confiscation of senators' possessions, the rehabilitation of the memory of Commodus, the importance assumed by the African clan among the imperial legates and other top people, the installation of a legion in Italy and the acknowledgement of the army's essential role there, the fact that the emperor permanently had the title of proconsul in Rome and Italy even though they were officially outside the provincial system, and his choice of new senators, promoted either by *adlectio* or by the award of the laticlave (they were all partisans of Severus, most often from equestrian circles).

The acceleration in the Senate's political decline may equally be observed in the converse ascendancy of the equestrian order. Three new legions and two recent provinces were entrusted to this order. It was granted numerous procuratorial posts, of which there were increasingly more (Severus himself created more than any other emperor – 50 posts between 197 and 211). Because of the admission into it of many centurions, the honors and titles distributed to members of the equestrian order were more numerous than ever. And the position of praetorian prefect, now invariably held by those of equestrian rank, had become the second most important in the Empire: the praetorian prefect, in addition to possessing immense power in virtue of his military functions, was head of the imperial administrative staff and the leading criminal judge in place of the emperor for all Italy (except Rome and central Italy). He was also the appeal judge for all sentences issued by provincial governors, and a member of the emperor's council, of which he was leader. Moreover, the position (which regularly had two joint-holders) came to be occupied by eminent men such as the jurist Papinian, a Syrian relative of the empress, whose students Ulpian and Paul, themselves great jurists, later became praetorian prefects.

In the hierarchy of equestrian offices the upper and lower ranks were those most affected by Severus' actions. The clearest example of Severus' plan to increase social mobility was that of the legionaries. A popular social policy was emerging, one that favored the less powerful – which again pointed to a rapid political decline of the Senate. For example, the emperor recommended that prefects of the city should listen as much to the complaints of slaves as to those of their masters, generally give a favorable response to petitions from peasants against local governors, and protect professional colleges against abuses. This aspect of imperial favor relating to the people was also reflected in public art: in the frontal arrangement of the bas-reliefs on the arch of Septimius in Rome or in that of Leptis Magna, the replacement of a deep landscape with superimposed episodes in several rows, the hieratic, simplified, and expressive aspect of characters and scenes, all proclaimed a new artistic taste. This new style was far removed from the intellectual art appreciated by the senators, and intended to recount imperial exploits directly to the people.

An absolute monarchy Starting with Severus, the imperial regime's inherent absolutism, hitherto concealed behind a screen of institutions and customs, was revealed with complete openness. For instance, the emperor's speeches to the

Box 12.1   Imperial constitutions

The first imperial edicts appeared with Augustus.

In the middle of the second century, jurists allowed imperial constitutions an authority comparable with that of the law.

In the third century, Ulpian identified the imperial will with the law.

There were four types of imperial constitutions:

1 *Imperial edicts:* texts of general application promulgated by the emperor by virtue of his *imperium;* they were obligatory throughout the Empire.
2 *Decrees:* decisions passed by the emperor (or his council) in civil or criminal trials; in principle, their force was restricted to individual cases, but in practice they had a formative effect on jurisprudence, and judges took a lead from them.
3 *Rescripts:* these were written replies given by the emperor to requests emanating from individuals in difficulties over points of law, whether litigants, or judicial officials in complicated cases; from the time of Hadrian, and above all under the Severi, they were a very important source of law; in theory, their effect was confined to the question posed, but, like the decrees, they assumed a normative value.
4 *Mandates:* instructions of an administrative nature addressed to magistrates or officials delegated by the emperor.

(from M. Humbert, *Institutions politiques et sociales de l'Antiquité, Dalloz, 8th edition, 2003*)

Senate became the official source of law. And the jurists surrounding the ruler put their knowledge to the service of his authority: "What pleases the emperor has the value of law," "the emperor is above the law," they said. Thousands of petitions (about 1,500 a year) flowed from all over the Empire to the emperor's council. The number of imperial offices and employees also grew, developing further the bureaucracy of the first century. Thus the administration of the emperor's personal wealth (*res privata*), swollen by the confiscation of his opponents' possessions, expanded to the point where it became a department of its own, distinct from the possessions of the crown (the *patrimonium*). Further examples were the development of the services connected with the *annona*, state intrusion into the organization of trade and craft companies, and the expansion of the phenomenon of peasant associations, all of which necessitated and promoted the growth of the central offices.

The birth of an unaccustomed style of court life further illustrates the absolutism of Severan power. Whether it was on the move or in one place, his court was characterized by an increasingly meticulous etiquette based on the eastern model: throne, crowns, robes, and attitudes were all codified. The emperor's formal entry (*adventus Augusti*) into various cities, especially Rome, unfolded according to a ceremonial of unprecedented formality. This new protocol also marked Severus' lavish funeral and apotheosis.

Two enemy brothers and an empress mother: Caracalla (211–217 CE), Geta (211–212 CE), Julia Domna

According to our sources, the two brothers (born in 188, 189) loathed each other. The elder, M. Aurelius Antoninus, had very little taste for intellectual matters, despite having received a thorough education. His main interest was in military life. He was loved by the soldiers, who gave him the nickname "Caracalla" after the Gaulish cloak he liked to wear. The literary tradition portrays Caracalla as a sickly, violent, and irascible devotee of Alexander the Great, who played the roughneck soldier, was hated by the senators, and was a follower of Serapis, in constant search of healing gods and miraculous cures. Conversely, L. Septimius Geta is portrayed as gentle and reflective, a narrative contrast to Caracalla recalling that between the Flavians Domitian and Titus. It appears that the senators were fairly favorable to Geta, and his mother also showed him preference.

The empress Julia Domna (perhaps around 40 in 211) exercised considerable influence on the emperor before losing power to Plautianus. She then turned to literature and philosophy, and became the leading light in a circle of scholars, jurists (Ulpian, Papinian), doctors (Galen), and writers. She surrounded herself with easterners, promoted her family (in particular, her sister Julia Maesa), and kept careful watch on the future of her sons. When Plautianus was murdered, she resumed her place alongside Severus, whom she accompanied to Britain.

The combined reign of the two brothers: February 4, 211, to February 26, 212 CE

The end of the campaign in Britain Caracalla made peace with the Caledonians, and withdrew the frontier (at this time or shortly afterwards) to Hadrian's Wall. He divided Britain into two provinces: Upper Britain in the south, with two legions and a governor of consular rank, probably installed in London, and Lower Britain in the north, governed by a former praetor, with one legion (in York) and numerous auxiliary troops.

The funeral ceremonies The return of Severus' ashes to Rome and his apotheosis created the illusion of unity between the two brothers. Issues of coinage saluted Concordia between the two *Augusti* under the approving gaze of Julia Domna. In reality, each was contemplating ridding himself of the other. On February 26, 212, the empress made an attempt to reconcile them. It was in vain: Caracalla had his brother murdered, allegedly in their mother's very arms (Herodian, 4.4; Cassius Dio, 78.2). He justified himself to the praetorians and the Senate on the grounds that his brother had been plotting against him. And in order to convince them, he promised the praetorians money and the Senate an amnesty for exiles. Executions (20,000 people, according to Cassius Dio) and confiscations took place. Geta's supporters and other possible competitors (including a grandson of Marcus Aurelius) were eliminated. The memory of Geta was

Plate 12.2 Doctor inspecting the eye of a seated woman. Detail of a sarcophagus of the Sosa family from Ravenna, third to fourth century CE. C. M. Dixon

damned – on a painted medallion from Upper Egypt representing the imperial family, Geta's face has been scratched out. Nothing was ever again allowed to recall his existence. Julia Domna turned to internal and administrative affairs and left the waging of war to her son.

Caracalla's reign: February 26, 212, to April 8, 217 CE

The army With a more easygoing recruitment policy, an increase in pay of perhaps 50 percent, and a raising of retirement gratuities, soldiers benefited from the reign, to the extent that the state incurred an additional expense, according to Cassius Dio, of some 70 million denarii per annum, which Julia Domna deplored but which must be set against an inflationary background.

The administration With a reorganization of the districts of the *res privata* and the responsibilities of the *iuridici*, as well as the appearance of a "controller," Italy lost a few more of its privileges. Additional procuratorial posts were created (16 between 211 and 214), and there was a further increase in the number of central officials. These actions suggest Caracalla's continuation of Severan policies regarding the management of the state.

Fiscal measures and monetary reform It seems that, in 194, Severus had carried out a devaluation of the denarius. Its silver content had been lowered in two stages to reach less than 50 percent. This devaluation of the basic currency had been a success. On the death of Severus the state's coffers were in a healthy condition. However, the new military and administrative expenses, the subsidies to be paid to the barbarian princes for their allegiance, and the expenditure on the large-scale public works that were undertaken (e.g. the Aventine baths, road maintenance) required the adoption of further measures. Certain taxes were increased (those on inheritances and enfranchisement went up from 5 to 10 percent, but these affected only Roman citizens). Extraordinary levies, such as the coronation gold (a "voluntary" contribution theoretically paid at the time of an accession), became more frequent, and the practice of exacting taxes in kind or in labor was extended. These fiscal measures were accompanied by a dual monetary reform. First, the gold coinage was devalued, with the weight of the *aureus* going down by 17 percent and the *aureus* itself rated at 50 denarii (25 in the Augustan system). Second, a new coin was created, the Antoninianus. This silver coin, heavier than the devalued traditional denarius, but also of low standard (c.50 percent), was worth 2 denarii in use (1.5 in real value) and was struck between 215 and 219. The later drop in its weight and standard (5 percent) explains its disappearance (though this was not permanent).

The Antonine Constitution of 212 This enactment (known also as the Edict of Caracalla) extended the right of Roman citizenship to all communities within the Empire. According to Cassius Dio and the jurist Ulpian (our main sources for the edict), Caracalla gave "all foreigners on earth [i.e. in the Roman Empire] the right of Roman citizenship, at the same time safeguarding that of their own cities, except for the *dediticii*." In other words, all the free inhabitants of the Roman world who had by this edict become Roman citizens were able to preserve their native rights and customs as long as they wished. Thus, Egypt after 212 has yielded numerous documents which suggest that the new Romans maintained their local traditions, Greek or Egyptian. Only the *dediticii* (who were perhaps irregular freedmen, though there is disagreement over the exact meaning of the term) did not benefit from this advantage, even when they too had become Roman citizens. This edict, a measure which marked the success of the Romanization policy, did not seek to impose Roman civil law, and did not need to.

The motives behind the Antonine Constitution have been widely argued, all the more so because the early authors had little to say about it. Several reasons underlay the edict. Cassius Dio assumed there was an economic and financial reason: foreigners-turned-citizens had to pay an inheritance tax, the one that had been increased. From an administrative and judicial point of view, an Empire in which the status of the inhabitants was more uniform would lighten the task of the offices and courts. Finally, the emperor's stated interest in religious unity might well have provided another motive for this grant of universal citizenship.

Frontier defense According to Dio, Caracalla proclaimed that he wished to end his days at war. And indeed, from 213 until his death, the emperor fought uninterruptedly on every frontier:

213   Caracalla campaigned against the Alemanni, mobilizing large forces (including the reserve force based in Italy) on the Rhine and Danube. Victorious on the Main, he took the name Germanicus Maximus and secured 20 years of peace on the western front.

214   After an inspection along the Danube, he departed for the East following the route taken by Alexander the Great.

215   At Antioch, he received proposals for peace from the Parthian king. In Alexandria, for reasons that are not clear (perhaps fear of a rebellion behind him during a Parthian campaign or rancor against a disaffected population) he came into conflict with the people, who were massacred.

216   In Syria, the cities of Emesa and Palmyra were promoted to Roman colonies with *ius Italicum*. Edessa in Osroëne became a colony. War was declared on the Parthian kingdom, an army was sent to Armenia, and the emperor led expeditions into Adiabene and Parthia, where he won the title of Parthicus Maximus.

217   On April 8, near Carrhae, he was stabbed to death by an officer of the praetorian guard on the orders of its prefect, M. Opellius Macrinus.

12.3 | Macrinus, Elagabalus, Severus Alexander

Macrinus: 217–218 CE: an interlude

After Caracalla's death at the hands of his praetorian prefect Macrinus, the soldiers, who did not suspect a conspiracy, acclaimed Macrinus emperor. It was the first time an equestrian had attained the throne. Herodian (5.1) relates the contents of a letter that Macrinus wrote to the Senate, in which he openly admitted the inferiority of his equestrian status but boldly asserted his claim to the throne on the basis of his moral virtues.

Born in Caesarea (Cherchel) in Mauretania in 164, Macrinus is described as a man of humble origins and exotic Moorish features, such as his pierced ear (Cassius Dio, 79.11). He had been a lawyer, and then procurator of Plautianus' possessions. He had subsequently followed a civil equestrian career, during which Caracalla had noticed him. In 212, he had become praetorian prefect. His reign as emperor was given up to seeking support in order to confront the urgent demands of the moment: to rally the soldiers, persuade the senators, neutralize the Parthians, and break the ambitions of the Syrian princesses who were related to the Severi.

In order to win the loyalty of partisans of the Severi (especially the soldiers), he took the *cognomen* Severus, had Caracalla proclaimed *divus* by the Senate, and bestowed the *cognomen* Antoninus on his young son Diadumenianus, together with the title of *Caesar*. But at the same time, in order to win over the opponents of the Severi, he repealed Caracalla's measures (reducing the inheritance tax to 5 percent once more), paid the Parthian king an indemnity of 200 million sesterces to maintain the Roman–Parthian frontier and unchanged areas of influence (Armenia), and reduced the pay of new recruits by half. This retrenchment brought on disaffection in the ranks of the legions in Syria. Moreover, his obscure origins and his clumsy tactics (his refusal, though justified, to come to Rome, the appointment of his colleague in the praetorian guard to the prefectship of the capital, etc.) alienated the little sympathy he gathered in the Senate. He thus found himself quite incapable of opposing the machinations of the Syrian princesses.

On the death of her son, after trying to incite against Macrinus the troops that he had sent to keep a watch on her, Julia Domna starved herself to death at Antioch. But the *Augusta* left an elder sister, Julia Maesa, who had two daughters, Julia Soaemias and Julia Mamaea. All three were descended from the great priestly family of Emesa who ruled over the temple of the local god, Elah-Gabal. Similarly, all three belonged to the *domus divina* of Caracalla, and nurtured imperial ambitions. They possessed immense wealth, the legitimacy of blood relations, a solid network of loyal supporters, and two heirs: the son of Julia Soaemias, Varius Avitus Bassianus, and the son of Julia Mamaea, Gessius Alexianus. The former was born in 204, the latter in 205 or 206. Thus, both were first cousins once removed of Caracalla, but Bassianus held the priesthood of the god of Emesa. Artfully superseding the rivalry between the two sisters, the boys' grandmother allowed the rumor to be put about that Bassianus was the illegitimate son of Caracalla, and that she had a great quantity of gold at her disposal. In April or May 218, Bassianus was acclaimed emperor by the Third Gallica under the names of his alleged father, M. Aurelius Antoninus. On June 8, the armies of Macrinus and Bassianus came face to face near Antioch. Macrinus and his son Diadumenianus were killed. The Severan dynasty retrieved the imperial throne. From being African it had now become Syrian.

Elagabalus: 218–222 CE: the East in Rome

It is under the name "Elagabalus," taken from the god of Emesa, that Bassianus is best known. A sculpted and inscribed relief discovered near Emesa (Homs, in Syria) explains it as meaning "mountain god." At Emesa, religion had a very marked solar nature, so the "mountain god" was also a Sun god known as Sol Elagabalus.

The temple idol was a huge, conical black stone, said to have fallen from the skies, which coins represent with an eagle on the front of it or perched on its summit. God of the summits? Sun god? At all events, in Rome no one knew if he should be regarded as Jupiter or the Sun, and "Elagabalus" was often translated as "Heliogabalus." Bassianus, as the high priest, would dance before this god to the sound of flutes and trumpets, dressed in a purple and gold Phoenician robe. His embrace of eastern customs and his rejection of Greek and Roman traditions (such as clothing), together with his luxurious ostentation and cruelty, greatly dismayed his subjects (Herodian, 5.5).

Several aspects of his reign should be remembered.

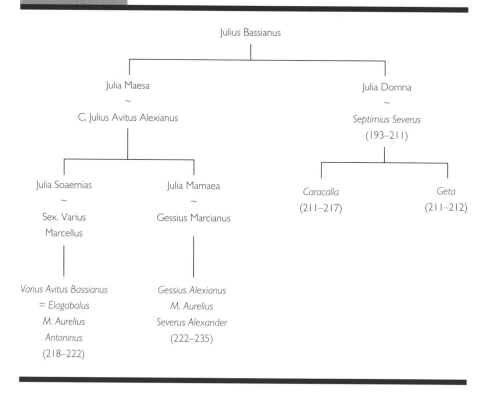

The new emperor's arrival in Rome

After a short stay in Antioch and a purge of Macrinus' colleagues in the administration, the Syrian princesses and their offspring set off for Rome. The journey took a year, and assumed the air of a religious procession because of its route and because they brought the black stone with them, since the young emperor did not wish to be parted from his idol. In the summer of 219, Elagabalus made his solemn entry into Rome. He seemed to have only one preoccupation – to install his god.

A Syrian high priest

On the Palatine, near the imperial palace, the emperor had a temple built for his god, the Elagabalium, inaugurated at the latest in 221. Inside, he is said to have assembled the emblems of Rome's traditional religion (the Vestal flame, Palladium, Salian shields, black stone of Cybele), as if to subordinate all other cults to the god of Emesa, who also now married Tanit–Dea Caelestis of Carthage. For the first time, a kind of tolerant and inclusive monotheism (henotheism) emerged at the heart of the Empire.

The princesses in power

The Syrian princesses were the ones who governed, especially Julia Maesa, Elagabalus' grandmother, and Julia Soaemias, his mother. They are even said to have taken part in sessions of the Senate. Julia Maesa's most important decision was to have Elagabalus adopt his cousin Gessius Alexianus (in 221). The future of the dynasty was thus assured. In 222, the emperor and the new "Caesar of the State and Elagabalus" were consuls together.

Numerous difficulties

The financial situation deteriorated, the Germani were aggressive once again, the hostility of the army and praetorians to the emperor was added to that of the Senate, and Julia Mamaea plotted in the interests of her son. Moreover, Elagabalus' provocative behavior, his excesses, eccentricities, marriages, courtesans, his passion for exotic animals, and his nepotism to his favorites (the prefect of the watch was a former coachman, the prefect of the *annona* a former hairdresser, and the prefect of the city a former dancer) all offended the Romans, fueled malicious gossip, and isolated the emperor. A refusal to sacrifice at the Capitol, a plan (real or imagined) to exile the Senate, and attempts to oust his cousin and rival provoked an uprising of the praetorians, plotted, it seems, by Julia Mamaea. Elagabalus, his mother, and those loyal to them were massacred in March 222. Their decapitated bodies were thrown into the Tiber, and their memory damned. Alexander was proclaimed emperor.

Severus Alexander: 222–235 CE: the good pupil

The denigration of an emperor's predecessor has a long tradition in Roman historiography. The more our sources condemn Elagabalus, the more they heap praise on the new emperor and father of all the virtues. Cassius Dio concludes his history praising Alexander for appointing him to the consulship (80.21), while the *Augustan History* (*Severus Alexander* 29–52) praises his character in great detail. Only Herodian has reservations, showing the gentle and amiable reader of Plato and Cicero as weak, cowardly, and lacking in authority. But, in any case, it was not the 15-year-old Alexander who governed; it was the Syrian women, Julia Maesa and Julia Mamaea, the latter on her own after her mother's death (in 223 or 226). Rejecting the escapades of the preceding reign, the new government subscribed to the Severan tradition, as expressed in the adoption of the *cognomen* Severus, added to the emperor's names, M. Aurelius Severus Alexander.

Domestic policies

The new policy was marked by a more or less sharp reaction in three domains.

Moral reaction Palace mores returned to a modest simplicity, and scandalous promotions were canceled, although a good many of the top people in Elagabalus' entourage remained in place, for example the prefect of the city, Valerius Comazon. Moreover, the jurists, students of Papinian, returned to the seat of power and gathered around the Syrian princesses. They included Ulpian (who died in 223, assassinated by the praetorians, whose prefect he was), Paul, and Modestinus. It is probably due to these jurists that a clearly perceptible humanitarian policy emerged at this time, including the limitation of treason trials, improvements in the condition of slaves, and the revival of institutions about food-provisioning. Ulpian's assertion that, in the matter of natural law, all men are equal was finding practical application under the Severans.

Senatorial reaction According to the *Augustan History*, Severus Alexander restored to the Senate some of its political power, but it now appears this was less than previously thought. The only fact that seems to point in this direction is his institution in 222 of a regency council (probably temporary) composed of 16 senators. Otherwise, following the Severan tradition, Severus Alexander did not institute measures favorable to the Senate but rather reforms strengthening the equestrian order. The *cursus honorum* for senators, for example, was tightened, prefects of the praetorian guard were legally admitted to the Senate, and, in place of senators, equestrians were appointed to govern imperial provinces.

Religious reaction All the statues and emblems that Elagabalus had assembled around the black stone of Emesa were returned to their proper temples: the Palladium went back to the temple of Vesta, Tanit–Dea Caelestis to her temple in Carthage, and even the black stone to its temple at Emesa. The gods of the capital had their rights re-established and Jupiter the Avenger was placed in the former Elagabalium. Severus Alexander wanted to be seen as welcoming all gods. He is said, though it is doubtful, to have worshiped Alexander the Great, Apollonius of Tyana, Abraham, Christ, and Orpheus in the palace shrines to the household gods. It is, however, certain that Julia Mamaea met leading Christian authors such as Origen and Julius Africanus, and that Hippolytus of Rome, a presbyter, dedicated a treatise on the Resurrection to her. Another of the century's trends, syncretism, thus revealed itself in place of Elagabalus' henotheism.

Foreign policies

Externally, new threats loomed. In the East, the Sassanid Persians were driving out the Parthians. These nationalists wanted to re-establish the Persian Empire within its former boundaries. They relied on a holy book, the *Avesta*, to impose the religion of Zoroaster, which was exclusive and intolerant. At their head was a remarkable prince, Ardashir (Artaxerxes). In 211/212, he had seized power in Persia, and since then had striven to recreate the former Achaemenid Empire. In 227, he became the king of Persia. He organized a strong, centralized, even totalitarian state, in which Mazdaism, the religion taught in the *Avesta*, was the official and compulsory religion, and whose army included an impressive, heavily armored cavalry, the cataphracts. In 230/231, the Persians invaded Mesopotamia and launched raids into the Syrias and Cappadocia. It was up to the emperor to intervene. He did so, but unwillingly and after attempts at negotiation.

In late 231, the emperor was at Antioch. Reinforced by large contingents drawn from the armies of Europe, the expeditionary force was divided into three corps. In the north, one was to attack Media through Armenia, Rome's ally. In the south, a second was to force its way down the Euphrates as far as its mouth. Between the two, the central corps, commanded by the emperor, was to make a frontal attack on the enemy troops. Only the army in the north fulfilled its mission, although it had difficulty getting back. The other two had to retreat. All in all, it was a half-success transformed by imperial propaganda into a victory. In the meantime, the Germans took advantage of the fact that the armies on the Danube and the Rhine had been depleted to supply troops for the campaign against Ardashir. They crossed the Rhine and the Danube, attacked camps in the Taunus, and threatened Raetia and Noricum. The emperor's presence on the Rhine was necessary. He returned to Rome, celebrated a triumph (see his supposed speech to the Senate after his triumph; *Augustan History, Severus Alexander* 56), and then left for Upper Germania.

Operations against the Alemanni began in 234. The emperor and his mother were in Mainz, where an army was assembled with numerous auxiliary corps (for the first time, cataphracts are mentioned among them). A bridge of boats was built on the Rhine, and a few small local successes were achieved, but the emperor vacillated and deferred the launching of a large expedition. Under the leadership of a Thracian trainer, Maximinus, who apparently resented Mamaea's influence with her son, the soldiers mutinied. Caught by surprise, Severus and his mother were killed in his tent by the mutineers (at some time between February 18 and March 9, 235). Thus the reign of the Severi, both African and Syrian, came to an end.

12.4 | Provincial Upsurge and the Orientalization of the Empire?

Africans, Syrians, and a Thracian at the head of the Empire: it is obvious that the provinces, and more especially those in the eastern part of the Empire, were providing political and military personnel who aspired to the highest offices. This pre-eminence is also apparent in the intellectual field. For example, we find Aelian (c.170–c.235), a Latin from Praeneste living in Rome, writing his *Animal Stories* in Greek. We shall now turn to the increasing influence of the East in the religious and intellectual life of the Empire under the Severi.

Religious life

The "easternization" of Roman religion has often been attributed to the Severi, which perhaps credits them with more power than they actually possessed or were willing to exercise in this field. However, it is true that, under the influence of the empresses, the traders, and the jurists of the Severan court, there was a noticeable expansion of the eastern religions in this period. In the countries where they had already been introduced, they gained more power, and they spread to places that they had not reached before. On the other hand, apart from the blatant practices of Elagabalus, the connection between imperial activities and these religions was not always clear.

The trends in religious thinking revealed by these easternizing activities constitute an even clearer connection between imperial policies and eastern cults. Put simply, these trends can be seen as exemplified, respectively, in the two religious policies of Elagabalus and Severus Alexander. Elagabalus promoted the increasingly popular idea of a single god with manifold powers, of whom the other divine figures were merely expressions. The Sun god (Sol, Helios) was the great

---

Box 12.2 Expansion of the eastern religions

- Cybele returned to favor everywhere. Bull and sheep sacrifices became more numerous at the end of the Antonine era and during the period of the Severi, and were frequently associated with the imperial cult.
- The cults of Isis and Serapis benefited from imperial favor. On Julia Domna's denarii, Isis suckles Horus, with the legend "Felicity of the century," an allusion to the motherhood of the empress. Caracalla vowed a special cult to Serapis, who in 212 figured on the reverse of his coinage. He was also known as the "Well-beloved of Serapis," and had a grandiose temple built to this god on the Quirinal.
- The cult of Jupiter Dolichenus reached its height under the Severi, before declining around 220 (according to the inscriptional evidence). As it was closely connected with soldiers, this cult was more or less confined to the various frontier defense lines.
- Under the Severi, Mithraic dedications "for the safekeeping of the emperor" were most numerous. But the importance of Mithraism needs to be qualified in two ways: first, all inscriptions, of whatever kind, followed the same formula; second, of all the gods invoked for the safeguarding of the *Augusti*, Jupiter Optimus Maximus was by far the most prominent.
- A strong indication of the link between the actions of the Severi and the easternization of religion was the promotion of the local gods connected with the origins of the imperial family: Aziz of Emesa was honored at Intercisa for the protection of Severus Alexander; Liber Pater and Hercules of Leptis Magna were the Latin names for the Semitic gods Shadrafa and Melqart.

divinity who benefited from the vast syncretist movement of the third century. With Severus Alexander, another sort of syncretism emerged: it placed the gods on the same level, without favoring one or excluding another, because, as the third-century philosophers saw it, they were all reflections of the higher divinity that they were seeking to define. At the heart of these two trends, the position occupied by philosophers grew ever stronger as philosophies became increasingly imbued with the religious spirit.

Finally, the last aspect of the easternization of religious life was the expansion of Christianity. In 202, Septimius Severus banned Jewish and Christian conversions (*Augustan History, Severus* 17). This was the first formal legal act directly aimed at the Christians, whose legal situation had not changed since the time of Marcus Aurelius. Was there also a Severan edict of persecution? Despite a passage from the *Augustan History*, it would not appear so. There were martyrs at this time, in Alexandria and Carthage (see the document known as *The Passion of Perpetua and Felicitas*, arguably written by the martyrs themselves), but they were the result of local pogroms (actions by mobs, overzealousness on the part of governors). No Christian author indicates the existence of a general decree authorizing such persecutions. Apart from the measure of 202, the Severi showed notable, and occasionally even benevolent, neutrality toward Christianity. Contemporary testimony reveals the growing number of Christians in every region and every class of society. They took part in economic, even political, life, but they also wanted to live as Christians. This caused several problems, over such matters as the use of the baths, attendance at certain spectacles, and the education of their children. On the whole, however, apart from radical elements (like the sectarian movement of the Montanists and the Christian apologist Tertullian, a Romanized African who wrote in Latin) who preached withdrawal from society and urged people to reject every sort of occupation, Christians shared in the daily life of their compatriots. In addition, they had the sense of belonging to another community, a community of faith, that was constantly growing and becoming better organized (with the first Christian cemeteries in Rome, the appointment of deaconesses, the appearance of Christian art, parishes, lower-rank clerics). Missions went out from three important centers: Rome, already at the head of all the churches, Carthage, and Alexandria. But the East remained the most important Christian land: the last king of Osroëne had himself baptized; at Dura-Europus the first building identifiable as a Christian church made its appearance; and in Alexandria the Didascalia, a school of Christian philosophy, flourished.

Intellectual life

Taken as a whole, the intellectual life of the Empire was influenced by the intellectual currents of the East and the court of the Syrian princesses, a real workshop for ideas and Greek-language authors. In history, Cassius Dio and Herodian dominated their period. Dio was from Nicaea, Herodian perhaps from Asia

Minor. Both (but chiefly Cassius Dio, who was twice consul) were privileged witnesses of the period of the Severi, whom they served before returning to their country of origin and consigning their experiences to writing. In the field of law, with Papinian and his students, who, as we have noted, impressed their views on the emperors, the school of Beirut emerged as an important intellectual center. In philosophy, again the contribution of the East was important. Philosophers turned to the past to seek models of ethical conduct. Philostratus of Athens wrote the *Lives of the Sophists* and, at the request of Julia Domna, a *Life of Apollonius of Tyana*, a neo-Pythagorean miracle-worker of the second half of the first century CE. This story, riddled with anachronisms, achieved great success: the mixture of the marvelous and the irrational revealed in this biography was aligned with the intellectual and spiritual quest of the times. Less imaginative, but proceeding from the same approach, were the compilations of Diogenes Laertius of Cilicia (*Lives, Doctrines, and Opinions of Illustrious Philosophers of Each Sect*) and Athenaeus of Naucratis (*The Sophists' Banquet*). The era also produced some outstanding philosophers: Alexander of Aphrodisias, known as "the interpreter" (Exegete), drew up the texts of the Aristotelian tradition, with variants and an ample commentary; Sextus Empiricus, a Greek doctor and skeptic, criticized all philosophical sects and supported a philosophy of experience; and Ammonius Saccas, the first great neo-Platonist, founded a philosophical school in Alexandria around 200 and had as his disciples Plotinus (204–270) and Origen (c.185–254/255), two of the greatest thinkers in the ancient world. Plotinus, a neo-Platonist, and Origen, an uncompromising Christian, introduce us to the intellectual universe of the third century CE, which is quite distinct from that of the two previous centuries of the Empire.

The final contribution of the East to the intellectual life of the Empire was the appearance of important Christian literature written in Greek. Such literature had existed since the late first century, but it really flourished at the end of the Antonines' reign and under the Severi, with four authors: Irenaeus, originally from Asia, the second bishop of Lyons and founder of Catholic theology (who died, probably as a martyr, in the reign of Septimius Severus); Hippolytus, a Roman presbyter (c.170–235), who composed, in Greek, the earliest exegetical treatise to have come down to us; Clement of Alexandria (c.150–c.215), who wrote under the Severi, a convert of staggering erudition who did not hesitate, as he said, "to make use of the finest elements of philosophy and culture" (*Stromateis* 1.1.15) in order to elaborate what was the first great synthesis of Christianity and philosophy; and Origen, the author of a gigantic *opus* (perhaps 2,000 books, of which 800 titles have come down to us), exegetist, philosopher, philologist, biblicist, ascetic, mystic, preacher, and teacher, in short one of the mightiest geniuses of early Christianity. Alongside these giants of Greek Christian literature stands the imposing figure of Tertullian (c.160–240), a writer in Latin. A radical Christian apologist, he was also a remarkable writer and theologian. With these writers, Christianity took on an intellectual dimension.

Two hundred and twenty years after the death of Augustus, the dynasty of the Severi was extinguished. The constituent elements of Augustus' imperial government were still at work, providing an illusion that little had changed since his time. But, in fact, the Empire had evolved greatly, adapting to new situations with extraordinary flexibility. It had been able to integrate the elites of the provinces within its senators and equestrians, and to maintain the prestige of the Senate as a political body without any real power. Absorbing assassinations of its rulers and civil wars, it had also extended Roman citizenship to all free inhabitants of its lands without, for the most part, suppressing their attachment to their own small homeland, and by bringing security and a certain prosperity to almost everyone. Of course, the system had shown some weaknesses, but it still worked. The modest tomb of an African killed in 238 at the time of the revolt against Maximinus, who was deemed barbarous and tyrannical, suggests eloquently a loyalty that testifies to Rome's success at universal integration. The inscription reads "He died for the sake of Rome."

PART III ANOTHER ROMAN WORLD
THIRD TO FIFTH CENTURY CE

Introduction to Part III: The Nature of the Times

The period that began in the year 235 CE can no longer be studied as it was some decades ago; advances in research have radically altered historians' interpretations of it. Still, however, it falls roughly into three stages delineated by traditional approaches. In the following chapters we look for changes and developments in the characteristics of each of these periods.

Thus, the years 235–284 (generally regarded as the last part of the early Roman Empire) were marked by numerous problems affecting all areas of public life: external invasions, internal civil war, economic collapse, societal change. Today there is more emphasis on the limits of this crisis, which varied in gravity according to regions and periods – Africa and the Iberian peninsula, for instance, suffered less than Gaul. Moreover, the general crisis of the times met with a sustained reaction on the part of the "Illyrian" emperors.

What is sometimes called the "late Empire" began in 284. This term ultimately acquired a pejorative sense and became a synonym for a general decadence or decline of Rome. Researchers now stress, on the contrary, the renaissance that occurred in many areas, where a different order was being established. Rejecting the fatalistic idea of a "high empire" followed by an inevitable decline and fall, most historians favor the term "late antiquity." During these years, the state was reorganized; political power, the army, and civil institutions were renewed by a strengthened monarchy, more imbued with the sacred and even more personal than in preceding centuries. Several sectors of the economy were energized, while social contrasts were accentuated but without giving rise to serious troubles. Culture and religious life also experienced a new surge, and the conflict between Christianity and paganism imparted great strength to both. The Christian church succeeded in adapting to the new conditions, becoming a major social and intellectual force in late antiquity.

In the last quarter of the fourth century, we may observe the beginning of a separation between the East and the West. A fresh crisis, serious and deep-rooted, began in the West, illustrated by two dates: in 406, the Vandals, Alani, and Suebi crossed the Rhine, and no one could stop them; and in 410, Alaric seized Rome. In contrast, a new empire and a different civilization emerged in the East, that of Byzantium.

13

EQUILIBRIUM: 235 CE

By the time that the last of the Severi died in 235, the Empire had attained a kind of equilibrium (these days it is no longer believed that the accession of Septimius Severus in 193 marked the start of a great and continuing crisis). The alarm and the terrible years of Marcus Aurelius were forgotten, and the difficulties that cropped up here and there were generally perceived as fairly normal and temporary nuisances. As for the pessimism that is to be discerned among writers, it stemmed from a literary commonplace – praise for times gone by. Of course, that equilibrium was in fact threatened; but at the time no one was aware of it, apart from certain cultivated intellectuals who felt they were living in a period of crisis which appeared to them to be both biological and moral.

13.1 | A Fragile Balance

Institutions

The Empire stretched from Scotland to the Sahara, from the Atlantic Ocean to Mesopotamia. One city, Rome, had conquered this immense expanse, supported by those it had defeated, Latins, then Italians, then various provincials. Its leader, the emperor, guided political life: the state became more and more an absolute monarchy.

Roman territory was still divided into provinces, some dependent on the Senate, others on the emperor. The senatorial provinces were administered by proconsuls, the others either by imperial propraetorian legates who came from the Senate (for the larger imperial provinces, and those where legions were garrisoned), or by equestrian prefects or procurators (for the smaller ones, where garrisons consisted only of auxiliaries).

Nevertheless, provincial administration left a certain amount of autonomy to the local urban communities that formed the cells of this immense body (colonies, *municipia*). Smaller clusters of habitation (*vici*, *pagi*, *castella*, etc.) were subordinate to these larger ones, and semi-nomadic peoples who escaped urban regulations were monitored by prefects. Since Caracalla's edict in 212, all free men had become Roman citizens.

Society

Senators had lost their political role, although they kept their position in provincial administration and the army. In the imperial council and the important departments of state, their role diminished to the advantage of the equestrians. Moreover, provincial elites were increasingly becoming visible, their members entering the Senate and the equestrian order. In the second century, there were signs of a reaction against this mobility. Another thing that fomented social conflict was the rise of Christianity.

The economy

Although the institutional order within which the economy operated can be described readily, more caution is needed regarding the economy itself, since we lack statistics.

Food supply depended mainly on bread-making cereals (the "grain") which, in combination with vineyards and olive groves, formed the basis of the Mediterranean diet. The breeding of livestock and regional differences, often linked with climate, must also be taken into account.

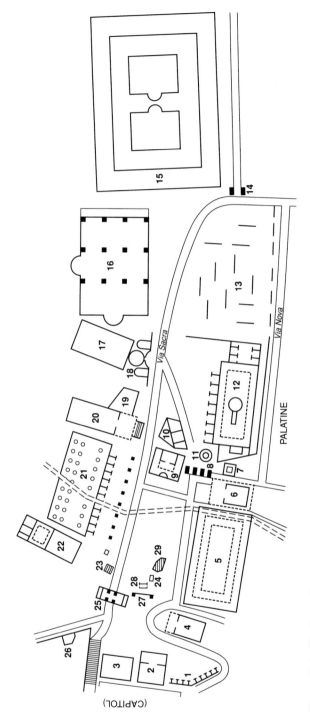

Figure 13.1 The Roman Forum in the imperial period. © Ruggiero Vanni/CORBIS

1 Portico of the Dii Consentes 2 Temple of the Divine Vespasian 3 Temple of Concord 4 Temple of Saturn 5 Basilica Iulia 6 Temple of the Dioscuri 7 Fountain of Iuturna 8 Arch of Augustus 9 Temple of the Divine Julius 10 Regia 11 Temple of Vesta 12 House of the Vestals 13 Portico of the jewelers 14 Arch of Titus 15 Temple of Venus and Rome 16 Basilica of Maxentius and Constantine 17 Library of Peace 18 Temple of Romulus Augustulus 19 Ancient cemetery 20 Temple of Antoninus and Faustina 21 Basilica Aemilia 22 Senate house 23 Lapis Niger 24 Column of Phocas 25 Arch of Septimius Severus 26 Mamertine prison 27 Reliefs of Trajan 28 Rostra 29 Lake Curtius

The period witnessed a great development in craft products and trade, both helped by an extensive and well-developed road network. A regional description will show things more clearly.

13.2 | Rome and Italy

Rome had preserved its traditional institutions, apart from the electoral assemblies, which had disappeared long before. The Senate, which still played the political role that the emperor allowed it, served as a permanent municipal council. Magistrates, too, still existed: quaestors were concerned with the finances, aediles with policing and buildings, and praetors administered the law; the consulship was no longer anything but a reward by the emperor for men who had passed through the three preceding stages of the senatorial *cursus*.

The emperor had long since tightened his control by means of appointed representatives. The streets of Rome were maintained by a council of four men. Curators were paired with the *aediles* and looked after buildings and aqueducts. Prefects supervised provisioning (prefect of the *annona*), the maintenance of good order in general (prefect of the city), and nocturnal policing and firefighting (prefect of the watch or *vigiles*).

A large number of staff were made necessary by the immensity of an overcrowded city with widely varying economic functions: Rome was still the political, commercial, and cultural capital, providing multiple financial services and opportunities. Epigraphy clearly shows that Rome teemed with urban life, and that all sorts of people made their living there – shopkeepers, craftsmen, soldiers, servants, and all the staff needed for the leisure pursuits of the masters of the world.

Associated with Rome in its extraordinary imperial venture, Italy profited from its situation in the field of institutions rather than in its material prosperity. The cities it comprised in fact enjoyed a great degree of autonomy and were for the most part subject only to the fairly relaxed control of the Senate and magistrates of Rome, and to the activities of the four *iuridici*, imperial nominees whose exact function is not entirely clear to us.

For the beginning of the third century, Italy's economic situation is most frequently judged as very poor: a fairly general decline is noted, marked by depopulation and regional imbalances. There is certainly much truth to this, but the peninsula's status in 238 was far from moribund. Four regions stand out.

Latium naturally benefited by its proximity to the capital city. Ostia was the busiest Italian port in that period, and numerous towns dotted the territory, such as Praeneste, Tibur, Alba, and Tusculum.

Campania had lost its splendor, and no longer possessed its remarkable balance between crafts and agriculture. It had chosen quantity rather than quality

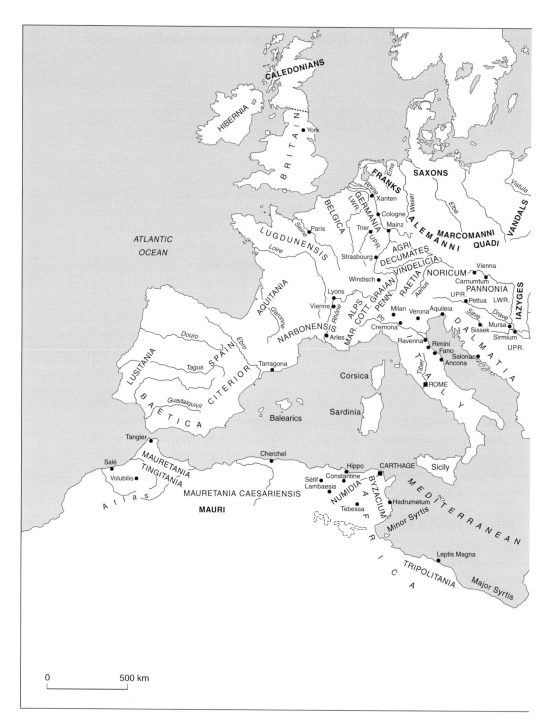

Map 13.1 The Roman Empire and the barbarians in 235 CE

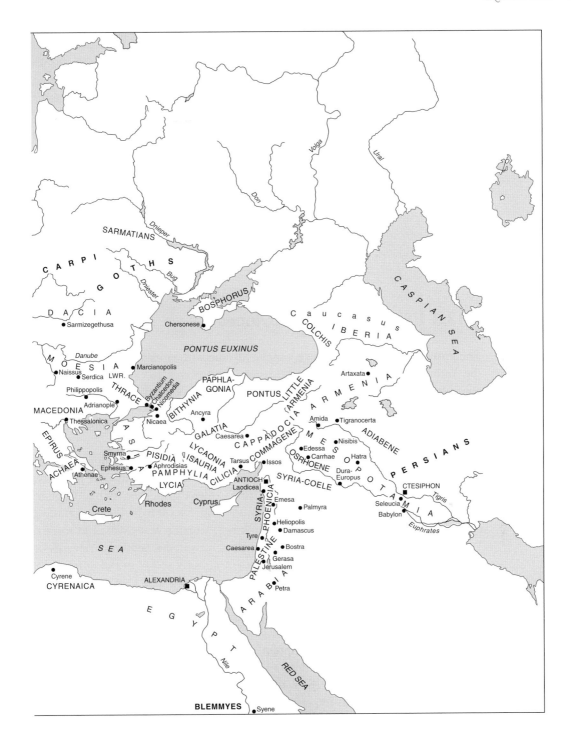

SARMATIANS

CARPI

G O T H S

DACIA

● Sarmizegethusa

Danube

M O E S I A

● Naissus
● Serdica
LWR.
● Marcianopolis

Philippopolis ●

THRACE

MACEDONIA

Adrianople ●

● Thessalonica

EPIRUS

ACHAEA

Smyrna ●

Ephesus ●

● Aphrodisias

Athenae ●

Crete

S E A

● Cyrene

CYRENAICA

ALEXANDRIA ■

E G Y P T

Nile

BLEMMYES   ● Syene

RED SEA

BOSPHORUS

Chersonese ●

PONTUS EUXINUS

C a u c a s u s

COLCHIS

IBERIA

CASPIAN SEA

Dnieper

Bug

Dniester

Volga

Don

Ural

PAPHLA-
GONIA

Byzantium
Chalcedon
Nicomedia

● Nicaea

● Ancyra

PONTUS

LITTLE ARMENIA

● Artaxata

A R M E N I A

GALATIA

● Caesarea

CAPPADOCIA

COMMAGENE

● Amida

● Tigranocerta

ADIABENE

LYCAONIA

ISAURIA

PISIDIA

PAMPHYLIA

LYCIA

CILICIA

● Tarsus

● Issos

OSRHOENE

● Edessa

● Carrhae

● Nisibis

M E S O P O T A M I A

Hatra ●

P E R S I A N S

ANTIOCH ■

Laodicea ●

SYRIA-COELE

Dura-
Europus ●

CTESIPHON ■

Rhodes

Cyprus

SYRIA

PHOENICIA

● Emesa

Heliopolis ●

Tyre ●

● Damascus

● Palmyra

Seleucia ●

● Babylon

Tigris

Euphrates

PALESTINE

Caesarea ●

● Bostra

● Gerasa

Jerusalem ●

A R A B I A

● Petra

for its oil and luxury wines, Falernian and Massican, harvested on the borders of the region. The main centers were Capua (for what was left of its crafts), Misenum, Cumae, and Pozzuoli for their ports, and Naples for its cultural role.

A fairly similar but certainly less prosperous region was Etruria. Populonia had lost its "industrial" base; the territory of Cosa was going through a rural crisis; and we must mention also Veii, the port of Luna, and Carrara for its marble. Etrurian wines remained a much-sought-after product, except for that of Veii, which was poor.

The Cisalpine region seems to have fared best. It produced wheat and wine, and raised cattle as well as the sheep which provided the raw material necessary for textile production in Milan, Padua, and Verona. Aquileia continued to develop as a commercial center. The other large towns of the region were Mantua, Piacenza, Modena, and Bologna.

13.3 | The Western Provinces

The provinces in the West, which supplied Rome with emperors – Spanish under the Antonines and African under the Severi – had played an extremely important role during the first two centuries of the Empire. Italy's relative decline highlights conversely their ascent.

Before we come to the three main groups (Africa, the Iberian peninsula, and the Gauls), we must mention the minor provinces of the islands in the Mediterranean and Atlantic. Sicily, a senatorial province, which still produced wheat, had Palermo and Syracuse as its chief centers. Sardinia, an imperial province, exported cereals, lead, gold, and silver; three towns stood out, Olbia, Cagliari (Carales), and Porto Torres (Turris Libisonis). More cut off from the great trading circuits, but like Sardinia an imperial province, Corsica was covered in forests. Lastly, Britain, divided into two imperial provinces under Septimius Severus or Caracalla, was also divided into two zones: a military sector in the north, with York (Eburacum) and Hadrian's and Antoninus' Walls, and a civilian region in the south, around London and Colchester (Camulodunum). In addition to the usual products, wheat, livestock, and pottery, it exported metals, in particular those of north Wales.

From the administrative standpoint, several regions may be distinguished within Roman Africa. Africa Proconsularis, whose name expresses its status, covered present-day Tunisia, the west of Libya, and an eastern fringe of Algeria. Numidia, entrusted to an imperial legate, spread around its two major towns, Constantine (Cirta) and Lambaesis, where the Third Augusta was stationed. The two Mauretanian provinces, both governed by equestrian procurators, and thus also imperial, had as their principal centers Tangier (Tingi) and Volubilis in Tingitana, Cherchel (Caesarea) and Bougie (Saldae) in Caesariensis.

It has recently been discovered that some African pottery was made locally, but Africa was essentially an agricultural region. It produced vast quantities of grain (mainly wheat in the valley of the Medjerda, the High Steppe, the High Plains), which it exported either in the form of the *annona* or for commercial purposes. Olive oil production and viticulture continued to develop. Racehorses and wild beasts for the amphitheaters were also exported to Rome and Italy.

Furthermore, Africa was a highly urbanized region, especially in the north-east (Zeugitana) around Carthage, one of the largest cities in the Empire. Today immense areas of ruins stretch around proconsular territory or the modern towns which have covered sites of antiquity: Utica, Hippo, El-Djem, Dougga, Tebessa, and Hadrumetum; in Tripolitania (in 235, still part of Africa Proconsularis) there is Leptis Magna and Sabratha; in Numidia, Timgad and Lambaesis in the south, Djemila and Constantine in the north; and the centers in Mauretania named above.

The Iberian peninsula, though larger than Roman Africa, was divided into only three provinces, shared between the Senate (Baetica) and the emperor (Citerior or Tarraconensis and Lusitania). Its economy also appears more balanced, since there was greater diversification. The Mediterranean triad (grain, olive oil, wine) was found along the eastern and southern coasts, especially in Baetica. The high quality of its olive oil and wine ensured the prosperity of Seville, Cadiz, and Cordoba. The Atlantic regions seem to have been less prosperous, given more to raising livestock (horses in the north and on the Meseta, sheep in the south). Lusitania yielded olive oil, but had opted for quantity.

The most distinctive feature of the peninsula lay in its mines: gold in the north-west (supervised by the Seventh Gemina, stationed at León, whose Latin name was Legio), gold, silver, and lead at Cartagena, copper at Cordoba, mercury at Almaden, iron, and tin. The main towns were agricultural centers, but they could also be administrative centers, like Mérida, or ports, like Barcelona and Tarragona.

Similarly to the Iberian peninsula, Gaul was divided into a rich senatorial province in the south, Narbonensis, and a range of imperial provinces, some civil and administered by legates (Aquitania, Lugdunensis, Belgica), others military and also entrusted to legates (Upper and Lower Germania), as well as the small procuratorian districts of the Alps (Maritime, Cottian, Graian, and Pennine).

Agriculture, moreover, showed the same contrast as on the Iberian peninsula: a Mediterranean front, where cooking was done with oil, and wine was consumed, beyond which, in the north, on the Atlantic coast and inland, butter and beer were predominant. As a whole, the Gauls produced plenty of wheat, partly thanks to efficient technical means (scythe, harvester, and wheeled swing plow). Horses were bred, and free-range pigs provided some renowned delicacies.

Gaulish pottery manufacture had definitively emigrated toward the Argonne region and the Rhineland, where it joined metalworking and glasswork. But the

Plate 13.1 Mosaic from Moknine, Tunisia, mid-third century CE. The "Telegenic" troupe kills leopards at a beast-hunt. Magerius, for whom it is staged, pays each performer 1,000 denarii, which a servant carries in bags on a plate. Sousse Museum. C. M. Dixon

Gaulish isthmus, between Britain and Germany to the north and Italy and Spain to the south, played an important commercial role. Its chief feature was its road network, complemented by navigable rivers, the Seine, Saône, and Rhône. From Boulogne, traders from Britain could reach Lyons, where they met those from Cologne, Trier, Strasbourg, Bonn, and Mainz, and from Germania across the Rhine, as well as from Mediterranean lands, by way of Marseilles and Arles.

In Narbonensis, the Rhône valley was lined with towns, Vienne, Orange, Arles, and Nîmes, and it was matched by the Mediterranean front, with Agde and Marseilles, a network completed by Narbonne and Toulouse. The Rhineland, too, was highly urbanized, with town development there connected with the presence of legionary camps, but Belgica was less densely populated (Reims, Metz), like Aquitania (Saintes, Bordeaux) and Lugdunensis (Autun and, of course, Lyons). As for the little Alpine provinces, they lived on a mountain economy, controlling the Alpine passes and, from Nice-Cimiez, access to the coast.

To the north, the Latin West was extended eastwards by the string of provinces along the Danube. This great river both provided a barrier against invasion and formed a major line of communication by lengthening the Rhineland route. In 235, these were all imperial provinces with legions, and therefore governed by imperial propraetorian legates.

Straddling Switzerland and Bavaria, Raetia, a poor plateau, possessed only two large centers, Augusta of the Vindelicians (Augsburg) in the south and Castra Regina (Regensburg) in the north.

Immediately to the east, Noricum lived better, thanks to the breeding of livestock, salt production, and, chiefly, the supplying of iron from Styria and of lead. There were several important centers, Virunum, Celeia, Solua, and Lauriacum.

Lying at an angle to these provinces, Dalmatia and Pannonia had attained an importance that became more marked in the following decades. Economic life prospered, with crops of the Mediterranean type on the coastal strip, and with the profits of livestock breeding and forestry in the interior. If the mining resources – iron, gold, silver – are also taken into account, as well as the trade in slaves imported from across the Danube, the density of population will be understood. This is explained by the presence of legionary camps in the north – Roman camps, wherever they were stationed, always became demographic magnets for the area – at Vienna (Vindobona), Carnuntum, Brigetio, and Aquincum; Salonae, situated in the south, was more civilian in character.

One province alone lay on the left bank of the Danube, Dacia – its modern name, Romania, suggests its deep Romanization since Trajan's wars. Dacia provided grain, gold, iron, and salt, and had a large population. Its main city was Sarmizegethusa, which had been king Decebalus' capital before Trajan's Dacian wars.

Lastly, on the right bank of the lower Danube, Moesia belonged partly to the Greek world, the East, mainly on its Black Sea coast, where the old Greek colonies of Tomi and Callatis lay. These ports were used for exporting the grain surpluses produced by the plains of the interior.

13.4 | The Eastern Provinces

The Greek-speaking East, like the West, had been organized into several great provincial areas, four of which stood out clearly: the Balkan peninsula, Anatolia, Syria, and Egypt.

Subject to Antony's rule during the Civil War that had ended with Actium in 31 BCE, these regions had not always been treated favorably by the central government under Augustus. But Athens, Macedonia, Pergamum, Galatia, Syria, and Egypt had a considerable cultural and economic heritage, and in 235 found themselves in a fairly good overall situation.

Augustus had left to the Senate the two provinces in the Balkan peninsula, Achaea (all the southern part) and Macedonia. Later, Thrace had been annexed, and in the reign of Trajan was entrusted to an imperial propraetorian legate. But within this imposed administrative framework lay a number of regional distinctions set up by history and geography.

Within the province of Achaea (from which the imperial equestrian province of Epirus had been separated), Aetolia was a sparsely populated and depressed region, troubled by brigandage, its economy dependent on meager cereal crops, wine, and top-quality olive oil. This also seems to have been the situation of Attica. Hymettus honey and cultural tourism, based mainly on Athens, would do little to change this state of affairs, although the public projects and benefactions of patrons such as Herodes Atticus in the second century illustrate that acquisition of large wealth was possible. The island of Euboea possessed marble (from Carystos), livestock, and the purple dye obtained from a type of shellfish, the murex. The Peloponnese appears to have been little more prosperous than Attica, but one may note the presence of some very wealthy and important men, especially in Sparta, Patras, and above all Corinth, the province's capital. North again of Attica, the regions of Boeotia and Phocis seem to have attained a satisfactory level of prosperity, mainly based on abundant and relatively diversified agricultural production (wheat, vines, olive trees, chiefly around Lake Copaïs). Thebes remained the principal town.

Thessaly maintained its reputation as good country, specializing in horse-breeding. This was also important in Macedonia itself, where gold and silver mining supplemented agricultural production. Famous Macedonian cities like Pella, Thessalonica, and Philippi dotted a territory crossed by the major route of the Via Egnatia.

As we saw, the kingdom of Thrace had been annexed to the Empire after all the other regions just listed. Despite the mountains that occupied part of its territory, this province possessed a healthy economy. Agriculture produced grain surpluses, horses were bred, pottery manufactured, and the subsoil yielded gold.

The Balkan peninsula thus had both strengths and weaknesses. A very different situation obtained in Anatolia, where, together with its Persian and Hellenistic heritage, geography formed a unifying element. This region is a vast plateau, high and arid; the climate is one of extremes, dry all year round but very hot in summer and very cold in winter, with a Mediterranean climate in the narrow coastal plains. Temples, often places of pilgrimage, were the owners of immense domains and centers of craft production, and they also acted as banks. This arrangement dated back to early antiquity together with a good part of the urban fabric and road network, much of which had been established under the Persians and Alexander's successors, if not earlier.

Confined to the western end of Anatolia, the senatorial province of Asia corresponded to the ancient kingdom of Pergamum. It was one of the richest regions of the Empire, and its level of urbanization reflected its wealth. Besides the capital, Ephesus, where the proconsul resided, other important cities included Pergamum, which produced *pergamena* (parchment), Miletus, Smyrna, Aphrodisias of Caria, Halicarnassus, and Clazomenae. Agriculture flourished in the coastal plains, the valley of the Menderes, and the islands, particularly on Chios, "the isle of wines." The textile industry was supplied with its main raw material by sheep-breeding, and the marble mines were still exploited.

Immediately to the north, Bithynia–Pontus, now an imperial province, benefited from its exceptional position between Europe and Asia, and between the

Black Sea and the Aegean. To the income derived from the land, it added that from the sea, both fishing and trade, all of which contributed to the prosperity of Nicaea, Nicomedia, Prusa, and Prusias.

In the remainder of Anatolia, divided into imperial provinces, populations experienced harsher living conditions because of the climate. There is scarcely any evidence of wine and oil production outside the coastal plains. Galatia, less urbanized than the more temperate regions, was divided into large domains devoted to the raising of sheep for wool (its capital was Ancyra, home of the *Res Gestae* inscription). The same applies to Cappadocia. But this also housed several great legionary fortresses, such as the one at Melitene, and the soldiers' pay favored the growth of a monetary economic sector. On the other hand, civil centers like Tyana also played an important part in the life of the province. Lycia–Pamphylia seemed like an extension of Galatia, but with access to the Mediterranean. This fortunate situation influenced agriculture and trade. Lastly, Cilicia, whose capital was Tarsus, produced goatskins from which a cloth (*cilicium*) was made, and saffron, as well as wine and oil on the plains.

Syria had a history at least as ancient as that of Anatolia and from this, as well as from its geography, came its particular diversity. Like Cappadocia, this imperial province was situated facing the Parthians, and it too had been supplied with legions, at Cyrrhus, Laodicea, Raphaneae, and Emesa. From here, the conquests of Septimius Severus had extended the Roman world as far as the Tigris, adding to it the province of Mesopotamia. Agriculture was developed in various ways. A Mediterranean front provided grain, wine, and oil. The mountains, which were carefully maintained, supplied wood for shipbuilding, and in the east, cultivated oases dotted the desert. Meager rainfall enforced operations to collect, conserve, and distribute water, with the Euphrates and Orontes playing an important role. Men's long experience was also an advantage to the craft industries. Textiles (linen and wool) benefited from the great inventiveness of the dyeworks (purple, extracted from the murex). Silk was imported from China. Glass was probably a local invention. These activities fed a coastal and caravan trade that, by this time, was more than 1,000 years old. Consequently, Antioch was one of the largest cities in the Empire. Other centers included Seleucia, Emesa, and the caravan cities in the east, Dura-Europus and Palmyra.

In the south-west, Phoenicia had been detached from Syria by Septimius Severus. Its agriculture was Mediterranean along the coast and mountainous to the east, where the cedars of Lebanon and other species of trees were used in the naval dockyards. Here, too, commercial traditions over a millennium old made the traders of Beirut and Tyre wealthy.

Farther south, two small provinces were caught between the sea and the desert. Judaea–Palestine lived very poorly, and religious or "nationalistic" motives were not entirely to blame for the risings in 66 and 132. An economy that was too exclusively agricultural (the Jordan valley) and overpopulation aggravated those difficulties. However, Caesarea and Jerusalem managed to attain some prosperity. East of the Jordan, Arabia had done better thanks to a greater diversification. The Hauran valley produced good harvests of wheat, and oil production was well developed. Livestock breeding, practiced by semi-nomads, complemented these agricultural resources. Perfumes and incense were exported, and the caravan trade assured Bostra and Petra of a substantial income.

To the south-west, we come to Egypt, which from an administrative viewpoint had been reduced to the ranks, only the title of its governor, the "prefect of Egypt," distinguishing it from other imperial provinces.

"Egypt," wrote Herodotus in the fifth century BCE, "is a gift of the Nile," meaning the god Nile, for the river was regarded by those who lived along its banks as a beneficent god. By 235 CE, little had changed: the farmers still depended on it for their livelihoods. In August, the floods arrived regularly and deposited silt that fertilized the edges of the desert. The country was in fact divided into three zones, the valley, the delta, and the oases, and together these produced great harvests of grain as well as wine, oil, flax, and, above all, papyrus, which sustained a craft. Crafts, in fact, were well developed in this province, which was dominated by a real "industrial triad," papyrus, textiles (linen and wool), and glass. To these we must add the rather meager products of a few mines. Luxury goods (perfumes, fabrics, and jewels) came from Alexandria, one of the principal cities in the Empire and a purely Greek city, like Naucratis, Ptolemais, and Antinoöpolis.

To return to the islands of the Mediterranean, Cyprus, close to Syria, was a senatorial province, making its living from the sea (fishing, coastal navigation) and from agriculture on its plains. Crete, which must have had similar means of existence, had been linked administratively with Cyrenaica, forming the senatorial province of Crete–Cyrenaica.

Cyrenaica, situated in North Africa between Egypt and Africa Proconsularis, completes our tour of the Empire. Here, there were both nomads and settlers, with traditional cultivation carried on around the towns (Cyrene) and trade from the ports (Apollonia).

Various governmental means were used to manage inter-provincial relations and to smooth out the differences between the various parts of the Empire stemming from history and geography. It is difficult, however, to speak of the unity of the Empire in the third century without mentioning its neighbors.

13.5 | Beyond the *Limes*

The development of Roman military strength on the frontiers of the Empire reveals which enemies were feared by army headquarters. Here we can distinguish three major sectors.

The north Possibly the most dangerous adversaries, in proportion to their numbers, were the Britons living beyond Hadrian's and Antoninus' Walls. Tribes of Picts (from the Latin *picti*, "painted, tattooed") and Scots could attack equally by land or sea. Against them it had been necessary to mobilize (and thus immobilize) three legions, almost one tenth of the imperial army.

The Germani, who lived beyond the Rhine and the Danube, constituted another threat. The size of their population and their effectiveness in combat made them fearsome enemies. Until the third century they had lived divided into small, aggressive tribes without any political or social coordination. But at the beginning of the century, leagues were formed. The Alemanni faced the angle formed by the upper courses of the Rhine and Danube, and the Franks waited behind the middle and lower Rhine. Moreover, the Goths (another Germanic people), organized notably by King Kniva, were coming down toward the south and southeast. It is possible, though not certain, that the movements of peoples at that time in the Far East had profound and swift consequences on this frontier. What is certain is that the Roman Empire was beginning to face serious threats on multiple fronts.

The imperial army headquarters had not failed to notice this deterioration, and military numbers continued to be reinforced on the lower Danube. Whereas the Germanies were defended by only four legions, 13 ensured the security of the provinces situated between present-day Switzerland and the Black Sea.

In the north-east, the Sarmatians were also on the move and increasingly often leaving the steppelands. Then they either settled in the Empire, merged into the Goths or, as in the case of the Iazyges and Alani, tried to preserve a certain autonomy.

The east The second major source of danger lay in the east. Perhaps less formidable on the battlefield than the barbarian leagues, Persia was nevertheless the only large organized state likely to countervail Rome, and the number of legions charged with keeping it under surveillance had hardly stopped growing since the time of Augustus – it was now 10. The threat was made all the more apparent by the fact that the heavy trade in expensive and precious goods from the Far East passed in part through Persian territory. Moreover, between Persia and Rome lay a constant source of discord, Armenia.

During the reign of the Severi, Persia had undergone a profound upheaval. Between 212 and 227, the Arsacid Parthians had been replaced by the Sassanid Persians: Artaban had been driven out by Ardashir (a descendant of Sassan), who had mapped out a precise program on two levels.

Politically, he intended to pursue a fierce nationalism. He aspired to re-establish the Achaemenid imperial tradition and gain control of the territories formerly dominated by Darius and Xerxes. He relied on solid institutions: the king, an absolute and divine monarch, was aided by a great commander and a high priest; territorial government was assured by the traditional military governors (satraps), who were more closely supervised than ever. The development of a heavily armored cavalry (cataphracts) rendered this enemy even more fearsome to the Romans.

In the religious field, the new government revealed a rather intolerant, even fanatical, attitude, imposing a kind of reformed Zoroastrianism as the state religion. Zoroastrianism or Mazdaism was Persia's oldest religion. It had been preached by Zoroaster, also called Zarathustra, and honored the god Ahura Mazda, the "Wise Lord." But other beliefs existed in the Persian lands. In the east, Buddhism was widespread. This was a form of wisdom, rather than a religion. It sought to teach people to perceive the reality behind appearances, and to break the cycle of reincarnation by the practice of virtue and asceticism. In the west lived large numbers of Jews (Babylonia was one of the great centers of the diaspora) and also, even at that early date, communities of Christians. And between 241 and 275, Mani preached a new dualistic theology of redemption, derived from Zoroastrianism, based on a belief in two fundamental spirits, one of good, Ahura Mazda, and one of evil. He suffered persecution because of his teachings and was eventually crucified.

The south The Roman emperor had fewer worries when dealing with his southern frontier. Possible enemies there had no political unity and little demographic potential, and represented a threat only through their mobility and nomadic way of life.

The Nobades and Blemmyes, well attested south of Aswan, posed a possible danger for Egypt. The decline of the kingdom of Meroë had been matched by the development of the state of Aksoum, where Hellenism spread, but which turned rather more to the Red Sea and trade than to Egypt and war. Lastly, in north-west Africa, the Berbers, chiefly Garamantes and Maures, lived on either side of the *limes*, on the edges of the desert or in the mountains. These days credence is no longer given to the idea of a "camel revolution," the sudden spread of that animal in the third-century Sahara, a spread that might have been connected with rebellious elements being driven into this arid zone. The chief danger lay in the close interweaving of these peoples with those already settled: one of the soldiers' tasks was to keep watch over the comings and goings of the nomads, and to guide traders safely through their lands.

13.6 | Balance and Instability

In 235, the Empire appeared to have achieved a balance. Despite some difficulties, order and prosperity ruled fairly generally. One might, however, pick out two possible sources of anxiety.

First, the East and the West, which formed two distinct entities, had not progressed at the same pace. The Latin West had perhaps started off earlier than the Greek East, in the time of Augustus. Perhaps its expansion had lasted a long time and was running out of steam; whereas the East, with its more ancient institutions and slower pace, experienced a great surge in the second and early third centuries.

Second, although the frontier system that separated Rome from the barbarians was still working satisfactorily, the Persians and Germani were altering and improving their own political, social, and military structures. On both sides of the Empire, difficulties appeared as early as under Marcus Aurelius; by 235, the last of the Severi had had to fight successively against the Persians and the Alemanni. Severus Alexander's killers, his own soldiers, were unaware that they were opening a new era.

14

A DISINTEGRATING ORDER: 235–284 CE

From 235, the Empire plunged into a crisis described by contemporary authors in tragic tones. These ancient descriptions have been so influential that modern historians often refer to this period as "the third-century crisis." Indeed, there can be no denying its gravity and general nature. Recent research, however, tends to set certain limits on this disintegration and notes a reaction to it. Therefore, it would be better not to yield to the absolute pessimism of the writers of that period. Of course, the Empire did not suddenly collapse. Its disintegration was gradual, slow, and prolonged. We must first look at this decline in its broad outlines, following its chronology; for its rhythm is marked by the reigns of the emperors. Let us not forget, however, that documentation relating to this period is scarce compared to that of the previous imperial centuries.

14.1 | Sinking into Crisis: 235–260 CE

Senatorial tradition depicts Maximinus Thrax (235–238) as a rough soldier who had emerged from the depths of society, "half-barbarian and scarcely speaking Latin, but rather almost pure Thracian" (*Augustan History, The Two Maximini* 2), a shepherd who became a soldier, then an officer, and then ascended all the ranks of the hierarchy. What is certain is that, having become emperor, he associated with himself his son, also Maximinus, as *Caesar*; and, having waged a long, hard war against the Alemanni, he installed himself at Sirmium in order to keep a watch on the Dacians and Sarmatians and to prepare for a counter-offensive against them. Some sources also mention his persecution of the Christians, especially church leaders, portraying it as the inadequate response of a feeble mind confronted with a complex problem.

Maximinus also reacted in another way: to cover the expenses of his war he demanded that taxes should be levied very strictly. By doing so, he unleashed the events of 238. It was at first a general rebellion of the Africans, both rich and poor, peasants and town-dwellers alike. At Thysdrus (El-Djem), a demanding procurator was murdered by some young men of good family. Stunned by their own audacity, they could see no salvation except in taking the initiative. They proclaimed the proconsul of the province and his son emperors (we know them as Gordian I and Gordian II). At first, the Third Augusta recognized their legitimacy; then, at the instigation of its legate Capelianus (a senator), it ended the rebellion in a bloodbath of the short-lived emperors and those loyal to them.

Next, Italy rebelled. The senators, appalled by the base origins of Maximinus, and further exasperated by his tax policies, decided to give the provincials their support. They deposed the man they regarded as a tyrant, and mobilized against him all the forces of the peninsula. For good measure, they entrusted the government to two of their own number, Pupienus and Balbinus. Maximinus then had to decide whether to turn his back on the barbarians and immediately march on Rome. When he later met with stout resistance on his way through Italy, the soldiers assumed control of the situation by assassinating Maximinus, his son, and, not long afterwards, Pupienus and Balbinus. According to other traditions, Maximinus committed suicide after he had seen his son murdered by the mutinous soldiers.

Power then fell into the hands of Gordian III (238–244), proconsul of Africa, who was forced to the throne at the insistence of the soldiers; however, caution is needed, as our sources disagree on the prosopography of the three Gordians, on the timing and circumstances of Gordian's accession (compare the versions in Herodian, 7.5, *Augustan History, The Three Gordians* 2; and *Augustan History, The Two Maximini* 14). Gordian III was an acceptable choice to all concerned: to the senators because he was one of their own, grandson of Gordian I and nephew of Gordian II; to the soldiers because, on account of his youth, he was under the thumb of the praetorian prefect, Timesitheus, who was no longer

Plate 14.1 Bust of
Maximinus Thrax.
c.235–238 CE.
Capitoline Museums,
Rome. Alinari
Archives, Florence

only a war commander but also the emperor's deputy and head of the entire army. In a way, Gordian III was the candidate of a fairly wide alliance.

In fact, in 241, responsibility for running the Empire fell to Timesitheus, whose daughter the emperor married. There was no shortage of work to be done. In 238, the Carpi and Goths had attempted to cross the Danube. The Goths were again repulsed in 242, while the Persians were defeated in 243. Gordian III was still on the Syrian front, at Dura-Europus, when he was assassinated.

Philip the Arab, Gordian's deputy who had probably engineered his murder, was then proclaimed emperor (244–249). He made various efforts to consolidate his power. He associated with him his small son, aged barely six, and gave responsibility for eastern affairs to his brother Priscus, who received the title *rector Orientis* ("governor of the East"). These two measures clearly show that Philip understood the importance of the succession, and that he sensed that the destinies of the two parts of the Mediterranean world were beginning to diverge. With an eye to propaganda, he also had Rome's millennium celebrated in great style, on April 21, 248, hoping thereby to strengthen his position.

But war continued to cause increasing difficulties. Philip had hardly become emperor before he had to buy peace with the Persians. In this way he hoped, first, to settle his position among his own followers, and then to gain the opportunity for military intervention elsewhere. For in the same year (244), the Alemanni invaded Alsace on the west bank of the Upper Rhine, and the Carpi and Goths were once again on the lower Danube.

The counter-offensives against the barbarians were impaired because in several places usurpers were declaring themselves emperor: Uranius in Syria, Pacatian in Moesia, Jotapian in Cappadocia, and then Decius, on the lower Danube, where he had repulsed the Goths.

Decius succeeded in seizing power from Philip and his son and keeping it for over two years. To give the impression that all was going well, he had baths constructed on the Aventine in Rome. He also unleashed a wave of persecutions against the Christians, inaugurating a decade of intense suffering for the adherents of the new faith.

In the meantime, the plague spread through the Empire, and Goths flooded the Balkans. In 250, they crossed Lower Moesia, and reached Beroea in Macedonia and Philippopolis in Thrace. Then, during the summer of 251, they subjected the Roman army to a disastrous rout in the Dobruja (eastern Romania). Decius died in the battle confronting the enemy.

The Empire was plunged into crisis. The barbarians became more and more of a threat, and Roman emperors increasingly temporary and unstable. Trebonianus Gallus (251–253) was partnered by his son Volusianus and applied feebly various measures against the Christians, who were rapidly becoming the scapegoats for the distress of the times. Volusianus doubtless had other worries, for by then wars were ravaging even the interior of the Roman world. In an extraordinary exploit in 253, Franks and Alemanni crossed the Rhine, pierced the *limes*, and pillaged Gaul and then Spain before returning home. And the Goths were embarking on new expeditions in the direction of Greece and Asia.

Let us make brief mention of the Moor Aemilianus (253), the governor of Moesia, who held on as emperor for just three months even though he had been recognized in the East. His attainment of power was evidence of the new importance assumed by his country's cavalry in the ranks of the Roman army. In fact, consequent upon developments in recruitment and tactics, Moorish horsemen represented an essential element of Rome's fighting forces. This military role, in a period of military crisis, allowed them to play a political role and favor the promotion of their compatriots.

The Empire experienced its most trying times under Valerian (253–259/260), who, unlike other pretenders of this era, came from a senatorial family. During his reign, foreign assaults were launched on several points along the frontier. The Goths attacked Greece and Asia in 252–253; in 256 they returned, and again in 258. In 253 and 256, the Franks and Alemanni returned to Gaul in search of riches; Valerian sent his son and partner Gallienus against them, and he succeeded in driving them back. The Saxons appeared on the shores of the North Sea, and Berber tribes were in revolt from 253 to 260. In the East, the troops of Sapor fell upon the province of Syria on at least three occasions, even reaching Antioch. The violent persecution of the Christians in 257 and 258 no more solved the Empire's problems than did the action of Ingenuus, the governor of Pannonia, who proclaimed himself emperor (258–260) after repulsing the Quadi and Marcomanni.

The most tragic phase of the crisis came in around 260, when invasions and usurpations mounted up in a disastrous tally. The Roxolani and Sarmatians descended on Pannonia. The Alemanni invaded Gaul and then threatened Italy, where Gallienus halted them only in the north of the peninsula. Under the sovereignty of Odaenathus, Palmyra seceded. In the East, again, there were at least two usurpers, Macrianus and Quietus. On the Danube, after defeating the Roxolani, Regalianus proclaimed himself emperor. In Cologne, Postumus also claimed the throne, but confined his empire to Gaul. Valerian the Younger, son and grandson of the official rulers, was assassinated.

But more was to come. The emperor Valerian, who had been captured by the Persians (perhaps in 259), was put to death (in 260 at the latest), and his remains (or the slave's garment he had been forced to wear) were put on display in the principal towns of Persia. Since our most extensive narrative of Valerian's life (the *Augustan History*) is fragmentary, we rely on an extraordinary non-Roman source for a better comprehension of this affair. This is the bas-relief of Bishapur (in Iran), showing Valerian kneeling humbly before king Sapor. Sapor was able to boast about this victory also in the reliefs and inscription of Naqs-i-Rustem, known as the *Res Gestae Divi Saporis* (by analogy with the *Res Gestae Divi Augusti*).

We shall now turn to the character, as well as the limits, of the crisis disclosed by these dramatic events.

14.2 | The Nature and Limits of the Crisis

The main characteristics of the third century's great crisis have long been known.

Military To a large extent it was a crisis of military origin. For the first time the enemy had attacked persistently and almost simultaneously on two fronts. The

Germani had to be driven back in the north, on both the Rhine and the Danube, and the Persians in the east. The emperors continually chased back and forth from one end of the Empire to the other, depleting one province to defend another. This vulnerability on the frontier encouraged peoples to rebel who would otherwise have remained confined in their territories.

Defeat revealed two further weaknesses in the Augustan strategy. First, when they had penetrated the *limes*, the barbarians met no other obstacles. The army had been deployed in a thin "curtain" separating the Roman from the barbarian world. Second, for both economic and demographic reasons, commanders had no reserves of men at their disposal. The policy of quality in recruitment limited choice and imposed the payment of suitable wages.

Political The defeats brought about a political crisis. The foreign war against barbarians was exacerbated by a civil war between Romans. Holding their supreme leader responsible for their woes, the soldiers frequently mutinied. They eliminated the titular ruler and appointed his successor following a familiar procedure: the praetorian prefect had the emperor assassinated, took his place, and appointed a praetorian prefect who, in his turn, became emperor in this way. The Empire, deprived of a dynasty, had become an absolute monarchy tempered by assassination, hence the brevity of the reigns. Moreover, such a situation aroused the desires of ambitious men with troops at their disposal, leading them to proclaim themselves emperor, sometimes successfully – a legitimate emperor was often a victorious usurper. Under these conditions, there could be no continuity necessary for a policy of recovery.

Economic The defeats also brought in their wake an economic crisis. In antiquity it was traditional for invaders to loot. Booty was their main aim, and they destroyed what they could not carry off. Thus, when they had taken everything they could, the barbarians sacked the towns, destroyed the herds, and burned the crops. Increased insecurity about transportation cut the trade routes and the subsequent disorder generated the return of brigandage and piracy.

The development of coinage allows us to trace the development of misfortune – indeed, through the obstruction in trade that they caused, the invasions were a prime factor in inflation, added to which were the rash promises made to soldiers by usurpers, the expenses inherent in long, hard wars, and payments made to the barbarians. But the Empire's monetary situation had long been unstable. Trading beyond the frontiers had been poor, and the wages paid to the army even in normal times were already devouring most of the state's budget.

Gold disappeared, hoarded by the wealthy. The silver Antoninianus dwindled in weight and standard. Even the bronze coinage was affected. The usurper Tetricus issued small bronze coins in Gaul which barely covered the little fingernail. Workshops stopped minting coins. Trade reverted in part to barter, a rather primitive form of economy. Military pay itself was affected, and the *aerarium militare*, whose duty it was to pay out a sum to each veteran, disappeared in the middle of the third century.

Social As might be expected, these economic difficulties resulted in a social crisis. The poor were further impoverished, directly by the invasions, but also by growing tax pressure. Evidence of these difficulties is provided by an inscription from Scaptopara in Thrace dating to the reign of Gordian III. It contains a complete text of a petition by the locals to Gordian for economic relief, and an evasive imperial response. This exchange between provincials and the emperor is echoed in the laments of the imperial colonists living at Aragoe in Phrygia during the reign of Philip – everyone was protesting against excessive demands. Municipal worthies, made responsible for the levying of taxes, at first slowed down and then completely halted their acts of public benefaction. The rich, though not all of them, also had to suffer the misfortunes of the times. Lastly, signs of a period of crisis, brigandage, piracy, and the plague reappeared.

Spiritual These misfortunes, worsened by contemporaries' perception of them, provoked a spiritual crisis. Not knowing how to ward off fate, people lived in a state of disarray. Their uncertainties were transposed to the religious plane, but very few questioned the will of the gods, still less their existence. The query was simple: "Why don't the gods give us better protection?" The reply was self-evident: "The peace of the gods has been shattered because in the bosom of the Empire lives an impious sect that does not worship them." It may be guessed that this referred to the Christians. Hence the persecutions.

In 250–251, the emperor Decius commanded a general sacrifice to the state gods. Some terrified Christians conformed (they were called the *lapsi*) and accepted what was proposed to them: the granting of an official document (*libellus*) that showed that they had performed what had been required made them *libellatici*, a term of contempt used for them by Christians who had not yielded. There was a new wave of harassment in 252–253, but it was relatively moderate. The worst occurred in 257–258. Under the influence of Macrianus, his "minister of finance," Valerian resumed the persecutions. In 257, he banned Christian worship and ordered the members of the church hierarchy to make sacrifices to the gods of the Empire. In 258, he had the refractory dignitaries executed, and stubborn rich Christians were deprived of their possessions. It was in this persecution that St Cyprian, bishop of Carthage, died.

Two further causes of the crisis

The war on two fronts thus resulted in the disorganization of the Empire's political, economic, and social life, and in a period of persecutions. Perhaps two other causes of this crisis should be added to these fairly generally accepted origins.

1   First, the economic circumstances, especially of the western provinces, played an important role. Since the period of Augustus, the economy had continually grown, and at an increasingly rapid pace: the slow expansion of the Julio-Claudian era had been followed by the acceleration due to the operations of the Flavians, with the peak achieved under the Antonines and Severi. Now, a long rising phase of expansion is usually followed by a sharp downward phase of contraction, and it may be that a downturn of this kind underlay the crisis. However, we lack the day-to-day accounts that would enable us to define better this cyclical phenomenon for this period. Moreover, it is not absolutely certain that ancient economies even followed that pattern. All we have, therefore, is a hypothesis.

2   Second, the third-century crisis seems also to have been a crisis of adaptation. The political, administrative, and military institutions of the Empire dated broadly from the period of Augustus, who had received the legacy of the Republic. Later emperors and citizens were faced with completely new problems and circumstances. The Principate had been succeeded by the Dominate, war had broken out on two fronts, and nobody knew what attitude to adopt toward the Christians, who had to be integrated somehow since they could not be destroyed. The Roman spirit was steeped in the law. To bring new solutions to new problems, it needed new institutions.

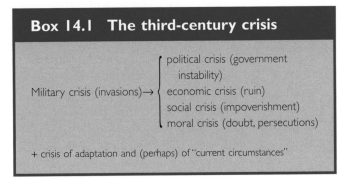

> ## Box 14.1   The third-century crisis
>
> Military crisis (invasions) →
>   - political crisis (government instability)
>   - economic crisis (ruin)
>   - social crisis (impoverishment)
>   - moral crisis (doubt, persecutions)
>
> + crisis of adaptation and (perhaps) of "current circumstances"

The limits of the crisis

Recent research has made it necessary to establish clearly the limits of this third-century crisis.

Chronology   Today, it is no longer accepted that the period of the Severi was part of this difficult time, apart from a few exceptional episodes. Indeed, for many provinces it marked a peak, for example in the economic field.

Difficulties did not begin until 235, and the Empire then sank into crisis until 260. Nevertheless, even in the midst of its worst problems, the government did not remain inactive. Military reaction was accompanied by other measures, such as the creation of outlying mints as early as 250.

Geography   The most dangerous enemies were the Persians and the Germani, especially the Franks, Alemanni, and Goths. The provinces most exposed to their attacks suffered more and earlier than the others. Egypt, for instance, was not seriously affected until around 260, when the countryside was depopulated, sub-desert land was abandoned, and the Faiyum region was hit. Moreover, even in the face of the enemy, some sectors resisted better than others. Olbia on the Black Sea, for example, was finally abandoned to the invading barbarians only at the end of the third century.

Among the regions least touched by the crisis were the Iberian peninsula, especially Lusitania, then in full expansion, and Africa, especially central and southern Proconsularis, although Mauretania Caesariensis suffered a wave of rebellions and these overflowed into Numidia (there is evidence of disturbances still taking place in 260).

The usurpations and secessions, notably those of Postumus in Gaul and Odae-nathus at Palmyra, reveal both the weakness of central government and the strength of the provincials' will to resist the invasions. It was not by chance that the two most important secessions erupted where the pressure was greatest: in Gaul, confronted with the Germani, and at Palmyra, confronted with the Per-sians. In 260, Postumus made himself master of the Gauls, and then gained the support of Britain and the Iberian peninsula. He was not rising against Rome, he said, but against the barbarians. The secession lasted until 274. The rule of Odaenathus and his wife Zenobia extended over Syria, Palestine, Arabia, and southern Anatolia.

It is possible that some large land-owners in sheltered provinces were able to profit from the misfortunes of others, selling scarce goods at exorbitant prices. At the end of the crisis, quite a few found themselves richer than when they started. This might explain the origin of certain vast fourth-century fortunes.

Sectors of activity Not all sectors were affected equally. There was some redis-tribution of wealth. Life changed. Towns surrounded themselves with defensive walls – covering, it is true, an area smaller than in preceding centuries, but the towns were nevertheless able to build them. Moreover, although it did not become marked until the following century, there was an exodus to the country-side, with the powerful installing themselves more permanently in their landed estates. Lastly, despite the persecutions, or perhaps because of them, Christianity continued to make progress. In the later third century, Dionysius of Alexandria (who wrote apologetics and pastoral poetry) and the school of Antioch contributed to the deepening of the doctrine. Gnosticism, which first came into prominence in the second century and was now flourishing divided into many sects, may itself be interpreted as a sign of spiritual vigor. Gnosticism set out the perfect knowledge (*gnosis* in Greek) of a God who was pure spirit, and claimed that the quest for the good leads to the rejection of the material, the source of all evil.

But the best proof of the vitality of the Roman world was supplied by the attitude of the central government.

14.3 | The Reaction of the Imperial Government: 260–284 CE

In fact, the period between 260 and 284 was marked by a sustained reaction to the crisis. Gallienus himself, who lived through some very dark days, did not remain inactive – contrary to what senatorial tradition would have us believe. And his successors, the "Illyrian" emperors, so called because of the geographical origin of most of them, gradually restored the situation.

Gallienus (259/260–268), who in 253 had become a partner in his father's rule, indeed inherited a disastrous state of affairs, mainly in the military field and in all parts of the Empire. Pirates pillaged the coasts of the North Sea, the Franks had entered Gaul, and the Alemanni had reached northern Italy. There was also unrest in Africa (the Moors) and Egypt (the Blemmyes). And in the East, after the death of Odaenathus in 267, his widow, Zenobia, assumed power on behalf of their young son, Vaballathus. Palmyra had seceded to defend itself better against Persia, and also to extend its trading ascendancy, but there was a pro-Roman faction, both among the desert Arabs and in the town itself.

But whatever our sources may say about him ("he administered the state similarly to boys who play at holding power"; *Augustan History, The Two Gallieni* 4), Gallienus was a resolute emperor. He personally took part in campaigns, and above all reorganized the army. He was responsible for the creation of a mobile reserve, composed of *vexillationes* of cavalry commanded by *duces* (generals) and quartered notably at Milan, and made systematic recourse to the *protectores* as bodyguards. Moreover, when the senators balked at rendering themselves vulnerable to the chances of war, their military posts were abolished. As a result, the prefect of the camp (*praefectus castrorum*), who had become first officer, was transformed into legion commander (*praefectus legionis*), and provincial legates gave way to equestrian governors (*praesides*). No one knows for certain where the new soldiers came from, but they were probably recruited from the sons of military men, from farmers, barbarians, and chiefly the inhabitants of Illyria, which soon became the pivot of the Empire.

Gallienus, the last great ruler to emerge from the aristocracy, considerably strengthened imperial absolutism by imparting to it a theocratic character. This was symbolized by the diadem, which later became an abstract and eternal figure.

This cultured man, who was strongly philhellenic, had been initiated into the Eleusinian mysteries. He lived surrounded by a court led by the empress Salonina, where the neo-Platonist philosopher Plotinus was conspicuous. His reign witnessed a blossoming of culture and the arts. The use of Latin, which was expanding, spread to the lower Danube. Painting (the Vault of the Flavii in the Catacomb of Domitilla) and especially sculpture produced some masterpieces (the arch on the Esquiline, imperial busts, and sarcophagi, e.g. the Ludovisi or "consul's" sarcophagus at Naples).

Plate 14.2 Stone slab from the Catacomb of Domitilla, with Christian iconography of anchor and fish. First half of third century CE. Foto Pontificia Commissione di Archeologica Sacra

Plate 14.3 Ludovisi Sarcophagus. The front shows a battle scene between Roman soldiers and Germans, who are distinguished by their hair and long beards. The Roman on horseback (center-top) has been identified as Hostilian, son of the emperor Decius, who died in 252 CE. The sarcophagus dates to that time. Museo Nazionale Romano. Photo © Bettmann/CORBIS.

In 260, to gain an advantage, or perhaps from conviction, Gallienus discontinued the persecutions of Christians, issuing a decree of toleration that opened a 40-year period known as the church's "little peace." In 267, the external situation again became troublesome. The Goths reached Athens, and Illyria was invaded. But there was also soon a fresh internal threat. Aureolus, commander of the troops in Milan, proclaimed himself emperor. Gallienus, besieging him there, was assassinated by his own officers in 268. His successors pursued his work of re-establishing order. These "Illyrian" emperors came mainly from the ranks of the army.

Claudius II (268–270), known as Gothicus, partly remedied this situation. He freed northern Italy from the Alemanni, who had once more invaded, by crushing them near Lake Garda. He also liberated Illyria by a great victory over the Goths near Naissus (270), which earned him his nickname. He nevertheless had to put up with the (fleeting) usurpation of Quintillus, and failed to prevent the empire of the Gauls passing from Marius to Victorinus. Worse still, he was forced to let Zenobia extend Palmyra's domination toward Egypt and Asia Minor. The *Augustan History* (*Claudius* 2) remarks nostalgically that Claudius possessed "the virtue of Trajan, the piety of Antoninus, the moderation of Augustus, and the good qualities of the great emperors."

It fell to Aurelian (270–275) to carry on the task of restoration, but in the military field Rome still had numerous active enemies. In 270, the Franks attacked on the Rhine; Alemanni and Juthungi reached the Po valley; Marcomanni, Vandals, and Sarmatians entered the valley of the Danube, where the Goths were defeated in 271; and it was probably during this reign that Dacia was finally abandoned for good. However, two lasting military successes must be credited to this ruler. He became the *restitutor Orientis* ("restorer of the East") after vanquishing Zenobia, and without combat obtained the surrender of Tetricus, the last emperor of the Gauls. He thus fully deserved the triumph celebrated in Rome in 274.

The war did not prevent his attending to works of construction and reform. Indeed, it was Aurelian who had Rome encircled by a new defensive wall, long sections of which are still prominently visible. In the provinces, he tried to restore the economic situation by the creation of mints and the circulation of a new Antoninianus.

But Aurelian is also remembered as a man of solar theology. His desire was to rebuild the moral unity of the Empire around the Sun god, and in 274 he proposed to his contemporaries a quasi-monotheism, or henotheism, something still alien to collective attitudes, though the forms of the cult remained close to traditional paganism (rites, the institution of priests of the Sun). The *Augustan History* (*Aurelian* 44) suggests the ambiguity of biographical traditions on this emperor: "Many place Aurelian among neither the good nor the bad emperors because he lacked mercy, the prime dowry of an emperor."

For contemporaries, it seems, the main feature that marked the brief reign of his successor, Tacitus (275–276), was a supposed late flowering of senatorial authority. Under his rule, or the one that followed, the *iuridici* of Italy created by Marcus Aurelius were replaced by *correctores* (a form of controller who ensured that everything was in order). What is certain is that this emperor was faced with difficult problems, the first of which was Florian's usurpation. Even more serious, in 275 the Goths fell on Asia and the Franks on Gaul.

It was thus a burdensome legacy that came down to Probus (276–282). This vigorous officer drove the Franks and Alemanni out of Gaul, the Burgundii and Vandals out of Raetia, and lastly the Goths and Getae out of the Danubian provinces. He went to Asia, and then to Egypt to fight the Blemmyes. Under his rule an episode occurred that was of little importance in itself but is suggestive of the state in which the Empire and its navy found themselves: Franks who had been deported to the shores of the Black Sea seized some vessels, sailed across the Mediterranean, looting on the way, passed the Straits of Gibraltar, and returned home by way of the Atlantic. To these misfortunes must be added the usurpation by Proculus and Bonosus in Gaul.

The energetic Probus had another good general as his successor, Carus (282–283), who was partnered in his government by his two sons, Carinus (283–285), who set off to repulse the Sarmatians, and Numerian (283–284), who went with his father to do battle with the Persians. Carus had just taken Ctesiphon from them when he died. Numerian was withdrawing westwards when he was assassinated. Carinus in his turn was killed in Moesia, after being defeated by Diocletian. At that point another chapter opened in Rome's history.

The Germani and Persians had severely damaged the organization of 235. Imperial power had needed to be strengthened, the army to acquire greater mobility. The economic system had been disrupted, as had social structures and collective attitudes.

There were still many problems to be resolved, and a whole new development had to be taken into account. It was up to the conqueror of Carinus to take charge of setting up a new order.

15

A DIFFERENT ORDER: 284–361 CE

The disorder and destruction of the third century involved the setting up of a fresh order, and allowed the building, or rebuilding, of a different world. Using and systematizing the work of their predecessors, the emperors Diocletian and, later, Constantine reorganized the state, the economy, and society. A new equilibrium was achieved in the mid-fourth century under Constantius II. In the same period, a new empire and a material and spiritual civilization emerged under the influence of Christianity, the Byzantine civilization. Considered for a long time a decline from the "classical" Roman splendor of the western Empire, Byzantium is now recognized as an original and brilliant offshoot of Rome and is studied in its own right.

15.1 | Diocletian and the Tetrarchy: 284–305 CE

Born around 245 in Illyria into a humble family, Diocletian pursued a military career that eventually placed him at the head of Numerian's *protectores*. After the assassination of this emperor in 284, Diocletian was merely the last in a long line of usurpers. But he was clever enough to profit from the void created by the third-century destruction, and also from the public safety measures taken by his predecessors, the "Illyrian" emperors, of whom he was also the last. Using his ingenuity and experience, he reaped the benefit of a long period (20 years) in power. His policies, apparently contradictory, made him both a reformer, even a creator of civilian and military institutions, and a reactionary who promoted a return to older institutions, particularly in the religious field.

A new political regime

On November 20, 284, Diocletian, proclaimed *Augustus*, became emperor. In order to solve military problems and to control the ever-diverging territories of the empire, he was the first to establish the rule of four emperors, which we call the First Tetrarchy. This consisted of two *Augusti* and two designated heirs, proclaimed *Caesares*.

In the spring of 285, after defeating his rival, Carinus in battle, Diocletian appointed Maximian first as *Caesar* and then (April 1, 286) as *Augustus*, his associate but nevertheless subordinate. In 293, Galerius and Constantius Chlorus both became *Caesares*. Each of these four received a town of residence, respectively Nicomedia, Milan, Sirmium, and Trier. However, they remained in close contact and were bound together in various other ways. A religiously based hierarchy was instituted: Diocletian, "Jupiterian," prevailed over Maximian, who was merely "Herculean" (in both cases it was the office that was sacred, not the person). Family links were also forged, through marriage and adoption. The absolutism of power was in no way less than it had been in the preceding centuries, but the two *Augusti* committed themselves to abdicating simultaneously after 20 years, in favor of the two *Caesares*, on condition that they then in turn appointed two *Caesares* in their own place. In principle, this system of the rule of four (Tetrarchy) was an efficient way for a safe and peaceful succession. The sculpted group of *The Tetrarchs*, preserved today in Venice, and the reliefs on the arch of Thessalonica celebrate Diocletian as the protector of imperial unity.

Box 15.1 Hierarchy of the Tetrarchs

East	West
DIOCLETIAN *Augustus*, Jupiterian (Nicomedia, Antioch)	
	MAXIMIAN *Augustus*, Herculean (Milan, Aquileia)
GALERIUS *Caesar* (Sirmium)	CONSTANTIUS CHLORUS *Caesar* (Trier)

Plate 15.1
Sculptured group of *The Tetrarchs*, dated to 305 CE, today at the left corner of the façade of San Marco in Venice. It is carved in porphyry, a rare purple stone reserved for imperial objects. The identical dress, height, and expression, as well as the embrace of the Tetrarchs, symbolize the equality and unity of their rule. akg-images/Erich Lessing

Plate 15.2 Palace of Diocletian, emperor 284–305 CE, at Split, near Salonae, Croatia. Ancient Art & Architecture Collection

The consequences of the Tetrarchy

This political system produced good results in the military field, where there were three imperatives: to cut down the number of usurpations, to pacify provincial uprisings, and to repulse external enemies.

In the West, Maximian suppressed the Bagaudes. These were Gaulish peasants who, unable to pay their taxes and condemned by the law, had turned to brigandage. Then Constantius Chlorus successfully fought Carausius and his successor, Allectus, who had formed an independent state for themselves in Britain and had even extended it to mainland Europe. Maximian once again drove back the Franks and Alemanni, and then went on to Africa to re-establish order (296–298).

Diocletian himself, and then Galerius, repulsed the Iazyges and the Carpi on the lower Danube. Diocletian went to Egypt, where he vanquished the Blemmyes and quelled the usurpers Achilleus and Domitius Domitianus. When Narses, king of Persia, attacked on the Euphrates (297), Galerius was again called on. He seized Nisibis and Ctesiphon, and defeated the nomadic Saraceni. The peace of Nisibis (298) acknowledged the Empire's possession of five provinces beyond the Tigris. The tetrarchic system had made these victories possible; they were facilitated or, at least, accompanied by the reorganization of institutions.

Plate 15.3 Gold medallion of Constantius Chlorus, minted at Trier, 297 CE, to celebrate his victory over Allectus in 296 CE. Constantius and his navy approach the gates of London, welcomed by Britannia. C. M. Dixon

In fact, Diocletian undertook the creation of a new army. He increased the number of soldiers, chiefly in the frontier army, favoring quantity over quality, created smaller legions, and set up a different hierarchy, placing divisional generals (*duces*) over the prefects of legions. He divided up the provinces (they went up from 47 to 85) following the example of the legions, brought Italy into line with the common regime, and grouped the provinces, together with the divisions of Italy, into 12 dioceses, each under the control of a deputy (*vicarius*). Each province was administered by an equestrian governor, except for Asia and Africa Proconsularis, which kept their proconsular status.

He similarly modified the central administration, where posts were created for *magistri* (heads of department), and he took even greater interest in finance. In 294, he reformed the monetary system, based on gold (the *aureus*), silver (the *argenteus*, which definitively supplanted the Antoninianus), and issues in good-quality bronze. In 301, his edict on maximum prices fixed an upper limit on prices and wages, more successfully than has sometimes been thought. Lastly, he set up a new fiscal organization, attested as early as 297 in Egypt, based on payment per head and per plot of land.

The last great persecution of the Christians is also attributed to Diocletian. Its true authors were in fact Maximian and even more Galerius (Constantius Chlorus, on the other hand, proved very moderate). At first, measures targeted the army: an entire Egyptian (Theban) legion was executed on the orders of Maximian, for

Chronology 15.1	**Principal events of Diocletian's reign**

284	Death of Numerian; Diocletian *Augustus*
285	Defeat of Carinus; Maximian *Caesar*
286	Maximian *Augustus*
293	Constantius Chlorus and Galerius appointed *Caesares*
294	Monetary reform
296	Reconquest of Britain
297	Persian attack; law against the Manicheans
298	Peace of Nisibis
301	Edict on maximum prices
303	*Vicennalia*
303–4	Principal persecution of the Christians
305	Abdication of Diocletian and Maximian

refusing to sacrifice to pagan gods (in 285–286); isolated martyrs, such as the recruit Maximilian, the veteran Typasius, and the centurion Marcellus, also came from the military. In 302, the soldiers were ordered to offer sacrifices, and in 303 and chiefly in 304, four general decrees were promulgated: confiscation of holy books and destruction of churches; imprisonment of community leaders; freeing of those who recanted; organization of sacrifices throughout the Empire.

The Christians were not, however, the only ones to be targeted. In 297, in connection with the war against Persia, and again in 302, the state also turned on the Manicheans.

After celebrating their 20 years in power (*vicennalia*) in 303, Diocletian and Maximian, partly pressed by Galerius, abdicated simultaneously on May 1, 305. Diocletian retired to his palace near Salonae.

15.2 | Constantine: 306–337 CE

Before re-establishing single government, Constantine, who also benefited from a long term of office, for the most part took up and completed or extended Diocletian's reforms. However, he departed from them radically in the religious field.

The son of Constantius Chlorus and Helena (possibly a former tavern waitress), Constantine was born at Naissus around 280. Like Diocletian, he was a soldier (war in Egypt in 295–296, then against the Sarmatians) and a pragmatist rather than a theorist or a theologian. Despite long sessions of explanation, the bishops who advised him do not seem to have persuaded him on the differences between orthodoxy and Arianism.

Plate 15.4 Bronze head from a colossal statue of Constantine, emperor 306–337 CE. C. M. Dixon

Seizing power

His accession to power was, unsurprisingly, the result of his military victory over his rivals. In 305, Galerius became *Augustus* in the East and Constantius Chlorus in the West. For their respective *Caesares* they took Maximinus Daia and Severus. But in 306 the death of Constantius Chlorus (from natural causes) prompted the army in Britain to proclaim his son Constantine emperor. Reacting against this, the praetorians in Rome chose Maxentius, the son of Maximian, while Severus was assassinated. The following year, Maximian came out of retirement to take up office again.

Galerius arranged a conference at Carnuntum (308). That gave rise to the constitution of the Second Tetrarchy, which left the East to Galerius and Maximinus Daia, and entrusted the West to Constantine and a newcomer, Licinius. Maximian and Maxentius, however, maintained their claims, and Domitius Alexander declared his own in Africa. Thus there were then seven emperors. The inevitable consequence of the Tetrarchy, this Heptarchy closely resembled anarchy.

Murder clarified the issue of succession. Maximian was the first to die, in 310, followed by Domitius Alexander and Galerius. In 312, in the battle of the Milvian Bridge (today's Ponte Molle on the Tiber), but in fact at Saxa Rubra, Constantine defeated Maxentius, and a victory at Adrianople in 313 gave Licinius success over Daia. In 324 Constantine defeated Licinius in the battle of Adrianople, and re-established the rule of one.

Reforms

His wars did not prevent Constantine from carrying out various reforms. In the military field, he organized a new officer corps (*magistri*, *comites*, and *duces*); and he developed the mobile field army or army of the interior, the *comitatus*, to the detriment of the frontier army. He put these reforms into effect before 325.

He also transformed the administration of the Empire. At the center, it had once again become a monarchy: the *Caesares*, much subordinate to the *Augustus*, enjoyed very little power. The sovereign made use of a larger number of staff, who were also far more hierarchized: the prefect of the sacred bedchamber (*praepositus sacri cubiculi*), the quaestor of the palace, *comites*, and *magistri*. Likewise, at regional level, Constantine introduced innovations. The praetorian prefects lost their former functions. While retaining their title, they now became responsible for territorial prefectures, which grouped together dioceses that were themselves collections of provinces.

Religious policy

Constantine is known today above all for his religious policy. The first problem, his conversion to Christianity, is inevitably mired in the tradition of imperial biography, with its plentiful miracles and premonitions, as well as in the new genre of Christian hagiography, the biography of martyrs and saints (in fact Constantine and his mother Helena are honored as saints in the Catholic and the Eastern Orthodox churches).

Constantine appears to have been originally a follower of the Sun god, led to henotheism by a vision of Apollo. On the eve of the battle of the Milvian Bridge, a second vision, Christian this time, caused him to make his troops carry a *labarum*, a standard on which were embroidered a *chi* and a *rho*, the first two letters in Greek of the name of Christ. The combination of these two symbols, one superimposed on the other, evoked the rays of the Sun, an iconography bound to appeal to Christian and pagan soldiers alike. We do not know precisely when Constantine decided that Christ was not to be regarded as a version of the Sun god (certainly not before 322). Nor do we know whether he eventually gained a clear understanding of Christian orthodoxy. But he certainly received counsel from Pope Miltiades and Ossius of Cordoba, a wealthy and cultured Christian. He had himself baptized only on his deathbed, which was not out of the ordinary for that period.

Regardless of the elusive personal motives behind his conversion, Constantine's Christian policies combined genuine sympathy for Christianity and a pragmatic acceptance of its growing popularity. Galerius had issued a decree of toleration in 311, and Maximinus Daia one of persecution in 312. By the Edict of Milan in 313, Licinius and Constantine established the "peace of the church:" freedom of worship was assured and confiscated possessions restored. Furthermore, the government intervened in two church conflicts: Donatism was condemned as a schism by the Synod of Arles in 314, and Arianism as a heresy by the Council of Nicaea in 325.

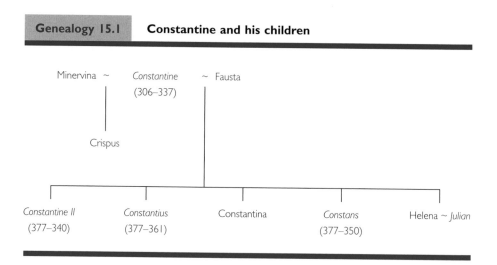

| **Genealogy 15.1** | **Constantine and his children** |

The founding of Constantinople

The emperor gave his name to the new city he founded in the East, Constantinople. The decision had been made in 324, and the inauguration took place on May 11, 330. The new town, covering the former Byzantium on the shores of the Bosporus strait, was laid out in a purposeful imitation of Rome: it lay on seven hills, was divided into 14 regions, and possessed a forum, a capitol, and a Senate.

Chronology 15.2	**Principal events of Constantine's reign**

306   Death of Constantius; Constantine *Augustus* (York); Maxentius *Augustus* (Rome)
308   Conference at Carnuntum
310   Usurpation of Domitius Alexander
311   Galerius' decree on Christianity; death of Galerius
312   Constantine's victory over Maxentius ("Milvian Bridge")
313   Edict of Milan; victory of Licinius over Daia
314   Synod of Arles
316   War between Constantine and Licinius
317   Crispus, Constantine (II), and Licinius (II) *Caesares*
324   Constantine's victory over Licinius; Constantius (II) *Caesar*
325   Council of Nicaea
326   Execution of Crispus and Fausta
330   Dedication of Constantinople
333   Constans *Caesar*
335   Dalmatius *Caesar*
337   Death of Constantine

Although it was merely the second capital of the Empire, headed at first by a proconsul and not a prefect of the city (its true period of expansion dates from Constantius II), there should be no misconception over the significance of the foundation of Constantinople. It was not an act of public benefaction, or an aesthetic choice, but the result of a careful consideration of a profound change: the Empire's center of gravity had shifted eastward in every area: politics, economy, religion, culture.

Constantine planned his succession early on. In 317, he appointed three *Caesares*, Crispus (whom he had executed in 326, on moral grounds, and/or to limit him as a rival), Constantine (II) the Younger, and Licinius the Younger, to whom he added Constantius (II) in 324, Constans in 333, and Dalmatius in 335, after celebrating the 30 years of his official reign (*tricennalia*). He died on May 22, 337.

15.3 | Constantine's Sons: 337–361 CE

In the middle of the fourth century, the history of the Empire was dominated by three problems: government, Christianization, and the barbarians.

From the political viewpoint, the major undertaking of the era was the re-establishment of a single ruler by the elimination of all the rival emperors until only one remained. In 337, after three months of intrigue, Dalmatius was

Chronology 15.3	The sons of Constantine

337	Accession of Constantine II, Constantius II, and Constans
338	Siege of Nisibis
340	Death of Constantine II
343	Constantius II in Adiabene
350	Usurpation of Magnentius; death of Constans
351	Battle of Mursa
353	Death of Magnentius
354	Execution of the *Caesar* Gallus
355	Julian *Caesar*
357	Battle of Strasbourg; Constantius II's journey to Rome
360	Julian acclaimed *Augustus*
361	Death of Constantius II

assassinated. The Empire was then divided into three: Constantine II, who was in authority over the imperial college, took charge of Gaul, Britain, and Spain; Constans of Africa, Italy, and Illyria; and Constantius II of the East. In 340 Constans reunified the West to his own advantage, after Constantine II had been defeated and killed. In 350, he in his turn was defeated and killed, by the usurper Magnentius, who was himself beaten at Mursa in 351 by Constantius II, although not eliminated until 353.

Constantius II is regarded as the first Byzantine emperor. He lived surrounded by a court of his trusted associates: Eusebius, the eunuch prefect to the sacred chamber (*praepositus sacri cubiculi*) under both Constantine and Constantius II and an ardent proponent of Arianism, exerted influence comparable to that of the infamous imperial freedmen of the first century CE. Constantius II gave pride of place to the East, and despite the solemn nature he imparted to his visit to Rome in 357, he did not attempt to keep up appearances regarding the relative importance of the two parts of the empire. He appointed two *Caesares*: Gallus, a cousin, whom he soon had executed, and another relation, Julian, whom he dispatched to Gaul to restore order there.

Two dangers threatened the Empire at this time.

1 The religious question: whereas Constans had sincerely supported the orthodox party, notably under the influence of Athanasius, Constantius II had ended by supporting Arianism, with equal sincerity. To this risk of conflict between Christians was added the real conflict that set Christians against pagans (edict of 356). We shall return later to these issues (chapter 18).

2 War: Persia attacked in Armenia at the end of Constantine's reign and in 337 Sapor II targeted Roman Mesopotamia. In Gaul, the *Caesar* Julian fought a series of campaigns against the Germani. The army of the West had suffered heavy losses at Mursa, but this did not prevent Julian from achieving a great

Plate 15.5 Greek Orthodox icon of St Constantine (called "the Great") and his mother St Helena, who is credited with recovering the True Cross from Jerusalem. St Luke's Cathedral, Hong Kong. akg-images

victory (battle of Strasbourg in 357) over the Alemanni, who had been ravaging Gaul since 352.

When Constantius II asked Julian for reinforcements to help him to repulse the Persians, the troops assembled at Lutetia (Paris) staged a rebellion, proclaiming a reluctant Julian as emperor (360). Constantius II died very opportunely (361).

15.4 | Three Emperors and their Achievements

The period from 284 to 361 was dominated by the three personalities of Diocletian, Constantine, and Constantius II. The measures each took contributed to the birth of a different Roman world, with new institutions, a fresh economy and fresh social structures, and a new civilization. In spite of everything, the dangers, mainly from barbarians, had become less pressing.

16

DIFFERENT INSTITUTIONS

Reorganization

In the fourth century CE more than ever, the Roman Empire remained an absolute monarchy. The fiction of the Principate had been abandoned, and there was no longer any hesitation in speaking openly of the Dominate. The sovereign made himself ubiquitous by means of a meticulous bureaucracy, and the army was still a fundamental instrument of power in his hands. However, in the face of mounting difficulties he was increasingly constrained to share his government and power.

16.1 | Central Government

The emperor

Inscriptions and coins bear the range of titles by which the emperor let it be known what he wanted from his sacred power. As under the early Empire, but with even fewer limitations, this was exercised in three principal areas.

1 The emperor intervened personally in civil matters, and he was the law through his edicts, which were applicable throughout the Empire, through his orders to governors, and through his responses to the petitions of private persons as well as to embassies from the towns. He was therefore fundamentally responsible for ensuring the maintenance of order and social stability – the avowed mission of the Principate. To this end, the sovereign appointed his representatives in the provinces, the governors, and set the amount of taxation.

2 As regards the army, which was his main supporter, he was its supreme commander, awarding honors and promotions, and determining the pay. His special charisma assured Rome of victory. Like Mithras, the pagan emperors bore the title *invictus* ("unconquered"), while from 324 CE Constantine, and from 337 his sons, had themselves called *victor*, abandoning only the polytheistic reference.

3 Religion was another fundamental element in the collective attitudes of the times, because success in combat was considered a gift from the gods and the manifestation of celestial support. Also, for the pagans, the safeguarding of Rome and the good fortune of the Empire depended on the "peace of the gods." The pagan emperors demanded that the sacred nature of their office be recognized, but imposed nothing concerning their person: in principle, people were at liberty to worship them or not, as they pleased. Obviously, the same did not apply to Christian rulers, who considered themselves only God's "vicars." This of course did not diminish their authority or even absolutism. The "peace of God" followed on quite easily from the pagan "peace of the gods."

Given these conditions, it may be seen how the victor's propaganda represented a rival usurper: he acted like a tyrant, abused his power in regard to his subjects; an impious man, he did not respect the gods.

The strengthening of imperial absolutism was reflected in the elaboration of an etiquette that had already existed under the early Empire. The sovereign no longer had anything in common with ordinary mortals. He lived in a palace and not necessarily in Rome (notably in Milan, Aquileia, Nicomedia, and Antioch). When he made his (epiphanic) appearances, he wore the insignia of his office, a diadem and a cloak adorned with precious stones; and, before any audience, he was separated from the public by a curtain. Later, it was required that he be venerated ("the adoration of the purple" had been demanded since 291 CE) and addressed as "lord," *dominus* (this appellation traced back to Domitian, who first institutionalized and intensified the cult of the imperial family, the *gens Flavia*). A ceremonial character was also conferred upon certain regular actions of his, such as a speech to the army (*adlocutio*) or an entry into a town (*adventus*).

Central administration

To take his decisions and transmit his orders, the emperor had at his disposal a central administration that was much larger than in preceding centuries and was becoming more militarized, at least as indicated by its vocabulary.

Diocletian made a few innovations in this field. The creation of the Tetrarchy brought in its wake the creation of four councils, already called "sacred"; the emergence and proliferation of the notorious imperial spies known as *agentes in rebus* dates back to this period; and vice-prefects (*vicarii*) were appointed to administer the newly created dioceses (groups of provinces). For the rest, Diocletian had retained the praetorian prefects, who were prime ministers and ministers of war simultaneously, and changed their titles: *magister memoriae* and *magistri scriniorum* in the chancellery, *rationalis rei summae* and *magister rei privatae* in finances. The heads of these departments ruled like despots over their numerous staff.

Constantine did the most in this field: the appearance of new high offices and a new praetorian prefectship, now territorial, date from his time and will be discussed later in this chapter.

The imperial household, overall control of which was entrusted to the prefect of the sacred bedchamber, was divided into two: the sacred chamber properly speaking, in the care of the *primicerius* or "chamberlain," and the palace, entrusted to a "military" assistant (*castrensis*).

Bureaucratic administration was divided into offices (*scrinia*), each under the command of a head or master (*magister*). The *magister* was subordinate to the quaestor of the palace, a person with extensive authority who replaced in this role the old praetorian prefect, and to a *primicerius*, or superintendent. The quaestor and the *primicerius* also controlled the "school" (*schola*) of notaries. The principal departments dealt with archives, correspondence, petitions, and official journeys. The increase and power of the bureaucrats were two characteristics of the new government.

Similarly growing in importance, the police were answerable to the commander of the imperial guard, that is, the master of the offices (*magister officiorum*). They were furnished by the "school" of *agentes in rebus*, a cross between imperial courier service and secret intelligence. The *agentes* monitored mail and other communications from and to the palace, and were entrusted with keeping potential plotters under surveillance.

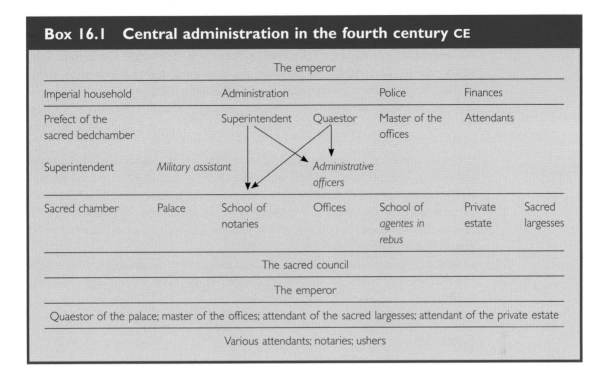

Box 16.1 Central administration in the fourth century CE

The emperor				
Imperial household	Administration		Police	Finances
Prefect of the sacred bedchamber	Superintendent	Quaestor	Master of the offices	Attendants
Superintendent	*Military assistant*	*Administrative officers*		
Sacred chamber	Palace	School of notaries	Offices	School of *agentes in rebus*	Private estate	Sacred largesses
The sacred council				
The emperor				
Quaestor of the palace; master of the offices; attendant of the sacred largesses; attendant of the private estate				
Various attendants; notaries; ushers				

Lastly, the two main treasuries, i.e. the private estate and sacred largesses, were each entrusted to a supervising attendant (*comes*).

On the fringes of these various "ministries," the emperor's council (*consilium principis*) was still active. Beside the seated emperor stood the quaestor of the palace, the master of the offices, and the two attendants assigned to finances. Various other attendants were also summoned to attend, together with notaries and ushers.

Limitations

The reinforcement of the imperial power and its administration explains why the sovereign's authority was exercised with practically no limitations.

Freeborn plebeians were rarely able to have their say. They could barely make themselves heard, except in Rome and Constantinople, and only then by mutterings and demonstrations, for instance at chariot races at the circus (see, for example, the *Nika* rebellion in Constantinople, 532 CE, as narrated by the historian Procopius of Caesarea (*Wars* 1.24), an eye-witness to the events).

Of the former Senate nothing remained but its name: the assembly was used only as a municipal council for Rome, or Constantinople. The political ladder (*cursus honorum*) still survived, but quaestors, aediles, praetors, and consuls did not have much real authority, contenting themselves with bearing titles that were void of power. Under Constantius II, three such career structures led to the consulship: civil, military, and bureaucratic. Valentinian I classified senators in three levels, *illustres* (illustrious) at the apex, *spectabiles* (worthy of respect) in the middle, and *clarissimi* (honorable) at the lowest, delimiting a strict hierarchy among them. Nevertheless, though not possessing real political power by virtue of their magistracies, some senators possessed great wealth and all were occasionally able to wield a certain moral authority, as in the affair of the altar of Victory, which the Christian emperor Gratian ordered to be removed from the Curia (see chapter 19 below).

It was, however, mainly the force of circumstances that set limits on the imperial power. The difficulties linked with the extent of the territory and the barbarian menace often imposed collegiality and cooperation. And even though heredity became increasingly the rule, the question of the succession still caused difficulties, so that the emperor had sometimes to tread carefully to guard against covert resentment and open rebellion.

Another element that enfeebled imperial power was the finances, which were still precariously balanced. They were organized on a system that was extremely bureaucratic, and thus not very profitable.

Finances

The army took the lion's share of the Empire's budget, followed by the administration, the court, imperial benefaction, and, finally, the projects needed to sustain the lives of the plebeians of Rome, joined now by those of Constantinople. As regards revenues, each reign added a new measure, further complicating a structure that had never been simple.

The *annona* still existed. The word indicated both a tax and the department responsible for levying it. Originally this land and personal tax, paid at least partly in kind, was intended to assure free men in the capital of the essential minimum of food. The military *annona*, which could be paid in coin (*adaeratio*), was the part of that payment hived off for the benefit of the army, beginning from the start of the third century. During the fourth century, yet another part was allocated to administrative staff. In the last two cases, it was hoped to compensate for dwindling salaries. The officer in charge, the prefect of the *annona*, eventually yielded his power to the praetorian prefect, assisted by the prefect of the city, the association of ship-owners, and a large staff. Under Diocletian, the method of levying such taxes was altered and the system of *iugatio–capitatio* perfected, extending now to Italy. The *iugatio* applied to land. But historians are divided about the *capitatio*: for some it had a strictly personal nature, whereas others consider, perhaps rightly, that it was a land tax calculated on a personal basis (the tax assessor took account of the number of people working on an estate). Depending on the province, only the *iugatio* counted (Syria), or only the *capitatio* (Gaul), or both methods of calculating were used (Asia Minor). Soldiers and veterans benefited from an immunity, but only for part of the *capitatio*. Responsibility for levying these two categories of revenue was at first entrusted to the master of the private estate (*magister rei privatae*), who was subordinate to the *rationalis rei summae*, a sort of finance minister. The property qualification assessment was revised every five years under Diocletian, and then, beginning with Constantine, through a cycle of 15 years ("indiction").

Another tax on land, the tribute, also persisted, and Theodosius again demanded that it should be paid in coin. In Constantine's time, an effort was made for the rich to pay their share. The senators were asked for land (*gleba*), municipal men for "coronation gold," which under Valentinian became obligatory, and merchants for gold and silver (*chrysargyre*).

The anonymous author of *De rebus bellicis*, writing in the late fourth century, suggested a lowering of taxes by means of a reduction in expenditure and, above all, waste. He does not appear to have been heard.

Law and justice

A high level of sophistication is found in the field of law and justice, and here the Roman tradition was truly respected. We know how a legal matter proceeded. Henceforth, only the procedure called "extraordinary" (*extra ordinem iudiciorum*, "outside the order of private judges") was applied, as only the administrative authority took a hand in it. Minor cases were heard by municipal magistrates. Every affair of any importance was within the competence of the governor of the province. And an appeal could be made only before the emperor or his representative, the praetorian prefect. Furthermore, any official in authority had jurisdiction.

The main points of the laws promulgated during the time of Constantine and his successors are to be found in the compilation of the Code of emperor Theodosius, made between 429 and 438 CE.

16.2 | The Army

The third-century crisis, which brought about profound alterations in the state, likewise affected the army, all the more so because it had been first and foremost a military crisis.

From an organizational viewpoint, Gallienus effected important changes: he developed the cavalry and created a mobile reserve to the rear of the frontier zone. Nor must we forget the role played by the army in public life, and above all in politics, where it had created and destroyed emperors. However, the strengthening of the sovereign's authority, and the parallel decline of that very army, caused it gradually to lose its power. On the other hand, the mere presence of a garrison was enough to alter the economic, cultural, and religious life of the surrounding area and thus the army as a whole wielded social and demographic power.

Under Diocletian

Diocletian was the creator of the new army (although we should note that some historians present his reforms as less extensive than those of Constantine).

His actions were inspired by the lessons learned from the failures of the third century. First, quality had to be replaced by quantity as the overriding criterion in the recruitment of soldiers. Second, large defensive projects, mainly walls, were urgently needed. Without going so far as to quadruple the numbers of men, as Lactantius accused him of doing, he certainly considerably increased, and perhaps even doubled, them.

He reorganized the different types of units, to the undeniable advantage of the frontier army. New, smaller legions of no more than 1,000 men were created (some legions, however, retained their 5,000 combatants), and two legions were posted in each frontier province. Their total number at the time went up from 39 to 60. The wings (*alae*) and detachments (*vexillationes*) of the cavalry assumed greater importance, from the point of view of numbers and prestige, as revealed in their pay (see below). The auxiliary infantry of the cohorts was still active, and agreements were made with neighboring peoples, who supplied temporary troops (*gentiles*).

In contrast, the place of the field army created by Gallienus seems to have been reduced, even to nothing, according to some historians, who think that it was gleaned in times of major wars from the troops assigned to the frontiers. Such a choice would not have been surprising on Diocletian's part. At all events, the campaign army, if it still existed, played a minor role during his reign.

On the other hand, he found it necessary to build up the navy once more, not only restoring it but even improving it after the decline it had experienced during the third century. It had a presence in the Mediterranean and on the rivers, and a new squadron was installed at Constantinople. Some historians consider that its numbers reached over 10 percent of the entire Roman army, that is, 45,000 men out of 435,000.

Pay, which helped to ensure the prosperity of military regions, also revealed the lines of the new hierarchy: horsemen of the *alae* obtained parity with legionaries (1,800 pieces of silver per year), and thus remained well above the cohort infantry men of the auxiliaries (1,200 pieces of silver per year).

The addition to personnel posed the question of recruitment. The principle of compulsory military service remained in force but, as under the early Empire, volunteers provided the initial source of recruits. When there were not enough of them, it was decided that large land-owners, by virtue of the extent of their estates, should supply men or, failing that, money (*aurum tironicum*). Soldiers' sons, practically born in the camps or near them, formed a good part of the troops, and when there was a shortage of traditional recruits, barbarian volunteers were accepted. These choices suggest that the quantity of recruits was a more important consideration than their quality. Naturally, such a policy impacted the efficiency of the Roman army in the long term.

The state was compelled to make equally rash choices of military officers, at least at the lower levels. Since the middle of the third century, senators had no longer wished to carry out military duties. Commanders of units (prefects of legions, prefects and tribunes of *alae* and cohorts, the commanders of *vexillationes*) came from the equestrian order or rose from the ranks. The Empire's *limes* was divided into short sectors each entrusted to a *praepositus*, and a province's army might, as an exception, be placed under a general (*dux*). Further up the hierarchy, the *vicarius* was in charge of the troops in his district, and higher still were the praetorian prefects. The supreme command belonged of course to the emperors, the Tetrarchs.

To make up for the mediocrity of the men, defense works were intensified. The Empire had for a long time erected physical barriers in places where no natural obstacle thwarted the barbarians (the walls of Hadrian and Antoninus in Britain, the so-called "Devil's Wall" in Germania). Those that already existed were now repaired or brought back into commission, and new ones were constructed. Moreover, many new fortresses were built, usually of modest size (they were called *centenaria*, a mysterious word), like the one discovered in the south of Algeria at Barika near Aqua Viva ("Living Spring"). These new camps were provided with rectangular corner towers that protruded externally; and accommodation abutted on the enclosing walls, as did sometimes the headquarters (*principia*). These characteristics are occasionally referred to as the "Diocletian type," although it is now known that the development of this type of fortress predates the period of the Tetrarchy. R. P. A. Poidebard, one of the pioneers of aerial photography, discovered in the Syrian desert several dozen of these enclosures which dated from the beginning of the fourth century. This strategic arrangement was complemented by a new road, the Strata Diocletiana, which ran from Damascus to Mesopotamia.

Under Constantine

Diocletian's military measures were completed or, on some points, reversed by those of Constantine.

The different types of units were reorganized. First, a new imperial guard had to be created, after the disbanding of the praetorian cohorts and the *equites singulares*, both of whom had sided with Maxentius. Thus, a corps of officers was set up, the *protectores et domestici*, and the five Palatine "schools" (*scholae palatinae*).

Gradually a field army (*comitatus*) was formed, perhaps from what Diocletian had left. This was an army of the interior, very mobile and intended for rapid intervention, comprising of legions and detachments (*vexillationes*) of horsemen. High standards were applied to its recruitment and training, so that it formed an elite.

By contrast, the frontier army, which was still made up of legions, auxiliaries (*alae*, cohorts, *numeri*), and *vexillationes*, seems to have been neglected.

Constantine has been accused of having "barbarized" the frontier soldiers (*limitanei*); but, as we have seen, this kind of reproach was commonly leveled against the emperors in the third century.

The new types of units called for a new organization and chain of command. Certain commands were assigned to particular army corps (for example, the *comitatus* infantry), others to a geographical area (for example, Gaul). This cross-checking of authority, which complicated military operations, must also have hampered excessive ambition and thus attempts at rebellion.

On the other hand, civilian and military powers were definitively and completely separated. Praetorian prefects and vice-prefects or deputies (*vicarii*) were restricted to purely administrative and judicial functions, and only for parts of the Empire. Similarly, provincial governors were released from all concerns of a military nature.

The imperial guard was therefore handed over to the master of the offices (Palatine schools) and to the attendant of the *domestici* (*protectores et domestici*). Two masters of the militia, one for the infantry and the other for the cavalry, were placed at the head of the *comitatus*. Three other masters of the militia shared the Empire (the East, Illyria, and Gaul). Groups of provinces received central administrators, who oversaw the governors of individual provinces. This last institution, already in practice under Gallienus and Diocletian, was thus generalized. The institution of the *praepositus limitis*, the officer responsible for a sector of the *limes* of a province, was also generalized. In contrast, the commands of units (prefects, tribunes, and *praepositi*) were left untouched.

All these reforms came about gradually – the first of them undertaken as a result of the *coup d'état* of 306 CE. But in this area everything was completed by 325.

Under Constantine's successors

Under Constantine's successors, modifications were minor.

The army corps were still further hierarchized. Within the *comitatus* a distinction was made between the Palatine and the ordinary units; legions (infantry) and *vexillationes* (units of cavalry) could come into either category. The frontier army, which was static, comprised, in descending order, *pseudocomitatenses* legions, *riparenses* legions and units of cavalry, and auxiliaries (*alae*, cohorts, and *numeri*). But it also relied a great deal, probably too much, on the "federates," barbarian peoples loosely bound to the Empire by a treaty.

The navy must not be omitted from this picture; it fulfilled its missions until at least the end of the fourth century.

Lastly, the policy of fortifications was continued. Even under Valentinian, large-scale works were carried out in Germania to strengthen Gaul's security. The establishment of Sponeck at Kaiserstuhl in the Black Forest was part of this system.

The *Notitia Dignitatum,* a document listing civil and military dignitaries and their areas of responsibility (dated to 420 CE), is a major source of information for the administrative organization of both the eastern and western Empire; at least as it was conceived if not as it was actually carried out.

As time passed, recruitment had recourse more and more frequently to the barbarians, chiefly the Franks. They gradually infiltrated the hierarchy, reaching even the highest ranks.

The role of the army

The historical significance of the army cannot, however, be reduced to its purely military function and activities. As under the early Empire, it played an important role in the life of the times.

From the material point of view, the presence of soldiers still had the same consequences (stability, peace, prosperity), but the nature of army pay had changed. The proportion paid in cash, the *stipendium,* was charged to the central treasury (*aerarium*), which had it distributed through the financial authorities in the provinces (*thesauri*) under the aegis of the attendant of the sacred largesses. Distributions in kind, the military *annona,* were carried out in the name of the praetorian prefect and deducted from the *arca.* In addition, soldiers and veterans benefited from tax exemptions, described on the bronze table found in Pannonia at Brigetio.

In the spiritual field, it appears that the army had developed little and remained one of the bastions of paganism and tradition. Tertullian had already said that Christians were cluttering the camps under Septimius Severus, but he was no doubt exaggerating. And the martyrdom of the Theban legion, which Maximian is supposed to have annihilated to punish it for its faith, needs to be reduced to more modest proportions: probably no more than a cohort was involved in the emperor's condemnation. Soldiers more willingly took sides with the persecutors than with the persecuted. Even so, geographical distinctions must be made: more Christians were to be found in the garrisons of the East than in those of the West.

Military treatises

After all the reforms of Gallienus, Diocletian, and Constantine and his successors, the situation of the army in the late fourth century, mainly in the West, appeared sufficiently grave to some intellectuals. Two works, arguing for contrasting solutions to the military problem, deserve mention here.

Vegetius, in his treatise *The Military Institutions of the Romans* (*Epitoma rei militaris,* also known as *De re militari*), proposed a simple and idealistic return to the past. He sketched a picture of the Roman army of the early Empire, at least as he believed it to have been, in the hope that this description would lead to a rediscovery of the key to success.

Box 16.2 The army in the fourth century CE

Units		
Imperial guard	Army of the interior (*comitatus*)	Frontier army (*limitanei, riparenses*)
Protectores et domestici Palatine schools (5)	Palatine and ordinary legions; Palatine and ordinary *vexillationes*	*Riparenses* and *pseudocomitatenses* legions; *vexillationes*; *alae*, cohorts, *numeri*; peasant auxiliaries; *gentiles*

NB: (1) Legions numbered either 1,000 or 5,000 men (2) The navy still existed: c. 10 percent of total numbers.

Officers		
Diocletian	Constantine and his successors	Extent of authority
Emperor	Emperor	Supreme command
Praetorian prefects	Masters of the militia (*comitatus*), infantry, cavalry	Emperor's direct aides
Praetorian prefects	Master of the offices and count of the *domestici*	Imperial guard
Vicarii	Masters of the militia, the East, Illyria, Gaul	Regional commands
Dukes	Dukes	Provinces
Praepositi limitum	*Praepositi limitum*	Sectors of the *limes*
Prefects, tribunes, *praepositi*	Prefects, tribunes, *praepositi*	Units

The anonymous author of *De rebus bellicis*, on the other hand, seems more inventive. To start with, he introduced the military problem into the overall political and social problems of his time. He went on to suggest extreme and largely unfeasible solutions: a raise in pay would improve the quality of recruitment and give greater motivation to the fighting troops; new fortifications would save more human lives; more intensive recourse to military engineering and machinery would give the Empire superiority over the barbarians.

The Roman army of the fourth century does indeed seem to have lost part of the efficiency possessed by its forerunner in the early Empire. And this development was no doubt due to a certain weakening in recruitment, itself the consequence of the financial difficulties of the state. The author of *De rebus bellicis* was correct about these matters.

16.3 | Territorial Authorities

The state had to ensure order on the frontiers and within the Empire. To this end, and in keeping with the Roman attention to law, it resorted to a complex system of institutions, partly inherited from the early Empire – although the same name often masked a quite different institutional structure.

The organization of land areas into provinces still existed, but Italy itself had lost all its privileges and had been brought into alignment with the administrative model used in other parts of the Roman world. Diocletian had broken up the provinces, raising their number from 47 to 85. We know that Byzacena and Tripolitania, taken from Africa Proconsularis, were created between 294 and 305 CE. The first *praeses* ("ruler," pl. *praesides*) of Byzacena bore the additional title *perfectissimus*; his successors, between 313 and 322, became *clarissimi*, and were sometimes called "consulars." In contrast, all their known counterparts in Tripolitania remained *perfectissimi*.

The governors received the title of *praesides*. Those in Asia and Africa Proconsularis remained proconsuls, others were called "consulars" or "correctors." Under Constantine they finally and completely lost their military powers. All that remained to their authority was an important judicial role, which they long performed – their presence is still attested at the beginning of the fifth century, chiefly in Africa.

It was also Diocletian who grouped the provinces into dioceses. Heading each one was a *vicarius*, an important official who was formally or technically a deputy of the praetorian prefect. The number and composition of these dioceses varied as time went on, although the number stayed in the region of 13.

In order to understand the overall structure of the dioceses, one must know that the implication of the expression "prefectship of the *praetorium*" changed radically. After 324 the title survived, but it covered a completely different function: the holders of this office were now confined to purely administrative and judicial activities, and their areas of responsibility restricted to groups of dioceses, forming territorial prefectures. There were most often three praetorian prefectships: the East, the Gauls, and Italy; but sometimes a fourth was added, Africa–Illyria.

Box 16.3 The dioceses after 381 CE

Prefectship of the praetorian guard (*praetorium*)	Number	Names
The East	4	Thrace, Asia, Pontus and the East, Egypt
Italy	6	Macedonia, Dacia, Pannonia, Africa, Italy, Rome
Gauls	3	Gauls, Spain, Britain

The hierarchy of province–diocese–praetorian prefecture no doubt matches a desire for uniformity, which may be taken for rationalization. But this arrangement also expresses the wish of the imperial power not to entrust extensive authority to anyone other than the emperor himself. Here, too, there was a fear of usurpation.

16.4 | Cities and Municipal Life

The Empire was still an immense body whose cells were the cities. The study of these cells and their activities, municipal life, forms one of the main centers of interest of current research. New evidence and interpretation temper the exaggeratedly pessimistic traditional picture of deserted *curiae*, impoverished municipal worthies, and the disappearance of autonomy under the weight of bureaucracy.

The two capitals

We shall begin with two special cases. Despite the general trend toward administrative uniformity, the two most important cities, the two capitals, largely preserved their peculiar administrative status.

In Rome, the Senate, as we have seen, found itself reduced to the role of a municipal council, and the "treasury of Saturn," which still existed in the fourth century, was no longer anything more than the city's funds.

The people of Rome had played no real part in the civic process for a long time. Their expressions of dissatisfaction were confined to demonstrations at public venues such as the circus.

The real administration was in the hands of a range of high officials, the prefects of the city, of the *annona*, and of the *vigiles* (night police and firemen), as well as such other officials as the curators of the aqueducts and public works. But, among these, the prefect of the city played the leading role. Still very rich, and often from the old aristocracy, he accumulated powers. At the end of the third century, he administered the city of Rome and the port of Ostia, and exercised his jurisdiction to a distance of the hundredth milestone around Rome. Constantine made him the city's grand master. Already chief of police and president of the Senate, he also became, after 331 CE, the supervisor of the curators and other prefects. But he possessed no legislative power and was himself kept under the eye of the prefect of the *praetorium*, an official appointed by the emperor.

Constantinople, conceived by its founder as an imitation of Rome, was also endowed with a staff of high officials and a Senate, though this conferred less prestige on its members than the Roman one. Because it was only the second capital of the Empire it received no prefect of the city, but rather a proconsul. As for its plebeians, they were put on an equal footing with those of Rome.

Italian and provincial cities

The civic arrangements of the rest of the Empire, that is, Italy and the provinces, had been drawn up on a common model. However, this standardization was accompanied by a difference in status. There were three separate cases:

1   Non-urbanized peoples, tribes, lived within the *limes*. Subject to their own laws and ruled by their chiefs, *principes* or *reguli*, they were nevertheless under the firm control of the governor.

2   Settlements that were not considered capable or worthy of complete autonomy, known as *vici*, *pagi*, or *castella*, were dependent on their nearest large center for a number of their needs, especially for the exercise of justice.

3   The true cities came into a single category, that of the *civitas*, although some retained their former title of colony or *municipium*. They had autonomy and a complete range of civic institutions.

The cities' institutions were broadly still those of the early Empire, modified to suit the changing times.

- The assembly of the citizens, the *populus*, still existed. It is attested in Africa until the end of the fourth century.

- The municipal council (*curia*), the *ordo* of the *curiales* (the new name for the decurions), played a more important role. In order to be admitted to it, one had to have a property qualification, although hereditary privilege was also involved in the process. The members of this assembly became responsible for the collection of taxes and for that reason were generally detested. This obligation weighed heavily enough on some for them, at least during difficult periods, to take refuge in the desert or in the clergy, all the more so since membership of the assembly was not confined to the rich.

- A variety of municipal posts existed, greater even than under the early Empire. The head of the magistrates, the curator of the city, had become the real mayor of the town, the *duumvir* serving only as his aide. The aedile and the quaestor no longer did anything much, except, as regards the second, in the financial field. The state also instituted the posts of "defender of the city" and, from 368 CE, "defender of the *plebs*," magistrates who had the duty of affording protection against oppressive provincial government. But the best protection lay in the backing of a good patron, especially against the abuses of tax collectors (*exactores*). Naturally, the most popular choices were priests – *flamines*, pontiffs, and augurs, and sometimes Christian clergy.

An inscription found at Orcistus in Phrygia (Anatolia) provides a good illustration of the importance of these institutions. The township, formerly a city, had been reduced to the rank of *vicus* and placed under the authority of its neighbor, Nacolia. It addressed a petition to Constantine, who re-established it in its former position of *civitas*. It could thus regain the bodies it had lost, *ordo*, *populus*, and magistracies.

Municipal life displayed an activity that can be measured, thanks to epigraphy, by following the development of public benefaction (see chapter 17). An examination of municipal life, as it was lived in these latter years, shows that the fourth-century towns enjoyed some prosperity, and that Romanization was more

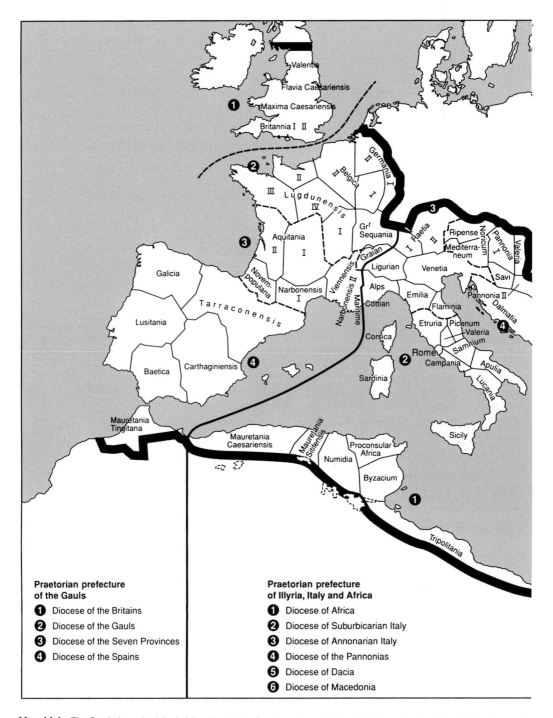

**Praetorian prefecture
of the Gauls**

❶ Diocese of the Britains
❷ Diocese of the Gauls
❸ Diocese of the Seven Provinces
❹ Diocese of the Spains

**Praetorian prefecture
of Illyria, Italy and Africa**

❶ Diocese of Africa
❷ Diocese of Suburbicarian Italy
❸ Diocese of Annonarian Italy
❹ Diocese of the Pannonias
❺ Diocese of Dacia
❻ Diocese of Macedonia

Map 16.1 The Empire's territorial administration in the fourth century CE (from R. Rémondon, *La Crise de l'Empire romain*, PUF, 1980)

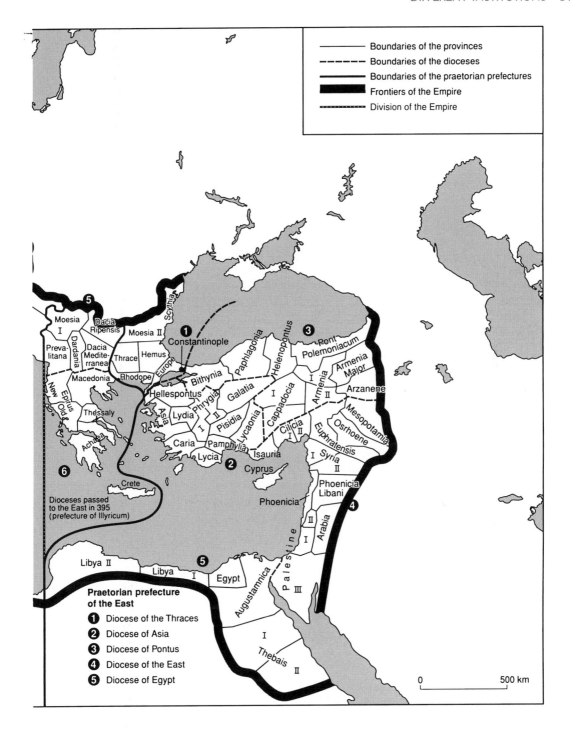

Boundaries of the provinces
Boundaries of the dioceses
Boundaries of the praetorian prefectures
Frontiers of the Empire
Division of the Empire

Dioceses passed
to the East in 395
(prefecture of Illyricum)

**Praetorian prefecture
of the East**

❶ Diocese of the Thraces
❷ Diocese of Asia
❸ Diocese of Pontus
❹ Diocese of the East
❺ Diocese of Egypt

0   500 km

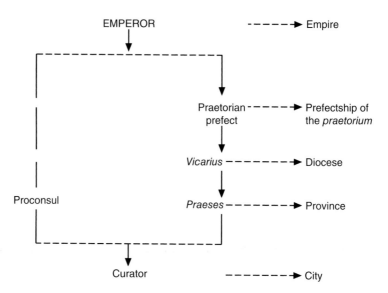

Figure 16.1 Territorial government

extensive than has often been believed. However, geographical, chronological, and social distinctions need to be made.

16.5 | An Absolute Monarchy

The Empire of the fourth century, like the early Empire, was ruled by an absolute monarchy. But imperial power now was more visible and oppressive. The number of employees in the service of the state certainly increased; bureaucracy became more meticulous and officious; and military men and state officials occupied a growing place in society.

17

A DIFFERENT SOCIO-ECONOMIC WORLD

Recovery and State Control

The economic recovery that was perceptible in the last quarter of the third century CE was furthered in the period of Diocletian. Signs of a fresh crisis, however, appeared after Julian's reign (361–363 CE). The legacy of the disorder of the third century, and the demands of the state, both civil and military, explain the characteristics peculiar to fourth-century society.

17.1 | The Economic Recovery

The character of economic life in the fourth century CE has more to do with the conditions in which it developed than with production itself.

Conditions

Because of the gaps in documentation, it is difficult to gauge the combination of circumstances that provided the general conditions of economic life. Nevertheless, one may trace the main outlines on the basis of the evidence of public benefaction and coinage.

Public benefaction This varied in inverse proportion to taxation, usurpations, and invasions. Therefore, it forms a good indicator of the prosperity of different periods and different regions.

In chronological terms, the case of Africa as shown by public benefactions is well known. Recovery is evident as early as 276, and was very clear under Diocletian. Civil war then caused a slowing down, which was followed by a new boom under Constantius II, and this reached its peak under Julian. Prosperity was then maintained until the time of Theodosius, but the late fourth century witnessed a return of crisis, which was plainly marked under his successor Honorius (395–423).

The study of public benefactions also allows us to discern the relative prosperity and vulnerability of various regions across the Empire. Gaul, Britain, and the provinces bordering the Rhine and Danube were particularly affected by the barbarian invasions. Egypt, except in Alexandria, had never developed a very active municipal life. Italy and Spain kept themselves going fairly well. In Anatolia, and also in the Syria of Libanius at Antioch, men still took a passionate interest in the affairs of their town. Africa too offers a good example of a healthy municipal condition. Three hundred and thirty-two construction sites have been counted there for the fourth century; and, in Proconsularis and Numidia, even the mountain areas were Romanized. On the other hand, these African projects were generally works of restoration, and the Mauretanias and Tripolitania did not keep up with the general trend.

Coinage Three dates mark important moments for the historian: 294, 301, and 311 CE. These punctuate the setting up of a new monetary order.

Under Aurelian, the failure of the Antoninianus became obvious. Gold and silver (real currency) had disappeared and the abundance of bronze (fiduciary currency) made all such issues unreliable. In response to these new circumstances, Aurelian deprived the Senate and the cities, with the exception of Alexandria, of the right to issue coinage. Instead, he had his own coins struck, mainly in provincial workshops, and with greater regularity. Gold reappeared, the Antoninianus was improved, and confidence in bronze was restored.

The first really major reform of the coinage took place under Diocletian in 294. A new system was set up, with new weights and new denominations. (The official maintenance of the bimetallic coinage should not hide the fact that, because of the greater commercial activity of the East, gold, which the East favored, assumed an increasing role in trade.)

The institution of this system provoked a serious financial crisis marked by a general rise in the cost of living. The state made efforts to react. In 300, it had an inquiry held throughout the Empire to establish the value of goods and labor. Then the edict on maximum prices (301), which we know from inscriptions, fixed a maximum for all prices and wages. The text of this edict, in Greek and Latin, was to be displayed in every province, and anyone contravening the regulations contained in it was liable to the death penalty. Whatever commentators may have written, this measure enjoyed some success: the rich were content because it contributed to stabilizing prices, the poor because it readjusted the lowest wages.

Box 17.1   Diocletian's monetary system: 294 CE

Metal	Name	Weight (in grams)	Remarks
Gold	*Aureus*	5.45	1/60 pound
Silver	*Argenteus*	3.41	1/96 pound
Bronze	*Follis*	>9	
	Neo-Antoninianus	2.90	1 neo-Antoninianus (real currency) = 2 denarii (account value)

The development that followed confirmed the trend that had begun toward the primacy of gold in trade, which was achieved around 309 and then embodied in official practice by Constantine, who decided in 311 to create the gold *solidus*, a coin of 4.55 g (1/72 pound) destined for a long future.

The monetary system of late antiquity stabilized. A sector of natural economy survived in the *annona*, and the monetary economy, which predominated, remained everywhere officially subject to the rule of the bimetallic system, even though it remained the case that the most used precious metals were silver in the West (outside of trade) and gold in the East.

Other conditions accompanied the fourth-century economic recovery. Unsurprisingly, there were few technological innovations. The only advance that deserves mention here is the spread of the water mill.

This advance was perhaps connected with a decline in population in those regions. Early authors frequently bewailed the depopulation that caused shortages of labor. Unfortunately, in the absence of population statistics, it is difficult to know what weight to attach to this stock literary theme of decline.

We have a better knowledge of the system of "colleges" or corporations, a social structure that formed a setting for economic life. A legacy from the early Empire, it underwent two major modifications in the fourth century, due mainly to Constantine: constraint and compulsory inheritance. These decisions are explained by the importance of certain associations, especially that of the ship-owners, for the provisioning of the two capitals. However, numerous workers, even in the towns, eluded this structure; and even in the case of the trade corpo-rations, it is essential to make a distinction between the political intentions, as revealed in the laws, and what really happened.

Activities

As a whole, these conditions seem to have been less favorable to economic activ-ity than those of the early Empire.

Agriculture Wheat still formed perhaps 90 percent of food consumption, and certainly still employed 90 percent of the agricultural workforce. Vineyards and olive groves, however, made progress. Vineyards were still spreading everywhere, but especially northward. Olive groves, which were far more delicate and sus-ceptible to climatic conditions, were developing mainly in Africa, which produced large surpluses for export, as indicated by discoveries of stamped amphorae. In the north, however, the consumption of beer and butter was far more common

Plate 17.1 Mosaic of a Roman country estate in Tunisia, fourth century CE. Bardo Museum, Tunis. C. M. Dixon

than that of wine and olive oil. And there were no new developments in livestock raising, except the propagation of the dromedary camel in Africa.

The change which had the greatest effect on agricultural life was the continuing concentration in the ownership of the land. Historians and sociologists (Max Weber as early as 1896) have long discussed this process. But some of the effects had been noted by the early authors, who lamented the fact that rural areas were becoming deserts and that some apparently productive lands had been abandoned.

There was still great diversity in the way the land was worked. Livestock raising was still partly carried on by semi-nomadic populations. For settled peoples, there was at first a great expansion of the colonist system, which after the third-century crisis became the usual form of working the land. The sons of *coloni* held onto the land by right of inheritance, but they were still tenants and remained sharecroppers. This entailed their supervision by the master, but at least it enabled them to escape the supervision of the state. Recent research reveals that they were less attached to the land than had once been believed, and notes a decline in the number of smallholdings. A series of wooden tablets discovered in modern Algeria and dating to the end of the fifth century CE contain estate records that show the persistence of this type of farm working in Africa. Written in cursive Latin, these are known as the Albertini tablets, after their discoverer, or as the Vandal tablets, after their authors, who belonged to the Germanic tribe of the Vandals. These peoples had crossed from Spain into north Africa earlier in the fifth century.

Though often subjected without distinction to the colonist regime, barbarians installed in the Empire were differentiated on the legal plane.

- The *dediticii*, those who had been conquered, had to pay a capital tax and perform military service; they lived on imperial or private estates.
- The "federates," those who had obtained a treaty (*foedus*) with Rome, had received the right of ownership (*commercium*).
- The *laeti* or "fortunate" (the Franks came into this category) provided recruits in exchange for land; they therefore occupied a position midway between the *dediticii* and federates.
- The *gentiles* (notably Sarmatians) enjoyed the same status as the *laeti*.

These newcomers supplied reinforcement to the workforce, but they also posed a problem, for they no longer became assimilated.

Craftsmanship The work of extracting precious and non- precious metals, stone and marble, etc., resumed its normal operation after the reunification of the Empire and the restoration of state authority.

Manufacturing activities, by contrast, went through considerable changes. Pottery production, in particular, was dispersed, with local, mediocre products having everywhere replaced the fine stamped pottery of the early Empire. The large Gaulish workshops had been swept away in the upheavals of the third century, with the exception of new centers of production in the Argonne. More generally, there were still private corporations of craftsmen. But they were increasingly subject to the requirements of the state, and independent businesses now coexisted with imperial workshops.

Trade State intervention in trade also became more insistent than before. A number of dealers were compelled to join corporations (*collegia*), where it was easier to keep an eye on them. Besides the *mercatores* (wholesale dealers, or merchants), who had to pay the *chrysargyre* (gold and silver), these included the mariners, water-carriers, and ship-owners who ensured Rome's food supplies, working with the department of the *annona*.

The return of peace favored trade. The barter system was still in use, although the monetary sector had never completely disappeared. Land and sea routes resumed the same traffic as under the early Empire. But although the West experienced a certain recovery, the East (Byzantium) showed the greatest dynamism: all roads no longer necessarily led to Rome.

On land, some new routes were developed. In northern Italy, Milan and Aquileia now played a leading role, and not only strategically. And a great northern road ran along the Rhine and Danube. Each region had its backbone: Tarragona–Cadiz in Spain, Carthage–Tebessa in Africa, Arles–Lyons–Boulogne or Trier in Gaul, the old Via Egnatia from Dyrrachium to Thessalonica in Macedonia, Nicomedia–Mopsuestia and Ephesus–Tarsus in Asia Minor, the coastal road and Strata Diocletiana (Damascus–Mesopotamia) in Syria, and lastly the valley of the Nile in Egypt.

Goods carried by sea used a more centralized network: Ostia was linked to Tarragona, Carthage, Cyrene, Alexandria, Antioch, and Ephesus. But the Red Sea, the Black Sea, and the Adriatic, by their comparative activity, threatened to alter the traditional balance.

17.2 | Society and the State

Main features

Society in the fourth century was more hierarchical than it had ever been. By means of proliferating laws the emperor defined, with increasing precision, the various hierarchies and the places within them. From the juridical point of view, there was a fundamental contrast between the elite of *honestiores* and the mass of *humiliores*, who did not have the right to equal treatment in the courts; for the same crime, the first were less severely punished than the second.

It was also undeniably a class society. The concentration of land properties already mentioned brought about a concentration of riches. An increasingly restricted minority grabbed a growing portion of the available possessions.

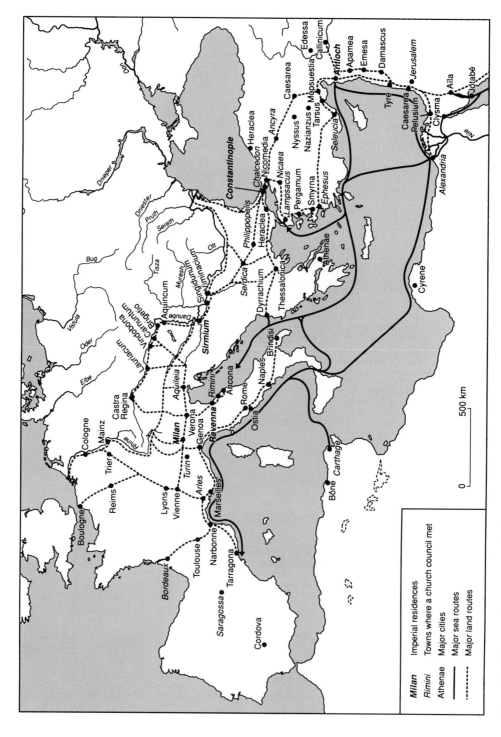

Map 17.1 Towns and the economy in the fourth century CE (from R. Rémondon, *La Crise de l'Empire romain*, PUF, 1980)

Milan Imperial residences
Rimini Towns where a church council met
Athenae Major cities
━━━ Major sea routes
┄┄┄ Major land routes

0   500 km

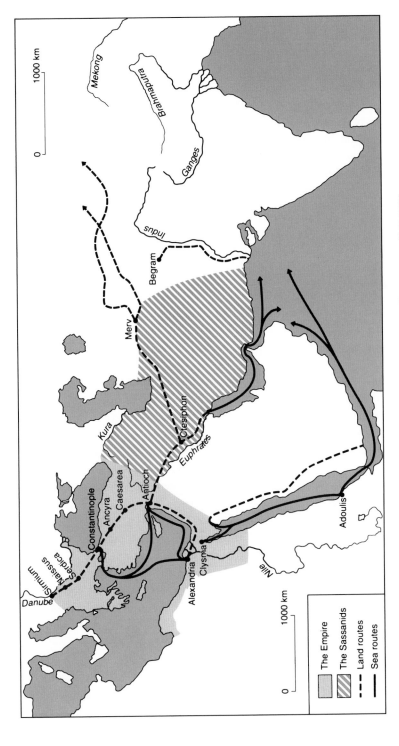

Map 17.2 Communication routes in the late fifth century CE (from R. Rémondon, *La Crise de l'Empire romain*, PUF, 1980)

The Empire

The Sassanids

Land routes

Sea routes

1000 km

1000 km

Danube
Sirmium
Naissus
Serdica
Constantinople
Ancyra
Caesarea
Antioch
Clysma
Alexandria
Nile
Adoulis
Euphrates
Ctesiphon
Kura
Merv
Begram
Indus
Ganges
Brahmaputra
Mekong

But the most striking feature was found elsewhere: the government, by its actions, seemed to be intent on forming a society of castes. The compulsory inheritance of occupation or place imposed by certain laws, for example, tended in this direction. Nevertheless, social mobility still existed, for many were not affected by such legislation, and it was also sometimes possible to evade it. However, bureaucracy, or rather the spying of the notaries, made state control increasingly pervasive and difficult to escape. In the face of pressures imposed by bureaucracy and the tax system, notables sometimes had no alternative but to enter the clergy or flee to the desert. Individual peasants, among others, might gain protection through patronage, entrusting themselves and their possessions to the governor, to high officials, or even to military officers, whose tenant farmers they became. The state attempted to limit this practice, even to ban it, but often in vain.

Social elites

A strict hierarchy had always been the defining characteristic of the Roman society, and it continued to be throughout this time. Social elites were defined by their role in the service of the state and by their wealth, which continued to grow.

At the apex was the imperial family, an extremely tiny minority who possessed power, immense fortunes, and various extraordinary honors.

A second exclusive group consisted of the rich, who were mainly land-owners. These were able to extend their influence over several cities and even over several provinces, gathering vast clienteles. Probus, for example, a member of the influential family of the Anicii (who held a praetorian prefectship almost uninterruptedly from 367 to 384) owned estates everywhere. Their vast geographical distribution enabled him to offset the disadvantage of weather hazards, so that he was assured of obtaining at least one good harvest each year. Quintus Aurelius Symmachus (a pagan senator and author in the predominantly Christian culture of the late fourth century) similarly possessed vast wealth.

The poet Ausonius was somewhat lower on the scale of riches. The owner of eight estates distributed across Aquitania, he was a provincial notable, and represents the more dynamic section of the municipal councils of the provinces. Men who belonged to the municipal elites could sometimes still penetrate to the heart of the Roman aristocracy.

The wealth sometimes survived well into the fifth century. The *Life* of the Christian saint Melania the Younger and the notes Palladius devoted to her familiarize us with the elites living in Spain at the time: immensely rich, they owned vast estates and were still very attached to classical culture. The hagiographers tell us that Melania plundered her inheritance to give to the poor. In the same period in Gaul, Sidonius Apollinaris of Lyons distinguished himself by the same characteristics of wealth and learning. In addition, he strove to serve both the church (becoming bishop of Clermont in 472) and the state.

Together with the possession of wealth, it was this service to the state in an official capacity which set one up to become a senator. Of course, birth still counted: theoretically, a *nobilis* had to be the son of a noble, although some newcomers had managed to work their way into the circle. Senatorial families still forged connections and alliances among themselves through marriage and adoption. Birth, wealth, and power – if they had these they might be tempted into the political game, as in their interventions in the usurpations of Maximus and Eugenius, and their opposition to the emperor in the affair of the altar of Victory (see chapter 19). Their relations with the current emperor were subject to variation – Diocletian, the "hammer of the aristocracy," curtailed their privileges by opening provincial posts to equestrians. Senators fared far better with Constantine.

Here we must distinguish between the two capitals of the Empire. The Roman Senate, the membership of which Constantine raised from 600 to about 2,000, made up of a minority of true Romans and a majority of Italians and provincials, still enjoyed great prestige, particularly the elite of this body – a prestige to which certain customs contributed, such as the holding of games on appointment to the rank of praetor, and the consuls' giving carved ivory tablets (diptychs) to a few privileged friends as New Year presents. The senators of Rome were attached to classical culture, which was still based on values such as *otium* (the refusal to do exacting paid work) and paganism (though Christianity slowly spread among the senatorial families).

An internal hierarchy was expressed in titles. Every senator was addressed as *clarissimus* ("most illustrious"). Constantine created the non-hereditary dignity of *patricius* (patrician) for the outstanding among them. And then, in the mid-fourth century, in the time of Valentinian I, senators were divided into three grades, *clarissimi* on the lowest rung, *spectabiles* at the intermediate level, and at the top *illustres*, who were few in number, spread then among only nine families. The instituting of this classification was no doubt connected with the fact that recruitment at that time had developed, with bureaucrats from Ravenna and German military men having come to join traditional Roman aristocrats. The title *clarissimus*, moreover, swiftly suffered devaluation, being conferred even on the elite of municipal notables.

Belonging to the Senate of Constantinople bestowed less prestige. First, the institution was relatively recent, something which mattered a great deal to the collective attitudes of the time. Second, entry to this assembly was comparatively easy. Certainly, the law demanded the exercise of an office; but it was necessary to allow co-optation. As a result, under Constantine and Constantius II, men who had emerged from the people – stenographers, fullers' sons, and so on – were to be found there. And again under Constantius, it was possible to become a senator and citizen of Constantinople at the same time. Themistius attempted to raise the standard of recruitment, calling on intellectuals and provincial notables as members, as the correspondence of Libanius shows.

Belonging to the Senate conferred greater prestige than did membership of the equestrian order. The equestrians had nevertheless assumed a large share in public life. In the course of the third century, and during the crisis, they had monopolized military duties; and at the beginning of the fourth century, when the bureaucracy started to develop on a large scale, they grabbed the posts of heads of department. As a result, under Diocletian, the smooth functioning of the state largely rested with them.

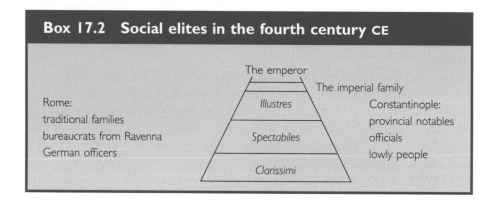

Box 17.2 Social elites in the fourth century CE

The emperor

The imperial family

Rome:
traditional families
bureaucrats from Ravenna
German officers

Constantinople:
provincial notables
officials
lowly people

Illustres

Spectabiles

Clarissimi

Paradoxically, it was between 312 and 326 CE that the equestrian order vanished. Early in the fourth century, many equestrians attained the rank of senator; and then, in 326, the main equestrian title, *vir egregius* ("distinguished man"), was abolished. There were then a good many equestrian *clarissimi*, and although the equestrian title *perfectissimus* survived, it was reserved for the holders of a few rare offices.

Historians have pondered over the causes of the disappearance of the equestrian order, and some have deemed it inexplicable. In fact, it would seem that it died of its own success and from the desertion of the state by the senatorial elites. The role played by equestrians, from Valerian to Diocletian, forced the state to recognize their merits; and the awarding of a prestigious title, without necessarily adding the material advantages linked with it, enabled the government to escape cheaply.

The middle classes

Here, the historian comes up against a methodological difficulty, for the very notion of a "middle" class is modern and raises problems in the absence of ancient statistics. Amount of wealth and participation in local government are considered criteria for this classification, but they are always to some extent arbitrary.

Among the easily identifiable groups are the *curiales* (members of a city council or *curia*), the new name for the former decurions. From the economic point of view, they are defined as land-owners whose estates rarely went beyond a city's boundaries. Because of that, they had a certain diversity: some lived fairly comfortably, others on the edge of poverty. All one needed to become a *curialis* was to own 25 *jugera* (6.25 ha), and the term in the end became a simple synonym for *possessor* (hereditary owner). Their situation deteriorated because of the burdens laid on them by the tax system, in addition to the consequences of the third-century crisis and obligatory benefaction. In each city, a commission of 10 members from among the decurions (*decemprimi* in the West, *dekaprotoi* in the East) had been charged at the end of the second century with the collection of taxes due from their municipality. Members of the assembly ended up being responsible for these payments out of their own pocket, so that they found themselves trapped between the government and their own citizens, who regarded them as "petty tyrants" (according to the fifth-century Christian writer Salvian). The honor became a burden, as revealed by a word play on *honos* ("honor") and *onus* ("burden"). Some fled, others entered the Senate or the clergy. Their plight varied greatly according to imperial policy: Constantine persecuted them, but Julian made efforts to lighten their burden.

To counterbalance those duties, prestige and honor accompanied the title of *curialis*, as is shown in the letters of Libanius, who lived in Antioch. The wealthiest ones, called *principales*, could enter the senatorial order, or could at least receive the title *clarissimus*. An inscription found at Timgad in Numidia indicates into which order those who had come to greet the governor had been admitted. This *ordo salutationis*, dating from the time of Julian, reveals the hierarchy that had been established in the province and in the municipal council.

> **Box 17.3 The *ordo salutationis* (provincial hierarchy)**
>
> Governor
>
> Senators
> Governor's cabinet
> Former priests of the imperial cult
> (Christian priests, excluded under Julian)
> Personnel of the provincial administration
> Simple *curiales*

Entry to the *curia* was prepared for by enrolling in a body of young people, the *iuvenes*. Here sons of notables, whether *honestiores* or *humiliores*, received paramilitary training, especially in the amphitheater – an inscription from Saldae (Bejaia, in modern Algeria) tells us that they were capable of manning the walls in the absence of regular troops and of repelling an enemy attack. They also celebrated pagan cults, and particularly honored Mars and Jupiter. Their cultic practiced involved transforming into sacrifices the executions of condemned men that took place in the arena.

Besides the land-owners, the members of other groups belonging to the middle class sometimes entered the *curiae*. In the lead were those officials who had some learning and were close to the government, which gave them some prestige. It is known that their numbers were increasing. To these should be added members of the liberal professions, lawyers, doctors, teachers, men esteemed for their culture but usually fairly poor, although the state financed a few professorial chairs.

The position of the Christian clergy depended largely on the attitude of the emperor. Emperors favorable to the new religion granted them exemption from duties (*munera*), and privileges such as the right to use the official postal service, the *cursus publicus*. The Christian clergy was a diverse body, including both sincere believers and fugitive *curiales*. Municipal priests enjoyed greater dignity than monks, at least in the eyes of their contemporaries.

The last group to be examined here are the soldiers. They served as government auxiliaries, which justified giving them a regular wage and exemption from certain charges. Their importance had grown with their numbers, but the entry of barbarians into the camps proportionately diminished the prestige traditionally attached to their profession. The soldiers belong to what we understand today as the lower strata of society.

The lower strata

The idea of the "lowly" or "humble" is equally difficult to define, again because of the gaps in documentation. Ancient biases, which conceptualized these out-groups as morally degenerate and socially dangerous, also complicate our understanding of the lower strata as presented in our historical texts. But, while bearing in mind the limitations of this subject, we can say that the term covers all those who lived in poverty or were excluded from power.

The working class included shopkeepers, artisans (either settled or itinerant), and peasants, the vast majority of whom had the status of *coloni*. The state embodied in corporations those crafts or trades that were essential to it for the provisioning of the capitals or for armaments. It was a novelty of the time that barbarians were settling in the Empire but no longer sought to integrate in it.

Slavery persisted, but its role in production had dwindled still further. It provided some farm workers, craftsmen, and tradesmen, as well as domestic servants and prostitutes. The church, which had never condemned the institution of slavery, had eventually resigned itself to its existence, confining itself to recommending masters to practice Christian charity. But harsh treatment increased, as legislation indicates. Heavy lead collars have been found for fugitive slaves who had been recaptured, bearing the inscription: "I am a fugitive slave; return me to my master."

The periods of crisis drove many men into itinerant groups that made their living without regular employment. Among them one could encounter charlatans, army deserters, landless peasants, magicians, astrologers, vagabonds, and brigands. Such a troupe were the Bagaudes, who ravaged Gaul between 284 and 286 CE led by Aelius and Amandus.

Africa witnessed the development of the much-discussed *Circumcellio* movement. The "Circumcellions" were agricultural day laborers without permanent employment, especially in the slack seasons. They first appear in a religious context as supporters of the heretical Christian Donatists, which earned them the condemnation of orthodox sources (Optatus of Milevis, and later St Augustine). Then, chiefly between 340 and 347, the movement was transformed into a peasant revolt, largely through the impetus provided by two local leaders, Axido and Fasir. Crossing Numidia, the Circumcellions incited slaves to rebel and terrorized masters and creditors, which caused the Donatist bishops themselves to call on the army. In light of this unexpected turnaround, the Circumcellions again gave a religious aspect to their actions, making a cult of their dead, whom they elevated to martyrdom.

Ultimately, fourth-century society seems to have been fragmented into groups, or cells, rather than stratified in horizontal layers. Another feature of the period was the new balance between town and country.

17.3 | Towns and Villas

On this subject there is a traditional image of the fourth century CE: the decline of the towns and a retreat to the countryside. Recent research has called that picture into question.

Urban centers

Urban life continued, though obviously accompanied by changes. The third-century crisis had caused much destruction and material difficulty, and had necessitated the creation of new administrative structures. After the return to order, towns displayed new features.

- Many towns surrounded themselves with a rampart or defensive wall. These walls were not all built at around the same time, but rather at various times during the second half of the third century and during the course of the fourth. Moreover, some, but not all, were built in haste using materials taken from previous buildings.
- In general, these structures enclosed a more limited surface area than that occupied under the early Empire, either because the town was smaller or because part of it was left outside. In some cases, we may note a revival of the suburbs in the fourth century; in others, it seems that excluded areas were abandoned for good (for example, at Aix-en-Provence the dead were buried in a place that had formerly been part of the town).
- The setting up of schools, encouraged and assisted by the municipal authorities, reflected the desire to defend classical culture and tradition. The survival of Roman paganism and the rebirth of native cults expressed the same sentiment.

- The expansion of Christianity brought about the appearance of complexes of episcopal buildings (cathedral, baptistery, and bishop's residence).

There were limits to this revival, however. Some areas were never rebuilt, there is no evidence of any new town, and restorations of monuments by far outstripped the building of new ones. Moreover, crisis reared its head again at the end of the fourth century, mainly in the West.

The two largest cities were, of course, the two capitals. In the middle of the fourth century, Rome still preserved its unchallenged primacy. The emperors continued to strive to beautify it (Diocletian's and Constantine's baths, the grandiose basilica of Maxentius and Constantine). In the midst of pagan Rome a Christian Rome was born. The first Roman churches, the *tituli*, were in fact private homes used for worship – there were 25 at the beginning of the fourth century. In Constantine's period came the great basilicas, St Peter's and chiefly the Lateran, then later Santa Maria Maggiore (p. 543–4). Outside the city, catacombs such as those of Domitilla and St Callistus became spaces of tribute to the dead, and especially the martyrs.

The Empire also possessed other great cities that were at least as active as they had been formerly.

In the East, Alexandria, still cosmopolitan (with Greek, Syrian, and Jewish populations) and prosperous (craftsmen, trade), remained a cultural capital. The spread of a Christianity at first heterodox (Gnosticism) and then more traditional (Dionysius, Athanasius) was marked in the landscape by the appearance of catacombs west of the town, and later by churches.

In the fourth century Antioch reached its peak, with an estimated population between 150,000 and 200,000. It owed its rise to the fact that it sometimes played the role of capital, and to its economic activities, notably trade with Mesopotamia and the non-Roman East. Like Alexandria, Libanius' Antioch was characterized by its cosmopolitanism and the presence of a good number of Christians.

The West also had its large centers, at the head of which was Carthage, which archaeologists continue to excavate. Its vitality may be explained chiefly by its port, which provided part of Rome's food supplies. Large dwellings have been found there (the "hunting house," probably the headquarters of an equestrian club, the "house with the *cachette*"), and many large and beautiful mosaics (the mysterious "lady of Carthage"). And in the time of St Augustine the town had no fewer than 12 churches.

In the far north, an important city was Trier (Augusta Treverorum), an imperial residence from the time of Constantine, where palaces, basilicas, temples, and then churches were built. A mint and arms-makers (siege weapons and shields) contributed to its prosperity. The praetorian prefectship of the Gauls had its headquarters there, and when it was transferred to Arles, in the fifth century, difficult times ensued.

Another great western town was Milan (Mediolanum). It owed its expansion to its position in the center of a prosperous region and the easy communications

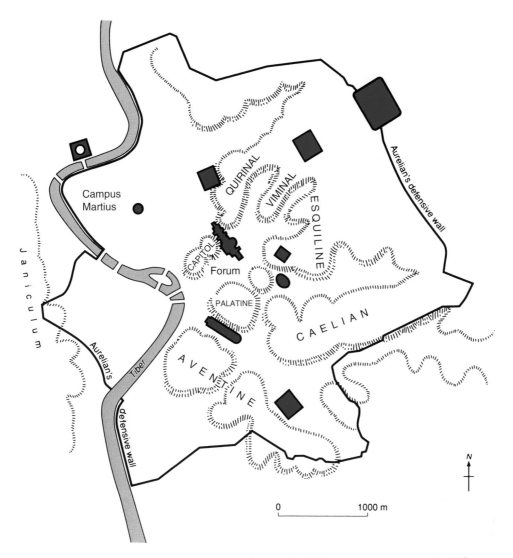

Figure 17.1   Rome in the fourth century CE (from A. Aymard and J. Auboyer, *Rome et son empire*, PUF, 1980)

it offered with the frontier regions on the Rhine and Danube. It too was used as an imperial residence.

Rural centers

In terms of the growth of economic centers, the most striking feature of the fourth century was the development, mainly in the West, of the rural villa. Although we must not imagine a vast exodus from the town to the country, it is

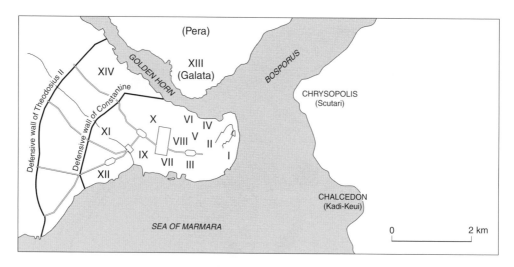

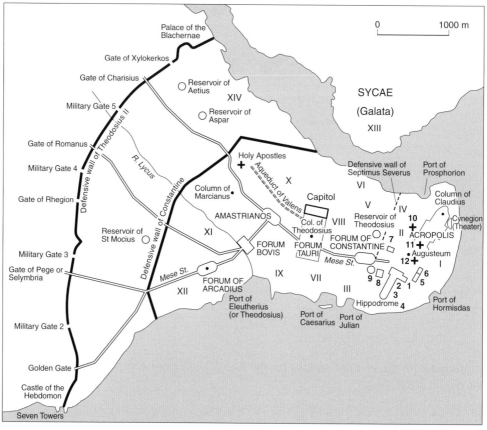

Figure 17.2 Constantinople in the fifth century CE (from R. Rémondon, *La Crise de l'Empire romain*, PUF, 1980) Figure key: I–XIV Regions of Constantinople 1 Chalke (vestibule of the Grand palace) 2 Grand palace 3 Daphne palace 4 Palace of Hormisdas 5 Magnaura (annex of the palace) 6 Meeting hall of the Senate 7 Basilica (tribunal and, from the time of Julian, a library) 8 Palace of Lausus (Museum of Art) 9 Cistern of Philoxenus 10 Theotokos of Chalkoprateia 11 Saint Irene 12 Saint Sophia

Plate 17.2 Roman mosaic from the hunting villa of the emperor Maximian, built 293–305 CE. A bullock-cart carries wild animals to the amphitheater. Piazza Armerina, Sicily. © Art Archive/Dagli Orti

nonetheless certain that this expansion reveals a shift of numerous centers of demographic gravity.

In Africa, archaeology reveals many fortified farms, or villas with towers, as depicted in the great mosaics of Carthage and Tabarka. In Sicily, there is the vast dwelling decorated with beautiful mosaics at Piazza Armerina. Despite the assumption that it was occupied by Maximian until 309, there is nothing to prove that it was in fact used as a retreat for the Tetrarch. Then there is the villa of Montmaurin in southern Gaul, which covered 4 ha in its central part, including over 200 rooms, and 18 ha overall. Many other examples of this type of residence could be quoted, such as the "small inheritance" of Ausonius or the villa of Nennig – the movement indeed reached as far as the Germanies.

17.4 | Expansion and Lifestyles

The fourth century experienced an economic recovery accompanied by a reorganization of society, both developments marked by much greater state intervention. Although many traditions endured in the ways that life was lived, with the town preserving a great importance, the powerful paid more attention to the countryside than ever before. This material expansion, with its limitations, was not, however, the only upheaval in an era that also had its renaissance.

18

BETWEEN PAGANISM AND CHRISTIANITY

For some decades now, historians studying the third and fourth centuries CE have for the most part been reaching the same conclusion: after the crisis of the third century, the limits of which can be put into perspective, we are in the presence not of a decline of civilization, but of a rebirth.

18.1 | The Fourth-Century CE Renaissance

The military, political, and economic difficulties of the third century did not result in a general decline in intellectual and artistic activities. Quite the reverse: in certain fields, creative artists improved their production techniques still further. This is especially so in the case of sculpted busts and sarcophagi. Some historians even consider the period to mark a kind of pinnacle in those fields. The art of mosaics especially developed throughout the fourth century: immense tessellated pavements with heavy ornamental foliage adorn the grand residences. The mosaics produced in North Africa, notably at Carthage and Tabarka, have encouraged a belief in the existence of an African school, to which the decoration of the villa at Piazza Armerina in Sicily, among others, has been attributed (at least five master craftsmen worked there early in the fourth century). We must, however, note the limits of this renaissance, which did not equally affect all sectors of intellectual and artistic production, as we shall see below.

Roman elements

Because of the many unifying elements that survived, it is certainly still possible to speak of Roman art and literature.

Fundamentally, classical culture remained an ideal to which all subscribed. Homer, Cicero, and Virgil were unreservedly admired. For a very long time Rome had been the model, and consolation for the real or imagined ills of the present was sought in a quest for the past. Consequently, the restoration of monuments and reading the works of earlier authors tended to prevail over the creation of new works.

Education went through four levels: a young man passed through the hands of a *litterator*, or primary school teacher; a *grammaticus*, or secondary school teacher; a *rhetor*, or teacher of rhetoric; and lastly a specialist teacher (law, philosophy, etc.). Students, like those of Libanius, generally belonged to the privileged social groups. Schools multiplied. For rhetoric, there was a choice between numerous centers, both in the West (Rome, Autun, Bordeaux, Milan, Carthage) and in the East (Athens, Constantinople, Antioch, Alexandria). For law, one still had to go to Rome or Beirut. The state created chairs and granted exemptions.

This spread of education did not prevent the proliferation of superstitious beliefs, a staple of Roman civilization for centuries. Many lives were ruled by astrology, which claimed that humans were ruled by the movements of heavenly bodies. The observation of nature also encouraged a belief in magic, which claimed to be able to compel the gods through the action of spirits. Alchemy sought to transform base metals into gold. Practices of theurgy ("divine-work") included meditation and invocation of the divine, and promised miracles and apparitions. Spell-casting tablets multiplied during the fourth century. At a mystical ceremony a magic text was inscribed on a papyrus, or a tablet of wood or metal, mostly lead, and then placed in a tomb or shaft. These tablets reveal what preoccupied people's thoughts – love, revenge, winning on the horses, and bumper harvests.

The emperors themselves were not immune to the spiritual challenges of the times. Constantius II is said to have lived permanently in superstitious fear. He banned anyone from casting his horoscope, on pain of death. And the pagan Julian, referred to by Christian sources as "the apostate" ("the rebel"), believed in theurgy.

A break in unity

Though all minds shared the same taste for the past and the supernatural, some elements of diversity were beginning to spread. Under the early Empire, unifying trends had prevailed: Rome, the emperor, and his family formed universal examples. A change in artistic production has been noted that came about in Constantine's period, which was one of transition. In the middle of the fourth century, there was great variety in works, not only between one region and another, but also between one studio and another.

Moreover, certain facts of life that had their origin in the early Empire became more pressing during the fourth century. First, artists and intellectuals were trapped between autonomy and dependence. Few had the means to be truly free; most depended on patrons. All had to reckon with the weight of political power, the church, and dominant attitudes, constraints that were more stifling than in the preceding centuries. Second, increasingly often, a choice had to be made between Greek and Latin. The Empire remained officially bilingual, but the inhabitants of the East became less interested in Latin, while fewer and fewer westerners used Greek.

Lastly, there was the conflict that set pagans against Christians, a divergence that most marked the spirit of the times, collective attitudes, literature, and art. However, in their struggle they also influenced each other: the pagans, turning away from the cheerfulness of popular Epicureanism, vied in austerity with Christian morality, justifying this attitude now by neo-Platonism rather than Stoicism. Meanwhile, the Christians tried, by "baptizing" pagan elements as Christian, to graft the new faith and culture onto the traditions of the pre-Christian world.

18.2 | Paganism on the Defensive

Here one must beware of a misleading anachronism: at the beginning of the fourth century all was not lost for paganism, which later even found itself in the role of persecutor once again, and which could rely on an increasingly elaborate philosophy.

The diversity of paganism

The same pantheon was to be found as under the early Empire, with the same rites, though with variations. If indigenous gods and traditional Roman gods (Jupiter) appear to be less venerated, that is perhaps because many of their worshipers lived in rural areas, where the use of inscriptions and sculptures was not as widespread as in urban centers.

The imperial cult persisted and developed, passing through three phases. At first it preserved all its political and religious strength, and was even reinforced under Diocletian. Next, under Constantine, it was maintained, but its content was less clearly defined, although its celebration could still include gladiatorial combats as well as sacrifices. The rescript of Hispellum, which created and organized this kind of celebration in Umbria at the time of Constantine and his sons, corresponds with this phase. Lastly, in the official Christian era, imperial cult was emptied of all sacred content and transformed into a civic and social demonstration. Even before then, in the time of Diocletian, the ecclesiastical Council of Elvira which took place in Baetica (dated to 300/303 CE) had permitted Christians to be pagan priests, allowing them to fulfill the civic, public part of their office, provided they abstained from performing sacrifices. And long after the Christianization of the Empire, *flamines* and *sacerdotales* are attested in Africa, up to the time of Vandal domination, although by then those titles meant nothing more than membership to the local social elite.

Pagan fervor also affected the eastern cults, which reached their peak early in the fourth century. At that time, they had more followers than ever, but only in urban and military circles, and became even more elitist. That aspect was strengthened by the adherence of intellectuals like the emperor Julian, who imparted a philosophical form to pagan myths.

The attack on paganism came mainly from a few emperors, and was thus an intensely political phenomenon. Although he did not completely adopt the Christian faith until fairly late, Constantine, in 331 CE, dealt paganism an unobtrusive but much harsher blow than has sometimes been thought. Inspired by piety and/or political expediency, the law of that year ordering an inventory of temple possessions resulted in confiscations that provided the funds for the building of Constantinople. It destroyed paganism's economic power, a weakening that had considerable consequences.

His son Constantius II was bold enough to attack pagan practices themselves. By a law of 356, he ordered the banning of sacrifices and the closure of certain temples. That decision, however, seems to have applied only to the East.

Under Valentinian I and Valens, there was a period of toleration; the first, despite his faith, did not wish to interfere in religious affairs, and the second was more concerned with heretics and schismatics than with pagans.

The imperial measures against paganism do not appear to have met with all the success hoped for, since they had to be renewed. They recur in a group of measures taken by Gratian and chiefly by Theodosius, the great enemy of paganism. In 381, sacrifices involving bloodshed were forbidden once again. In 385, the ban was extended to the reading of entrails. This policy encouraged fanatical Syrian monks who in 386 set about destroying pagan sanctuaries, provoking a protest from Libanius (his discourse *On Behalf of the Temples*). The Syrians had their imitators in Egypt and Africa. Finally, in 391, the emperor banned the celebration of pagan cults in Rome and Alexandria, and in 392 throughout the Empire.

The concept of martyrdom had never been part of pagan traditions. Nevertheless, a pagan backlash occurred. Intellectuals displayed their contempt for Christianity as a religion that was deemed foreign, simplistic, and popular, not to mention dangerous to the state. They proclaimed their respect for pagan traditions, and showed their capacity for renewal through philosophy. Henotheism is a result of the philosophical quests of the times.

Here we must establish some geographical distinctions. It is agreed that the West remained more faithful to pagan traditions, especially Gaul and Illyria, but that Africa was more receptive to Christianity.

Similarly, in social terms, some groups showed greater attachment to the pagan past, and thus rejected Christianity. These groups included aristocrats from the highest nobility (Symmachus) and intellectuals (Iamblichus, Libanius), but also humble peasants (the word "pagan" originates with *paganus*, meaning "country dweller") – an inscription from Arykanda in Lycia informs us of a petition by such folk against the Christians. It was the same with the soldiers, especially in the West – Constantine's army at the "Milvian Bridge" and Julian's in Gaul certainly did not worship Christ. This is doubtless explained by soldiers' attachment to tradition, and the fact that recruitment took place mainly in rural areas and among barbarians.

Chronology 18.1	The persecution of paganism

331	Inventory of temple possessions, confiscations.
341	First ban on pagan sacrifices.
356	In the East, ban on sacrifices, closing of temples.
381	Ban on sacrifices.
after 382	Paganism rejected as state religion: the altar of Victory is removed from the Curia.
385	Ban on sacrifices and examination of the victims' entrails.
386	Destruction of temples in Syria, Egypt, and Africa.
391	Ban on private pagan worship in Rome; destruction of the Serapeum in Alexandria.
392	Ban on all forms of pagan cult in the Empire.
399	Destruction of rural pagan temples and the temple of Caelestis in Carthage.
435	Renewed ban on pagan sacrifices.

Consequently, this pagan resistance was fitful (see also chapter 19). Julian's policy, which re-established paganism in 361 and persecuted Christians from 362, did not outlive him. The affair of the altar of Victory and the senatorial resistance to its removal from the *curia* by Gratian (382), marked paganism's last great battle (382–402). In 384, Quintus Aurelius Symmachus, prefect of Rome, sent an unsuccessful petition to Gratian's successor, Valentinian II, asking for the restoration of the altar in the senate house. Symmachus' request for religious tolerance was strongly opposed by Ambrose, the bishop of Milan, and the debate between the two constitutes an invaluable source on the intellectual struggles between paganism and Christianity in the fourth century. The usurpation of Eugenius (393–394) must be placed in this context. He was supported, if not pushed, by pagan aristocrats hoping for the re-establishment of their religion. The battle of the River Frigidus, in which Eugenius died, marked the end of polytheism's political and military hopes.

Having lost its wealth in 331, and the state in 394, paganism took refuge in the souls of soldiers and peasants and the hearts of a few intellectuals. It nevertheless achieved some important work in the fourth century, in both the literary and the artistic field.

The works of pagan intellectuals

When we look at the written works, the first notable characteristic is the language of our texts.

Philosophers wrote primarily in Greek. In Gallienus' court, Plotinus created the neo-Platonism that pervades his *Enneads*. He influenced the Athenian rhetorician Longinus and had many disciples, chiefly Porphyry and Iamblichus. This doctrine, characterized by an elevated spirituality and austere morality, permeated the entire fourth century.

The emperor Julian was also among the Hellenists. He wrote theoretical treatises (*Against the Galileans*, *On Helios, the King*, *On the Mother of the Gods*), speeches (*Panegyrics*), and letters (see also chapter 19).

Libanius, a teacher of rhetoric from Antioch, moderate in all things, left mostly speeches (65 are known, including *On the Death of Julian*) and letters. Thanks to him we have been able to describe the student world and municipal life of his homeland, and his works contain much information about the culture of his times.

The output of works in Latin was far larger and may be separated into three main genres: oratory, history, and poetry.

Oratory This is illustrated by *Twelve Latin Panegyrics*, a collection of eulogies of emperors composed in a fairly pure Latin, for the most part in Gaul, notably by Eumenius of Autun. In the late fourth century, Symmachus, who attained the prefectship of Rome in 384, was renowned not only for his wealth but for his eloquence, which pervaded his speeches and letters.

History This inspired Latin writers even more. The *Augustan History* is presented as a series of biographies aiming to extend the work of Suetonius. These are ostensibly composed by six senators living under Diocletian and Constantine. We now know that, in fact, the whole work was written in about 400 by a modest *grammaticus* who was expressing the viewpoint of the moderate pagan aristocracy. Aurelius Victor aspired to continue the work of Livy. Prefect of Rome under Theodosius, he wrote a work on the *Caesars*, which was abridged in an *Epitome*, as was often done at the time. It was the historical works of Tacitus that were used as a model and starting-point by Ammianus Marcellinus, an army officer from Antioch. The perspective that permeates his *Histories*, which extends Tacitus' narrative up to 378 (only his narrative between 353 and 378 remains), shows that he was a moderate pagan.

Poetry Here, three names attract attention. According to certain authors, Ausonius was converted to Christianity; but there is no trace of this faith in his little poems (*The Moselle, Roses*). Originally from Bordeaux, he had been private tutor to Gratian, who made him governor of Gaul and later of other provinces. Claudian, though born in Egypt, wrote biting satires in Latin, in the service of Stilicho (see chapter 19). Rutilius Namatianus, a Gaul from a great family, returning from Rome to his native country in 417, related his *Return* in a poem in which he eulogizes Rome and its civilization.

Lastly, in Macrobius we have a different perspective. A friend of Symmachus, he left in the *Saturnalia* a series of dissertations that aim to summarize his encyclopedic knowledge.

Art in pagan tradition

We must first recall the renaissance that took place in Gallienus' time in spite of the crisis. As we have seen, it was outstanding chiefly for the production of busts and sarcophagi. The sarcophagi fall into two major categories: those featuring a philosopher, and Dionysiac sarcophagi, which are characterized by lively, baroque ornamentation for the rich, and by a *pointilliste* style and strigils (striated lines) for the less well-off.

Artistic development did not cease in the fourth century. Under Diocletian, Rome remained the city of cities (evidenced by public projects such as Diocletian's baths). But the provincial palaces (Diocletian's residence at Salonae) and great country villas (Piazza Armerina with its famous mosaics) assumed importance. At the time, there was both a court art (as suggested by the sculptural complex of *The Tetrarchs*; see plate 15.1) and a private art (sarcophagi were now adorned with scenes from everyday life; the Dionysiac carvings, still baroque, showed processions).

Rome maintained its urban pre-eminence in the time of Constantine (arch and baths), but Constantinople gained the rank of second capital, and towns such as Trier, Arles, Autun, Antioch, and Alexandria underwent great development.

The late fourth century produced several major works. African mosaics, already flourishing at the beginning of the century, continued to do well (Carthage, Tabarka). Sculpture is illustrated by the bronze statue known as the Colossus of Barletta (from its current location in the namesake Apulian city), which probably represents the emperor Honorius (395–423). And a new form of art, ivory work, made its appearance with the consular diptychs, New Year gifts given by consuls to their friends.

Plate 18.1 Colossus of Barletta, identified with various eastern emperors of the fifth century CE, and dated to that time. Alinari Archives-Anderson Archive, Florence

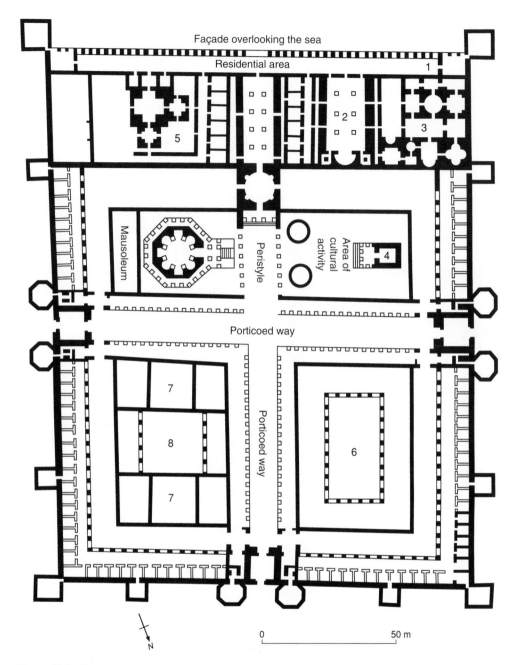

Figure 18.1 The palace of Diocletian near Salonae (from R. Bianchi-Bandinelli, *Rome, la fin de l'art antique*, Gallimard, 1970)

Figure key: 1 Promenade 2 Library 3 Apartments 4 Temple 5 Dining room 6 Imperial guard 7 Stables 8 Outbuildings

However, it would not be fair to reduce fourth-century civilization to its pagan aspect. Christianity, too, played an important role in the culture of the times. But as is the case in the early centuries of Christianity, it cannot be understood without an account of Judaism.

18.3 | Judaism between the Empire and the Church

In Roman eyes, belonging to Judaism meant belonging to both a nation and a religion. The defeats of 68–70 and 132–135 CE had two consequences for Judaism. First, Pharisaism prevailed, combining strictness in the monotheistic faith and rites with toleration in politics (although Rome had been universally detested by Pharisaism's adherents). Second, the diaspora grew and spread. It had always been strong in the East in Mesopotamia, and thus among the Persians, and in the Roman sphere at Alexandria and Antioch and in Anatolia and Greece. It now reached the West – although Rome itself had had a large Jewish colony for a long time – with Italy and Africa (Carthage) seeming to have received more Jews than Spain and Gaul. Each community (this is the primary meaning of the Greek word *synagogē*, "synagogue") had a hierarchy of dignitaries: the *archon* (leader), clerk, and "father" and "mother" of the synagogue (honorific titles).

From the economic point of view, there is nothing to make us think that the Jews were any different from the other inhabitants of the Empire. They expended their energies in the religious field. It was agreed that the writing down of the Law had been completed. From the second to the fourth century, a commentary was undertaken, and together these made up the Talmud. This work of commentary was carried out by two schools, one at Tiberias, the other in Mesopotamia, who collected the opinions of the rabbis and rearranged them into several treatises. The first produced the Talmud of Jerusalem (in fact, of Tiberias), and the second the Talmud of Babylon ("Talmud" thus refers to the Gemara as well as to the whole).

Box 18.1   The Talmud

Talmud =
1   Mishna ("recital" of the Law) + Gemara ("commentaries" on the Law)
2   Halaka ("rules" of conduct) or prescriptive parts + Aggada ("story") or narrative parts
Midrash = collection (of homilies)

Plate 18.2 Arch of Constantine in the Roman Forum, constructed 312–315 CE. The emperor makes a state sacrifice of the ox, boar, and ram. The panel was taken from a monument of Marcus Aurelius, with the face of the emperor re-cut to represent Constantine. C. M. Dixon

The synagogues (the word means both the assembly and the place in which it meets) resembled vast private homes; but there was a room for prayer, with benches, and a throne for the rolls of the Torah. The one at Dura-Europus is from before 256; those at Tiberias and Hammam-Lif in Tunisia seem to be later. The cemeteries were catacombs (Villa Torlonia in Rome) or groups of underground chambers (Palestine, Gamarth near Carthage).

The aesthetic quality of Jewish art, which borrowed much from paganism (mosaics of Hammam-Lif), influenced Christianity. Among its iconographic

Plate 18.3 Ivory leaf of a diptych, c.450 CE, showing the apotheosis of an emperor, possibly Antoninus Pius. C. M. Dixon

subjects, only the seven-branched candelabra, the menorah, remained a purely Jewish symbol; it is found on mosaics and lamps. Old Testament scenes (paintings at Dura-Europus) were also used by Christians.

Relations between the Jews and Christians had always been hostile, and they did not improve in the fourth century. Before the time of Constantine, the Jews had sometimes been the persecutors; subsequently, they often became the persecuted.

18.4 | Christianity Takes the Offensive

Between Christians, Jews, and pagans, relations were complex, turning now to confrontation, now to appeasement, with the three religions always influencing one another. Everything depended on the balance of power. The "new faith" achieved swifter and greater success in the East. Persecuted under the Tetrarchy, the church found "peace" under Constantine, and then in its turn changed into an agent of persecution, chiefly under Gratian and Theodosius (as we shall see in chapter 19).

The development of Christian doctrine

The Christians believed that Christ is God. It had then to be explained how he could be simultaneously also the Son of God and part of a Holy Trinity completed by the Father and the Holy Ghost. Strict Christian monotheism forbade any compromise with paganism in such matters, as well as any worship of the gods in Rome's traditional pantheon and any acceptance of the imperial cult.

The Christians' fundamental beliefs were set out in two series of books. They preserved the message of the Jewish scriptures in the Old Testament (on condition that it was interpreted according to the teachings of Christ). Christ's teaching, the "Good News" (*evangelia*, in Greek), and some treatises that accompanied it formed the New Testament. However, the Christians rejected any contribution from Judaism later than the birth of Christ, placing the Talmud on the same level as pagan mythology.

Theory brought about a deepening of the doctrine, embodied most enduringly in the works of the Fathers of the Church, notably Basil, John Chrysostom, Gregory of Nazianzus, and Augustine. The golden age of this movement occurred

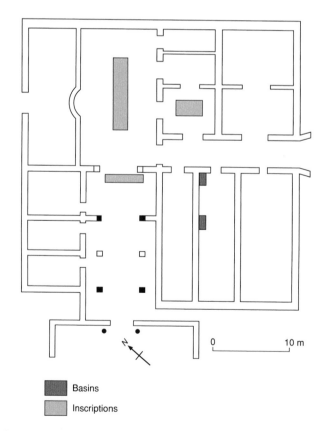

0   10 m

Basins

Inscriptions

Figure 18.2   Plan of synagogue at Hammam-Lif

in the second half of the fourth century. Points of argument could be debated in assemblies that brought together the elite of clerics, in regional synods and councils, or in ecumenical councils, where there gathered, in theory, bishops from the whole inhabited world (in Greek, *ecumene*). This lively and multifaceted interaction, however, also brought divergences in its wake, leading to schisms and heresies.

A break within the church over disciplinary matters was called a "schism": a minority would break away to signify its disagreement over a practical measure. African Donatism belonged to this category. One Caecilian had been ordained bishop of Carthage in 312. Because one of his consecrators had previously "yielded" sacred objects at the time of a persecution and was thus considered a "traitor," some members of the African church considered the ceremony to be worthless, and eventually elected Donatus as a rival bishop. The movement spread. The Donatists denied that sacraments given by "traitors" had any validity. They provoked riots over the possession of churches, and, reinforced by the Circumcellions, they waged a real war of religion (347). However, contrary to what has sometimes been written, their movement never had an ethnic or a social motive. They had been condemned in 314 at the Synod of Arles; they were then attacked by Optatus of Milevis in around 360–365, and later by St Augustine; and the great episcopal conference of 411 in Carthage ended in the dissolution of their movement.

The fourth century was also marked by heresies, that is breaks within the church over theological matters. The most important was Arianism. Arius, a priest in Alexandria, claimed that only the Father was God, and the Son merely a man. Arius was condemned by the Council of Nicaea in 325, but his message spread. It reached the West much earlier than has sometimes been said, extending through northern Italy, Illyria, and the Danubian provinces, and secondarily in Gaul and Spain. The doctrine was deepened in the middle of the fourth century, notably by the theologian Maximinus. It reached the Goths as a result of the preaching of Wulfila, beginning in 350, but it was not the Goths who brought Arianism into northern Italy (on their arrival in the fifth century it had long been present there). After numerous debates and conflicts, Arianism was definitively condemned, and ultimately disappeared.

Box 18.2   The Arian heresy

1	Strict Arians (homoeans)	Father is God, Son is man, Son is subordinate to Father.
2	Extremist Arians (anomoeans)	Father is totally different from Son.
3	Strict Nicaeans (homoousians)	Father and Son are same substance.
4	Moderate Nicaeans (homoiousians)	Father and Son are alike but not consubstantial.

A different source of heresy left its mark on the fifth century, the Monophysite argument. Egyptian clerics had affirmed "the single composite nature," human and divine, of Christ (Monophysitism). In Antioch, Nestorius took the side of the duality of Christ's nature, saying that Christ possessed both a human *and* a divine nature. Two ecumenical councils were convened. The first, at Ephesus (431), condemned Nestorianism; the second, at Chalcedon (451), rejected Monophysitism.

Box 18.3   Ecumenical councils

325	Nicaea	Arianism	Condemned (homoousian success)
360	Constantinople I	Arianism	Accepted (homoean success)
381	Constantinople II	Arianism	Condemned (return to Nicaea)
431	Ephesus	Monophysitism	Adopted (Nestorianism condemned)
451	Chalcedon	Monophysitism	Rejected

Christian practice

Christians followed these arguments with passionate interest. In social terms, the majority belonged to the poorer classes, *tenuiores* and slaves who expected alms from their more fortunate brothers. Notables had, however, joined them. There is evidence of these early in the fourth century, when some Christians wanted to enjoy the prestige attached to the title of *flamen*, and on this point consulted the Council of Elvira, which, as we have seen, gave them permission on condition that they refrained from making sacrifices. Within the church, the rich formed only a minority, whether clerics like St Cyprian or laymen. They were those who could have the advantage of a "privileged burial," for example having their tomb placed under a mosaic inside a church.

All were united for a certain number of ceremonies that punctuated Christian life. Several sacraments existed at that time. Entry into the community could be marked by baptism, which was, however, commonly deferred until one's death-bed, as in Constantine's case, because it erased sins. But infant baptism was also practiced. In all instances, baptism involved immersion in a vat of water. The eucharist, a communion meal at which bread and wine were consumed, regularly gathered the faithful together, and penance was performed in public.

Other ceremonies drew the pious to pilgrimages in the tombs of saints or sites of martyrdom, and the councils of the church made efforts to replace the *concilia* of the imperial cult.

The organization of the church was hierarchical and, as usual in the Roman world, employed institutions modeled on those of the state. The clergy comprised numerous grades, first and foremost the hierarchy of bishops. The pope, the bishop of Rome, continued to extend his authority, although this was still largely moral, based on his prestige alone. The primates, from 381, controlled several provinces, and the metropolitans a single province. The local bishop carried out his responsibilities in a city, over which he had an almost monarchical power. With his subordinates, he formed a sort of select assembly similar to the *curia*. Ordination was perceived as entry into an *ordo*, and the state reinforced this structure by granting exemptions from duties and awarding civil jurisdiction. A regular *cursus honorum* was set up, as is shown by the inscription of Flavius Latinus in Brescia: starting as an exorcist, he became a priest and finally a bishop. The three upper grades in the hierarchy of the clergy subordinate to the local bishop were priests or elders, deacons placed in the service of the bishop, and subdeacons. The lower grades were divided into four levels: acolytes to assist the subdeacons, exorcists to drive out the devil, lectors to read during ceremonies, and porters to attend to material tasks. The laity, the faithful, among whom there were some privileged members, including ascetics, confessors, virgins, and widows, corresponded to the *populus*.

On the fringes of the church's organization in the cities, monasticism began to expand. Founded by St Anthony (d. 356), at first it was most successful in the East. Anthony himself lived as a hermit in the Theban desert of Egypt. Extreme ascetics called the stylites lived on the tops of pillars. Saints Pachomius and Basil, on the other hand, recommended a communal life (cenobitism), an idea which spread in Upper Egypt, east of Alexandria, and in Palestine, in the form of the *laura* or groups of recluses' cells.

The life of the church had sometimes been troubled by persecutions. These had often had to do with politics: rejection of the imperial cult and traditional gods had placed authority in jeopardy. The legal aspect had always been involved: by obstinately practicing their faith, Christians disobeyed the emperor and the governor. Sometimes, competition between religions had played a part (Cybele, Judaism), as had communal enmity and the provocation of tactless fanatics. But though at first they were persecuted, Christians later became the persecutors, of Judaism and, above all, paganism.

Christianity in literature and art

The new religion imposed itself first in the field of literature, by way of an output that was soon plentiful and often polemical, for it felt obliged to do battle against Judaism, paganism, and heresies.

There are four distinct groups of Christian authors, writing in Greek.

1   Origen (c.185–254/255), born in Alexandria, emigrated to Palestine, most probably to Caesarea and Tyre. He wrote erudite treatises on the scriptures, and a work of apologetics, *Against Celsus*, criticizing pagan neo-Platonism.
2   The Arian conflict was in part the inspiration for the works of both Eusebius and Athanasius. Eusebius (260–340), bishop of Caesarea in Palestine, has left

Plate 18.4 Early Christian baptismal bath in the Basilica, originally a Roman temple, at Sbeitla (Roman Sufetela), Tunisia. C. M. Dixon

Speeches, religious treatises (*Evangelical Preparation*), and historical works (the *Chronicles* retrace the history of the world, and the *Ecclesiastical History* is concerned with church government and the persecutions). The commitment of Athanasius (295–373) against the Arians revealed itself more plainly. This bishop of Alexandria was an unbending opponent of the heresy that was born in his own city.

3 The Cappadocians. Born in Caesarea, St Basil (330–379) studied at Athens and Antioch, notably under Libanius, and became a bishop. He fought against Arianism and made efforts to organize monasticism. His friend St Gregory of Nazianzus (329–390) had been a rhetorician before he too became a bishop. He was above all a contemplative, and wrote *Speeches* and *Letters*. St Gregory of Nyssa (340–394) was Basil's brother. In his writings he sought to use Platonic philosophy in the service of Christianity.

4 The school of Antioch was made illustrious mainly by St John Chrysostom (345–407). This son of a master of the militia was possibly a student of Libanius. Bishop and monk, moralist and preacher (his name means "golden mouthed"), he was the author of many works, including speeches, treatises, and letters.

In the case of Latin authors too, there are four distinct groups – although let us first mention St Hilary of Poitiers, who also fought against Arianism.

1 The African school proved especially fruitful. St Cyprian, bishop of Carthage, who was martyred in 258, left letters and treatises. Arnobius, who lived in

the time of Diocletian, was a convert, and a rhetorician by profession. He attempted to prove that the ills of the period were not attributable to Christianity, and pointed out the absurd features of pagan mythology. His student Lactantius, who went on to teach in Nicomedia, composed a *History of the Persecutions* and a work *Concerning Divine Institutes*. Undoubtedly, the most important member of this group was St Augustine. Born a pagan at Thagaste, in the province of Africa Proconsularis but in Numidian country, he studied at Carthage, Rome, and Milan, where he became a rhetorician in 383. He was converted, returned to Africa, became the bishop of Hippo in 395, and died in 430. He left a considerable number of works directed against the Jews, pagans, heretics, and schismatics, chiefly the Donatists, the most outstanding of his works being the *City of God* and his *Confessions*.

2   History was not neglected. Orosius, a Spanish priest of passionate temperament, took up Arnobius' arguments in favor of his religion and against polytheism, while Eutropius, under Valens, wrote an *Abridged History* which began with the founding of Rome.

3   Besides those already mentioned, the group of the Fathers of the Church includes two more great names. The illustrious St Ambrose (c.330–397), bishop of Milan, dominated both church councils and emperors (Theodosius). He was the author of *Funeral Orations*, a *Treatise on the Duties of the Clergy*, and a collection of sermons, the *Hexameron*. No less famous was St Jerome, who was born c.348 in Dalmatia or Pannonia. After studying in Rome, he withdrew to the Syrian desert and later founded the monastery of Bethlehem. He left extensive works (lives of saints, letters, and, above all, the Vulgate, the Latin translation of the Bible). He died in 420.

4   Christianity inspired poetry as well, chiefly the verses of the *Instructions* and *Carmen Apologeticum* by Commodian. Prudentius (348–410), a Spanish lawyer, was converted at the age of 57; his work *Peristephanon*, as its title indicates, "weaves the crowns" for the martyrs. Sidonius Apollinaris, bishop of Clermont-Ferrand in 472, also left poems as well as a collection of letters.

The emergence of Christian art is not seen until after that of Christian literature. This delay can be accounted for in several ways – biblical mistrust of visual art, the caution necessary in a hostile environment, and also poverty. In Rome, the great Christian buildings did not begin to be built until the time of Constantine. But before then the conversion of a few wealthy people brought about a change in the nature of Christian art, as did the needs of worship and catechesis, as well as the unobtrusive influence of paganism. For Christian art had been produced initially for ordinary people.

Among the iconographic subjects, the best known, apart from the dove, is the fish, the Greek word for which, *ichthus*, comprises the initial letters of the words of the phrase *(I)esous (Ch)ristos, (Th)eou H(u)ios, (S)oter* ("Jesus Christ, son of God, savior"). Other subjects were borrowed from Judaism (Isaac and Daniel)

Plate 18.5
Christian mosaic,
c. fourth century CE,
from the catacombs
of Hermes in Sousse,
Tunisia. The dolphin
and anchor symbolize
Christ on the Cross;
the fish represent his
faithful followers.
C. M. Dixon

and paganism (the Good Shepherd), but received a new meaning (the sacrifice of Isaac prefigures that of Christ).

Christian art became renowned in the same fields as pagan art. Painting was used very early on, in the church and baptistery of Dura-Europus before 256, and in the Roman catacomb of Domitilla. Sculpture produced sarcophagi illustrated with scenes from the Old Testament, sometimes separated by columns, or ornamented with simple strigils. The sarcophagus of Junius Bassus, found in Rome and dated 359, sets biblical and evangelic subjects side by side. Mosaics, chiefly African, brought figured representations and inscriptions together. They were used in particular for the tombs of leading clerics and wealthy people who had themselves buried in a church ("privileged interment").

There was also the gradual development of a Christian architecture. The church was at first a room in a house, then the house itself, and finally a special building constructed on a basilican plan. With the development of large Christian communities, the episcopal group was born, comprising at least three distinct parts – a cathedral, a round or octagonal baptistery, and the bishop's house. In

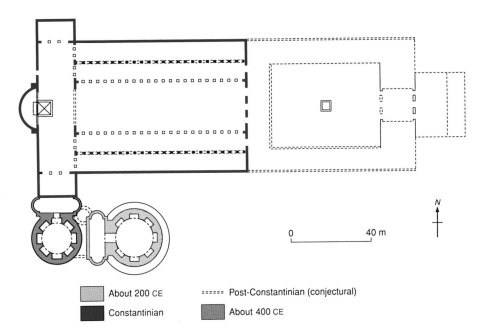

Figure 18.3 Plan of Constantine's Vatican basilica (from R. Bianchi-Bandinelli, *L'arte dell'antichità classica*, Gallimard, 1976)

0 _____ 40 m

N

| | About 200 CE | | Post-Constantinian (conjectural) |
| | Constantinian | | About 400 CE |

Rome the construction of the basilica of the Lateran and its baptistery (around 319) was followed by Santa Maria Maggiore, St Peter's (in the Vatican, after 326), St Paul-outside-the-Walls (with some rebuilding under Valentinian II), and Santa Pudenziana (late fourth century). Constantinople did not follow this example until later, like Alexandria, Trier, Aquileia, and Milan (church of San Nazaro, basilica of the Martyrs). In Palestine, it was St Helena, Constantine's mother, who built the church of the Nativity in Bethlehem and the sanctuary of Golgotha in Jerusalem. The latter, which covers an area of 36 m by 140 m, includes a church of basilican plan with five naves and an exedra. Conceived as a place for the worship of Christ the Martyr, it was built against the mount of Calvary. The whole also included a rotunda, corresponding to the Holy Sepulcher, and a baptistery.

Cemeteries were at first above ground (Vatican), then subterranean chambers, and lastly catacombs (in Rome, St Callistus, Domitilla). Their decoration was particularly careful and abundant.

18.5 | Boom and Decline

In the fields of religion, intellectual life, and the arts, the situation was not as has been described for the economy. Pagans, Jews, and Christians were in opposition to one another, but were also mutually enriched. Without doubt, however, it was paganism and, to a lesser degree, Judaism which were the eventual losers, although their decline was by no means total.

From the point of view of language, one could already distinguish the Latin West and the Greek East. When these actually divided, the break chiefly affected the West, especially after the events of 406 and 410. These dates, however, have little significance for Christianity, and chiefly concern political and military matters.

19

THE END OF THE ROMAN WORLD?

There is no easy way to fix a date at which to close a history of Rome. One can but observe a complex process that differed according to the sectors of activity and the regions involved. However, at least the symbolic importance of certain events, and the emergence of a crisis starting in 364 CE, must be noted.

19.1 | Julian: 361–363 CE

The man Christians called "the apostate" had a tragic destiny, perceived as such even as late as the sixteenth century. Modern thinkers explain it variously: psychoanalysts emphasize the traumas he suffered in his childhood; historians see him as an exceptional man, trapped in the transition between two worlds, who tried to resolve many serious difficulties. Our most extensive source for Julian is Ammianus Marcellinus, the last pagan historian of antiquity. Ammianus' narrative, often referred to as *Res Gestae*, is also our last major narrative of Roman history. Marcellinus intends his work as a continuation of Tacitus' *Annals*, and so begins with Nerva's accession in 96 CE, finishing with the death of Valens at the battle of Adrianople in 378 (on these events see below). Today, only the latter part of the work survives, covering the period 353–378. Ammianus attributes to Julian classic Roman military, political, and moral virtues: the emperor surpasses Alexander the Great in intellectual pursuits; he shares the labors and food of his soldiers while on campaign; he is well versed in both military and civilian duties; and he despises material wealth and physical pleasures while upholding strict ethical principles (*History* 16.5, 25.2, 25.4).

His education

The grandson of Constantius Chlorus, Julian was born in 331, and for his tutors had Eusebius, bishop of Nicomedia, and the Scythian eunuch Mardonios.

His childhood was spent on the estates of Chalcedon, where he studied Homer, and at Macellum in Cappadocia, where he came under the influence of the Arian bishop George. Constantius II, who distrusted all family members as possible rivals, exiled him to Nicomedia. There he discovered the works of Libanius and, following a vision, was converted to paganism.

Julian was a pagan intellectual with a passion for Hellenism, especially neo-Platonism (Plotinus, Porphyry, and Iamblichus). His conversion came in a period of difficulty for Christianity (Catholics against Arians) and during a renaissance of culture in the East.

He left plentiful literary works, which are both profound and yet not without a touch of humor. His *Misopogon* is a satire against the inhabitants of Antioch who had made fun of his beard. In his *Caesars* he eulogizes Marcus Aurelius and criticizes Constantine.

Julian Caesar

In 355, Constantius II appointed Julian *Caesar*, his successor to the throne. There was danger both on the domestic front (with six usurpers having declared themselves) and from external pressure. Sapor II was preparing a new offensive in the

Genealogy 19.1	Julian's parentage

Constantius Chlorus ~ Theodora

|

Julius Constantius ~ Basilina

|

Julian ~ Helena

East despite the threats that lay over his northern frontier, and in Europe there were as many dangers as there were foreign peoples. There was fear of the Franks on the lower Rhine, the Alemanni in the angle of the Rhine and Danube, the Quadi and Marcomanni facing Pannonia, the Goths on the lower Danube, and the Huns (the advance guard of the Turks), who were driving the Scythians before them.

Julian left for Gaul in 357. There he won a great victory over the Alemanni near Strasbourg, and made incursions into Germania. He set up his winter quarters at Lutetia, where he read Caesar and Plutarch, and was there when Constantius II asked him to bring reinforcements to the East. The army refused to leave and proclaimed him emperor. He hesitated, then accepted, and was marching on Sirmium when Constantius fell ill and died.

Julian Augustus

Julian had defined his political philosophy in a eulogy of Constantius II entitled *On Royalty* and published in 358. To the Roman traditional virtues of piety, justice, and clemency, he added that of kindness, an addition dictated by his humanism.

Julian is mainly known for his religious policy. A devotee of theurgy and initiated at Eleusis, a worshiper of the Sun (*Discourse on King Helios*) and Cybele (*Discourse on the Mother of the Gods*), he first restored paganism by decree, and then attacked Christianity (treatise *Against the Galileans*): Christians were banned from teaching, holding public office, and performing funerals in daylight.

A few other reforms were made: he simplified court etiquette, alleviated the tasks of the *curiales* by quashing exemptions from taxes and reducing coronation gold, and cancelled the authorization that had been given to private citizens to use the state postal service, the *cursus publicus*.

Meanwhile, he had to confront the Persian problem inherited from Constantius II. He marched against Sapor II, advanced toward Ctesiphon, but then had to

Plate 19.1 Statue of Julian the Apostate. Louvre, Paris. C. M. Dixon

retreat. During this episode he was mortally wounded. A Christian legend ascribes to him the famous last words: "You have won, Galilean!" Nevertheless, once again an emperor had died confronting the enemy.

Jovian was proclaimed as Julian's successor. This Pannonian officer, a moderate Christian, capitulated to Persia: he abandoned the left bank of the Tigris, which had been occupied since 298, and gave up all influence over Armenia. He also annulled Julian's measures against the Christians. He died in 364, a year after becoming emperor.

19.2 | A New Crisis: 364–395 CE

The period that then began was marked by a crisis similar to that of the third century. Its origins, too, lay in wars. But the fresh wave of invasions was, though there were exceptions, more a matter of slow and gradual infiltrations. The barbarians admired Rome, yet were unable or unwilling to assimilate with it. This situation brought about a division of the Empire; but while the West then foundered in disorder, the East rode out the storm and molded a new civilization.

The single unifying element came from the dynastic policy that was followed at the time. From 364 until the beginning of the fifth century, the same blood ran through the veins of all the emperors except Theodosius.

For convenience' sake, three periods may be distinguished, each marked by a personality: those of Valentinian I, Theodosius, and Stilicho.

The period of Valentinian I

Valentinian I soon opted for a division: he kept the West, with Milan as its capital, and in 364 entrusted the East to his brother Valens, who installed himself in Constantinople. In 367, his son Gratian was proclaimed a third *Augustus*, and sent to Trier. He was only eight years old, but was betrothed to Constantia, the daughter of Constantius II, which conferred additional legitimacy on the dynasty.

Valentinian I (364–375) acceded to the Empire at the age of 44. Like Jovian a Pannonian officer, and a tolerant Catholic, he was vigorous and honest, quick-tempered and cultured (he chose Ausonius as tutor to Gratian).

He made efforts to improve the situation of all strata of society. To win over the Senate, he instituted the *defensor senatus* ("defender of the senate"), who was responsible for the protection of senators in Constantinople from the abuses of tax collectors; but a split developed and this brought executions in its wake, which explains the criticisms leveled at him by the aristocratic Ammianus Marcellinus. He also tried to improve the lot of the *curiales* by transferring to the state part of their responsibilities in the areas of taxation and the official postal service. He took an equal interest in the plebeians, increasing free food distributions in Rome, and appointed a *defensor plebis* ("defender of the *plebs*"), a lawyer protecting the city's poor from the exactions by powerful citizens. But he was unable to do anything against the owners of great landed estates or against corruption.

The gravest difficulties came from the barbarians, and Valentinian I's period was marked by several wars. The Scots and Saxons who were ravaging Britain

Genealogy 19.2   **Fourth-century emperors**

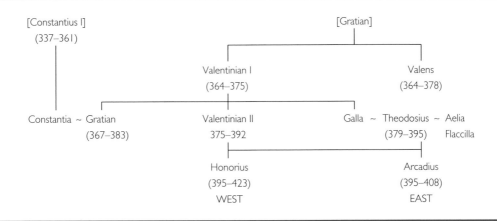

were repulsed in 368–369 by the Spanish officer Theodosius. In 366–374, Valentinian I fought in person in the Gauls against the Alemanni, who finally obtained a treaty after suffering defeat. Africa, too, was troubled by raids, directed at the ports of Tripolitania (364), and by the rebellion of Firmus (372–375), a movement combining indigenous demands, weariness with taxation, and religious confrontation, Donatist in this instance. This situation was brought under control by the same Theodosius, who was beheaded shortly afterwards for an unknown reason.

In the East, responsibility for running affairs had fallen to Valens (364–378), a fanatical Arian. The crisis there seems, paradoxically, both more complex and less serious than in the West. In 365, there was a usurpation in Constantinople. The claimant, Procopius, was related to Julian, and his movement was simultaneously political and religious. Moreover, social difficulties became apparent in outbreaks of brigandage.

But it was the accompanying military problems that were the main cause for concern. In 372–373, the war against the Persians resumed. In 374–375, the Quadi and Sarmatians were defeated by Valens and Theodosius (the son of Valentinian's Spanish general). In the meantime, it had been necessary to fight the Goths (who were themselves harassed by the Huns), as attested in 364 and 367–369 (when they ended by negotiating). Finally, in 378, Valens was defeated and killed by the Goths at Adrianople. It was the first great defeat for the Empire since the third century, but the scale of the disaster must not be exaggerated, as it was by Ammianus Marcellinus. The East was still capable of striking back.

The period of Theodosius

At this point the Empire was once more divided into three. The young Gratian, based in Trier, found himself compelled to face the Alemanni in that same year, 378. In 375, Valentinian II had succeeded his father, but he was only four years old and was placed under the tutelage of a Frankish general, Arbogast, who took Milan for his capital. From there he kept watch on Illyria and protected Italy. This moderate pagan is said to have been a morally upright man. Meanwhile, the younger Theodosius, a man endowed with a powerful personality, impressed everyone. He had attained the rank of master of cavalry, and was appointed *Augustus* in 379 after the disaster of Adrianople. To legitimize his dynasty, he married one of Valentinian I's daughters, Galla, the future mother of Galla Placidia, then set himself up in Trier. Of Spanish origin, he was a good general, described by our sources as a fervent, or even fanatical, Orthodox Christian. He had to confront the two great troubles of the Empire's crisis, barbarians and usurpations, to which he added religious conflict.

In the military field, Theodosius achieved success in three theaters of operations. After a new thrust, the Goths were settled in the Empire in 380, with a treaty (*foedus*) – although they became restless again in 386. In 387 and (by the treaty of Constantinople) 390, Theodosius came to an agreement with Persia on the division of Armenia. And, in the end, war and victory restored peace on the Rhine.

Theodosius showed himself much more active in the religious field. After Constantine's conversion, his reign marked the most important change in the relations between the government and the gods; for the state now renounced paganism. As early as 379, Gratian had refused to wear the mantle of *pontifex maximus*. Then, in 382, he had rescinded the privileges granted to pagan priests and had ordered the altar of Victory to be removed from the Curia. But the strongest measure against paganism came directly from Theodosius. In 391–392, under the influence of St Ambrose, he banned private pagan worship, and prohibited the adoration of statues and the performance of pagan rites.

Additionally, Theodosius had to solve domestic problems, notably two attempts at usurpation. In 383, a pretender named Maximus emerged in Britain. He soon extended his authority over Gaul, where he eliminated Gratian and proclaimed himself *Augustus*. At that point, Theodosius could do nothing to stop him. In 388, Maximus defeated Valentinian II and ousted him. But Theodosius was now able to take action – he did so and was victorious.

The ban on paganism in 391–392 provoked discontent that crystallized around a new usurper. In 392, Arbogast had Valentinian II strangled, and proclaimed Eugenius emperor. This reaction by traditionalism lasted until just after the battle of the River Frigidus (394), when Eugenius and Arbogast were defeated.

Theodosius had associated his two sons with his rule: Arcadius had taken charge of the East; Honorius of the West (under the supervision of the Vandal general Stilicho). Theodosius died in 395. By then, Christianity had won, peace reigned, and the Empire was divided.

The period of Stilicho

Flavius Stilicho was born in around 360 to a family of Vandals who were settled in the Empire and had been converted to Christianity, but were Arian. There has been much argument about this man: he is sometimes presented as a barbarian friend of the Goths' leader, Alaric; others see him as a Roman and the defender of the city. In fact, he behaved like a Romanized barbarian, as is evidenced by his career and his relations with the poet Claudian.

Claudian, originally from Egypt, had remained a pagan, although he had lived in a largely Christian court. He gave up his mother tongue, Greek, for Latin, and for 10 years (394–404) he acted as Stilicho's spokesman, a task which inspired part of his abundant polemical and other writings.

Stilicho had a family connection with Theodosius, whose niece Serena he had married. The ivory diptych of Monza represents him and his wife with one of their children, Eucher. Appointed in 395 to supervise the education of Honorius, who lived in Milan, he became even closer to the ruling dynasty in 398, when his daughter Maria married the young emperor.

Pedagogy and intrigue, however, were not the main part of the Vandal Stilicho's activities; he was chiefly concerned with war. First there was an internal conflict. In 395, Stilicho had to face the rebellion of the count of Africa, Gildo, who, at the instigation of Eutropius, the favorite of Arcadius, sought to gain independence for the provinces of Africa. Gildo, the brother of Firmus, whom he had betrayed, blocked the provisioning of Rome. He repulsed the troops sent to fight him in 397, but was in his turn betrayed by another of his brothers, Maczel. He was captured and executed in 398. The role played by Eutropius in this affair shows that relations between Rome and Constantinople were far from friendly. Campaigns fought by Stilicho in Thessaly (395) and the Peloponnese (397) aimed at weakening the influence of Arcadius more than at driving out the Goths who had infiltrated there.

While the imperial forces weakened themselves in internal struggles, the barbarians were preparing to launch fresh attacks. In the East, Eutropius repulsed the Huns in 398 – though he could not stop this fearsome race from being a recurrent threat. In 401, Alaric's Visigoths were beaten by Stilicho near Aquileia. And in 406 it was the turn of the Ostrogoths under Radagais to experience defeat at his hands (near Florence). But the danger was coming nearer to Rome. The Romans, however, felt reassured by Stilicho's actions. They gave him a triumphal welcome on two occasions, in 403 and 406. Statues were erected to him and inscriptions carved in his honor.

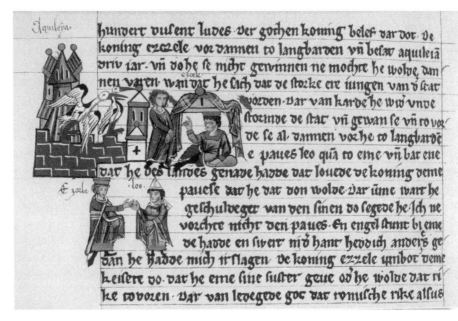

Plate 19.2
Thirteenth-century
book painting of Attila
besieging Aquileia.
AKG, London

19.3 | The End of Rome?

For historians seeking the end of Rome, the point at which to end a history of Rome, the question "at what moment did it happen?" gives rise to two prior questions. What happened? How did it happen?

Several answers have been given to the first question. Many writers have long talked about decadence. Even in antiquity this idea was a literary commonplace, and the Christians reinforced it: the end of Rome was a punishment sent by God. During the Renaissance, moral reasons were again sought, and the decline of the population was considered an additional reason. Other writers have blamed the failure of institutions to adapt, or a general crumbling of institutions, followed, as it were, by a "natural death" of the Empire. Still others have supported the notion that the situation in the provinces was less somber than previously considered, and that the barbarians killed a perfectly healthy Roman world. Several recent researchers, rejecting the model of a decline and fall which implies modern sensitivities and expectations about "the grandeur that was Rome," have claimed that there was no decline, still less a decadence, but merely a succession of historical developments and transformations.

To get a better answer to the first question, the second must be asked: how did it happen? The fourth century was in fact characterized by its complexity: features of the early Empire coexisted with new elements; and the latter may be seen as creative, and thus elements of strength, or as tending to weakness and crisis. The complexity even forces us to make distinctions and to give our attention to three sets of contrasts.

1   East and West, indeed, cannot be regarded in the same light. While the Byzantine Empire was being born in the East, provincials in the West saw the state growing weaker and the army unable to prevent the barbarians crossing the Rhine in 406 or capturing Rome in 410. The might of the Germani partly explains this decline. The reinforcements they received through further migrations from the east and their improved organization in federations of peoples contributed just as much to their success as did the enfeeblement of Rome by bureaucracy and the economic crisis, the lack of currency, and an imbalance between town and country.

2   The second contrasting pair, town and country, experienced opposing and no longer complementary fortunes. It is widely agreed that there was at least a comparative preservation of the towns, but the unequal distribution of taxes weighed more heavily on rural dwellers than on townspeople, and on the poor more than on the rich. This economic inequality certainly contributed to the "end" of the Roman world, at least in the western provinces.

3   Lastly, we must distinguish between two cultures, paganism and Christianity, which were certainly not totally alien to each other but had clashed bitterly. Pagan tradition survived in cultural circles, to be sure, but only by becoming the subject of study; it no longer created socio-cultural products, apart from academic works (Martianus Capella). In contrast, Christianity continued to progress, and this expansion was accompanied by new forms of art and thought. Moreover, according to Piganiol, this religion favored the formation of an internationalist ideology that knew no boundaries.

Of course, all these changes did not come about simultaneously. Hence the third question: when?

In the late fourth century, an economic crisis occurred and was accompanied by a slowing down in public benefaction. East and West were already following their separate destinies. Thereafter, a few major events have captured the attention of historians. These occurred at the beginning and end of the fifth century.

Stilicho's last years were marked by a drama that began on the night of December 31, 406, when the Vandals, Alani, and Suebi crossed the Rhine, which had frozen over. They traversed Gaul, Spain, and Africa (crossing the Straits of Gibraltar in 429). Nothing could stop them.

This invasion led to a usurpation by Constantine III, who declared himself western emperor in Gaul (407 CE); a fresh offensive by Alaric's Visigoths, more successful this time; and a general reaction: the councilor Olympus, the emperor's sister Galla Placidia, and the army united against Stilicho, who was arrested and beheaded, together with his wife and children, on August 23, 408. Galla Placidia then revealed herself as a major figure at the center of her times.

The death of Stilicho did not prevent Alaric from taking Rome in 410; the city was sacked, and this pillaging also marks an essential date for our consideration. From then on, the Roman West had in actual fact become the barbarian West.

For the main part of the fifth century (from 410 to 471–472), the destinies of the two parts of the Empire diverged.

In the West, the weak Honorius (d. 423) had enabled Constantius to emerge (411–421), fleetingly as Constantius III (421). Next it was the turn of Valentinian III (425–455) to be eclipsed, this time by the master of the militia Aetius. Their initial adversaries were the count of Africa, Boniface, and then Attila, king of the Huns, who was defeated in 451 at the Campus Mauriacus. But the central government functioned only in fits and starts: the Visigoths moved from Italy to Aquitaine; the Franks and Burgundians installed themselves in Gaul; Vandals, Alani, and Suebi pursued their ventures. From 457 to 472, it was a Suebian, Ricimer, master of the militia, who imposed his protectorate on the West.

In the East, and even though it sometimes had characteristics similar to those described for the West, the general situation, both internal and external, improved under Theodosius II (408–450), chiefly thanks to the many undertakings of

Plate 19.3 Roman Forum, seen from the Capitoline hill. C. M. Dixon

Anthemius, praetorian prefect of the East and regent to the young emperor. It was then that the Code of Theodosius was worked out. The lull on the frontiers even allowed internal conflicts to arise: the murder of the pagan philosopher Hypatia by the Alexandrian mobs in 415; the Monophysite dispute (see chapter 18); the Council of Ephesus, in 431, which condemned Nestorianism. But then, between 450 and 471, the East experienced the same fate as the West, with one difference: it was a member of the Alani, Aspar, who imposed his protectorate.

The end of the century was marked by two events with a strong symbolic content.

In 475, Orestes, Attila's former secretary, had driven the emperor Nepos out of Rome and given the purple to his own son, Romulus Augustulus. The Scirian Odoacer, who had also frequented Attila's court, became king of the Heruli and asked for federate status. When he was refused, he drove Romulus Augustulus out and sent the imperial insignia back to Constantinople (476). Odoacer became "patrician" and "king of barbarian peoples," carving out a domain for himself in Italy, Sicily, and Dalmatia.

The emperor Zeno, in 488, gave the Ostrogoth Theodoric the task of reconquering the West; after the assassination of Odoacer in 493, Theodoric made himself master of Rome and Italy, and henceforth the Roman West became *in law* the barbarian West.

Even the fifth century did not mark the end, for there was a legacy.

In the East, a new Roman Empire was built up, linked with Byzantine civilization, and this lasted until 1453. In the West, the idea of empire remained very strong. This is borne out by the creation of the German Holy Roman Empire and the diffusion of the title "Caesar," which lasted in Russia until 1917 (abdication of "Tsar" Nicholas II), until 1918 in Germany (abdication of "Kaiser" Wilhelm II), and as late as 1946 with the Tsars of Bulgaria.

In the early years of the twenty-first century, what we understand collectively as the "western world" is a largely Roman inheritance bequeathed to modern Europe through the Renaissance. The values, aesthetics, and traditions of the West are in turn spreading rapidly throughout the world through the globalization of technology and communications. Some of the most commonly spoken languages are based on Latin, which is also strongly present in English, today's global *lingua franca*. Christianity, another offshoot of the Roman world, also defines the West, while the connections and conflicts between East and West are still timeless and timely cultural issues. Studying the Roman past is a most fruitful way to understand our present, and, in this sense, it is neither sentimentalism nor exaggeration to say that Rome still lives.

CHRONOLOGICAL TABLE

MILITARY EVENTS	POLITICAL AND SOCIAL EVENTS	CULTURAL AND RELIGIOUS EVENTS
BCE	BCE	BCE
	2nd millennium Arrival of the Indo-Europeans in Italy.	
	8th century The Etruscans in central Italy. Greek colonization in Sicily and south Italy.	
	754/753 Foundation of Rome (according to tradition); the first villages.	
	753–717 The Latin and Sabine kings.	
	650–510/509 The Etruscan kings (Servius Tullius).	
540 Battle of Aleria between Etruscans and Carthaginians.		
	509 Expulsion of the Etruscan kings. Annual magistrates (praetors, then consuls) replace them.	**509** The first Capitoline temple.
496 Battle of Lake Regillus		**496–484** First temple to Saturn, at the foot of the Capitol. Temple of Ceres, Liber, and Libera. Temple of Mercury. Temple of Castor and Pollux in the Forum.
	494 Secession of the *plebs*.	

MILITARY EVENTS	POLITICAL AND SOCIAL EVENTS	CULTURAL AND RELIGIOUS EVENTS
485? Coriolanus' victory over the Volsci.		
474 Cumae, Greek victory (Syracuse) over the Etruscans and Carthaginians.	**471** The first four tribunes of the plebeians.	
	451–450 Laws of the twelve tables.	
	445 *Lex Canuleia*: equality of patricians and plebeians. Creation of the censorship.	
406–396 Siege and capture of Veii.	**421** The first quaestors.	
c.400 The Celts in north Italy.		
390 The Gauls sack Rome.		
	367 Death of Dionysius of Syracuse. Licinio-Sextian plebiscite: sharing of the consulship between patricians and plebeians.	**367** Camillus' temple of Concordia at the foot of the Capitol.
		362 The first *ludi scaenici*.
	348 Agreement between Rome and Carthage.	**348** The first Secular Games.
341 First Samnite War.		
340–337 Revolt and end of the Latin League (the Latin War).		
	338 Antium (Anzio), Roman colony.	
	335 Foundation of Ostia.	
327–304 Second Samnite War.	**328** Rome in control of Latium, Etruria, and Campania.	
	318–313 Ovinian plebiscite.	
	312 Via Appia, Rome–Capua.	
	312–308 Censorship of Appius Claudius.	
	306 Roman–Carthaginian treaty.	
	300 *Lex Ogulnia*: the pontificate open to plebeians.	
298–291 Third Samnite War.		
280–272 War against Tarentum and Pyrrhus.		
		275 Theocritus at Syracuse.
272 Capture of Tarentum.		**272** The Romans in contact with Greek civilization.

MILITARY EVENTS	POLITICAL AND SOCIAL EVENTS	CULTURAL AND RELIGIOUS EVENTS
	278 Agreement between Rome and Carthage.	
	270–265 Rome in control in Italy except Cisalpine Gaul.	
265 Capture of Volsinii.		
264–241 First Punic War.		264 First recorded gladiatorial fights in Rome.
256–255 Regulus' expedition in Africa.		249 Secular Games.
	244 Brindisi a Roman colony (Brundisium).	
242 Victory in the Aegates Islands.	242 The first praetor (*peregrinus*) for non-Romans.	
	241 Reform of the *comitia*.	241 Via Aurelia (Rome–Pisa).
240–237 Rebellion of the mercenaries against Carthage.		240 The first tragedy in Latin (Livius Andronicus of Tarentum).
		239 Birth of Ennius near Tarentum.
238 Carthage yields Corsica and Sardinia to Rome.		
237 Hamilcar founds the Barcine empire in Spain.		
		235 First play by Naevius.
230 Illyrian pirates raid in the Adriatic.		
	227 Sicily, first Roman province. Creation of the provinces of Corsica and Sardinia.	
225 Roman intervention in Illyria. Gaulish offensive in north Italy.		
221 Hannibal in Spain.		
		220 Via Flaminia (Rome–Ariminum). Building of the Circus Flaminius in Rome.
218–201 Second Punic War.		219 First Greek surgeon in Rome.
218 Roman defeat at the Trebia.	218 *Lex Claudia* on trade.	
217 Trasimene.	217 Fabius Cunctator dictator.	217 First Plebeian Games.
216 Cannae.		
215–205 First Macedonian War against Philip.	215 First companies of *publicani* (tax-gatherers).	
213 Hannibal takes Tarentum.		
		212 *The Menaechmi* by Plautus.

MILITARY EVENTS	POLITICAL AND SOCIAL EVENTS	CULTURAL AND RELIGIOUS EVENTS
211 Recapture of Capua.		
210 Scipio in Spain, recaptures Cartagena.		
207 Victory of the Metaurus.		
205 Peace with Philip V of Macedon.		
204 Scipio in Africa.		204 *Miles gloriosus* by Plautus.
202 Victory of Zama.		
200–196 Second Macedonian War.		c.200 Birth of Polybius.
198 Flamininus in Greece.		
197 Victory of Cynoscephalae.	197 Spain a Roman province (two praetors).	
	196 Flamininus proclaims Greece's freedom.	
	195 Consulship of Cato.	
		193 Construction of the *emporium* (port) at Rome.
192–188 War against Antiochus III of Syria. Victory of Thermopylae.		
		c.190 Birth of Terence.
189 Victory of Magnesia.		189 Tragedy by Ennius.
188 Treaty of Apamea.	187 Trial of Scipio.	
	186 Affair of the Bacchanalia.	186 Last comedies of Plautus.
		185 Basilica Porcia on the Forum.
	184–182 Censorship of Cato the Elder.	
	183 Death of Scipio and Hannibal.	
		181 Temple of the Erycine Venus on the Capitol. Birth of the philosopher Panaetius.
	180 *Lex Villia Annalis* on the *cursus honorum*.	180 Birth of Lucilius at Suessa Aurunca.
		179 Basilica Aemilia in the Forum.
		175 Epicurean philosophers driven from Rome.
171–168 Third Macedonian War.		170 Basilica Sempronia in the Forum.
168 Victory of Pydna over Perseus.		167 Polybius at Rome as a hostage.
	166 Delos a free port.	166 Terence's *Andria*.
		160 Terence's *Adelphi*. Cato the Elder's *On Agriculture*.

MILITARY EVENTS	POLITICAL AND SOCIAL EVENTS	CULTURAL AND RELIGIOUS EVENTS
		155 Embassy of the Athenians Carneades, Diogenes, and Critolaus.
154–152 Campaign by Marcellus against the Celtiberi.		
150 Massinissa's war against Carthage.		
149–146 Third Punic War.	149 Death of Cato. Creation of the *quaestiones perpetuae*.	
147–139 War with Viriathus in Spain.		
146 Capture of Carthage. War against the Achaean League. Capture of Corinth.	146 Roman provinces of Macedonia and Africa.	146 Secular Games. First use of Greek marble for Roman temples.
		145 Panaetius in Rome.
		144 Aqua Marcia.
		142 Pons Aemilius.
	140 *Lex Aebutia* on formulary procedure.	
137–133 Scipio Aemilianus against Numantia.		
135–132 Slave war in Sicily.		
	133 Tribunate of Tiberius Gracchus. Agrarian reforms (*lex Sempronia*). Legacy of the kingdom of Pergamum to Rome.	131 *Satires* by Lucilius.
	128–126 Creation of the province of Asia.	
125 Legions in Transalpine Gaul.	123–122 Tribunates of Gaius Gracchus.	
	122 Foundation of Aquae Sextiae (Aix-en-Provence).	
	120/119 Creation of the province of Gallia Transalpina (known as Narbonensis from 118)	
	119 Tribunate of Marius.	
	119/118 Foundation of Narbo Martius (Narbonne).	
		116 Birth of Varro.
113 Invasion of Noricum by the Cimbri and Teutones.		

MILITARY EVENTS	POLITICAL AND SOCIAL EVENTS	CULTURAL AND RELIGIOUS EVENTS
112 Massacre of the Italians in Cirta.		
		109 Pons Milvius.
107 Military reforms of Marius.	107 Marius' first consulship.	
106 Marius against Jugurtha.	106 Birth of Pompey.	106 Birth of Cicero at Arpinum.
105 Roman defeat at Orange.		
101 Second slave war in Sicily and Campania.		
102–101 Victories of Marius at Aquae Sextiae and Vercellae.	100 Birth of Caesar. Disorders in Rome (Saturninus). Expedition against the Cilician pirates; creation of the province of Cilicia.	c.94 Birth of Lucretius.
	90–89 *Lex Julia and lex Plautia Papiria* on citizenship rights.	
91–88 Social War.		
88 Massacre of Italians by Mithridates.	88 Sulla's consulship; end of the Social War.	
	86 Marius' seventh consulship.	86 Birth of Sallust.
85 Sulla negotiates with Mithridates.		84 Birth of Catullus at Verona.
82 Sulla returns to Rome. Anti-Marian proscriptions.	82 Sulla's measures against the reforms of the Gracchi.	
80 Rising by Sertorius in Spain.		
75–65 Third war against Mithridates.	75–62 Provinces of Bithynia and Pontus.	
	74–67 Creation of the provinces of Crete and Cyrenaica.	
73–71 War with Spartacus; Pompey victorious.		
		70 Birth of Virgil near Mantua. Cicero's *Verrines*.
67 Pompey against the pirates.		
		65 Birth of Horace. Poems by Catullus.
63 Pompey defeats Mithridates.	63 Creation of the province of Syria.	63 Cicero's *Against Catiline*.
61 Germani (Helvetii) in Gaul.		
	60 First Triumvirate.	
	59 Consulship of Caesar.	59 Birth of Livy (or 64 BCE).
58–51 Gallic war.		
	56 Lucca agreements.	
		55 Pompey's theater, the first stone-built theater in Rome. Birth of Tibullus (or 48 BCE).

MILITARY EVENTS	POLITICAL AND SOCIAL EVENTS	CULTURAL AND RELIGIOUS EVENTS
		54 Basilica Julia in the Forum. Birth of Propertius (or 47 BCE).
53 The disaster at Carrhae.		
52 Rebellion of Vercingetorix.	52 Assassination of Clodius. Trial and exile of Milo. Pompey sole consul.	52 Cicero's *Pro Milone*.
	51 Celtic Gaul becomes a Roman province.	51 Caesar's *Gallic Wars*.
49 Caesar crosses the Rubicon.	49 Marseilles becomes a Roman town.	
48 Pharsalus; Pompey defeated; assassinated in Egypt.		
47 Caesar victorious at Zela.		
46 Caesar defeats the supporters of Pompey at Thapsus.	46 Caesar dictator for 10 years. Foundation of Arles.	
45 Caesar's victory at Munda.		45–37 Virgil's *Eclogues*.
	44 Caesar dictator for life. Ides of March, assassination of Caesar.	44–43 Cicero's *Philippics*.
	43 Second Triumvirate. Foundation of Lyons.	43 Birth of Ovid.
42 Philippi; defeat and death of Brutus and Cassius.		
	40 Treaty of Brundisium.	40 Sallust's *Jugurthine War*.
39–36 Negotiations and war with Sextus Pompey		
		38 Horace presented to Maecenas.
		37 Varro's treatise *On Agriculture*.
		mid-30s Horace's first book of *Satires*.
31 Victory at Actium.		
30 Occupation of Egypt.	30 Octavian in Egypt; suicide of Antony and Cleopatra. Egypt becomes a Roman province.	
29 Beginning of the Spanish campaigns.	29 Octavian's triple triumph.	29 Virgil: the *Georgics*. Dedication of the temple to the deified Caesar. Start of the imperial religion. Completion of the first stone amphitheater in Rome, and Augustus' mausoleum and triumphal arch.

MILITARY EVENTS	POLITICAL AND SOCIAL EVENTS	CULTURAL AND RELIGIOUS EVENTS
	28 *Census* and *lectio senatus* of Octavian and Agrippa. Octavian becomes *princeps senatus*.	
	27 "Sharing out" of the provinces between the Senate and Octavian, who receives the title "Augustus."	27 Dedication of Agrippa's Pantheon.
25 Start of the Alpine campaigns. Expedition by the Romans in Arabia. Indian embassy to Rome.	25 Galatia becomes a Roman province.	25 Foundation of Aosta and Merida. c.25 Livy begins his *Roman History*.
	23 Political crisis in Rome. Augustus quits the consulship, receives tribunician power for life, renewable each year.	
20 Return of the insignia by the Parthians.		20 "All roads lead to Rome," capital of the Empire. 19 Death of Tibullus and Virgil.
	18 Agrippa associated with the Empire. Julian laws on morals.	
		17 Secular Games. Horace: *Carmen saeculare*.
15 Combined campaigns of Tiberius and Drusus in the Alps.	15 Raetia and Noricum Roman provinces.	
12 Tiberius in Pannonia. Drusus' campaigns in Germania.	12 Augustus, *pontifex maximus*. Death of Agrippa.	
		11 Marcellus' theater. 10 Dedication of the altar of the Three Gauls. 9 Dedication of the Ara Pacis Augustae. 8 Death of Maecenas and Horace.
9–7 Tiberius' campaigns in Germania.	7 Creation of the 14 districts in Rome and perhaps the 11 regions in Italy.	
7/6 Surrender of the Alps.		6 Trophy of La Turbie.
2 Revival of the Armenian question.	2 Augustus, father of his country.	2 Dedication of Augustus' Forum.

MILITARY EVENTS	POLITICAL AND SOCIAL EVENTS	CULTURAL AND RELIGIOUS EVENTS
CE	CE	CE
4–6 Tiberius' campaigns in Germania.	4 Adoption of Tiberius by Augustus.	
6–9 Dalmatian–Pannonian rising; Tiberius' campaign.	6 Judaea becomes a Roman province.	
		8 Ovid exiled to Tomis.
9 Varus' disaster.		
9–12 Tiberius' campaigns in Germania.	10 Province of Pannonia.	
	14 Death of Augustus. Accession of Tiberius.	
15–16 Germanicus' campaigns in Germania.	15 Sejanus, prefect of the praetorian guard.	
17 Germanicus in the East (to 19). Tacfarinas' rising.	17 Province of Cappadocia.	17 Death of Livy (or 12 CE) and Ovid.
	19 Death of Germanicus.	
21 Revolt of Sacrovir and Florus.		
		after 21 Death of Strabo.
	26 Tiberius in Campania. Pontius Pilate prefect of Judaea.	
		c.30 Preaching and death of Christ.
	31 Downfall and death of Sejanus.	
		32 Temple of Bel at Palmyra.
	33 Financial crisis in Rome.	
34 The Parthians control Armenia.		c.34 Martyrdom of Stephen. Subterranean monument of the Porta Maggiore.
	37 Death of Tiberius. Accession of Caligula.	
39 Caligula in Gaul, on the Rhine.		
	41 Assassination of Caligula. Accession of Claudius.	
	42 Organization of Mauretania into two provinces.	
43 Start of the conquest of Britain.	43 Establishment of the port of Ostia.	
	46 Province of Thrace.	
	47/8 Censorship of Claudius.	47 Reconstruction of the college of *haruspices*. Reform of the cult of Cybele.

MILITARY EVENTS	POLITICAL AND SOCIAL EVENTS	CULTURAL AND RELIGIOUS EVENTS
	48 Claudius' speech for the admission of Gauls into the Senate.	
		49 "Apostolic Council" of Jerusalem. Seneca appointed Nero's tutor. 50 Foundation of Cologne.
	54 Death of Claudius. Accession of Nero. 55 Death of Britannicus.	54 Expulsion of the Jews (Rome).
58–9 Campaigns of Corbulo in Armenia. War against the Parthians. 61 Boudicca's (Boadicea's) rebellion. 63 End of the war against the Parthians. Agreement on Armenia.	59 Assassination of Agrippina.	60 First celebration of the *Neronia*.
	64 Burning of Rome. Monetary reform. 65 Piso's conspiracy.	64 Start of building of the Domus Aurea. 65 Suicide of Seneca, Lucan, and Petronius.
66 Revolt of the Jews. Start of the Jewish War. 68 Rising of Vindex in Gaul, Galba in Tarraconensis. 69 German–Gaulish rebellion of Civilis.	66 Nero in Greece. 68 Suicide of Nero. Accession of Galba. 69 Year of the four emperors: Galba, Otho, Vitellius, and Vespasian, who triumphed.	before 70–80 The Synoptic Gospels.
70 Capture of Jerusalem. Assembly of Reims and end of the "Gaulish Empire."		70 Destruction of the Temple (Jerusalem). Rebuilding of the temple of Jupiter Capitolinus in Rome.
	71 Titus sole commander of praetorian guard. 72–8 Reorganization of the East. 73–4 Vespasian and Titus appointed censors. The Iberian peninsula receives Latin rights.	
74–90 Subjection and organization of the Agri Decumates.		74 Expulsion of philosophers and astrologers (Rome).
	77–84 Agricola in Britain. 79 Death of Vespasian. Accession of Titus. Vesuvius erupts.	79 Death of Pliny the Elder.

MILITARY EVENTS	POLITICAL AND SOCIAL EVENTS	CULTURAL AND RELIGIOUS EVENTS
		80 Dedication of the Colosseum.
	81 Death of Titus. Accession of Domitian.	80–120 Literary activity of Plutarch.
83 Domitian's campaigns in Germania.		
c.85 Formation of the first *limes* (frontier defense line) in Upper Germania.	c.85 Creation of the two provinces of Germania.	
85–6 War against the Dacians.	86 Moesia divided into two.	
89 Rising of Saturninus.		c.88–97 Clement I pope.
89–92 Campaigns on the Danube.	92 Decrees on viticulture.	92 Quintilian, *Institutes of Oratory*.
		94/5 Expulsion of philosophers (Rome and Italy), including Epictetus.
		c.95 St John's Gospel and Revelation.
	96 Assassination of Domitian. Accession of Nerva.	
96–7 Operations in Germania.	97 Poor relief project.	
98 First attestation of the word *limes* as meaning a defense system.	98 Death of Nerva. Accession of Trajan.	98 Tacitus, *Agricola*.
		100 *Panegyric of Trajan* by Pliny the Younger. Foundation of Timgad.
		c.100 Tacitus, *Germania*.
101–2 First Dacian War.		
	102–5 Development of the port of Ostia.	
105–6 Second Dacian War.		
106 Annexation of Arabia.		
	107 Dacia becomes a Roman province.	
		109 Tacitus, *Histories*. Trophy of Adamklissi.
		112 Dedication of Trajan's Forum. Pliny's letter on the Christians.
		113 Dedication of Trajan's Column.
114–17 Parthian wars.	114 Trajan receives the title of *Optimus*. Armenia becomes a Roman province.	

MILITARY EVENTS	POLITICAL AND SOCIAL EVENTS	CULTURAL AND RELIGIOUS EVENTS
115–17 Jewish rising in the East.		
117 In the East, evacuation of Trajan's conquests. Frontier on the Euphrates.	**117** Death of Trajan. Accession of Hadrian.	**117** Tacitus, *Annals*.
	118 Execution of the four ex-consuls.	**118** Start of work on Hadrian's villa at Tibur (Tivoli). Rebuilding of the Pantheon.
	120 Creation of the *consulares* of Italy.	**120** Suetonius, *Lives of the Caesars*.
	121–5 First journey by Hadrian in the provinces.	
122 Hadrian's Wall.		
123 Peace with the Parthians.		
	128–34 Second journey of Hadrian in the provinces.	
		130 Jerusalem becomes *colonia Aelia Capitolina*. Death of Antinous.
		131 Perpetual Edict of the Praetor.
132–5 Revolt of Bar Kochba.		
		134 Dedication of the temple of Rome and Venus (Rome).
	138 Death of Hadrian. Accession of Antoninus.	
142 Building of Antoninus' Wall.		
		143 Aelius Aristides, *Eulogy of Rome*.
		160 First known *taurobolium* (sacrifice of a bull) in the West.
		c.160 Gaius, *Institutes*.
161 Parthian invasion of Syria and Armenia.	**161** Death of Antoninus. Accession of Marcus Aurelius, who has Lucius Verus as his associate.	
162 Campaigns of L. Verus in the East.		
	163 Institution of the *iuridici* in Italy.	
167–75 First "Germanic" War.	**167** The plague in Rome and in the Empire.	
	169 Death of Lucius Verus.	

MILITARY EVENTS	POLITICAL AND SOCIAL EVENTS	CULTURAL AND RELIGIOUS EVENTS
		c.170 Appearance of Montanism.
175 Revolt of Avidius Cassius.		
177–80 Second "Germanic" War.	177 Commodus appointed co-emperor.	177 Persecution in the Empire (martyrs of Lyons).
		c.178 Celsus, *The True Account*.
180 Peace with the Quadi and Marcomanni.	180 Death of Marcus Aurelius. Accession of Commodus.	between 180 and 196 The Aurelian column.
186 Rising of Maternus.		
	192 Assassination of Commodus.	
193 Two military rebellions: Septimius Severus, Pescennius Niger.	193 Pertinax becomes emperor and is killed. Didius Julianus buys the Empire.	
194–5 First war against the Parthians.	194 Septimius Severus sole emperor.	
	196 Clodius Albinus declares himself *Augustus*.	
197 Clodius Albinus beaten at Lyons.		197 Tertullian, *Apology*.
197–200 Campaigns of Severus in the East and journey in Egypt.	198 Caracalla becomes *Augustus*.	c.200 Christian School of Alexandria (Clement, Origen). Neo-Platonic school (Ammonius Saccas).
		202 Ban on all Jewish and Christian proselytism.
208–11 Campaigns in Britain.	209 Geta becomes *Augustus*.	
	211 Death of Septimius Severus. Caracalla and Geta co-emperors.	
	212 Assassination of Geta. Antonine Constitution.	212–16 Baths of Caracalla.
213–14 Campaigns on the Danube.		
215–17 Campaigns in the East.		
	217 Assassination of Caracalla. Macrinus emperor.	
	218 Death of Macrinus. Elagabalus emperor.	
		219 The Baal of Emesa is received in Rome.

MILITARY EVENTS	POLITICAL AND SOCIAL EVENTS	CULTURAL AND RELIGIOUS EVENTS
		220 House-church of Dura-Europus.
	222 Assassination of Elagabalus. Accession of Severus Alexander.	
227 Sassanid dynasty in Persia.		
		c.229–30 Cassius Dio, *Roman History*.
231–2 Campaigns against the Sassanids.		
234–5 Campaigns in Germania.	235 Assassination of Severus Alexander at Mainz. Maximinus proclaimed emperor.	
Wars: Alemanni, Dacians, and Sarmatians, Carpi and Goths.	235–8 Maximinus Thrax.	
Wars: Carpi and Goths.	238 Civil war (Africa: Gordian I and Gordian II; Italy: Pupienus and Balbinus).	
240 Capture of Nisibis by the Persians.	238–44 Gordian III.	241 Beginning of Mani's preaching.
Wars: Carpi and Goths, Persians, Alemanni.	244–9 Philip the Arab. Usurpations: Uranius, Pacatian, Jotapian.	
Wars: Carpi and Goths.	249–51 Decius. The plague in the Empire.	
Wars: Franks and Alemanni, Goths and Persians.		248 (**April 21**) Rome's millennium. 249 Aventine baths.
	251–3 Trebonianus Gallus.	250–1 Persecution of Christianity.
Wars: Goths, Persians, Saxons, Moors, Quadi and Marcomanni, Roxolani and Sarmatians.	253–9/60 Valerian. Usurpation: Ingenuus (258–60). Secession of Palmyra (Odaenathus) and Gaul (Postumus).	
		257–8 Persecution of Christianity (death of St Cyprian). Plotinus. Ludovisi sarcophagus.
	259/260–8 Gallienus. Vaballathus (son of Zenobia) replaces Odaenathus. Postumus replaced by Laelianus, then Marius. Usurpations by Macrianus, Quietus, Regalianus, and Aureolus.	260 Decree of toleration of Christianity.

MILITARY EVENTS	POLITICAL AND SOCIAL EVENTS	CULTURAL AND RELIGIOUS EVENTS
253 Franks and Alemanni in Gaul.		
258 Alemanni in north Italy.		
259–60 Capture and death of Valerian.		
	268–70 Claudius II.	
Wars: Franks and Alemanni, Persians and Goths.	269 Appearance of the Bagaudes. Usurpation by Quintillus. Victorinus replaces Marius in Gaul.	
Wars: Alemanni, Persians.	270–5 Aurelian.	
270 Victory at Naissus over the Goths.		
Wars: Franks, Juthungi and Alemanni, Carpi and Goths, Marcomanni, Vandals, Sarmatians.		
271 Withdrawal from Dacia.		
	273 Palmyra returned to the Empire.	
	274 Surrender of Tetricus, Victorinus' successor. Monetary reform.	274 Primacy of the cult of the Sun.
275 Evacuation of the Agri Decumates.	275–6 Tacitus. Hypothetical senatorial restoration. Usurpation: Florian.	275 Death of Mani.
Wars: Goths and Franks.		
Wars: Burgundii and Vandals, Goths and Getae, Blemmyes.		
276–8 Franks and Alemanni in Gaul.	276–82 Probus.	
	282–3 Carus.	
	283–4 Numerian.	
	283–5 Carinus.	
	284–6 Bagaudes in Gaul.	
	284–305 Diocletian.	
	285 Maximian *Caesar*.	
	286 (**April 1**) Maximian *Augustus*.	
	288 Insurrection of Carausius in Britain.	

MILITARY EVENTS	POLITICAL AND SOCIAL EVENTS	CULTURAL AND RELIGIOUS EVENTS
Wars: Sarmatians and Persians.	293 (**March 1**) Galerius and Constantius Chlorus appointed *Caesares*.	
Other wars: Franks and Alemanni, Iazyges and Carpi.	294 Monetary reform.	c.295 Arnobius, *Against the Nations*.
	296 Britain reconquered from Allectus, the successor of Carausius.	
		297 Law against the Manicheans.
298 War against the Moors. Treaty of Nisibis with the Persians.		
		303 Celebration of the *vicennalia*.
		303–4 Persecution of the Christians.
	305 (**May 1**) Abdication of the two *Augusti*.	c.305 Lactantius, *Divine Institutes*. The Tetrarchs (now in Venice). Baths in Rome. Arch of Thessalonica.
	306 Death of Constantius; Constantine is *Augustus*; Maxentius *Augustus*.	
	306–37 Constantine.	
	308 Conference of Carnuntum ("Second Tetrarchy").	
	310 Usurpation of Domitius Alexander.	
	311 Monetary reform (gold *solidus*).	311 Decree of Galerius (toleration of Christianity).
	312 Defeat of Maxentius in the battle of the Milvian Bridge.	312 Daia's decree against the Christians.
	312–26 Disappearance of the equestrian order.	
	313 Victory of Licinius over Daia.	313 Edict of Milan.
		314 Synod of Arles (Donatism).
	317 Crispus, Constantine II, and Licinius II appointed *Caesares*.	
		c.319 Church of St John Lateran.
	324 Licinius defeated at Adrianople; Constantius II appointed *Caesar*.	

MILITARY EVENTS	POLITICAL AND SOCIAL EVENTS	CULTURAL AND RELIGIOUS EVENTS
		325 Council of Nicaea (Arianism).
	326 Execution of Crispus and Fausta.	328 Athanasius bishop of Alexandria.
	333 Constans appointed *Caesar*.	330 (**May 11**) Inauguration of Constantinople.
	335 Dalmatius appointed *Caesar*.	
337 Attack by the Persians.	337 Baptism and death of Constantine. Constantine's sons in power; assassination of Dalmatius.	331 Inventory of temples' possessions, the first confiscations.
338 Siege of Nisibis.		
	340 Death of Constantine II.	340 Death of Eusebius of Caesarea.
	340–7 Circumcellions in Africa.	341 First ban on pagan sacrifices.
343 Constantius II in Adiabene.		
	350 Usurpation by Magnentius; death of Constans.	c.350 Preaching of Wulfila. *Chronicler of 354*.
	351 Battle of Mursa.	
	353 Death of Magnentius.	
	354 Death of Gallus *Caesar*.	356 Death of St Anthony.
	355 Julian *Caesar*.	
357 Battle of Strasbourg (Alemanni).	357 Journey to Rome by Constantius II.	
		358 Julian, *On Royalty*.
		359 Sarcophagus of Junius Bassus.
	360 Julian acclaimed *Augustus*.	360 First Council of Constantinople.
	361 Death of Constantius II.	361 Re-establishment of paganism; first measures against the Christians.
	361–3 Julian.	
363 War against the Persians. Peace with the Persians.	363–4 Jovian.	
	364–75 Valentinian I.	
	364–78 Valens.	
	364–95 Valentinian dynasty; Theodosius.	
	365 Usurpation by Procopius.	
	367–83 Gratian.	366–84 Damasius pope.
	368 Creation of the "defender of the *plebs*."	
	372–5 Rebellion of Firmus.	372 St Martin bishop of Tours.
		373 Death of Athanasius; St Ambrose bishop of Milan.
	375–92 Valentinian II.	
	379–95 Theodosius.	

MILITARY EVENTS	POLITICAL AND SOCIAL EVENTS	CULTURAL AND RELIGIOUS EVENTS
364 Troubles in Tripolitania.		
366–74 Attacks by the Alemanni.		
367–9 Attacks by the Goths.		
368–9 Wars of Theodosius the Elder against the Scots and Saxons.		
372–3 War against the Persians.		
374–5 War against the Quadi and Sarmatians.		
378 Disaster of Adrianople.		
		379 Consulship of Ausonius; St Jerome becomes a priest; death of St Basil.
380 Treaty with the Goths.		380 Decree against the Arians.
		381 Second Council of Constantinople; renewed ban on pagan sacrifices.
	383–8 Usurpation by Maximus.	382–402 Affair of the altar of Victory (Symmachus).
		386 Destruction of temples.
		387 Baptism of St Augustine.
390 Treaty of Constantinople with the Persians.		390 Libanius, *On Behalf of the Temples*; death of St Gregory of Nazianzus.
	392–4 Usurpation by Eugenius.	391–2 Ban on pagan worship.
	394 Battle of the River Frigidus.	394 Death of St Gregory of Nyssa and St Martin.
	395–408 Arcadius (East).	394–404 Claudian, propagandist for Stilicho.
	395–423 Honorius (West).	395 St Augustine bishop of Hippo.
	395–8 Gildo's revolt.	397 Death of St Ambrose.
398 Invasion by the Huns.		397–8 St Augustine, *Confessions*.
		c.400 *The Augustan History*.
		407 Death of St John Chrysostom.
	408 Execution of Stilicho.	
	408–50 Theodosius II in the East.	410 Death of Commodian.

MILITARY EVENTS	POLITICAL AND SOCIAL EVENTS	CULTURAL AND RELIGIOUS EVENTS
401 Victory of Aquileia over the Visigoths.		
406 Victory of Fiesole over the Ostrogoths.		**415** Murder of Hypatia.
		417 Rutilius Namatianus, *The Return*.
406 (December 31) Vandals, Alani, and Suebi cross the Rhine.		**420** Death of St Jerome.
410 Capture of Rome by Alaric.		
	411–21 Constantius in command of the West (as Constantius III in 421).	**411** Conference of Carthage (end of Donatism).
		413–26 St Augustine, *The City of God*.
	425–55 Valentinian III in the West, with the master of the militia Aetius.	**429–38** Theodosian Code.
		430 Death of St Augustine.
		431 Council of Ephesus (Monophysitism).
		435 Renewed ban on pagan sacrifices.
451 Battle of the Campus Mauriacus.	**450–71** Aspar in command of the East.	**451** Council of Chalcedon (Monophysitism).
		472 Sidonius Apollinaris bishop of Clermont-Ferrand.
	457–72 Ricimer master of the militia in the West.	
	476 Deposition of Romulus Augustulus.	
	488 Theodoric sent to the West.	
	493 Theodoric in Rome.	
		533 *Digest*.
		534 Code of Justinian.

GLOSSARY

aediles	Patrician (curule) and plebeian magistrates, who superintended the provisioning of Rome, trade, markets (especially weights and measures), public games, roadways, sanitation, and police.
album senatorium	Roll of senators drawn up by the censors every five years, later by the emperor. The senators were classed in order of seniority according to the offices they had held: first former consuls, next former praetors, aediles, and tribunes, lastly former quaestors.
amphitheater	Venue for gladiatorial combats and animal spectacles (e.g. the Colosseum (Flavian Amphitheater) at Rome). Included arena, subchambers, and seating for spectators.
annales	Annual account of events concerning Rome and Roman life drawn up by the pontiffs and recorded on whitened boards set up in the Regia. Included records of magistrates and events of cult importance.
apotheosis	Ceremony whereby a mortal was admitted to the number of the gods (*divus*). It was customary under the Empire, decided by the Senate as the prerogative of "good" emperors. "Bad" emperors (those who had persecuted the Senate) were subjected to the condemnation of their memory (*damnatio memoriae*); their names were struck off inscriptions and their enactments canceled.
Arianism	The theory of Arius which resulted in one of the first major doctrinal divisions in the early Church. Condemned as a heretic at the Council of Nicaea in 325 CE, he asserted that Christ was a man, distinct from and subordinate to God.
Arval Brethren	A college of 12 priests, devoted to the worship of Dea Dia, a corn deity. Their place of worship was a sacred wood (*lucus*), on the road from Rome to Ostia. They were held to have drawn up their *Records* no later than between 30 and 28 BCE.
Arx	Rome's citadel, on the Capitol.
augurs	College of priests skilled in interpreting the flight of birds, and from that determining the will of the gods. They were consulted before any official action and could interrupt any discussion or decision if they had perceived a divine sign: two words were enough: *alio die* ("till another day").
auspices	Signs of the divine will, observed by the augurs in a *templum*, a "space marked out" with the help of a curved stick (*lituus*). Most frequent were the flights of birds, but also thunder and lightning, the behavior of the sacred chickens, and threatening omens. Under the Empire only the emperor had the right to take the auspices; all victories were thus won under his auspices.
Calends	The first day of the month; belonged to Janus.
Capitoline Triad	Jupiter, Juno, and Minerva, the triad that replaced the initial triad of Jupiter, Mars, and Quirinus. Worshiped on the Capitol in Rome and all the capitols of the Roman world.

carmen	An incantatory formula, magical and usually in verse, uttered on a certain note and with a certain rhythm.
censor	Magistrate charged with the task of conducting a *census* every five years of citizens and their possessions, and of drawing up a list of senators.
circus	Racetrack for chariot racing (e.g. the Circus Maximus at Rome). Chariots started from starting gates (*carceres*) and raced seven laps down and back around a central barrier (*euripus*) and conical turning posts (*metae*).
comitatus	Campaign army, starting with Constantine.
comitia centuriata	Assembly of the people, gathered for the election of senior magistrates, voting on laws and justice. Voting was by *centuria*, according to classes established on the basis of their wealth at the time of the *census*.
comitia curiata	Ancient assembly of the people (voting was by *curia*), which retained only a religious role; it conferred the *imperium* on magistrates.
comitia tributa	Plebeian assembly charged with the election of aediles, tribunes, and quaestors, and voting on plebiscites. Voting was by tribe.
consul	Head of state under the Republic; survived under the Empire with reduced powers. The office was annual and collegial: two consuls under the Republic; two ordinary and eponymous consuls plus normally two substitute consuls under the Empire.
conventus	A district of a province in which citizens assembled, and where the governor administered justice.
curia	A voting group in the *comitia curiata*. Also, the customary meeting place of the Senate in the Forum. There was also a *curia* in Pompey's theater on the Campus Martius. In the colonies and townships in the provinces, the meeting place of the municipal council, generally in the open on the Forum.
curialis	A member of a *curia*, a municipal notable; the term was used in the fourth century to designate decurions.
cursus honorum	Ascending order of Roman magistracies. The political career ladder.
curule seat	Folding X-shaped seat, reserved for senators.
decemviri, decemvirs	Legislators who replaced the consuls in 451 and 450 BCE; the compilers of the Law of the Twelve Tables.
devotio	Ceremony during which a general devoted (offered) himself and his army to the *Manes* (benevolent spirits) and the Earth by reciting a formula, dictated to him by the *pontifex maximus*, to ward off a major peril to the army and obtain victory from the gods on the occasion of a battle.
dictator	Magistrate appointed legally with full powers, but for a specified period (less than six months) and in order to accomplish a precise task, when grave danger threatened the state.
diocese	Administrative division comprising several provinces, entrusted to the authority of a *vicarius* (vicar).
epulones	College of seven priests whose duty was to organize the sacred banquets (*epula*); created in 196 BCE.
evocatio	Religious ceremony intended to compel a divinity to abandon the city he or she protected in order to take up residence in the city that wanted to extend a welcome.
factions	Professional chariot racing business associations; groupings of spectators according to the "color" or team they supported.
familia	Group of gladiators under a trainer (*lanista*).

fasces	A bundle of rods bound round an axe. Carried by the lictors accompanying the magistrates *cum imperio* (senior magistrates with civil and military powers).
Fathers (of the Church)	Post-classical designation of the many first–sixth-century theologians who developed the doctrine of the Church.
fetiales	College of 20 diplomat-priests entrusted with international affairs: declarations of war, making of peace and treaties.
flamines	College of 15 priests attached to the worship of a divinity: 3 major *flamines* (Jupiter, Mars, and Quirinus) and 12 minor. In Italy and provincial towns, the *flamines* administered the imperial cult.
genius	A god's power of creation. Each man also had his protective *genius*, as each woman had her *Juno*.
gens (pl. *gentes*)	A Roman clan or group of families linked by a common name and by a belief in a common ancestor.
gladiator	A skilled, trained, and well-armored weapons fighter who performed in public combats against another gladiator. Various types (Samnite, *Retiarius*, etc.).
haruspices	Of Etruscan origin, college of 60 councilors (later priests) who were specialists in examining the entrails of sacrificial victims, notably the liver and heart. They also interpreted the 11 categories of lightning that could occur.
Ides	Day of the month: the 15th in March, May, July, and October; the 13th in the other months; belonged to Jupiter.
imperium	Sovereign civil and military power; under the Republic was held by dictators, consuls, and praetors. Under the Empire, only the emperor could hold it; he could delegate it.
inauguration	When the augurs took the auspices to consecrate the investiture of a magistrate, or the opening of a temple or a public place (= dedication).
lectio senatus	A reading or calling of the roll of the senators, carried out by the censor, who could strike from the list the names of those he considered unworthy.
loca sanctorum	All the places in which relics of martyrs were honored.
ludi	Public games or shows; gladiatorial schools.
lupercalia	February 15, when animals were sacrificed in the Lupercal (the cave where the she-wolf was supposed to have suckled Romulus and Remus); the festival combined fertility and purificatory rituals, and included flagellation. The Luperci or priests of Lupercus were a fraternity of 12 (later 24) priests attached to the worship of Faunus.
lustration	Performance of a purificatory ceremony, e.g. of a body of people, a piece of land, a city.
lustrum	Five-yearly purification performed by the censors after carrying out the *census*; hence the space of five years (*lustrum*) between two purifications.
martyrium	Church constructed around a burial of relics.
missio	Release from combat, public decision (of sparing or killing defeated gladiator) at end of combat.
munus (pl. *munera*)	A duty or obligation to the dead, often in the form of funeral games; an arena spectacle (combat of gladiators or beasts).
munera legitima	Proper or regular shows in a tripartite format: *matutina*, beast shows with hunting or fighting of beasts; *meridiani*, "lunchtime shows" with public executions of criminals; gladiatorial combats in the afternoon.
naumachia	A staged naval battle; the basin dug for such a show.
Nones	Day of the month: the 7th in March, May, July, and October; the 5th in other months. The Nones were related to the Nundinae, the market days which fell on the eighth day of the eight-day market week (the Nundinae are so called because in the Roman system of inclusive counting they came every nine days).

numen	A divinity's power of decision; often meant the divinity himself or herself.
Nundinae	A market day. Also used to denote a weekly market.
optimates	Roman political group, through not an organized party. Aristocratic and conservative, members of the Senate, they opposed the *populares*.
pagus	The smallest recognized territorial unit, often subordinate to an urban community (*oppidum*, *municipium*).
patrician	Originally a member of the *de facto* nobility providing senators (*patres*), then a member of the nobility by birth, for whom access to certain priesthoods and the consulate was initially reserved. The republican patriciate was defined and formed in the fifth century BCE.
patron	Important personage with whom, by a bilateral commitment, individuals (*clientes*) or public collectives (cities, peoples, provinces) were linked. The patron ensured the daily security and legal defense of his clients, who in return owed him respect, help, and their votes. He acted as intermediary between the state and the public collectives to whom he was patron.
plebs, **plebeians**	Political grouping, which appeared in 494/493 BCE, of all those in Rome, of any class, who opposed the patrician organization of the state. Made up of rich and poor, patrons and clients, native Romans and foreigners (Latins, Sabines, etc.) who had come into the city. At first their sole point in common was their opposition to the privileges of the patricians. Subsequently plebeian *gentes* were formed, in opposition to the patrician *gentes*. At the end of the Republic, the word defined the common people.
pomoerium	Sacred boundary of Rome. The land that lay inside it could not receive the tombs of the dead, temples to foreign gods, or the army except for triumphs. Magistrates with *imperium* lost it by crossing the boundary.
pontiffs (*pontifices*)	College of six, later nine, and then 16 priests with the duty of administering sacred and family law, religious jurisdiction, and keeping the *Annales*. They set the calendar, and their Books were a liturgical manual. At their head was the great pontiff (*pontifex maximus*), who also had authority over all the other priests, whom he appointed and inaugurated. Under the Empire, the emperor was the *pontifex maximus*.
populares	Roman political group, though not an organized party, who worked through and supposedly on behalf of the people, challenging the *optimates* in the Senate.
potestas	Power, especially civil (executive) powers of a magistrate, inferior to *imperium*.
praetor	Senior magistrate specially responsible for justice. Performed some of the functions of the consuls in their absence.
princeps (pl. *principes*)	Simply, "first" or "leader." The word was used generally to denote a man of great prestige and authority. In the senate, influential men such as Caesar or Cicero could at times act as *principes*, by speaking first on the topic discussed and thus influencing subsequent debate.
princeps iuventutis	Leader of the equestrian order. Under the emperors, the probable successor to the throne (i.e. the crown prince).
princeps senatus	Leader of the Senate. Inscribed first on the official list drawn up by the censors, and had the privilege of speaking first at meetings of the Senate. Under the Empire, the emperor was *princeps senatus*.
prodigy	Spontaneous and unusual manifestation of the divine will, for example rain of blood or ashes, lightning in a clear sky, etc. Gave rise to an expiatory ceremony.
proletarii, **proletarians**	Those whose only belongings were their offspring (*proles*).

publicani	Private individuals who "farmed" public services (*publica*); levying taxes, contracting for public works and for equipping armies and the navy. In the late third century BCE they formed companies and soon large joint stock companies (*societates*).
quaestor	Minor magistrate whose special task was finance.
quindecimviri *sacris faciundis*	College of two (*duumviri*), later ten (*decemviri*), then 15 (*quindecimviri*) priests charged with custody and interpretation of the Sibylline Books, the worship of Apollo, and overseeing foreign cults established in Rome.
quirites	Denomination of the Roman people, i.e. members of the civilian body: as opposed to *milites*, which designated citizens under arms.
Regia	Abode of the king on the Forum, near the temple of Vesta, and then frequently the dwelling of the *pontifex maximus*. Religious center of Rome.
rex sacrorum	First of the Roman priests, successor to the kings, from whom he inherited religious authority. Entrusted with the worship of Janus.
rostra	A platform from which speakers delivered their addresses, situated near the Curia under the Republic and subsequently moved farther west. Decorated with the prows of boats captured at the Battle of Antium (338 BCE), whence its name *rostra* (cutwaters).
sacer	Sacred, thus reserved for the gods (as opposed to profane), whence taboo, sacrosanct (e.g. the tribunes of the *plebs*).
sacramentum	Solemn oath taken by the conscript on his enrolment. It bound the soldier to the state and his superiors and rendered "accursed" anyone who broke it.
Salii, Salians	Fraternity of 12, later 24 priests of Mars and Quirinus. They opened and closed the war cycle of the year: March–October.
Senate	Assembly of 300 members, then 600 under Sulla, 900 under Caesar, again 600 from Augustus, composed of former magistrates, a list of whom was drawn up every five years by the censors, later by the emperor, who carried out the *lectio senatus* (calling the roll). It was the government of the republican state. Under the Empire it maintained its prestige, but its role diminished to the point where it became Rome's municipal council.
senatus *consultum*	Decision of the Senate which, under the Empire, had the force of a law. In the event of major danger, under the Republic, the *senatus consultum ultimum*, or ultimate senatorial decree, gave full powers to the consuls.
seviri augustales **(priests of Augustus)**	Associations of six people, generally freedmen, formed to celebrate imperial worship at municipal level. See *flamines*.
Sibylline Books	Collection of prophecies attributed to the Sibyl, preserved by the *Quindecimviri sacris faciundis*, who were specialists in the interpretation of these writings. From 38 BCE they were kept in the Palatine temple of Apollo.
sodales, *sodalities*	Colleges of priests, generally attached to the worship of archaic divinities: Arvales, Luperci, Salians.
taurobolium	Sacrifice of a bull, followed by a "baptism" accomplished by sprinkling the blood in a trench. Practiced in the worship of Cybele.
tribunes of the plebs	College of 10 magistrates whose task was the protection of the *plebs*; they were inviolable (*sacri*) and had the right of intercession (= veto) over decisions of the magistrates, with the exception of dictators. Starting with Augustus, the emperor held the power of the tribunes (*tribunicia potestas*).
triumph	A public processional entrance of a general into Rome in celebration of military victory.

venatio	Spectacle with beasts, staged as a hunt with hunters or as a combat of beasts against humans or other beasts.
vestals	College of six priestesses whose duty was to watch over the flame, the guarantee of Rome's power, a flame that must never be extinguished, kept in the temple of Vesta on the Forum.
vexillatio	Military detachment, a unit formed temporarily with soldiers taken from other bodies of troops.
vicarius	High functionary responsible for a diocese.
vicus	A village or hamlet; or a district or quarter of a city.
vow	Promise which religiously committed whoever made it (*votum susceptum*) and which it was imperative that he carry out (*votum solutum*).

GUIDE TO GREEK AND ROMAN WRITERS

The works of classical authors are preserved mainly in manuscripts, which were re-copied by hand, often many times, over the course of the Middle Ages. They were written continuously, and normally without punctuation; their division into "books" (referred to below) and "chapters" is a modern editorial convention meant to facilitate citation.

The two most complete and authoritative collections of Greek and Latin works are the Oxford Classical Texts (Oxford University Press) and the Bibliotheca Teubneriana (B. G. Teubner). Reliable translations of most works can be found in the Loeb Classical Library, and in the Penguin Classics series. A growing number of Internet sites, of varying quality, act as repositories for classical texts and translations; a good place to start is the site entitled "Electronic Resources for Classicists," maintained by the University of California at Irvine.

In what follows, authors like Appian, who lived in the second century CE but wrote about the republican era, have been grouped according to the period they describe, rather than the one in which they lived.

The Roman Republic (to 31 BCE)

Appian (c.95–165 CE) A Greek from Alexandria, Appian spent much of his working life at Rome, as a lawyer and civil servant. His ethnographically arranged *Roman History* is partially preserved. An admirer of Roman imperialism, he is perhaps most important for what he reveals of political and social conditions at Rome in the period from the Gracchi to the end of the Republic, mainly in books 13–17 (covering 133–35 BCE), which are often cited separately as *Civil Wars*, books 1–5.

Julius Caesar (100–44 BCE) The most important political and military leader of his time, Gaius Julius Caesar wrote primarily for political reasons – to justify his actions and to defend his policies. His *Gallic War*, which describes his conquest of Gaul in the period 58–52 BCE, is the earliest surviving account of the culture and customs of the Gauls and

Germans. His *Civil War*, in three books, is a transparently partisan account of the events of 49–48 BCE.

Cato the Elder (234–149 BCE) Marcus Porcius Cato, born at Tusculum, in central Italy, was a vocal proponent of traditional Roman virtues, and spokesperson of a conservative and patriotic ideology. His sole surviving work is *On Agriculture*, a manual on farming and estate management written about 160 BCE. It is an important source of information on contemporary social and economic institutions, including agricultural slavery.

Catullus (c.84–54 BCE) Gaius Valerius Catullus of Verona (in northern Italy) spent much of his short life at Rome, where he moved in fashionable circles. Passionate and immediate, his poems range across a wide variety of styles and subjects, including his tempestuous and sometimes debilitating affair with a woman whom he addresses as "Lesbia," and who was, in real life, Clodia, the sister of Publius Clodius, tribune in 58 BCE.

Cicero (106–43 BCE) Marcus Tullius Cicero of Arpinum (in central Italy), consul in 63 BCE, and self-styled defender of republican institutions, is probably better known through his own works than any other writer of classical antiquity. Most of his 57 surviving speeches, which belong to the period 81–43 BCE, deal with civil and criminal cases, and with the doings of the politically active. An extensive set of his letters, 864 in all (774 written by Cicero, 90 by his correspondents), was published after his death, in four collections: one to friends and members of his household (*Letters to his Friends*), a second to his friend Atticus, a third, in three books, to his brother Quintus, the fourth to Brutus, Caesar's assassin. He also wrote extensively about political theory, rhetoric, and philosophy.

Diodorus Siculus (c.80–after 21 BCE) Pedestrian and occasionally inaccurate, Diodorus' *Historical Library*, of which books 1–5 and 11–20 are fully preserved, is a general world history from mythological times to 54 BCE, important mainly for what it records about developments at Rome in the period 480–302.

Dionysius of Halicarnassus (c.60/55–after 7 BCE) A literary critic and teacher of rhetoric, Dionysius lived at Rome from 30 BCE. Given to long and unhistorical speeches, his *Roman Antiquities*, a history of Rome from its foundation to 264 BCE, is sometimes insightful, more often tedious and antiquarian. The whole of books 1–10 and most of 11 (to 446 BCE) are extant; the rest survives in fragments.

Fabius Pictor (c.254 BCE–?) One of the earliest Roman prose historians, he is considered the father of Roman history. A member of the prominent Fabii family, he was the grandson of Gaius Fabius, who received the nickname Pictor ("painter"). His works, written in Greek, consist of *Annales Maximi*, the chronicles of the great consular families, and his own experiences in the Second Punic War (218–201). After the defeat of the Romans by Hannibal at the battle of Cannae (216), he was sent by the Romans to consult the oracle of Apollo at Delphi. Later historians such as Polybius, Dionysius of Halicarnassus, and Livy use Fabius as a source.

Livy (59 BCE–17 CE or 64 BCE–12 CE) In many ways the pre-eminent historian of the Republic, Titus Livius was raised at Patavium (modern Padua) in northern Italy. A skillful story-teller, fond of idealized (and sometimes fictionalized) examples of old-fashioned heroism, he is rarely critical of his sources. Of his *History of Rome*, from its origins to 9

BCE (in 142 books), books 1–10 (to 293) and 21–45 (218–167) are preserved more or less intact. The rest are known from the later *Epitomes* of them.

Lucan (39–65 CE)   Born at Corduba (modern Córdoba), Spain, a nephew of the philosopher Seneca the Elder, Marcus Annaeus Lucanus lived at Rome until he was forced to commit suicide for having plotted against the emperor Nero. His only surviving work, *Civil War*, is an unfinished, and staunchly anti-Caesarian, epic poem on the causes and course of the war between Caesar and Pompey.

Lucretius (c.94–55 BCE)   Almost nothing is known of the life of the poet and philosopher Titus Lucretius Carus, whose only work, *On the Nature of Things*, borrows from Epicurus to construct a mechanical and atomic view of the universe, intended to allay fears of the gods' intervention in human affairs, and of the after-life.

Cornelius Nepos (c.99–24 BCE)   A correspondent of Cicero, and acquaintance of Catullus, Cornelius Nepos is important for having authored the earliest surviving Latin biographies (*On Illustrious Men*), eulogizing and sometimes careless accounts of the lives of writers, kings, and generals.

Plautus (died after 184 BCE)   Credited in one tradition with having authored 130 plays, of which 21 are extant, Titus Maccius Plautus was born at Sarsina in Umbria, a proverbially backward region of north-central Italy. Set in Greece, and based on Greek models (like Menander), but informed by Roman ideas and practices, his imaginative, and sometimes fantastic, comedies afford a tantalizing glimpse into the social conventions and attitudes of the middle Republic.

Polybius (c.200–after 118 BCE)   A politically active Greek from Megalopolis, Polybius was taken hostage in 167 BCE and deported to Rome, where he befriended the Roman general and statesman Publius Cornelius Scipio Aemilianus. Of the 40 books of his *Histories*, a general history of the Mediterranean world written mainly to explain the rise of Rome to his fellow Greeks, only the first five (to 216 BCE) survive intact. Unromantic and explicitly unrhetorical, he is easily our most reliable source for the period from the beginning of the Second Carthaginian War to about the middle of the second century BCE.

Sallust (86–c.35 BCE)   A partisan of Julius Caesar from 50 BCE, Gaius Sallustius Crispus of Amiternum (in central Italy) retired from political life after Caesar's assassination to write history. Two monographs are preserved: the *Jugurthine War*, which recounts the incompetence and venality of the senatorial generals sent to North Africa to campaign against the renegade Jugurtha in the period 112–107 BCE, and *The Conspiracy of Catiline*, which accepts, for the most part, Cicero's tendentious account of Catiline's alleged attempt to overthrow the government in 63. We have only fragments of Sallust's *Histories*, which probably described what he considered to be the moral decline of the Republic.

Terence (c.190–159 BCE)   Brought to Rome as a slave from his native North Africa, and subsequently freed, Publius Terentius Afer is known to have written six comedies, all of which were produced in the period 166–160 BCE. Heavily dependent on Hellenistic models, especially Menander, his plays are almost entirely Greek in subject and manner.

Varro (116–27 BCE)   An antiquarian, and uncommonly prolific writer, Marcus Terentius Varro of Reate (in central Italy) was at one time a partisan of Pompey; subsequently restored to favor by Caesar, he was later outlawed by Antony. Of the 74 works attributed to him, only two survive: a manual on farm management (*On Agriculture*), published in 37 BCE, and a much cited but probably little read treatise *On the Latin Language*, in 25 books, of which 5–10 are partly extant.

The Roman World, 31 BCE–235 CE

Apuleius (born c.123 CE) Born to a wealthy family at Madaurus, North Africa, Apuleius was educated at Carthage, Athens, and Rome. A lawyer, poet, rhetorician, philosopher, and lecturer, his extant works include the only Latin novel to have survived intact, the *Metamorphoses* (or *Golden Ass*), the charming story of a young man named Lucius, who, having been turned into an ass, endures a series of strange and amusing adventures before being restored to human form by the goddess Isis.

Cassius Dio (164/165–after 229 CE) A native of Nicaea, in Asia Minor, and a senator from the time of Commodus, Cassius Dio Cocceianus is said to have spent 22 years writing his *Roman History*, an annalistic narrative of events from the foundation of Rome to his own day, of which only books 36–54, covering the period 68–10 BCE, survive intact. (Others are partially preserved, in the epitomes made by the Byzantine compilers Xiphilinus and Zonaras, or, like 55–60, on the period 9 BCE–46 CE, in abbreviated form.) It is valuable chiefly for its account of the age of Augustus, and of Dio's own time.

Celsus (time of Tiberius) Aulus Cornelius Celsus wrote an encyclopedia covering agriculture, medicine, rhetoric, and military science (possibly also philosophy and law), of which only the medical books are preserved. *On Medicine* is important mainly for what it reveals about Hellenistic medical theories.

Columella (mid-first century CE) Lucius Iunius Moderatus Columella, born to a land-owning family at Gades (modern Cádiz), Spain, became an army officer and the owner of several estates in Italy. *On Agriculture* (written 60–5 CE), which draws mainly from his own experience, is easily our most comprehensive source of information about agricultural practices and farm management.

Dio Chrysostom (c.40–after 112 CE) An orator and popular philosopher, once banished by the emperor Domitian, Dio Cocceianus Chrysostomos is a valuable source of information about society and civic affairs in the Greek cities of his native Asia Minor. The 80 speeches attributed to him cover a wide variety of themes, including popular morality, Stoic (and Cynic) ideals, mythology, and literary criticism.

Florus (time of Hadrian?) All that is known of Lucius Annaeus Florus is that he was born in North Africa. He may be the Florus who is said to have been a poet and friend of the emperor Hadrian. His short, almost exclusively military, history of Rome, from its origins to the time of Augustus (*Epitome bellorum omnium annorum DCC*), is derivative, unimaginative, and often inaccurate.

Fronto (c.100–166 CE) Marcus Cornelius Fronto of Cirta, North Africa, was the leading orator of his day, and, for a time, tutor of the future emperor Marcus Aurelius. His correspondence (*Epistulae*) is concerned mostly with the study of rhetoric, but also reveals something of the character of the imperial court.

Gaius (mid-second century CE) Nothing at all is known of Gaius, not even his full name. His *Institutes*, written probably about 160 CE, is easily our best surviving introduction to

Roman civil law. Lucid and economical, it was later used as a kind of textbook for first-year students at law schools in the East, and served as the model for the emperor Justinian's *Institutes*, published in 533 CE.

Galen (129–c.199 CE)   Galen of Pergamum was physician to the imperial court at Rome in the time of Marcus Aurelius. An accomplished anatomist and physiologist, he is also a valuable source of information about earlier theories of pathology, pharmacology, and dietetics.

Aulus Gellius (c.130–180 CE)   An antiquarian about whom little is known, Aulus Gellius wrote *Attic Nights*, in 20 books, to entertain and educate his children. Ranging over a great variety of subjects, including history, law, grammar, and philosophy, it is valuable partly because it quotes extensively from earlier writers whose works have not survived.

Herodian (c.165–255 CE)   A Syrian-born Greek, Herodian worked as a civil servant at Rome. His *History*, a narrative of events 180–238 CE, is moralizing and superficial, useful only because it covers a period which is otherwise badly documented.

Horace (65–8 BCE)   Born at Venusia, in southern Italy, the son of an ex-slave, Quintus Horatius Flaccus became part of the literary circle patronized by Augustus' friend Maecenas. His surviving works include the *Epodes*, 17 poems written in imitation of the Greek poet Archilochus, and the *Satires*, published probably in the mid-30s BCE, broadly autobiographical reflections on life, literature, food, family, and friends. The *Odes* (*Carmina*), the first three books of which were published probably about 23 BCE, are generally agreed to be his greatest accomplishment. Vivid and sophisticated, technically and stylistically flawless, they tackle a remarkably wide variety of topics, including death, love, and even politics. The *Epistles*, verse letters published probably in 20 BCE, are conversational set pieces warning against greed, and extolling, among other things, the virtues of the "simple life." He also wrote a hymn (*Carmen saeculare*) for Augustus' celebration of the Secular Games in 17 BCE, and the disappointingly unimaginative *Art of Poetry*.

Josephus (37/38–c.100 CE)   A Jewish priest of aristocratic birth, assigned to defend Galilee against the Romans in the Jewish rebellion of 66–70 CE, Flavius Josephus was captured in 67, pardoned by the future emperor Titus, and later awarded Roman citizenship. His *Jewish War*, written originally in Aramaic, is a narrative of the revolt that draws mainly on his own knowledge of it. His other surviving works are an *Autobiography*, written to defend his conduct during the rebellion, the *Jewish Antiquities*, a full-scale history of the Jews from creation to 65 CE, and *Against Apion*, which defends Judaism against the misrepresentations of anti-Semitic writers.

Juvenal (c.60–140 CE)   Little is known with certainty about the life or career of Decimus Iunius Iuvenalis of Aquinum (in central Italy). Consumed, it seems, by a bitter sense of failure and injustice, he is said to have been banished at one point for lampooning a favorite of the imperial court. His 16 *Satires*, which ruthlessly ridicule the vices and vulgarities of the wealthy, include (6) a famously savage and unfunny denunciation of women.

Lucian (c.120–after 180 CE)   A native of Samosata (modern Samsât, Turkey) who made his living first as an advocate in court, and later as a traveling lecturer, Lucian moved eventually (probably when he was about 40) to Athens, where he abandoned rhetoric for philosophy. His 80 or so surviving works, many of which are in dialogue form, satirize a variety of contemporary institutions and manners, including popular religion and philosophical pretensions.

Martial (c.40–104 CE)   A penetratingly keen observer of human nature, Marcus Valerius Martialis of Bilbilis, Spain, lived at Rome from 64 CE until a few years before his death. His verse *Epigrams* (in 12 books) are succinct, and sometimes obscene, portraits of contemporary men and women. They are a rich source of information about private life and social customs in the last decades of the first century CE.

Ovid (43 BCE–17 CE)   Born at Sulmo, in central Italy, Publius Ovidius Naso was a prominent part of the literary culture of Rome in the time of Augustus. In 8 CE, for reasons that are unclear, he was banished by Augustus to Tomis, on the Black Sea, where he spent the rest of his life, complaining (in *Letters from the Black Sea* and *Tristia*) about his isolation. His other surviving works include two collections of love poems, the *Amores* and the *Heroides*, the *Art of Love*, a cleverly subversive guide to seduction and intrigue, its companion-piece, the *Remedies of Love*, the *Metamorphoses*, an epic and original collection of stories about changes of shape, and the *Fasti*, a verse calendar of religious festivals and anniversaries.

Pausanius (mid-second century CE)   Nothing is known about the life of Pausanius, a Greek geographer and traveler whose *Description of Greece*, in 10 books, was meant to be a kind of tourist's guide to Greece, including its historical and religious artifacts.

Petronius (first century CE)   Possibly the Petronius who is said to have been "arbiter of elegance" at the court of the emperor Nero, Petronius wrote both poetry (a small collection of which survives) and a novel, the *Satyricon*, which is only partially preserved. It recounts the adventures of two rather dissolute young men, Encolpius (the narrator) and Giton, including a fantastically extravagant dinner they attend at the home of a wealthy and comically vulgar ex-slave named Trimalchio. Petronius committed suicide in 66 CE.

Philo (c.30 BCE–45 CE)   Commonly known as Philo Judaeus, Philo was the head of the Jewish community in his native Alexandria. A theologian and philosopher, he is important mainly for his political writings *Against Flaccus*, which catalogs Jewish complaints about the governor of Egypt, and the *Embassy to Gaius*, his first-hand account of a delegation sent to Rome in 39/40 CE to ask Caligula to exempt the Jews from the duty of worshiping the emperor.

Pliny the Elder (23/24–79 CE)   Uncle and adoptive father of Pliny the Younger, Gaius Plinius Secundus was born at Comum, in northern Italy. At one time commander of a cavalry squadron on the Rhine, he later held a series of prominent posts under the emperors Vespasian and Titus, culminating in his appointment as commander of the fleet stationed at Misenum (on the bay of Naples). He died observing the eruption of Mt. Vesuvius in 79 CE. His only surviving work is the *Natural History*, an encyclopedic collection of pseudo-scientific lore, wondrous, and sometimes fanciful, stories about natural phenomena, people, animals, plants, metals, and stones.

Pliny the Younger (c.61–112 CE)   Like his uncle, Gaius Plinius Caecilius Secundus was born at Comum. A wealthy and well-connected lawyer, he had a long and distinguished public career, culminating in his appointment as governor of the province of Bithynia-Pontus (in modern Turkey) in about 111/112 CE. His *Letters*, 368 in all, are mostly formal and literary, many of them short essays on contemporary political and social issues. The tenth book, written when he was governor of Bithynia-Pontus, consists of his official correspondence with the emperor Trajan; it is an important source of information about Roman provincial administration. We possess also his *Panegyricus*, a ponderously effusive speech in praise of Trajan that he delivered in the Senate in 100 CE.

Plutarch (before 50–after 120 CE)   Philosopher, priest (at Delphi), and occasional lecturer, Plutarch spent most of his life in his native Chaeronea, in central Greece. Most of his surviving works are contained in the *Moralia*, a collection of more than 60 short essays on a variety of topics, many of them ethical and religious. Extant also is the deservedly famous *Parallel Lives*, 50 biographies of Greek and Roman generals and political leaders, most of them organized in Greek–Roman pairs. They are adulatory, anecdotal, moralizing, vivid, and irresistibly readable.

Propertius (54/47–before 2 BCE)   Born to a prominent family at Assisi, Sextus Propertius became part of the literary circle at Rome patronized by Maecenas. His self-consciously elegant love poems, addressed to a woman he calls Cynthia (and whose real name is said to have been Hostia), are a window on Augustan thought and society.

Quintilian (c.30/35–100 CE)   A distinguished teacher of oratory, reportedly the first to be paid a salary by the state, Marcus Fabius Quintilianus was born at Calagurris (modern Calahorra), Spain. His painstakingly detailed (and often lumbering) *Institutes of Oratory*, in 12 books, is easily our most comprehensive source of information about the nature and ideals of Roman education.

Seneca the Elder (c.55 BCE–37/41 CE)   Little is known of the life of Lucius Annaeus Seneca, father of the philosopher Seneca the Younger. Born at Corduba (modern Córdoba), Spain, he acquired a considerable fortune, perhaps through trade, and probably spent much of his life at Rome. His surviving works on rhetoric, five books of *Controversiae* ("Debates") and one of *Suasoriae* ("Pleadings"), are a valuable source for the literary history of the early Empire.

Seneca the Younger (4 BCE/1 CE–65 CE)   Born, like his father, at Corduba, Lucius Annaeus Seneca served as tutor and adviser to Nero until 65 CE, when he was implicated in a conspiracy against the emperor and forced to commit suicide. His many surviving works, which constitute our fullest guide to Roman Stoicism, include *Dialogues* on various ethical topics (e.g. anger), 124 *Moral Epistles*, 7 technical and tiresome books *On Benefits*, and 2 others, *On Clemency*, that he presented to Nero in 56 CE. He also wrote *Natural Questions*, on physics and cosmology, 8 (perhaps 9) uninspired tragedies, and the *Apocolocyntosis* ("Pumpkinization"), a clever and original satire on the deification of the emperor Claudius.

Strabo (64/63 BCE–after 21 CE)   A Greek historian and geographer, Strabo seems to have spent most of his life at his native Amaseia, in the province of Pontus. His *Geography*, which covers (in 17 books) the whole of Europe, western Asia, and North Africa, is an important source of information not only about historical geography, but also about economic and political history.

Suetonius (c.69–150 CE)   Born to a wealthy and politically active Roman family, Gaius Suetonius Tranquillus was a lawyer and, for a time, a secretary to the emperor Hadrian. His surviving works include several biographies of grammarians, rhetoricians, and poets (in the partially preserved *On the Lives of Illustrious Men*), and *The Lives of the Caesars*, biographies of Julius Caesar and of the first 11 emperors (i.e. from Augustus to Domitian). Anecodotal, credulous, and not infrequently gossipy, they present a fascinating and often arresting picture of the imperial court.

Tacitus (c.56–after 113 CE)   Arguably the greatest Roman historian, Cornelius Tacitus was born probably in southern Gaul or in northern Italy. He was consul in 97 CE, and later (probably in 112/113) governor of the province of Asia. The earliest of his surviving works is the *Dialogue on Orators*, a pessimistic account of the decline of oratory. The *Agricola*, a biography of his father-in-law, Gnaeus Julius Agricola, governor of Britain, 78–84 CE, provides valuable information about the pacification and Romanization of the province. The *Germania*, written about 100 CE, is a fascinating account of the ethnography, military and political institutions, religion, and customs of the Germanic tribes. The *Annals*, a full-scale history (in 18 books) of the period 14–68 CE, is only partially preserved: we have the whole of books 1–4, the beginning of 5, all of 6, the last part of 11, and all of 12–16 (covering the periods 14–29, 31–37, and 47–66 CE). Eloquently incisive, often cynical, too narrowly focused on Rome and on the person of the emperor, it is far and away our most reliable source for the history of the early Empire. Of his *Histories*, which covered the period 69–96 CE, only books 1–4 and the beginning of 5 survive (69–70 CE).

Tibullus (55/48–19 BCE)   Little is known about Tibullus (an anonymous biography makes him out to be something of a dilettante). His surviving love poetry, much of it addressed to a woman he calls Delia, and to a boy, Marathus, is a valuable source for the social and literary climate of Augustan Rome.

Valerius Maximus (time of Tiberius)   Nothing at all is known about the life of Valerius Maximus, whose *Memorable Deeds and Sayings*, published probably soon after 31 CE, is a collection of moralizing anecdotes for the use of teachers and rhetoricians. Simple and uncritical, it preserves some valuable information about famous people and about Roman institutions.

Velleius Paterculus (c.19 BCE–after 30 CE)   An army officer from Campania (in central Italy), Velleius Paterculus wrote a *History of Rome* in two books, of which only the second, covering the period 146 BCE–30 CE, is intact. It is valuable as a counter-narrative to the perspectives of Tacitus, Suetonius, and Cassius Dio on Tiberius.

Virgil (70–19 BCE)   Publius Vergilius Maro was born at Andes, a village near Mantua, in northern Italy. He studied rhetoric at Rome, where he befriended Horace, and became a prominent part of the literary circle of Maecenas. The *Eclogues*, written probably 45–37 BCE, are 10 pastoral poems (about shepherds and the like) set in Greece and modeled on Greek originals (especially Theocritus). The *Georgics*, written probably 36–29 BCE to praise agriculture and Italy, deal in turn with crops, fruit trees, animals, and bees. It was, however, the *Aeneid*, begun in 26 BCE and not quite finished at Vergil's death in 19, which established his reputation as the greatest Latin poet. Modeled on Homer, but infused with a nationalistic Roman patriotism, it recounts, in epic style, the adventures and travails of the legendary Trojan hero Aeneas.

Vitruvius (time of Augustus)   An architect and military engineer, about whom little is known, Vitruvius Pollio is the author of the *Treatise on architecture*, the only surviving Roman work on architecture. Written probably about 25–23 BCE, it also discusses town planning, water supply, and machines.

The Later Roman Empire

Ammianus Marcellinus (c.330–395 CE)   A career military officer, Ammianus Marcellinus was born to a moderately wealthy family at Antioch, in Syria. Of the 31 books of his *History*, written in Latin (though his native language was Greek), only the last 18 survive, covering the period 353–378 CE. A pagan who greatly admired the emperor Julian, he writes tolerantly of Christianity.

The Augustan History (fourth century CE?)   Written perhaps in the middle of the fourth century CE, probably by a single author, the *Augustan History* (or *Lives of the Later Caesars*) is a collection of 30 biographies of the emperors (and usurpers) from Hadrian to Carinus and Numerianus (117–284 CE). They are entertaining, anecdotal, uncritical, and generally unreliable.

Aurelius Victor (mid-/late fourth century CE)   Governor of the province of Pannonia (Secunda) in 361 CE, and prefect of the city of Rome in 389, Sextus Aurelius Victor of North Africa was the author of *The Caesars*, a moralizing and biographically inspired history of the period from Augustus to Constantius (360 CE), which is much concerned with prodigies, and generally not of much value.

Ausonius (died c.395 CE)   Decimus Magnus Ausonius taught grammar and rhetoric at his native Bordeaux for 30 years, before being appointed tutor to the future emperor Gratian; he was later governor of Gaul, and, in 379 CE, consul. His surviving works include 25 letters, and many poems, of which the most important, and charming, is the *Mosella*, written in praise of the river (it describes, in some detail, the various kinds of fish that could be found in it).

Claudian (c.370–404 CE)   A Greek-speaking native of Alexandria, Claudius Claudianus moved to Italy sometime before 395 CE, where he served as court-poet to the emperor Honorius, and propagandist of Honorius' minister, Stilicho. A number of his poems survive, many of them political in purpose; they are a useful (if tendentious) guide to the history of the period.

Eutropius (late fourth century CE)   Little is known of Eutropius, whose *Breviarium ab urbe condita* narrates the whole of Roman history from Romulus to 364 CE. Drawn mainly from secondary materials, it is valuable chiefly for filling gaps in other sources.

Julian (332–363 CE)   Caesar from 355 CE, and emperor 361–363, Flavius Claudius Julianus is probably best known for his attempt to revive paganism. His surviving works include *The Beard-Hater*, a satirical defense of his policies, *The Banquet* (or *The Caesars*), a waggish account of Constantine's reception on Mt. Olympus, 8 speeches, and about 80 *Letters*, many of which are anti-Christian.

Libanius (314–c.393 CE)   Libanius spent much of his life at his native Antioch (in Syria), where he taught rhetoric. A pagan who admired the emperor Julian, he was not altogether unsympathetic to Christianity. A great many of his works are preserved, including 64 speeches, most of which are concerned with public and municipal affairs, and about 1,600 letters, which constitute a storehouse of information about the social, cultural, and political life of the urban elite of the eastern half of the empire in the fourth century CE.

Macrobius (late fourth/early fifth centuries CE)   Little is known about the life of Ambrosius Theodosius Macrobius; he may have been North African. His most important work is the antiquarian *Saturnalia*, a fictitious symposium, in seven books, which deals mainly with philology, history, and literary criticism (especially of Virgil).

Procopius (c.500–after 562 CE)   Born at Caesarea in Palestine, trained in law and rhetoric, Procopius held a series of military and administrative posts under the emperor Justinian, culminating in his appointment as prefect of the city of Constantinople in 562 CE. His main works are the generally reliable *History of the Wars of Justinian*, in eight books, and the *Secret History*, written about 550 CE, a sustained and scurrilous attack on Justinian and his policies.

Symmachus (c.340–402 CE)   Widely acknowledged to be the greatest orator of his day, Quintus Aurelius Symmachus held a number of prominent positions in the imperial administration, including a consulship in 391 CE. A vigorous opponent of Christianity, he wrote numerous letters (many of which survive) and speeches, including two in praise of the emperors Valentinian I and Gratian, which are important sources for the history of the period.

Zosimus (late fifth century CE)   Not much is known about the life of Zosimus, who is said to have held several imperial posts. His *New History*, which covers the period from Augustus to 410 CE, is valuable mainly for its account of the years after 305, and for its interpretation of the decline of the Empire, which Zosimus attributes to neglect of the pagan gods.

Christian Writers

Augustine (354–430 CE)   Born at Thagaste (modern Souk Ahras, Algeria), Aurelius Augustinus taught rhetoric at Carthage and in Italy (at Rome and Milan), where he converted to Christianity. From 395 CE, he was bishop of Hippo (modern Bône, Algeria). More than 100 of his works are preserved, including many letters and sermons, and what are probably his two most important works, the *City of God*, a reply to anti-Christian propaganda (in 22 books), and the *Confessions*, a vivid and highly personal account of his life (to 388), and of his conversion.

Cyprian (c.200–258 CE)   The son of a wealthy and well-connected family, Thascius Caecilius Cyprianus became bishop of Carthage in 248 CE. His surviving works include *On the Unity of the Catholic Church* and *On Those Who Have Lapsed*, which deal mainly with the consequences of the persecutions that began under the emperor Decius in 249, *To Donatus*, a denunciation of worldliness, and *Letters*, most of which are concerned with the organization and management of the Church.

Eusebius (c.260–340 CE)   Born in Palestine, Eusebius became bishop of Caesarea about 314 CE. His most important work is the *Ecclesiastical History*, which describes, in 10 books, the development of the Church to 324 CE. He also wrote an adulatory *Life of Constantine*, and a chronology of universal history, which is preserved in an Armenian version and in a Latin adaptation by Jerome.

Jerome (c.348–420 CE)   A vocal champion of asceticism, Eusebius Hieronymus was widely considered to be the most learned man of his time. Best known for his Latin translation of the Bible (the Vulgate), he also wrote *On the Lives of Illustrious Men*, an introduction to 135 Christian writers, an historical chronology (*Chronicle*), based on Eusebius, and numerous letters.

Lactantius (c.240–320 CE)   Born probably at Carthage, Lucius Caecilius Firmianus, who was known also as Lactantius, taught rhetoric for a time at Nicomedia (near modern Istanbul); he was later appointed tutor to the emperor Constantine's eldest son, Crispus. His most important surviving works are the *Divine Institutes*, a reply, in seven books, to pagan attacks on Christianity, and *On the Deaths of the Persecutors*, an account of the sufferings of the persecutors, written probably about 318 CE.

Minucius Felix (early/mid-third century CE)   Nothing is known of the life of Marcus Minucius Felix. His only surviving work is the *Octavius*, a dialogue between a Christian, Octavius, and a pagan, Caecilius Natalis, whose case against Christianity borrows heavily from Fronto.

Origen (c.185–254/255 CE)   Origenes Adamantius spent much of his life as a teacher, first at his native Alexandria, later at Caesarea (in Palestine). His writing, which included commentaries on the Bible and an exposition of Christian doctrine (*De principiis*), is preserved only in bits and pieces. The main surviving work is *Against Celsus*, written, probably about 249 CE, to counter anti-Christian propaganda.

Orosius (early fifth century CE)   A native of Spain, Paulus Orosius was a student of Augustine from 414 CE. His *History Against the Pagans* is a history of the world, in seven books, from creation to 417 CE. Rhetorical, and not infrequently mistaken, it was written to demonstrate that the calamities of the imperial period were not a consequence of the spread of Christianity.

Prudentius (348–410 CE)   Aurelius Clemens Prudentius of Spain abandoned a distinguished administrative career to write Christian poetry. His surviving works include hymns, allegories, and *Against Symmachus*, a polemic against paganism.

Tertullian (c.160–240 CE)   Born at (or near) Carthage, Quintus Septimius Florens Tertullianus was trained as a lawyer, but converted to Christianity about 195 CE. His more than 30 surviving works include *To the Pagans* and *Apology*, both written (in about 197) to defend Christianity against popular charges of atheism and black magic.

GUIDE TO FURTHER READING

General

Reference works

Bang, P. F., Ikeguchi, M., and Ziche, H. G. *Ancient Economies, Modern Methodologies: Archaeology, Comparative History, Models and Institutions*. Bari, 2006.

Boatwright, M. T., Gargola, D. J., and Richard, J. A. *The Romans from Village to Empire*. New York, 2004.

Cary, M. *The Geographic Background of Greek and Roman History*. Oxford, 1949.

Crawford, M. H. *Roman Republican Coinage*, 2 vols. Cambridge, 1987.

Cuomo, S. *Technology and Culture in Greek and Roman Antiquity: Key Themes in Ancient History*. New York, 2007.

Dilke, O. A. W. *Greek and Roman Maps*. London, 1985.

Erdkamp, P. (ed.). *A Companion to the Roman Army*. Oxford, 2007.

Hammond, N. G. L. (ed.). *Atlas of the Greek and Roman World in Antiquity*. Park Ridge, NJ, 1981.

Hammond, N. G. L. and Scullard, H. H. (eds.). *The Oxford Classical Dictionary*, 2nd edn. Oxford, 1970.

Keppie, L. *Understanding Roman Inscriptions*. Baltimore, 1991.

King, H. *Health in Antiquity*. London, 2005.

Raaflaub, K. A (ed.). *War and Peace in the Ancient World*. Oxford, 2007.

Rives, J. B. *Religion in the Roman Empire*. Oxford, 2007.

Rüpke, J. (ed.). *A Companion to Roman Religion*. Oxford, 2007.

Stillwell, R., MacDonald, W. L., and McAllister, M. H. (eds.). *The Princeton Encyclopedia of Classical Sites*. Princeton, 1976.

Sutherland, C. H. V. and Carson, R. A. G. (eds.). *The Roman Imperial Coinage*, 9 vols. London, 1984.

General studies

Boardman, J., Griffin, J. and Murray, O. (eds.). *The Oxford History of the Roman World*. Oxford, 1991.

Kenney, E. J. (ed.). *Latin Literature*. Vol. 2 of *The Cambridge History of Classical Literature*. Cambridge, 1982.

Wacher, J. (ed.). *The Roman World*, 2 vols. London, 1987.

The Roman Republic to 133 BC

General histories

Astin, A. E., Walbank, F. W., Fredericksen, M. W., and Ogilvie, R. M. (eds.). *Rome and the Mediterranean to 133 B.C.* Vol. 8 of *The Cambridge Ancient History*, 2nd edn. Cambridge, 1989.

Brunt, P. A. *Social Conflicts in the Roman Republic*. New York and London, 1971.

Cornell, T. J. *The Beginnings of Rome: Italy and Rome from the Bronze Age to the Punic Wars (c. 1000–264 BC)*. London and New York, 1995.

Forsythe, G. *A Critical History of Early Rome: From Prehistory to the First Punic War*. Berkeley, 2005.

Heurgon, J. *The Rise of Rome*. Trans. J. Willis. Berkeley, 1973.

Scullard, H. H. *A History of the Roman World, 753–146 B.C.*, 4th edn. London and New York, 1980.

Walbank, F. W., Astin, A. E., Fredericksen, M. W., Ogilvie, R. M., and Drummond, A. (eds. *The Rise of Rome to 220 B.C.* Vol. 7, Part 2 of *The Cambridge Ancient History*, 2nd edn. Cambridge, 1989.

Pre-Roman Italy

Barker, G. *Landscape and Society: Prehistoric Central Italy*. London, 1981.

Boardman, J. *The Greeks Overseas: Their Early Colonies and Trade*, new and enlarged edn. London, 1980.

Bonfante, L. *Etruscan Life and Afterlife: A Handbook of Etruscan Studies*. Detroit, 1986.

Hencken, H. *Tarquinia and Etruscan Origins*. New York and Washington, 1968.

Pallottino, M. *The Etruscans*, rev. and enlarged edn. Trans. J. Cremona. Bloomington, 1975.

Pallottino, M. *A History of Earliest Italy*. Trans. M. Ryle and K. Soper. Ann Arbor, 1991.

Ridgway, D. and Ridgway, F. R. (eds.). *Italy before the Romans: The Iron Age, Orientalizing and Etruscan Periods*. London, 1979.

Scullard, H. H. *The Etruscan Cities and Rome*. Ithaca, NY, 1967.

Pre-republican Rome

Alföldi, A. *Early Rome and the Latins*. Ann Arbor, 1965.

Bloch, R. *The Origins of Rome*. New York and Washington, 1960.

Bremmer, J. N. and Horsfall, N. M. *Roman Myth and Mythography*. London, 1987.

Ogilvie, R. M. *A Commentary on Livy, Books 1–5*. Oxford, 1965.

Politics and government

Eckstein, A. M. *Rome Enters the Greek East: From Anarchy to Hierarchy in the Hellenistic Mediterranean, 230–170 BC*. Oxford, 2008.

Kunkel, W. *An Introduction to Roman Legal and Constitutional History*, 2nd edn. Trans. J. M. Kelly. Oxford, 1972.

Millar, F. "The Political Character of the Classical Roman Republic, 200–151 B.C." *Journal of Roman Studies*, 74 (1984), 1–19.

Mitchell, R. E. *Patricians and Plebeians: The Origin of the Roman State*. Ithaca, NY, 1990.

Nicolet, C. *The World of the Citizen in Republican Rome*, 2nd edn. Trans. P. S. Falla. Berkeley and Los Angeles, 1980.

Raaflaub, K. A. (ed.). *Social Struggles in Archaic Rome: New Perspectives on the Conflict of the Orders*. Berkeley and Los Angeles, 1986.

Scullard, H. H. *Roman Politics, 220–150 B.C.*, 2nd edn. Oxford, 1973.

Sherwin-White, A. N. *The Roman Citizenship*, 2nd edn. Oxford, 1973.

The army, war, and imperialism

Caven, B. *The Punic Wars*. New York, 1980.

Curchin, L. A. *Roman Spain: Conquest and Assimilation*. London, 1991.

David, J.-M. *The Roman Conquest of Italy*. Trans. A. Nevill. Oxford, 1996.

Dyson, S. *The Creation of the Roman Frontier*. Princeton, 1985.

Eckstein, A. M. *Mediterranean Anarchy, Interstate War, and the Rise of Rome*. Berkeley, 2006.

Harris, W. V. *Rome in Etruria and Umbria*. Oxford, 1971.

Harris, W. V. *War and Imperialism in Republican Rome, 327–70 B.C.* Oxford, 1979.

Harris, W. V. (ed.). *The Imperialism of Mid-Republican Rome*. Rome, 1984.

Lazenby, J. F. *Hannibal's War: A Military History of the Second Punic War*. Warminster, 1978.

Lazenby, J. F. *The First Punic War: A Military History*. London, 1996.

Richardson, J. S. *Hispaniae: Spain and the Development of Roman Imperialism, 218–82 B.C.* Cambridge, 1986.

Salmon, E. T. *Samnium and the Samnites*. Cambridge, 1967.

Salmon, E. T. *Roman Colonization under the Republic*. Ithaca, NY, 1970.

Salmon, E. T. *The Making of Roman Italy*. Ithaca, NY, 1982.

Toynbee, A. J. *Hannibal's Legacy: The Hannibalic War's Effect on Roman Life*, 2 vols. London, 1965.

Foreign policy and external relations

Badian, E. *Foreign Clientelae (264–70 B.C.)*. Oxford, 1958.

Badian, E. "Notes on Roman Policy in Illyria (230–201 B.C.)," in E. Badian, *Studies in Greek and Roman History* (Oxford, 1964), 1–33.

Crawford, M. H. "Rome and the Greek World: Economic Relations," *Economic History Review*, 30 (1977), 42–52.

Eckstein, A. M. *Senate and General: Individual Decision-Making and Roman Foreign Relations, 264–194 B.C.* Berkeley and Los Angeles, 1987.

Gruen, E. S. *The Hellenistic World and the Coming of Rome*, 2 vols. Berkeley and Los Angeles, 1984.

Religion

Dumézil, G. *Archaic Roman Religion: With an Appendix on the Religion of the Etruscans.* Trans. P. Krapp, 2 vols. Chicago and London, 1970.
Michels, A. K. *The Calendar of the Roman Republic.* Princeton, 1967.
Scullard, H. H. *Festivals and Ceremonies of the Roman Republic.* Ithaca, NY, 1981.

Intellectual life

Bonfante, L. and Swaddling, J. *Etruscan Myths.* London and Austin, 2006.
Gruen, E. S. *Studies in Greek Culture and Roman Policy.* Leiden, 1990.
Gruen, E. S. *Culture and National Identity in Republican Rome.* London, 1993.
Momigliano, A. *Alien Wisdom: The Limits of Hellenization.* Cambridge, 1975.
Segal, E. *Roman Laughter: The Comedy of Plautus*, 2nd edn. London, 1987.
Wardman, A. *Rome's Debt to Greece.* London, 1976.

Historians and historiography

Badian, E. "The Early Historians," in T. A. Dorey (ed.), *Latin Historians* (London, 1966), 1–38.
Walbank, F. W. *Polybius.* Berkeley and Los Angeles, 1972.
Walsh, P. G. *Livy: His Historical Aims and Methods*, 2nd edn. Bristol, 1989.

Law

Bauman, R. A. *Lawyers in Roman Republican Politics: A Study of the Roman Jurists in their Political Setting, 316–82 B.C.* Munich, 1983.
Watson, A. *Roman Private Law around 200 B.C.* Princeton, 1971.
Watson, A. *Rome of the Twelve Tables: Persons and Property.* Princeton, 1976.

Biography

Astin, A. E. *Scipio Aemilianus.* Oxford, 1967.
Astin, A. E. *Cato the Censor.* Oxford, 1978.
Scullard, H. H. *Scipio Africanus: Soldier and Politician.* Ithaca, NY, 1970.

The Roman world, 133 BCE–235 CE

General histories

Beard, M. and Crawford, M. H. *Rome in the Late Republic: Problems and Interpretations.* Ithaca, NY, 1985.
Bowman, A. K., Champlin, E., and Lintott, A. (eds.). *The Augustan Empire, 43 B.C.–A.D. 69.* Vol. 10 of *The Cambridge Ancient History*, 2nd edn. Cambridge, 1996.

Bringmann, K. *A History of the Roman Republic*. Cambridge, 2007.

Crook, J. A., Lintott, A., and Rawson, E. (eds.). *The Last Age of the Roman Republic, 146–43 B.C.* Vol. 9 of *The Cambridge Ancient History*, 2nd edn. Cambridge, 1994.

Eck, W. *The Age of Augustus*, 2nd edn. Oxford, 2007.

Flower, H. I. *The Cambridge Companion to the Roman Republic*. Cambridge, 2004.

Galinsky, K. *Augustan Culture*. Princeton, 1996.

Galinsky, K. *The Cambridge Companion to the Age of Augustus*. Cambridge, 2005.

Garzetti, A. *From Tiberius to the Antonines: A History of the Roman Empire, A.D. 14–192*. Trans. J. R. Foster. London, 1976.

Millar, F. et al. *The Roman Empire and its Neighbors*, 2nd edn. New York, 1981.

Scullard, H. H. *From the Gracchi to Nero: A History of Rome from 133 B.C. to A.D. 68*, 5th edn. London and New York, 1982.

Wells, C. M. *The Roman Empire*, 2nd edn. London, 1992.

General studies

Potter, D. S. (ed.). *A Companion to the Roman Empire*. Oxford, 2006.

Rosenstein, N. and Morstein-Marx, R. (eds.). *A Companion to the Roman Republic*. Oxford, 2006.

Politics and government

Badian, E. *Publicans and Sinners: Private Enterprise in the Service of the Roman Republic*, rev. edn. Ithaca, NY, and London, 1983.

Bispham, E. *From Asculum to Actium: The Municipalization of Italy from the Social War to Augustus*. Oxford, 2007.

Bowersock, G. W. *Augustus and the Greek World*. Oxford, 1965.

Brunt, P. A. *The Fall of the Roman Republic and Related Essays*. Oxford, 1988.

Brunt, P. A. *Roman Imperial Themes*. Oxford, 1990.

Earl, D. *The Moral and Political Tradition of Rome*. Ithaca, NY, 1967.

Earl, D. *The Age of Augustus*. London, 1968.

Farney, G. D. *Ethnic Identity and Aristocratic Competition in Republican Rome*. Cambridge, 2007.

Flower, H. I. *The Art of Forgetting: Disgrace and Oblivion in Roman Political Culture*. Chapel Hill, 2006.

Gelzer, M. *The Roman Nobility*. Trans. R. Seager. Oxford, 1969.

Gordon P. K. *A History of Exile in the Roman Republic*. Cambridge, 2006.

Gowing, A. M. *Empire and Memory: The Representation of the Roman Republic in Imperial Culture*. Cambridge, 2005.

Gruen, E. S. *The Last Generation of the Roman Republic*. Berkeley and Los Angeles, 1974.

Hollander D. B. *Money in the Late Roman Republic*. Leiden, 2007.

Hopkins, K. *Death and Renewal: Sociological Studies in Roman History*, vol. 2. Cambridge, 1983.

Keaveney, A. *The Army in the Roman Revolution*. London and New York, 2007.

MacMullen, R. *Enemies of the Roman Order: Treason, Unrest and Alienation in the Empire*. Cambridge, MA, 1966.

Millar, F. *The Emperor in the Roman World, 31 B.C.–A.D. 337*, 2nd edn. London, 1992.

Osgood, J. *Caesar's Legacy*. Oxford, 2006.

Raaflaub, K. and Toher, M. (eds.). *Between Republic and Empire: Interpretations of Augustus and his Principate*. Berkeley, 1990.

Seager, R. (ed.). *The Crisis of the Roman Republic: Studies in Political and Social History*. Cambridge, 1969.

Shatzman, I. *Senatorial Wealth and Roman Politics*. Brussels, 1975.

Stockton, D. *The Gracchi*. Oxford, 1979.

Syme, R. *The Roman Revolution*. Oxford, 1939.

Syme, R. *Roman Papers*, 7 vols. New York, 1979–91.

Talbert, R. J. A. *The Senate of Imperial Rome*. Princeton, 1984.

Taylor, L. R. *Party Politics in the Age of Caesar*. Berkeley and Los Angeles, 1949.

Wirszubski, C. *Libertas as a Political Idea at Rome during the Late Republic and Early Principate*. Cambridge, 1950.

Wiseman, T. P. *New Men in the Roman Senate 139 B.C.–A.D. 14*. London, 1971.

Yavetz, Z. *Plebs and Princeps*. Oxford, 1969.

Zanker, P. *The Power of Images in the Age of Augustus*. Trans. A. Shapiro. Ann Arbor, 1988.

The army and the frontiers

Badian, F. *Roman Imperialism in the Late Republic*, 2nd edn. Ithaca, NY, 1968.

Birley, E. *The Roman Army: Papers, 1929–1986*. Amsterdam, 1988.

de Blois, L. and Cascio, E. L. (eds.). *Impact of the Roman Army (200 BC–AD 476): Economic, Social, Political, Religious, and Cultural Aspects*. Leiden and Boston, 2007.

Breeze, D. J. *Roman Frontiers in Britain*. London, 2007.

Breeze, D. J. and Dobson, B. *Roman Officers and Frontiers*. Stuttgart, 1993.

Brunt, P. A. "The Army and the Land in the Roman Revolution," in P. A. Brunt, *The Fall of the Roman Republic and Related Essays* (Oxford, 1988), 240–80.

Brunt, P. A. "Laus Imperii," in P. A. Brunt, *Roman Imperial Themes* (Oxford, 1990), 288–323.

Campbell, J. B. *The Emperor and the Roman Army, 31 B.C.–A.D. 235*. New York, 1984.

Campbell, J. B. *Greek and Roman Military Writers: Selected Readings*. London and New York, 2004.

Davies, R. W. *Service in the Roman Army*, eds. D. J. Breeze and V. A. Maxfield. New York, 1989.

Dixon, K. R. and Southern, P. *The Roman Cavalry: From the First to the Third Century A.D.* London, 1992.

Gabba, E. *Republican Rome: The Army and the Allies*. Trans. P. J. Cuff. Berkeley and Los Angeles, 1976.

Goldsworthy, A. K. *The Roman Army at War, 100 BC–AD 200*. Oxford, 1996.

Isaac, B. *The Limits of Empire: The Roman Army in the East*, 2nd edn. Oxford, 1992.

Kennedy, D. L. *The Roman Army in Jordan*, 2nd rev. edn. London, 2004.

Keppie, L. *The Making of the Roman Army: From Republic to Empire*. Totowa, NJ, 1984.

Keppie, L. *Colonization and Veteran Settlement in Italy, 47–14 B.C.* London, 1985.

Luttwak, E. N. *The Grand Strategy of the Roman Empire: From the First Century A.D. to the Third*. Baltimore, 1976.

Mann, J. C. *Legionary Recruitment and Veteran Settlement during the Principate*, ed. M. M. Roxan. London, 1983.

Maxfield, V. A. et al. "The Frontiers," in J. Wacher (ed.), *The Roman World* (London, 1987), vol. 1, 139–325.

Osborn, G. *Hadrian's Wall and its People*. Exeter, 2006.

Phang, S. E. *Roman Military Service: Ideologies of Discipline in the Late Republic and Early Principate*. Cambridge and New York, 2008.

Robinson, H. R. *The Armour of Imperial Rome*. New York, 1975.

Saddington, D. B. *The Development of the Roman Auxiliary Forces from Caesar to Vespasian (49 B.C.–A.D. 79)*. Harare, 1982.

Smith, R. E. *Service in the Post-Marian Roman Army*. Manchester, 1958.

Watson, G. R. *The Roman Soldier*. London, 1969.

Webster, G. *The Roman Imperial Army of the First and Second Centuries A.D.*, 3rd edn. Totowa, NJ, 1985.

Whittaker, C. R. *Frontiers of the Roman Empire: A Social and Economic Study*. Baltimore, 1994.

Regional histories

Adams, C. *Land Transport in Roman Egypt: A Study of Economics and Administration in a Roman Province*. Oxford and New York, 2007.

Alföldy, G. *Noricum*. Trans. A. R. Birley. London, 1974.

Bagnall, R. S. *Hellenistic and Roman Egypt*. Aldershot, 2006.

Bekker-Nielsen, T. (ed.). *Rome and the Black Sea Region: Domination, Romanisation, Resistance*. Aarhus, 2006.

Birley, A. R. *The Roman Government of Britain*. Oxford and New York, 2005.

Blagg, T. and Millett, M. (eds.). *The Early Roman Empire in the West*. Oxford, 1990.

Bowersock, G. *Roman Arabia*. Cambridge, MA, 1983.

Collingwood, R. G. and Richmond, I. A. *The Archaeology of Roman Britain*, rev. edn. London, 1969.

Creighton, J. *Britannia: The Creation of a Roman Province*. London and New York, 2006.

Curchin, L. A. *The Romanization of Central Spain: Complexity, Diversity, and Change in a Provincial Hinterland*. London and New York, 2004.

Dmitriev, S. *City Government in Hellenistic and Roman Asia Minor*. Oxford and New York, 2005.

Drinkwater, J. F. *Roman Gaul: The Three Provinces, 58 B.C.–A.D. 260*. Ithaca, NY, 1983.

Frere, S. S. *Britannia: A History of Roman Britain*, 3rd edn. London, 1987.

Goodman, M. *State and Society in Roman Galilee, A.D. 132–212*. Totowa, NJ, 1983.

Howgego, C., Heuchert, V., and Burnett, A. (eds.). *Coinage and Identity in the Roman Provinces*. Oxford, 2005.

Keay, S. J. *Roman Spain*. Berkeley, 1988.

Lewis, N. *Life in Egypt under Roman Rule*. New York, 1983.

Magie, D. *Roman Rule in Asia Minor to the End of the Third Century after Christ*, 2 vols. London, 1950.

Mattingly, D. *An Imperial Possession: Britain in the Roman Empire*. London, 2006.

Millar, F. *The Roman Near East, 31 B.C.–A.D. 337*. Cambridge, MA. and London, 1993.

Millett, M. *The Romanization of Britain: An Essay in Archaeological Interpretation*. Cambridge, 1990.

Mitchell, S. and Katsari, C. *Patterns in the Economy of Roman Asia Minor*. Swansea and Oakville, CT, 2005.

Mócsy, A. *Pannonia and Upper Moesia: A History of the Middle Danube Provinces of the Roman Empire*. Trans. S. S. Frere. Boston, 1974.

Potter, T. W. *Roman Italy*. Berkeley, 1987.

Raven, S. *Rome in Africa*, 3rd edn. New York, 1993.

Richardson, J. S. *The Romans in Spain*. Oxford, 1996.

Salway, P. *Roman Britain*. Oxford, 1981.

Schäfer, P. *History of the Jews in the Greco-Roman World: The Jews of Palestine from Alexander the Great to the Arab Conquest*. London and New York, 2003.

Schürer, E. *The History of the Jewish People in the Age of Jesus Christ (175 B.C.–A.D. 135)*, rev. edn., 3 vols. Trans. T. A. Burkill et al. Edinburgh, 1973–87.

Sherwin-White, A. N. *Roman Foreign Policy in the East, 168 B.C.–A.D. 1*. Norman and London, 1984.

Sullivan, R. *Near Eastern Royalty and Rome, 100–30 B.C.* Toronto, 1990.

Todd, M. (ed.). *Research on Roman Britain, 1960–89*. London, 1989.

Todd, M. (ed.). *A Companion to Roman Britain*. Oxford, 2004.

Wightman, E. M. *Gallia Belgica*. Berkeley, 1985.

Wilkes, J. J. *Dalmatia*. Cambridge, MA, 1969.

Wilson, R. J. A. *Sicily under the Roman Empire: The Archaeology of a Roman Province, 36 B.C.–A.D. 535*. Warminster, 1990.

Economy, demography, and material conditions

Andreau, J. *Banking and Business in the Roman World*. Cambridge, 1999.

Bagnall, R. S. and Frier, B. W. *The Demography of Roman Egypt*. Cambridge, 1994.

Barker, G. and Lloyd, J. (eds.). *Roman Landscapes: Archaeological Survey in the Mediterranean Region*. London, 1991.

Brunt, P. A. "Free Labour and Public Works," *Journal of Roman Studies*, 70 (1980), 81–100.

Brunt, P. A. *Italian Manpower 225 B.C.–A.D. 14*, reprinted edn. Oxford, 1989.

Clarke, J. R. *Roman Life: 100 B.C. to A.D. 200*. New York, 2007.

Cool, H. E. M. *Eating and Drinking in Roman Britain*. New York, 2006.

Crawford, M. H. *Coinage and Money under the Roman Republic: Italy and the Mediterranean Economy*. London, 1985.

D'Arms, J. and Kopff, E. C. (eds.). *The Seaborne Commerce of Ancient Rome: Studies in Archaeology and History*. Rome, 1980.

Duncan-Jones, R. P. *The Economy of the Roman Empire: Quantitative Studies*, 2nd edn. Cambridge, 1982.

Duncan-Jones, R. P. *Structure and Scale in the Roman Economy*. Cambridge, 1990.

Duncan-Jones, R. P. *Money and Government in the Roman Empire*. Cambridge, 1994.

Erdkamp, P. *The Grain Market in the Roman Empire: A Social, Political and Economic Study*. Cambridge and New York, 2005.

Finley, M. I. (ed.). *Studies in Roman Property*. Cambridge, 1976.

Finley, M. I. *The Ancient Economy*, 2nd edn. Berkeley, 1985.

Garnsey, P. *Famine and Food Supply in the Graeco-Roman World: Responses to Risk and Crisis*. Cambridge, 1988.

Garnsey, P. and Saller, R. P. *The Roman Empire: Economy, Society and Culture*. Berkeley, 1987.

Garnsey, P. and Whittaker, C. R. (eds.). *Trade and Famine in Classical Antiquity*. Cambridge, 1983.

Garnsey, P., Hopkins, K., and Whittaker, C. R. (eds.). *Trade in the Ancient Economy*. Berkeley, 1983.

Goodman, P. J. *The Roman City and its Periphery from Rome to Gaul*. London and New York, 2007.

Greene, K. *The Archaeology of the Roman Economy*. Berkeley, 1986.

Grünewald, T. *Bandits in the Roman Empire: Myth and Reality*. London and New York, 2004.

Hopkins, K. "Taxes and Trade in the Roman Empire (200 B.C.–A.D. 400)," *Journal of Roman Studies*, 70 (1980), 101–25.

Jongman, W. *The Economy and Society of Pompeii*. Amsterdam, 1988.

Kehoe, D. P. *The Economics of Agriculture on Roman Imperial Estates in North Africa*. Göttingen, 1988.

Laurence, R. *Roman Pompeii: Space and Society*, 2nd edn. London and New York, 2007.

Lomas, K. and Cornell, T. *Bread and Circuses: Euergetism and Municipal Patronage in Roman Italy*. London and New York, 2003.

Parker, A. J. *Ancient Shipwrecks of the Mediterranean and the Roman Provinces*. Oxford, 1992.

Parkin, T. G. *Demography and Roman Society*. Baltimore and London, 1992.

Peacock, D. P. S. and Williams, D. F. *Amphorae and the Roman Economy: An Introductory Guide*. London, 1986.

Raschke, M. G. "New Studies in Roman Commerce with the East," *Aufstieg und Niedergang der römischen Welt*, 9.2 (1978), 604–1378.

Rich, J. and Wallace-Hadrill, A. (eds.). *City and Country in the Ancient World*. London, 1991.

Rostovtzeff, M. *The Social and Economic History of the Roman Empire*, 2nd edn, ed. P. M. Fraser, 2 vols. Oxford, 1957.

Spurr, M. S. *Arable Cultivation in Roman Italy, c. 200 B.C.–A.D. 100*. London, 1986.

Veyne, P. *Bread and Circuses: Historical Sociology and Political Pluralism*. Trans. B. Pearce. London, 1990.

White, K. D. *Roman Farming*. Ithaca, NY, 1970.

Whittaker, C. R. (ed.). *Pastoral Economies in Classical Antiquity*. Cambridge, 1988.

Whittaker, C. R. *Land, City and Trade in the Roman Empire*. Brookfield, VT, 1993.

Society

Allen, J. *Hostages and Hostage-Taking in the Roman Empire*. New York and Cambridge, 2006.

Atkins, E. M., and Osborne, R. (eds.). *Poverty in the Roman World*. Cambridge, 2006.

Balsdon, J. P. V. D. *Life and Leisure in Ancient Rome*. London, 1974.

Bradley, K. R. *Slavery and Rebellion in the Roman World, 140 B.C.–70 B.C.* Bloomington, 1989.

Bradley, K. R. *Slavery and Society at Rome*. Cambridge, 1994.

Brunt, P. A. "The Roman Mob," in M. I. Finley (ed.), *Studies in Ancient Society* (London and Boston, 1974), 74–102.

Cohen, A. and Rutter, J. B. (eds.). *Constructions of Childhood in Ancient Greece and Italy*. Princeton, 2007.

D'Arms, J. *Romans on the Bay of Naples: A Social and Cultural Study of the Villas and their Owners from 150 B.C. to A.D. 400*. Cambridge, MA, 1970.

D'Arms, J. *Commerce and Social Standing in Ancient Rome*. Cambridge, MA, and London, 1981.

Dench, E. *Romulus' Asylum: Roman Identities from the Age of Alexander to the Age of Hadrian*. Oxford and New York, 2005.

Dyson, S. L. *Community and Society in Roman Italy*. Baltimore, 1992.

Edwards, C. *Death in Ancient Rome*. New Haven, 2007.

Finley, M. I. (ed.). *Classical Slavery*. Totowa, NJ, 1987.

Gardner, J. F. *Being a Roman Citizen*. London and New York, 1993.

Garnsey, P. *Social Status and Legal Privilege in the Roman Empire*. Oxford, 1970.

Hallett, J. P. and Skinner, M. B. (eds.). *Roman Sexualities*. Princeton, 1997.

Hopkins, K. *Conquerors and Slaves: Sociological Studies in Roman History*, vol. I. Cambridge, 1978.

Kaster, R. A. *Emotion, Restraint, and Community in Ancient Rome*. Oxford and New York, 2005.

Kyle, D. G. *Spectacles of Death in Ancient Rome*. London and New York, 1998.

Langlands, R. *Sexual Morality in Ancient Rome*. Cambridge, 2006.

Lintott, A. W. *Violence in Republican Rome*. New York, 1968.

McDonnell, M. A. *Roman Manliness: Virtus and the Roman Republic*. Cambridge and New York, 2006.

MacMullen, R. *Roman Social Relations, 50 B.C. to A.D. 284*. New Haven, 1974.

MacMullen, R. *Changes in the Roman Empire: Essays in the Ordinary*. Princeton, 1990.

MacMullen, R. *Romanization in the Time of Augustus*. New Haven and London, 2000.

Morgan, T. *Popular Morality in the Early Roman Empire*. Cambridge, 2007.

Roller, M. B. *Dining Posture in Ancient Rome: Bodies, Values, and Status*. Princeton, 2006.

Roth, U. *Thinking Tools: Agricultural Slavery between Evidence and Models*. London, 2007.

de Ste Croix, G. E. M. *The Class Struggle in the Ancient Greek World from the Archaic Age to the Arab Conquests*. Ithaca, NY, 1981.

Saller, R. P. *Personal Patronage under the Early Empire*. Cambridge, 1982.

Sebesta, J. L. and Bonfante, L. (eds.). *The World of Roman Costume*. Madison, 1994.

Sherwin-White, A. N. *Racial Prejudice in Imperial Rome*. Cambridge, 1970.

Snowden, Jr, F. M. *Before Color Prejudice: The Ancient View of Blacks*. Cambridge, MA, 1983.

Swain, S., Harrison, S., and Elsner, J. (eds.). *Severan Culture*. Cambridge, 2007.

Thompson, L. A. *Romans and Blacks*. Norman, 1989.

Treggiari, S. *Roman Freedmen during the Late Republic*. Oxford, 1969.

Treggiari, S. *Roman Social History*. London and New York, 2002.

Veyne, P. (ed.). *From Pagan Rome to Byzantium*. Vol. 1 of *A History of Private Life*, eds. P. Ariès and G. Duby. Trans. A. Goldhammer. Cambridge, MA, 1987.

Vout, C. *Power and Eroticism in Imperial Rome*. Cambridge, 2007.

Wallace-Hadrill, A. "Patronage in Roman Society: From Republic to Empire," in A. Wallace-Hadrill (ed.), *Patronage in Ancient Society* (London and New York, 1989), 63–87.

Wallace-Hadrill, A. *Houses and Society in Pompeii and Herculaneum*. Princeton, 1994.

Weeber, K.-W. *Luxus im alten Rom: Die öffentliche Pracht*. Darmstadt, 2006.

Spectacles

Auguet, R. *Cruelty and Civilization: The Roman Games*. London, 1972.

Barton, C. A. *Sorrows of the Ancient Romans: The Gladiator and the Monster*. Princeton, 1993.

Beacham, R. C. *Spectacle Entertainments in Early Imperial Rome*. New Haven and London, 1999.

Bell, A. *Spectacular Power in the Greek and Roman City*. Oxford and New York, 2004.

Bergmann, B. and Kondoleon, C. (eds.). *The Art of Ancient Spectacle*. New Haven and London, 1999.

Coleman, K. M. "Fatal Charades: Roman Executions Staged as Mythological Enactments," *Journal of Roman Studies*, 80 (1990), 33–73.

Futrell, A. *Blood in the Arena: The Spectacle of Roman Power*. Austin, 1997.

Futrell, A. *The Roman Games: A Sourcebook*. Oxford, 2006.

Gabucci, A. (ed.). *The Colosseum*. Los Angeles, 2001.

Humphrey, J. *Roman Circuses: Arenas for Chariot Racing*. Berkeley and Los Angeles, 1986.

Köhne, E. and Ewigleben, C. (eds.). *Gladiators and Caesars: The Power of Spectacle in Ancient Rome*. Berkeley and Los Angeles, 2000.

König, J. *Athletics and Literature in the Roman Empire*. Cambridge and New York, 2005.

Kyle, D. G. *Spectacles of Death in Ancient Rome*. London and New York, 1998.

Mahoney, A. *Roman Sports and Spectacles: A Sourcebook*. Newburyport, 2001.

Plass, P. *The Game of Death in Ancient Rome: Arena Sport and Political Suicide*. Madison, 1995.

Potter, D. S. and Mattingly, D. J. (eds.). *Life, Death and Entertainment in the Roman Empire*. Ann Arbor, 1999.

Toner, J. P. *Leisure and Ancient Rome*. Cambridge, 1995.

Versnel, H. S. *Triumphus: An Inquiry into the Origin, Development and Meaning of the Roman Triumph*. Leiden, 1970.

Wiedemann, T. *Emperors and Gladiators*. London and New York, 1992.

Women and the family

Bradley, K. *Discovering the Roman Family: Studies in Roman Social History*. New York, 1991.

Dixon, S. *The Roman Mother*. Norman and London, 1988.

Dixon, S. *The Roman Family*. Baltimore, 1992.

Dixon, S. (ed.). *Childhood, Class and Kin in the Roman World*. London and New York, 2001.

Evans, J. K. *War, Women and Children in Ancient Rome*. London and New York, 1991.

Fantham, E., Foley, H. P., Kampen, N. B., Pomeroy, S. B., and Shapiro, H. A. *Women in the Classical World: Image and Text*. Oxford, 1994.

Gardner, J. F. *Women in Roman Law and Society*. Bloomington, 1986.

Gardner, J. F. and Wiedemann, T. E. J. *The Roman Household: A Sourcebook*. London and New York, 1991.

Hallett, J. *Fathers and Daughters in Roman Society: Women and the Elite Family*. Princeton, 1984.

Kampen, N. *Image and Status: Roman Working Women in Ostia*. Berlin, 1981.

Pomeroy, S. *Goddesses, Whores, Wives and Slaves: Women in Classical Antiquity*. New York, 1975.

Rawson, B. (ed.). *The Family in Ancient Rome: New Perspectives*. Ithaca, NY, 1986.

Rawson, B. (ed.). *Marriage, Divorce and Children in Ancient Rome*. Oxford and New York, 1992.

Rawson, B. and Weaver, P. (eds.). *The Roman Family in Italy: Status, Sentiment, Space*. Canberra and Oxford, 1997.

Saller, R. P. *Patriarchy, Property and Death in the Roman Family*. Cambridge, 1994.

Treggiari, S. *Roman Marriage: Iusti Coniuges from the Time of Cicero to the Time of Ulpian*. Oxford, 1991.

Wiedemann, T. E. J. *Adults and Children in the Roman Empire*. New Haven and London, 1989.

Pagan religion

Ando, C. *The Matter of the Gods: Religion and the Roman Empire*. Berkeley, 2008.

Ando, C. and Rüpke, J. *Religion and Law in Classical and Christian Rome*. Stuttgart, 2006.

Beck, R. *The Religion of the Mithras Cult in the Roman Empire: Mysteries of the Unconquered Sun*. Oxford and New York, 2006.

de Blois, L., Funke, P., and Hahn, J. (eds.). *The Impact of Imperial Rome on Religions, Ritual and Religious Life in the Roman Empire*. Leiden and Boston, 2006.

Clark, A. J. *Divine Qualities: Cult and Community in Republican Rome*. Oxford, 2007.

Cumont, F. *Les Religions orientales dans le paganisme romain*. Turin, 2006.

Ferguson, J. *The Religions of the Roman Empire*. London, 1970.

Heyob, S. K. *The Cult of Isis among Women in the Graeco-Roman World*. Leiden, 1975.

Hinnells, J. R. (ed.). *Mithraic Studies: Proceedings of the First International Congress of Mithraic Studies*, 2 vols. Totowa, NJ, 1975.

Liebeschuetz, J. H. W. G. *Continuity and Change in Roman Religion*. New York, 1979.

Lightfoot, J. L. (trans. and comm.). *The Sibylline Oracles: With Introduction, Translation, and Commentary on the First and Second Books*. Oxford, 2007.

MacMullen, R. *Paganism in the Roman Empire*. New Haven, 1981.

Ogilvie, R. M. *The Romans and their Gods in the Age of Augustus*. London, 1969.

Price, S. R. F. *Rituals and Power: The Roman Imperial Cult in Asia Minor*. Cambridge, 1984.

Schultz, C. E. *Women's Religious Activity in the Roman Republic*. Chapel Hill, 2006.

Schultz, C. E and Harvey, P. B. (eds.). *Religion in Republican Italy*. Cambridge and New York, 2007.

Takács, S. A. *Vestal Virgins, Sibyls, and Matrons: Women in Roman Religion*. Austin, 2008.

Turcan, R. *The Cults of the Roman Empire*. Trans. A. Nevill. Oxford, 1996.

Vermaseren, M. J. *Cybele and Attis: The Myth and Cult*. Trans. A. M. H. Lemmers. London, 1977.

Wardman, A. *Religion and Statecraft among the Romans*. London, 1982.

Weinstock, S. *Divus Iulius*. Oxford, 1971.

Wildfang, R. L. *Rome's Vestal Virgins: A Study of Rome's Vestal Priestesses in the Late Republic and Early Empire*. London and New York, 2006.

Judaism and Christianity

Ben Zeev, M. P. *Diaspora Judaism in Turmoil, 116/117 CE: Ancient Sources and Modern Insights*. Leuven and Dudley, MA, 2005.

Benko, S. *Pagan Rome and the Early Christians*. Bloomington, 1984.

Chadwick, H. *The Early Church*. Grand Rapids, MI, 1967.

Edwards, D. R. *Religion and Society in Roman Palestine: Old Questions, New Approaches*. London and New York, 2004.

Frend, W. H. C. *Martyrdom and Persecution in the Early Church: A Study of Conflict from the Maccabees to Donatus*. Oxford, 1965.

Frend, W. H. C. *The Rise of Christianity*. London, 1984.

Lane Fox, R. *Pagans and Christians in the Mediterranean World from the Second Century A.D. to the Conversion of Constantine*. Harmondsworth and New York, 1986.

Leon, H. J. *The Jews of Ancient Rome*. Philadelphia, 1960.

Lieu, J., North, J. A., and Rajak, T. (eds.). *The Jews among Pagans and Christians in the Roman Empire*. London, 1992.

MacMullen, R. *Christianizing the Roman Empire (A.D. 100–400)*. New Haven, 1984.

Meeks, W. A. *The First Urban Christians: The Social World of the Apostle Paul*. New Haven, 1983.

Musurillo, H. (ed.). *The Acts of the Christian Martyrs*. Oxford, 1972.

Wilcken, R. L. *The Christians as the Romans Saw Them*. New Haven, 1984.

Intellectual life (literature, philosophy, education)

Barnes, T. D. *Tertullian: A Historical and Literary Study*. Oxford, 1971.

Beard, M. et al. (eds.). *Literacy in the Roman World*. Ann Arbor, 1991.

Bonner, S. F. *Education in Ancient Rome: From the Elder Cato to the Younger Pliny*. Berkeley and Los Angeles, 1977.

Bowersock, G. W. *Greek Sophists in the Roman Empire*. Oxford, 1969.

Bowman, A. K. and Woolf, G. (eds.). *Literacy and Power in the Ancient World*. Cambridge, 1994.

Cameron, A. *Greek Mythography in the Roman World*. Oxford and New York, 2004.

Champlin, E. *Fronto and Antonine Rome*. Cambridge, MA, 1980.

Clackson, J. and Horrocks, G. *The Blackwell History of the Latin Language*. Oxford, 2007.

Corbier, M. *Donner à voir, donner à lire: Mémoire et communication dans la Rome ancienne*. Paris, 2006.

Dominik, W. and Hall, J. (eds.). *A Companion to Roman Rhetoric*. Oxford, 2007.

Feeney, D. C. *Caesar's Calendar: Ancient Time and the Beginnings of History*. Berkeley, 2007.

Fitch, J. G. (ed.). *Seneca*. Oxford and New York, 2008.

Fitzgerald, W. *Martial: The World of the Epigram*. Chicago, 2007.

Fox, M. *Cicero's Philosophy of History*. Oxford, 2007.

Gaisser, J. H. (ed.). *Catullus*. Oxford, 2007.

Gale, M. R. (ed.). *Lucretius*. Oxford, 2007.

Gildenhard, I. *Paideia Romana: Cicero's Tusculan Disputations*. Cambridge, 2007.

Griffin, J. *Latin Poets and Roman Life*. Chapel Hill, 1986.

Harris, W. V. *Ancient Literacy*. Cambridge, MA, 1986.

Inwood, B. *Reading Seneca: Stoic Philosophy at Rome*. Oxford and New York, 2005.

Jaeger, M. *Archimedes and the Roman Imagination*. Ann Arbor, 2008.

Jones, C. P. *Plutarch and Rome*. Oxford, 1972.

Jones, C. P. *The Roman World of Dio Chrysostom*. Cambridge, MA, 1978.

Kennedy, G. *The Art of Rhetoric in the Roman World 300 B.C.–A.D. 300*. Vol. 2 of G. Kennedy, *A History of Rhetoric*. Princeton, 1972.

König, J. and Whitmarsh, T. (eds.). *Ordering Knowledge in the Roman Empire*. Cambridge, 2007.

Marshall, C. W. *The Stagecraft and Performance of Roman Comedy*. Cambridge, 2006.

Powell, J. and Paterson, J. *Cicero the Advocate*. Oxford and New York, 2004.

Rawson, E. *Intellectual Life in the Late Roman Republic*. Baltimore, 1985.

Rosen, R. M. *Making Mockery: The Poetics of Ancient Satire*. Oxford, 2007.

Ross, D. O. *Virgil's Aeneid: A Reader's Guide*. Oxford, 2007.

Sandbach, F. H. *The Stoics*, 2nd edn. Bristol, 1989.

Sherwin-White, A. N. *The Letters of Pliny: A Historical and Social Commentary*. Oxford, 1985.

Sorabji, R. and Sharples, R. W. (eds.). *Greek and Roman Philosophy 100 BC–200 AD*, 2 vols. London, 2007.

Spisak, A. L. *Martial: A Social Guide*. London, 2007.

Steel, C. *Roman Oratory*. Cambridge, 2006.

Wiseman, T. P. *Roman Studies: Literary and Historical*. Liverpool, 1987.

Woodman, A. J. and West, D. (eds.). *Poetry and Politics in the Age of Augustus*. Cambridge, 1984.

Ziolkowski, J. M. and Putnam, M. C. J. (eds.). *The Virgilian Tradition: The First Fifteen Hundred Years*. New Haven, 2008.

Art, architecture, and engineering

Andreae, B. *The Art of Rome*. Trans. R. E. Wolf. New York, 1977.

Blake, M. E. *Ancient Roman Construction in Italy from the Prehistoric Period to Augustus*. Washington, 1949.

Blake, M. E. *Roman Construction in Italy from Tiberius through the Flavians*. Washington, 1959.

Blake, M. E. and Bishop, D. T. *Roman Construction in Italy from Nerva through the Antonines*. Philadelphia, 1973.

Boatwright, M. T. *Hadrian and the City of Rome*. Princeton, 1987.

Bruun, C. *The Water Supply of Ancient Rome: A Study of Roman Imperial Administration*. Helsinki, 1991.

Chevallier, R. *Roman Roads*, rev. edn. Trans. N. H. Field. London, 1989.

Clarke, J. C. *Looking at Laughter: Humor, Power, and Transgression in Roman Visual Culture, 100 B.C.–A.D. 250*. Princeton, 2007.

Clarke, J. R. *The Houses of Roman Italy, 100 B.C.–A.D. 250: Ritual, Space and Decoration*. Berkeley, 1991.

Clarke, J. R. *Art in the Lives of Ordinary Romans: Visual Representation and Non-Elite Viewers in Italy, 100 B.C.–A.D. 315*. Berkeley, 2003.

Dillon, S. and Welch, K. E. (eds.). *Representations of War in Ancient Rome*. New York and Cambridge, 2006.

Dunbabin, K. M. D. *The Mosaics of Roman North Africa: Studies in Iconography and Patronage*. New York, 1978.

Elsner, J. *Roman Eyes: Visuality and Subjectivity in Art and Text*. Princeton, 2007.

Henig, M. (ed.). *A Handbook of Roman Art: A Comprehensive Survey of All the Arts of the Roman World*. Ithaca, NY, 1983.

Higgins, R. *Greek and Roman Jewellery*, 2nd edn. Berkeley, 1980.

Hodge, A. T. *Roman Aqueducts*. London, 1992.

Humphrey, J. H. *Roman Circuses: Arenas for Chariot Racing*. Berkeley, 1986.

Kleiner, D. E. E. *Roman Sculpture*. New Haven, 1992.

Kleiner, F. S. *A History of Roman Art*. Belmont, 2006.

Ling, R. *Roman Painting*. New York, 1991.

MacDonald, W. L. *The Architecture of the Roman Empire*, 2 vols. New Haven, 1982–6.

Marvin, M. *The Language of the Muses. The Dialogue between Roman and Greek Sculpture*. Los Angeles, 2008.

Nash, F. *Pictorial Dictionary of Ancient Rome*, rev. edn, 2 vols. London, 1968.

Newby, M. and Painter, K. (eds.). *Roman Glass: Two Centuries of Art and Invention*. London, 1991.

O'Connor, C. *Roman Bridges*. Cambridge, 1993.

Peacock, D. P. S. *Pottery in the Roman World: An Ethnoarchaeological Approach*. London, 1982.

Percival, J. *The Roman Villa: An Historical Introduction*. Berkeley, 1976.

Ramage, N. H. and Ramage, A. *Roman Art: Romulus to Constantine*. Englewood Cliffs, NJ, 1991.

Rea, J. A. *Legendary Rome: Myth, Monuments and Memory on the Palatine and Capitoline*. London, 2007.

Rehak, P. *Imperium and Cosmos: Augustus and the Northern Campus Martius*, ed. J. G. Younger. Madison, 2006.

Richardson, Jr, L. *A New Topographical Dictionary of Ancient Rome*. Baltimore and London, 1992.

Sear, F. *Roman Theatres: An Architectural Study*. New York and Oxford, 2006.

Smith, R. R. R. *Roman Portrait Statuary from Aphrodisias*. Mainz, 2006.

Stewart, P. *Statues in Roman Society: Representation and Response*. Oxford and New York, 2003.

Strong, D. E. *Roman Art*, 2nd edn. New York, 1988.

Strong, D. E. and Brown, D. (eds.). *Roman Crafts*. New York, 1976.

Ward-Perkins, J. B. *Cities of Ancient Greece and Italy: Planning in Classical Antiquity*. New York, 1974.

Ward-Perkins, J. B. *Roman Imperial Architecture*, 2nd edn. Harmondsworth, 1981.

Wheeler, M. *Roman Art and Architecture*. London, 1964.

White, K. D. *Greek and Roman Technology*. Ithaca, NY, 1984.

Yegül, F. K. *Baths and Bathing in Classical Antiquity*. Cambridge, MA, 1992.

Historians and historiography

Ash, R. *Tacitus*. Bristol, 2006.

Cameron, A. (ed.). *History as Text: The Writing of Ancient History*. Chapel Hill, 1990.

Earl, D. *The Political Thought of Sallust*. Cambridge, 1961.

Edmondson, J., Mason, S., and Rives, J. *Flavius Josephus and Flavian Rome*. Oxford and New York, 2005.

Lintott, A. *Cicero as Evidence: A Historian's Companion*. Oxford and New York, 2008.

Marincola, J. (ed.). *A Companion to Greek and Roman Historiography*, 2 vols. Oxford, 2007.

Martin, R. *Tacitus*. Berkeley, 1981.

Mellor, R. *Tacitus*. New York and London, 1993.

Millar, F. *A Study of Cassius Dio*. Oxford, 1964.

Morgan, M. G. *69 A.D.: The Year of Four Emperors*. Oxford, 2007.

Pagán, V. E. *Conspiracy Narratives in Roman History*. Austin, 2005.

Rajak, T. *Josephus: The Historian and his Society*. Philadelphia, 1983.

Ramsey, J. T. *Sallust's Bellum Catilinae*, 2nd edn. Oxford, 2007.

Sacks, K. *Diodorus Siculus and the First Century*. Princeton, 1990.

Syme, R. *Tacitus*, 2 vols. Oxford, 1958.

Syme, R. *Sallust*. Berkeley and Los Angeles, 1964.

Wallace-Hadrill, A. *Suetonius: The Scholar and his Caesars*. New Haven, 1983.

Wiseman, T. P. "Practice and Theory in Roman Historiography," in T. P. Wiseman, *Roman Studies: Literary and Historical* (Liverpool, 1987), 244–62.

Woodman, A. J. *Rhetoric in Classical Historiography: Four Studies*. Portland, 1988.

Yarrow, L. M. *Historiography at the End of the Republic: Provincial Perspectives on Roman Rule*. Oxford and New York, 2006.

Law

Brunt, P. A. "Judiciary Rights in the Republic," in P. A. Brunt, *The Fall of the Roman Republic and Related Essays* (Oxford, 1988), 194–239.

Buckland, W. W. *A Text-Book of Roman Law from Augustus to Justinian*, 3rd edn, ed. P. Stein. Cambridge, 1963.

Champlin, E. *Final Judgments: Duty and Emotion in Roman Wills, 200 B.C.–A.D. 250.* Berkeley, 1991.

Crawford, M. H. (ed.). *Roman Statutes*, 2 vols. London, 1996.

Crook, J. A. *Law and Life of Rome, 90 B.C. to A.D. 212.* Ithaca, NY, 1967.

Crook, J. A. *Legal Advocacy in the Roman World.* London, 1995.

Daube, D. *Forms of Roman Legislation.* Oxford, 1956.

Daube, D. *Roman Law: Linguistic, Social and Philosophical Aspects.* Edinburgh, 1969.

Frier, B. W. *Landlords and Tenants in Imperial Rome.* Princeton, 1980.

Frier, B. W. *The Rise of the Roman Jurists: Studies in Cicero's Pro Caecina.* Princeton, 1985.

Harries, J. *Cicero and the Jurists: From Citizen's Law to the Lawful State.* London, 2006.

Jones, A. H. M. *The Criminal Courts of the Roman Republic and Principate.* Oxford, 1972.

Kelly, J. M. *Roman Litigation.* Oxford, 1966.

Kelly, J. M. *Studies in the Civil Judicature of the Roman Republic.* Oxford, 1976.

Nicholas, B. *An Introduction to Roman Law.* Oxford, 1962.

Sherwin-White, A. N. *Roman Society and Roman Law in the New Testament.* Oxford, 1963.

Watson, A. *The Law of Persons in the Later Roman Republic.* Oxford, 1967.

Watson, A. *The Law of Property in the Later Roman Republic.* Oxford, 1968.

Watson, A. *Law Making in the Later Roman Republic.* Oxford, 1974.

Watson, A. *Roman Slave Law.* Baltimore, 1987.

Williamson, C. *The Laws of the Roman People: Public Law in the Expansion and Decline of the Roman Republic.* Ann Arbor, 2005.

Biography

Barrett, A. A. *Caligula: The Corruption of Power.* New Haven, 1989.

Birley, A. R. *Marcus Aurelius: A Biography*, rev. edn. New Haven, 1987.

Birley, A. R. *Septimius Severus: The African Emperor*, rev. edn. New Haven, 1989.

Canfora, L. *Julius Caesar: The Life and Times of the People's Dictator.* Trans. M. Hill and K. Windle. Berkeley and Los Angeles, 2007.

Carney, T. F. *A Biography of Marius.* Salisbury, 1962.

Clarke, M. L. *The Noblest Roman.* Ithaca, NY, 1981.

Fantham, E. *Julia Augusti: The Emperor's Daughter.* London and New York, 2006.

Gelzer, M. *Caesar: Politician and Statesman*, 6th edn. Trans. P. Needham. Cambridge, MA, 1968.

Ginsburg, J. *Representing Agrippina: Constructions of Female Power in the Early Roman Empire.* New York and Oxford, 2006.

Greenhalgh, P. *Pompey*, 2 vols. Columbia, 1980–1.

Griffin, M. T. *Seneca: A Philosopher in Politics*. Oxford, 1976.

Griffin, M. T. *Nero: The End of a Dynasty*. New Haven, 1984.

Huzar, E. *Mark Antony: A Biography*. London, 1986.

Jones, B. W. *The Emperor Titus*. New York, 1984.

Jones, B. W. *The Emperor Domitian*. London, 1992.

Keaveney, A. *Sulla: The Last Republican*. London, 1982.

Keaveney, A. *Lucullus: A Life*. London and New York, 1992.

Levick, B. *Tiberius the Politician*. London, 1976.

Levick, B. *Claudius*. New Haven, 1990.

Levick, B. *Julia Domna: Syrian Empress*. London, 2007.

Rawson, E. *Cicero: A Portrait*. Ithaca, NY, 1975.

Seager, R. *Tiberius*. Berkeley, 1972.

Seager, R. *Pompey: A Political Biography*. Berkeley and Los Angeles, 1979.

Shackleton Bailey, D. R. *Cicero*. New York, 1971.

Spann, P. O. *Quintus Sertorius and the Legacy of Sulla*. Fayetteville, 1987.

Stockton, D. *Cicero: A Political Biography*. London, 1971.

Tatum, W. J. *Always I am Caesar*. Oxford, 2008.

Walker, S. and Ashton, S.-A. *Cleopatra*. London, 2006.

Ward, A. M. *Marcus Crassus and the Late Roman Republic*. Columbia and London, 1977.

The Later Roman Empire

General studies

Brown, P. *The World of Late Antiquity*, A.D. 150–750. New York, 1971.

Bury, J. B. *History of the Later Roman Empire from the Death of Theodosius I to the Death of Justinian (A.D. 395 to A.D. 565)*, 2 vols. London, 1923.

Cameron, A. *The Later Roman Empire*, A.D. 284–430. Cambridge, MA, 1993.

Cameron, A. *The Mediterranean World in Late Antiquity*. London, 1993.

Cameron, A. and Garnsey, P. (eds.). *The Late Empire*, A.D. 337–425. Vol. 13 of *The Cambridge Ancient History*, 2nd edn. Cambridge, 1998.

Garnsey, P. and Humfress, C. *The Evolution of the Late Antique World*. Cambridge, 2000.

Jones, A. H. M. *The Decline of the Ancient World*. London, 1966.

Lenski, N. E. (ed.). *The Cambridge Companion to the Age of Constantine*. Cambridge and New York, 2006.

Little, L. K. (ed.). *Plague and the End of Antiquity: The Pandemic of 541–750*. New York and Cambridge, 2007.

MacMullen, R. *Corruption and the Decline of Rome*. New Haven, 1988.

Maxwell, J. L. *Christianization and Communication in Late Antiquity: John Chrysostom and his Congregation in Antioch*. Cambridge, 2006.

Mitchell, S. *A History of the Later Roman Empire*, AD 284–641. Oxford, 2007.

Walbank, F. W. *The Awful Revolution: The Decline of the Roman Empire in the West*. Liverpool, 1978.

Politics and government

Barnes, T. D. *Constantine and Eusebius*. Cambridge, MA, 1981.

Barnes, T. D. *The New Empire of Diocletian and Constantine*. Cambridge, MA, 1982.

de Blois, L. *The Policy of the Emperor Gallienus*. Leiden, 1976.

Dignas, B. and Winter, E. *Rome and Persia in Late Antiquity: Neighbours and Rivals*. Cambridge, 2007.

Haarer, F. K. *Anastasius I: Politics and Empire in the Late Roman World*. Cambridge, 2006.

Kelly, C. *Ruling the Later Roman Empire*. Cambridge, MA, 2004.

MacMullen, R. *Roman Government's Response to Crisis*, A.D. 235–337. New Haven, 1976.

Matthews, J. *Western Aristocracies and Imperial Court*, A.D. 364–425. Oxford, 1975.

Millar, F. *A Greek Roman Empire: Power and Belief under Theodosius II (408–450)*. Berkeley, 2006.

O'Flynn, J. M. *Generalissimos of the Western Roman Empire*. Edmonton, 1983.

The army, war, and foreign relations

Burns, T. S. *A History of the Ostrogoths*. Bloomington, 1984.

Dodgeon, M. H. and Lieu, S. N. C. (eds.). *The Roman Eastern Frontier and the Persian Wars (A.D. 226–363)*. London, 1990.

Drinkwater, J. F. *The Alamanni and Rome, 213–496: Caracalla to Clovis*. Oxford, 2007.

Elton, H. *Warfare in Roman Europe*, A.D. 350–425. Oxford, 1996.

Feld, K. *Barbarische Bürger: Die Isaurier und das Römische Reich*. Berlin and New York, 2005.

Ferrill, A. *The Fall of the Roman Empire: The Military Explanation*. London, 1986.

Gardner, A. *An Archaeology of Identity: Soldiers and Society in Late Roman Britain*. Left Coast Press, 2007.

Goffart, W. *Barbarians and Romans*, A.D. 418–584. Princeton, 1980.

Heather, P. *Goths and Romans, 332–489*. New York, 1991.

Kulikowski, M. *Rome's Gothic Wars: From the Third Century to Alaric*. New York and Cambridge, 2007.

Lee, A. D. *War in Late Antiquity: A Social History*. Oxford, 2007.

Lewin, A. and Pellegrini, P. (eds.). *The Late Roman Army in the Near East from Diocletian to the Arab Conquest*. Oxford, 2007.

MacMullen, R. *Soldier and Civilian in the Later Roman Empire*. Cambridge, MA, 1963.

Maenchen-Helfen, O. *The World of the Huns*. Berkeley and Los Angeles, 1973.

Potter, D. S. *The Roman Empire at Bay*, AD 180–395. London and New York, 2004.

Thompson, E. A. *Romans and Barbarians: The Decline of the Western Empire*. Madison, 1982.

Regional and local histories

Bagnall, R. S. *Egypt in Late Antiquity*. Princeton, 1993.

Brock, S. P. *Syriac Perspectives on Late Antiquity*. London, 1984.

Drinkwater, J. F. *The Gallic Empire: Separatism and Continuity in the North-Western Provinces of the Roman Empire*. Stuttgart, 1987.

Drinkwater, J. F. and Elton, H. (eds.). *Fifth-Century Gaul: A Crisis of Identity?* Cambridge, 1992.

Esmonde Cleary, A. S. *The Ending of Roman Britain*. Savage, MD, 1989.

Johnson, S. *Later Roman Britain*. London, 1980.

King, A. and Henig, M. (eds.). *The Roman West in the Third Century: Contributions from Archaeology and History*. Oxford, 1981.

Liebeschuetz, J. H. W. G. *Antioch: City and Imperial Administration in the Later Roman Empire*. Oxford, 1972.

Rousseau, P. *Pachomius: The Making of a Community in Fourth-Century Egypt*. Berkeley, 1985.

Sivan, H. *Palestine in Late Antiquity*. Oxford and New York, 2008.

Van Dam, R. *Leadership and Community in Late Antique Gaul*. Berkeley, 1985.

Warmington, B. H. *The North African Provinces from Diocletian to the Vandal Conquest*. Cambridge, 1954.

Economy and trade

Crawford, M. H. "Finance, Coinage, and Money from the Severans to Constantine," *Aufstieg und Niedergang der römischen Welt*, 2.2 (1975), 560–93.

King, C. E. (ed.). *Imperial Revenues, Expenditure and Monetary Policy in the Fourth Century A.D.* Oxford, 1980.

Stevens, C. E. "Agriculture and Rural Life in the Later Roman Empire," in M. M. Postan (ed.), *The Cambridge Economic History of Europe*, 2nd edn (Cambridge, 1971), vol. 1, 92–124.

Walbank, F. W. "Trade and Industry under the Later Roman Empire in the West," in M. M. Postan and E. Miller (eds.), *The Cambridge Economic History of Europe*, 2nd edn (Cambridge, 1987), vol. 2, 71–131.

Society

Arjava, A. *Women and Law in Late Antiquity*. Oxford, 1996.

Brown, P. *The Making of Late Antiquity*. Cambridge, MA, 1978.

Brown, P. *Society and the Holy in Late Antiquity*. Berkeley, 1982.

Brown, P. *Power and Persuasion in Late Antiquity: Towards a Christian Empire*. Madison, 1992.

Cameron, A. *Circus Factions*. Oxford, 1976.

Clark, G. *Women in Late Antiquity: Pagan and Christian Life-Styles*. Oxford, 1993.

Cooper, K. *The Fall of the Roman Household*. Cambridge, 2007.

Drake, H. A. *Violence in Late Antiquity: Perceptions and Practices*. Aldershot and Burlington, VT, 2006.

Little, L. K. (ed.). *Plague and the End of Antiquity: The Pandemic of 541–750*. New York and Cambridge, 2007.

MacCormack, S. G. *Art and Ceremony in Late Antiquity*. Berkeley, 1981.

Matthews, J. *The Journey of Theophanes: Travel, Business, and Daily Life in the Roman East*. New Haven, 2006.

Sarris, P. *Economy and Society in the Age of Justinian*. Cambridge, 2006.

Shaw, B. D. "Latin Funerary Epigraphy and Family Life in the Later Roman Empire," *Historia: Zeitschrift für alte Geschichte*, 33 (1984), 457–97.

Shaw, B. D. "The Family in Late Antiquity: The Experience of Augustine," *Past and Present*, 115 (1987), 3–51.

Swain, S. and Edwards, M. (eds.). *Approaching Late Antiquity: The Transformation from Early to Late Empire*. Oxford and New York, 2004.

Van Dam, R. *The Roman Revolution of Constantine*. Cambridge, 2007.

Whittaker, C. R. "Circe's Pigs: From Slavery to Serfdom in the Later Roman World," *Slavery and Abolition*, 8 (1987), 88–123.

Religion

Brown, P. *Religion and Society in the Age of Saint Augustine*. London, 1972.

Brown, P. *The Cult of the Saints: Its Rise and Function in Latin Christianity*. Chicago, 1982.

Brown, P. *The Body and Society: Men, Women and Sexual Renunciation in Early Christianity*. New York, 1988.

Cameron, A. *Christianity and the Rhetoric of Empire*. Berkeley and Los Angeles, 1991.

Chuvin, P. *A Chronicle of the Last Pagans*. Cambridge, MA, 1990.

Clark, G. *Ascetic Piety and Women's Faith*. Lewiston, NY, 1986.

Croke, B. and Harries, J. (eds.). *Religious Conflict in Fourth Century Rome*. Sydney, 1982.

Dodds, E. R. *Pagan and Christian in an Age of Anxiety*. Cambridge, 1965.

Elsner, J. and Rutherford, I. *Pilgrimage in Graeco-Roman and Early Christian Antiquity: Seeing the Gods*. Oxford and New York, 2005.

Frend, W. H. C. *The Donatist Church: A Movement of Protest in Roman North Africa*. Oxford, 1952.

Hunt, E. D. *Holy Land Pilgrimage in the Later Roman Empire*. Oxford, 1982.

Maxwell, J. L. *Christianization and Communication in Late Antiquity*. Cambridge, 2006.

Momigliano, A. (ed.). *The Conflict between Paganism and Christianity in the Fourth Century*. Oxford, 1963.

Tougher, S. *Julian the Apostate*. Edinburgh, 2007.

Williams, R. L. *Arius, Heresy and Tradition*. London, 1987.

Intellectual life (literature and philosophy)

Binns, J. W. (ed.). *Latin Literature of the Fourth Century*. London, 1974.

Bowersock, G. W. *Hellenism in Late Antiquity*. Ann Arbor, 1990.

Cameron, A. *Claudian: Poetry and Propaganda at the Court of Honorius*. Oxford, 1970.

Cox, P. *Biography in Late Antiquity: A Quest for the Holy Man*. Berkeley, 1983.

Kaster, R. A. *Guardians of Language: The Grammarian and Society in Late Antiquity*. Berkeley, 1988.

Palmer, A.-M. *Prudentius on the Martyrs*. New York, 1989.

Rist, J. M. *Plotinus: The Road to Reality*. Cambridge, 1967.

Art and architecture

Bandinelli, R. B. *Rome, The Late Empire: Roman Art, A.D. 200–400*. Trans. P. Green. New York, 1971.

Ben Khader, A. B. A. *Tunisian Mosaics: Treasures from Roman Africa*. Los Angeles, 2006.

Bowersock, G. W. *Mosaics as History: The Near East from Late Antiquity to Islam*. Cambridge, MA, 2006.

Dorigo, W. *Late Roman Painting*. Trans. J. Cleugh and J. Warrington. New York, 1970.

Milburn, R. *Early Christian Art and Architecture*. Berkeley, 1988.

Historians and historiography

Barnes, T. D. *The Sources of the Historia Augusta*. Brussels, 1978.

Bird, H. W. *Sextus Aurelius Victor: A Historiographical Study*. Liverpool, 1984.

Blockley, R. C. *Ammianus Marcellinus: A Study of his Historiography and Political Thought*. Brussels, 1975.

den Boer, W. *Some Minor Roman Historians*. Leiden, 1972.

Croke, B. and Emmett, A. M. (eds.). *History and Historians in Late Antiquity*. Sydney, 1983.

Liebeschuetz, J. H. W. G. *Decline and Change in Late Antiquity: Religion, Barbarians and their Historiography*. Aldershot and Burlington, VT, 2006.

Marasco, G. (ed.). *Greek and Roman Historiography in Late Antiquity: Fourth to Sixth Century A.D.* Leiden and Boston, 2003.

Matthews, J. *The Roman Empire of Ammianus*. Baltimore, 1989.

Syme, R. *Ammianus and the Historia Augusta*. Oxford, 1968.

Syme, R. *Emperors and Biography: Studies in the Historia Augusta*. Oxford, 1971.

Syme, R. *Historia Augusta Papers*. New York, 1983.

Biography

Athanassiadi, P. *Julian: An Intellectual Biography*, rev. edn. London, 1992.

Bowersock, G. W. *Julian the Apostate*. Cambridge, MA, 1978.

Bregman, J. *Synesius of Cyrene: Philosopher-Bishop*. Berkeley, 1982.

Brown, P. *Augustine of Hippo*. London, 1967.

Clark, G. *The Life of Melania the Younger*, Lewiston, NY, 1984.

MacMullen, R. *Constantine*. New York, 1969.

Rousseau, P. *Basil of Caesarea*. Berkeley, 1994.

Williams, S. *Diocletian and the Roman Recovery*. New York, 1985.

INDEX

Page numbers in *italics* refer to illustrations.